ECONOMIC WELL-BEING AND INEQUALITY: PAPERS FROM THE FIFTH ECINEQ MEETING

RESEARCH ON ECONOMIC INEQUALITY

Series Editors:

John A. Bishop
East Carolina University, USA

Juan Gabriel Rodríguez
Universidad Complutense de Madrid, Spain

RESEARCH ON ECONOMIC INEQUALITY VOLUME 22

ECONOMIC WELL-BEING AND INEQUALITY: PAPERS FROM THE FIFTH ECINEQ MEETING

EDITED BY

JOHN A. BISHOP
East Carolina University, Greenville, NC, USA

JUAN GABRIEL RODRÍGUEZ
Universidad Complutense de Madrid, Madrid, Spain

Emerald

United Kingdom – North America – Japan
India – Malaysia – China

Emerald Group Publishing Limited
Howard House, Wagon Lane, Bingley BD16 1WA, UK

First edition 2014

British Library Cataloguing in Publication Data
A catalogue record for this book is available from the British Library

ISBN: 978-1-78350-567-8
ISSN: 1049-2585 (Series)

CONTENTS

LIST OF CONTRIBUTORS

Olga Alonso-Villar	Departamento de Economía Aplicada, Universidade de Vigo, Vigo, Spain
João Sousa Andrade	Faculty of Economics, University of Coimbra, Coimbra, Portugal
Francisco Azpitarte	Melbourne Institute of Economic and Social Research and Brotherhood of St. Laurence, University of Melbourne, Melbourne, Australia
Sanghamitra Bandyopadhyay	Queen Mary, University of London, London, UK
Elena Bárcena-Martín	Department of Applied Economics, Universidad de Málaga, Málaga, Spain
John A. Bishop	East Carolina University, Greenville, NC, USA
Florent Bresson	CERDI, Université d'Auvergne, Clermont-Ferrand, France
Shiyi Chen	Department of Economics, University of Colorado Denver, Denver, CO, USA
Karina Doorley	IZA, Bonn, Germany
Adelaide P. S. Duarte	Faculty of Economics, University of Coimbra, Coimbra, Portugal
Uwe Fachinger	Department of Economics and Demography, University of Vechta, Vechta, Germany
Jürgen Faik	Department of Economics and Demography, University of Vechta and FaSo (Faik Sozialforschung), Frankfurt (Main), Germany

Gertrudes Saúde Guerreiro	Department of Economics, University of Évora, Évora, Portugal
Luis J. Imedio-Olmedo	Department of Applied Economics, Universidad de Málaga, Málaga, Spain
Barbara Jancewicz	Institute of Sociology, University of Warsaw, Warsaw, Poland
Vanesa Jordá	Department of Economics, University of Cantabria, Santander, Spain
Haiyong Liu	East Carolina University, Greenville, NC, USA
Michel Lubrano	Aix-Marseille University, CNRS & EHESS, Marseille, France
Joachim Merz	Research Institute on Professions (FFB), Department of Economics, Leuphana University Lüneburg, Lüneburg, Germany
Abdoul Aziz Junior Ndoye	Aix-Marseille University and CNRS & EHESS, Marseille, France
Encarnación M. Parrado-Gallardo	Department of Applied Economics, Universidad de Málaga, Málaga, Spain
Faustino Prieto	Department of Economics, University of Cantabria, Santander, Spain
Juan Gabriel Rodríguez	Department of Economic Analysis I, Universidad Complutense de Madrid, Madrid, Spain
José María Sarabia	Department of Economics, University of Cantabria, Santander, Spain
Bettina Scherg	Research Institute on Professions (FFB), Department of Economics, Leuphana University Lüneburg, Lüneburg, Germany
Carsten Schröder	Kiel Institute for the World Economy, University of Kiel, Kiel, Germany

Eva Sierminska	CEPS/INSTEAD, Luxembourg; IZA, Germany; DIW Berlin, Germany
Jacques Silber	Department of Economics, Bar-Ilan University, Israel; CEPS/INSTEAD, Luxembourg
Marta C. N. Simões	Faculty of Economics, University of Coimbra, Coimbra, Portugal
Simon Alain Song Ntamack	Faculty of Economics and Management, University of Yaoundé II, Yaoundé, Cameroon
Edward N. Wolff	Department of Economics, New York University, New York, NY, USA
Buhong Zheng	Department of Economics, University of Colorado Denver, Denver, CO, USA

INTRODUCTION

Research on Economic Inequality, Volume 22, *Economic Well-Being and Inequality: Papers from the Fifth ECINEQ Meeting*, is primarily a collection of papers presented at the July 2013 Bari, Italy meeting. As is typical with volumes in this series, the contributions range from senior scholars to emerging scholars in the field of income distribution and poverty studies.

Great interest for inequality researchers lies in the use of wealth data. The volume begins with three papers that employ wealth data. The first of these papers is by the leading U.S. wealth inequality scholar, Edward N. Wolff. Wolff's paper focuses on the impact of the Great Recession on the distribution of U.S. household's wealth and its components. While median U.S. wealth fell "by a staggering 47 percent …, black households much harder hit than whites" and Hispanics also suffered disproportionately as a high percentage of bought homes close to the housing cycle peak. Finally, Wolff reports that "young households also got pommelled by the Great Recession."

In the second paper, Karina Doorley and Eva Sierminska use harmonized households level wealth data from four European countries, the United States, and Canada to investigate the role of observable household characteristics in explaining cross-national asset mixes. They find that the "differences in the level of financial assets between the U.S. and Canada, and Europe is largely driven by household characteristics." In contrast, European and Canadians hold higher levels of debt (primarily mortgage debt) than U.S. households "for reasons unrelated to their household characteristics." Finally, they conclude that the investment decisions made by younger households are "more sensitive to institutions, culture, or other country differences than older households."

Following the lead of the Stiglitz Commission on Social Progress, Jürgen Faik and Uwe Fachinger evaluate German inequality on three dimensions: income, consumption, and wealth. The authors find that the inequality of potential income is "strikingly driven by annualized wealth," which is mainly a function of the inequality of real estate holdings. By decomposing material well-being in great detail they shed light on its many dimensions. For example, they observe that attempts to improve generational justice are likely to lead to an increase in within group inequality.

A second topic included in this volume is the measurement and evaluation of poverty and inequality in the world. Vanesa Jordá, José María Sarabia, and Faustino Prieto offer an innovative approach to exploiting the limited information available in the national income statistics to make distributional judgments. These authors propose the Lamé 1 and 2 distributions, together with the published Gini coefficients and mean incomes, to estimate national distributions. Furthermore, they generate global and regional distributions and their associated inequality statistics for the 1990s.

In the next paper, Florent Bresson extends the literature on stochastic dominance poverty orderings. Specifically, the paper considers the case where we are interested in excluding a particular group, here the very poorest. Using the World Bank's Povcal Net data, she finds an increase in moderate poverty between 1990 and 2005, as households in moderate poverty appear to be climbing the ladder out of poverty at a somewhat slower rate than those in extreme poverty.

Sanghamitra Bandyopadhyay, in her paper, asks the intriguing question, has the spread of mass communication had a beneficial effect on income inequality? She constructs an index of information and communication technologies (ICT) using World Bank indicator data factor analysis. She concludes that "the evidence obtained in the paper is convincing that there exists significant association between media and communication infrastructures, and inequality and poverty" while recognizing that identifying the specific political economy routes of causation will require future research.

The third topic of the volume presents papers from the emerging field of using self-reported status and perception data to study economic well-being. In their paper, Shiyi Chen and Buhong Zheng address the question of inequality of happiness in the United States. Their paper adopts Zheng's earlier work on accessing inequality using ordinal health data. Under very general conditions, they show how happiness and inequality can be measured and they then apply their approach to U.S. data. Interestingly, they conclude that 2010 (the year after the Great Recession began) was the low point in recent American happiness.

John A. Bishop, Haiyong Liu, and Juan Gabriel Rodríguez use self-reported social status data to examine the relationship between inequality and intergenerational social status mobility. In particular, they would like to know if there is a social status Great Gatsby Curve similar to the association Alan Krueger popularized between earnings and inequality. They find a positive but weak relationship between past inequality and status immobility. An extension of their model suggests that social status mobility is positively related to economic freedom.

Barbara Jancewicz examines the extensive body of work on perceptions of income inequality. She notes that the researchers typically find that people do not perceive inequality in accordance with the traditional axioms. Her paper attempts to move beyond what people do not perceive and examine how respondents actually perceive inequality. Using the tools of multidimensional scaling, she provides a preference map, revealing that respondents' decisions are driven by the biggest gaps in income and whether some groups have equal income.

Joachim Merz and Bettina Scherg present a new measure of multidimensional polarization based on a CES-type well-being function, the mean minimum polarization gap. These authors quantify their new approach for the polarization development of the working poor and the working rich in Germany. They find that not only income but also leisure time is an important polarization attribute. In addition, they observed that multidimensional polarization increased over the 1990s in Germany.

The next paper addresses the question of regional convergence in Portugal. Adelaide P. S. Duarte, Jacques Silber, João Sousa Andrade, and Marta C. N. Simões measure regional convergence in Portugal by applying the method decomposition developed by Silber in an earlier paper. This approach decomposes convergence into an inequality component, a pure mobility component, and a re-ranking component. Studying the period 1985–2006, they find "regional real convergence of average real earnings," a deterioration of mobility among Portuguese NUT3 regions, and "reranking [that] was not in favor of poorer regions."

Gertrudes Saúde Guerreiro, in her paper, approaches the study of Portuguese convergence by observing spatial error dependence and estimating spatial econometric models to test for convergence. Her findings confirm spatial correlation in wage and growth for municipalities but not in NUT3 regions. She suggests that spatial correlation applies at the intra-regional rather than inter-regional level. Her convergence results are mixed, absolute β-convergence occurs in GDP per capita, but not in wages. However, wages do converge in conditional models.

The next two papers propose new methodologies to represent social preferences regarding income distributions and to measure intermediate inequality. First, Encarnación M. Parrado-Gallardo, Elena Bárcena-Martín, and Luis J. Imedio-Olmedo, using the distributions of order statistics, construct a set of social welfare functions from which the generalized Gini coefficients and the family of indices proposed by Aaberge (2000) are derived. Thus, inequality measures can be interpreted in terms of the statistics computed from a randomly selected sample and the identification of unbiased estimators of the Social Welfare Functions. This methodology is particularly appropriate for those distributions with heavy tail and pronounced positive skew.

Second, Francisco Azpitarte and Olga Alonso-Villar introduce a unit-consistent Lorenz dominance criterion that allows ranking income distributions according to centrist measures à la Seidl and Pfingsten (1997). In particular, they define the α-Lorenz curve which generalizes the absolute Lorenz curve and allows implementing unanimous rankings for a broad set of centrist inequality notions. In their empirical illustration, these authors find that despite the reduction of relative inequality for Australian-born people between 1999 and 2003, their inequality increased for most centrist value judgments.

In its influential 2001 report, the Canberra expert group on household income statistics argued that the lack of a uniform accounting period across micro databases may introduce "an element of non-comparability." Following this advice, Carsten Schröder, in his paper, explores systematically the sensitivity of inter-temporal and inter-regional inequality comparisons to the length of the accounting period. He finds that there is no general rule for the size of the Shorrocks effect, the negative relationship between inequality and the accounting period. In fact, the Shorrocks effect depends on the inequality index and varies over time and regions.

During the last three decades, the U.S. economy has experienced a marked increase in wage inequality in the upper tail of the distribution. To understand this fact, Abdoul Aziz Junior Ndoye and Michel Lubrano propose to approximate the upper tail of a wage distribution by a mixture of two Pareto distributions. Applying this mixture model to the data from the CPS (1992 through 2009), they find that the increase of wage inequality in the upper tail of the distribution is in accordance with the explanations combining the model of superstars and the model of tournaments in hierarchical organization structure.

The volume ends with a specific study on inequality for non-wage earners in Cameroon. Simon Alain Song Ntamack analyzes the determinants of inequality in income among non-waged employees using the regression-based decomposition technique and data obtained from the 2005 *Employment and Informal Sector Survey* in Cameroon. The level of income inequality is primarily determined by human capital endowments like education and the age-experience relationship.

John A. Bishop
Juan Gabriel Rodríguez
Editors

THE ASSET PRICE MELTDOWN AND HOUSEHOLD WEALTH OVER THE GREAT RECESSION IN THE UNITED STATES

Edward N. Wolff

ABSTRACT

I find that median wealth plummeted over the years 2007–2010, and by 2010 was at its lowest level since 1969. The inequality of net worth, after almost two decades of little movement, was up sharply from 2007 to 2010. Relative indebtedness continued to expand from 2007 to 2010, particularly for the middle class, though the proximate causes were declining net worth and income rather than an increase in absolute indebtedness. In fact, the average debt of the middle class actually fell in real terms by 25 percent. The sharp fall in median wealth and the rise in inequality in the late 2000s are traceable to the high leverage of middle-class families in 2007 and the high share of homes in their portfolio. The racial and ethnic disparity in wealth holdings, after remaining more or less stable from 1983 to 2007, widened considerably between 2007 and 2010. Hispanics, in particular, got hammered by the Great Recession in terms of net worth and net equity in their homes. Households under age 45 also

Economic Well-Being and Inequality: Papers from the Fifth ECINEQ Meeting
Research on Economic Inequality, Volume 22, 1–42

ISSN: 1049-2585/doi:10.1108/S1049-258520140000022001

got pummeled by the Great Recession, as their relative and absolute wealth declined sharply from 2007 to 2010.

Keywords: Household wealth; inequality; racial inequality; portfolio composition

JEL classifications: D31; J15

INTRODUCTION

The last two decades have witnessed some remarkable events. Perhaps, most notable is the housing value cycle which first led to an explosion in home prices and then a collapse, affecting net worth and helping to precipitate the Great Recession. The housing bubble, in turn, was based on questionable mortgage practices and then speculative over-building.

The paper focuses mainly on how the middle class fared in terms of wealth over the years 2007–2010 during one of the sharpest declines in stock and real estate prices. As discussed later, the debt of the middle class exploded from 1983 to 2007, already creating a very fragile middle class in the United States. The main interest here is whether their position deteriorated even more over the Great Recession. The paper also investigates trends in wealth inequality, and changes in the racial wealth gap and wealth differences by age. The period covered spans the years from 1962 to 2010. The choice of years is dictated by the availability of survey data on household wealth. By 2010, we are able to see what the fall-out was from the financial crisis and associated recession and, in particular, which groups were impacted the most.

There are five specific issues addressed in the paper. (1) Did the inequality of household wealth rise over time, particularly during the Great Recession? (2) Did median household wealth continue to advance over time or did it fall? (3) Did the debt of the middle class increase over time, especially over the Great Recession? (4) What are the time trends in home ownership and home equity? (5) How did time trends in median wealth, household debt, the home ownership rate, and home equity vary among different racial and ethnic groups and by age group?

Previous work of mine (see Wolff, 1994, 1998, 2002, 2011a), using data from the Survey of Consumer Finances (SCF) over years from 1983 to 2007, presented evidence of sharply increasing household wealth inequality between 1983 and 1989 followed by little change between 1989 and 2007. Both mean and median wealth holdings climbed briskly during the 1983–1989 period as well as from 1989 to 2007. However, most of the wealth gains from 1983 to 2007 were concentrated among the richest 20 percent of households. Moreover, despite the buoyant economy over the 1990s and 2000s, the overall indebtedness continued to rise among American families.

The ratio of mean wealth between African-American and white families was very low in 1983, at 0.19 and about the same in 2007. In 1983, the richest households were those headed by persons between 45 and 74 years of age, and the relative wealth holdings of both younger and older families fell between 1983 and 2007, particularly those of the former.

In this study, I look at wealth trends from 1962 to 2010. The most telling finding is that median wealth plummeted over the years 2007 to 2010, and by 2010 was at its lowest level since 1969. The inequality of net worth, after almost two decades of little movement, was up sharply between 2007 and 2010. Relative indebtedness continued to expand during the late 2000s, particularly for the middle class, though the proximate causes were declining net worth and income rather than an increase in absolute indebtedness. In fact, the average debt of the middle class in real terms was down by 25 percent. The sharp fall in median net worth and the rise in its inequality in the late 2000s are traceable to the high leverage of middle-class families in 2007 and the high share of homes in their portfolio. The racial and ethnic disparity in wealth holdings widened considerably in the years between 2007 and 2010. Hispanics, in particular, got hammered by the Great Recession in terms of net worth and net equity in their homes. Finally, young households (under age 45) also got pummeled by the Great Recession, as their relative and absolute wealth declined sharply from 2007 to 2010.

The paper is organized as follows. The next section provides some historical background. The section "Data Sources and Methods" discusses the measurement of household wealth and describes the data sources used for this study. The next three sections present results on time trends in median and average wealth holdings, on changes in the concentration of household wealth, and on the composition of household wealth, respectively. After this, I provide an analysis of the effects of leverage on wealth movements over time, particularly over the Great Recession. The next section investigates changes in wealth holdings by race and ethnicity; and the section that follows reports on changes in the age-wealth profile. The final section provides a summary and concluding remarks.

THE CONTEXT

The median house price remained virtually the same in 2001 as in 1989 in real terms.[1] However, the home ownership rate shot up from 62.8 percent in 1989 to 67.7 percent in 2001 according to data from the SCF. Then, 2001 saw a recession (albeit a short one). Despite this, house prices suddenly took off. The median sales price of existing one-family homes nationwide rose by 17.9 percent in real terms nationwide. However, from 2004 to 2007 housing prices slowed, with its median value advancing by only 1.7 percent in real terms. Over the years 2001 to 2007 real housing prices gained 18.8 percent. The home ownership rate continued to expand, though at a somewhat slower rate, from 67.7 to 68.6 percent.

Then, the Great Recession and the associated financial crisis hit at the end of 2007 and asset prices plummeted. From 2007 to 2010, in particular, the median price of existing homes nosedived by 24 percent in real terms.[2] Moreover, for the first time in 30 years, the share of households owning their own home fell, from 68.6 to 67.2 percent.

The housing price bubble was fueled in large part by a generous expansion of credit available for home purchases and refinancing. This took a number of forms. First, many home owners re-financed their primary mortgage. However, because of the rise in housing prices, these home owners increased the outstanding mortgage principal and thereby extracted equity from their homes. Second, many home owners took out second mortgages and home equity loans or increased the outstanding balances on these instruments. Third, among new home owners, credit requirements were softened, and so-called "no-doc" loans were issued requiring none or little in the way of income documentation. Many of these loans, in turn, were so-called "sub-prime" mortgages, characterized by excessively high interest rates and "balloon payments" at the expiration of the loan (i.e., a non-zero amount due when the term of the loan was up). All told, average mortgage debt per household expanded by 59 percent in real terms between 2001 and 2007 according to the SCF data, and outstanding mortgage loans as a share of house value rose from 0.334 to 0.349, despite the 19 percent gain in real housing prices (see the section "Household Debt Continues to Remain high").

In contrast to the housing market, the stock market boomed during the 1990s. On the basis of the Standard & Poor (S&P) 500 index, stock prices surged 59 percent in real terms between 1989 and 2001.[3] Stock ownership spread and by 2001 over half of U.S. households owned stock either directly or indirectly. However, the stock market peaked in 2000 and dropped steeply from 2000 to 2003, recovered somewhat in 2004, and then rebounded from 2004 to 2007. Over the period from 2001 to 2007, the S&P 500 was up 6 percent in real terms. However, the share of households who owned stock either directly or indirectly fell somewhat to 49 percent from 52 percent in 2001. Then came the Great Recession. Stock prices, based on the S&P 500 index, crashed from 2007 to 2009 and then partially recovered in 2010 for a net decline of 26 percent in real terms. The stock ownership rate also once again declined, to 47 percent.

Real wages, after stagnating for many years, finally grew in the late 1990s. According to BLS figures, real mean hourly earnings gained 8.3 percent between 1995 and 2001. From 1989 to 2001, real wages rose by 4.9 percent (in total), and median household income in constant dollars inched up by 2.3 percent.[4] Employment also surged over these years, growing by 16.7 percent.[5] The (civilian) unemployment rate remained relatively low over these years, at 5.3 percent in 1989 and 4.7 percent in 2001, with a low point of 4.0 percent in 2000, and averaging 5.5 percent over these years.[6] Real wages then rose very slowly from 2001 to 2007, with the BLS real mean hourly earnings up by only 2.6 percent, while median household income gained only 1.6 percent. Employment also grew more slowly over these years, gaining 6.7 percent. The unemployment rate remained low again, at 4.7 percent in 2001 and 4.6 percent in 2007 and an average value of 5.2 percent.

Real wages, on the other hand, picked up from 2007 to 2010, with the BLS real mean hourly earnings increasing by 3.6 percent. In contrast, median household income in real terms declined sharply over this period, by 6.4 percent. Moreover, employment contracted as well, by 4.8 percent, and the unemployment rate surged from 4.6 percent in 2007 to 10.5 percent in 2010, though it has since come down to 6.7 percent in February 2014.

There was also an explosion of consumer debt leading up to the Great Recession. Between 1989 and 2001, total consumer credit outstanding in constant dollars surged by 70 percent and then from 2001 to 2007 it rose by another 17 percent.[7] There were a number of factors responsible for this. First, credit cards became more generally available for consumers. Second, credit standards were relaxed considerably, making more households eligible for credit cards. Third, credit limits were generously increased by banks hoping to make profits out of increased fees from late payments and from higher interest rates.

Another source of new household indebtedness was from a huge increase in student loans. According to the SCF data, the share of households reporting an educational loan rose from 13.4 percent in 2004 to

15.2 percent in 2007 and then surged to 19.1 percent in 2010.[8] The mean value of educational loans in 2010 dollars among loan holders only increased by 17 percent from $19,410 in 2004 to $22,367 in 2007 and then by another 14 percent to $25,865 in 2010. The median value of such loans first went up by 19 percent from $10,620 in 2004 to $12,620 in 2007 and then by another 3 percent to $13,000 in 2010. These loans were heavily concentrated among younger households and, as we shall see later, was one of the factors (though not the principal one) which led to a precipitous decline in their net worth between 2007 and 2010.

Another important change over the last three decades affecting household wealth was a major overhaul of the private pension system in the United States. As documented in Wolff (2011b), in 1989, 46 percent of all households reported holding a defined benefit (DB) pension plan. DB plans are traditional pensions, such as provided by many large corporations, the federal government, and state and local governments, which guarantee a steady flow of income upon retirement. By 2007, that figure was down to 34 percent. The decline was more pronounced among younger households, under the age of 46, from 38 to 23 percent, as well as among middle-aged households, ages 47–64, from 57 to 39 percent.

Many of these plans were replaced by defined contribution (DC) pension accounts, most notably 401(k) plans and Individual Retirement Accounts (IRAs). These plans allow households to accumulate savings for retirement purposes directly. The share of all household with a DC plan skyrocketed from 24 percent in 1989 to 53 percent in 2007. Among younger households, the share rose from 31 to 50 percent, and among middle-aged households it went from 28 to 64 percent.

This transformation is even more notable in terms of actual dollar values. While the average value of DB pension wealth among all households crept up by 8 percent from $56,500 in 1989 to $61,200 in 2007, the average value of DC plans shot up more than sevenfold from $10,600 to $76,800 (all figures are in 2007 dollars).[9] Among younger households, average DB wealth actually fell in absolute terms, while DC wealth rose by a factor of 3.3. Among middle-aged households, the value of DB pensions also fell in absolute terms while the value of DC plans mushroomed by a factor of 6.5.

These changes are important for understanding trends in household wealth because DB pension wealth is *not* included in the measure of marketable household wealth, whereas DC wealth *is* included (see the section "Data Sources and Methods"). Thus, the substitution of DC wealth for DB wealth is likely to lead to an overstatement in the "true" gains in household wealth, since the displacement in DB wealth is not captured (see Wolff, 2011b, for more discussion).

The other big story was household debt, particularly that of the middle class, which skyrocketed during these years, as we shall see later. Despite the recession, the relative indebtedness of American families continued to rise from 2007 to 2010.

What have all these major transformations wrought in terms of the distribution of household wealth, particularly over the Great Recession? How have these changes impacted different demographic groups, particularly as defined by race, ethnicity, and age? This is the subject of the remainder of the paper.

DATA SOURCES AND METHODS

The primary data sources used for this study are the 1983, 1989, 1992, 1995, 1998, 2001, 2004, 2007, and 2010 SCF conducted by the Federal Reserve Board. Each survey consists of a core representative sample combined with a high-income supplement. The high-income supplement was selected as a list sample derived from tax data from the IRS Statistics of Income. This second sample was designed to disproportionately select families that were likely to be relatively wealthy (see, e.g., Kennickell, 2001, for a discussion of the design of the list sample in the 2001 SCF). The advantage of the high-income supplement is that it provides a much "richer" sample of high income and therefore potentially very wealthy families. Typically, about two-thirds of the cases come from the representative sample and one-third from the high-income supplement. In the 2007 SCF, the standard multi-stage area-probability sample contributed 2,915 cases while the high-income supplement contributed another 1,507 cases.

The principal wealth concept used here is marketable wealth (or net worth), which is defined as the current value of all marketable or fungible assets less the current value of debts. Net worth is thus the difference in value between total assets and total liabilities or debt. Total assets are defined as the sum of (1) owner-occupied housing; (2) other real estate; (3) demand deposits; (4) time and savings deposits, certificates of deposit, and money market accounts; (5) government, corporate, and foreign bonds and other financial securities; (6) the cash surrender value of life insurance plans; (7) the cash surrender value of pension plans, including IRAs, Keogh, and 401(k) plans; (8) corporate stock and mutual funds; (9) net equity in unincorporated businesses; and (10) equity in trust funds. Total liabilities are the sum of (1) mortgage debt, (2) consumer debt, including auto loans, and (3) other debt such as educational loans.

This measure reflects wealth as a store of value and therefore a source of potential consumption. I believe that this is the concept that best reflects the level of well-being associated with a family's holdings. Thus, only assets that can be readily converted to cash (i.e., "fungible" ones) are included. As a result, consumer durables, such as automobiles, televisions, and furniture, are excluded here, since these items are not easily marketed, with the possible exception of vehicles, or their resale value typically far understates the value of their consumption services to the household. Another justification for their exclusion is that this treatment is consistent with the national accounts, where purchase of vehicles is counted as expenditures, not savings.[10] As a result, my estimates of household wealth will *differ* from those provided by the Federal Reserve Board, which includes the value of vehicles in their standard definition of household wealth (see, e.g., Kennickell & Woodburn, 1999).

Also excluded is the value of future Social Security benefits the family may receive upon retirement (usually referred to as "Social Security wealth"), as well as the value of retirement benefits from DB pension plans ("pension wealth"). Even though these funds are a source of future income to families, they are not in their direct control and cannot be marketed.[11]

Two other data sources are used in the study. The first of these is the 1962 Survey of Financial Characteristics of Consumers (SFCC), also conducted by the Federal Reserve Board (see Projector & Weiss, 1966). This is also a stratified sample which oversamples high-income households. Though the sample design and questionnaire are different from the SCF, the methodology is sufficiently similar to allow comparisons with the SCF data (see Wolff, 1987, for details on the adjustments). The second is a synthetic dataset, the 1969 MESP database. A statistical matching technique was employed to assign income tax returns for 1969 to households in the 1970 Census of Population. Property income flows (such as dividends) in the tax data were then capitalized into corresponding asset values (such as stocks) to obtain estimates of household wealth (see Wolff, 1980, for details).

MEDIAN WEALTH PLUMMETS OVER THE LATE 2000s

Fig. 1 documents a robust growth in wealth from 1983 to 2007, even back to 1962. From 1962 to 1983, median wealth in real terms increased at an

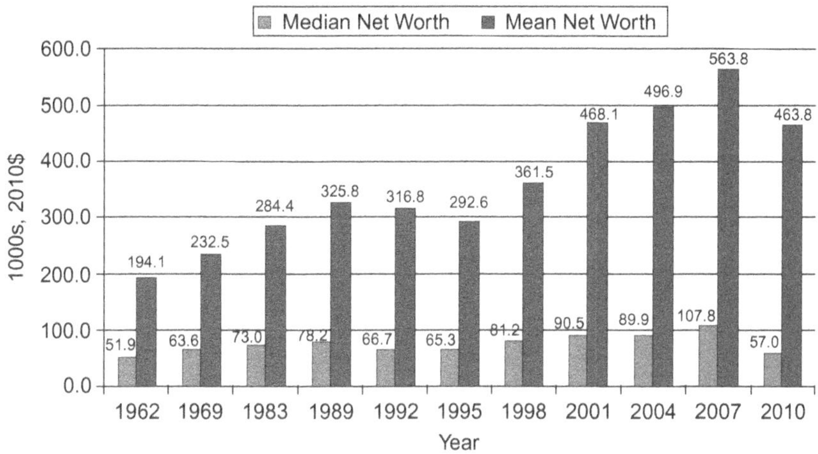

Fig. 1. Mean and Median Net Worth, 1962–2010.

annual rate of 1.63 percent. The annual growth rate fell a bit to 1.13 percent between 1983 and 1989, then rose to 1.32 percent between 1989 and 2001, and then to 2.91 percent from 2001 to 2007. Then between 2007 and 2010, median wealth plunged by a staggering 47 percent (in total)! Indeed, median wealth was actually lower in 2010 than in 1969 (in real terms). The primary reasons, as we shall see later, were the collapse in the housing market and the high leverage of middle-class families.[12]

Mean net worth also grew vigorously from 1962 to 1983, at an annual rate of 1.82 percent, then 2.27 percent from 1983 to 1989, 3.02 percent from 1989 to 2001, and 3.10 from 2001 to 2007. An important point of note is that mean wealth grew about twice as fast as the median between 1983 and 2007, indicating widening inequality of wealth over these years.

The Great Recession also saw an absolute decline in mean household wealth. However, whereas median wealth plunged by 47 percent, mean wealth fell by (only) 18 percent.[13] In this case, both falling housing and stock prices were the main causes. However, here, too, the relatively faster growth in mean wealth than median wealth (i.e., the latter's more moderate decline) was coincident with rising wealth inequality.

Median household income in real terms, based on the Current Population Survey (CPS), advanced at a fairly solid pace, by 20 percent, from 1962 to 1983 (see Fig. 2). Then, after gaining 11 percent between 1983 and 1989, it grew by only 2.3 percent from 1989 to 2001 and another 1.6 percent from 2001 to 2007. From 2007 to 2010, it fell off by 6.4 percent.

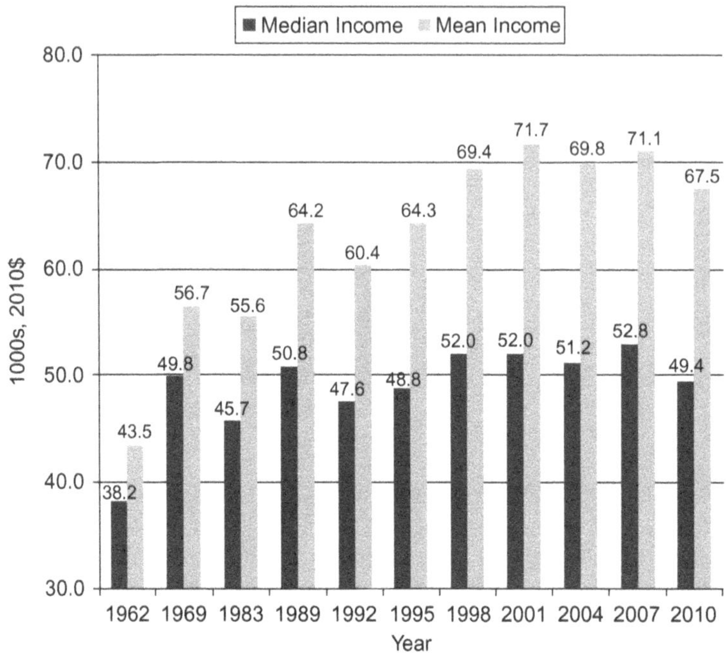

Fig. 2. Mean and Median Household Income, 1962–2010.

This reduction over the Great Recession was not nearly as great as that in median wealth. Mean income also dropped in real terms from 2007 to 2010, by 5.0 percent, slightly less than that of median income.

In sum, while median household income virtually stagnated for the average American household over the 1990s and 2000s, median net worth grew strongly over this period. From 2001 to 2007, mean and median income changed very little while mean and median net worth grew strongly. The Great Recession, on the other hand, saw a massive reduction in median net worth but much more modest declines in mean wealth and both median and mean income.

WEALTH INEQUALITY JUMPS IN THE LATE 2000s

The results in Fig. 3 show that wealth inequality in 1983 was quite close to its level in 1962. However, it then rose steeply between 1983 and 1989, with

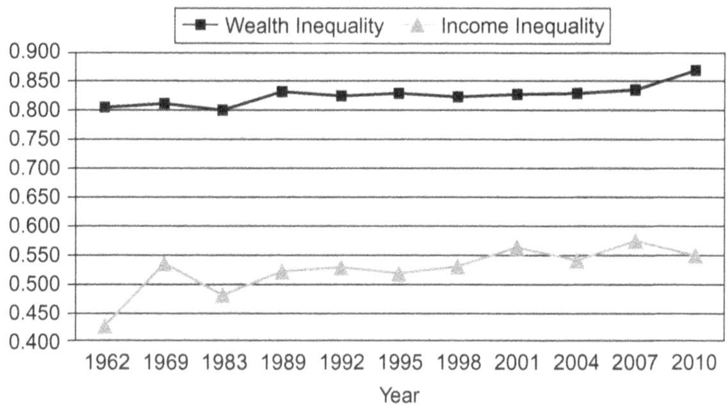

Fig. 3. Wealth and Income Inequality, 1962–2010 (Gini Coefficients).

the share of wealth held by the top 1 percent rising by 3.6 percentage points and the Gini coefficient increased from 0.80 to 0.83. What was behind the sharp rise in wealth inequality? There are two principal factors accounting for changes in wealth concentration (also see the section "The Role of Leverage"). The first is the change in income inequality and the second is the change in the ratio of stock prices to housing prices. As we shall see later, there was a huge increase in income inequality between 1983 and 1989, with the Gini coefficient rising by 0.041 points. Second, stock prices increased much faster than housing prices. The stock market boomed and the S&P 50 Index in real terms was up by 62 percent, whereas median home prices increased by a mere 2 percent in real terms. As a result, the ratio between the two climbed by 58 percent. Wealth inequality then remained virtually unchanged from 1989 to 2007, with a Gini coefficient of 0.832 in 1989 and 0.834 in 2007.

In contrast, the years of the Great Recession saw a very sharp elevation in wealth inequality, with the Gini coefficient rising from 0.83 to 0.87. Interestingly, the share of the top percentile showed less than a one percentage point gain. Most of the rise in wealth share took place in the remainder of the top quintile, and overall the share of wealth held by the top quintile climbed by almost four percentage points. The shares of the other quintiles, correspondingly, dropped, with the share of the bottom 20 percent falling from 0.2 percent to −0.9 percent.

The top 1 percent of families (as ranked by income on the basis of the SCF data) earned 17 percent of total household income in 2009 and the top

20 percent accounted for 59 percent – large figures but lower than the corresponding wealth shares.[14] The time trend for income inequality also contrasts with that for wealth inequality. Income inequality showed a sharp rise from 1961 to 1982, with the Gini coefficient expanding from 0.43 to 0.48 and the share of the top 1 percent from 8.4 to 12.8 percent.[15] Income inequality increased sharply again between 1982 and 1988, with the Gini coefficient rising from 0.48 to 0.52 and the share of the top 1 percent from 12.8 to 16.6 percent. There was then very little change between 1988 and 1997. However, between 1997 and 2000, income inequality again surged, with the share of the top percentile rising by 3.4 percentage points, the shares of the other quintiles falling again, and the Gini index advancing from 0.53 to 0.56.[16] This was followed by a modest uptick in income inequality, with the Gini coefficient advancing from 0.562 in 2000 to 0.574 in 2006. All in all, years 2001 to 2007 witnessed moderate rises in both wealth and income inequality.

Perhaps, somewhat surprisingly, the Great Recession witnessed a rather sharp contraction in income inequality. The Gini coefficient fell from 0.574 to 0.549 and the share of the top 1 percent dropped sharply from 21.3 to 17.2 percent. Property income and realized capital gains (which is included in the SCF definition of income), as well as corporate bonuses and the value of stock options, plummeted over these years, a process which explains the steep decline in the share of the top percentile. Real wages, as noted earlier, actually rose over these years, though the unemployment rate also increased. As a result, the income of the middle class was down but not nearly as much in percentage terms as that of the high-income groups. In contrast, transfer income such as unemployment insurance rose, so that the bottom also did better in relative terms than the top. As a result, overall income inequality fell over the years 2006–2009.[17] One of the puzzles we have to contend with is the fact wealth inequality rose sharply over the Great Recession while income inequality fell sharply. I will return to this question in the section "The Role of Leverage."

The Share of Overall Wealth Gains, 1983–2010

Over the years 1983–2010, the largest gains in wealth and income in relative terms were made by the wealthiest households (see Table 1). The top 1 percent saw their average wealth (in 2010 dollars) rise by 71 percent. The remaining part of the top quintile experienced increases from 52 to

Table 1. Mean Wealth Holdings and Income by Wealth or Income Class, 1983–2010 (in Thousands, 2010 Dollars).

Variable	Top 1.0%	Next 4.0%	Next 5.0%	Next 10.0%	Top 20.0%	4th 20.0%	3rd 20.0%	Bottom 40.0%	All
(A) *Net worth*									
1983	9,599	1,588	690.5	372.9	1,156.5	178.7	74.2	6.3	284.4
2010	16,439.4	3,192.5	1,263.4	567.0	2,061.6	216.9	61.0	−10.6	463.8
% change	71.3	101.1	83.0	52.1	78.3	21.4	−17.9	−269.7	63.1
% of gain[a]	38.1	35.8	16.0	10.8	100.7	4.3	−1.5	−3.8	100.0
(B) *Income*									
1982	827.1	213.7	132.7	99.6	167.1	69.7	45.6	19.9	64.4
2009	1,318.2	317.2	164.0	112.0	226.2	72.0	41.7	17.3	76.9
% change	59.4	48.4	23.6	12.5	35.4	3.3	−8.4	−12.9	19.3
% of gain[a]	39.4	41.6	12.7	10.1	103.7	3.6	−3.1	−4.1	100.0

Source: Own computations from the 1983 and 2010 SCF.
Notes: For the computation of percentile shares of net worth, households are ranked according to their net worth; and for percentile shares of income, households are ranked according to their income.
[a]The computation is performed by dividing the total increase in wealth of a given group by the total increase of wealth for all households over the period, under the assumption that the number of households in each group remains unchanged over the period. It should be noted that the households found in a given group (such as the top quintile) may be different in each year.

101 percent and the fourth quintile by 21 percent, while the middle quintile lost 18 percent and the poorest 40 percent lost 270 percent!

Another way of viewing this phenomenon is afforded by calculating the proportion of the total increase in real household wealth between 1983 and 2010 accruing to different wealth groups. This is computed by dividing the increase in total wealth of each percentile group by the total increase in household wealth, while holding constant the number of households in that group. If a group's wealth share remains constant over time, then the percentage of the total wealth growth received by that group will equal its share of total wealth. If a group's share of total wealth increases (decreases) over time, then it will receive a percentage of the total wealth gain greater (less) than its share in either year. However, it should be noted that in these calculations, the households found in a given group may be different in the two years.

The results indicate that the richest 1 percent received over 38 percent of the total gain in marketable wealth over the period from 1983 to 2010.

This proportion was greater than the share of wealth held by the top 1 percent in any of the 9 years. The next 4 percent received 36 percent of the total gain and the next 15 percent 27 percent, so that the top quintile collectively accounted for a little over 100 percent of the total growth in wealth.

A similar calculation using the SCF income data reveals that the greatest gains in real income over the period from 1982 to 2009 were made by households in the top 1 percent of the income distribution, who saw their incomes grow by 59 percent. Mean incomes increased by almost half for the next 4 percent, over a quarter for the next highest 5 percent and by 13 percent for the next highest 10 percent. The fourth quintile of the income distribution experienced only a 3 percent growth in income, while the middle quintile and the bottom 40 percent had absolute declines in mean income. Of the total growth in real income between 1982 and 2009, 39 percent accrued to the top 1 percent and over 100 percent to the top quintile. These figures are very close to those for wealth.

These results indicate rather dramatically that the growth in the economy during the period from 1983 to 2010 was concentrated in a surprisingly small part of the population – the top 20 percent and particularly the top 1 percent.

HOUSEHOLD DEBT CONTINUES TO REMAIN HIGH

In 2010, owner-occupied housing accounted for 31 percent of total assets (see Table 2). However, net home equity – the value of the house minus any outstanding mortgage – amounted to only 18 percent of total assets. Other real estate and business equity comprised 30 percent, liquid assets (demand and time deposits, money market funds, CDs, and the cash surrender value of life insurance) made up 6 percent and pension accounts 15 percent. Corporate stock, including mutual funds, amounted to 11 percent, while stocks directly or indirectly owned made up 18 percent. Debt as a proportion of gross assets was 17 percent, and the debt-equity ratio (the ratio of household debt to net worth) was 0.21.

There were some significant changes in the composition of household wealth over the years 1983–2010. First, the share of gross housing wealth in total assets increased from 30.1 percent in 1983 to 33.5 percent in 2004 and then fell off to 31.3 percent in 2010. There are two main factors behind this – the home ownership rate and housing prices. According to the SCF, the home ownership rate increased from 63.4 percent in 1983 to a peak of 68.6 percent in 2007 but then fell to 67.2 percent in 2010. Median house

Table 2. Composition of Total Household Wealth, 1983–2010 (Percent of Gross Assets).

Wealth Component	1983	1989	1992	1995	1998	2001	2004	2007	2010
Principal residence	30.1	30.2	29.8	30.4	29.0	28.2	33.5	32.8	31.3
Other real estate	14.9	14.0	14.7	11.0	10.0	9.8	11.5	11.3	11.8
Unincorporated business equity	18.8	17.2	17.7	17.9	17.7	17.2	17.1	20.1	18.0
Liquid assets[a]	17.4	17.5	12.2	10.0	9.6	8.8	7.3	6.6	6.2
Pension accounts	1.5	2.9	7.2	9.0	11.6	12.3	11.8	12.1	15.3
Financial securities	4.2	3.4	5.1	3.8	1.8	2.3	2.1	1.5	1.8
Corporate stock and mutual funds	9.0	6.9	8.1	11.9	14.8	14.8	11.9	11.8	11.4
Net equity in personal trusts	2.6	3.1	2.7	3.2	3.8	4.8	2.9	2.3	2.4
Miscellaneous assets	1.3	4.9	2.5	2.8	1.8	1.8	1.8	1.7	1.7
Total[b]	100.0	100.0	100.0	100.0	100.0	100.0	100.0	100.0	100.0
Debt on principal residence	6.3	8.6	9.8	11.0	10.7	9.4	11.6	11.4	12.9
All other debt	6.8	6.4	6.0	5.3	4.2	3.1	3.9	3.9	4.5
Total debt[b]	13.1	15.0	15.7	16.3	15.0	12.5	15.5	15.3	17.4
Selected ratios in percent									
Debt/equity ratio	15.1	17.6	18.7	19.4	17.6	14.3	18.4	18.1	21.0
Debt/income ratio	68.4	87.6	88.8	91.3	90.9	81.1	115.0	118.7	127.0
Net home equity/total assets	23.8	21.6	20.1	19.5	18.2	18.8	21.8	21.4	18.4
Principal residence debt as ratio to house value	20.9	28.6	32.7	36.0	37.0	33.4	34.8	34.9	41.2
Stocks, directly or indirectly owned as a ratio to total assets[c]	11.3	10.2	13.7	16.8	22.6	24.5	17.5	16.8	17.8

Source: Own computations from the 1983, 1989, 1992, 1995, 1998, 2001, 2004, 2007, and 2010 SCF.

[a]Checking accounts, savings accounts, time deposits, money market funds, certificates of deposits, and the cash surrender value of life insurance.

[b]Here and in subsequent tables totals may differ from the sum of individual components due to rounding error.

[c]Includes direct ownership of stock shares and indirect ownership through mutual funds, trusts, and IRAs, Keogh plans, 401(k) plans, and other retirement accounts.

prices for existing homes rose by 19 percent in real terms between 2001 and 2007 but then plunged by 26 percent from 2007 to 2010. A substantial share of the movement of the proportion of housing in gross assets can be traced to these two time trends.[18]

Second, net equity in owner-occupied housing as a share of total assets, after falling from 24 percent in 1983 to 19 percent in 2001, rose to

21 percent in 2007 but then declined to 18 percent in 2010. The difference between gross and net housing as a share of total assets can be traced to the changing magnitude of mortgage debt on homeowner's property, which increased almost continuously over time from 21 percent in 1983 to 41 percent in 2010. The decrease in net home equity as a proportion of assets from 2007 to 2010 is attributable to the sharp decline in housing prices.

Third, relative indebtedness increased, with the debt-equity ratio climbing from 15 percent in 1983 to 21 percent in 2010 and the ratio of debt to total income surging from 68 percent in 1983 to 127 percent in 2010, its high for this period. If mortgage debt on principal residence is excluded, the ratio of other debt to total assets actually fell off from 6.8 percent in 1983 to 4.5 percent in 2010. The rise in *relative* indebtedness between 2007 and 2010 could be due to a rise in the absolute level of debt and/or a fall off in net worth and income. As discussed in the section "Median Wealth Plummets over the Late 2000s," both mean net worth and mean income fell over the three years. There was also a slight contraction of debt in constant dollars, with mortgage debt declining by 5.0 percent, other debt by 2.6 percent, and total debt by 4.4 percent. Thus, the increase in the debt to equity ratio (3.1 percentage points) and the debt to income ratio (8.3 percentage points) over the three years was entirely due to the reduction in wealth and income.

A fourth change is a dramatic increase in pension accounts, which rose from 1.5 percent of total assets in 1983 to 15 percent in 2010. There was a huge increase in the share of households holding these accounts between 1983 and 2001, from 11 to 52 percent. The mean value of these plans in real terms climbed dramatically. It almost tripled among account holders and skyrocketed by a factor of 13.6 among all households. These time trends partially reflect the history of DC plans. IRAs were first established in 1974. This was followed by 401(k) plans in 1978 for profit-making companies (403(b) plans for non-profits are much older). However, 401(k) plans and the like did not become widely available in the workplace until about 1989.

From 2001 to 2007 the share of households with a DC plan leveled off and then from 2007 to 2010 the share fell modestly, from 52.6 to 50.4 percent. The average value of DC plans in constant dollars continued to grow after 2001. Overall, it advanced by 21 percent from 2001 to 2007 and then by 11 percent from 2007 to 2010 among account holders and by 22 percent and 7 percent, respectively, among all households. Thus, despite the stock market collapse of 2007–2010 and the 18 percent decline of overall mean net worth, the average value of DC accounts continued to grow after 2007.

The reason is that households shifted their portfolio out of other assets and into DC accounts.

Fifth, the value of stocks directly owned or indirectly owned through mutual funds, trusts, IRAs, 401(k) plans, and other retirement accounts as a share of total assets more than doubled from 11 percent in 1983 to 25 percent in 2001 but then tumbled to 18 percent in 2010. The rise during the 1990s reflected the bull market in corporate equities as well as increased stock ownership, while the decline in the 2000s was a result of the sluggish stock market as well as a drop in stock ownership.

Portfolio Composition by Wealth Class

The tabulation in Table 2 provides a picture of the average holdings of all families in the economy, but there are marked class differences in how middle-class families and the rich invest their wealth. As shown in Table 3, the richest 1 percent of households (as ranked by wealth) invested over three-quarters of their savings in investment real estate, businesses, corporate stock, and financial securities in 2010. Corporate stocks, either directly or indirectly owned, comprised 21 percent. Housing accounted for only 9 percent of their wealth, liquid assets 5 percent, and pension accounts 8 percent. The debt-equity ratio was only 3 percent and the ratio of debt to income was 61 percent.

Among the next richest 19 percent of U.S. households, housing comprised 30 percent of their total assets, liquid assets 7 percent, and pension assets 21 percent. Investment assets – non-home real estate, business equity, stocks, and bonds – made up 41 percent and 20 percent was in the form of stocks directly or indirectly owned. Debt amounted to 14 percent of their net worth and 118 percent of their income.

In contrast, almost exactly two-thirds of the wealth of the middle three quintiles of households was invested in their own home in 2010. However, home equity amounted to only 32 percent of total assets, a reflection of their large mortgage debt. Another 20 percent went into monetary savings of one form or another and pension accounts. Together housing, liquid assets, and pension assets accounted for 87 percent of total assets, with the remainder in investment assets. Stocks directly or indirectly owned amounted to only 8 percent of their total assets. The debt-equity ratio was 0.72, substantially higher than that for the richest 20 percent, and their ratio of debt to income was 1.35, also much higher than that of the top

Table 3. Composition of Household Wealth by Wealth Class, 2010 (Percent of Gross Assets).

Asset	All Households	Top 1 Percent	Next 19 Percent	Middle 3 Quintiles
Principal residence	31.3	9.4	30.1	66.6
Liquid assets (bank deposits, money market funds, and cash surrender value of life insurance)	6.2	5.5	6.8	5.9
Pension accounts	15.3	7.8	20.6	14.2
Corporate stock, financial securities, mutual funds, and personal trusts	15.7	25.4	14.9	3.1
Unincorporated business equity; other real estate	29.8	50.3	25.6	8.9
Miscellaneous assets	1.7	1.6	2.0	1.3
Total assets	100.0	100.0	100.0	100.0
Memo (selected ratios in percent)				
Debt/equity ratio	21.0	3.5	13.7	71.5
Debt/income ratio	127.0	60.6	117.9	134.5
Net home equity/total assets[a]	18.4	7.7	21.0	32.4
Principal residence debt/house value	41.2	18.9	30.1	51.3
All stocks/total assets[b]	17.8	20.6	20.1	8.2
Ownership rates (percent)				
Principal residence	67.2	98.1	96.3	68.4
Other real estate	18.6	75.1	48.9	12.4
Pension assets	50.4	90.2	82.7	45.8
Unincorporated business	12.1	74.1	30.3	8.1
Corporate stock, financial securities[c], mutual funds, and personal trusts	22.9	88.8	61.2	15.4
Stocks, directly or indirectly owned[b]	46.9	94.9	84.4	41.4
(1) $5,000 or more	35.5	94.3	79.7	29.4
(2) $10,000 or more	31.1	93.1	77.2	24.0

Source: Own computations from the 2010 SCF.

Notes: Households are classified into wealth class according to their net worth. Brackets for 2010 are: Top 1 percent: Net worth of $6,616,000 or more. Next 19 percent: Net worth between $373,000 and $6,616,000. Quintiles 2 through 4: Net worth between $0 and $373,000.

[a]Ratio of gross value of principal residence less mortgage debt on principal residence to total assets.

[b]Includes direct ownership of stock shares and indirect ownership through mutual funds, trusts, and IRAs, Keogh plans, 401(k) plans, and other retirement accounts.

[c]Financial securities exclude U.S. government savings bonds in this entry.

quintile. Finally, their mortgage debt amounted to a little more than half the value of their principal residences.

Almost all households among the top 20 percent of wealth holders owned their own home, in comparison to 68 percent of households in the middle three quintiles. Three-quarters of very rich households (in the top percentile) owned some other form of real estate, compared to 49 percent of rich households (those in the next 19 percent of the distribution) and only 12 percent of households in the middle 60 percent. Eighty-nine percent of the very rich owned some form of pension asset, compared to 83 percent of the rich and 46 percent of the middle. A somewhat startling 74 percent of the very rich reported owning their own business. The comparable figures are 30 percent among the rich and only 8 percent of the middle class.

Among the very rich, 95 percent reported owning stock either directly or indirectly, compared to 84 percent of the rich and 41 percent of the middle. If we exclude small holdings of stock, then the ownership rates drop off sharply among the middle three quintiles, from 41 percent to 29 percent for stocks worth $5,000 or more and to 24 percent for stocks worth $10,000 or more.

The rather staggering debt level of the middle class in 2010 raises the question of whether this is a recent phenomenon or whether it has been going on for some time. Table 4 shows the wealth composition for the middle three wealth quintiles from 1983 to 2010. Houses as a share of assets remained virtually unchanged from 1983 to 2001 but then increased from 2001 to 2010. It might seem surprising that despite the steep drop in home prices from 2007 to 2010, housing as a share of total assets actually increased slightly. The reason is that the other components of wealth fell even more than housing. While housing fell by 30 percent in real terms, other real estate was down by 39 percent, liquid assets by 48 percent, and stocks and mutual funds by 47 percent.

Pension accounts rose as a share of total assets by almost 13 percentage points from 1983 to 2010 while liquid assets declined as a share by 16 percentage points. This set of changes paralleled that of all households. The share of all stocks in total assets mushroomed from 2.4 percent in 1983 to 12.6 percent in 2001 and then fell off to 8.2 percent in 2010 as stock prices stagnated and then collapsed and middle-class households divested themselves of stock holdings. The proportion of middle-class households with a pension account surged by 41 percentage points between 1983 and 2007 but then fell off sharply by almost 8 percentage points in 2010.

Table 4. Composition of Household Wealth of the Middle Three Wealth Quintiles, 1983–2010 (Percent of Gross Assets).

Asset	1983	1989	1998	2001	2004	2007	2010
Principal residence	61.6	61.7	59.8	59.2	66.1	65.1	66.6
Liquid assets (bank deposits, money market funds, and cash surrender value of life insurance)	21.4	18.6	11.8	12.1	8.5	7.8	5.9
Pension accounts	1.2	3.8	12.3	12.7	12.0	12.9	14.2
Corporate stock, financial securities, mutual funds, and personal trusts	3.1	3.5	5.5	6.2	4.2	3.6	3.1
Unincorporated business equity; other real estate	11.4	9.4	8.8	8.5	7.9	9.3	8.9
Miscellaneous assets	1.3	2.9	1.8	1.2	1.4	1.3	1.3
Total assets	100.0	100.0	100.0	100.0	100.0	100.0	100.0
Memo (selected ratios in percent)							
Debt/equity ratio	37.4	41.7	51.3	46.4	61.6	61.1	71.5
Debt/income ratio	66.9	83.0	101.6	100.3	141.2	156.7	134.5
Net home equity/total assets[a]	43.8	39.2	33.3	33.8	34.7	34.8	32.4
Principal residence debt/house value	28.8	36.5	44.4	42.9	47.6	46.6	51.3
All stocks/total assets[b]	2.4	3.3	11.2	12.6	7.5	7.0	8.2
Ownership rates (percent)							
Principal residence	71.6	71.5	73.3	75.9	78.2	76.9	68.4
Other real estate	15.4	15.5	13.7	13.2	13.6	14.7	12.4
Pension assets	12.2	27.3	48.5	52.9	51.4	53.4	45.8
Unincorporated business	8.5	8.4	8.5	7.9	8.1	8.8	8.1
Corporate stock, financial securities[c], mutual funds, and personal trusts	21.6	24.2	26.7	27.5	27.1	23.1	15.4

Source: Own computations from the SCF.
Note: Households are classified into wealth class according to their net worth. Also, see notes to Table 3.
[a]Ratio of gross value of principal residence less mortgage debt on principal residence to total assets.
[b]Includes direct ownership of stock shares and indirect ownership through mutual funds, trusts, and IRAs, Keogh plans, 401(k) plans, and other retirement accounts.
[c]Financial securities exclude U.S. government savings bonds in this tabulation.

Changes in debt, however, represent the most dramatic movements. There was a sharp rise in the debt-equity ratio of the middle class from 0.37 in 1983 to 0.61 in 2007, with all of the increase occurring between 2001 and 2004, a reflection mainly of a steep rise in mortgage debt. The debt to income ratio more than doubled from 1983 to 2007. Once again, much of the increase happened between 2001 and 2004. The rise in the debt-equity ratio and the debt to income ratio was much steeper than for all households. In 1983, for example, the debt to income ratio was about the same for middle class as for all households, but by 2007 the ratio was much larger for the middle class.

Then, the Great Recession hit. The debt-equity ratio continued to rise, reaching 0.72 in 2010 but there was actually a retrenchment in the *debt to income* ratio, falling to 1.35 in 2010. The reason is that from 2007 to 2010, the mean debt of the middle class in constant dollars actually contracted by 25 percent. There was, in fact, a 23 percent reduction in mortgage debt as families paid down their outstanding balances, and an even larger drop in other debt of 32 percent as families paid off credit card balances and other forms of consumer debt. The steep rise in the debt-equity ratio of the middle class between 2007 and 2010 was due to the sharp drop in net worth, while the decline in the debt to income ratio was almost exclusively due to the sharp contraction of overall debt.

As for all households, the ratio of net home equity to assets fell for the middle class from 1983 to 2010 and mortgage debt as a proportion of house value rose. The decline in the ratio of net home equity to total assets between 2007 and 2010 was relatively small despite the steep decrease in home prices, a reflection of the sharp reduction in mortgage debt. On the other hand, the rise in the ratio of mortgage debt to house values was relatively large over these years because of the fall off in home prices.

The "Middle Class Squeeze"

Nowhere is the middle class squeeze more vividly demonstrated than in their rising debt. As noted earlier, the ratio of debt to net worth of the middle three wealth quintiles rose from 0.37 in 1983 to 0.46 in 2001 and then jumped to 0.61 in 2007. Correspondingly, their debt to income rose from 0.67 in 1983 to 1.00 in 2001 and then zoomed up to 1.57 in 2007. This new debt took two major forms. First, because housing prices went up over these years, families were able to borrow against the now enhanced value of their homes by refinancing their mortgages and by taking out home equity loans. In fact, mortgage debt on owner-occupied housing (principal residence only) as a proportion of total assets climbed from 29 percent in 1983 to 47 percent in 2007, and home equity as a share of total assets fell from 44 to 35 percent over these years. Second, because of their increased availability, families ran up huge debt on their credit cards.

Where did the borrowing go? Some have asserted that it went to invest in stocks. However, if this were the case, then stocks as a share of total assets would have increased over this period, which it did not (it fell from 13 to 7 percent between 2001 and 2007). Moreover, it did not go into other assets. In fact, the rise in housing prices almost fully explains the increase in the net worth of the middle class from 2001 to 2007. Of the $16,400 rise in median wealth, gains in housing prices alone accounted for $14,000 or 86 percent of the growth in wealth. Instead, it appears that middle-class households, experiencing stagnating incomes, expanded their debt in order to finance normal consumption expenditures.

The large build-up of debt set the stage for the financial crisis of 2007 and the ensuing Great Recession. When the housing market collapsed in 2007, many households found themselves "underwater," with larger mortgage debt than the value of their home. This factor, coupled with the loss of income emanating from the recession, led many home owners to stop paying off their mortgage debt. The resulting foreclosures led, in turn, to steep reductions in the value of mortgage-backed securities. Banks and other financial institutions holding such assets experienced a large decline in their equity, which touched off the financial crisis.

THE ROLE OF LEVERAGE IN EXPLAINING THE STEEP FALL IN MEDIAN WEALTH AND THE SHARP RISE IN WEALTH INEQUALITY OVER THE GREAT RECESSION

Two major puzzles emerge from the preceding analysis. The first is the steep plunge in median net worth between 2007 and 2010 of 47 percent. This happened despite a moderate drop in median income of 6.4 percent in real terms and steep but less steep declines in housing and stock prices of 24 and 26 percent in real terms, respectively.

The second is the steep increase of wealth inequality of 0.035 Gini points. It is surprising that wealth inequality rose so sharply, given that income inequality dropped by 0.025 Gini points (at least according to the SCF data) and the ratio of stock prices to housing prices was essentially unchanged. In fact, as shown by Wolff (2002), wealth inequality is positively related to the ratio of stock to house prices, since the former is heavily concentrated among the rich and the latter is the chief asset of the middle class.

A regression run of the share of wealth held by the top 1 percent of households (WLTH) on the share of income received by the top 5 percent of families (INC), and the ratio of the Standard and Poor 500 index to housing prices (RATIO), with 21 data points between 1922 and 1998, yields:

$$\underset{}{\text{WLTH}} = \underset{(0.9)}{5.10} + \underset{(4.2)}{1.27\,\text{INC}} + \underset{(2.5)}{0.26\,\text{RATIO}}, \quad R^2=0.64, \quad N=21 \qquad (1)$$

with t-ratios shown in parentheses. Both variables are statistically significant (INC at the 1 percent level and RATIO at the 5 percent level) and with the expected (positive) sign. Also, the fit is quite good, even for this simple model.

Changes in median wealth and wealth inequality from 2007 to 2010 can be explained to a large extent by leverage (the ratio of debt to net worth). The steep fall in median wealth was due in large measure to the high leverage of middle-class households. The spike in wealth inequality was largely due to *differential leverage* between the rich and the middle class.

Two Arithmetic Examples

A simple arithmetical example might illustrate the effects of leverage. Suppose average assets are 50 and average debt is zero. Also, suppose that asset prices rise by 20 percent. Then average net worth also rises by 20 percent. However, now suppose that average debt is 40 and asset prices once again rise by 20 percent. Then average net worth increases from a base of 10 (50 minus 40) to 20 (60 minus 40) or by *100 percent*. Thus, leverage amplifies the effects of asset price changes. However, the converse is also true. Suppose that asset prices decline by 20 percent. In the first case, net worth falls from 50 to 40 or by 20 percent. In the second case, net worth falls from 10 to 0 (40 minus 40) or by 100 percent. Thus, leverage can also magnify the effects of an asset price bust.

Another arithmetical example can illustrate the effects of differential leverage. Suppose the total assets of the very rich in a given year is 100, consisting of 50 in stocks and 50 in other assets, and its debt is zero, for a net worth of 100. For the "middle class," suppose total assets are 70, consisting of 60 in housing and 10 in other assets, and their debt is 30, for a net worth of 40. The ratio of net worth between the very rich and the middle is then 2.5 (100/40).

Suppose the value of both stocks and housing falls by 20 percent but the value of "other assets" remains unchanged. Then, the total assets of the rich fall to 90 (40 in stocks and 50 in other), for a net worth of 90. The total assets of the middle falls to 58 (48 in housing and 10 in other) but its debt remains unchanged at 30, for a net worth of 28. As a result, the ratio of net worth between the two groups *rises* to 3.21 (90/28). Here it is apparent that even though housing and stock prices fall at the *same rate*, wealth inequality goes up. The reason is differential leverage between the two groups. If asset prices decline at the same rate, net worth decreases at an even greater rate for the middle than the rich, since the debt-equity ratio is higher for the former than the latter. The converse is also true. A proportionate increase in house and stock prices will result in a decrease in wealth inequality.

Rates of Return

Fig. 4 shows estimated average annual real rates of return for both gross assets and net worth over the period from 1983 to 2010. Results are based

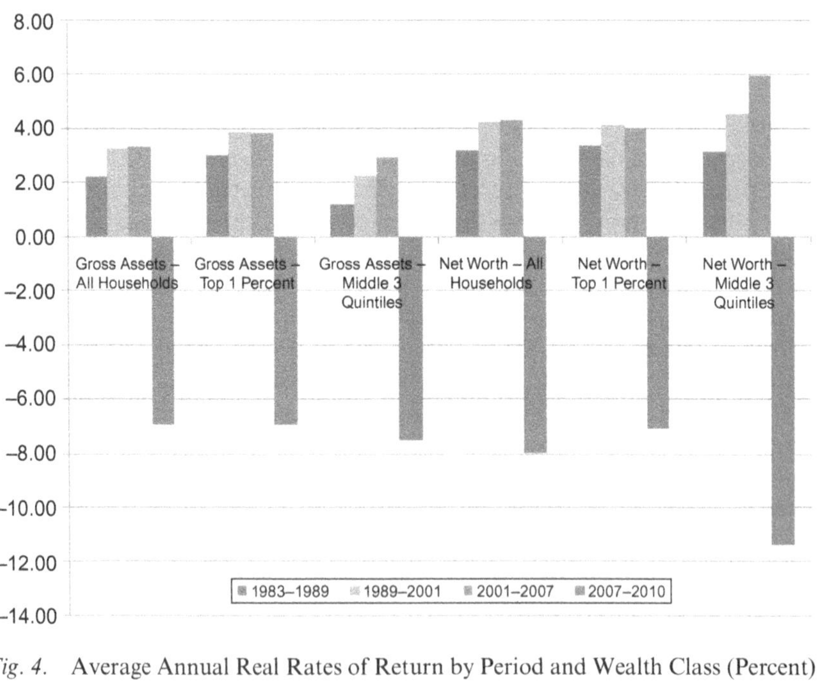

Fig. 4. Average Annual Real Rates of Return by Period and Wealth Class (Percent).

on the average portfolio composition over the period. It is first of interest to look at the results for all households. The overall average annual real rate of return on gross assets rose from 2.20 percent in the 1983–1989 period to 3.25 percent in the 1989–2001 period and then to 3.34 percent in the 2001–2007 period before plummeting to –6.95 percent over the Great Recession. The largest declines in asset prices over the years 2007–2010 occurred for residential real estate and the category businesses and non-home real estate. The value of financial assets, including stocks, bonds, and other securities, registered an annual rate of return of "only" –2.23 percent because interest rates on corporate and foreign bonds continued to remain strong over these years. The value of pension accounts had a –2.46 percent annual real rate of return, reflecting the mixture of bonds and stocks held in pension accounts.

The average annual real rate of return on net worth among all households also increased from 3.17 percent in the first period to 4.25 percent in the second and then to 4.31 percent in the third but then fell off sharply to –7.98 percent in the last period. It is first of note that the annual rates of return on net worth are uniformly higher – by about one percentage point – than those of gross assets over the first three periods, when asset prices were generally rising. However, in the 2007–2010 period, the opposite was the case, with the annual return on net worth 0.44 percent lower than that on gross assets. These results illustrate the effect of leverage, raising the return when asset prices rise and lowering the return when asset prices fall. Over the full 1983–2010 period, the annual return on net worth was 0.87 percentage points higher than that on gross assets.[19]

There are striking differences in returns by wealth class. The highest returns on gross assets were registered by the top 1 percent of wealth holders and the lowest by the middle three wealth quintiles. The differences are quite substantial. Over the full 1983–2010 period, the average annual rate of return on gross assets for the top 1 percent was 1.39 percentage points greater than that of the middle quintiles. The differences reflect the greater share of high yield investment assets like stocks in the portfolios of the rich and the greater share of housing in the portfolio of the middle class (see Table 3 for details on portfolio composition).

This pattern is almost exactly reversed for rates of return for net worth. In this case, in the first three periods when asset prices were generally rising, the highest return was recorded by the middle three wealth quintiles but in the 2007–2010 period, when asset prices were declining, the middle three quintiles registered the lowest (i.e., most negative) return. The exception was the first period when the top 1 percent had the highest return. The reason was the substantial spread in returns on gross assets between the top 1 percent and the middle three quintiles – 1.79 percentage points.

Differences in returns between the top 1 percent and the middle three quintiles were quite substantial in some years. In the 2001–2007 period, the return on net worth was 5.95 percent per year for the latter and 4.03 percent per year for the former – a difference of 1.92 percentage points. Over the Great Recession the rate of return on net worth was −7.10 percent for the top 1 percent and, astonishingly, −11.37 percent for the middle three quintiles – a differential of 4.27 percentage points. The spread in rates of return between the top 1 percent and the middle three quintiles reflects the much higher leverage of the middle class. In 2010, for example, the debt-equity ratio of the middle three quintiles was 0.72 while that of the top 1 percent was 0.04. Indeed, except for years 2007 to 2010, the rate of return on net worth for the middle quintiles was *more than double* its return on gross assets.

The huge negative rate of return on net worth of the middle three wealth quintiles was largely responsible for the precipitous drop in median net worth between 2007 and 2010. This factor, in turn, was due to the steep drop in asset prices, particularly housing, and the very high leverage of the middle wealth quintiles. Likewise, the very high rate of return on net worth of the middle three quintiles over the 2001–2007 period (5.95 percent per year) played a big role in explaining the robust advance of median net worth, despite the sluggish growth in median income. This in turn, was a result of their high leverage coupled with the boom in housing prices.

The substantial differential in rates of return on net worth between the middle three wealth quintiles and the top quintile (over four percentage points) helps explain why wealth inequality rose sharply between 2007 and 2010 despite the decline in income inequality. Likewise, this differential over the 2001–2007 period (a spread of about two percentage points in favor of the middle quintiles) helps account for the stasis in wealth inequality over these years despite the increase in income inequality.

THE RACIAL DIVIDE WIDENS OVER THE GREAT RECESSION

Striking differences are found in the wealth holdings of different racial and ethnic groups. In Tables 5 and 6, households are divided into three groups: (i) non-Hispanic whites ("whites" for short), (ii) non-Hispanic African-Americans ("blacks" for short), and (iii) Hispanics.[20] In 2007, while the

Table 5. Household Income and Wealth by Race, 1983–2010 (in Thousands, 2010 Dollars).

Year	Means			Medians		
	Whites	African-Americans	Ratio	Whites	African-Americans	Ratio
(A) *Income*						
1982	68.2	36.7	0.54	48.0	26.7	0.56
1988	74.7	33.2	0.45	49.7	18.9	0.38
2000	93.4	45.3	0.48	54.2	30.8	0.57
2006	97.1	46.9	0.48	52.6	31.6	0.60
2009	86.8	41.4	0.48	51.0	30.0	0.59
(B) *Net worth*						
1983	332.3	62.5	0.19	95.7	6.4	0.07
1989	393.2	65.9	0.17	113.6	2.9	0.03
2001	573.5	81.7	0.14	131.0	13.1	0.10
2007	685.8	129.0	0.19	151.1	9.7	0.06
2010	593.3	84.5	0.14	97.0	4.9	0.05
(C) *Home ownership rate (in percent)*						
1983	68.1	44.3	0.65			
1989	69.3	41.7	0.60			
2001	74.1	47.4	0.64			
2007	74.8	48.6	0.65			
2010	74.6	47.7	0.64			
(D) *Percent of households with zero or negative net worth*						
1983	11.3	34.1	3.01			
1989	12.1	40.7	3.38			
2001	13.1	30.9	2.35			
2007	14.5	33.4	2.30			
2010	18.6	33.9	1.83			

Source: Own computations from the 1983, 1989, 2001, 2007, and 2010 SCF.
Notes: Households are divided into four racial/ethnic groups: (i) non-Hispanic whites; (ii) non-Hispanic blacks; (iii) Hispanics; and (iv) American Indians, Asians, and others. For 2001, the classification scheme does not explicitly indicate non-Hispanic whites and non-Hispanic blacks for the first two categories so that some Hispanics may have classified themselves as either whites or blacks.

ratio of mean incomes between white and black households was an already low 0.48 and the ratio of median incomes was 0.60, the ratios of mean and median wealth holdings were even lower, at 0.19 and 0.06, respectively.[21] The home ownership rate for black households was 49 percent in 2007, a little less than two-thirds that among whites, and the share of black

Table 6. Family Income and Wealth for Non-Hispanic Whites and Hispanics, 1983–2010 (in Thousands, 2010 Dollars).

Year	Means			Medians		
	Non-Hispanic Whites	Hispanics	Ratio	Non-Hispanic Whites	Hispanics	Ratio
(A) *Income*						
1982	68.2	41.2	0.60	48.0	31.8	0.66
1988	74.7	34.0	0.46	49.7	23.8	0.48
2000	93.4	46.3	0.50	54.2	29.6	0.55
2006	97.1	48.8	0.50	52.6	36.8	0.70
2009	86.8	49.1	0.57	51.0	34.0	0.67
(B) *Net worth*						
1983	332.3	54.0	0.16	95.7	3.7	0.04
1989	393.2	64.7	0.16	113.6	2.4	0.02
2001	573.5	98.6	0.17	131.0	3.6	0.03
2007	685.8	179.2	0.26	151.1	9.6	0.06
2010	593.3	90.3	0.15	97.0	1.3	0.01
(C) *Home ownership rate (in percent)*						
1983	68.1	32.6	0.48			
1989	69.3	39.8	0.57			
2001	74.1	44.3	0.60			
2007	74.8	49.2	0.66			
2010	74.6	47.3	0.63			
(D) *Percent of households with zero or negative net worth*						
1983	11.3	40.3	3.01			
1989	12.1	39.9	3.38			
2001	13.1	35.3	2.69			
2007	14.5	33.5	2.30			
2010	18.6	35.8	1.93			

Source: Own computations from the 1983, 1989, 2001, 2007, and 2010 SCF.
Note: See the note to Table 5 for details on racial/ethnic categories.

households with zero or negative net worth stood at 33 percent, more than double that among whites.

Between 1982 and 2006, while the average real income of white households increased by 42 percent and the median by 10 percent, the former rose by only 28 percent for black households but the latter by 18 percent. As a result, the ratio of mean income slipped from 0.54 in 1982 to 0.48 in 2006, while the ratio of median income rose from 0.56 to 0.60.[22] The contrast in time trends between the ratio of means and that of medians reflects the huge increase in income for a relatively small number of white households – a result of rising income inequality among whites.

Between 1983 and 2001, average net worth in constant dollars climbed by 73 percent for whites but rose by only 31 percent for black households, so that the net worth ratio fell from 0.19 to 0.14. However, between 2001 and 2007, mean net worth among blacks gained an astounding 58 percent while white wealth advanced by 29 percent, so that by 2007 the net worth ratio was back to 0.19, the same level as in 1983.

It is not clear how much of the sharp drop in the racial wealth gap between 1998 and 2001 and the turnaround between 2001 and 2007 is due to actual wealth changes in the African-American community and how much is due to sampling variability (since the sample sizes of African-Americans are relatively small in all years). However, one salient difference between the two groups is the much higher share of stocks in the white portfolio and the much higher share of homes in the portfolio of black households. In 2001, the gross value of principal residences formed 46 percent of the total assets of black households, compared to 27 percent among whites, while (total) stocks were 25 percent of the total assets of whites and only 15 percent that of black households. In the case of median wealth, the black-white ratio fluctuated over time but was almost exactly the same in 2007 as in 1983, 0.06 compared to 0.07.

The home ownership rate of black households grew from 44 to 48 percent between 1983 and 2007 and relative to white households, the ratio of home ownership rates stayed at 0.65. The share of black households with zero or negative net worth fell slightly from 34 percent in 1983 to 33 percent in 2007.

The picture is rather different for Hispanics (see Table 6). The ratio of mean income between Hispanics and non-Hispanic whites in 2007 was 0.50, almost the same as that between black and white households. However, the ratio of median income was 0.70, much higher than the ratio between black and white households. The ratio of mean net worth was 0.26 compared to a ratio of 0.19 between blacks and whites. However, the ratio of medians was 0.06, almost identical to that between blacks and whites. The Hispanic home ownership rate was 49 percent, almost identical to that of black households, and 34 percent of Hispanic households reported zero or negative wealth, almost the same as African-Americans.

Hispanic households made considerable progress over the years1983 to 2007. Mean income grew by 18 percent and median income by 16 percent, so that while the ratio of mean income slid from 60 to 50 percent, that of median income advanced from 66 to 70 percent. Between 1983 and 2001, mean wealth doubled for Hispanic households and the ratio of mean net worth increased slightly from 16 to 17 percent. Mean net worth among Hispanics then climbed by another 82 percent between 2001 and 2007, and the corresponding ratio advanced to 26 percent, quite a bit higher than that between black and white households. The surge in Hispanic wealth from 2001 to 2007 can be traced to a five percentage point jump in the Hispanic home ownership rate (see below).

From 1983 to 2007, median wealth among Hispanics remained largely unchanged, so that the ratio of median wealth between Hispanics and whites stayed virtually the same. In contrast, the home ownership rate among Hispanic households surged from 33 to 44 percent between 1983 and 2001, and the ratio of home ownership rates between the two groups grew from 0.48 in 1983 to 0.60 in 2001. Between 2001 and 2007, the Hispanic home ownership rose once again, to 49 percent, about the same as black households, and the home ownership ratio rose sharply to 0.66. The percentage of Hispanic households with zero or negative net worth fell rather steadily over time, from 40 percent in 1983 to 34 percent in 2007 (about the same as black households), and the share relative to white household tumbled from a ratio of 3.0 to 2.3.

Despite some progress from 2001 to 2007, the respective wealth gaps between minorities and whites were still much greater than the corresponding income gaps in 2007. While mean income ratios were of the order of 50 percent, mean wealth ratios were of the order of 20–25 percent and the share with zero or negative net worth was around a third, in contrast to 15 percent among white households (a difference that appears to mirror the gap in poverty rates). While blacks and Hispanics were left out of the wealth surge of the years 1989 to 2001 because of relatively low stock ownership, they actually benefited from this (and the relatively high share of houses in their portfolio) in the 2001–2007 period. However, all three racial/ethnic groups saw an increase in their debt to asset ratio from 2001 to 2007.

The racial picture really changed radically by 2010. While the ratio of both mean and median income between black and white households changed very little between 2007 and 2010 (mean income, in particular, declined for both groups), the ratio of mean net worth dropped from 0.19 to 0.14. The proximate causes were the higher leverage of black households and their higher share of housing wealth in gross assets (see Table 7). In 2007, the debt-equity ratio among blacks was an astounding 0.55, compared to 0.15 among whites, while housing as a share of gross assets was 0.54 for the former as against 0.31 for the latter. The ratio of

Table 7. Composition of Household Wealth by Race and Ethnicity, 2007 (Percent of Gross Assets).

Asset	Non-Hispanic Whites	African-Americans	Hispanics
Principal residence	30.8	54.0	52.5
Liquid assets (bank deposits, money market funds, and cash surrender value of life insurance)	6.6	7.6	3.9
Pension accounts	12.5	12.3	7.7
Corporate stock, financial securities, mutual funds, and personal trusts	17.1	3.4	2.5
Unincorporated business equity; other real estate	31.3	20.9	32.9
Miscellaneous assets	1.7	1.8	0.4
Total assets	100.0	100.0	100.0
Memo (selected ratios in percent)			
Debt/equity ratio	15.4	55.3	51.1
Debt/income ratio	109.0	152.2	187.9
Net home equity/total assets[a]	20.8	27.3	28.8
Principal residence debt/house value	32.4	49.4	45.2
All stocks/total assets[b]	18.3	5.0	5.1
Annual rate of return on net worth (in percent)			
2001–2007	4.14	6.35	6.74
2007–2010	−7.74	−10.90	−11.82

Source: Own computations from the 2007 SCF.
[a]Ratio of gross value of principal residence less mortgage debt on principal residence to total assets.
[b]Includes direct ownership of stock shares and indirect ownership through mutual funds, trusts, and IRAs, Keogh plans, 401(k) plans, and other retirement accounts.

mortgage debt to home value was also much higher for blacks, 0.49, than for whites, 0.32. The sharp drop in home prices from 2007 to 2010 thus led to a relatively steeper loss in home equity for the former, 25 percent, than the latter, 21 percent, and this factor, in turn, led to a much steeper fall in mean net worth for black households than white households.[23] Indeed, in terms of rates of return, while the overall annual real rate of return on net worth among white households plummeted from 4.1 percent in the 2001–2007 period to −7.7 percent in the 2007–2010 period, it collapsed from 6.4 percent to −10.9 percent among black households. It is of note that black households had a much higher return on net worth than white households in the 2001–2007 period but a much lower return in 2007–2010.

The Great Recession actually hit Hispanic households much harder than blacks in terms of wealth. The mean net worth in 2010 dollars of Hispanics fell almost *in half*, and the ratio of this to the mean wealth of whites plummeted from 0.26 to 0.15. The same factors were responsible as in the case of black households. In 2007, the debt-equity ratio for Hispanics was 0.51, compared to 0.15 among whites, while housing as a share of gross assets was 0.53 for the former as against 0.31 for the latter (see Table 7). The ratio of mortgage debt to home value was also higher for Hispanics, 0.45, than for whites, 0.32. As a result, net home equity dropped by 48 percent among Hispanic home owners, compared to 21 percent among white home owners, and this factor, in turn, was largely responsible for the huge decline in Hispanic net worth both in absolute and relative terms. In terms of the real annual return on net worth, it nosedived from 6.7 percent in years 2001 to 2007 to −11.8 percent in years 2007 to 2010. The drop was even steeper than that for black households. In fact, while Hispanic households had a higher return than white or black households in 2001–2007, it had the lowest return in 2007–2010.

There are two reasons that might explain the extreme drop in Hispanic net worth. First, a large proportion of Hispanic home owners bought their home in the interval from 2001 to 2007, when home prices were peaking. This is reflected in the sharp increase in their home ownership rate over this period. As a result, they suffered a disproportionately large percentage drop in their home equity. Second, it is likely that Hispanic home owners were more heavily concentrated than whites in parts of the country like Arizona, California, Arizona, and Nevada (the "sand states") and Florida, where home prices plummeted the most.

There was also a steep drop in the home ownership rate among Hispanic households of 1.9 percentage points from 2007 to 2010. Indeed, after catching up on white households in this dimension from 1983 to 2007, Hispanic households fell back in 2010 to the same level as in 2004.

WEALTH SHIFTS FROM THE YOUNG TO THE OLD

As shown in Table 8, the cross-sectional age-wealth profiles generally follow the predicted hump-shaped pattern of the life-cycle model (also see Fig. 5). Mean wealth increases with age up through age 65 or so and then falls off. Home ownership rates have a similar profile, though the fall-off after the peak age is much more attenuated than for the wealth numbers

Table 8. Age-Wealth Profiles and Home Ownership Rates by Age, 1983–2010.

Age	1983	1989	1992	1995	1998	2001	2004	2007	2010
(A) *Mean net worth (ratio to overall mean)*									
Under 35	0.21	0.29	0.20	0.16	0.22	0.19	0.14	0.17	0.10
35–44	0.71	0.72	0.71	0.65	0.68	0.64	0.65	0.58	0.41
45–54	1.53	1.50	1.42	1.39	1.27	1.25	1.21	1.19	1.14
55–64	1.67	1.58	1.82	1.81	1.91	1.86	1.91	1.69	1.81
65–74	1.93	1.61	1.59	1.71	1.68	1.72	1.57	1.86	1.74
75 and over	1.05	1.26	1.20	1.32	1.12	1.20	1.19	1.16	1.36
(B) *Home ownership rate (in percent)*									
Overall	63.4	62.8	64.1	64.7	66.3	67.7	69.1	68.6	67.2
Under 35	38.7	36.3	36.8	37.9	39.2	40.2	41.5	40.8	37.5
35–44	68.4	64.1	64.4	64.7	66.7	67.6	68.6	66.1	63.8
45–54	78.2	75.1	75.5	75.4	74.5	76.1	77.3	77.3	75.2
55–64	77.0	79.2	77.9	82.3	80.6	83.2	79.1	80.9	78.1
65–74	78.3	78.1	78.8	79.4	81.7	82.5	81.2	85.5	82.5
75 and over	69.4	70.2	78.1	72.5	76.9	76.2	85.1	77.0	81.3

Source: Own computations from the 1983, 1989 1992, 1995, 1998, 2001, 2004, 2007, and 2010 SCF.
Note: Households are classified according to the age of the householder.

(and in 2004 they actually show a steady rise with age). In 2010, the wealth of elderly households (age 65 and over) was 2.1 times as high as that of the non-elderly and their home ownership rate was 19 percentage points higher. Despite the apparent similarity in the profiles, there were notable shifts in the relative wealth holdings by age group from 1983 to 2007. The relative wealth of the youngest age group, under 35 years of age, declined from 21 percent of the overall mean in 1983 to 17 percent in 2007. In 2007, the mean wealth of the youngest age group was $95,900 (in 2010 dollars), which was only slightly more than the mean wealth of this age group in 1989 ($93,100). Though as noted in the section "Introduction," educational loans expanded markedly over the 2000s and by 2007 one-third of households in this age group reported a student loan outstanding, still 74 percent of the total debt of this age group was mortgage debt and only 10 percent took the form of student loans.

The mean net worth of the next youngest age group, 35–44, relative to the overall mean, collapsed from 0.71 in 1983 to 0.58 in 2007. The relative wealth of the next youngest age group, 45–54, also declined, from 1.53 in

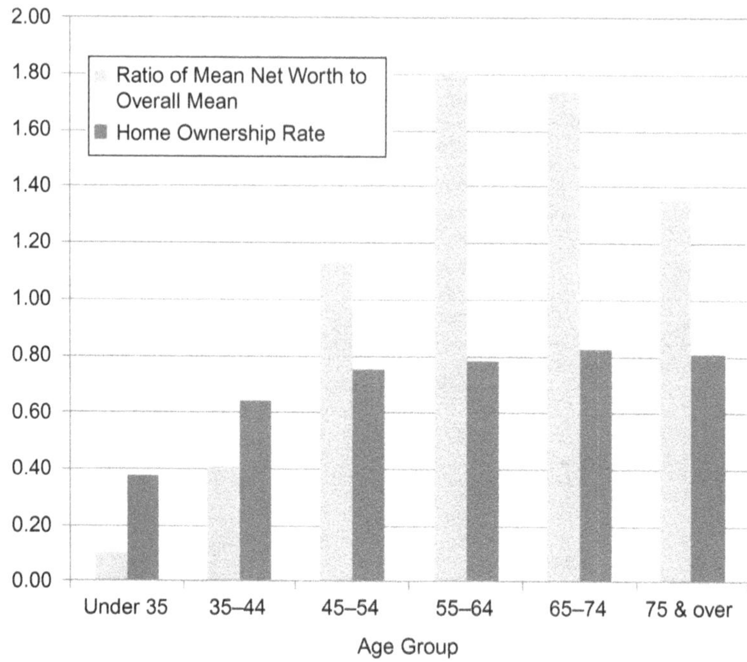

Fig. 5. Household Net Worth and Home Ownership Rate by Age Group, 2010.

1983 to 1.19 in 2007. The relative wealth of age group 55–64 was about the same in 2007, 1.69, as in 1983, 1.67. The relative net worth of age group 65–74 plummeted from 1.93 in 1983 to 1.61 in 1989 but recovered to 1.86 in 2007. The wealth of the oldest age group, age 75 and over, gained ground, from only 5 percent above the mean in 1983 to 16 percent in 2007.

Changes in home ownership rates tend to mirror these trends. While the overall ownership rate increased by 5.2 percentage points from 63.4 to 68.6 percent between 1983 and 2007, the share of households in the youngest age group owning their own home increased by only 2.1 percentage points. The home ownership rate of households between 35 and 44 of age actually fell by 2.3 percentage points, and that of age group 45–54 years declined by 0.9 percentage points. Big gains in home ownership were recorded by the older age groups: 3.9 percentage points for age group 55–64, 7.1 percentage points for age group 65–74, and 7.6 percentage points for the oldest age group.[24] The statistics point to a relative shifting of home ownership away from younger towards older households between 1983 and 2007.

Changes in relative wealth were even more dramatic from 2007 to 2010. The relative wealth of the under 35 age group plummeted from 0.17 to 0.10 and that of age group 35–44 from 0.58 to 0.41, while that of age group 45–54 fell somewhat from 1.19 to 1.14. In actual (2010) dollar terms, the average wealth of the youngest age group collapsed from $95,500 in 2007 to $48,400 in 2010, is second lowest point over the 27 year period (the lowest occurred in 1995),[25] while the relative wealth of age group 35–44 shrank from $325,00 to $190,000, its lowest point over the whole 1983 to 2010 period. One possible reason for these steep declines in wealth is that younger households were more likely to have bought homes near the peak of the housing cycle.

In contrast, the relative net worth of age group 55–64 increased sharply from 1.69 to 1.81 (though it shrank in actual 2010 dollar terms from $950,400 to $841,000) and that of the oldest age group from 1.16 to 1.36 (though once again it was down in absolute terms from $653,700 to $629,100), while the relative wealth of age group 65 to 74 declined from 1.86 to 1.74 (and fell in absolute dollars as well, from $1,048,600 to $808,500). Home ownership rates fell for all age groups from 2007 to 2010 (except the very oldest) but the percentage point decline (3.3 percentage points) was greatest for the youngest age group.

Changes in the relative wealth position of different age groups depend in large measure on relative asset price movements and differences in asset composition. The latter are highlighted in Table 9 for the year 2007. Homes comprised over half the value of total assets for age group 35 and under, and the share fell off with age to about a quarter for age group 55–64 and then rose to 30 percent for the oldest age group. Liquid assets as a share of total assets remained relatively flat with age group at around 6 percent except for the oldest group for whom it was 11 percent, perhaps reflecting the relative financial conservativeness of older people. Pension accounts as a share of total assets rose from 4 percent for the youngest group to 16 percent for age group 55–64 and then fell off to 5 percent for the oldest age group. This pattern reflects the build-up of retirement assets until retirement age and then a decline as these retirement assets are liquidated.[26] Corporate stock and financial securities showed a steady rise with age, from a 4 percent share for the youngest group to a 26 percent share for the oldest. A similar pattern was evident for total stocks as a percentage of all assets. Unincorporated business equity and non-home real estate were relatively flat as a share of total assets with age, about 30 percent. There was a pronounced fall off of the debt-equity ratio with age, declining from 0.93 for the youngest group to 0.02 for the oldest, as well as the debt to income ratio

Table 9. Composition of Household Wealth by Age Class, 2007 (Percent of Gross Assets).

Asset	All	Under 35	35–44	45–54	55–64	65–74	75 and over
Principal residence	32.8	54.3	43.7	33.8	25.6	28.2	30.2
Liquid assets (bank deposits, money market funds, and cash surrender value of life insurance)	6.6	5.7	5.4	6.4	6.3	6.1	10.5
Pension accounts	12.1	6.0	10.7	13.0	15.8	12.9	5.0
Corporate stock, financial securities, mutual funds, and personal trusts	15.5	4.2	8.6	13.1	16.4	20.5	25.6
Unincorporated business equity; other real estate	31.3	28.7	30.1	32.0	34.4	30.2	27.1
Miscellaneous assets	1.7	1.2	1.5	1.7	1.5	2.1	1.6
Total assets	100.0	100.0	100.0	100.0	100.0	100.0	100.0
Memo (selected ratios in percent)							
Debt/equity ratio	18.1	92.7	41.3	20.2	11.9	7.1	2.1
Debt/income ratio	118.7	167.5	156.5	118.2	100.0	79.7	29.9
Net home equity/total assets[a]	21.4	18.8	21.3	20.9	18.1	23.4	28.7
Principal residence debt/house value	34.9	65.4	51.4	38.3	29.2	16.9	4.9
All stocks/total assets[b]	16.8	5.9	11.2	15.1	19.4	21.5	20.0
Annual rate of return on net worth (in percent)							
2001–2007	4.31	8.12	5.92	4.56	4.00	3.62	2.64
2007–2010	−7.98	−15.00	−10.53	−8.36	−7.38	−7.07	−6.72

Source: Own computations from the 2007 SCF.
Note: Households are classified into age class according to the age of the household head.
[a]Ratio of gross value of principal residence less mortgage debt on principal residence to total assets.
[b]Includes direct ownership of stock shares and indirect ownership through mutual funds, trusts, and IRAs, Keogh plans, 401(k) plans, and other retirement accounts.
[c]Financial securities exclude U.S. government savings bonds in this tabulation.

from 1.68 to 0.30 and mortgage debt as a share of house value from 0.65 to 0.05. As a result of the latter, net home equity as a proportion of total assets rose from 19 to 29 percent from the youngest to oldest age group.

Younger households were thus more heavily invested in homes and more heavily in debt, whereas the portfolio of older households was more heavily skewed to financial assets, particularly corporate stock. As a result, younger households benefit relatively when housing prices rise and inflation is strong while older households benefit relatively from rising stock prices. Changes in the relative net worth position of age groups over the 1983–2007 period were thus largely due to these relative asset price movements. In particular, as with minority households, the higher leverage of younger age groups made them vulnerable when asset prices, particularly housing prices, declined. The steep decline in house prices from 2007 to 2010 thus led to a relatively steeper loss in home equity for the youngest age group, 59 percent, than overall, 26 percent, and this factor, in turn, led to a much steeper fall in net worth. Indeed, the annual real return on the net worth of this age group nosedived from a considerable 8.1 percent in the 2001–2007 period, the highest of any age group, to −15.0 percent(!) in the 2007–2010 period, the lowest of any age group.

The story is very similar for age group 35–44. Their debt-equity ratio was 0.41 in 2007, their ratio of mortgage debt to house value was 0.51, and their share of housing in gross assets was 0.44, all much higher than overall. As with the youngest age group, the drop in home prices from 2007 to 2010 caused a large fall in home equity of 49 percent, which in turn caused a steep fall off in their relative net worth. The annual rate of return on net worth for this group tumbled from 5.9 percent in years 2001 to 2007, the second highest of any age group, to −10.5 percent in years 2007 to 2010, the second lowest of any age group.

SUMMARY AND CONCLUDING REMARKS

Median wealth showed robust growth during the 1980s and 1990s and an even faster advance from 2007 to 2010. Then the Great Recession hit. From 2007 to 2010, house prices fell by 24 percent in real terms, stock prices by 26 percent, and median wealth by a staggering 47 percent. Median income also dropped but by a relatively modest 6.4 percent. The percent of households with non-positive net worth rose sharply from 18.6 to 22.5.

Wealth inequality after remaining relatively stable from 1989 to 2007 showed a steep increase over the Great Recession. The Gini coefficient climbed from 0.834 to 0.870 and the share of the top 20 percent from 85 to 89 percent. The share of the bottom 40 percent experienced a precipitous drop from 0.2 to −0.9 percent. In contrast, income inequality, after rising moderately from 2000 to 2007 (an increase of 0.012 Gini points), dropped substantially from 2006 to 2009 (a decrease of 0.025 Gini points).

The percentage increase in net worth (also income) from 1983 to 2010 was much greater for the top wealth (and income) groups than for those lower in the distribution. The greatest gains were enjoyed by the upper 20 percent, particularly the top 1 percent, of the respective distributions. Between 1983 and 2010, the top 1 percent received 38 percent of the total growth in net worth and 39 percent of the total increase in income. The figures for the top 20 percent are 101 percent and 104 percent, respectively – that is to say, the upper quintile got it all!.

The years 2001 to 2007 also saw a sharply rising debt to income ratio, reaching its highest level in almost 25 years, at 1.19 among all households in 2007. The debt-equity ratio was also way up, from 0.14 to 0.18. Most of the rising debt was from increased mortgages on homes. From 2007 to 2010 both ratios rose, the former moderately from 1.19 to 1.27 and the latter more steeply from 0.18 to 0.21. This was true despite a moderate retrenchment of overall average debt of 4.4 percent and reflected the drop in both mean wealth and income.

Home values as a share of total assets among all households remained relatively unchanged from 1983 to 2010 (around 30 percent). However, net home equity as a share of total assets fell from 0.24 in 1983 to 0.18 in 2010, reflecting rising mortgage debt on homeowner's property, which grew from 21 percent in 1983 to 35 percent in 2007 and then jumped to 41 percent in 2010. The large increase in the ratio from 2007 to 2010 was a result of falling home values (average mortgage debt actually declined by 5.0 percent in absolute terms).

Trends are more pronounced for the middle class. Among the middle three wealth quintiles, there was a huge increase in the debt-income ratio from 1.00 in 2001 to 1.57 in 2007 and an almost doubling of the debt-equity ratio from 0.32 to 0.61 percent. The debt-equity ratio was also much higher among the middle 60 percent of households in 2007, at 0.61, than among the top 1 percent (0.028) or the next 19 percent (0.121). However, from 2007 to 2010, while the debt-equity ratio continued to advance to 0.72, the debt to income ratio actually fell off to 1.35. The reason is the substantial retrenchment of average debt among the middle class over these years. Overall debt fell by 25 percent in real terms, mortgage debt by 23 percent, and other debt by 32 percent. The fact that the debt-equity ratio rose over these years was a reflection of the steep drop in median net worth.

Despite the 24 percent plunge in house prices (in real terms) from 2007 to 2010, the share of home owners who were "underwater" was "only" 8.2 percent in 2010. However, average home equity among home owners did decline by 26 percent. This reduction would have been higher except for the contraction of mortgage debt noted earlier. Hispanics, younger households, and middle income households were hit particularly hard in terms of the loss of home equity.

The key to understanding the plight of the middle class over the Great Recession was their high degree of leverage and the high concentration of assets in their home. The steep decline in median net worth between 2007 and 2010 was primarily due to the very high negative real rate of return on net worth among the middle three wealth quintiles (−8.9 percent per year). This, in turn, was attributable to the precipitous fall in home prices and their very high degree of leverage. High leverage, moreover, helps explain why median wealth fell more than house (and stock) prices over these years and declined much more than median household income.

The large spread in rates of return on net worth between the middle three wealth quintiles and the top quintile (over a point and a half lower) also largely explained why wealth inequality increased steeply from 2007 to 2010 despite the decline in income inequality. Indeed, the middle class took a bigger relative hit on their net worth from the decline in home prices than the top 20 percent did from the stock market plunge. This factor is also reflected in the fact that median wealth dropped much more in percentage terms than mean wealth over the Great Recession.

The racial disparity in wealth holdings, after fluctuating over the years from 1983 to 2007, was almost exactly the same in 2007 as in 1983. However, the Great Recession hit black households much harder than whites and the ratio of mean wealth between the two groups plunged from 0.19 in 2007 to 0.14 in 2010, mainly due to a 34 percent decline (in real terms) in African-American wealth. The relative (and absolute) losses suffered by black households from 2007 to 2010 are ascribable to the fact that blacks had a higher share of homes in their portfolio than did whites and much higher debt-equity ratios (0.55 and 0.15, respectively).

Hispanic households made sizeable gains on (non-Hispanic) white households from 1983 to 2007. The ratio of mean net worth grew from 0.16 to 0.26 and the home ownership rate among Hispanic households climbed from 33 to 49 percent. However, in a reversal of fortunes, Hispanic households got hammered by the Great Recession. Their mean net worth plunged in half, the ratio of mean net worth with white households fell from 0.26 to 0.15, their home ownership rate fell by 1.9 percentage points, and their net home equity plummeted by 48 percent. The relative (and absolute) losses suffered by Hispanic households over these three years are also mainly due to the much larger share of homes in their wealth portfolio and their much higher debt-equity ratio (0.51 vs. 0.15). Another likely factor is that a high percentage of Hispanics bought their homes close to the housing cycle peak.

Young households also got pummeled by the Great Recession. The ratio of net worth between households under age 35 and all households fell from 0.21 in 1983 to 0.17 in 2007 and then plunged to 0.10 in 2010. In (real) dollar terms, their mean net worth declined by 49 percent from 2007 to 2010. Among age group 35–44, the ratio of their net worth to the overall figure fell from 0.71 in 1983 to 0.58 in 2007 and then declined precipitously to 0.41 in 2010. In dollar terms, their wealth fell by 42 percent over the latter three years. The same two factors explain the losses suffered by young households – the higher share of homes in their wealth portfolio and their much higher leverage ratios.

NOTES

1. The source for housing price data, unless otherwise indicated, is Table 935 of the *2009 Statistical Abstract*, US Bureau of the Census, available at http://www.census.gov/compendia/statab/

2. The source is National Association of Realtors, "Median Sales Price of Existing Single-Family Homes for Metropolitan Areas," available at http://www.realtor.org/sites/default/files/reports/2012/embargoes/2012-q1-metro-home-prices-49bc10b1efdc1b8cc3eb66dbcdad55f7/metro-home-prices-q1-single-family-2012-05-09.pdf

3. The source for stock price data is Table B-96 of the *Economic Report of the President, 2012*, available at http://www.gpoaccess.gov/eop/tables12.html

4. The wage figures are based on the Bureau of Labor Statistics (BLS) hourly wage series. The source is Table B-47 of the *Economic Report of the President, 2012*, available at op. cit. The source for the income data is Table B-33 of the *Economic Report of the President, 2012*, available at op. cit.

5. The figure is for civilian employment. The source is Table B-36 of the *Economic Report of the President, 2012*, available at op. cit.

6. The source is Table B-42 of the *Economic Report of the President, 2012*, available at op. cit.

7. These figures are based on the Federal Reserve Board's Flow of Funds data, Table B.100, available at http://www.federalreserve.gov/releases/Z1/

8. Unfortunately, no data on educational loans are available in the 2001 SCF.

9. The computation of DB pension wealth is based on the present value of expected pension benefits upon retirement (see Wolff, 2011b, for details).

10. Another rationale is that if cars are included in the household portfolio, their "rate of return" would be substantially negative since cars depreciate very rapidly over time (see the section "The Racial Divide Widens over the Great Recession" for calculations of the overall rate of return on the household portfolio).

11. See Wolff (2011b) for estimates of Social Security and pension wealth.

12. The percentage decline in net worth from 2007 to 2010 is lower when vehicles are included in the measure of wealth – "only" 39 percent. The reason is that automobiles comprise a substantial portion of middle class wealth.

13. The decline in mean net worth is 15 percent when vehicles are included in net worth.

14. It should be noted that the income in each survey year (say 2007) is for the preceding year (2006 in this case).

15. The 1969 MESP data suggest a huge expansion in income inequality from 1962 to 1969, but it is likely that the income data in the MESP file are flawed.

16. It should be noted that the SCF data show a much higher level of income inequality than the CPS data. In the year 2000, for example, the CPS data show a share of the top *five* percent of 22.1 percent and a Gini coefficient of 0.462. The difference is primarily due to three factors. First, the SCF oversamples the rich (as noted earlier), while the CPS is a representative sample. Second, the CPS data are top-coded (i.e., there is an open-ended interval at the top, typically at $75,000 or $100,000), whereas the SCF data are not. Third, the SCF income definition includes realized capital gains whereas the CPS definition does not. However, the CPS data also show a large increase of inequality between 1989 and 2000, with the share of the top five percent rising from 18.9 to 22.1 percent and the Gini coefficient from 0.431 to 0.462.

17. The CPS data, in contrast, shows little change in household income inequality, with the Gini coefficient falling slightly from 0.470 in 2006 to 0.468 in 2009. The source for the CPS data is: http://www.census.gov/hhes/www/income/data/historical/household/2010/H04_2010.xls. However, the work of Emmanuel Saez and Thomas Piketty, based on IRS tax data, reveals a sizeable decline in income inequality from 2007 to 2010. In particular, incomes at the 99.99th, 99.9th, and 99th percentile dropped sharply over these years (the source is the World Top Incomes Database, available at http://topincomes.parisschoolofeconomics.eu/).

18. It may seem surprising that the share of housing in gross assets declined very little between 2007 and 2010, given the steep drop in housing prices, but the price of other assets also fell over this period, particularly those of stocks and business equity.

19. An earlier analysis was conducted by the author for the 1969–1975 period in the United States (see Wolff, 1979, for details).

20. The residual group, American Indians and Asians, is excluded here because of its small sample size.

21. It should be noted that the unit of observation is the household, which includes both families (two or more related individuals living together), as well as single adults. As is widely known, the share of female-headed households among African-Americans is much higher than that among whites. This difference partly accounts for the relatively lower income and wealth among African-American households.

22. The 1988 income figure for black households appears to be an outlier. The low income for blacks in that year probably reflects the small sample size for blacks (and Hispanics as well) and the survey-to-survey sample variability.

23. There was almost no change in the relative home ownership rates of the two groups – both experienced moderate losses – while the share of households with non-positive net worth actually increased more in relative terms for white

households than black ones. Unfortunately, there are no data available to separate out actual declines in house prices for white, black, and Hispanic homeowners.

24. As with racial minorities, the sample size is relatively small for the oldest age group, so that the nine percentage point increase in their home ownership rate from 2001 to 2004 may be due to sampling variation.

25. As in 2007, the principal source of debt was mortgage debt, which comprised 70 percent of the total debt for the youngest age group in 2010. However, educational loans now amounted to 15 percent of their total liabilities, up from 10 percent in 2007, and 40 percent of households in this age group had an outstanding student loan in 2010.

26. This pattern may also be partly a cohort effect since 401(k) plans and other defined contribution plans were not widely introduced into the workplace until after 1989.

REFERENCES

Kennickell, A. B. (2001, October). *Modeling wealth with multiple observations of income: Redesign of the sample for the 2001 Survey of Consumer Finances*. Retrieved from http://www.federalreserve.gov/pubs/oss/oss2/method.html

Kennickell, A. B., & Woodburn, R. L. (1999). Consistent weight design for the 1989, 1992, and 1995 SCFs, and the distribution of wealth. *Review of Income and Wealth*, *45*, 193–216.

Wolff, E. N. (1979). The distributional effects of the 1969–75 inflation on holdings of household wealth in the United States. *Review of Income and Wealth Series*, *25*(2), 195–207.

Wolff, E. N. (1980). Estimates of the 1969 size distribution of household wealth in the U.S from a synthetic data base. In J. Smith (Ed.), *Modeling the distribution and intergenerational transmission of wealth* (pp. 223–271). Chicago, IL: University of Chicago Press.

Wolff, E. N. (1987). Estimates of household wealth inequality in the United States, 1962–83. *Review of Income and Wealth*, *33*, 231–256.

Wolff, E. N. (1994). Trends in household wealth in the United States, 1962–1983 and 1983–1989. *Review of Income and Wealth*, *40*, 143–174.

Wolff, E. N. (1998). Recent trends in the size distribution of household wealth. *Journal of Economic Perspectives*, *12*, 131–150.

Wolff, E. N. (2002). *Top heavy: A study of increasing inequality of wealth in America* (Newly updated and expanded edition.). New York, NY: The New Press.

Wolff, E. N. (2011a). Recent trends in household wealth in the U.S.: Rising debt and the middle class squeeze. In J. M. Gonzales (Ed.), *Economics of wealth in the 21st century* (pp. 1–41). New York, NY: Nova Science Publishers.

Wolff, E. N. (2011b). *The transformation of the American pension system: Was it beneficial for workers?* Kalamazoo, MI: W.E. Upjohn Institute for Employment Research.

CROSS-NATIONAL DIFFERENCES IN WEALTH PORTFOLIOS AT THE INTENSIVE MARGIN: IS THERE A ROLE FOR POLICY?

Karina Doorley and Eva Sierminska

ABSTRACT

Using harmonized wealth data and a novel decomposition approach in this literature, we show that cohort effects exist in the income profiles of asset and debt portfolios for a sample of European countries, the United States, and Canada. We find that the association between household wealth portfolios at the intensive margin (the level of assets) and household characteristics is different from that found at the extensive margin (the decision to own). Characteristics explain most of the cross-country differences in asset and debt levels, except for housing wealth, which displays large unexplained differences for both the under-50 and over-50 populations. However, there are cohort differences in the drivers of wealth levels. We observe that younger households' levels of wealth, given participation, may be more responsive to the institutional setting than mature households. Our findings have important implications, indicating a scope for policies which can promote or redirect investment in

Economic Well-Being and Inequality: Papers from the Fifth ECINEQ Meeting
Research on Economic Inequality, Volume 22, 43–85

ISSN: 1049-2585/doi:10.1108/S1049-258520140000022000

housing for both cohorts and which promote optimal portfolio allocation for mature households.

Keywords: Wealth portfolios; decomposition; institutions; demographics

INTRODUCTION

Assets have been playing an increasingly important role in measuring material well-being and in determining welfare program eligibility and take-up. The traditional approach to measuring economic well-being via income and labor market participation does not shed much light on other important aspects of welfare that can be measured via wealth. Wealth data can be used to study the way in which households acquire assets and the role they play in improving living standards and creating future opportunities for the owner and their children. In our previous work on wealth participation (Sierminska & Doorley, 2013), we find that income and household composition explain a lot of the cross-country differences in asset and liability ownership for young households. For older households, education and household composition seem to be the main observable drivers. However, many of the cross-country differences in asset and liability ownership cannot be explained by observable household characteristics and may be attributable to the institutional framework, cultural or other differences. In the younger cohort, more of the cross-country differences in asset ownership seem unexplained and leave scope for policy interventions. For the older cohort, it is the decision to hold debt which seems to leave more room for policy interventions. These findings are important as they give us an idea of how policy can affect household well-being through a different channel, namely wealth/debt ownership.

In this paper, we continue our exploration of differences in wealth holdings across countries and focus on the level of assets and liabilities held. Once a household has decided to purchase a particular asset or liability, the next decision is how much to invest and whether or not to diversify the portfolio. This outcome will certainly depend on household characteristics as well as the institutional environment. Particularly for the elderly, the level of wealth may prove an important supplement to income, as current income may otherwise understate the amount of resources that are at hand to be used to maintain the desired level of economic well-being.[1] For the young, wealth is important in ensuring future opportunities either for education, for their children, for retirement or as a safety net in case of an unexpected loss of income. Comparing these in a cross-national perspective and by cohort could lead to important policy implications.

The literature which advocates incorporating wealth into economic well-being measures is not abundant, but is certainly present. For example, several decades ago, Weisbrod and Hansen (1968) proposed a wealth-augmented income definition, which led to different policy prescriptions than if the income alone measure is used. Due to the lack of reliable data on wealth, wealth has not been universally incorporated as proposed. More recently, due to additional data availability, there has been more interest in incorporating wealth in the measurement of economic well-being (e.g., Brandolini, Magri, & Smeeding, 2010; Haveman & Wolff, 2004). Population aging has also raised questions about the long-term sustainability of pension systems and the need to assess the adequacy of savings for retirement through the study of the level and composition of assets with which households retire (e.g., Chiuri & Jappelli, 2010; Gornick, Sierminska, & Smeeding, 2009). Nevertheless, the literature on incorporating wealth portfolios in the measurement of well-being is not abundant. Single or two-country studies are more common than cross-country comparisons due to data availability and difficulties in performing cross-national comparisons. Comparable cross-country data is not easily available. For example, the Survey of Health, Aging and Retirement in Europe (SHARE) captures individuals 50 and over. The Household Finance and Consumption Survey (HFCS) is available for euro-zone countries only. Another option for researchers is to rely on data in the Luxembourg Wealth Study, which has thoroughly examined and harmonized comparable and non-comparable components of wealth and has made a detailed study of country wealth components and institutions. This approach facilitates an insightful analysis of wealth portfolios across countries and allows comparisons across European, as well as non-European countries.

In this paper, we follow the conceptual framework developed by the Luxembourg Wealth Study and apply it to independent data. We use two datasets that are used in the Household Finance and Consumption Survey (Italy and Spain) and are publicly available. In addition, we use data for Canada, Germany, Luxembourg, and the United States, and thus are able to provide a unique view on household wealth portfolios in a cross-national perspective.

Our paper is novel in several ways. We use data for a unique set of countries and identify differences in their wealth portfolio levels and their determinants, focusing on differences between younger and older cohorts. We also introduce a novel way of decomposing asset levels across the distribution. In this way, we extend the literature methodologically by integrating methods typically used in discrimination analysis and labor studies to the study of differences in portfolio choices by applying a "distributionally sensitive" approach to the decomposition of wealth levels. As the absolute levels of wealth across countries can be very different, we favor the distribution regression (DR) approach of Chernozhukov, Fernandez-Val, and Melly (2009) over the Machado and Mata (2005) quantile regression methodology in order to highlight the extent of the wealth gap in the tails of each distribution. Correlating the "unexplained gap" in wealth levels across countries with institutional features of those countries allows us to make inferences about which policies promote asset and debt accumulation. Our focus is on the main assets and liabilities held by households – financial assets, main residence, investment real estate, and debt – with a focus on mortgages and non-housing debt.[2]

Past research suggests a large role for institutions in explaining cross-national differences in portfolios. Christelis, Georgarakos, and Haliassos (2012) find that characteristics play a small or negligible role in generating observed international differences for households 50 years and over. We show that the role of characteristics is more important than previously thought for particular assets and for the younger population.

We find that, given participation, cross-country differences in the level of financial assets and debt are largely driven by household characteristics. Real estate differences are, however, somewhat unexplained and could be attributable to cross-country differences in institutions. The level of wealth, given participation, varies more in response to characteristics and other unobservables for the older cohort than the younger one for financial assets and risky assets. Mortgage debt levels across countries vary more for the young while we see mixed cross-country cohort results for non-housing debt. There is a strong effect of both characteristics and unexplained factors for both cohorts' levels of investment in real estate.

Our results suggest that institutional (or other unobserved) differences between countries predominantly affect the portfolio composition for younger households' levels of housing and mortgage debt. We take a preliminary look at some institutional features that could drive cross-country differences in these instruments. For older households, there are unexplained factors affecting levels of housing and financial assets at the top of this asset's distribution. These findings have important implications, indicating a scope for policies which can promote or redirect investment in housing for both cohorts, which target debt levels of young households and which promote optimal portfolio allocation for mature households.

In the next section we describe the data. The section "Methodology" overviews the methods and provides basic descriptive statistics. The results are presented next and the conclusions are in the last section.

DATA

In our sample, we use data for two North American countries: Canada and the United States, and several European countries with varying institutional and welfare regimes: Germany, Italy, Luxembourg, and Spain. At the time of data collection, all of these countries were experiencing low unemployment and positive GDP growth (Table 1).[3] The data for Canada come from the 2005 Survey of Financial Security, for Germany the 2007 wealth module of the Socio-Economic Panel (SOEP), for Italy the 2008 Survey of Household Income and Wealth (SHIW), for Luxembourg from the 2007 wealth module of the PSELL3/EU-SILC, for Spain from the 2008 EFF, and the data for the United States come from the 2007 Survey of Consumer Finances (SCF).

The data contain detailed information on multiple income sources and financial and non-financial assets and debts. On the basis of this detailed information, we use the conceptual framework developed by the

Table 1. Country Sample Macroeconomic Conditions.

	2002	2003	2004	2005	2006	2007	2008	2009
(A) *Real GDP growth*								
Canada	2.9	1.9	3.1	3.0	2.9	2.5	0.4	−2.7
Germany	0.0	−0.2	0.7	0.9	3.4	2.6	1.0	−4.9
Italy	0.5	0.1	1.4	0.8	2.1	1.4	−1.3	−5.1
Luxembourg	4.1	1.5	4.4	5.4	5.6	6.5	0.0	−3.4
Spain	2.7	3.1	3.3	3.6	4.0	3.6	0.9	−3.6
United States	1.8	2.5	3.6	3.1	2.7	2.1	0.4	−2.4
(B) *Harmonized unemployment rates*								
Canada	7.7	7.6	7.2	6.8	6.3	6.0	6.1	8.3
Germany	8.4	9.3	9.8	10.6	9.8	8.4	7.3	7.5
Italy	8.6	8.5	8.0	7.7	6.8	6.2	6.8	7.7
Luxembourg	2.6	3.8	5.0	4.6	4.6	4.2	4.9	5.4
Spain	11.1	11.1	10.6	9.2	8.5	8.3	11.4	18.0
United States	5.8	6.0	5.5	5.1	4.6	4.6	5.8	9.3

Source: OECD (2010), Annex Tables 1 and 14.

Luxembourg Wealth Study (described by Sierminska, Brandolini, & Smeeding, 2006) for creating harmonized variables of net worth (total assets: financial assets, principal residence, investment real estate, and business equity minus liabilities: mortgages and non-housing debt) and income. Each of the wealth variables has been bottom and top coded at their 1% and 99% levels to stop outliers from over-influencing our results, and monetary variables have been converted to 2007 euros using PPP and price indices.

The data are collected at the household level and individual level variables that are reported (such as age, gender, education) refer to the respondent/household head. In most cases, this person is the person most knowledgeable about household finances. Table A1 shows the instruments that are available in each country. A comparison of this harmonized cross-country database to other sources (the HFCS data and the SHARE data for the over-50 population) was undertaken by Sierminska and Doorley (2013) which indicates that the LWS framework adopted here to harmonize the different surveys leads to similar participation rates in each of the instruments in the wealth portfolio.

METHODOLOGY

The Level of Wealth Holdings

Just as the decision to participate in different components of wealth portfolios may differ across countries (Sierminska & Doorley, 2013), so too may the level of holding, given participation, differ across countries. The top panel of Table 2 shows the mean level of each portfolio instrument held in each country by the whole population. For financial assets, we find the largest mean holdings in the United States. Canada and European countries have similar, lower levels with Luxembourg leading this group. Taking participation rates from Table 3 into account, we can conclude that the differences with the United States stem both from higher participation and higher levels of this asset, given participation, in the United States. In all of the countries examined, a large portion of wealth is held in the form of real estate. The highest levels can be observed in Luxembourg and Spain, with Canadian households holding the lowest levels of real estate. Debt levels are mostly composed of mortgages and are the highest in the United States and Luxembourg.

In further panels of Table 2, the sample is partitioned by cohorts. For the younger cohort, the patterns are similar to the ones described above for the

Table 2. Mean Level of Each Instrument in the Wealth Portfolio for the Whole Population, 25 to 49 Year Olds and 50 and over by Country.

	United States	Canada	Germany	Italy	Luxembourg	Spain	Total
All							
Total financial assets	176,020	16,835	22,243	22,064	33,446	22,235	69,758
Deposit accounts	19,510	7,607	NA	11,846	NA	19,480	8,043
Risky assets	51,013	8,191	NA	9,318	NA	1,871	16,828
Main residence	206,655	68,364	101,139	188,389	381,255	227,195	145,330
Other property	56,090	11,790	27,318	38,578	126,962	94,656	39,910
Business equity	57,570	5,098	8,952	22,471	17,917	30,282	25,844
Total assets	544,560	109,413	168,087	281,325	570,226	380,630	301,575
Total debt	96,811	26,838	31,016	10,381	48,678	36,704	50,190
Mortgage	69,184	17,620	17,899	9,157	48,678	24,048	32,952
Other home debt	7,649	2,176	6,924	NA	NA	8,434	6,566
Non-housing debt	13,732	4,090	3,920	1,131	NA	3,197	6,736
25 to 49 year olds							
Total financial assets	92,840	8,843	13,081	15,073	24,520	15,902	40,455
Deposit accounts	13,334	3,747	NA	9,632	NA	14,627	6,018
Risky assets	22,800	4,978	NA	5,081	NA	1,010	8,360
Main residence	173,637	62,973	77,606	153,986	327,936	208,027	121,570
Other property	35,830	10,180	17,228	21,679	72,421	66,483	26,163
Business equity	43,288	4,953	9,547	26,321	18,473	30,233	22,932
Total assets	367,063	92,916	124,171	223,285	453,052	323,897	222,651
Total debt	115,656	35,635	43,456	19,449	80,536	60,007	67,313
Mortgage	85,549	24,778	29,174	NA	80,536	43,400	47,390
Other home debt	7,552	2,405	6,056	NA	NA	11,079	6,283
Non-housing debt	17,353	5,101	5,577	1,701	NA	3,954	9,255
50 and over							
Total financial assets	257,549	26,678	28,895	26,576	43,125	27,884	93,642
Deposit accounts	25,564	12,361	NA	13,276	NA	23,808	9,695
Risky assets	78,667	12,149	NA	12,054	NA	2,639	23,730
Main residence	239,019	75,003	118,227	210,596	439,071	244,294	164,697
Other property	75,950	13,772	34,646	49,488	186,102	119,787	51,115
Business equity	71,568	5,277	8,520	19,985	17,314	30,325	28,218
Total assets	718,537	129,732	199,975	318,791	697,280	431,238	365,904
Total debt	78,339	16,003	21,983	4,527	14,133	15,918	36,233
Mortgage	53,144	8,804	9,712	NA	14,133	6,786	21,183
Other home debt	7,744	1,894	7,555	NA	NA	6,075	6,798
Non-housing debt	10,184	2,844	2,718	762	NA	2,521	4,682

Source: 2005 SFS, 2007 SCF, 2007 SOEP, 2008 SHIW, 2007 PSELL3, and 2008 EFF.
Note: The levels are in 2007 euros and include zeros.

Table 3. Portfolios Participation Rates for the Whole Population, 25 to 49 Year Olds and 50 and over.

	United States	Canada	Germany	Italy	Luxembourg	Spain	Total
All							
Total financial assets	94.29	88.50	57.65	77.08	67.82	92.95	73.11
Deposit accounts	92.70	87.00	NA	76.48	NA	92.95	41.39
Risky assets	34.22	26.55	NA	21.15	NA	3.37	13.14
Main residence	71.86	65.47	41.15	70.25	71.03	83.10	55.57
Other property	19.99	16.75	13.21	22.02	27.84	36.43	17.17
Business equity	12.57	17.18	6.14	16.78	5.64	12.25	9.53
Total assets	95.46	94.44	71.52	91.20	88.55	98.33	82.40
Total debt	77.34	69.86	36.55	25.79	35.14	46.28	50.10
Mortgage	48.30	35.95	18.45	12.71	35.14	26.05	28.34
Other home debt	5.80	4.71	5.88	NA	NA	8.02	5.50
Non-housing debt	66.47	56.99	21.08	15.59	NA	23.20	36.09
25 to 49 year olds							
Total financial assets	91.97	86.17	52.32	79.73	64.40	92.05	70.97
Deposit accounts	90.25	84.64	NA	79.23	NA	92.05	43.77
Risky assets	32.55	24.85	NA	16.50	NA	2.48	13.30
Main residence	62.61	59.59	32.02	57.66	64.09	77.00	47.52
Other property	15.46	14.39	10.31	15.95	21.48	29.19	13.56
Business equity	12.87	18.91	7.36	21.41	5.60	14.94	10.95
Total assets	93.53	93.17	64.97	88.62	86.58	98.08	79.06
Total debt	86.56	81.86	50.36	40.64	53.91	66.61	64.34
Mortgage	55.46	46.48	24.93	22.76	53.91	45.41	37.28
Other home debt	6.21	4.98	5.62	NA	NA	10.05	5.67
Non-housing debt	77.31	68.07	31.22	22.59	NA	30.23	47.91
50 and over							
Total financial assets	96.56	91.37	61.51	75.37	71.85	93.76	74.85
Deposit accounts	95.09	89.91	NA	74.71	NA	93.76	39.45
Risky assets	35.86	28.65	NA	24.15	NA	4.17	13.01
Main residence	80.93	72.71	47.78	78.38	78.40	88.53	62.13
Other property	24.43	19.66	15.31	25.94	34.97	42.89	20.12
Business equity	12.27	15.06	5.25	13.80	5.67	9.85	8.37
Total assets	97.36	96.00	76.28	92.87	90.70	98.56	85.12
Total debt	68.31	55.08	26.53	16.21	14.95	28.14	38.50
Mortgage	41.29	22.98	13.74	6.22	14.95	8.78	21.05
Other home debt	5.40	4.38	6.07	NA	NA	6.20	5.37
Non-housing debt	55.84	43.35	13.72	11.08	NA	16.92	26.46

Source: 2005 SFS, 2007 SCF, 2007 SOEP, 2008 SHIW, 2007 PSELL3, and 2008 EFF.

whole population. For the older cohort, in the bottom panel, we find differences, particularly when it comes to liabilities. In all countries, the level of debt is lower for this group but this is particularly true in Europe, where the participation rate is also substantially lower (Table 3). In Canada, we observe a drop in participation in debt as well as the level of debt, but not to such a great extent as that observed in Europe. This points to substantial cohort differences among the groups of countries.

Fig. 1 plots the aggregate level of each wealth component across the income distribution. To make holdings across countries more comparable, we scale each component by median annual income in each country. The top left panels in Fig. 1 show the level of Total Financial Assets held by households across the income distribution for the under-50 and over-50 population. The subsequent panels show Risky Assets, Principal Residence, Investment Real Estate, Mortgage Debt, and Non-Housing Debt.

There is a strong positive relationship documented between income and wealth. We also find this to be the case in our selection of countries when examining the relationship between income and the various components of the wealth portfolio. The level of each portfolio instrument increases as we move up the income distribution. In terms of total financial assets, the four European countries and Canada show similar holdings, which peak at around 4 times the median income at the very top of the income distribution for both the under-50 and over-50 population. In the United States, the total financial asset holdings are similar to European levels up to median earnings, after which they shoot up to a maximum of 12 times median earnings for the top earners under 50 years of age and 32 times median earnings for the top earners over 50. So, not only is participation in financial assets higher in the United States, but the level of financial assets given participation is higher, particularly at the top of the income distribution. Risky assets show a similar pattern, although the top level for the United States is less than half of that of total financial assets.

In terms of real estate, we find that the Spanish and Luxembourgish holdings of both principal property and investment real estate are consistently higher than those of other countries across the earnings distribution. Italian households hold higher levels of principal residence than Germany, the United States, or Canada, while these four countries hold comparable levels of investment real estate across the income distribution, with the United States holding the least amount of either real estate asset.

Looking at debt, Spanish households hold the highest level of debt at the bottom of the income distribution, while the United States, Germany, and Luxembourg hold the most debt at the top of the income distribution. The vast majority of this debt is made up of mortgages in each country.

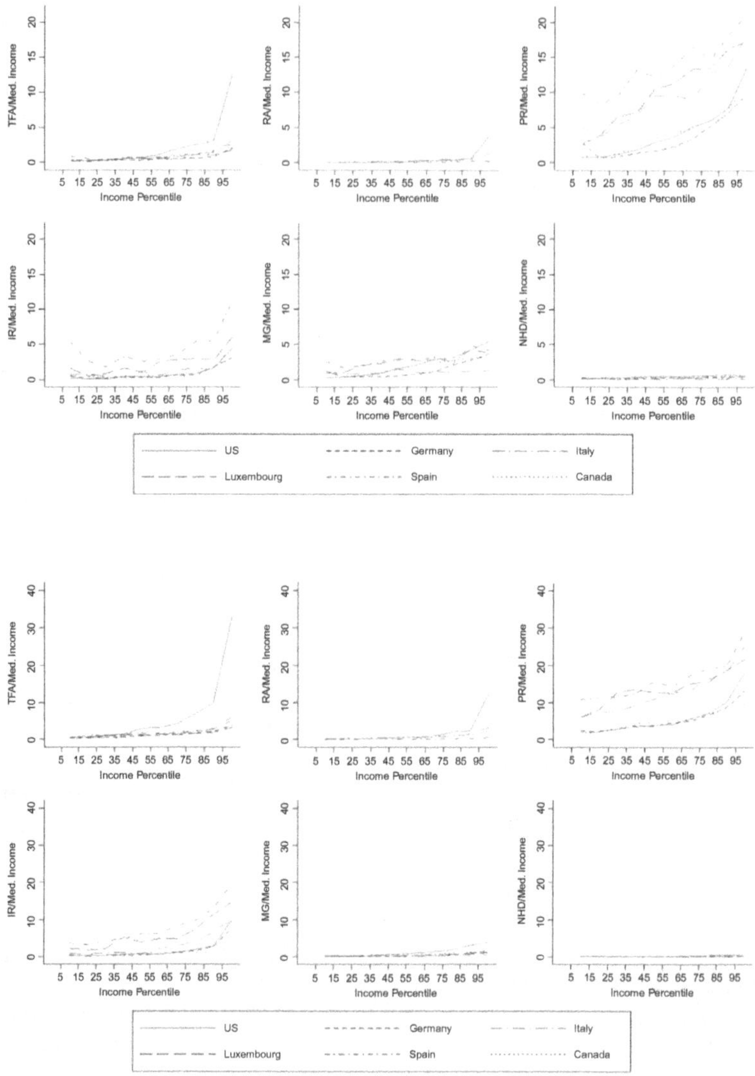

Fig. 1. Level of Each Wealth Component (Excluding Zeros) across the Income Distribution for the 25 to 49 Population (Top) and 50 and over (Bottom). *Notes*: Weighted statistics. Lowess curve applied for smoothing purposes. TFA is Total Financial Assets; RA is Risky Assets; PR is Principal Residence; IR is Investment Real Estate; MG is Mortgage; NHD is Non-Housing Debt. *Source*: 2005 SFS, 2007 SCF, 2007 SOEP, 2008 SHIW, 2007 PSELL3, and 2008 EFF.

There are some noticeable differences between the sub-populations of under-50 and over-50. The under-50 population holds higher levels of principal residence and total debt in each country, given participation. In the United States, the highest level of financial assets is confined to the over-50 population at the top of the income distribution. However, the level of financial assets held by the under and over-50 population is similar throughout the rest of the income distribution.

Decomposing the Cross-Country Level of Wealth Holdings

The previous discussion of wealth levels is based on raw distributions of wealth components. To study marginal distributions, that is, controlling for characteristics across countries across the distribution, we employ DR, following Chernozhukov et al. (2009) and Fortin, Lemieux, and Firpo (2011). In practical terms, this involves running a series of probit models at each point in the distribution of each wealth component, w, in each country. The dependent variable is binary and takes the value of 1 if the household's wealth holding is less than or equal to w, and 0 otherwise, where w takes the value of each point of the wealth distribution sequentially. Contrary to the Machado-Mata decomposition, which models conditional wealth levels at specific quantiles, DR models the conditional probability that a household has a wealth holding below w in the distribution, hence mapping the whole conditional cumulative distribution function. We use demographics, labor market status, marital status, and education to model the level of wealth held.[4] Using DR, we predict the probability that *each* household has a wealth holding below *each* w in the distribution. This allows us to construct predicted cumulative distribution functions for each component of the wealth portfolio. We can also predict what this probability would be if the household accumulated wealth in the same way as a similar household in the United States, that is, if the model coefficients of each country were identical to those of the US model. This allows us to construct counterfactual cumulative distribution functions for each instrument in the wealth portfolio. We employ a Blinder-Oaxaca style decomposition of the marginal wealth distributions in each country (using the United States as the baseline) to identify what portion of the difference between wealth distributions is due to characteristics and what portion is unexplained, or due to institutional or other unobserved differences.

Starting from estimates of the conditional distribution of each wealth component (w) in country j, given household characteristics (X), we recover estimates of the marginal distribution by integration of the conditional distributions over household characteristics:

$$F_j^j(w) = \int_{\Omega_X} F^j(w|X)h_j(X)\,\mathrm{d}X \tag{1}$$

where $F^j(\cdot|X)$ is the conditional cumulative wealth distribution function for household characteristics X in country j and h_j is the density distribution of household characteristics for this country.

We can separate the household characteristics from the conditional cumulative wealth distribution to construct counterfactual wealth distributions for country j, if they chose wealth portfolios in the same way as similar US households (i.e., if the institutional setting in country j was that of the United States). For example:

$$F_j^{\mathrm{US}}(w) = \int_{\Omega_X} F^{\mathrm{US}}(w|X)h_j(X)\,\mathrm{d}X \tag{2}$$

estimates the counterfactual wealth distribution that would prevail in country j if portfolio decisions followed the US model, where $F^{\mathrm{US}}(\cdot|X)$ is the conditional cumulative wealth distribution function for household characteristics X in the United States and h_j is the density distribution of household characteristics in country j.

Estimates are obtained by replacing $F^{\mathrm{US}}(\cdot|X)$ by estimates $\hat{F}^{\mathrm{US}}(\cdot|X)$ in Eq. (2), and by averaging over our sample of N households w in country j:

$$\hat{F}_j^{\mathrm{US}}(w) = \sum_{t=1}^{N_j} \hat{F}^{\mathrm{US}}(w|x_t) \tag{3}$$

In order to represent the explained and unexplained gaps graphically in terms of the level of each asset, we invert the conditional and counterfactual distributions to obtain quantiles.[5] Consider $Q_{j,\tau}^{\mathrm{US}}(w)$, the τth quantile of the counterfactual distribution $F_j^{\mathrm{US}}(w)$. The estimated counterfactual quantile is:

$$\hat{Q}_{j,\tau}^{\mathrm{US}}(w) = \left[\hat{F}_{j,\tau}^{\mathrm{US}}(w)\right]^{-1} \tag{4}$$

Performing an Oaxaca-Blinder style decomposition to isolate the difference in wealth distributions that is due to household characteristics and the difference that is unexplained, or can be attributed to institutional differences and unobservables across countries, we have:

$$Q_{\mathrm{US},\tau}^{\mathrm{US}}(w) - Q_{j,\tau}^{j}(w) = \left[\hat{Q}_{\mathrm{US},\tau}^{\mathrm{US}}(w)\right] - \left[\hat{Q}_{j,\tau}^{\mathrm{US}}(w)\right] + \left[\hat{Q}_{j,\tau}^{\mathrm{US}}(w)\right] - \left[\hat{Q}_{j,\tau}^{j}(w)\right] \quad (5)$$

The first expression on the right hand side of Eq. (5) identifies the unexplained contribution to differences in wealth levels, while the second expression identifies the difference that can be accounted for by different household characteristics across countries. We perform this decomposition for each wealth component in each country.

RESULTS

Country Differences in Asset Level Determinants

To model country differences in asset levels, we use the DR approach elaborated in the section "Methodology." Model results for the median of each asset's distribution for the population under 50 years of age are displayed in Tables A3–A5. Interpretation of these coefficients is as follows. The negative coefficient on age for the US portfolio of total financial assets shows that, as age increases, households are less likely to hold less than the median level of this asset, that is, age has the traditionally positive effect on this measure of wealth. We generally see similar effects of age across countries, except for non-housing debt, which decreases with age. In all countries, a male or more educated household head increases wealth levels compared to a female or low educated household head.

There are differences in the direction of the effect of marital status, labor market status, number of children, and income across countries. In our reference country, the United States, we find that being married (compared to single or divorced), having no children, being employed or self-employed, and having higher income and other wealth all positively affect wealth holdings.

Decomposition of Wealth Levels across the Distribution

To begin examining wealth level differences across the distribution, we first plot (Fig. 2) the predicted cumulative distributions of each item in the wealth

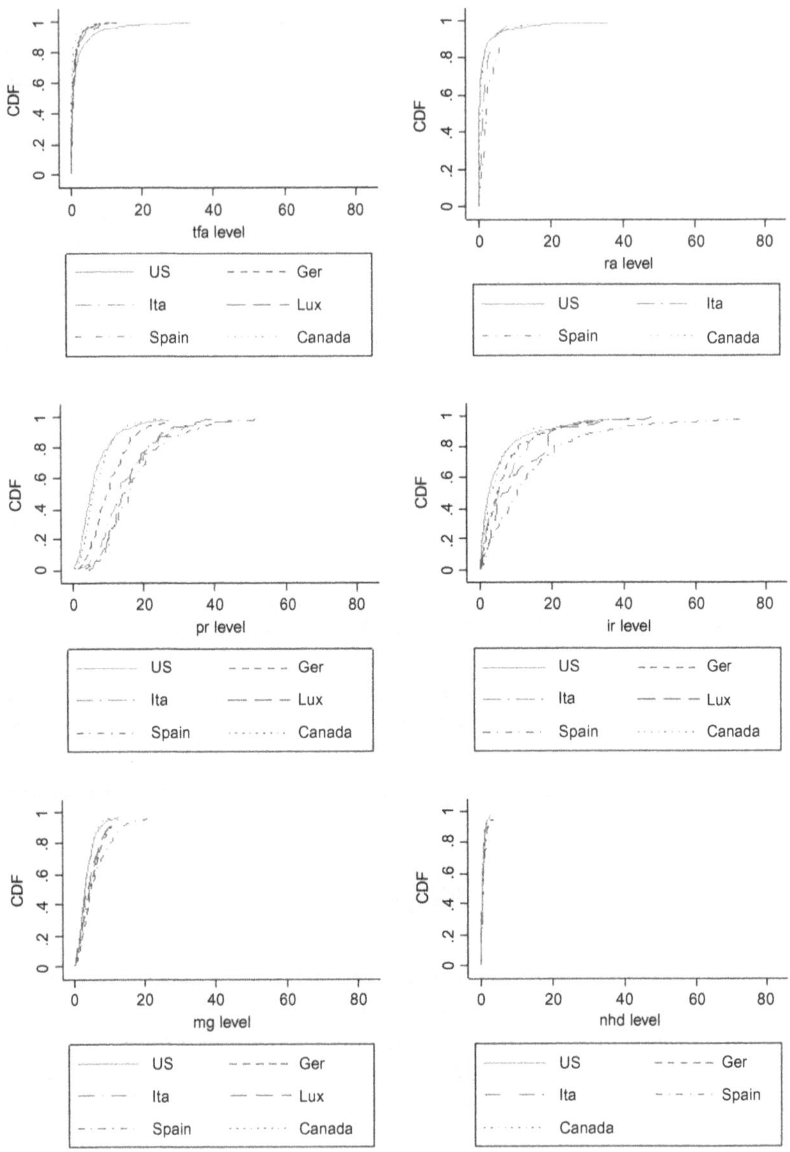

Fig. 2. Predicted Levels of Assets/Liabilities in the Total Asset Portfolio for the u-50 Population. *Notes*: Asset levels are scaled by the median income. TFA is Total Financial Assets; RA is Risky Assets; PR is Principal Residence; IR is Investment Real Estate; MG is Mortgage; NHD is Non-Housing Debt. *Source*: 2007 SCF, 2005 SFS, 2007 SOEP, 2008 SHIW, 2007 PSELL3, and 2008 EFF.

portfolio by country for the younger cohort. These graphs show the distribution of the level of wealth conditional on participation. The monetary value of the relevant wealth component is scaled by the median income in each country to facilitate cross-country comparisons. The fit of the DR model is excellent as the predicted distributions follow the actual wealth distributions very closely (results available from authors upon request).

From the top panels of Fig. 2, we note that the level of financial assets and risky assets is highest and affects a larger share of the population in the United States (in line with our observations in Fig. 1). The level of these assets is lower and more similar in the other countries. Levels of investment real estate and principal residence are highest in the European countries, particularly in Spain and Luxembourg and lowest in the United States and Canada. Mortgage debt is highest in Spain and lowest in the United States and Canada. These phenomena are likely to be related to the high housing prices in Spain and Luxembourg, relative to income, and the high availability of loans in Spain in pre-crisis times. Non-housing debt levels are similar across countries.

Decomposition Example

To graphically represent the decomposition elaborated in Eq. (5), in Fig. 3, we present a graphical example of the decomposition. Here, we show the conditional distributions of principal residence, given participation, for the younger cohort for the United States and Germany. The United States has lower levels of principal residence than Germany, as evidenced by the fact that the "US" line is consistently closer to the vertical axis than the line for Germany. Only about 20% of US households hold a level of principal residence that is more than 10 times the median income of the country. By contrast, at least 50% of German households hold a level of principal residence that is more than 10 times the median income of the country. The counterfactual distribution of principal residence in Germany, if the institutional/other settings were the same as the United States, is shown by the line "Germany with US coefficients." The horizontal difference between the lines "US" and "Germany with US coefficients" shows the difference in the level of principal residence that is explained by the different characteristics of German and US households. The horizontal difference between the lines "Germany with US coefficients" and "Germany" is the unexplained/institutional gap. In this example, the unexplained/institutional gap is small. Thus, the characteristics are able to explain almost all of the difference in principal residence levels between these two countries for the under-50 cohort.

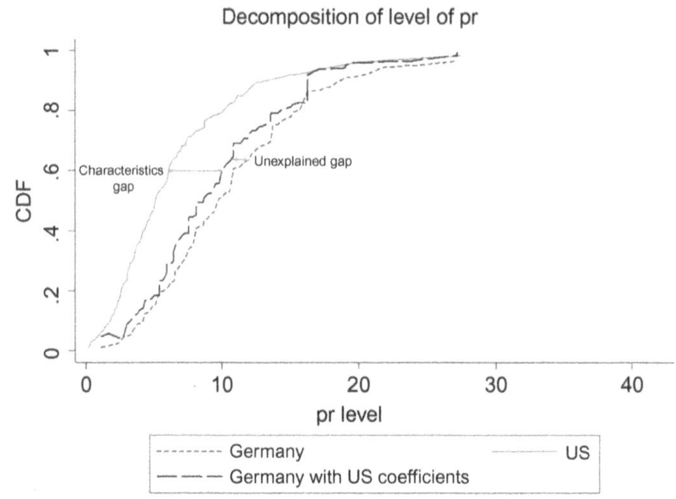

Fig. 3. Example: Decomposition of the Principal Residence Gap across the Distribution of Principal Residence for the u-50 Households. *Note*: Principal residence levels are scaled by the median income. *Source*: 2007 SOEP.

In what follows, we will only graph these horizontal gaps in order to facilitate interpretation.

Components of Wealth Portfolios

The main components of wealth portfolios and, therefore, those examined in detail in the remainder of this paper, include financial assets, non-financial assets and liabilities. In our case, in additional to total financial assets, we are also able to distinguish a sub-component of risky assets for some countries. Non-financial assets refer to real estate and businesses. Here we focus on the main residence and investment real estate. The largest share of liabilities is composed of mortgages and non-housing debt. Table 4 shows the proportion each instrument in the portfolio represents compared to total assets. As discussed, a majority of wealth is held in the form of real estate. Across countries, 52% of total assets are composed of principal residence while 14% are investment real estate. These shares are even larger for the younger than the older cohort. For the older cohort in the United States and Canada, a larger share is held in financial assets (40% for the United States and 22% in Canada). We do not see a very large change across cohorts in wealth composition in European countries indicating that

Table 4. Mean Level of Each Instrument in the Wealth Portfolio as a Proportion of Total Assets for the Whole Population, 25 to 49 Year Olds and 50 and over by Country.

	United States	Canada	Germany	Italy	Luxembourg	Spain	Total
All							
Total financial assets	35	16	14	8	6	6	25
Deposit accounts	4	7	NA	4	NA	5	3
Risky assets	10	8	NA	3	NA	0	6
Main residence	42	67	63	69	68	61	52
Other property	11	12	17	14	23	25	14
Business equity	12	5	6	8	3	8	9
Total assets	100	100	100	100	100	100	100
Total debt	20	26	19	4	9	10	18
Mortgage	14	17	11	3	9	6	12
Other home debt	2	2	4	NA	NA	2	2
Non-housing debt	3	4	2	0	NA	1	2
25 to 49 year olds							
Total financial assets	27	10	11	7	6	5	19
Deposit accounts	4	4	NA	4	NA	5	3
Risky assets	7	6	NA	2	NA	0	4
Main residence	50	72	66	71	74	65	58
Other property	10	12	15	10	16	21	12
Business equity	13	6	8	12	4	9	11
Total assets	100	100	100	100	100	100	100
Total debt	33	41	37	9	18	19	32
Mortgage	25	28	25	8	18	14	23
Other home debt	2	3	5	NA	NA	3	3
Non-housing debt	5	6	5	1	NA	1	4
50 and over							
Total financial assets	40	22	15	9	6	7	28
Deposit accounts	4	10	0	4	0	6	3
Risky assets	12	10	0	4	0	1	7
Main residence	37	62	62	69	64	58	49
Other property	12	11	18	16	27	28	15
Business equity	11	4	4	7	3	7	8
Total assets	100	100	100	100	100	100	100
Total debt	12	13	12	1	2	4	11
Mortgage	8	7	5	1	2	2	6
Other home debt	1	2	4	NA	NA	1	2
Non-housing debt	2	2	1	0	NA	1	1

Source: 2005 SFS, 2007 SCF, 2007 SOEP, 2008 SHIW, 2007 PSELL3, and 2008 EFF.
Note: The levels are in 2007 euros and include zeros.

most of their wealth remains locked in real estate, although we do see diminishing levels of debt compared to total assets.

Total Financial Assets. First, we examine total financial assets. Fig. 4 shows the total gap between the level of total financial assets in the United States and each of the other countries. This total gap is decomposed into a characteristic gap and an institutional gap. The total gap is always positive meaning that the United States has higher levels of total financial assets, given participation, than each of the other countries. This gap is largest at the top of the total financial asset distribution and is largely composed of characteristic differences. In fact, the institutional gap between the United States and the other countries is negative, meaning that the total gap would even be larger if the European countries and Canada did not have certain institutional (or other) features which encouraged investment in financial assets. This institutional gap, present particularly at the top of the distribution, is larger for the older cohort. Taxation, investment incentives, and differences in the culture of inheritances could be some of the factors affecting these differences.

In comparison to the participation decision in financial assets, for which characteristics explain just a small part of the cross-country gap (Sierminska & Doorley, 2013), the level of financial assets held, conditional on participation, is almost entirely explained by household characteristics although there are some unexplained factors driving the gap at the top of the asset distribution suggesting that, for most households, once they make the decision to own financial assets, the levels are mostly driven by their family and economic characteristics.

Risky Assets. Risky assets are an important component driving the results for financial assets at the top of the distribution. We find a similar characteristics gap as for total financial assets throughout the distribution and a virtually non-existent institutional gap, except in Canada, in Fig. 5. This gap suggests that there is an unobserved reason for Canadian households to increase their risky asset holdings, particularly older households at the top of the risky asset distribution. The participation gap in risky assets was also found to be driven by the characteristics such as income and education (Sierminska & Doorley, 2013).

Principal Residence. As we saw in Table 3, main homeownership is higher in the United States that in every other country examined except Spain. We turn next to the difference in the distribution of principal residence, given

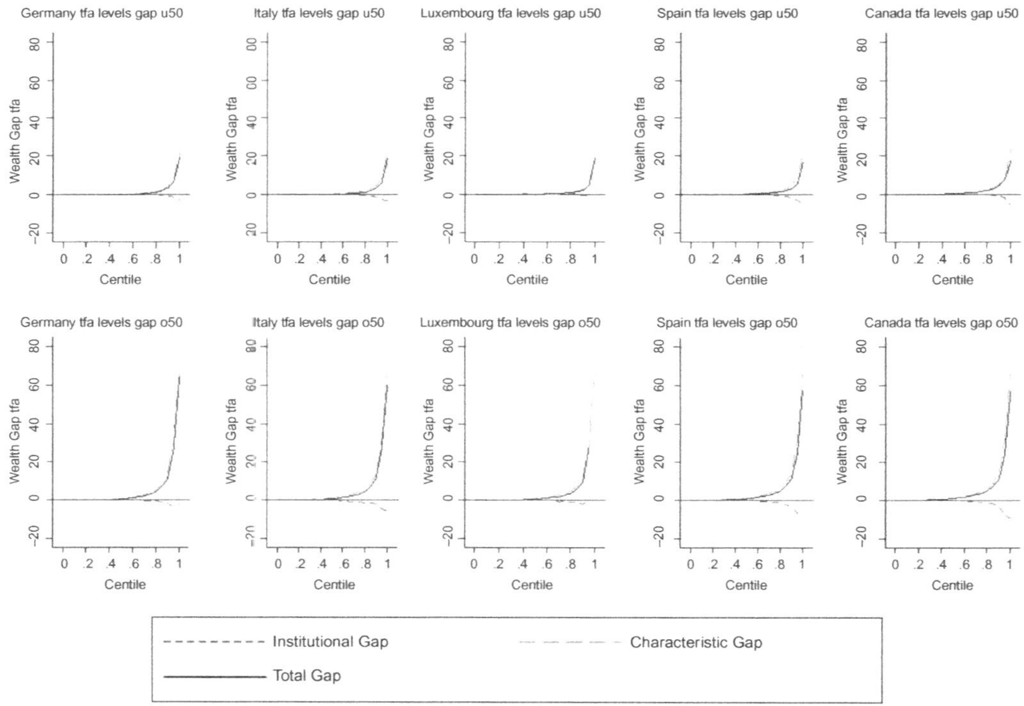

Fig. 4. Coefficient and Institutional Gaps across the Distribution of Total Financial Assets. *Notes*: The wealth gaps are scaled by the median income. The characteristics gap shows the level of difference between the US and each country's investment in total financial assets which is accounted for by household characteristics. The institutional gap shows the gap which is unexplained. The total gap is the sum of these two. *Source*: 2007 SCF, 2005 SFS, 2007 SOEP, 2008 SHIW, 2007 PSELL3, and 2008 EFF.

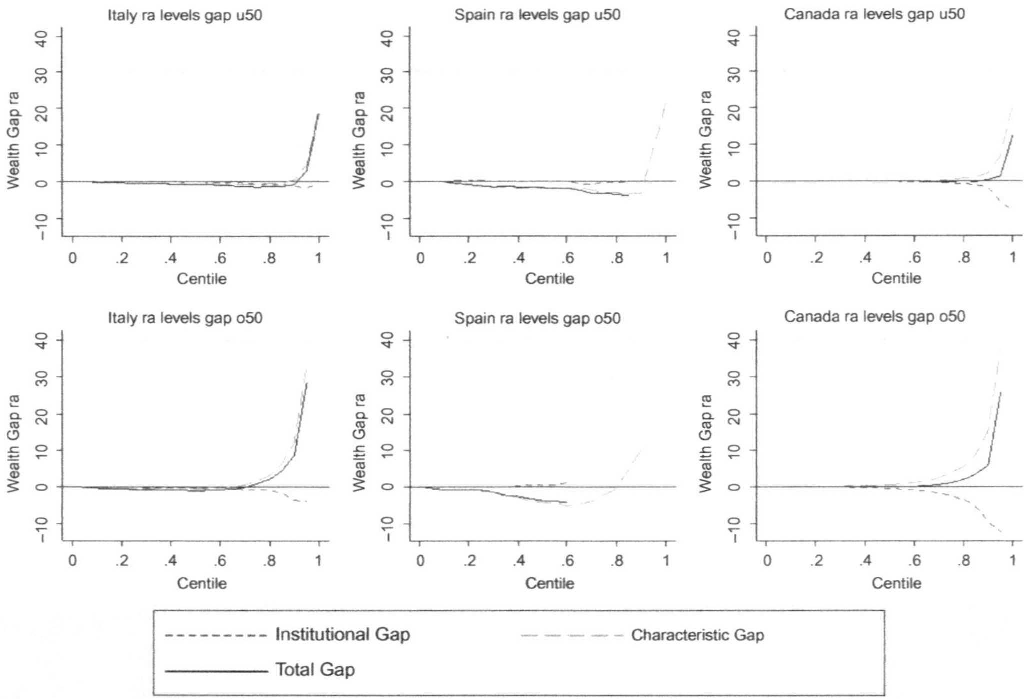

Fig. 5. Coefficient and Institutional Gaps across the Distribution of Risky Assets. *Notes*: The wealth gaps are scaled by the median income. The characteristics gap shows the level of difference between the US and each country's investment in risky assets which is accounted for by household characteristics. The institutional gap shows the gap which is unexplained. The total gap is the sum of these two. *Source*: 2007 SCF, 2005 SFS, 2007 SOEP, 2008 SHIW, 2007 PSELL3, and 2008 EFF.

participation. From Fig. 6, the total gap between the US distribution and the European countries is negative while there is a small positive gap between the United States and Canada. This implies that, given participation, the US holds lower levels of principal residence (or that housing is cheaper relative to the median income) than the European countries and a slightly higher level than Canada (toward the top of the distribution). Unlike other components of the wealth portfolio, these gaps are similar for both cohorts. A negative characteristic gap makes up most of this difference indicating that US households hold less valuable principal residences due in large part to their household characteristics. This could include their level of investment in other assets. However, there is also a negative institutional gap for Germany, Italy, Spain, and Canada indicating that households in these countries also hold higher levels of wealth in their principal residence (relative to their income) due to institutional or other features of their country compared to the United States.

Investment Real Estate. The results for the difference in the level of investment real estate between the United States and the other countries in Fig. 7 indicate a small, but negative gap in every country but Canada. The gap is larger for the older cohort and is the largest in Spain and Luxembourg. For most countries, the total gap is composed of a negative characteristics gap and a smaller negative unexplained gap indicating that households from other countries invest in higher levels of real estate than US households due both to household characteristics and to institutional or other country features. One exception is Canada which displays a positive characteristics gap.

To compare these results to the participation decision (Sierminska & Doorley, 2013), we find that, in both the participation and levels decision, a mix of explained and unexplained factors contribute to the cross-country gaps.

Mortgage Debt. Mortgages are a very interesting case (Fig. 8). The total gap in mortgage debt levels between the United States and the European countries is negative for the younger cohort, as is the value of real estate, and, except for Canada, is smaller for the older cohort. There is a small positive gap between the United States and Canada at the top of the distribution and at the bottom of the distribution between the United States and Italy and the United States and Luxembourg. Most of these gaps are unexplained and negative (in contrast to the participation decision for this group), indicating that US households hold lower mortgage debt levels

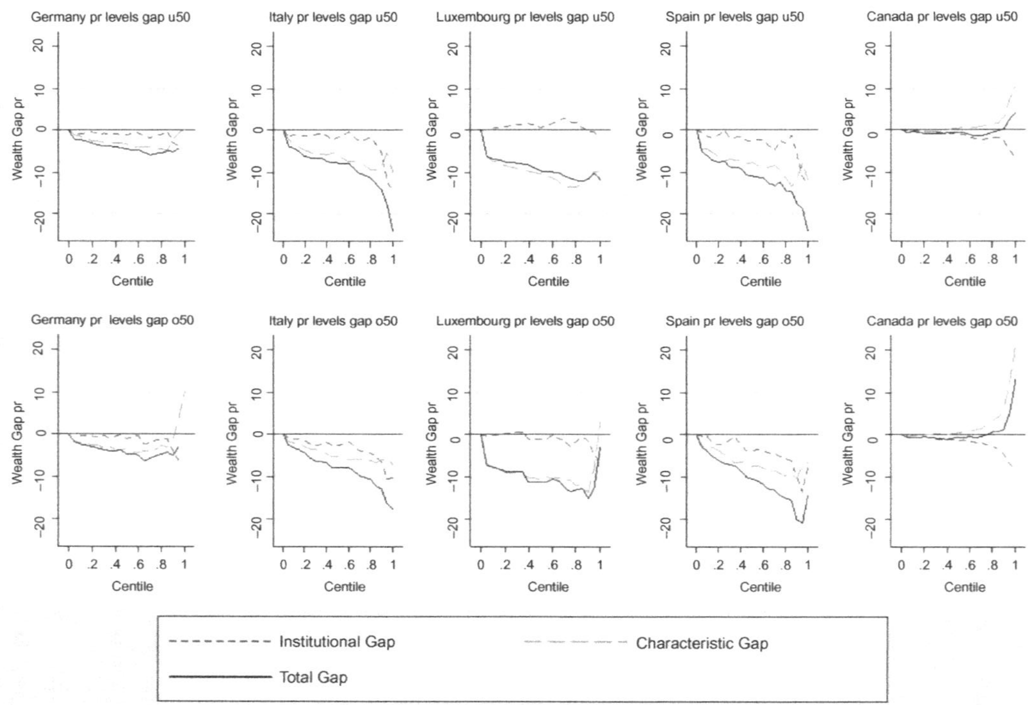

Fig. 6. Coefficient and Institutional Gaps across the Distribution of Principal Residence. *Notes*: The wealth gaps are scaled by the median income. The characteristics gap shows the level of difference between the US and each country's investment in principal residence which is accounted for by household characteristics. The institutional gap shows the gap which is unexplained. The total gap is the sum of these two. *Source*: 2007 SCF, 2005 SFS, 2007 SOEP, 2008 SHIW, 2007 PSELL3, and 2008 EFF.

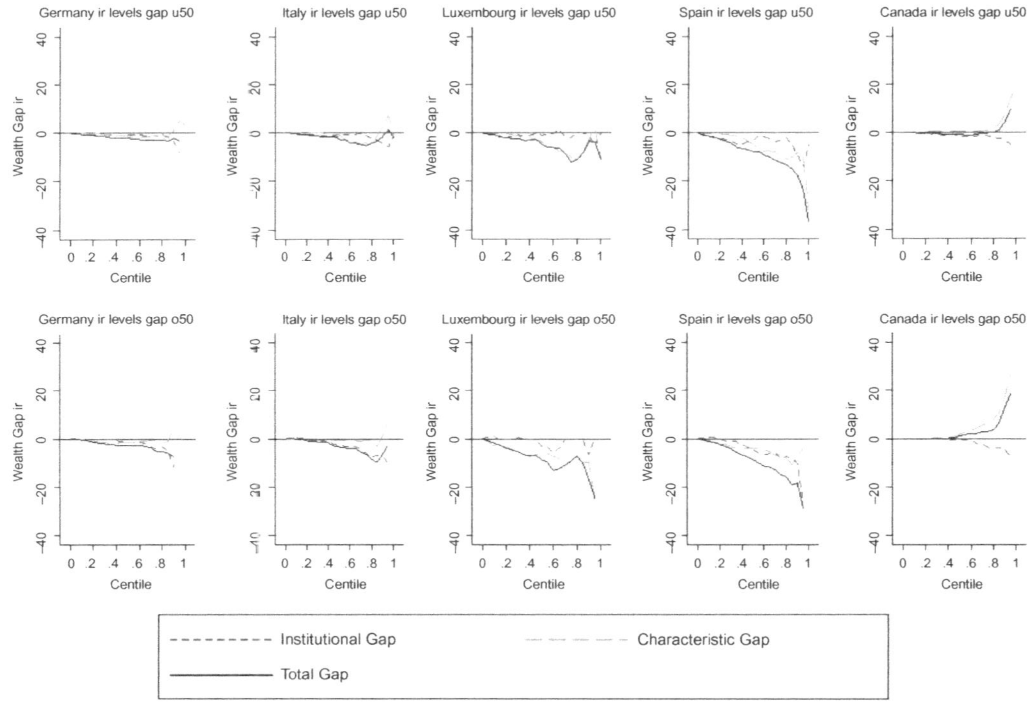

Fig. 7. Coefficient and Institutional Gaps across the Distribution of Investment Real Estate. *Notes*: The wealth gaps are scaled by the median income. The characteristics gap shows the level of difference between the US and each country's investment in investment real estate which is accounted for by household characteristics. The institutional gap shows the gap which is unexplained. The total gap is the sum of these two. *Source*: 2007 SCF, 2005 SFS, 2007 SOEP, 2008 SHIW, 2007 PSELL3, and 2008 EFF.

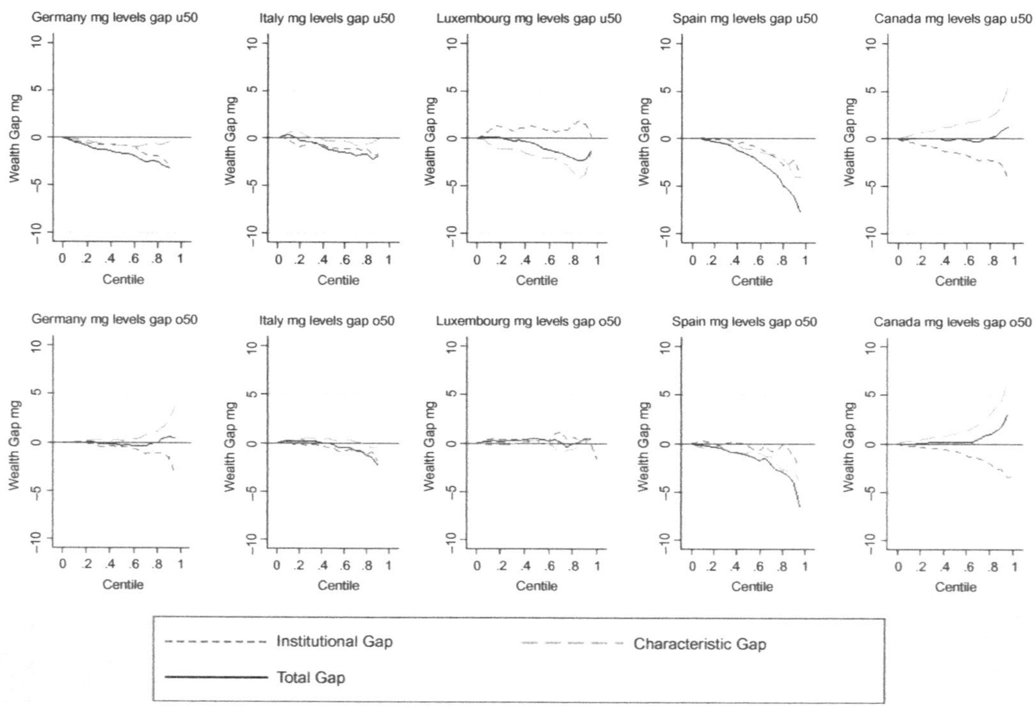

Fig. 8. Coefficient and Institutional Gaps across the Distribution of Mortgage Debt. *Notes*: The wealth gaps are scaled by the median income. The characteristics gap shows the level of difference between the US and each country's investment in mortgage debt which is accounted for by household characteristics. The institutional gap shows the gap which is unexplained. The total gap is the sum of these two. *Source*: 2007 SCF, 2005 SFS, 2007 SOEP, 2008 SHIW, 2007 PSELL3 and 2008 EFF.

than European households due to the institutional environment or other unobserved factors (Luxembourg is an exception). There is also a negative institutional gap between the United States and Canada but a larger positive characteristic gap between these countries leads to a small positive overall gap.

For the older cohort, the total gaps are smaller indicating that cross-country differences in mortgage levels are more similar across countries for older households than younger households. The characteristic gap in Germany and Canada remains positive.

Non-Housing Debt. Finally, we turn to non-housing debt (Fig. 9). Here we observe two patterns: a negative gap between the United States and Germany and Spain, increasing at the top of the distribution and a positive almost non-existent gap for Italy and Canada. The gaps become larger for the older cohort for Germany and Spain and smaller for Italy and Canada. In all countries, except Germany, the characteristic effect dominates the unexplained effect. In Germany, for the younger cohort the institutional gap is driving the results and is still present for the older cohort.

Cohort Differences

Comparing the results for the two cohorts we find total gaps and characteristic gaps to be larger for the older cohort's level of financial assets across countries. Unexplained/institutional gaps are more important in determining the share of financial assets in the younger cohort's portfolio (although they are smaller in level terms). This contrasts to the participation decision, for which the characteristic and institutional gaps are larger for the younger cohort. The gaps for both cohorts are larger at the top of the distribution, thus only the very rich seem to be sensitive to the institutional setup, possibly via tax incentives.

Housing is a big part of the wealth portfolio, often reaching about two-thirds of total assets. Thus, a specific housing enhancing institutional policy can potentially play a large role in wealth accumulation. We find similar gaps in the level of principal residence for the two cohorts. However, the older cohort shows larger between-country differences in the distribution of investment real estate. We find institutional effects and other unobservables to play a similar role in the housing wealth for the two cohorts leaving scope for more targeted policy overall.

On the other hand, we find a smaller role of institutions for the older rather than the younger cohort in the level of mortgage debt. As the younger cohort has higher average levels of mortgage debt than the older

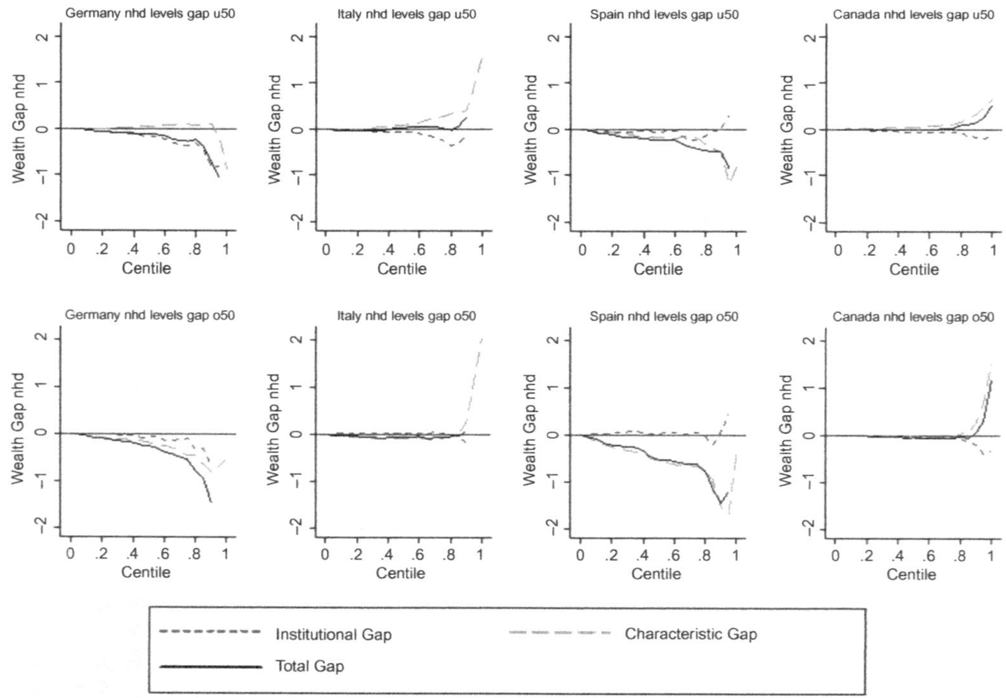

Fig. 9. Coefficient and Institutional Gaps across the Distribution of Non-Housing Debt. *Notes*: The wealth gaps are scaled by the median income. The characteristics gap shows the level of difference between the US and each country's investment in non-housing debt which is accounted for by household characteristics. The institutional gap shows the gap which is unexplained. The total gap is the sum of these two. *Source*: 2007 SCF, 2005 SFS, 2007 SOEP, 2008 SHIW, 2007 PSELL3, and 2008 EFF.

cohort (Table 2), this is unsurprising. Given the decision to take out a mortgage, the amount borrowed may be more sensitive to lending terms or other institutional factors for the younger cohort.

The Intensive versus the Extensive Margin of Investment

Comparing asset participation rates across countries, as was done by Sierminska and Doorley (2013), informs us of the prevalence of each instrument in the population. The decision to own or not to own can be considered as the extensive margin of investment. In this paper, we examine the intensive margin or the magnitude of investment in each instrument separately by country and deduce the differences in relative investment levels across countries. This provides us with a more complete picture of portfolios and shows us the extent to which wealth could be used to supplement well-being cross-nationally. For example, large unexplained differences in housing levels indicate there are probably differences in housing affordability. Large characteristic gaps for most instruments indicate that most of the cross-national variation in these can be explained. Unexplained gaps suggest there is room for policy intervention via, for example, tax rates. Here, we summarize our findings for the main wealth instruments: financial assets, principal residence, investment real estate, and mortgage debt and compare the results to those on the participation decision by Sierminska and Doorley (2013).

The participation gap in financial assets between the United States and the other countries is largely unexplained. By contrast, almost all of the levels gap, given participation, are explained by characteristics, with institutions contributing a small negative gap at the top of the income distribution, indicating that institutions are more conducive to investing in high levels of financial assets for high income people outside the United States.

In terms of risky assets, both the participation and the amount that is invested are mostly driven by characteristics (income and education for the participation decision). Education is often used as a proxy for financial literacy and, as such, could serve as a proxy of financial sophistication, leading households to invest in risky assets that are known, on average, to yield higher returns.

The cross-national differences in housing wealth (given participation) are explained by differences in characteristics to a large extent. The value of this housing in the United States is also lower than those of similar households in most countries (except Canada) due to institutional or other features. Thus, in the United States, home value represents a lower proportion of the total asset portfolio than in Europe. Homeownership is also more prevalent in the United States than in the other countries, but this is due once again to characteristics. The institutional effect is also negative for homeownership indicating that Canadian and European households would still have higher homeownership rates than the United States if they had the same characteristics.

The United States has higher participation in mortgage debt than either Canada or the European countries. This participation gap is a mixture between explained and unexplained components. The unexplained part of the gap is dominant and larger for the older cohort than for the younger one. Although there is higher prevalence of mortgage debt in the United States, the levels are higher in European countries and this is unexplained by characteristics, especially for the younger cohort. The gaps are negative and unexplained for the younger cohort (except in Luxembourg). The variation in these outcomes suggests there are a lot of institutional differences at play here (as discussed in the next section) and scope for policy related to debt take-up for the older cohort, but to a smaller extent at the intensive margin (the amount, given take-up).[6]

The participation gaps for non-housing debt are large (except for Canada), largely unexplained and present for both cohorts. For levels this is also true except for the fact that the gaps are driven by characteristics for the older cohort. Thus once households commit to having debt, the levels depend on household characteristics. The decision to have debt in the first place may stem from institutional or cultural factors.

The Role of Institutions and Culture

In this section, we take a more in-depth look at institutional differences in the countries in our sample and try to draw a link between the sign and magnitude of the unexplained (institutional) gaps in wealth levels across countries and the institutional setting. Institutional differences across countries may be responsible for different investment patterns and an understanding of which institutions drive investment decisions will be invaluable to policymakers who are, for example, interested in further market integration at the EU level or, indeed, in promoting certain types of investment over others depending on the labor market, dependency ratio, and other characteristics of the country concerned.

Ideally, we would like to include institutional measures in our decomposition framework but, for compatibility with a cross-country decomposition, we would need regional variation in these measures within a country so that the measure can be incorporated into each country's wealth level regressions. In the same way as we can draw inferences about the effect of household composition and labor market status on wealth accumulation, the coefficients on these institutional variables would then also tell us something about how they affect wealth accumulation. However, in the absence of regional variation in most institutions or of data relating to any suitable regional variations, we limit ourselves to robust bivariate linear regressions of the unexplained gap in wealth levels at the median for each component of wealth on country institutional features.

In our analysis, we use a number of indices, summarized in Table 5. A number of these directly relate to the economy. The Financial Development Index is a score for the breadth, depth, and efficiency of each country's financial system and capital markets (Bilodeau, 2008). Next, the Index of Economic Freedom measures the economic freedom in each country, with higher scores indicating lower government interference in the economy (Kane, 2007). The banking regulation index measures the degree of banking regulation in each country, including enforcement power (Andrews, Sánchez, & Johansson, 2011). The marginal tax rate measures the tax due on an extra dollar of income for a single person earning either 67% or 167% of the average wage. Household equity in pensions measures the net equity (in euros per capita) of households in life insurance and pension funds reserves. Dividend tax is a measure of the top rate of tax on corporate dividends. Tax as a percentage of GDP measures current taxes on income, wealth, etc., as a proportion of GDP. The same ratio for capital tax is also used.

As our analysis looks at a number of aspects of the housing market, principal residence, investment real estate, and mortgage debt, we also use three features of mortgages in each country (see Andrews et al., 2011): the maximum loan-to-value (LTV) ratio, the prevalence of fixed rate mortgages, and the typical maturity rate of mortgages. Lastly, we use a measure of mathematical literacy from the PISA project as a proxy for the education system.

The results of these simple regressions are depicted in Table 6 for five components of the wealth portfolio. We exclude Risky Assets from this analysis as we do not have information on this wealth component in either Germany or Luxembourg.

The dependent variable is the unexplained gap in the level of each component of the wealth portfolio in turn. To visualize this gap, we can look at

Table 5. Institutional Indices.

Index	Description	Scale	Source
Financial development	Measures the breadth, depth, and efficiency of financial systems and capital markets	1–7 with higher values indicating more development	Financial Development Report 2008
Economic freedom	Measures the level of government interference in the economy	0–100 with higher values indicating more freedom	2007 Index of Economic Freedom
Bank regulation	Measures anticompetitive regulations in banking taking into account regulatory barriers on domestic and foreign entry, restrictions on banking activities, and the extent of government ownership	0–5 with higher values indicating more regulation	Andrews et al. (2011)
Marginal tax rate	Net personal marginal tax rate of a single person earning 67% or 167% of the average wage in 2007	%	OECD Stat
HH equity in pensions	Net equity of households in life insurance and pension funds reserves in 2007	Euro/capita	OECD Stat
Tax/GDP	2007 taxes on income, wealth, etc. as a percentage of GDP	%	OECD Stat
Capital tax/GDP	2007 capital taxes as a percentage of GDP	%	OECD Stat
Tax on dividends	Net top statutory rate to be paid at the shareholder level in 2007	%	OECD Stat
Mortgage maturity	Typical mortgage maturity term	Years	Andrews et al. (2011)
Fixed rate mortgages	Prevailing type of interest rate. Measured as the proportion of fixed rate mortgages	%	Andrews et al. (2011)
Maximum LTV ratio	Regulatory limit on mortgage LTV limits	%	Andrews et al. (2011)
Mathematical literacy	Measures the mathematical skills of 15 year olds	The average score among OECD countries is 500 points and the standard deviation is 100 points	PISA 2006

Fig. 3. The unexplained gap in principal residence between Germany and the United States is the horizontal distance between the lines "Germany with US coefficients" and "Germany" or, more formally:

$$\left[\hat{Q}^{\mathrm{US}}_{j,\tau}(w)\right] - \left[\hat{Q}^{j}_{j,\tau}(w)\right] \tag{6}$$

For the purpose of this exercise and to facilitate interpretation, we multiply this gap by −1. That is, we define:

$$gap = \left[\hat{Q}^{j}_{j,\tau}(w)\right] - \left[\hat{Q}^{\mathrm{US}}_{j,\tau}(w)\right] \tag{7}$$

Our simple model becomes:

$$\hat{gap} = \alpha + \beta I \tag{8}$$

where I takes the value of each of the institutional indices in turn. A positive β in Table 6 indicates a positive correlation between the unexplained gap in the level of a particular wealth component (and, therefore, a positive correlation between the level of a particular wealth component, given household characteristics) and the institutional index. We summarize the results by index below.

Financial Development

This index measures the breadth, depth, and efficiency of each country's financial system across a range of factors including the institutional environment, financial stability, banking and non-banking financial services, financial markets, and financial access. Regressing the unexplained gap in the level of either type of housing (principal residence or investment real estate) on this index yields negative coefficients both for households under 50 years of age and over. An increase of one point in the financial development index is associated with a decrease in the level of principal residence or investment real estate of about twice the median income, with a larger effect for older households. Financial development, therefore, seems to be negatively associated with homeownership. It is possible that countries with more developed and stable financial systems substitute real estate investment for investment in more liquid financial assets although we see no direct evidence of this in our regression for total financial assets. It is

Table 6. Coefficients from a Bivariate Regression of the Unexplained Wealth Gap on Institutional Indices.

	TFA u-50	TFA o-50	PR u-50	PR o-50	IR u-50	IR o-50	MG u-50	MG o-50	NHD u-50	NHD o-50
Financial development	−1.72**	−2.24*	−1.46	−2.57	−0.50	−0.15	−0.09***	−0.22**	−0.02	0.04
Economic freedom	−0.15**	−0.15*	−0.09	−0.15	−0.06	−0.02	−0.01***	−0.02**	−0.00	0.00
Bank regulation	−0.33	−0.81	−0.81	−1.67	0.58	0.48	0.03	−0.02	−0.07	−0.03
Mortgage maturity	−0.16	−0.22**	−0.14	−0.26*	−0.03	−0.01	−0.01**	−0.02*	−0.00	0.00
Proportion of fixed rate mortgages	−0.00	−0.02	−0.01	−0.03**	0.01	0.01	−0.00	−0.00	0.00	0.00*
Maximum LTV ratio	−0.04	−0.02	−0.01	−0.01	−0.03	−0.01	−0.00	−0.01	−0.00**	−0.00
Mathematical literacy	−0.01	−0.02	−0.01	−0.03	0.01	0.01	−0.00	−0.00	0.00	0.00
Marginal tax rate (low earner)	0.00	−0.01	−0.02	0.00	0.07*	0.04***	0.00	0.00	0.01*	0.00
Marginal tax rate (high earner)	−0.05	−0.05	−0.05	−0.02	−0.04	−0.00	0.00	−0.00	0.00	−0.00
HH equity in pensions	−0.02*	−0.01	−0.01	0.00	−0.02***	−0.01*	−0.00	−0.00*	−0.00	−0.00
Tax/GDP	0.13	0.04	0.02	−0.09	0.13**	0.05	0.00	0.01	−0.02	−0.01
Capital tax/GDP	2.50	3.51	3.24	3.68	0.49	−0.55	−0.03	0.12	−0.03	−0.00
Tax on dividends	−0.11	−0.18	−0.10	−0.25	0.04	0.03	−0.01*	−0.01	0.00	0.01*

Source: 2005 SFS, 2007 SCF, 2007 SOEP, 2008 SHIW, 2007 PSELL3, and 2008 EFF.

Notes: The dependent variable is the unexplained gap, measured in times the median income, in the level of wealth between the United States and the reference country. TFA is Total Financial Assets; PR is Principal Residence; IR is Investment Real Estate; MG is Mortgage; NHD is Non-Housing Debt. u-50 refers to households whose head is under 50 years of age while o-50 refers to those whose head is over 50 years of age.

also possible that financial development leads to a lower need for precautionary savings/investments altogether.

Economic Freedom
We observe similar patterns with the index of Economic Freedom. Economic Freedom measures the degree of government interference in each economy and captures business freedom, trade freedom, fiscal freedom, freedom from government, monetary freedom, investment freedom, financial freedom, property rights freedom, freedom from corruption, and labor freedom. The higher this index is, the less the government interferes in the economy. As such, we might expect more economically free countries to provide less subsidies for housing. Our results confirm this theory with economic freedom associated with less investment in housing.

Bank Regulation
Banking regulation measures the degree of banking regulation, including enforcement power, in each country. We expect that countries with higher levels of bank regulation will have stricter lending policies but, also, more banking stability. This may lead to higher trust in institutions. We observe that the degree of regulation is positively correlated with the level of mortgage debt, particularly for the over-50 population which is in line with the idea that more regulation promotes lending through its effect on stability rather than hindering it through its effect on regulatory capital adequacy ratios and LTV measures. We also observe a negative correlation between the level of real estate held, particularly investment real estate, and the degree of banking regulation which could indicate that lending for this purpose is curtailed in more regulated banking systems or that higher trust in institutions encourages households to invest in financial products more than in real estate.

Tax Rate
We also use a number of tax measures in our analysis. The marginal tax rate measures the tax due on an extra dollar of income for a single person earning either 67% or 167% of the average wage. Higher marginal tax rates indicate less disposable income and less incentive to earn investment income as more of it will have to be paid over in tax. However, we find little association between the marginal tax rate and the various portfolio instruments, except for a positive correlation between the marginal tax rate for low earners and investment real estate and non-housing debt. The dividend tax rate measures the net top statutory rate to be paid at the shareholder level and

should indicate how attractive/profitable shareholdings are in each country. We find no association between the top rate of dividend taxation and the level of total financial assets, but there is a negative relationship between this tax rate and housing wealth. Tax as a proportion of GDP and capital tax as a proportion of GDP provide markers for how redistributive the tax-benefit system in a country is. It is unclear how we might expect these indices to be related to wealth accumulation as redistribution may encourage poorer households to invest while discouraging richer households. In general, we find a positive association between these measures and the level of assets and mortgages held, indicating that the net result of redistribution may be more wealth accumulation.

Household Equity in Life Insurance and Pension Fund Reserves

This measure indicates how prepared households are for retirement and/or unexpected losses of earnings. We expect that higher equity will result in lower wealth accumulation for precautionary reasons. We do indeed find a negative correlation between this measure and the level of assets (and debt) held by households.

Mortgage Characteristics

We use three measures relating to mortgages in each country: the typical maturity length, the prevalence of fixed rate mortgages, and the maximum LTV ratio. We find that longer mortgage maturities are associated with lower levels of real estate wealth. That is, the lower the monthly repayments (through longer mortgage terms) the lower the value of housing held. This could be due to the fact that longer mortgage terms mean higher overall interest payments, increasing the total cost of real estate and making it less affordable.

Mathematical Literacy

We use a measure of mathematical literacy from the 2006 PISA test which evaluates the mathematical literacy of 15 year olds across countries in a harmonized way. Financial literacy has been found to be negatively associated with non-housing debt (Lusardi & Tufano, 2009) and positively associated with mortgage participation (Brown & Graf, 2012). However, we find no association between mathematical literacy and any of the portfolio instruments.

CONCLUSIONS

In this paper, we apply novel techniques to the analysis of wealth portfolios. We decompose the wealth portfolio at the intensive margin (given participation in a particular instrument) for a selection of assets and liabilities across countries. We focus on households whose head is under 50 years of age and compare them to those over 50 years old. We compare our findings to our previous results relating to the participation decision itself.

We first show the positive relationship between income and asset and liability levels for various components of the wealth portfolio. The US households are found to have higher levels of financial and risky assets than European or Canadian households, especially at the top of the income distribution. European households, conversely, have higher levels of real estate investments than US households throughout the income distribution. The debt-income profile of our sample of countries shows that, among poor households, it is the Spanish that have the highest level of debt while, among rich households, the US, Luxembourgish, and German households have the highest level of debt.

The differences, we see that the difference in the level of financial assets between the United States, Canada, and Europe is largely driven by household characteristics. There is actually a small negative unexplained effect which indicates that European and Canadian households would have higher levels of financial assets than US households if their characteristics were the same. Differences in levels of real estate across countries are found to be only partly explained with European and Canadian households holding higher levels of housing wealth than US households for unexplained reasons, likely linked to the institutional environment. We see similar patterns for levels of debt (primarily mortgage debt) with the European countries and Canada holding higher levels of debt than US households for reasons unrelated to their household characteristics. Most of the unexplained cross-country differences that we observe occur at the top of the asset/debt distribution, indicating that if institutional factors are behind them, investment policies may be most effective if targeted at wealthier households.

Cohort effects exist in the cross-country differences in asset levels. Cross-country differences in asset and liability levels are generally larger for the older cohort but most of these differences are explained by household characteristics. The unexplained gap in investment and borrowing levels is larger for the younger cohort than the older cohort. This indicates that levels of investment and borrowing for younger households may be more influenced by the institutional environment. This contrasts to the participation decision across cohorts. Unexplained participation differences in assets are found to be larger for the younger cohort while unexplained differences in participation rates for debt are found to be larger for the older cohort. It seems that, once the decision to invest or to borrow is taken, the level of investment made by younger households is more sensitive to institutions, culture, or other country differences than older households.

In an attempt to explain part of the unexplained differences in asset and liability levels across countries, we examined the association between unexplained wealth gaps and a number of institutional indices. We found some consistent patterns with financial development, economic freedom, mortgage maturity, and bank regulation negatively correlated with housing wealth. Housing wealth is the instrument for which we found the largest unexplained differences across countries, so these results indicate that the institutional environment may be a driver of cross-country investment patterns in this instrument.

Clearly, the degree of participation in wealth and the level of wealth held across countries vary widely and for many observable and unobservable reasons. The incorporation of some measure of wealth into traditional poverty or well-being measures may, therefore, change the conclusions of such measure about at-risk populations, particularly older households. This is something that can be expected to happen in the future as the quality of data on wealth improves.

Future research could try to control for observable institutional factors to examine to what degree these affect the unexplained gap in portfolio participation and levels across countries.

NOTES

1. Income generating annuities (such as public and occupational pensions) may end with the death of a worker or spouse, while stocks or mutual funds can be passed on to children. Similarly, houses can be transferred to children, but their value is usually not captured in flow measures of economic well-being. Thus, wealth may also be a better measure than income, both of the economic well-being of older persons and their ability to assist children through inter vivo transfers and bequests.

2. Although we do not take into account other factors such as different risks and returns for financial assets, it has been shown that the majority of households have only a few types of assets. Less than 35% of households hold risky assets in the form of stocks or mutual funds and this number is much lower for the other countries.

3. One exception is Italy which registers a small decrease in GDP per capita in 2008, the year of data collection.
4. The variable list can be seen in Tables A3–A5.
5. See Fortin et al. (2011) for a more detailed discussion of this inversion.
6. For the older cohort, pension income may have a large effect on the extensive margin, as it determines their needs for debt.

ACKNOWLEDGMENTS

This research is part of the WealthPort project (*Household Wealth Portfolios in a Comparative Perspective*) supported by the Luxembourg "Fonds National de la Recherche" (contract CORE C09/LM/04) and by core funding for CEPS/INSTEAD by the Ministry of Higher Education and Research of Luxembourg.

REFERENCES

Andrews, D., Sánchez, A. C., & Johansson, Å. (2011). *Housing markets and structural policies in OECD countries*. OECD Economics Department Working Paper No. 836. OECD Publishing.

Bilodeau, J. (Ed.). (2008). *The financial development report 2008*. World Economic Forum.

Brandolini, A., Magri, S., & Smeeding, T. M. (2010). Asset-based measurement of poverty. *Journal of Policy Analysis and Management*, *29*(2), 267–284.

Brown, M., & Graf, R. (2012). *Financial literacy, household investment and household debt: Evidence from Switzerland*. Working Papers on Finance 1301. University of St. Gallen, School of Finance, Switzerland.

Chernozhukov, V., Fernandez-Val, I., & Melly, B. (2009). *Inference on counterfactual distributions*. CeMMAP Working Paper No. CWP09/09. Centre for Microdata Methods and Practice, Institute for Fiscal Studies, London.

Chiuri, M., & Jappelli, T. (2010). Do the elderly reduce housing equity? An international comparison. *Journal of Population Economics*, *23*(2), 643–663.

Christelis, D., Georgarakos, D., & Haliassos, M. (2012). Differences in portfolios across countries: Economic environment or household characteristics? *The Review of Economics and Statistics*, *95*(1), 220–236.

Fortin, N., Lemieux, T., & Firpo, S. (2011). Decomposition methods in economics. In *Handbook of labor economics* (Chap. 1, Vol. 4, pp. 1–102). Amsterdam: Elsevier.

Gornick, J. C., Sierminska, E., & Smeeding, T. M. (2009). The income and wealth packages of older women in cross-national perspective. *The Journals of Gerontology: Social Sciences*, *64B*(3), 402–414.

Haveman, R., & Wolff, E. (2004). The concept and measurement of asset poverty: Levels, trends and composition for the U.S., 1983–2001. *Journal of Economic Inequality*, *2*(2), 145–169.

Kane, T. (2007). *2007 Index of economic freedom*. Washington, DC: Heritage Foundation and the Wall Street Journal.

Lusardi, A., & Tufano, P. (2009). *Debt literacy, financial experiences, and overindebtedness*. NBER Working Paper No. 14808. National Bureau of Economic Research, Inc.

Machado, J. A. F., & Mata, J. (2005). Counterfactual decomposition of changes in wage distributions using quantile regression. *Journal of Applied Econometrics*, *20*, 445–465.

OECD. (2010). *OECD employment outlook 2010: Moving beyond the jobs crisis*. Paris: OECD Publishing.

Sierminska, E., Brandolini, A., & Smeeding, T. (2006). The Luxembourg wealth study: A cross-country comparable database for household wealth research. *Journal of Economic Inequality*, *4*(3), 375–383.

Sierminska, E., & Doorley, K. (2013). *To own or not to own? Household portfolios, demographics and institutions in a cross-national perspective*. IZA Discussion Paper No. 7734. Institute for the Study of Labor (IZA).

Weisbrod, B. A., & Hansen, W. L. (1968). An income-net worth approach to measuring economic welfare. *American Economic Review*, *58*(5), 1315–1329.

APPENDIX

Table A1. Overview of Wealth Portfolio Components across the Sample Surveys.

Components	United States	Canada	Germany	Italy	Luxembourg	Spain
Financial assets	Sum	Sum	X	Sum	Collected in brackets	Sum
Deposit accounts	X	X	Not included	X	NA	X
Risky assets	X	X	NA	X	NA	X
Principle residence: current value of own home	X	X	X	X	X	X
Investment real estate	X	X	X	X	Net of mortgages	X
Business equity	X	X	X	X	X	X
Total debt	Sum	Sum	Sum	Sum	Sum	Sum
Total mortgage	Sum	Sum	Sum	X	NA	Sum
Mortgages (main home)	X	X	X	NA	X	X
Other mortgages	X	X	X	NA	NA	X
Non-housing debt	X	X	X	X	NA	X

Source: 2005 SFS, 2007 SCF, 2007 SOEP, 2008 SHIW, 2007 PSELL3, and 2008 EFF.

Table A2. Descriptive Statistics (Means) by Country and Age Groups.

	United States	Canada	Germany	Italy	Luxembourg	Spain	Total
25 to 49 year olds							
Age	38.04	37.37	38.70	39.63	38.75	38.74	38.48
Male (0/1)	0.78	0.61	0.52	0.66	0.45	0.50	0.62
Number of children less than 18 years of age (or under 18)	1.34	0.42	0.79	0.94	1.00	0.93	0.98
S × 100	20.59	33.42	36.51	27.50	24.08	19.21	29.41
SP × 100	15.18	7.92	11.02	6.47	6.52	9.59	11.96
CP × 100	15.74	22.11	16.53	16.26	15.06	11.32	16.15
CPK × 100	48.49	36.55	35.94	49.78	54.34	59.88	42.28
Married	0.53	0.56	0.42	0.66	0.58	0.71	0.49
Divorced	0.22	0.08	0.20	0.12	0.13	0.10	0.19
Low education	0.14	0.13	0.11	0.50	0.30	0.38	0.16
High education	0.32	0.31	0.22	0.13	0.34	0.22	0.26
Employed	0.78	0.81	0.71	0.67	0.80	0.63	0.73
Self-employed	0.11	0.07	0.07	0.21	0.05	0.11	0.09
Retired	0.00	0.00	0.00	0.01	0.00	0.01	0.00
Income	11.32	10.47	10.25	10.59	11.52	10.53	10.66
Wealth (non-PR)	3.61	−0.25	2.66	6.81	7.86	6.86	3.35
50 and over							
Age	64.89	63.94	67.28	67.12	64.69	65.54	66.41
Male (0/1)	0.67	0.60	0.58	0.62	0.51	0.52	0.61
Number of children less than 18 years of age (or under 18)	0.36	0.04	0.08	0.12	0.19	0.05	0.16
S × 100	35.60	40.41	48.17	40.56	35.82	29.67	42.84
SP × 100	8.84	0.67	0.90	1.10	4.58	12.37	3.70
CP × 100	39.12	54.91	45.78	50.32	36.62	28.61	43.54
CPK × 100	16.44	3.64	4.02	8.01	22.98	29.35	9.67
Married	0.52	0.53	0.48	0.58	0.58	0.58	0.51
Divorced	0.41	0.01	0.43	0.33	0.34	0.34	0.40
Low education	0.17	0.32	0.19	0.74	0.46	0.70	0.25
High education	0.30	0.20	0.20	0.08	0.22	0.14	0.22
Employed	0.40	0.37	0.24	0.16	0.24	0.19	0.28
Self-employed	0.11	0.06	0.05	0.10	0.03	0.07	0.07
Retired	0.47	0.48	0.50	0.68	0.43	0.39	0.50
Income	11.21	10.37	10.58	10.71	11.44	10.40	10.76
Wealth (non-PR)	8.53	4.97	5.88	8.13	9.46	8.99	6.93

Note: S – singles; SP – single parents; CP – couples without kids; CPK – couples with kids.

Table A3. Coefficients from DR at the Median Wealth Variable Level for Households Whose Head Is under 50 Years of Age in the United States and Canada.

	(1) TFA	(2) PR	(3) IR	(4) MG	(5) RA	(6) NHD
United States						
Age	−0.061**	0.089**	−0.253***	−0.079*	0.039	0.086***
Age^2	0.036	−0.129**	0.297***	0.168***	−0.073	−0.091**
Male	−0.074	0.111	−0.028	0.159*	−0.482***	−0.041
Child	0.371***	−0.070	0.331***	−0.057	0.275***	0.107***
Low education	0.925***	0.040	−0.210	0.379***	0.495**	0.216***
High education	−0.796***	−0.637***	−0.579***	−0.088*	−0.639***	−0.233***
Married	−0.348***	0.135*	−0.437***	0.114	0.237**	−0.361***
Divorced	0.067	0.429***	−0.332**	0.266***	0.249**	−0.229***
Employed	−0.471***	0.044	0.382	−0.643***	0.265	−0.162*
Self-employed	−0.269**	−0.097	−0.093	−0.447***	−0.044	−0.034
Retired	0.024	0.228	0.604*	−0.645**	−0.244	0.091
Income	−0.253***	−0.450***	−0.183***	−0.097***	−0.074**	−0.060***
Other wealth	−0.034***	−0.020***	−0.005		−0.068***	
Constant	5.434***	3.776***	7.595***	14.102***	1.440	−0.194
Observations	8,581	6,025	2,090	5,170	3,637	6,716
Canada						
Age	0.043	−0.122	0.109	0.057	0.063	0.202***
Age^2	−0.069	0.155	−0.126	−0.019	−0.093	−0.254**
Male	0.088	0.006	0.151	−0.001	0.227	0.156
Child	0.214**	−0.037	−0.356	0.041	−0.003	−0.158
Low education	0.259*	0.519***	0.411	0.138	0.055	0.124
High education	−0.375***	−0.384***	−0.229	−0.194*	−0.154	−0.183*
Married	−0.367***	−0.582***	−0.003	−0.217	0.317	−0.175
Divorced	0.038	−0.320	0.661	−0.134	1.192***	0.087
Employed	−0.135	0.266	0.119	−0.186	1.465***	−0.225
Self-employed	−0.193	−0.224	−0.641	0.127	1.179***	−0.517**
Income	−0.147	−0.203	0.021	−0.027	−0.531***	−0.174*
Other wealth	−0.040***	−0.019***	0.003		−0.050***	
Constant	1.452	4.903**	−2.393	12.011***	3.477	−1.657
Observations	2,087	1,599	425	1,191	683	1,650

Robust standard errors in parentheses.
TFA is Total Financial Assets; RA is Risky Assets; PR is Principal Residence; IR is Investment Real Estate; MG is Mortgage; NHD is Non-Housing Debt.
***$p < 0.01$, **$p < 0.05$, *$p < 0.1$.

Table A4. Coefficients from DR at the Median Wealth Level for Households Whose Head Is under 50 Years of age in Germany and Luxembourg.

	(1) TFA	(2) PR	(3) IR	(4) MG	(5) NHD
Germany					
Age	−0.094***	−0.259***	0.103	−0.097*	−0.145***
Age^2	0.097**	0.315***	−0.138	0.174***	0.179***
Male	0.034	−0.074*	0.066	−0.086*	−0.204***
Child	0.160***	−0.365***	0.210**	0.035	0.009
Low education	0.389***	0.226***	0.171	−0.225***	−0.137**
High education	−0.501***	−0.197***	−0.276***	−0.140***	0.042
Married	−0.116**	−0.545***	−0.157	−0.362***	−0.353***
Divorced	−0.014	0.038	−0.351***	−0.323***	−0.047
Employed	−0.070	−0.215***	0.015	0.028	0.234***
Self-employed	−0.289***	−0.233***	0.024	0.060	−0.301***
Income	0.005	0.015***	0.015	−0.002	−0.019**
Other wealth	−0.021***	−0.016***	−0.021***		
Constant	2.444***	6.024***	−1.726	11.848***	3.293***
Observations	13,315	9,395	2,870	7,430	7,575
Luxembourg					
Age	−0.080*	−0.152***	−0.169	0.036	
Age^2	0.078	0.152**	0.273*	0.054	
Male	−0.163***	−0.040	0.516***	−0.038	
Child	0.304***	0.035	−0.461***	0.265***	
Low education	0.435***	0.371***	−0.383**	−0.074	
High education	−0.316***	0.067	−0.467***	−0.384***	
Married	−0.189**	−0.193**	0.511**	−0.045	
Divorced	−0.350***	−0.254**	−0.339	−0.476***	
Employed	−0.217**	0.180**	0.165	−0.041	
Self-employed	0.015	−0.086	−0.080	0.069	
Income	−0.102**	−0.646***	0.443***	0.017	
Other wealth	−0.014***	−0.008	−0.289***		
Constant	3.317***	11.115***	25.341***	1.639	
Observations	6,068	5,256	2,272	4,635	

Robust standard errors in parentheses.

TFA is Total Financial Assets; RA is Risky Assets; PR is Principal Residence; IR is Investment Real Estate; MG is Mortgage; NHD is Non-Housing Debt.

***$p<0.01$, **$p<0.05$, *$p<0.1$.

Table A5. Coefficients from DR at the Median Wealth Variable Level for Households Whose Head Is under 50 Years of Age in Italy and Spain.

	(1) TFA	(2) PR	(3) IR	(4) MG	(5) RA	(6) NHD
Italy						
Age	0.037	−0.058	−0.430**	0.229	−0.247	0.251*
Age^2	−0.062	0.057	0.525**	−0.207	0.303	−0.318*
Male	−0.130	−0.108	−0.026	−0.096	−0.150	−0.022
Child	0.072	−0.049	0.127	0.054	0.362	−0.040
Low education	0.450***	0.343***	0.505**	0.078	0.114	0.025
High education	−0.074	−0.382***	−0.918***	−0.226	−0.151	−0.540*
Married	0.346**	0.162	−0.025	−0.086	0.047	−0.354
Divorced	0.230	0.249	0.269	−0.555	−0.717**	−0.006
Employed	0.313*	0.095	0.358	−0.414	0.049	−0.151
Self-employed	0.166	−0.046	0.295	−0.706**	−0.139	−0.222
Retired	0.443	0.389				−0.541
Income	−0.910***	−0.156**	−0.038	0.076	−0.667***	−0.035
Other wealth	−0.026***	−0.011	−0.016		0.008	
Constant	8.989***	3.185	8.941**	−1.499	12.266***	−3.118
Observations	2,001	1,476	400	519	430	584
Spain						
Age	0.089	0.082	−0.381**	0.186	0.388	0.097
Age^2	−0.137	−0.147	0.458**	−0.196	−0.495	−0.134
Male	−0.215**	0.087	−0.031	−0.091	−0.014	0.461***
Child	0.228**	−0.130	0.229	0.056	0.230	0.080
Low education	0.431***	0.480***	0.294	0.232	−0.646	0.269
High education	−0.344***	−0.255*	−0.380*	0.032	0.060	−0.043
Married	−0.169	−0.074	0.113	0.474**	0.112	−0.328
Divorced	0.327*	−0.084	0.012	0.055	−0.606	0.280
Employed	−0.204*	−0.259**	−0.248	−0.080	1.978	−0.411**
Self-employed	−0.066	−0.106	−0.811**	0.020	1.123	−0.968***
Retired	0.445	−0.003	−2.083***			−1.321**
Income	−0.026	−0.013	−0.034	0.006	−0.241	0.039
Other wealth	−0.043***	−0.003	0.045***		−0.152	
Constant	−0.547	−0.728	7.760**	1.466	−4.844	−1.749
Observations	1,698	1,417	637	741	90	514

Robust standard errors in parentheses.
TFA is Total Financial Assets; RA is Risky Assets; PR is Principal Residence; IR is Investment Real Estate; MG is Mortgage; NHD is Non-Housing Debt.
***$p < 0.01$, **$p < 0.05$, *$p < 0.1$.

THE DECOMPOSITION OF WELL-BEING DIMENSIONS: AN APPLICATION TO GERMANY

Jürgen Faik and Uwe Fachinger

ABSTRACT

In the wake of the Stiglitz Commission, we assess German economic well-being by considering income, wealth and consumption. A decomposition approach is used to test for corresponding inequality differences of these well-being dimensions. Total inequality is decomposed into within- and between-group inequality (via a normalised coefficient of variation). The decompositions are categorised into those that refer to socio-demographic characteristics (place of residence, age, household type) and those belonging to different well-being (sub-)categories (potential and net income, expenditure and wealth categories). The empirical analyses are performed for Germany using the 2008 German Sample Survey of Income and Expenditure. By decomposing German well-being inequality in great detail, we shed light on its dimensions. Our analyses illustrate that it is necessary to consider all well-being

Economic Well-Being and Inequality: Papers from the Fifth ECINEQ Meeting
Research on Economic Inequality, Volume 22, 87–113

ISSN: 1049-2585/doi:10.1108/S1049-258520140000022002

dimensions to make statements about the material well-being of private households or individuals.

Keywords: Decomposition; distribution; inequality; shift-share analysis; well-being

JEL classifications: D30; D31; D60

INTRODUCTION

In principle, from an economic point of view, three main categories of material well-being exist: income, consumption expenditure and wealth. In the following, a decomposition approach is used to test for differences of these alternative measures of inequality. This approach consists of decompositions of inequality with respect to socio-demographic groups and well-being categories.

The research question is twofold: First, is the inequality of material well-being dominated by within-group or by between-group inequality? Additionally, does consideration of the three main dimensions of material well-being produce different results for the distribution of inequality?

To measure inequality, the decomposable, normalised coefficient of variation is applied. This allows comparisons between the various well-being categories. The analyses include sensitivity calculations, performed as shift-share analyses by varying the population shares.

The paper is organised as follows: First, we discuss the relevance of the use of income, wealth and consumption data. The next section describes the database and its limitations. After a description of our methods, the results of the empirical analyses of several well-being dimensions are presented. Finally, we draw some conclusions.

BACKGROUND

The measurement of the distribution of well-being has a long tradition in economics (Fleurbaey, 2008; Osberg & Sharpe, 2005). However, there is no agreement on how to perform this measurement precisely, as different approaches can produce different results. Recently, the Stiglitz Commission recommended the consideration of income as well as of consumption expenditure and wealth to measure the material living standard of individuals or households at a particular point in time (Stiglitz, Sen, & Fitoussi, 2009, pp. 29 f.).[1]

Hence, material well-being (WB) can be written as a function of income Y, consumption C and wealth W at a particular point in time t:

$$WB_t = U_t(Y_t, C_t, W_t) \tag{1}$$

Other approaches that point in the direction of relatively comprehensive well-being indicators are the Levy Institute Measure of Economic Well-being (LIMEW), which consists of base income, income from wealth (including annuity from non-home wealth), net government expenditure and household production (Sharpe, Murray, & Evans, 2011; Wolff, Zacharias, & Masterson, 2012); the Human Development Index (HDI), which is composed of life expectancy, education and per capita income (United Nations Development Programme [UNDP], 2011, pp. 167 ff.); and the Index of Economic Well-being (IEWB), which consists of per capita consumption, per capita wealth, economic inequality and economic security (Osberg & Sharpe, 2009). Furthermore, the multidimensionality of material well-being was focused by a report published by the OECD where the 'Framework for Statistics on the Distribution of Household Income, Consumption and Wealth' – the so-called ICW Framework – was presented (Organisation for Economic Co-Operation and Development [OECD], 2013).

Although the Stiglitz Commission report received a lot of attention, there are other opinions on how to obtain appropriate information about material well-being. For example, Eurostat does not take into account wealth or consumption in its proposal for an EU-wide well-being indicator set (Eurostat, 2010, Table 4).

In the following sections, the three dimensions are considered for the decomposition of inequality of private households' material well-being. For illustration purposes, the decomposition is differentiated by socio-demographic variables: place of residence, age and type of household.

Despite the large body of literature, it is not easy to formulate hypotheses about the impact of those factors on the inequality of well-being. Following von Weizsäcker (1996), even the relation between population ageing and the distribution of well-being is very complex (Bishop, Formby, & Smith, 1997; Deaton & Paxson, 1998) since many channels exist by which the factor population ageing potentially influences the distribution of well-being.

However, at least some hypotheses can be drawn out of the extensive literature on the distribution of material well-being. Such a hypothesis can be deduced regarding place of residence; it is well documented that in Germany an adverse selection has taken place since 1989 as many young and well-educated people have migrated from East to West Germany, leaving behind people who are old and poorly trained. Therefore, it can be assumed that material well-being in West Germany will be higher than in East Germany (Schwarze, 1996).

This paper does not deduce or analyse an explanatory model but empirically considers differences between and within those groups defined by age, residence and type of household regarding the inequality of income, wealth and consumption.

In this context, to consider well-being relatively comprehensively, an approach is needed that exceeds a pure income-based or a pure wealth-based analysis. A possibility to reach this aim is the construction of a well-being indicator that covers the multidimensionality of well-being in a single variable (Atkinson, 2003). Theoretically, both material and immaterial aspects could be considered in such an indicator, but this would raise many problems (e.g. the evaluation of differently scaled aspects). Thus, a less ambitious procedure seems appropriate. In concrete terms, we follow a proposal by Weisbrod and Hansen (1968) simply to combine both income and wealth information (i.e. a restriction of analysis on material aspects of well-being). In this approach, wealth is discounted to a certain (base) year, and afterwards these discounted values are added to the (net) income; concretely, we chose a discount rate of 5 per cent, and the calculations of the (ordinary) annuities are based on the official German mortality table from 2007 to 2009 (Eisenmenger & Emmerling, 2011). Thus, this well-being variable called 'potential income' is a combination of income and wealth values in the sense of a flow variable.

DATA

The data used in this study are from the 2008 German Sample Survey of Income and Expenditure (*Einkommens- und Verbrauchsstichprobe*; hereafter, *EVS*) of private households (Statistisches Bundesamt, 2012). The *EVS* is, to a large extent, a representative sample that has been drawn by the German Statistical Office as a cross-sectional database since 1962 (in intervals of five years). Participation in the survey is voluntary, and the 2008 *EVS* comprises 55,100 households and 125,714 persons.

The survey units are persons living in private households (Statistisches Bundesamt, 2005, p. 3). This comprises people living by themselves as well as groups of people living together and sharing a common budget. Thus, the survey contains information at the individual and at the household level. As a result, people with no fixed residence (e.g. homeless persons and those living in public establishments or institutions such as residential care homes, prisons, common housings, community homes or social housings) are excluded from the survey. Additionally, households with a monthly net income of more than EUR 18,000 are also omitted to guarantee their anonymity.

The *EVS* contains detailed information about the socio-demography of private households, especially about income sources, wealth and expenditure (Statistisches Bundesamt, 2010). The data are collected in two different ways (Statistisches Bundesamt, 2005, pp. 5 f.):

- By an introductory interview with two questionnaires to gather socio-economic information, information about household durables and about the households' financial and tangible assets;
- by means of written surveys that include a household log book. All households keep the household log book for one quarter of a year. In each quarter, about 25 per cent of the respondents have to write down all of their receipts and expenses. Therefore, information about the expenses and receipts of households for a period of one year is available but not for the same household. Additionally, the log book covers the expenditures for food, beverages and tobacco in great detail for one month.

Socio-Demographic Information

As mentioned above, the *EVS* contains information both at the household and the individual level. Collected characteristics at the household level include place of residence (*Bundesland*), which can be categorised into West and East Germany, as well as type of household; the numerous types are aggregated into singles, single-parent households, two adults and parents with children (as well as 'other household types'). Additionally, the *EVS* provides personal characteristics from up to eight household members.

Of these, we refer to the year of birth to control for age-related impacts on well-being.

Income Sources

One main goal of the *EVS* is to obtain detailed information about all income sources; therefore, income data are also collected in great detail at the individual and at the household level. At the household level, income is recorded for different ways of aggregation: Information is given for household gross income and household net income as well as disposable household income. There are also several subcategories which are important in our income-related considerations:

- earned income from dependent employment,
- earned income from self-employment (e.g. as a farmer or as a businessman),
- capital income,
- income from public transfers and
- income from private transfers.

In our empirical analyses, the two first mentioned income subcategories are aggregated to the category 'labour income', and income from private transfers is added to income from public transfers, resulting in the category 'transfers'. It should be noted that individual income is even more differentiated, as the *EVS* covers all possible income sources.[2]

To obtain a complete picture of the financial situation of individuals and households, additionally, all taxes and contributions are recorded in the *EVS* (and they are summarised as 'taxes and contributions' in our empirical analyses).

Consumption Expenditure

Consumption expenditure is arranged in 12 categories in the *EVS*.[3] To reduce complexity, we have decreased the number of expenditure categories to only seven expenditure groups.

The categories are, to some degree, quite heterogeneous and, for example, the category transport comprises goods with low prices (e.g. bus tickets) up to very expensive goods (e.g. cars). Another problem is the mix of durable and non-durable goods. As durable goods are, on average, expensive, those expenditures may skew their distribution in a quarter but likely level out over a year. A further problem is that durables are not consumed over a short period of time, and, thus, consumption may stretch over several years. This, in general, leads to an overestimation of consumption within the period in which the corresponding product was purchased and to an underestimation in other periods. While, from a theoretical point of view, it is necessary to use actual consumption for well-being measurement (see e.g. OECD, 2013, pp. 104 ff.), the corresponding information is not available for Germany.

Wealth

The overall wealth of private households is measured in the *EVS* as the sum of monetary assets, tangibles and real estate, including the estimated value of house property.[4] In our empirical analyses, we divide private wealth into monetary assets and real estate. All wealth variables used are defined as net values (i.e. by subtracting debts from gross-wealth values).

The financial accounts of the *Deutsche Bundesbank* (2012) suggest that the *EVS* comprises only around 50 per cent of total financial assets (Bartzsch & Stöss, 2007, p. 221). The differences are mainly the result of the omission of several items from the *EVS*. For example, currency and transferable deposits, claims on insurance corporations and claims from company-pension commitments are not included in the questionnaire. Also not recorded as wealth subcategories are the market values of equities in private businesses (except current values of quoted shares), consumer durables, jewellery and objets d'art.

Furthermore, in the financial accounts of the *Deutsche Bundesbank*, the wealth of non-profit institutions that serve households also are taken into account (Deutsche Bundesbank, 2012, p. 8) but not in the *EVS*. Thus, the total wealth of private households is not recorded in the *EVS*; however, the most common elements of private households' wealth are covered.

Limitations

There are some analytical limitations of the *EVS* regarding the representativeness of the results (Becker & Hauser, 2003, pp. 71 ff.):

1. Institutionalised and homeless persons are not included in the *EVS*.
2. Households with a non-German head are underrepresented.

3. The *EVS* is not a randomised but a quota sample. Households with a (very) high income of EUR 18,000 per month are excluded, and households with very low incomes are underrepresented. Furthermore, participation in the survey is voluntary. All of these aspects lead to the so-called 'middle-class bias'.
4. The participants are not asked about their expenditures and incomes during a complete year but only – in a rotation procedure – during a quarter.

We note that points 1–3 tend to reduce the degree of inequality of well-being, whereas point 4 has a tendency to produce the opposite effect. This is because of special payments in single quarters (e.g. Christmas bonuses). Nevertheless, it may be that such special payments in particular quarters offset each other over a one-year period, so that the assumed bias is not large.

METHOD

The Inequality Indicator

To capture socio-demographic and other impacts on the inequality of well-being, we use a decomposable inequality measure. A very popular class of decomposable indicators is the family of Generalised Entropy (GE) measures. For these measures, groups' population shares as well as their well-being shares serve as weighting factors. Thus, it is possible to analyse within-group and between-group influences of inequality in which the assumed groups must be disjointed from each other. The within-group component measures the weighted sum of the indicator for the different groups. For the between-group component, each member of a group is given the average well-being level of his or her group.

We exemplarily chose the normalised coefficient of variation (HSCV) as a member of the GE family. It is defined as the half of the well-being variance σ^2 divided by the squared well-being mean μ^2:

$$\text{HSCV} = \frac{1}{2} \cdot \left(\frac{\sigma}{\mu}\right)^2 \tag{2}$$

HSCV is decomposable as follows (Faik, 2010, pp. 13 f.):

$$\mathrm{HSCV} = \underbrace{\sum_{g=1}^{G} v_g^2 \cdot w_g^{-1} \cdot \mathrm{HSCV}_g}_{\text{within-group inequality}} + \underbrace{\frac{1}{2} \cdot \left\{ \left[\sum_{g=1}^{G} w_g \cdot \left(\frac{\mu_g}{\mu} \right)^2 \right] - 1 \right\}}_{\text{between-group inequality}} \tag{3}$$

where $v_g^2 \cdot w_g^{-1}$ corresponds with $w_g \cdot (\mu_g/\mu)^2$.

The weighting factors w_g represent the population shares of the several groups of persons g ($g = 1, 2, \ldots, G$), μ_g is the mean of well-being levels within group g, v_g ($= w_g \cdot \mu_g/\mu$) denotes the group-specific share of the aggregated well-being level, and HSCV_g symbolises the within-group HSCV inequality measure and $\mathrm{HSCV_B}$ the between-group HSCV well-being indicator.

In our context, a further issue is relevant: the role of the different well-being components, as they are of different importance during the individual lifecycle. Labour income, for instance, plays an outstanding role during the individual working life, whereas during the times before and after working life (childhood or old age) it is of less importance than other kinds of income. Amidst the backdrop of demographic changes, shifts in the societal importance of various kinds of income are realistic (with corresponding changes in income/well-being distribution and income/well-being inequality).

Methodically, the inequality of an overall well-being variable (in our context: potential and net income, consumption expenditure and wealth) can be, principally, decomposed as follows (for HSCV: alternative decomposition rules may be found e.g. in Sastre & Trannoy, 2002):

$$\mathrm{HSCV_{WB}} = \mathrm{HSCV_A} \cdot \left(\frac{\mu_\mathrm{A}}{\mu_\mathrm{WB}} \right)^2 + \mathrm{HSCV_B} \cdot \left(\frac{\mu_\mathrm{B}}{\mu_\mathrm{WB}} \right)^2 + \frac{\mathrm{cov}(A, B)}{\mu_\mathrm{WB}^2} \tag{4}$$

where HSCV = normalised coefficient of variation, WB = the overall well-being variable (e.g. wealth), A = a concrete well-being component (e.g. real estate as a wealth subcategory), B = another well-being component (e.g. money assets as another wealth subcategory), cov = covariance, and μ = arithmetic mean.[5]

Equivalence Scales

All variables used are defined as *equivalent* household well-being variables (including economies of scales within a household) with the exception of net wealth and its components. Net wealth and its components are calculated as *per capita* variables because needs do not play an important role in this context. All other well-being categories are, in concrete terms, calculated as equivalent variables by normalising the corresponding well-being levels for all households via the 'new OECD equivalence scale' (OECD, 2009).[6] In the next step, the equivalent household well-being levels are assigned to each household member. This is because the individuals and not the households are the ultimate units of well-being (for corresponding conceptual issues see Atkinson, 1983, pp. 52 f.).

The Shift-Share Method

In many cases, comparative-static analyses of the influence of socio-demography on income inequality are conducted (for Germany; Faik, 2011; Peichl, Pestel, & Schneider, 2012) such that over-time changes of the population structure are analysed under the assumption of constant economic conditions. This simplified so-called 'shift-share approach' (Dinwiddy & Reed, 1977, pp. 115 ff.) implies that changes in the population structure do not affect the degree of inequality within the subgroups nor the differences in mean incomes between the several subgroups. However, shift-share analyses also are possible in another way: variability of economic parameters and constancy of population shares (Faik, 2011). For illustrative purposes, however, the empirical analyses (discussed in the next section) are restricted to pure demographic shift-share calculations (with varying population shares and constant economic parameters).

RESULTS

This section is divided into four parts: general inequality findings, subcategory-specific decompositions, socio-demographic decompositions and shift-share analyses. The section 'General Inequality Findings' presents HSCV results for the whole German population and for our main well-being dimensions (potential and net income, consumption expenditure and wealth). Based on this, the differences between these dimensions – and their underlying components – are analysed. In the another part, the corresponding analyses are extended by socio-demographic decomposition considerations which allow for the discrimination of total inequality values into within-group and between-group inequality. In the final part, our empirical (age-related) findings are used for inequality projections for Germany up to 2060.

General Inequality Findings

We calculate HSCV for different sub-indicators of material well-being. Table 1 shows the corresponding results. These results are quite familiar and match, in general, well-known results of previous analyses of the distribution of income, wealth and consumption expenditure for Germany (Hauser, Becker, & Grabka, 2007; Sabelhaus & Schneider, 1997). Wealth is distributed more unequally than income, the HSCV of real estate is higher than that for money assets, gross income is distributed more unevenly than net income, and so on.

Table 1. Inequality Results for the Whole of Germany Based on Half of the Squared Coefficient of Variation for Various Well-Being Dimensions, 2008.

Well-Being Category	Inequality Value
Potential income	*0.3922*
Annualised wealth	1.9251
Net income	*0.1633*
Gross income	0.1988
Labour income	0.5009
Capital income	1.1364
Transfers	0.6976
Taxes and contributions	0.5390
Consumption expenditure	*0.1589*
Food and the like	0.0820
Clothing and shoes	0.4962
Housing rent, water, electricity, gas and other fuels	0.1158
Health care	3.7829
Transport and communication	1.7859
Education and leisure, entertainment and culture	0.6944
Other goods and services	0.7090
Wealth	*1.9561*
Real estate	3.1876
Money assets	2.7029

Source: Authors' calculations.

In detail, the following results can be observed:

- Because wealth inequality (and, derived from this, annualised-wealth inequality) is much higher than net income inequality, potential income inequality is 2.4 times greater than net income inequality.
- Compared with gross income inequality, net income inequality is markedly lower for the whole of Germany (by about 18 per cent).
- The differentiation into various kinds of incomes reveals the highest inequality level for capital income in Germany, followed by transfers and labour income.
- The inequality levels for net income versus consumption expenditure are at a similar level, with a slightly higher value for net income.

In order to show the well-being implications of our four main well-being measures, Table 2 presents the correlation matrix for these variables. Pairwise, all well-being variables correlate positively with each other. This means that, in principle, all well-being variables, more or less (due to the level of Pearson's correlation coefficient), point into the same direction regarding the measurement results of well-being inequality. Net income and wealth correlate to a relatively high degree with each other: Pearson's correlation coefficient is +0.692, whereas e.g. the correlation between expenditure and wealth is considerably lower (indicated by a Pearson's correlation coefficient in the amount of +0.287).

Subcategory-Specific Decompositions

Decomposition of Potential Income

Decomposition of the well-being index of Weisbrod & Hansen called the 'potential income' – based on Eq. (4) – into its (net) income and its

Table 2. Pearson's Correlation Coefficients for Well-Being Categories, Germany, 2008.

Well-Being Category	Potential Income	Net Income	Wealth	Expenditure
Potential income	+1.000***	+0.692***	+0.834***	+0.445***
Net income	+0.692***	+1.000***	+0.384***	+0.576***
Wealth	+0.834***	+0.384***	+1.000***	+0.287***
Expenditure	+0.445***	+0.576***	+0.287***	+1.000***

Source: Authors' calculations.
***Significant at a significance level of 99 per cent (two-sided).

annualised wealth component yields for Germany on one hand a positive interaction term (covariance) between these two components (in the amount of €110,437,958 or, measured in a normalised way by Pearson's correlation coefficient, in the amount of +0.352 where the latter is significant at a significance level of 99 per cent). On the other hand, the within-subcategory inequality element of both components is much stronger than the inequality aspect of interaction between the subcategories (77.2 vs. 22.8 per cent).

Around 77 per cent of within-subcategory inequality of potential income is determined by annualised wealth. In other words, about 59 per cent (= 77.2 · 77.1 per cent) of potential income inequality is directly influenced by annualisation of wealth, which demonstrates the dominant role of this variable. The latter is a reflection of the relatively high degree of inequality of the distribution of personal wealth in Germany.

Decomposition of (Net) Income

Based on Table 1 and with additional information on specific covariance values, it is possible to decompose the HSCV values for gross and net income (see Eq. (4)). For Germany as a whole, this kind of decomposition leads to negative influences of the covariance terms, which means that the HSCV value for gross income, ceteris paribus, is diminished by 0.0629, and the one for net income even by 0.4080 through the interacting terms between the different income subcategories. In other words, considering only the effects of labour income, capital income and transfers (or transfers minus taxes) without the interacting terms would have resulted in HSCV values of the amount of 0.2617 (gross income) and of 0.5713 (net income), which are much higher than the ones stated in Table 1. The correlation matrix – in the sense of normalised covariance values (since Pearson's correlation coefficients transform absolute covariance values into ratios) – is shown in Table 3.

The signs of the correlation coefficients point in the expected directions. For example, as taxes are paid out of labour income and with progressive taxation in Germany, the correlation should be positive and very high, which it is. However, it seems a bit astonishing that the correlation between capital income and taxes is quite low, though it is positive. The sign of the correlation between labour income and transfers is also plausible: It should be negative as transfers should compensate for missing labour income, and the higher the labour income, the lower the transfers should be. This also corresponds to the correlation between transfers and taxes as it should not

Table 3. Pearson's Correlation Coefficients for Different Types of Incomes, Germany, 2008.

Type of Income	Labour Income	Capital Income	Transfers	Taxes	Transfers – Taxes
Labour income	+1.000***	+0.136***	−0.434***	+0.896***	−0.835***
Capital income	+0.136***	+1.000***	+0.165***	+0.215***	−0.016***
Transfers	−0.434***	+0.165***	+1.000***	−0.206***	+0.810***
Taxes	+0.896***	+0.215***	−0.206***	+1.000***	−0.741***
Transfers – taxes	−0.835***	−0.016***	+0.810***	−0.741***	+1.000***

Source: Authors' calculations.
***Significant at a significance level of 99 per cent (two-sided).

be the case that a household that receives high transfers should pay high taxes.

The within-subcategory inequality of (gross) income is dominated by labour income. The corresponding share is 77 per cent. Transfers have a share of 18 per cent, and capital income with 5 per cent only plays a minor role. One reason for the dominance of labour income may be that the majority of households receive labour income but no transfers and only a small amount of capital income. The last-mentioned finding may result from the fact that households with a monthly income of more than EUR 18,000 are excluded from the survey, and, with that, very high capital incomes are also excluded. Therefore, the inequality of (gross) income can be seen as an (at least slightly) distorted image of the inequality of labour income.

Decomposition of Consumption Expenditure

The following list shows consumption expenditure decomposed into the categories:

- food, non-alcoholic and alcoholic beverages and tobacco,
- clothing and shoes,
- housing rent, water, electricity, gas and other fuels,
- health care,
- transport and communication,
- education and leisure, entertainment and culture and
- other goods and services.

This decomposition generates the inequality results already shown in Table 1. Overall, the results are in line with those of previous research (e.g. Fachinger, 2001, p. 166).

Based on these inequality results and on the following (weak, continuously positive) correlations between the several expenditure categories (see Table 4), we calculate that, for all of Germany, 64.1 per cent of the overall inequality of consumption expenditure can be ascribed to the within-subcategory inequality levels of the several expenditure categories.

As illustrated in Fig. 1, the most important influences on the inequality of consumption expenditure arise from the category transport and communication, followed by other goods and services and housing rent, water, electricity, gas and other fuels. Altogether, these three categories amount to 81 per cent of the corresponding within-subcategory inequality. One reason for this, especially for the high shares of the categories transport and communication and other goods and services, may lie in the character of such goods and services. These two categories are very heterogeneous in that they include both products with very low market prices for daily living that only cost a few cents and luxury goods, such as very expensive cars and power cruisers.

Decomposition of Wealth

The relatively high inequality level of wealth is mainly driven by inequality within the wealth categories real estate and money assets (about 82 per cent) and less by inequality between these wealth components (approximately 18 per cent; Pearson's correlation coefficient between real estate and money assets is +0.251, which is significant at a significance level of 99 per cent; the covariance between both wealth subcategories amounts to €1,691,715,217).

The share of real estate is 75 per cent of the total within-subcategory inequality and, accordingly, the figure for money assets is only 25 per cent. This demonstrates the high importance of the distribution of personal real estate in the inequality of wealth (and, additionally, in the inequality of potential income which was already discussed in the section 'Decomposition of Potential Income'). However, as the measurement of real estate is by no means easy and often estimated by data from self-assessment of the households on the basis of incomplete and sometimes incorrect information (bear in mind the incomplete representation of total wealth in Germany via the *EVS*), the dominance of this wealth category may lead to misinterpretations about the total wealth situation. It is a

Table 4. Pearson's Correlation Coefficients for Various Expenditure Categories, Germany, 2008.

Expenditure Category	Food and the Like	Clothing and Shoes	Housing Rent, Water, Electricity, Gas and Other Fuels	Health Care	Transport and Communication	Education and Leisure, Entertainment and Culture	Other Goods and Services
Food and the like	+1.000***	+0.278***	+0.173***	+0.102***	+0.071***	+0.166***	+0.218***
Clothing and shoes	+0.278***	+1.000***	+0.163***	+0.117***	+0.114***	+0.277***	+0.330***
Housing rent, water, electricity, gas and other fuels	+0.173***	+0.163***	+1.000***	+0.156***	+0.086***	+0.182***	+0.241***
Health care	+0.102***	+0.117***	+0.156***	+1.000***	+0.035***	+0.120***	+0.144***
Transport and communication	+0.071***	+0.114***	+0.086***	+0.035***	+1.000***	+0.093***	+0.108***
Education and leisure, entertainment and culture	+0.166***	+0.277***	+0.182***	+0.120***	+0.093***	+1.000***	+0.243***
Other goods and services	+0.218***	+0.330***	+0.241***	+0.144***	+0.108***	+0.243***	+1.000***

Source: Authors' calculations.
***Significant at a significance level of 99 per cent (two-sided).

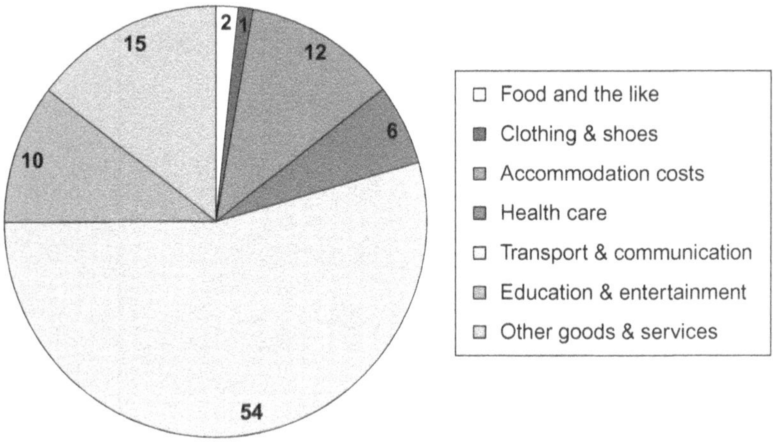

Fig. 1. Shares of Expenditure Categories on Within-Inequality of Consumption Expenditure (HSCV), Germany, 2008 (in Per Cent). *Source*: Authors' calculations.

naïve belief that information about real estate provides objective evidence. The high dependence of the inequality of the wealth distribution on information about real estate shows how problematic and sometimes even arbitrary the evidence for wealth of households may be. With good reason, Buiter suggested the exclusion of real estate from the analysis of people's wealth or, at least, to analyse it separately from other wealth subcategories (Buiter, 2008).

Socio-Demographic Decompositions

Inequality Levels and Relative Positions

Table 5 reveals inequality levels as well as relative positions of our four main well-being variables (potential income, net income, consumption expenditure and wealth) concerning socio-demographic characteristics. Relative positions are defined as the ratio between group-specific and overall (arithmetic) means.

For our *spatially differentiated* decomposition, we distinguish between West and East Germany. In the 2008 *EVS*, the population shares were 82.5 per cent (West Germany) and 17.5 per cent (East Germany). The HSCV values show that East Germany has lower inequality levels than

Table 5. Socio-Demographic Inequality Results (Half of the Squared Coefficient of Variation) and Relative Positions for Various Well-Being Dimensions in Germany, 2008.

Variable	HSCV Inequality Level				Relative Position			
	Potential income	Net income	Consumption expenditure	Wealth	Potential income	Net income	Consumption expenditure	Wealth
Place of residence								
West Germany	0.3892	0.1627	0.1587	1.8377	1.0630	1.0380	1.0302	1.1038
East Germany	0.2320	0.1294	0.1380	1.8287	0.7028	0.8206	0.8573	0.5102
Individual age								
Less than 29 years	0.3007	0.1277	0.1311	1.5586	0.8523	0.9221	0.9118	0.6024
30–59 years	0.2851	0.1675	0.1602	1.7217	0.9775	1.0645	1.0226	0.9320
60 years and older	0.5242	0.1835	0.1730	1.6081	1.2275	0.9810	1.0702	1.6258
Household type								
Single, female	0.5129	0.2011	0.1697	4.1916	0.7075	0.8153	0.9130	1.0241
Single, male	0.5121	0.2761	0.2484	2.4608	0.8297	0.9389	0.9467	1.2206
Single-parent household	0.2926	0.1175	0.1563	5.7088	0.5250	0.6798	0.7995	0.2995
Couple without children	0.4137	0.1802	0.1708	1.3262	1.2242	1.1223	1.1366	1.3984
Couple with child(ren)	0.2090	0.1148	0.1140	1.0915	0.9380	1.0082	0.9500	0.6565
Other type	0.3484	0.1160	0.1313	1.1684	1.0960	1.0112	0.9865	0.9556

Source: Authors' calculations.

West Germany in terms of all four well-being dimensions. With respect to the relative positions in West and East Germany, in all cases, the relative positions for East Germany are lower than the ones for West Germany, which reflects the lower (average) material well-being level in East Germany.

Regarding the variable *age*, we differentiate the population into three age groups (i.e. generations): up to 29 years, 30 to 59 years and 60 years and older. Their population shares in the *EVS* are: 30.9 per cent (up to 29 years), 44.6 per cent (30 to 59 years) and 24.5 per cent (60 years and older).

Referring to well-being dimensions points to the fact that the oldest generation has, on average, in three of four cases (with the exception of net income) the highest economic status indicated by the relative positions. This is, however, typically accompanied by relatively high group-specific inequality levels for the oldest age group, at least concerning potential and net income as well as expenditure.[7]

Furthermore, we differentiated six *household types* from each other (with the corresponding population shares in parentheses, in per cent):[8]

- female singles (12.3),
- male singles (7.0),
- single-parent households (3.9),
- couples without children (28.5),
- couples with children (27.8) and
- other household types (20.6).

The HSCV values of single-parent households are relatively low with respect to net and gross income and for consumption expenditure, but the opposite is the case for wealth. Across all well-being categories, couples with children exhibit lowest within-group inequality; thus, this group appears relatively homogeneously structured in terms of economic well-being.

For relative positions, the highest well-being levels are assigned to couples without children in nearly all cases. In contrast, single-parent households have the lowest relative positions.

Decomposition by Socio-Demographic Variables and Well-Being Dimensions

Table 6 shows the inequality decomposition by socio-demographic variables for each of the well-being dimensions. As is demonstrated in Eq. (2), HSCV can be decomposed in a between- and a within-group component. It becomes obvious that in all cases the within-group component clearly

Table 6. Within-Group Inequality Shares (HSCV) in Germany, 2008, for Different Socio-Demographic Groups (in Per Cent).

	Potential Income	Net Income	Consumption Expenditure	Wealth
Place of residence				
Sum	*97.6*	*97.9*	*98.6*	*98.7*
West Germany	92.5	88.6	89.0	94.4
East Germany	5.1	9.3	9.6	4.3
Individual age				
Sum	*97.5*	*98.8*	*98.8*	*96.2*
Less than 29 years	17.2	20.6	24.1	8.9
30 to 59 years	31.0	51.8	65.0	34.1
60 years and older	49.3	26.5	9.7	53.2
Household type				
Sum	*95.1*	*96.1*	*97.3*	*97.4*
Single, female	8.1	10.1	11.0	27.7
Single, male	6.3	10.4	11.3	13.1
Single-parent household	0.8	1.3	1.3	1.0
Couple without children	45.0	39.5	37.3	37.7
Couple with child(ren)	13.0	19.9	21.2	6.7
Other type	21.9	14.9	15.2	11.2

Source: Authors' calculations.

dominates the between-group component indicating a very high degree of heterogeneity within the socio-demographic groups.

In a *spatial-related* differentiation, for the within-group components, it is evident that they are clearly dominated by the within-group inequality in West Germany with shares ranging from 88.6 per cent (net income) to 94.4 per cent (wealth). Thus, despite the differences between West and East Germany for HSCV values and relative positions, the overall inequality levels are clearly dominated more by within-group inequality than by between-group inequality.

The results provide no evidence to support the hypothesis that the inequality of well-being results from differences between West and East Germany. On the contrary, we find an indication that the inequality within each part of Germany is the main driving factor for total inequality. Therefore, we obtain similar results twenty years after Schwarze stated that 'inequality was clearly dominated by income inequality within the western states' (Schwarze, 1996, p. 6) in which income redistribution from West to East Germany by political measures was seen as the main influencing source. Those measures were undertaken to cushion the impact of the accession of the New Laender in Germany on the well-being of households in East Germany.

In an *age-related* perspective, total HSCV inequality is dominated by the within-group inequality levels of the persons in the age of 30 to 59 concerning net income and consumption expenditure. Contrary to that, the age group 60 years and older and its within-group inequality predominates in the dimensions 'potential income' and 'wealth'. This reflects the relevance of (annualised) wealth. Apart from that, the within-group inequality of the elderly with respect to consumption expenditure is very low (only 9.7 per cent). This reflects relative homogenous consumption behaviour of the elderly.

Regarding *household type*, total within-group inequality is dominated by within-group inequality of couples without children (across all well-being dimensions).

Shift-Share Analyses

To illustrate the scope of decomposable inequality indicators, pure demographic shift-share analyses are applied (for a similar analysis for Germany with the 1995–2009 Socio-Economic Panel, see Faik, 2012a and 2012b, pp. 31 ff.). These analyses are based on forecasts of the German Statistical Office on the basis of the 12th coordinated population forecast, which gives evidence of a more or less distinct reduction of the German population size in the future (Statistisches Bundesamt, 2009). We do not take into account all scenarios but concentrate on two distinctly different variants, one with a relatively young population and another with a relatively old population, to provide some hints about the range in which the data may vary:

- A relatively young population (variant 3-W2): increasing birth frequency, on average, up to 1.6 children per woman in 2025 and subsequent constancy of this level until 2060; increasing life expectancy at birth to 89.2 years for girls and to 85.0 years for boys in 2060; life expectancy at the age of 60 years: 30.1 additional years for women and 26.6 additional years for men; migration at balance: +200,000 persons p.a.;

- a relatively old population (variant 6-W1): decreasing birth frequency, on average, up to 1.2 children in 2060; increasing life expectancy at birth to 91.2 years for girls and to 87.7 years for boys in 2060; life expectancy at the age of 60 years: 32.1 additional years for women and 29.2 additional years for men; migration at balance: +100,000 persons p.a.

As shown in Fig. 2 for Weisbrod and Hansen's well-being indicator, in both population variants, an inequality increase is to be expected. In this context, the following holds true: The more pronounced ageing in variant 6-W1 results in higher inequality at every point in time. Concerning potential income, this is primarily a result of the higher relative well-being positions and the higher group-specific HSCV values of the elderly (both of which are held constant in our shift-share analyses; see Table 5, column 1, concerning these values).

In contrast, the time-related projection of (net) income inequality remains more or less unchanged. For 2014, for the variant 3-W2, we calculate a net income inequality level in the amount of 0.1576, whereas the calculated inequality level will be 0.1569 in 2060. For variant 6-W1, the corresponding income inequality levels are 0.1568 (2014) and 0.1592 (2060). The discrepancy between the projections for potential income on one hand

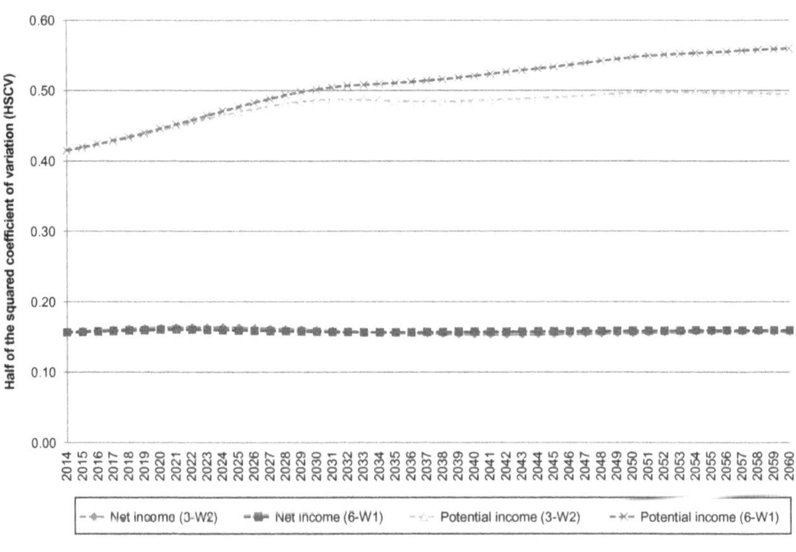

Fig. 2. Projections of Potential and Net Income Inequality for Germany, 2014–2060. *Source*: Authors' calculations.

and those for net income on the other hand arise from relatively small, age-related differences for group-specific HSCV values and group-specific relative positions with respect to net income. This holds true compared to the clear-cut dominance of the elderly's HSCV value and relative position in the context of potential income (see the corresponding values in Table 5).

CONCLUSIONS

The paper primarily dealt with the decomposition of material well-being inequality in Germany based on the database of the 2008 *EVS*. The analysed well-being categories were: equivalent household well-being following a proposal made by Weisbrod and Hansen called 'potential income' (Weisbrod & Hansen, 1968), equivalent household net income, equivalent household consumption expenditure and per capita household net wealth. As socio-demographic characteristics, we used: a spatial differentiation between West and East Germany (relative to residence), three age groups (up to 29 years, 30 to 59 years and 60 years and older) and six household types (female single, male single, single-parent household, couple without children, couple with child or children and other household types).

As main results from the categorial decompositions, we obtained:

- The inequality level of potential income is strikingly driven by annualised wealth, which in turn is mainly influenced by the within-category inequality of (net) real estate which, therefore, also influences wealth inequality most.
- For household net income inequality, labour income's within-category inequality plays the major role, followed by transfers and capital income (for which its relatively high inequality level is broadly balanced by the very low share of capital income on total income).
- Approximately two-thirds of expenditure inequality can be accounted for by within-subcategory inequality with the greatest importance of the expenditure subcategories transport and communication, other goods and services, and housing rent, water, electricity, gas and other fuels.

With respect to the socio-demographic characteristics used in this paper, the following decomposition results were found:

- As a general finding, all decompositions reveal the overwhelming role played by within-group inequality.

- The decomposition between West and East Germany shows that within-group inequality in West Germany clearly predominates (over all well-being categories).
- For age-related decompositions, the within-group inequality levels of the elderly are the most important components of potential income and wealth inequality. Regarding net income and consumption expenditure, the within-group inequality levels of the middle-aged persons are predominant.
- Regarding household type, total inequality (of all well-being categories) is predominated by within-group inequality of the household type couples without children.

Overall, by decomposing (material) well-being inequality in great detail for Germany, we shed light on its dimensions and showed that decomposition by income, wealth and expenditure, as well as by socio-demographic characteristics, is important to obtain adequate solutions for socio-political measures. For example, the restructuring of the old-age pension system in Germany since 2001, which should lead to more generational justice by, inter alia, reducing the benefit level of the statutory pension systems (Schmähl, 2004) and fostering private pensions, will affect the distribution of all well-being categories. However, the measures taken may not lead to more generational justice but will increase the within-group inequality even more. Not considering the true source of the real inequality is like barking up the wrong tree and bears the danger of false political measures for social and distributional policy.

NOTES

1. These three aspects only measure the material living standard (Stiglitz et al., 2009, p. 14) and ignore immaterial dimensions of well-being.
2. For a list of all income sources, see Statistisches Bundesamt (2010, pp. 12 ff.).
3. See Statistisches Bundesamt (2010); for an English translation, see for example, Bönke, Schröder, and Werdt (2010, pp. 24 ff.).
4. However, it is disputed whether housing wealth can be seen as wealth by itself (Buiter, 2008).
5. An alternative decomposition proposal, for the Gini coefficient, is from Lerman and Yitzhaki (1985, pp. 152 f.):

$$G = \sum_{k=1}^{K} s_k \cdot G_k \cdot R_k$$

where G = overall Gini coefficient; s_k = share of well-being component k on the total well-being value; G_k = Gini coefficient of well-being component

k; R_k = value of the correlation between well-being component k and total well-being; $k = 1, 2, \ldots, K$. This formula demonstrates that the Gini coefficient is very clearly decomposable by subcategories (i.e. without any interacting term between the several subcategories). Contrary to that, however, the Gini coefficient cannot be decomposed by population groups simply into a within-group and a between-group inequality component as with a GE indicator (regarding this disadvantage of the Gini coefficient, see e.g. Shorrocks, 2013, pp. 116 f.).

6. Alternatively, one might use variable (i.e. reference) income-dependent equivalence scales but, as illustrated by Faik (2012b) this would only affect the level and not the structure (or time course) of inequality. By the way, for linguistic simplification, we do not use the full terms *per capita wealth* or *equivalent household net income*, and so on.

7. For corresponding empirical age-related evidence for Germany, based on 1995–2009 Socio-Economic Panel, see Faik (2012a).

8. Children are defined as up to the age of 18 years.

REFERENCES

Atkinson, A. B. (1983). *The economics of inequality*. Oxford: Clarendon.

Atkinson, A. B. (2003). Multidimensional deprivation: Contrasting social welfare and counting approaches. *Journal of Economic Inequality*, *1*, 51–65.

Bartzsch, N., & Stöss, E. (2007). Measuring German household debt: Financial accounts data and disaggregated survey data as complementary statistics. In *Proceedings of the IFC conference on measuring the financial position of the household sector*, Bank for International Settlements, Basel (pp. 214–233), 30–31 August 2006.

Becker, I., & Hauser, R. (2003). *Anatomie der Einkommensverteilung. Ergebnisse der Einkommens – und Verbrauchsstichproben 1969–1998*. Berlin: Edition Sigma.

Bishop, J. A., Formby, J. P., & Smith, W. J. (1997). Demographic change and income inequality in the United States, 1976–1989. *Southern Economic Journal*, *64*, 34–44.

Bönke, T., Schröder, C., & Werdt, C. (2010). *Compiling a harmonized database from Germany's 1978 to 2003 sample surveys of income and expenditure*. FDZ-Arbeitspapier 32, Statistische Ämter des Bundes und der Länder, Düsseldorf.

Buiter, W. H. (2008). *Housing wealth isn't wealth*. NBER Working Paper Series 14204. National Bureau of Economic Research, Cambridge, MA.

Deaton, A. S., & Paxson, C. H. (1998). Aging and inequality in income and health. *AEA Papers and Proceedings*, *88*, 248–253.

Deutsche Bundesbank. (2012). *Financial accounts for Germany 2006 to 2011*. Frankfurt (Main): Deutsche Bundesbank.

Dinwiddy, R., & Reed, D. (1977). *The effects of certain social and demographic changes on income distribution*. London: H.M. Stationery Office.

Eisenmenger, M., & Emmerling, D. (2011). Amtliche Sterbetafeln und Entwicklung der Sterblichkeit. *Wirtschaft und Statistik*, *63*, 219–238.

Eurostat. (2010). *Feasibility study for well-being indicators*. Task 4: Critical review. Brussels: Eurostat.

Fachinger, U. (2001). *Einkommensverwendungsentscheidungen privater Haushalte. Eine alters – und kohortenspezifische Längsschnittanalyse auf der Grundlage der Einkommens – und Verbrauchsstichprobe des Statistischen Bundesamtes*. Berlin: Duncker & Humblot.

Faik, J. (2010). *Methodical settings in analyses of the income distribution – Some simple mathematical comments*. FaMa-Diskussionspapier 1/2010. Frankfurt (Main): FaMa.

Faik, J. (2011). Demografie und Einkommensungleichheit. *WSI – Mitteilungen*, *64*, 19–25.

Faik, J. (2012a). *Socio-economic influences on income inequality – Projections for Germany*. FaMa-Diskussionspapier 4/2012. Frankfurt (Main): FaMa.

Faik, J. (2012b). Variable equivalence scales and trends in German income inequality. In J. A. Bishop & R. Salas (Eds.), *Inequality, mobility and segregation: Essays in honor of Jacques Silber* (Vol. 20, pp. 311–336). Binglay, UK: Emerald Group Publishing Limited.

Fleurbaey, M. (2008). *Beyond GDP. Is there progress in the measurement of individual well-being and social welfare?* Paris: Commission on the Measurement of Economic Performance and Social Progress (CMEPSP).

Hauser, R., Becker, I., & Grabka, M. M. (2007). *Integrierte Analyse der Einkommens – und Vermögensverteilung*. Abschlussbericht zur Studie im Auftrag des Bundesministeriums für Arbeit und Soziales, Bonn (VKZ 06 01 03), der Bietergemeinschaft Deutsches Institut für Wirtschaftsforschung Berlin (DIW Berlin, Koordinator: Dr. Markus M. Grabka), Zentrum für Europäische Wirtschaftsforschung GmbH (ZEW Mannheim, Koordinator: Dr. Peter Westerheide), Prof. Dr. Richard Hauser, Universität Frankfurt am Main, Dr. Irene Becker, Riedstadt. Bonn: Bundesministeriums für Arbeit und Soziales.

Lerman, R. I., & Yitzhaki, S. (1985). Income inequality effects by income source: A new approach and applications to the United States. *The Review of Economics and Statistics*, *67*, 151–156.

Organisation for Economic Co-Operation and Development. (2009). What are equivalence scales? In *Organisation for economic co-operation and development*. Paris: OECD.

Organisation for Economic Co-Operation and Development. (2013). *OECD framework for statistics on the distribution of household income, Consumption and wealth*. Paris: OECD.

Osberg, L. S., & Sharpe, A. (2005). How should we measure the "economic" aspects of well-being? *Review of Income and Wealth*, *51*, 311–336.

Osberg, L. S., & Sharpe, A. (2009). *New estimates of the index of economic well-being for selected OECD countries, 1980–2007*. Ottawa: Centre for the Study of Living Standards Research (CSLS).

Peichl, A., Pestel, N., & Schneider, H. (2012). Does size matter? The impact of changes in household structure on income distribution in Germany. *Review of Income and Wealth*, *58*, 118–141.

Sabelhaus, J., & Schneider, U. (1997). Measuring the distribution of well-being: Why income and consumption give different answers. *Konjunkturpolitik*, *43*, 153–177.

Sastre, M., & Trannoy, A. (2002). Shapley inequality decomposition by factor components: Some methodological issues. *Zeitschrift für Nationalökonomie*. [*Journal of Economics*.], *9*, 51–89.

Schmähl, W. (2004). Paradigm shift in German pension policy: Measures aiming at a new public-private mix and their effects. In M. Rein & W. Schmähl (Eds.), *Rethinking the welfare state – The political economy of pension reform* (pp. 153–204). Cheltenham: Edward Elgar.

Schwarze, J. (1996). How income inequality changed in Germany following reunification: An empirical analysis using decomposable inequality measures. *Review of Income and Wealth*, *42*, 1–11.

Sharpe, A., Murray, A., & Evans, B. (2011). *The Levy Institute measure of economic well-being: Estimates for Canada, 1999 and 2005*. Levy Economics Institute Working Paper No. 680. Levy Economics Institute, Annandale-on-Hudson, NY.

Shorrocks, A. F. (2013). Decomposition procedures for distributional analysis: A unified framework based on the Shapley value. *Journal of Economic Inequality*, *11*, 99–126.

Statistisches Bundesamt. (2005). *Sample survey of income and expenditure 2003*. Wiesbaden: Statistisches Bundesamt.

Statistisches Bundesamt. (2009). *Bevölkerung Deutschlands bis 2060. Ergebnisse der 12. koordinierten Bevölkerungsvorausberechnung*. Wiesbaden: Statistisches Bundesamt.

Statistisches Bundesamt. (2010). *Wirtschaftsrechnungen. Einkommens-und Verbrauchsstichprobe – Einnahmen und Ausgaben privater Haushalte 2008*. Wiesbaden: Statistisches Bundesamt.

Statistisches Bundesamt. (2012). *Einkommens-und Verbrauchsstichprobe 2008*. Wiesbaden: Statistisches Bundesamt.

Stiglitz, J. E., Sen, A., & Fitoussi, J.-P. (2009). *Report by the commission on the measurement of economic performance and social progress*. Paris: Commission on the Measurement of Economic Performance and Social Progress (CMEPSP).

United Nations Development Programme. (2011). *Sustainability and equity: A better future for all*. New York, NY: UNDP.

von Weizsäcker, R. K. (1996). Distributive implications of an aging society. *European Economic Review*, *40*, 729–746.

Weisbrod, B. A., & Hansen, W. L. (1968). An income-net worth approach to measuring economic welfare. *The American Economic Review*, *58*, 1315–1329.

Wolff, E. N., Zacharias, A., & Masterson, T. (2012). *A comparison of inequality and living standards in Canada and the United States using an expanded measure of economic well-being*. Levy Economics Institute Working Paper No. 703. Levy Economics Institute, Annandale-on-Hudson, NY.

ON THE ESTIMATION OF THE GLOBAL INCOME DISTRIBUTION USING A PARSIMONIOUS APPROACH

Vanesa Jordá, José María Sarabia and Faustino Prieto

ABSTRACT

This paper aims to estimate the global income distribution during the nineties using limited information. In a first stage, we obtain national income distributions considering a model with two parameters. In particular, we propose to use the so-called Lamé distributions, *which are curved versions of the Sigh-Maddala and Dagum distributions. The main feature of this family is that they represent parsimonious models which can fit income data adequately with just two parameters and whose Lorenz curves are characterized by only one parameter. In a second stage, global and regional distributions are derived from a finite mixture of these families using population shares. We test the validity of the model, comparing it with other two-parameter families. Our estimates of different inequality measures suggest that global inequality presents a decreasing pattern mainly driven by the fall of the differences across*

Economic Well-Being and Inequality: Papers from the Fifth ECINEQ Meeting
Research on Economic Inequality, Volume 22, 115–145

ISSN: 1049-2585/doi:10.1108/S1049-258520140000022003

countries during the course of the study period that offsets the increase in disparities within countries.

Keywords: Limited information; Singh-Maddala and Dagum distributions; Gini index; national income distribution; regional income distribution

JEL classifications: C13; C18; D31

INTRODUCTION

Inequality, poverty and growth, as well as the links between these concepts have received an increasing amount of attention from economists, analysts and policymakers around the world. The exponential growth of China over the last 20 years, the relationship between globalization and inequality or the financial crisis and its consequences to the real economy, are contexts where these variables play a crucial role for assessing the new economic and social context and for evaluating the efficacy of the policies implemented.

Even when there is nearly consensus that per capita GDP is not an adequate measure of well-being, it is the most widely used indicator to make international comparisons as well as intertemporal evaluations of living standards. National incomes inform about the mean and hence about economic progress, but say nothing regarding other intrinsic features of this distribution. Consequently, aspects such as poverty and inequality would be completely ignored.

Despite their relevancy, the global income distribution was not investigated intensely until the nineties mainly due to the scarcity of data on individual incomes for a wide number of countries over reasonably long periods of time. However, there has been a great effort in the last 20 years to collect data on individual incomes (Deininger & Squire, 1996; LIS, 2000; Transmonee, 1999; UNU-WIDER, 2008), which come from surveys conducted every five years in most cases. Note that long time is required to complete the collection of the database, which is resource intensive. Consequently, the access to individual data is restricted, but instead, descriptive statistics of surveys such as mean, mode or income shares are freely available.

In this context, the derivation of income distributions from the pieces of information readily available is essential to analyze national and regional patterns of wealth.[1] This estimation is relatively simple for individual countries, however, a more complex methodological procedure is required for the estimation of regional and global distributions, whose summary statistics are not accessible. In that sense there have been many attempts to develop regional and global estimates from limited data, mainly based on two distinct methodologies.

On the one hand, non-parametric techniques have been applied to estimate income distributions based on kernel estimates (Minoiu, 2007; Sala-i-Martin, 2006). On the other hand, parametric models of the global income distribution have been estimated using conventional inference techniques. Numerous functional forms have been suggested in the literature. Chotikapanich, Valenzuela, and Rao (1997) assume a lognormal distribution for modeling national income distributions, which is the most commonly used family along with the gamma (Chotikapanich & Griffiths, 2008) and Pareto distributions. Other two-parameter distributions have been extensively used, including the beta, the Fisk and the Weibull distributions (Chotikapanich & Rao, 1998; Pinkovskiy & Sala-i-Martin, 2009). Three-parameter distributions have also been proposed. Along these lines, we find special cases of the generalized beta distribution: the beta of the second kind (Chotikapanich, Griffiths, & Rao, 2007; Chotikapanich, Grifiths, Rao, & Valencia, 2009), the Singh-Maddala and the Dagum distributions (Bresson, 2009).

As the number of parameters increases, the model becomes more flexible, thus improving the goodness of fit. It should also be noted that more information is needed and highly complex expressions are employed to estimate the parameters and other characteristics of the distribution. However, it is possible to model national income distributions based on a more parsimonious approach, using two-parameter families without a significant loss of reliability. Specifically, we propose to use the so-called Lamé family of distributions, which comprises two versions of the Singh-Maddala and the Dagum distributions. The adequacy of these distributions has been studied in the work by Sarabia, Jordá, and Trueba (2014), with the conclusion that the inclusion of an additional parameter does not significantly improve the performance of the model. Thus, this framework offers simple instruments to construct global and regional distributions as well as to report reliable estimates of inequality measures.

The objective of this paper is to obtain global and regional income distributions using limited information. The methodology is applied using data on the Gini index and per capita GDP of each country. Our study focuses on the period from 1990 to 2000 with three point estimates in 1990, 1995 and 2000. The proposed methodology to estimate regional income distributions from country level data is made up of two steps. In a first stage, we estimate individual distributions of 127 countries included in the sample. Global and regional distributions are derived from a finite mixture of these families using population shares. We provide different inequality indices for each region to assess the evolution of disparities over the nineties.

The remaining paper is structured as follows. The next section describes the methodology used to estimate global and regional distributions. Inequality measures and their decomposition in within- and between-country components are also presented. Following this, the data are presented. The performance of the estimated models is discussed next, also comparing the Lamé distributions with other two-parameter families. The section "Results" presents the evolution of the global and regional income distributions, and the inequality trends during the nineties are also presented. The main conclusions of the study are included in the final section.

MODELING INCOME USING THE LAMÉ FAMILY OF DISTRIBUTIONS

In this section, we describe the methodology used to obtain regional and global income distributions as well as the estimates of inequality measures. As a starting point, we compute national distributions of 127 countries for each benchmark year. Despite the long list of candidates,[2] the choice of the model is limited by the nature and availability of income data. In this case, we work with the per capita GDP and the value of the Gini index.[3] This implies that we need a simple two-parametric distribution with scale and shape parameters. Notwithstanding its simplicity, the proposed distribution must be sufficiently flexible to fit zero-mode – characteristic of income distributions in developing countries – and one-mode data. Moreover, it should be derived from a simple economic model and, at the same time, the distribution should be connected with the previous economic literature about income distributions.

It should be recalled that a large number of probability distributions have been proposed in the literature for modeling income and wealth distributions (for a review, see Kleiber & Kotz, 2003). Among the two-parameter distributions, we find the lognormal, Pareto, Weibull, gamma or Fisk. The most commonly used is the lognormal distribution, but its performance has been questioned with respect to other parametric forms (see e.g. Bresson, 2009). We propose to use the family of income distributions made up of two models called Lamé distributions of the first and second kind (see Sarabia et al., 2014). These models are described in terms of the cumulative distribution functions (CDFs) as:

$$F_1(x; a, \mu) = 1 - \frac{1}{[1 + (x/\mu)^{a/(1-a)}]^{1/a}}, \quad 0 \leq x < \infty \tag{1}$$

and $F_1(x;a,\mu) = 0$ if $x < 0$, where $0 < a \leq 1$ and $\mu > 0$, and

$$F_2(x; a, \mu) = \frac{1}{[1 + (x/\mu)^{a/(a-1)}]^{1/a}}, \quad 0 \leq x < \infty \tag{2}$$

and $F_2(x;a,\mu) = 0$ if $x < 0$, where $a \geq 1$ and $\mu > 0$. In both cases μ represents the mathematical expectation of the population.

This family is connected with the flexible model given by the GB2 distribution (McDonald, 1984) by the following relationships:

$$X_1 \sim \text{GB2}\left(A = \frac{a}{1-a}, P = 1, Q = \frac{1}{a}, \mu\right)$$

$$X_2 \sim \text{GB2}\left(A = \frac{a}{a-1}, P = \frac{1}{a}, Q = 1, \mu\right)$$

Note that Eqs. (1) and (2) are curved versions of the Singh-Maddala and Dagum distributions, respectively. These two models have been applied in several occasions to estimate income distributions, and their superiority over other three-parameter families was concluded (Bandourian, McDonald, & Turley, 2002). This feature makes the Lamé family especially suitable to model income distributions. The performance of these models to fit Lorenz curves has been tested in the work of Henle, Horton, and Jakus (2008), with the conclusion that the estimates provided by these distributions yield low mean square error. The main limitation of this model seems to be the assumption of the symmetry. Sarabia et al. (2014) compared the adequacy of this Lorenz curve with a more flexible proposal. The overall conclusion was that the inclusion of an additional parameter improved the goodness of fit but at the expense of overfitting the data. This model is a recently developed distribution which has not been applied extensively. The sole application to income data can be seen in the study by

Sarabia, Jordá, and Trueba (2013), which investigates the evolution of income distribution in Latin America and the Caribbean.

These distributions are derived from two well-known economic theories, namely trickle-up and trickle-down effects (Henle, Hortin and Jakus, 2008). The first approach assumes that an increase in income of the lower-middle class would be more advantageous for the economy given that they spend their wealth faster than the upper class. The trickle-down theory assumes that if the income of the upper class rises, this fact would stimulate the investment, thus resulting in a fall of unemployment and hence benefiting the society as a whole. Then, the trickle-up effect is related to the following expression:

$$\frac{\partial I}{\partial t} = \frac{(A/N)L}{N(1-r)} \tag{3}$$

whereas the trickle-down effect verifies that:

$$\frac{\partial I}{\partial t} = \frac{(A/N)(1-L)}{Nr} \tag{4}$$

where L is the Lorenz curve, I is the income of a family at rank r. As a consequence, $(A/N)L$ is the aggregate income of poorer citizens, and $N(1 - r)$ is the number of wealthy individuals. Conversely, $(A/N)(1 - L)$ is the income of the wealthiest citizens and Nr is the number of individuals at a lower rank. Assuming that L is adequately represented by the so-called Lamé Lorenz curves (see Eqs. (9) and (10)), the CDFs (1) and (2) are the solutions of Eqs. (3) and (4). According to Eq. (3), an increase in the income of any individual of the society can be achieved with an improvement of the economic situation of poorer citizens. In contrast, Eq. (4) states that an increase in the income of the upper class would lead to economic progress of the whole population.

The quantile functions associated with the previous distributions (Eqs. (1) and (2)) are respectively:

$$X_1(p_i; a, \mu) = \mu(1-(1-p)^a)^{-1+\frac{1}{a}}(1-p)^{a-1} \tag{5}$$

$$X_2(p_i; a, \mu) = \mu(1-p^a)^{1-\frac{1}{a}}p^{1-a} \tag{6}$$

To study the evolution of income inequality, the Lorenz curve is an extremely useful resource, which relates the income share ($\eta(x)$) with its respective population share ($F(x)$). For the Lamé income distributions, income shares are given by:

$$\eta_1(x; a, \mu) = \frac{1}{[1 + (x/\mu)^{-a/(1-a)}]^{1/a}}, \quad 0 \leq x \leq \infty \tag{7}$$

with $0 < a < 1$ and

$$\eta_2(x; a, \mu) = \frac{1}{[1 + (x/\mu)^{a/(1-a)}]^{1/a}}, \quad 0 \leq x \leq \infty \tag{8}$$

if $a > 1$.

Accordingly, Lamé Lorenz curves associated with Eqs. (1) and (2) are expressed respectively, as follows (see Sarabia, Jordá and Trueba, 2014):

$$L_1(p; a) = [1 - (1 - p)^a]^{1/a}, \quad 0 \leq p \leq 1 \tag{9}$$

$$L_2(p; a) = 1 - (1 - p^a)^{1/a}, \quad 0 \leq p \leq 1 \tag{10}$$

and the corresponding Gini index of each curve is given by:

$$G_1(a) = 1 - \frac{\Gamma(1/a)^2}{a\Gamma(2/a)}, \quad 0 \leq a \leq 1 \tag{11}$$

$$G_2(a) = \frac{\Gamma(1/a)^2}{a\Gamma(2/a)} - 1, \quad a \geq 1 \tag{12}$$

Estimation with Limited Information

In this section, we present the procedure to estimate the parameters of the distribution for each country when few pieces of information are available.

The estimation using limited information is based on solving a system of linearly independent equations. In the case of Lamé distributions, a plausible estimation method for the parameters consists of solving the following system:

$$\mu = \overline{X}$$

$$G_k(a) = g; \quad k = 1, 2$$

where $\overline{X}$ and g represent the per capita GDP and Gini index values, respectively and $G_k(a)$, $k = 1, 2$, are the theoretical Gini indices given, respectively, by Eqs. (11) and (12). Therefore, the estimated values of μ and a are:

$$\hat{\mu} = \overline{X}$$

$$\hat{a} = G_k^{-1}(g); \quad k = 1, 2 \tag{13}$$

It is worth noting that, as the right hand side of Eq. (13) is a monotonic function of parameter g, this system has only one solution. The standard errors of the parameters can be estimated using a parametric bootstrap, thus providing a measure of the accuracy of the estimation.

Modeling Regional and Global Income Distributions

The regional and global income distributions are defined as a mixture of the national distributions using population weights. Assume that the region under study comprises $M^{(r)}$ countries, where r denotes the world or any of the subsamples considered in this study.[4] The number of countries varies across regions but, for simplicity, we remove the superscript r, assuming that the rest of the methodology applies for each territory specifically.

Each country has an associated probability density function (PDF) and a cumulated distribution function (CDF) previously defined as $f_k(x)$ and $F_k(x)$, respectively, $k = 1, 2, \ldots, M^{(r)}$. The demographic weights are given by $\pi_k = N_k/N$, where N_k is the population of the k-th country and $N = \sum_{k=1}^{M} N_k$ is the total population of the region under study. Then, the regional income distribution is given by the finite mixture:

$$f_X(x) = \sum_{k=1}^{M} \pi_k f_k(x)$$

Assuming that $f_k(x)$ follows a Lamé I distribution (Eq. (1)), the regional PDF is given by:

$$f_X(x) = \sum_{k=1}^{M} \pi_k \frac{(x/\mu_k)^{(2a_k - 1)/(1 - a_k)}}{(1 - a_k)\mu_k \left(1 + (x/\mu_k)^{a_k/(1 - a_k)}\right)^{1/a_k + 1}} \tag{14}$$

Conversely, the regional CDF follows the expression:[5]

$$F_X(x) = \sum_{k=1}^{M} \pi_k \left\{ 1 - \frac{1}{\left(1 + (x/\mu_k)^{a_k/(1 - a_k)}\right)^{1/a_k}} \right\} \tag{15}$$

On the other hand, regional cumulative income shares are also a weighted average of the country income shares, given by the following expression:

$$\eta_X(x) = \sum_{k=1}^{M} \frac{\pi_k \mu_k}{\mu} \eta_{X_k}(x)$$

where $\eta_{X_k}(x)$, $k = 1, \ldots, n$, are defined in Eqs. (7) and (8) for each family and μ denotes the regional mean which is expressed as a population weighted average of country means. Once we have derived income shares and their corresponding population shares from $F_X(x)$, the regional Lorenz curve can be graphed using a grid of values of x to calculate the points $(F_X(x), \eta_X(x))$.

To analyze the evolution of inequality, we propose to use generalized entropy (GE) measures given that they allow us to decompose total inequality in two different components, namely within-country inequality and between-country inequality. The first term informs about the level of inequality in each country, assuming that there are no differences across nations. Conversely, the second component states the level of inequality if countries were totally equal, only presenting differences in the mean income of nations.

The regional GE measure can be specified in a simple form using the decomposability of this index. Accordingly, if X represents the regional income distribution we have:

$$I_X^{(\theta)} = \sum_{k=1}^{M} \pi_k^{1-\theta} s_k^{\theta} I_{X_k}^{(\theta)} + \frac{1}{\theta(\theta - 1)} \left(\sum_{k=1}^{M} \pi_k^{1-\theta} s_k^{\theta} - 1 \right)$$

where θ is a parameter that states the weight attached to the top of the distribution. High positive values of this parameter yield indices more sensitive to changes in the upper tail, whereas values lower than 1 make this measure more sensitive to redistributions at the lower tail. s_k is the proportion of the mean income of each country in the regional mean, $s_k = \pi_k\mu_k / \sum_{k=1}^{M} \pi_k\mu_k,\quad j = 1, 2, \ldots, M$ and $I_{X_k}^{(\theta)}$ is the GE index of the k-th country, expressed as follows for the Lamé I and Lamé II distributions respectively:

$$I_{X_k}^{(\theta)} = \frac{\left[\Gamma\left(1 + \frac{\theta(1-a_1)}{a_1}\right)\Gamma\left(\frac{1-\theta(1-a_1)}{a_1}\right)/\Gamma\left(\frac{1}{a_1}\right)\right] - 1}{\theta(\theta - 1)}$$

$$I_{X_k}^{(\theta)} = \frac{\left[\Gamma\left(\frac{1-\theta(a_2-1)}{a_2}\right)\Gamma\left(1 - \frac{\theta(a_2-1)}{a_2}\right)/\Gamma\left(\frac{1}{a_1}\right)\right] - 1}{\theta(\theta - 1)}$$

with $\theta \neq 0,1$ and $\theta \in [-a_1/(1-a_1), 1/(1-a_1)]$ in the case of Lamé I and $\theta \in [1/(a_2-1), a_2/(a_2-1)]$ in the case of Lamé II. These results are obtained using the raw moments developed in the work by Sarabia et al. (2014).

GE measures are additively decomposable in two terms – inequality within and between countries – given, respectively, by the following expressions:

$$I_W^{(\theta)} = \sum_{k=1}^{M} \pi_k^{1-\theta} s_k^{\theta} I_{X_k}^{(\theta)}$$

$$I_B^{(\theta)} = \frac{1}{\theta(\theta - 1)}\left(\sum_{k=1}^{M} \pi_k^{1-\theta} s_k^{\theta} - 1\right)$$

We also have considered the limit case of $\theta = 1$, that is the so-called Theil index, which can be decomposed as,

$$T_X = T_W + T_B$$

where

$$T_W = \sum_{k=1}^{M} \pi_k T_k; \quad T_B = \sum_{k=1}^{M} \pi_k \log\left(\frac{\mu}{\mu_k}\right)$$

T_k is the Theil index of the k-th country which, for the Lamé I and Lamé II, is given respectively by:

$$T(X) = \frac{1-a_1}{a_1}\left\{\psi\left(\frac{1}{a_1}\right) - \psi(1)\right\}, \quad 0 < a_1 < 1$$

$$T(X) = \frac{a_2-1}{a_2}\left\{\psi(1) - \psi\left(\frac{1}{a_2}\right)\right\}, \quad a_2 > 1$$

where $\psi(z) = \Gamma'(z)/\Gamma(z)$ is the digamma function.

DATA AND ESTIMATION

The data used in this analysis come from two main data sources: national accounts to obtain data on per capita GDP and surveys, which provide Gini index values. Per capita GDP in constant international US$ and population is drawn from Penn World Tables 7.1 (Heston, Summers, & Aten, 2012). These data are used to construct income and population shares for deriving regional distributions.

The World Bank has been a major provider of income data for cross-country comparisons. In fact, recent works that examined global income distributions used the *World Income Inequality Database* (WIID) compiled by the United Nations (Chotikapanich et al., 2007; Milanovic, 2002). However, the data contained in WIID come from a variety of sources, including Deininger and Squire (1996), the Trasmonee project (Transmonee, 1999); the Luxembourg Income Study (LIS, 2000) and national statistical offices. Therefore, this database reports a mix of observations regarding unity of analysis, income concept and population coverage, thus resulting in a lack of comparability.

Due to the high heterogeneity that characterizes the WIID data, we opt for using the Standardized World Income Inequality Database (Solt, 2009),[6] which provides comparable Gini indices based on gross income definition for 153 countries over the period 1960–2009. This database homogenizes the observations of WIID, taking LIS observations as a benchmark. After this procedure, more than 4,500 observations are provided, although the majority of them are concentrated in the period from 1985 to 2000, especially for developing countries. Our sample comprises

127 countries for three benchmark years in the nineties: 1990, 1995 and 2000. When there is no available data for the exact year, the closest observation is used only if it is within the previous two years or in the two following ones.[7] The percentage of coverage for each region in the three years considered is presented in Table 1.

In global terms, we cover nearly 93 percent of the world population over the whole period. Note, however, that this percentage is not achieved for each of the regions. Therefore, despite the large coverage of world population, many African and Eastern European countries are not included in the sample due to the scarcity of data. Given that practically all absentees are developing countries, our estimates can be biased downward. Consequently, the conclusions derived from this analysis should be cautiously interpreted, especially in the regions with low levels of representativeness.

TESTING THE VALIDITY OF THE MODEL

Before analyzing the distributional patterns over the nineties, we should investigate whether Lamé distributions provide the best approximation possible, given the data available. In this paper, we use two pieces of information, namely the mean and the Gini index, to estimate the income distribution of a particular country.[8] In this section, we compare the fit provided by different two-parameter models in order to achieve some conclusions about the adequacy of Lame distributions. In particular, we propose to evaluate the performance of the Weibull, the lognormal and the Fisk distributions with respect to the two kinds of Lamé distributions.

Since the aim of this paper is to provide estimates of inequality indicators, a valid method for comparing distributions is to use measures of the quality of the fit. In this sense, the higher the accuracy of the distribution, the closer the estimated inequality measures are to their real value. Then, we compare the performance of the models estimated using a score-based approach (Klugman, Panjer, & Willmot, 2012). We focus on five different scores: the lowest value of the chi-square, the Kolmogorov Smirnov, the Cramer-von Mises and the Anderson-Darling statistics and the highest *p*-value of the chi-square statistic.

Given that we estimate with limited information, there is no sample to perform the goodness of fit measures in the classical way. A valid

Table 1. Regional and Global Population Coverage.

	1990			1995			2000		
	Total	Included	Covered	Total	Included	Covered	Total	Included	Covered
EAP	1,821.36	1,568.78	0.8613	1,940.03	1,675.65	0.8637	2,045.00	1,761.20	0.8612
EECA	842.51	451.75	0.5362	855.78	458.68	0.5360	862.19	461.51	0.5353
LAC	442.07	430.69	0.9743	481.54	470.06	0.9762	520.37	507.06	0.9744
MENA	253.29	190.46	0.7520	283.43	210.74	0.7435	312.51	230.05	0.7361
SSA	512.73	392.91	0.7663	585.95	444.52	0.7586	666.68	502.24	0.7534
SA	1,146.78	1,088.11	0.9488	1,272.29	1,198.09	0.9417	1,398.31	1,315.70	0.9409
WENAO	852.53	852.17	0.9996	884.55	884.18	0.9996	912.10	911.71	0.9996
World	5,296.21	4,974.88	0.9393	5,714.72	5,341.91	0.9348	6,118.05	5,689.48	0.9299

procedure is to compare the empirical shares provided by WIID (UNU-WIDER, 2008) with their theoretical estimates for the five models (Chotikapanich et al., 2007). In this sense, the functional form that is supposed to provide the most precise estimates of inequality measures is the one that minimizes the differences between the observed and the estimated income shares. In this context, the chi-square statistic is the most intuitive indicator if we use grouped data, which is defined as:

$$\chi^2 = \sum_{k=1}^{K} \frac{(O_i - E_i)^2}{E_i}$$

where $O_i \; \forall i = 1, \ldots, K$, are the empirical shares and $E_i \; \forall i = 1, \ldots, K$, are the theoretical shares of each model which are calculated substituting the distribution of the incomplete moment in the expression:

$$s_i = \eta(x_i; a, \mu) - \eta(x_{i-1}; a, \mu) \quad \forall i = 1, 2, \ldots, K \tag{16}$$

$K = 5$, 10 depending on the number of points that we estimate. x_i is the estimate of the theoretical quantile derived using Eqs. (5) and (6) for the Lamé I and Lamé II distributions, respectively. Substituting x_i and the parameter estimates in $\eta(x; a, \mu)$ we obtain the estimated income shares.

On the other hand, we can also use a class of tests based on the empirical distribution function (EDF) to analyze the robustness of the conclusions achieved using the chi-square statistic. In this context, the Kolmogorov-Smirnov (KS) is the most widely used statistic, given by:

$$D = \sup_x \left| F_n(x) - F(x) \right|$$

where $F_n(x)$ are the empirical shares and $F(x)$ are the theoretical values derived from the distribution function of the incomplete moment. Given the nature of this statistic, its distribution under the null when the parameters of the theoretical distribution are estimated needs to be simulated (Babu & Rao, 2004).

The Cramer-von Mises test is also a goodness of fit measure based on the EDF, which belongs to the quadratic class of EDF test statistics, which are of the form:

$$Q = n \int_{-\infty}^{\infty} (F_n(x) - F(x))^2 \phi(x) \mathrm{d}F(x)$$

where $\varphi(x)$ is a function of weights of $(F_n(x)-F(x))^2$. For the Cramer-von Mises test, the weight function is equal to 1:

$$W^2 = n \int_{-\infty}^{\infty} (F_n(x) - F(x))^2 \mathrm{d}F(x)$$

Following Henze (1996), the discrete version of the previous statistic is:

$$W^2 = n \sum_{k=1}^{\infty} (F_n(x_k) - F(x_k))^2 (F(x_k) - F(x_{k-1}))$$

The main limitation of the two previous statistics is that they tend to be insensitive to the tails of the distribution. The Anderson-Darling test solves this deficiency considering a weight function of the form $\phi(x) = [F(x)\,(1 - F(x))]^{-1}$, which emphasizes the differences at the tails. As a result, this statistic follows the expression:

$$A^2 = n \int_{-\infty}^{\infty} \frac{(F_n(x) - F(x))^2}{[F(x)(1 - F(x))]} \mathrm{d}F(x)$$

whose discrete version was given by (Bracquemond, Cretois, & Gaudoin, 2002):

$$A^2 = n \sum_{k=1}^{\infty} \frac{(F_n(x_k) - F(x_k))^2}{[F(x_k)(1 - F(x_k))]} (F(x_k) - F(x_{k-1}))$$

As in the case of the KS statistic, the distributions of the Cramer-von Mises and the Anderson-Darling statistics need to be bootstrapped.

We perform these four tests of goodness of fit to investigate which model yields the most satisfactory fit of the income distribution of the country *i*. It is worth noting that the data on income shares are available for a lower number of countries than the Gini and the mean. We have performed 39 tests for the year 1990, 54 for 1995 and 61 for 2000, whose main results are summarized in Table 2. The top panel shows the first quartile of each statistic for the five models considered, the middle panel presents the median value and the bottom part includes the third quartile.

The results presented in Table 2 point out that we cannot establish universal conclusions about the best performing distribution. The rankings of

Table 2. Goodness of Fit Statistics and p-Values; Mean and Median Values.

	χ^2 Statistic	χ^2 p-Value	KS Statistic	A^2 Statistic	W^2 Statistic
First quartile					
Lognormal	3.28656	0.01330	0.17094	3.90022	0.00813
Weibull	2.22305	0.30784	0.12189	2.25656	0.00473
Fisk	0.42087	0.40334	0.05977	0.31092	0.00118
Lamé I	0.43377	0.35211	0.05843	0.36424	0.00107
Lamé II	0.50481	0.32853	0.05877	0.36883	0.00113
Median					
Lognormal	10.56234	0.09256	0.30269	42.56555	0.03044
Weibull	3.86960	0.67366	0.20024	8.28393	0.01246
Fisk	1.26648	0.90603	0.12016	1.39891	0.00512
Lamé I	1.35130	0.91604	0.13893	2.41400	0.00653
Lamé II	1.61828	0.90322	0.13550	2.61189	0.00671
Third quartile					
Lognormal	16.96169	0.59538	0.43123	125.32962	0.06878
Weibull	7.12861	0.90946	0.31298	27.53895	0.03611
Fisk	6.01349	0.99857	0.29311	10.07806	0.03967
Lamé I	6.26871	0.99708	0.28406	12.51349	0.03742
Lamé II	6.36723	0.99465	0.27707	13.24238	0.03674

the different functional forms are not robust to the goodness of fit criterion, although the competition is focused on three models: the Fisk distribution and the two kinds of Lame distributions. These three parameterizations present similar values of the five statistics, while the lognormal and the Weibull distributions show significant differences with respect to the other models. Specifically, the chi-square and the Anderson-Darling statistics point out that the Fisk distribution outperforms the rest of the models considered. However, the Kolmogorov-Smirnov and the Cramer-von Mises statistics support the superiority of the Lamé family over the Fisk distribution. Finally, the criterion of the highest p-value shows different results depending on the countries. We observe that, in the case of Lamé distributions, this test confirms that the estimations perform adequately in more than 90 percent of the countries, thus reinforcing the validity of our estimates.

In sum, the previous results suggest that the Lamé family of income distributions is a valid model to fit limited data. These models present low goodness of fit statistics, thus implying that the estimated shares are close to the theoretical ones reported by the Lamé distributions. Even when the Fisk distribution yields lower values of the four statistics in some cases, the differences with the Lamé distributions are negligible. Therefore, these models are competing and all three are good candidates for modeling income distributions with limited information.

RESULTS

Regional and Global Income Distributions

After looking at inequality trends during the nineties decade, it is worth focusing on the estimated regional and global distributions, which are obtained from a mixture of national Lamé distributions using the population weight of each country. The evolution of regional and global density functions over the study period is presented in Fig. 1. Before going any further, it should be emphasized that the Lamé family can only represent unimodal and zero modal distributions.[9] At the regional level, in contrast, several poles can be modeled since we use a mixture of these families which are able to represent such a distributional shape.

In fact, the distribution of EECA showed two different modes in 1990 at 1,700 and 7,000 international dollars. Over the nineties, a decrease in polarization was observed in this region (Ezcurra, Pascual, & Rapún, 2007) which led to a unimodal shape at the end of the decade. However, the effects of the transition from planned to market economy in communist countries moved the income distribution to the left which showed a more peaked shape with thinner tails at the end of the decade. In contrast, the nineties were characterized as a period of astonishing economic growth in EAP. Its income distribution shifted to the right and became less peaked. SA presented a similar evolution over this decade, but its improvements were less appreciable. The positive evolutions of these regions were mainly promoted by the so-called *Asian Dragons* such as China and India, characterized by growth rates that ranged from 5 to 8 percent (Ravallion, 2003; Ravallion & Chen, 2003).

In line with previous studies, income distribution in SSA remained almost unchanged over the nineties (Pinkovskiy & Sala-i-Martin, 2009). The mode of the income distribution was close to zero over the whole period, characterizing this region as the least developed territory. For the LAC region, after the periods of volatility and stagnation characteristic of the

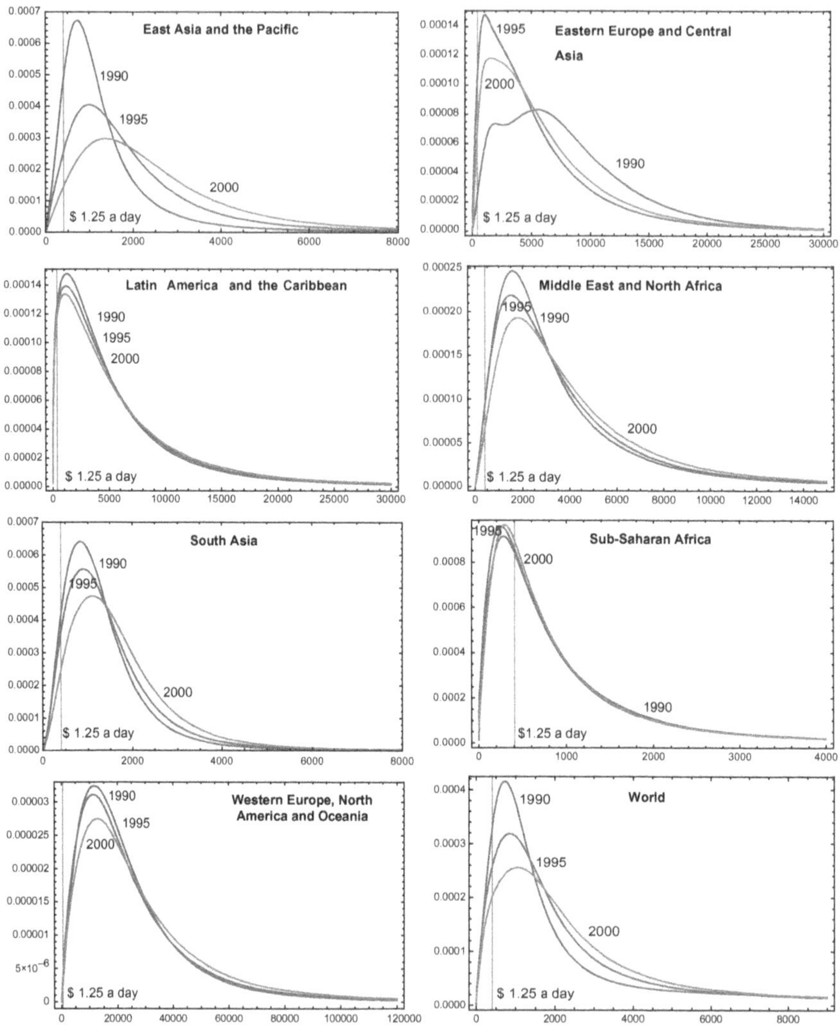

Fig. 1. Intertemporal Evolution of Regional and Global Density Functions (Lamé I).

eighties (Londoño & Székely, 2000), the nineties were characterized by macroeconomic stability and recovery. However, no remarkable progress is observed in the shape of the income distribution, which remains practically stagnant except for a slight increase in the mode.

The long-term effects of the oil-fired economic boom were still present during the course of the nineties in MENA. After two decades of intense economic progress with annual growth rates close to 4.5 percent (Adams & Page, 2003), the economic development of this region was slowed down during the nineties. In fact, income distribution presented only a modest increase of the mode and a less peaked shape in 2000. In the same line, WENAO, which comprises most of the advanced economies, showed a less skewed distribution at the end of the decade.

To analyze how these changes affected the position of each region in relative terms, Fig. 2 plots regional and global CDFs in 1990 and 2000.

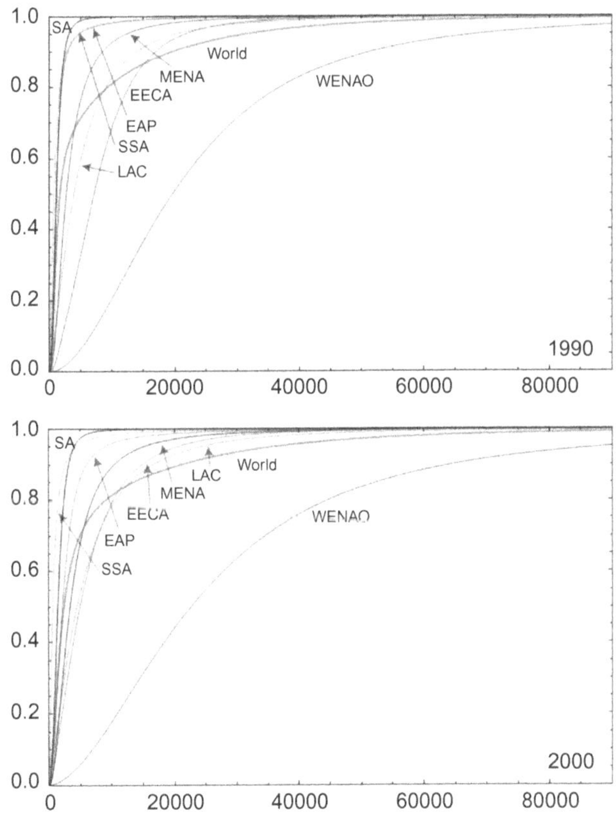

Fig. 2. Regional and Global Cumulative Distribution Functions in 1990 and 2000 (Lamé I).

SSA showed the worst economic performance, being relegated to the last position. The stagnation phase that characterized this territory during the nineties made it difficult to improve its economic situation with respect to other regions. The African tragedy contrasts with the outstanding progress achieved by EAP. At the beginning of the decade, it presented a similar situation to those observed for SA and SSA. The outstanding development of this region during the nineties placed its income distribution close to LAC. Conversely, EECA reported a poor economic performance over the nineties. Its distribution worsened to the point to be close to Latin America, while at the beginning of the period, it was closer to the distribution of the advanced economies. For the rest of the regions, their relative situation did not change considerably over the study period.

Inequality Patterns During the Nineties

In this section, we analyze the evolution of inequality at regional and global levels. The study of income inequality has received an increasing amount of attention and numerous inequality measures have been proposed in the literature.[10] Note that different measures attach different weights to some sections of the distribution. As a consequence, it is worth checking the robustness of the results to the choice of the inequality index. In this study, we focus on the Generalized Entropy (GE) measures because they are additively decomposable in within-country and between-country inequality, which is a desirable property for the study of income dynamics. Inequality within-country is a weighted average of the internal disparities of each nation. The between-country component is the amount of inequality that would exist if there were no internal disparities, in the sense that all citizens of a particular country had the same level of income. The decomposition in these components would provide additional information about the distributional patterns during the nineties.

Another desirable feature of these measures is that they have a sensibility parameter which attaches different weights to the top of the distribution depending on its value. In this study, this parameter is set to 0.5, 0.75, 1.5 and 1. The last case corresponds to the limit case of the GE measures called the Theil index which gives the same weight to all parts of the distribution. To save space, we present the complete results for the global distribution, whereas only the Theil index is reported for the regions.[11]

The estimates of the different GE measures considered and the decomposition in the components between- and within-countries during the nineties are presented in Table 3 for the global distribution of income. The evolution of the sample mean suggests that the nineties were characterized as a period of economic growth at global level, given that the world per capita GDP increased by nearly 18 percent. With regard to global inequality, we observe that if we attach larger weight at the upper tail ($\theta = 1.5$), the inequality tends to increase over the study period. In contrast, if we value more the transfers among the poor population, inequality decreases by 1 to 7 percent. The contrasting trends observed for different values of the sensitivity parameter suggest that no unambiguous conclusions can be achieved regarding the evolution of global inequality. This result is derived from the fact that we cannot establish a complete stochastic ordering for

Table 3. Global Income Inequality.

	1990		1995		2000		Change
	Value	%	Value	%	Value	%	
Mean	7,013.06		7,298.6		8,242.43		17.53
Theil	1.1077	100	1.0646	100	1.0292	100	−7.09
	(0.1753)		(0.2113)		(0.2477)		
Within	0.2896	26	0.3374	32	0.3273	32	13.02
	(0.0960)		(0.1194)		(0.1191)		
Between	0.8181	74	0.7271	68	0.7019	68	−14.20
	(0.1452)		(0.1660)		(0.1970)		
Generalized entropy	0.9701	100	0.9584	100	0.9379	100	−3.32
(θ=0.5)	(0.0627)		(0.0787)		(0.0968)		
Within	0.2389	25	0.2836	30	0.2803	30	17.35
	(0.0343)		(0.0413)		(0.0429)		
Between	0.7312	75	0.6748	70	0.6576	70	−10.08
	(0.0492)		(0.0603)		(0.0729)		
Generalized entropy	0.9805	100	0.9846	100	0.9697	100	−1.10
(θ=0.75)	(0.0459)		(0.0598)		(0.0775)		
Within	0.2620	27	0.3107	32	0.3093	32	18.04
	(0.0274)		(0.0337)		(0.0389)		
Between	0.7185	73	0.6740	68	0.6604	68	−8.09
	(0.0317)		(0.0398)		(0.0488)		
Generalized entropy	1.4051	100	1.5161	100	1.5348	100	9.23
(θ=1.1)	(0.0808)		(0.4775)		(0.7016)		
Within	0.6197	44	0.7494	49	0.7709	50	24.40
	(0.0781)		(0.4757)		(0.6881)		
Between	0.7854	56	0.7667	51	0.7639	50	−2.74
	(0.0113)		(0.0152)		(0.0198)		

Note: Bootstrapped standard errors based on 1,000 replications.

the income distributions in 1990 and 2000[12] and, therefore, the inequality measures do not necessarily present the same dynamics.

Moving onto the decomposition, it is observed that within-country inequality tended to increase over the course of the decade irrespective of the value of the parameter. This result is consistent with previous studies which point out that the internal disparities of the countries soared since 1960 (Bourguignon & Morrison, 2002; Milanovic, 2005; Sala-i-Martin, 2006). Note, however, that this trend was not monotonic. In fact, the value of this component rose sharply during the first half of the period, peaked in 1995 – reaching values from 0.33 to 0.77 – and then declined slightly in the second half of the nineties. Conversely, a continuously decreasing trend is observed for inequality between countries.

It is worth noting that the intensity of the variation of both components strongly depends on the weight assigned to the top of the distribution, determined by the θ parameter. Regarding within-country inequality, it is observed that the increase has been remarkably higher when the parameter is set to 1.5 (close to 25 percent), while the lowest rate was achieved by the Theil index with an increase of 13 percent. For the between-country component, the greatest decline is observed for the Theil index, which reports a reduction of 14 percent. The lowest fall is achieved when we set the sensitivity parameter to 1.5 (about 3 percent). In general terms, the decline of the between-country inequality offset the increase in within-country disparities, thus resulting in a reduction of overall inequality. However, if we attach a high weight to the top incomes, the increase in within-country inequality is so intense and that the reduction of the differences between countries was not enough to avoid the increase in global inequality.

The opposite evolution of both components affected the proportion of total inequality represented by each one. Note that, at the beginning of the period, inequality across countries accounted for nearly 75 percent of the global disparities in all cases, except for GE ($\theta = 1.5$). Ten years later, the within-country component gained weight at the expense of between-country inequality. Notwithstanding this fact, differences between countries played a predominant role in the evolution of global inequality over the whole period when the more (or equal) weight is attached at the lower tail of the income distribution. In contrast, if we give more weight to the upper tail both components present an equal weighting scheme.

Let us focus on regional inequality patterns. The values of the Theil index and its decomposition in the components within- and between-country are presented in Table 4 for each of the regions during the nineties.

Table 4. Regional Income Inequality: The Theil Index.

	1990		1995		2000		Change
	Value	%	Value	%	Value	%	
East Asia and the Pacific							
Mean	1,757.43		2,619.27		3,350.72		90.66
Theil	0.4679	100	0.4779	100	0.4319	100	−7.70
	(0.0325)		(0.0419)		(0.0411)		
Within	0.2525	54	0.3095	65	0.3027	70	19.89
	(0.0321)		(0.0450)		(0.0442)		
Between	0.2154	46	0.1684	35	0.1292	30	−40.04
	(0.0233)		(0.0208)		(0.0152)		
Eastern Europe and Central Asia							
Mean	8,792.88		6,427.31		7,195.83		−18.16
Theil	0.3129	100	0.5095	100	0.4480	100	43.20
	(0.0220)		(0.0530)		(0.0423)		
Within	0.1983	63	0.3815	75	0.3133	70	58.01
	(0.0166)		(0.0419)		(0.0345)		
Between	0.1146	37	0.1281	25	0.1347	30	17.59
	(0.0112)		(0.0159)		(0.0126)		
Latina America and the Caribbean							
Mean	6,539.32		7,038.05		7,699.79		17.75
Theil	0.5938	100	0.6066	100	0.6334	100	6.67
	(0.0776)		(0.0847)		(0.0682)		
Within	0.5302	89	0.5492	91	0.5557	88	4.80
	(0.0713)		(0.0763)		(0.0639)		
Between	0.0636	11	0.0574	9	0.0777	12	22.25
	(0.0167)		(0.0157)		(0.0187)		
Middle East and North Africa							
Mean	4,200.2		4,586.12		5,247.04		24.92
Theil	0.4183	100	0.4394	100	0.4317	100	3.19
	(0.0382)		(0.0430)		(0.0398)		
Within	0.2802	67	0.2955	67	0.2899	67	3.45
	(0.0289)		(0.0326)		(0.0298)		
Between	0.1381	33	0.1439	33	0.1418	33	2.66
	(0.0181)		(0.0201)		(0.0197)		
South Asia							
Mean	1,362.21		1,526.47		1,783.03		30.89
Theil	0.2235	100	0.2412	100	0.2302	100	3.02
	(0.0351)		(0.0355)		(0.0376)		

Table 4. (*Continued*)

	1990		1995		2000		Change
	Value	%	Value	%	Value	%	
Within	0.2040	91	0.2200	91	0.2052	89	0.58
	(0.0331)		(0.0337)		(0.0346)		
Between	0.0195	9	0.0212	9	0.0250	11	28.59
	(0.0046)		(0.0052)		(0.0059)		
Sub-Saharan Africa							
Mean	1,448.93		1,393.25		1,479.74		2.13
Theil	0.7483	100	0.7521	100	0.7573	100	1.21
	(0.0888)		(0.0875)		(0.1147)		
Within	0.4574	61	0.4443	59	0.4336	57	−5.20
	(0.0373)		(0.0396)		(0.0399)		
Between	0.2909	39	0.3077	41	0.3238	43	11.28
	(0.0646)		(0.0640)		(0.0861)		
Western Europe, North America, and Oceania							
Mean	26,393.7		28,194		32,326.5		22.48
Theil	0.3434	100	0.3899	100	0.4025	100	17.22
	(0.0318)		(0.0392)		(0.0407)		
Within	0.3186	93	0.3703	95	0.3818	95	19.85
	(0.0274)		(0.0331)		(0.0340)		
Between	0.0248	7	0.0196	5	0.0207	5	−16.50
	(0.0075)		(0.0092)		(0.0106)		

Note: Bootstrapped standard errors based on 1,000 replications.

Our results point out that SSA was the most unequal region in the world. Its inequality levels continuously increased during the nineties, thus intensifying the unequal situation of this region. As a positive trend, we can highlight that the mean income increased by 2 percent over this decade. Our estimates suggest a decrease in the within-country component due to the fall of disparities in highly populated nations such as Ethiopia, Tanzania and Kenya with reductions of 18, 38, and 32 percent, respectively.[13] In contrast, differences in income levels between countries sharply increased over the study period. As a result, this component gained weight in overall inequality at the expense of the disparities within countries. These trends reflect the fact that the increase in African inequality is a direct consequence of this process of divergence in income levels between countries.

Similar dynamics were observed for LAC which was characterized as the second most unequal region. Despite the economic recovery that followed the lost decade and the macroeconomic stability, inequality levels soared during the course of the nineties. Such an upward trend was mainly due to the increase in differences in income between countries. This pattern was reinforced by the rise of disparities within countries, which was driven by the increase of inequality in Colombia, Argentina and Peru. Note that the described trends of both components did not alter the proportions of each component significantly. The within-country inequality is the predominant factor in the overall disparities in LAC, which accounts for the 90 percent of inequality, while the differences between countries are seen as a residual component. This result emphasizes the fact that the rise of inequality in Latin America over the nineties was derived from important redistributions of wealth occurring within the borders of each nation.

EAP inequality levels declined due to the decrease in inequality between countries during the nineties. This sharp reduction offset the increase in disparities within countries, which were mainly driven by the substantial rise of inequality in China. As a consequence, the proportion of between-country inequality declined substantially. It was 30 percent in 2000 whereas at the beginning of the period it accounted for almost 50 percent. Therefore, overall inequality in this region was principally determined by internal disparities of the nations. The other Asian region (SA) was characterized as the most equal territory over the whole period. Its level of inequality remained constant, not experiencing significant changes in the weighting scheme of both inequality components. According to our estimates, most of the inequality in SA was due to internal inequalities of the countries, whereas only 10 percent came from differences in the income levels between countries.

MENA slightly increased its inequality due to the rise of both disparities within and between countries by 3 percent. Note that this variation did not affect the proportion of inequality represented by each of the components, which was dominated by the differences within countries. The rise of this component was driven by the increase of disparities in Morocco, Tunisia, Egypt, and Jordan which was quantified between 20 and 25 percent during the nineties.

In 1990, EECA showed inequality levels close to the disparities that we observed in other developed regions such as WENAO. The fall of the communist regime and the subsequent transition to a market economy led to a sharp increase in disparities in the first half of the nineties while the second part of the period was characterized by a decrease in inequality levels. Note, however, that this evolution resulted in a growth rate of disparities by 50 percent in just ten years. The remarkable increase in inequality was driven by large income redistributions within each nation that led to the expansion of within-country inequality by 58 percent. In fact, only four out of 29 countries reduced their internal disparities. It should be also noted that differences across countries rose during the nineties (by slightly over 17 percent), also playing an important role in the increase in inequality of EECA. According to our estimates, overall inequality in this region mainly came from the within-country component that represented the 70 percent of total disparities.

Finally, WENAO, the region that comprises most of the advanced economies, was characterized by low levels of inequality. Differences between countries were reduced by 16 percent, though not sufficient to offset the increase in inequalities with counties. As a result, this region became more unequal at the end of the nineties. The upward trend presented by the within-country factor was caused by the rise in internal disparities in most countries. Note that these trends did not alter the proportion of total inequality represented by each component, which is strongly dominated by inequality within countries.

CONCLUSIONS

In this study, we derive income distributions for 127 countries in three benchmark years: 1990, 1995 and 2000, using the two versions of Singh-Maddala and Dagum distributions. We use limited data on mean income, extracted from national accounts, and the Gini index, which comes from microeconomic surveys. In a second stage, global and regional distributions are computed using a mixture of the two families considered in this study. The aim of this paper is twofold. On the one hand, we try to shed more light on the study of the world distribution of income and its dynamics, using two-parameter families that are able to represent its main features adequately. Secondly, we examine the evolution of inequality during the nineties.

We propose to use the Lamé family of income distributions, which are curved versions of the Singh-Maddala and Dagum distributions. This feature makes these models especially suitable to fit income data. Moreover, they are sufficiently flexible to model zero-mode and one-mode distributions. On the other hand, they are strongly connected with two well-known economic theories, namely trickle-up and trickle-down effects (Henle et al., 2008). The fit of these models was evaluated in Henle et al. (2008), concluding that the estimates provided by these distributions yield low mean square error. These models were also compared with more flexible proposals, concluding that the inclusion of an additional parameter led to an overfitting of the data.

The proposed methodology allows us to analyze the inequality trends during the nineties. In particular, we compute GE measures, considering different values for the sensitivity parameter. Our results show a reduction of between-country inequality derived from the convergence in income experienced by some of the most populous countries, such as China and India, which presented an astonishing growth of their per capita GDP over the study period. However, inequality within countries increased notably during the nineties although not enough to eclipse the improvement in cross-country disparities. Consequently, our findings suggest a reduction in global inequality.

The global patterns, however, cannot be extrapolated to all regions that are characterized by a mix of experiences. In fact, EAP is the only region that brought down its inequality over the study period, mainly due to the decrease in between-country inequality. WENAO presented a process of convergence among countries, but it was too weak to offset the increase in internal disparities of nations. Conversely, SSA showed a modest decrease in the within-country component, which was not enough to bring down the inequality levels driven by the divergence process among African economies. The rest of the regions presented an increase in overall inequality derived from the increase in the within-county component, a trend that was reinforced by the enhancement of disparities between countries.

NOTES

1. In this paper, the word "regional" refers to supranational regions of the world instead of the classical conception of regions within a particular country.

2. These families include the classical Pareto distribution (Arnold, 1983), the lognormal, gamma (Salem & Mount, 1974), beta, Singh-Maddala (Singh & Maddala, 1976), Dagum (Dagum, 1977), Weibull, and the different generalized versions of each. Many of the above distributions can be embedded in the generalized gamma and generalized beta of first (GB1) and second kind (GB2) distributions, which were proposed by McDonald (1984). McDonald and Xu (1995) developed a generalized beta distribution with five parameters and the generalized beta-exponential (EGB), as extensions of the previous families.

3. Other studies used data on income shares which are the points associated with the Lorenz curve (see, e.g., Chotikapanich et al., 2009; Grüen & Klasen, 2008). In all cases 5 or 10 data points are available, making it possible to estimate distributions with several parameters. However, the availability of this data is substantially limited with respect to the mean and the Gini index, thus restricting notably the sample of countries and the possibility to consider long temporal periods.

4. In this study, we consider the following macro-regions: East Asia and the Pacific (EAP), Latin America and the Caribbean (LAC), South Asia (SA), Western Europe, North America and Oceania (WENAO), the Middle East and North Africa (MENA), Sub-Saharan Africa (SSA) and Eastern Europe and Central Asia (EECA).

5. Similar expressions of the CDF and the PDF are obtained for the Lamé II distribution.

6. It should be emphasized that we are merging limited information from surveys with national accounts to estimate the regional distribution. Note that it is a common practice and an accepted procedure in this field (Bhalla, 2002; Bourguignon & Morrison, 2002; Chotikapanich et al., 1997, 2007; Grüen & Klasen, 2008).

7. For the benchmark year 1990 the Gini indices of Burundi, Central African Republic, Gambia, Niger, Laos, Vietnam, Guyana, Nicaragua, Yemen, and Iceland correspond to 1992. This statistic in the case of Guinea, Guinea-Bissau, Senegal and Bosnia and Herzegovina corresponds to 1991. For the benchmark year 2000, the Gini index of Guyana corresponds to 1999.

8. The use of other kinds of limited information such as the income quantiles would allow for the estimation of more flexible models. However, this data would restrict our sample considerably in terms of population coverage. Furthermore, the aim of this paper is to present a simple model, which is able to represent the main characteristics of the distributions when only two pieces of information are available.

9. For countries where a bimodal distribution pattern is observed (as is the case of India, the United States, or Brazil (Andrade, Laurini, Madalozzo, & Valls Pereira, 2004; Bandyopadhyay, 2011; Quah, 1997)), the Lamé distribution approximates this shape by one mode.

10. See Cowell (2011) for a detailed description of a broad range of inequality measures and the properties attributable to each one.

11. The values of the different inequality measures considered in the study for regions are available from authors upon request.

12. The lack of stochastic dominance can be easily observed when comparing graphically the global cumulative distribution function in 1990 and 2000. The distribution in 2000 cross the distribution in 1990, thus implying that no complete ordering can be achieved between both years. (Results available upon request.)

13. The estimated inequality measures for each of the countries included in the study during the nineties are available from authors upon request.

ACKNOWLEDGMENTS

The authors thank the Ministerio de Economía y Competitividad (Project ECO2010-15455) and the Ministerio de Educación (AP2010-4907) for partial support of this work. Authors are grateful for the constructive suggestions provided by the reviewers, which improved the paper substantially.

REFERENCES

Adams, R. H., & Page, J. (2003). Poverty, inequality and growth in selected Middle East and North Africa countries, 1980–2000. *World Development*, *31*(12), 2027–2048.

Andrade, E., Laurini, M., Madalozzo, R., & Valls Pereira, P. L. (2004). Convergence clubs among Brazilian municipalities. *Economics Letters*, *83*(2), 179–184.

Arnold, B. C. (1983). *Pareto distributions*. Fairland, MD: International Cooperative Publishing House.

Babu, J. G., & Rao, C. R. (2004). Goodness-of-fit tests when parameters are estimated. *Sankhya: The Indian Journal of Statistics*, *66*, 63–74.

Bandourian, R., McDonald, J. B., & Turley, R. S. (2002). *A comparison of parametric models of income distribution across countries and over time*. Luxembourg Income Study Working Paper No. 305.

Bandyopadhyay, S. (2011). Rich states, poor states: Convergence and polarisation in India. *Scottish Journal of Political Economy*, *58*(3), 414–436.

Bhalla, S. (2002). *Imagine there is no country*. Washington, DC: Institute for International Economics.

Bourguignon, F., & Morrison, C. (2002). Inequality among world citizens: 1820–1992. *American Economic Review*, *92*, 727–744.

Bracquemond, C., Cretois, E., & Gaudoin, O. (2002). *A comparative study of goodness-of-fit tests for the geometric distribution and application to discrete time reliability*. Technical Report. Laboratoire Jean Kuntzmann, Applied Mathematics and Computer Science.

Bresson, F. (2009). On the estimation of growth and inequality elasticities of poverty with grouped data. *Review of Income and Wealth*, *55*(2), 266–302.

Chotikapanich, D., & Griffiths, W. E. (2008). *Estimating income distributions using a mixture of gamma densities*. Department of Economics – Working Papers Series No. 1034. The University of Melbourne.

Chotikapanich, D., Griffiths, W. E., & Rao, D. P. (2007). Estimating and combining national income distributions using limited data. *Journal of Business and Economic Statistics*, *25*(1), 97–109.

Chotikapanich, D., Grifiths, W., Rao, D. S. P., & Valencia, V. (2009). *Global income distribution and inequality: 1993 and 2000*. University of Melbourne Research Paper No. 1062.

Chotikapanich, D., & Rao, D. S. P. (1998). Inequality in Asia 1975–1990: A decomposition analysis. *The Asia Pacific Journal of Economics and Business*, *2*, 63–78.

Chotikapanich, D., Valenzuela, M. R., & Rao, D. S. P. (1997). Global and regional inequality in the distribution of income: Estimation with limited incomplete data. *Empirical Economics*, *20*, 533–546.

Cowell, F. A. (2011). *Measuring inequality* (5th ed.). New York, NY: Oxford University Press.

Dagum, C. (1977). A new model a personal income distribution: Specification and estimation. *Economie Appliquée*, *30*, 413–437.

Deininger, K., & Squire, L. (1996). New data set measuring income inequality. *World Bank Economic Review*, *10*, 565–591.

Ezcurra, R., Pascual, P., & Rapún, M. (2007). The dynamics of regional disparities in Central and Eastern Europe during transition. *European Planning Studies*, *15*(10), 1397–1421.

Grüen, C., & Klasen, S. (2008). Growth, inequality, and welfare: Comparisons across space and time. *Oxford Economic Papers*, *60*(2), 212–236.

Henle, J. M., Horton, N. J., & Jakus, S. J. (2008). Modelling inequality with a single parameter. In D. Chotikapanich (Ed.), *Modeling income distributions and Lorenz curves* (Vol. 5, pp. 255–269). Economic Studies in Inequality, Social Exclusion and Well-Being. New York, NY: Springer Verlag.

Henze, N. (1996). Empirical-distribution-function goodness-of-fit tests for discrete models. *Canadian Journal of Statistics*, *24*(1), 81–93.

Heston, A., Summers, R., & Aten, B. (2012). *Penn world table version 7.1*. Center for International Comparisons of Production, Income and Prices at the University of Pennsylvania.

Kleiber, C., & Kotz, S. (2003). *Statistical size distributions in economics and actuarial sciences*. Hoboken, NJ: Wiley.

Klugman, S. A., Panjer, H. H., & Willmot, G. E. (2012). *Loss models: From data to decisions* (Vol. 715). Hoboken, NJ: Wiley.

LIS. (2000). *Luxembourg income study*. Retrieved from http://www.lisproject.org/

Londoño, J. L., & Székely, M. (2000). Persistent poverty and excess inequality: Latin America, 1970–1995. *Journal of Applied Economics*, *1*, 93–134.

McDonald, J. B. (1984). Some generalized functions for the size distribution of income. *Econometrica*, *52*, 647–663.

McDonald, J. B., & Xu, Y. J. (1995). A generalization of the beta distribution with applications. *Journal of Econometrics*, *66*, 133–152.

Milanovic, B. (2002). True world income distribution, 1988 and 1993: First calculation based on household surveys alone. *Economic Journal*, *112*, 51–92.

Milanovic, B. (2005). *Worlds apart: Measuring international and global inequality*. Princeton, NJ: Princeton University Press.

Minoiu, C. (2007). *Poverty analysis based on kernel density estimates from grouped data*. Mimeo.

Pinkovskiy, M., & Sala-i-Martin, X. (2009). *Parametric estimations of the world income distribution*. NBER Working Paper No. 15433.

Quah, D. T. (1997). Empirics for growth and distribution: Stratification, polarization, and convergence clubs. *Journal of Economic Growth*, *2*(1), 27–59.

Ravallion, M. (2003). Measuring aggregate welfare in developing countries: How well do national accounts and surveys agree? *Review of Economics and Statistics*, *85*(3), 645–652.

Ravallion, M., & Chen, S. (2003). Measuring pro-poor growth. *Economics Letters*, *78*(1), 93–99.

Sala-i-Martin, X. (2006). The world distribution of income: Falling poverty and … convergence, period. *Quarterly Journal of Economics*, *121*, 351–397.

Salem, A. B., & Mount, T. D. (1974). A convenient descriptive model of income distribution: The gamma density. *Econometrica*, *42*, 1115–1127.

Sarabia, J. M., Jordá, V., & Trueba, C. (2013). Estimating the income distribution in Latin America using limited information. *International Advances in Economic Research*, *20*, 1–2.

Sarabia, J. M., Jordá, V., & Trueba, C. (2014). The Lamé class of Lorenz curves. *Communications in Statistics, Theory and Methods*, forthcoming.

Singh, S. K., & Maddala, G. S. (1976). A function for the size distribution of incomes. *Econometrica*, *44*, 963–970.

Solt, F. (2009). Standardizing the world income inequality database. *Social Science Quarterly*, *90*(2), 231–242.

TransMonee. (1999). *Monitoring social conditions and public policy in central and Eastern Europe*. UNICEF. Retrieved from http://eurochild.gla.ac.uk/Documents/monee/

UNU-WIDER. (2008). World income inequality database, version 2.0c. Retrieved from http://www.wider.unu.edu/research/Database/en_GB/database/. Accessed on May 2008.

POVERTY HAS DECLINED, BUT WHAT ABOUT THE BURDEN OF NON-EXTREME POVERTY? GENERALIZED DOMINANCE CRITERIA FOR CONVEX SUBSETS WITHIN THE POVERTY DOMAIN

Florent Bresson

ABSTRACT

This paper deals with poverty decompositions into subgroups defined with respect to intervals of income and the robustness of comparisons of the absolute contribution of such groups to poverty. For instance, world poverty estimates by the World Bank often distinguish between the extreme poor whose incomes are lower than $1.25 a day (in PPP terms) and the other poor with incomes between $1.25 and $2.5 a day. Existing dominance conditions can tell whether overall poverty and extreme poverty have declined in a robust manner when comparing countries at two points of time, but they cannot say anything for the contribution of the non-extreme poor to overall poverty. In the present paper we propose

---

Economic Well-Being and Inequality: Papers from the Fifth ECINEQ Meeting
Research on Economic Inequality, Volume 22, 147–184

ISSN: 1049-2585/doi:10.1108/S1049-258520140000022004

stochastic generalized dominance criteria to perform robust poverty ordering when the focus is placed on some interval of the poverty domain. Using generated data based on grouped data from World Bank's PovcalNet tool, the paper finally investigates whether the robust decline of extreme poverty around the world during the last decades was also accompanied by a decline of the contribution of non-extreme poverty.

Keywords: Poverty comparisons; stochastic dominance; world poverty; non-extreme poverty; poverty decompositions

JEL classifications: D63; I3

INTRODUCTION

Recent estimates of world poverty show a considerable decline of monetary poverty since 1990, hence a potential success with respect to the first target of the first MDGs, namely halving extreme poverty around the world between 1990 and 2015. For instance, Chen and Ravallion (2012) estimated that the share of the developing world population living with less than \$1.25 a day (in 2005 PPP terms) declined from 43.1% in 1990 to 25.1% in 2005. The picture is roughly the same if we consider a broader definition of monetary poverty. For instance, Chen and Ravallion (2010) showed that the value of the headcount index fell from 70.4% in 1990 to 56.6% in 2005 with a \$2.5 a day poverty line. A quick calculation then enables us to note that the share of the developing world population within the \$1.25–\$2.50 a day interval has increased from 27.3% to 31.5% during the same period around the developing world.[1] So it looks like the absolute contribution of moderate poverty to overall poverty has raised during the last two decades.

Of course, the headcount index is just one index within the set of indices that have been proposed in the poverty measurement literature (Zheng, 1997), so we may ask whether this result holds with other indices. Moreover, it is widely recognized that the headcount index is a crude and rather deceiving measure (Sen, 1976) so that the use of more refined indices is highly recommended. Most poverty indices used to track poverty changes are additive. Using additive poverty indices, one can easily compute the contribution of different groups to poverty since overall poverty is simply the sum of their absolute contributions. Decomposing the poor population into different groups based on intervals along the poverty domain is relatively unusual in empirical studies but there may be good reasons for doing it. First, provided the range of income in the poverty domain is not too narrow, it is quite trivial to assume that the needs of the extreme poor slightly differ from those of the non-extreme poor and thus call for different policy measures (Sachs, 2005). While improving health and securing a sufficient and balanced diet is generally the highest priority for those individuals who do not fulfill the basic needs for survival, expending economic opportunities is the challenging issue for the moderately poor. If multiple poverty traps can be observed, so that different groups are stuck below different income thresholds, it is of course valuable to estimate where poverty bunches up. Finally, social benefits are often distributed with respect to income and individuals falling into different income intervals are given specific benefits. So, for policy purposes, it may be helpful to know where the most important part of the burden of poverty is located on the income ladder and how this burden changes.

Of course, we support the claim that increasing the income of an extremely poor person should be given priority with respect to improving the situation of a non-extremely poor person as long as we believe in the monotonicity and continuity axioms on which are based most poverty indices (except the headcount index).[2] However, observing the decrease of both overall poverty and its extreme component does not necessarily entail a fall in the non-extreme component of poverty, though such results could also be desirable as we may wish all boats on the sea of poverty to lift up with the rising tide of economic growth. So, the reduction of the burden of non-extreme poverty deserves our interest as a secondary objective and should not be conducted without analyzing changes for the extreme poor as non-extreme poverty shrinks when individuals are lifted out of poverty and also when they fall into extreme poverty.

Nevertheless, assessing the extent of poverty in a given population is a complex exercise if one intends to take into account the different shades of poverty below the poverty line. Most people would agree that a poor person living with \$2 a day is better off than the same person with only 1\$ a day. However, there would be endless discussions about how much poorer the \$1-a-day person is with respect to the \$2-a-day person. The answer would of course depend on the level of the threshold used to separate the poor from the non-poor but also on value judgments that are essentially subjective and reflect notably the sensitivity of the social evaluator with respect to severe forms of deprivations. Blackorby and Donaldson (1980), Clark, Hemming, and Ulph (1981), and Chakravarty (1983b) have studied the ethical foundations of poverty indices and shown that a great variety of poverty indices could be admitted. In practice, a very limited number of poverty indices are used to assess poverty in both scholar and non-scholar studies, notably the first three elements of the family of poverty indices proposed by Foster, Greer, and Thorbecke (1984), but we should always be aware that poverty orderings are likely to be contingent to the choice of a specific functional form for the poverty measure.

Atkinson's (1987) seminal work has challenged this issue and demonstrated that stochastic dominance techniques could be used to assess the ethical robustness of poverty comparisons. First and second order dominance conditions hence make it possible to obtain comparisons that do not hinge on specific poverty indices within broad classes of poverty indices and/or specific values for the poverty line. A subsequent literature has followed Atkinson's paper and has highlighted and enriched the power of the dominance approach.[3] However, none of these contributions has proposed dominance criteria for any limited portion of the poverty domain, so that existing tools cannot be used to state whether the burden of poverty within the $1.25 to $2.50 a day interval has increased in a robust manner during the last decades. This specific issue is challenged in the present paper.

The paper is organized as follows. The section "Poverty Measurement and Generalized Dominance Conditions" introduces stochastic dominance criteria for components of poverty when the focus is put on convex subsets of the poverty domain. In the section "What about Non-Extreme Poverty Changes in the Developing World?," we address the issue of the post-1990 changes in non-extreme monetary poverty. To this end, we first estimate the aggregate distribution of income for low- and middle-income countries using World Bank's PovcalNet data. As income distribution data are provided as grouped data in PovcalNet, each country–year distribution is first assessed as in the study by Bresson (2009), choosing for each observation the most appropriate functional form. Generated micro-dataset are then "corrected" using Shorrocks and Wan's (2008) procedure so that the obtained distributions perfectly fit the data provided by PocalNet regarding the Lorenz curve for each observation. We provide estimates of monetary poverty and non-extreme poverty in 1990, 1995, and 2005 using the usual members from Foster et al.'s (1984) family of poverty indices. Proposed generalized dominance criteria are thereafter applied on the generated distribution of income to check the robustness of the trends observed with our estimates. It is notably shown that the contribution of non-extreme monetary poverty has increased during the first half of the 1990s and declined after 1995 considering the broad class of monotone poverty indices.

However, no conclusive result regarding the whole period of 1990–2005 can be obtained unless we focus on the narrow class of transfer-sensitive poverty indices. As in the case of overall poverty, we also emphasize the role of Chinese economic progress in these results, notably for the post-1995 period. The last section concludes.

POVERTY MEASUREMENT AND GENERALIZED DOMINANCE CONDITIONS

The General Framework

Let x describe an individual attribute defined on the domain $\boldsymbol{K}:=[\kappa^-,\kappa^+]\subset\Re$. For the sake of simplicity, x will generally be called the income, but we may also consider expenditures, wealth or any relevant non-monetary attribute that can be described by a continuous variable. Whatever x refers to, a person's well-being is supposed to be a non-decreasing function of this attribute. As noted by Sen (1976), poverty measurement is basically a two-step procedure. Firstly, we have to separate the poor from the non-poor, that is to choose a poverty line $z\in\boldsymbol{K}\backslash\{\kappa^-\}$ below which an individual is deemed poor and non-poor if individual income is above that line. Secondly, we assess the poverty level of each individual and aggregate the corresponding index over the whole population to get an estimate of the overall poverty level. In the present paper, we will consider additive poverty indices P that are the kernel of large classes of subgroup-consistent poverty indices.[4] More specifically, considering population A and poverty line z, a general expression for the poverty level $P_A(z)$ is:

$$P_A(z) := \int_{\kappa^-}^{\kappa^+} \pi(x,z)\,\mathrm{d}F_A(x) \tag{1}$$

where F_A is the cumulative distribution function (cdf) for population A and $\pi:\boldsymbol{K}\times\boldsymbol{K}\backslash\{\kappa^-\}\to\Re_+$ is an individual poverty index that is non-increasing in x and such that:

$$\pi(x,z)\begin{cases} >0 & \text{if } x<z, \\ =0 & \text{otherwise} \end{cases} \tag{2}$$

The index P is population invariant since replicating each income level in the observed distribution a given number of times does not change the poverty level. It also fulfils the focus axiom as the index is not sensitive to income increments for the non-poor population for a given value of the poverty line. Finally, P is additively decomposable since it is the weighted mean of poverty levels $\pi(x,z)$ over the population. This means that overall poverty is for instance the sum of the estimated contributions for the male and female subgroups, or for the active and inactive populations. With respect to our own issue, additive decomposability is also interesting as it means that overall poverty is also the sum of contributions within the different intervals of the poverty domain. If we suppose that incomes are non-negative real values and that the poverty line is fixed at $100, poverty is for instance the sum of poverty within the intervals [0,50[, [50,80[and [80,100]. Such decompositions by intervals can be very useful in the case where bounds within the poverty domain correspond to administrative thresholds for specific social benefits or income taxation. Famous additive poverty indices of the type (1) are for instance the Watts's (1968), Chakravarty's (1983a) and Foster et al. (1984) poverty indices where the individual poverty index $\pi(x,z)$ is respectively equal to:

$$\log z - \log x, \quad 1 - \left(\frac{x}{z}\right)^{\beta} \quad \text{with } \beta \in]0,1], \text{ and } \left(1 - \frac{x}{z}\right)^{\alpha} \quad \text{with } \alpha \geq 1.$$

We can now define the following classes of poverty indices in a similar way as (Duclos & Makdissi, 2004):

$$\Pi^{s}(z^{+}) := \left\{ P(z) \left| \begin{array}{l} z \leq z^{+}, \{z, z^{+}\} \subset \boldsymbol{K} \\ \pi(x,z) \in \hat{\mathscr{C}}^{s} \\ (-1)^{k} \pi^{(k)}(x;z) > 0, \forall x < z, k = 1 \dots s \end{array} \right. \right\} \tag{3}$$

where $\hat{\mathscr{C}}^{s}$ is the set of functions that are s times piecewise differentiable on $\boldsymbol{K}$ and $\pi^{(}k)(x;z) := \frac{\partial^k \pi}{\partial^k \pi}$ with $\pi^{(0)}(x;z) := \pi(x;z)$. Members from $\Pi^1(z^+)$ comply with a monotonicity property that states that increasing the income level of a poor individual should decrease poverty. Poverty indices from $\Pi^2(z^+)$ constitute a subset of $\Pi^1(z^+)$ and satisfy the Pigou–Dalton principle of transfers, that is, any sequence of progressive transfers within the poverty domain should result in reduced poverty. The last commonly used set of poverty indices, $\Pi^3(z^+)$, is a subset of $\Pi^2(z^+)$ and brings together poverty indices that respect the axiom of transfer sensitivity (Foster & Shorrocks, 1987; Kolm, 1976). In the context of poverty measurement

(Foster & Shorrocks, 1988b; Kakwani, 1980), transfer sensitivity means that a progressive transfer of a given amount between two poor persons showing a given income difference reduces poverty the more the lower is their income. Members from $\Pi^3(z^+)$ are hence associated with a marked aversion for extreme poverty as returns to income increments decrease at a decreasing speed.

As indicated in the introduction, we are not directly interested in the value of P, but in the absolute contribution of different groups to P, with groups being defined with respect to their income levels. For any set of values v and w within $\boldsymbol{K}$, this contribution, thereafter also called a component, is simply:

$$C(P_{\mathrm{A}}(z); v, w) = \int_{v}^{w} \pi(x, z)\mathrm{d}F_{\mathrm{A}}(x) \tag{4}$$

where C is an absolute contribution to overall poverty. Using additive poverty indices, C is thus the product of the poverty level for those individuals within the corresponding interval times the share of these individuals in the whole population. By definition, we have $C(P_{\mathrm{A}}(z);\kappa^{-},z)=P_{\mathrm{A}}(z)$. More generally, let us assume that the poverty domain can be split into m relevant intervals using different thresholds $v_0, v_1, \ldots, v_m$, with $v_0=\kappa^{-}$, $v_m=z$, and $v_k<v_{k+1}\ \forall k\in\{0, \ldots, m-1\}$ we have $P_{\mathrm{A}}(z)=\sum_{k=1}^{m} C(P_{\mathrm{A}}(z); v_{k-1}, v_k)$.

Usually, researchers are interested in comparing poverty levels between different groups because they want to identify the characteristics of those individuals that are the more severely hurt by poverty and so target the individuals who show the largest average return per (received) dollar in terms of poverty reduction. Turning to components induce a change in perspective as components take the relative size of groups into account. Roughly speaking, instead of asking whether it is better to help an extreme poor than a moderately poor person – this is of course a trivial question – contributions help finding for instance whether it would be preferable to foster public action on few extreme poor person instead of numerous moderately poor person regarding the objective of maximizing poverty alleviation.

Dominance Conditions for the Upper Part of the Poverty Domain and Continuous Poverty Indices

Here, we first suppose that we are only interested in the component C corresponding to the upper part of the poverty domain, that is income level below the poverty line z but above some meaningful threshold $\kappa^- < v < z$. For the sake of simplicity, we will call this set the non-extreme poverty domain though any individual whose income is below v shall not necessarily be deemed being in extreme poverty.

In order to ease the exposition of the next proposition, we define the following generalized dominance curves $D^1(x;v):=F(x)-F(v)$ and $D^s(x;v) := \int_v^x D^{s-1}(y;v)\,dy$ for all integer $s > 1$. We also suppose that an agreement can be met about the maximum value z^+ for the poverty line, with $v \le z \le z^+$. We then can introduce our first result.

Proposition 1.

$$C(P_A(z); v, z) \le C(P_B(z); v, z) \quad \forall P \in \Pi^s(z^+) \text{ and } z \in [v, z^+] \tag{5}$$

$$\text{iff} \quad D_A^s(x; v) \le D_B^s(x; v) \quad \forall x \in [v, z^+] \tag{6}$$

Proof: See appendix. ■

Proposition 1 states that the non-extreme component of poverty has not increased as a result of a move from distribution B to distribution A considering any poverty index from the class $\Pi^s(z^+)$ and any poverty line within the interval $[v,z^+]$ if and only if the generalized dominance curve for distribution A is nowhere greater than the generalized dominance curve for population B within this interval. Fig. 1 illustrates Proposition 1 in the case of monotone poverty indices, that is for members of $\Pi^1(z^+)$. In that case,

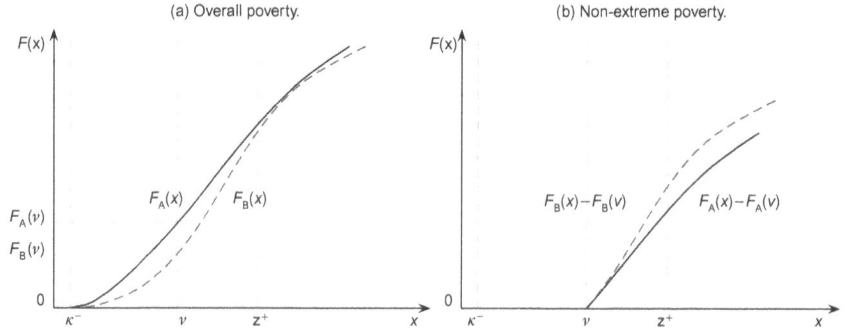

Fig. 1. First-Order and First-Order Generalized Dominance Conditions.

the generalized dominance curve $D^1(x;v)$ is simply the difference between the headcount index at x and that index at the lower bound v of the non-extreme poverty domain. The graphical representation then simply entails shifting down the two cdf values to be compared by their respective value at v as in panel 1b. Here, we can see that the non-extreme component of poverty can be said to be lower for population A when compared with population B in a robust manner considering monotone poverty indices. Panel 1a provides the traditional poverty test for the same distributions A and B and shows that observing poverty dominance of B over A is consistent with having simultaneous dominance for the non-extreme component of poverty of A over B.

It can easily be seen that the limiting case $v = \kappa^-$ corresponds to the usual s-order dominance tests investigated by Atkinson (1987), Foster and Shorrocks (1988a, 1988b), Zheng (2000), and Duclos and Makdissi (2004) since $F(\kappa^-)=0$, so that Proposition 1 can be seen as a generalization of traditional poverty dominance tests. In order to stress this relationship, we can rewrite the function $D^s(x;v)$ in a more tractable form. More specifically, it can be shown using the work by Fishburn (1976) that:[5]

$$D^s(x; v) = \frac{1}{(s-1)!} \int_v^x (x-y)^{s-1} \, \mathrm{d}F(y) \tag{7}$$

As the term $\frac{1}{(s-1)!}$ is constant, it can be dropped when performing dominance tests. We then obtain the non-extreme component of the absolute version of Foster et al.'s (1984) P^s poverty index. Indeed, if $D^s_{\mathrm{A}}(x, v) \leq D^s_{\mathrm{B}}(x; v)$, we necessarily should also observe $\frac{(s-1)!}{z} D^s_{\mathrm{A}}(x, v) \leq \frac{(s-1)!}{z} D^s_{\mathrm{B}}(x, v)$, where $C(P^s(z); v, z) := \frac{(s-1)!}{z} D^s(x; v) = \int_v^x \left(\frac{x-y}{z}\right)^{s-1} \mathrm{d}F(y)$ is simply the non-extreme component of the sth member P^s of the family of FGT poverty indices.[6] The equivalence emphasized by Foster and Shorrocks (1988a) between the stochastic dominance ordering and the ordering provided by the family of FGT poverty indices can thus be extended to the ordering of the non-extreme part of poverty.

It is worth stressing the conceptual differences between our present approach and the restricted dominance techniques investigated by Davidson and Duclos (2013) as the two involve a specific treatment for the bottom poor. With restricted dominance techniques, it is supposed that individuals below some income threshold are completely deprived so that income decrements for those individuals do not result in increasing poverty.[7] Such a line of reasoning can be motivated by ethical arguments but restricted dominance techniques are usually chosen for practical reasons since results of stochastic dominance tests heavily depend on the income values of the very poorest individuals. In practice this means censoring the distribution so that those individuals who are regarded as completely deprived are pushed up to the maximum income value associated with complete deprivation. In the present paper, censoring is not applied and v is not considered as the upper threshold for total deprivation. Indeed, we do not take the situation of the extreme poor into account for comparisons of the non-extreme component of poverty and consequently do not distinguish them from the non-poor. In other words, if censoring was applied for our approach, we would be lifting the income of the extreme poor up to some income level above the poverty line z! The difference should not be seen as a matter of concern since the two procedures have been designed to address different issues: while restricted dominance has been proposed for poverty orderings, our approach focuses on the ordering of poverty components.

An important issue with Proposition 1 is that the lower limit of the non-extreme poverty domain is regarded as known with certainty. That assumption can be regarded as not questionable when the line v refers to some administratively defined threshold. However, as for the poverty line, it may often be subject to discussion as the distinction between extreme and non-extreme poverty is rarely clear-cut. Nevertheless, we may suppose that an agreement can be met about the interval $[v^-, v^+]$ where that lower bound should be located. Generalizing Proposition 1 then straightforwardly yields the following proposition.

Proposition 2.

$$C(P_A(z); v, z) \leq C(P_B(z); v, z) \quad \forall P \in \Pi^s(z^+), z \in [v^+, z^+], \text{ and } v \in [v^-, v^+] \tag{8}$$

$$\text{iff} \quad D^s_A(x; v) \leq D^s_B(x; v) \quad \forall x \in [v, z^+], \ v \in [v^-, v^+] \tag{9}$$

Proof: See appendix. ■

Proposition 2 states that when the value of the lower limit of the non-extreme poverty domain is unknown, the same criterion as for Proposition 1 has to be observed, but for each potential value v of the non-extreme poverty threshold v within the interval $[v^-,v^+]$. The procedure may thus be computationally demanding when numerous values are chosen for v and x. Modern computers can handle such computing loads quite efficiently when the procedure is appropriately coded, but we may be desiring a quicker way of performing the dominance check, in particular when many distributions have to be compared. Fortunately, an alternative procedure that is operationally much simpler and more informative can be proposed. Noting f the probability density function (pdf), an alternative expression for Proposition 2 is thus:

Proposition 3.

$$C(P_{\mathrm{A}}(z); v, z) \leq C(P_{\mathrm{B}}(z); v, z) \quad \forall P \in \Pi^s(z^+),\ z \in [v^+, z^+],\ \text{and}\ v \in [v^-, v^+] \tag{10}$$

$$\text{iff} \quad D^s_{\mathrm{A}}(x; v^+) \leq D^s_{\mathrm{B}}(x; v^+) \quad \forall x \in [v^+, z^+] \tag{11}$$

$$\text{and} \quad f_{\mathrm{A}}(v) \leq f_{\mathrm{B}}(v) \quad \forall v \in [v^-, v^+] \tag{12}$$

Proof: See appendix. ■

Proposition 3 introduces a two-step procedure that transforms the bidimensional dominance procedure of Proposition 2 into a unidimensional procedure and therefore makes its graphical representation much easier. The first step described by condition (11) is essentially the same as condition (6) of Proposition 1, but with the lower bound v set equal to its maximum admissible value v^+. The second condition (12) is surely the most demanding condition as it requires the pdf for population A to be never larger than the pdf of population B for each income value between v^- and v^+. Fig. 2 illustrates Proposition 3 in the case where distribution A exhibits less non-extreme poverty than distribution B. Indeed, we can see from panel 2a that the adjusted curve $F_{\mathrm{A}}(x)-F_{\mathrm{A}}(v^+)+F_{\mathrm{B}}(v^+)$ is nowhere above the curve referring to $F_{\mathrm{B}}(x)$ for each income value between v^+ and z^+, and panel 2b shows that the pdf for A is everywhere lower than the value of the pdf for B for each income value within the interval $[v^-,v^+]$. From a technical point of view, we can note that condition (11) vanishes when the uncertainty about the appropriate value for the lower bound v is so large that

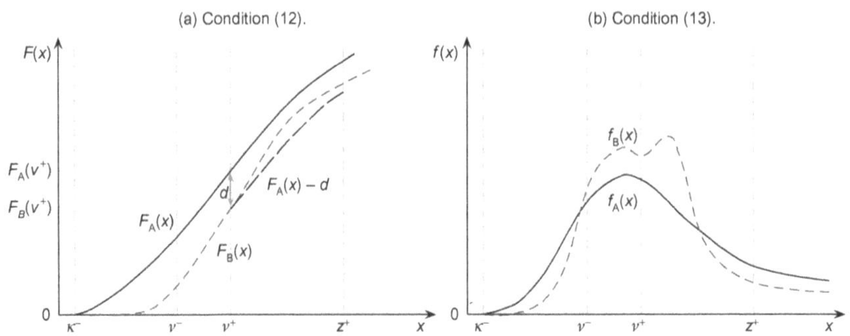

Fig. 2. First-Order Generalized Dominance Conditions with Uncertain Extreme Poverty Threshold.

$v^+ = z^+$, so that Proposition 3 boils down to comparing the two pdfs over the interval $[v^-,z^+]$.

It is worth emphasizing that condition (12) does not depend on the considered class $\Pi^s(z^+)$, so that failing to observe generalized dominance at the first order of dominance entails failing to obtain generalized dominance at any higher order. Consequently, contrary to traditional poverty dominance conditions and Proposition 1 that provide a complete ordering of income distributions at infinite order of dominance, Proposition 2 can only give a partial ordering when $s \rightarrow +\infty$. Finally, condition (12) shows that relaxing the assumption of a known value for v may lower in a substantial manner of the ordering power of our generalized dominance procedure. More specifically, considering broad intervals $[v^-,v^+]$ may dramatically raise the probability of obtaining non-conclusive results.

Dominance Conditions for any Convex Subset of the Poverty Domain and/or Non-Continuous Poverty Indices

For the present paper, we are mainly interested in the whole set of the poor above a given threshold $v \leq z$, but it may be worth considering the case where it is needed to focus on any continuous interval within the poverty domain, that is $C(P_A(z);v,w)$ where $w \in]v,z[$. If we suppose that the precise value of w is somehow uncertain but that it is known it should be within the interval $[w^-,w^+]$, we then can show that:

Proposition 4.

$$C(P_A(z); v, w) \leq C(P_B(z); v, w) \quad \forall P \in \Pi^s(z^+) \text{ and } w \in [w^-, w^+] \tag{13}$$

$$\text{iff} \quad D_A^s(x; v) \leq D_B^s(x; v) \quad \forall x \in]v, w^+] \tag{14}$$

$$\text{and} \quad D_A^k(w; v) \leq D_B^k(w; v) \quad \forall w \in [w^-, w^+], \ k = 1 \ldots \max\{1, s-1\} \tag{15}$$

Proof: See appendix. ■

The condition (14) in Proposition 4 is roughly the same as the one presented in Proposition 1 except that dominance curves have to be compared only up to w^+. Considering first-order dominance checks, condition (15) does not add anything to condition (14) so that the ordering power of Proposition 4 should be greater than with Proposition 1 for $w^+ < z^+$ and a given value for v. However, once we turn to higher dominance orders ($s \geq 2$), the ordering power is likely to decrease significantly as dominance is required at all lower orders $1 \ldots s-1$ for each value of w within $[w^-, w^+]$. That result is due to the fact that $\pi(w,z)>0$ and is reminiscent of the conditions developed for poverty dominance tests with discontinuity at the poverty line (Zheng, 1999) and welfare dominance checks (Duclos & Makdissi, 2004). Consequently, if $D_A^1(w; v) - D_B^1(w; v)$ shows alternating signs in ∈ $[w^-, w^+]$, no robust ordering of $C(P_A(z);v,w)$ and $C(P_B(z);v,w)$ can be achieved, even at infinite order.

Proposition 4 will also be helpful considering classes of poverty indices that exhibit discontinuities within the poverty domain and/or such that certain properties are assumed to be relevant only for some intervals of the poverty domain. The arguments in favor of introducing discontinuities in the individual poverty measure π are essentially the same as those put forward by Bourguignon and Fields (1997). Some functionings are dichotomous, or more generally show a discrete nature, so that marginal increases in resources may have non-marginal effects in terms of well-being for the poor when such increments make it possible to achieve some basic functioning. The usual way to illustrate this is to call for the widely quoted linen-shirt example used by Sen (1983) and that traces back to Adam Smith. In the work of Bourguignon and Fields (1997), the argument was used to justify the possible existence of a discontinuity at the poverty line, but we may also find it convincing for discontinuities within the poverty domain.

Of course, the introduction of discontinuities within the poverty domain violates the continuity axiom that is usually invoked for poverty measurement. However, it is worth reminding that continuity is generally not invoked on the basis of any ethical justification but merely for practical purpose as continuous functions π are less sensitive to measurement errors. In fact, the introduction of discontinuities within the poverty domain can be a matter of concern when considering "core" axioms like transfer sensitivity. With usual continuous poverty indices, transfer sensitivity is fulfilled when the second-order derivative of the individual poverty index is positive, but, as can be seen in Fig. 3, this condition does not ensure the satisfaction of the transfer axiom with a discontinuity, even if function π is piecewise twice differentiable with the second-order right derivative being non-negative. Indeed, it can be observed in Fig. 3 that the average level of poverty is lower with two individuals having respectively income levels equal to a and b than what is obtained after full equalization of income (that is with income level c). In this case, it is thus necessary to decide whether we prefer giving up the possibility of having meaningful discontinuities or fulfilment of the transfer axiom. If one decides to save the existence of discontinuities for the design of poverty indices, it deserves to be noted that we still can assume that progressive transfers between two individuals will not raise poverty, provided that the initial income of the two individuals are from the same interval where π is continuous. Dominance conditions can then be obtained for the corresponding classes of poverty indices using Propositions 1–4. For this purpose, it is first necessary to split the poverty

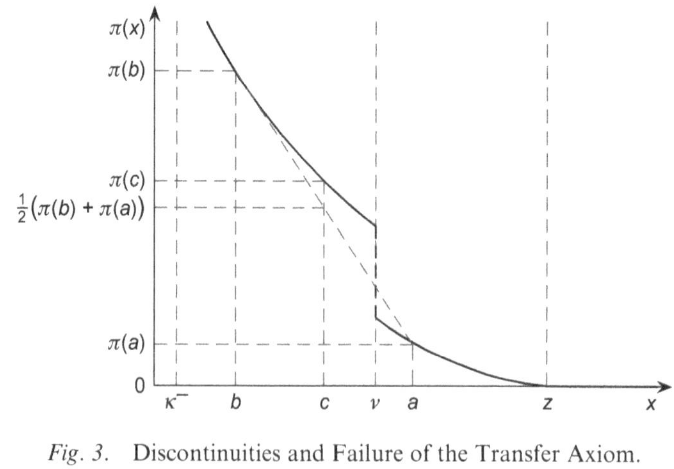

Fig. 3. Discontinuities and Failure of the Transfer Axiom.

domain into subintervals where the individual poverty index is assumed to be continuous and piecewise *s* times differentiable. In a second step, we can then use the corresponding dominance test on each subinterval.[8] It can easily be shown that the fulfilment of the conditions for each dominance test is a sufficient condition for robust comparisons of overall poverty to be concluded.[9]

WHAT ABOUT NON-EXTREME POVERTY CHANGES IN THE DEVELOPING WORLD?

In the next pages, we apply the tools proposed in the section "Dominance Conditions for the Upper Part of the Poverty Domain and Continuous Poverty Indices" to assess the ethical robustness of our initial observation that non-extreme poverty has increased between 1990 and 2005. Since no internationally comparable household surveys are available for that purpose, we choose to generate synthetic income series using grouped data. We first describe our procedure before showing our results.

Estimating a Developing World Distribution of Income

Estimating the world distribution of income is a complex task as no internationally comparable set of household surveys with a comprehensive coverage of the world's population is available. As a consequence, researchers have to rely on secondary datasets (see for instance Bourguignon & Morrisson, 2002; Dhongde & Minoiu, 2010; Milanovic, 2002; Sala-i-Martin, 2006) that provide grouped data information regarding the distribution of domestic income.[10] Here, we chose to use the raw data on mean income and the Lorenz curve given by World Bank's poverty calculator and the platform PovcalNet for which we had observations for both the periods 1987–1993, 1992–1998 and 2002–2008, so as to get estimates of the developing world distribution of income for the years 1990, 1995, and 2005.[11] We then obtain distributional information for 57 developing countries that accounted for approximately 85% of the population from low- and middle-income countries for the period 1995–2005.[12] In the case of China, India, and Indonesia that represent about 50% of the developing world's population, PovcalNet provides separate information for rural and urban areas. Since average income is also available for each area, the estimations of rural and urban distributions can be treated separately in the present paper. As the availability of household survey data has greatly improved during the 1990s, a larger sample of 76 countries has also been used for the comparison of the income distributions in 1995 and 2005. These additional data made it possible to extend the coverage to about 90% of the low- and middle-income countries' population.[13] For each observation, PovcalNet provides the mean income expressed in Purchasing Power Parity using the 2005 ICP, so that income values are directly comparable. Like most studies that estimate the world distribution of income using household survey data, we could not avoid the simultaneous use of both income and consumption data, so that, as stressed by Anand and Segal (2008, p.74), "it is therefore not clear exactly what type of global distribution emerges from combining these surveys [based on either income or consumption expenditures]." This may be a serious limitation, not only for estimating the extent of poverty or some of its components, but also to assess the sign of poverty changes notably because income and consumption are imperfectly correlated. Here, we tried to circumvent that problem by selecting data for each country in a consistent manner so that all corresponding distributions either refer to income or to consumption. So for a given country, observed distributional changes are generally not due to changes in the underlying concept.[14] Regarding the estimated global income distribution, the mixture of both income and consumption surveys may still be a matter of concern as the relative share of income and consumption data are not constant in our series. Indeed, these variations are prominently caused by demographic changes and there is no way of proving that results presented in the next section are not partly due to the imperfect structure of our initial dataset.

For each country, the income distribution is estimated using a two-step procedure. First, the distribution of income is assessed parametrically using different functionals. In the present paper, our attention is confined to the lognormal, Singh-Maddala, Dagum and Beta 2 distributions as well as Maddala and Singh's (1977) parametric Lorenz curve that proved to be the most interesting functional form in the work by Bresson (2009). The estimation showing the best fit as expressed by the sum of squared residuals is chosen for each distribution and a random sample of 10,000 values is then generated from the parametric distribution and adjusted using Shorrocks and Wan's (2008) procedure so as get a perfect fit with respect to the information on the Lorenz curve available from PovcalNet. Generated individual incomes are then taken together and weighted using population size data from the World Bank. Estimates and dominance checks are thus performed on fictive samples of 600,000 individuals (790,000 in the case of the extended sample).

Results

We first report in Table 1 our estimates of poverty as well as its non-extreme component for the first three members of the FGT family of poverty indices, namely the headcount, the poverty gap and squared poverty gap indices, and the two largest poverty lines used in the work of Chen and Ravallion (2010), that is the $2 and $2.5 a day poverty lines. The upper panel of Table 1 shows figures that are consistent with Chen and Ravallion's (2010) estimates regarding the headcount index. Estimates for the poverty gap and squared poverty gap indices with the $2 a day poverty line are also close to those presented by these authors. The authors do not provide such estimates with the 2.5$ poverty line, but estimates provided by PovcalNet for these measures and this poverty line are roughly equal to our estimates.[15] Differences in coverage with respect to our study – poverty estimates by PovcalNet are not obtained using a fixed set of countries – are likely to explain to a large extent these slight differences.

The non-extreme part of poverty is now assessed using the usual $1.25 a day poverty line as the lower bound for non-extreme poverty. As can be stressed from Chen and Ravallion's (2010) results, we first observe that the share of the developing countries' population whose daily per-capita income or consumption level is between $1.25 and $2.5 has increased during the period 1990–2005. The same increase can be observed for South Asia (SA), East Asia and Pacific (EAP), and Sub-Saharan Africa (SSA), while the incidence of non-extreme poverty declined in Europe and Central Asia (ECA), Latin America and Caribbean (LAC), and Middle East and North Africa (MENA). As noted in the introduction, the headcount index is a rather crude poverty indicator as it does not take into account the depth of poverty, so that it is highly recommended to turn to more refined poverty indicators. Using either the poverty gap or the squared poverty gap index, we also observe that the absolute contribution of non-extreme poverty has worsened during the period 1990–2005. However, we note that this result is contingent to the choice of the poverty line as estimates with a $2 a day poverty line show conversely a small decline of the non-extreme poverty component using the squared poverty gap index during the same period. The regional decomposition also shows an increase in the SA and

Table 1. Poverty Estimates and the Absolute Contribution of Non-Extreme Poverty (×100).

Poverty Line	$2.5 a Day							$2 a Day						
	EAP	ECA	LAC	MENA	SA	SSA	Total	EAP	ECA	LAC	MENA	SA	SSA	Total
Headcount index														
1990	87.8	11.7	26.5	30.8	91.0	78.8	74.0	80.4	7.5	21.0	19.0	84.3	71.5	67.0
1995	76.7	16.4	24.6	31.0	89.4	79.8	69.5	65.9	10.7	18.4	18.1	81.5	72.7	60.6
2005	49.9	6.4	21.7	24.4	83.9	77.6	56.5	38.4	3.6	16.1	13.2	74.0	70.1	47.0
Poverty gap index														
1990	47.3	3.9	12.2	8.6	48.0	46.5	39.1	38.1	2.5	9.4	4.6	38.2	39.4	31.3
1995	36.9	5.5	10.7	8.0	44.7	46.2	33.9	28.3	3.5	8.0	4.0	34.5	38.8	26.2
2005	19.0	1.7	9.5	5.9	38.7	43.5	24.8	12.7	1.0	7.2	2.7	28.6	36.0	18.0
Squared poverty gap index														
1990	29.2	1.9	7.6	3.5	28.7	32.2	24.0	21.5	1.2	5.8	1.7	20.5	26.1	17.6
1995	21.6	2.7	6.6	3.0	25.5	31.2	19.9	15.3	1.7	5.1	1.3	17.5	24.7	14.2
2005	9.4	0.7	6.0	2.1	20.9	28.7	13.5	5.7	0.4	4.7	0.9	13.7	22.4	9.0
Headcount index (non-extreme component)														
1990	32.0	8.9	14.7	26.6	34.5	25.8	28.6	24.5	4.7	9.2	14.8	27.9	18.5	21.7
1995	37.6	12.4	15.1	27.9	39.3	26.4	32.9	26.8	6.7	8.9	15.0	31.4	19.4	24.0
2005	34.1	5.4	13.3	22.4	44.0	28.0	32.4	22.6	2.6	7.7	11.1	34.1	20.4	22.9
Poverty gap index (non-extreme component)														
1990	9.9	2.0	3.8	6.1	11.2	7.5	8.8	5.3	0.8	1.7	2.5	6.3	3.9	4.7
1995	10.9	2.8	3.6	6.2	12.7	7.9	9.8	5.6	1.2	1.6	2.5	7.1	4.2	5.1
2005	9.2	1.1	3.2	4.7	13.7	8.3	9.3	4.4	0.4	1.4	1.7	7.3	4.3	4.7
Squared poverty gap index (non-extreme component)														
1990	3.6	0.6	1.3	1.9	4.3	2.7	3.2	1.4	0.2	0.4	0.6	1.7	1.0	1.3
1995	3.9	0.9	1.2	1.9	4.8	2.9	3.5	1.5	0.3	0.4	0.6	1.9	1.1	1.4
2005	3.1	0.3	1.0	1.4	5.1	3.0	3.3	1.1	0.1	0.3	0.4	2.0	1.1	1.2

Notes: The lower bound for non-extreme poverty is set at $1.25 a day. EAP stands for Eastern Asia and Pacific, ECA for Europe and Central Asia, LAC for Latin America and Caraibes, MENA for Middle East and Northern Africa, SA for Southern Asia, and SSA for SubSaharan Africa.

SSA regions, and a decrease in the remaining areas. In terms of relative contribution, the picture shows logically a soaring weight of moderate poverty in total poverty. For instance, non-extreme poverty accounted for 38% of total poverty in 1990 but 57% of total poverty in 2005 using the $2.5 a day poverty line. Figures are lower with poverty indices that exhibit aversion to extreme poverty, but also indicate dramatic increases for this relative contribution. This is not bad news since total and extreme poverty have decreased but it stresses the need to adapt poverty reduction strategies to changes in the distribution of income deprivations, that is changes in the living conditions of the poor.

Turning to subperiod decompositions, we see that the contribution of non-extreme poverty has rapidly increased during the period 1990–1995 and then more moderately decreased afterwards. That inverse U-shaped pattern of non-extreme poverty variations can be observed for every region and every poverty index except for SSA where the burden of non-extreme poverty worsened during the period 1995–2005. Latin America also registered a small decrease between 1990 and 1995 considering the poverty gap and squared poverty gap indices. Using the $2 poverty line instead of the $2.5 poverty line does not alter these results and considering the extended sample (Table 2) does not change the picture regarding variations of the non-extreme component of poverty during the period 1995–2005. Whatever the chosen region, index or income threshold for the poverty line, we can finally note the increase of the relative contribution of non-extreme poverty to overall poverty.

Now, we try to assess the ethical robustness of these findings with the help of the generalized stochastic dominance procedures described in Section "Poverty Measurement and Generalized Dominance Conditions." Before focusing on the non-extreme poor, we first consider the whole poverty domain as the interpretation of changes in the contribution of non-extreme poverty crucially depends on observed changes for the whole poverty domain. Fig. 4(a) plots the cdf for the years 1990, 1995, and 2005. Since the curves do not cross for any income level below $3, usual poverty dominance criteria are fulfilled and we can unambiguously conclude that poverty has declined during the period 1990–2005 as well as for the subperiods 1990–1995 and 1995–2005 whatever the chosen poverty index within the broad class Π^1 and the value for the poverty line below $3 a day. As for the poverty estimates, our results are once again in line with those presented by Chen and Ravallion (2010).

Generalized dominance curves are shown in Fig. 4(b). In order to ease the reading of the results, it is preferable to plot the difference

Table 2. Poverty Estimates and the Absolute Contribution of Non-Extreme Poverty (×100), Extended Sample.

Poverty line	$2.5 a day							$2 a day						
	EAP	ECA	LAC	MENA	SA	SSA	Total	EAP	ECA	LAC	MENA	SA	SSA	Total
Headcount index														
1995	76.7	17.5	25.0	32.6	89.4	82.3	69.4	65.9	11.5	18.8	19.7	81.5	75.6	60.6
2005	50.1	7.8	22.1	27.6	83.9	79.0	57.0	38.6	4.5	16.3	16.2	74.0	70.9	47.4
Poverty gap index														
1995	36.9	5.9	10.9	8.9	44.7	48.3	34.1	28.3	3.8	8.2	4.7	34.5	40.7	26.4
2005	19.1	2.2	9.5	7.4	38.7	42.6	25.0	12.8	1.2	7.2	3.9	28.6	34.6	18.3
Squared poverty gap index														
1995	21.6	2.9	6.7	3.5	25.5	32.7	20.1	15.3	1.8	5.2	1.7	17.5	26.0	14.4
2005	9.4	0.9	5.9	2.9	20.9	27.2	13.7	5.7	0.5	4.6	1.4	13.7	20.8	9.2
Headcount index (non-extreme component)														
1995	37.6	13.2	15.3	28.6	39.3	26.1	32.5	26.9	7.2	9.0	15.7	31.4	19.4	23.7
2005	34.1	6.5	13.7	24.1	44.0	31.2	32.5	22.6	3.2	7.9	12.7	34.1	23.1	23.0
Poverty gap index (non-extreme component)														
1995	10.9	3.0	3.7	6.5	12.7	7.9	9.6	5.6	1.3	1.6	2.6	7.1	4.2	5.0
2005	9.2	1.4	3.3	5.3	13.7	9.3	9.3	4.4	0.5	1.5	2.1	7.3	4.9	4.7
Squared poverty gap index (non-extreme component)														
1995	3.9	1.0	1.2	2.0	4.8	2.9	3.5	1.5	0.3	0.4	0.6	1.9	1.1	1.3
2005	3.2	0.4	1.1	1.6	5.1	3.4	3.3	1.1	0.1	0.4	0.5	2.0	1.3	1.2

Notes: The lower bound for non-extreme poverty is set at $1.25 a day. EAP stands for Eastern Asia and Pacific, ECA for Europe and Central Asia, LAC for Latin America and Caraibes, MENA for Middle East and Northern Africa, SA for Southern Asia, and SSA for SubSaharan Africa.

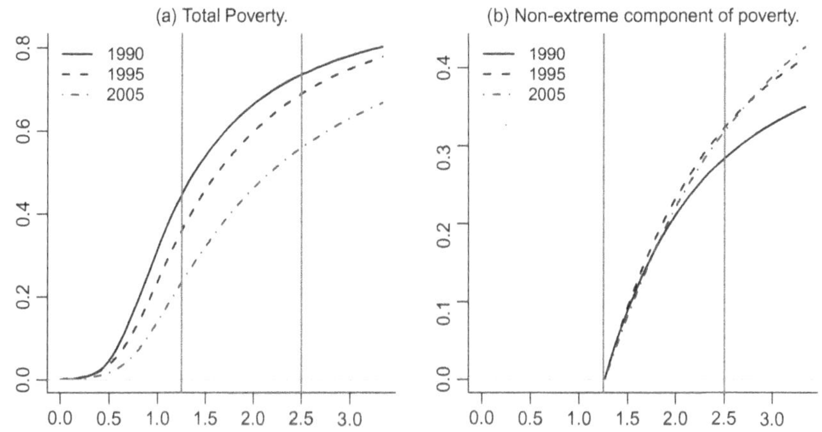

Fig. 4. First-Order Dominance Test: Whole Population.

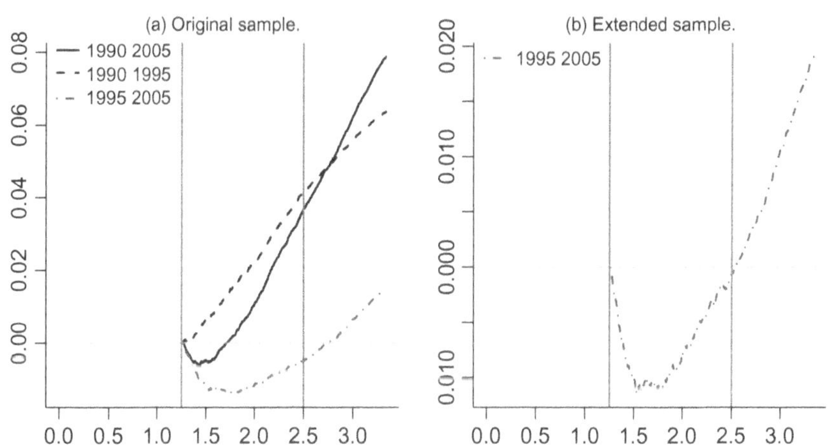

Fig. 5. Generalized First-Order Dominance Tests: The Whole Population.

$D^s_B(x; v) - \hat{D}^s_A(x; v)$ for each pair of distributions to be compared with A (B) being the initial (final) distribution and $\hat{D}^s(x; v)$ the empirical counterpart of $\hat{D}^s(x; v)$. When this difference is non-positive for each income level within $[v,z^+]$, we thus can conclude in a robust manner that the non-extreme part of poverty has declined during the corresponding period. In the present case, the resulting curve reported in Fig. 5(a) for the period 1990–2005 does not make it possible to conclude that the increase in non-extreme poverty observed in Table 1 is not contingent to choices with respect to the poverty index and the poverty line as the curve first shows negative values below $1.7 and positive values above that threshold. However, when applied to the subperiods 1990–1995 and 1995–2005, the dominance procedures show that the two observed trends, that is a worsening during the first period and an improvement during the second period, are ethically robust considering the whole class of monotone poverty indices and poverty lines within the range [1.25,2.7]. Moreover, as we have previously observed an unambiguous decline of overall poverty for the period 1995–2005, we can be sure that the alleviation of the burden of non-extreme poverty is not due to a net move from non-extreme poverty to extreme poverty. Extending the sample (cf. Fig. 5(b)) leaves this result unchanged though the curve exhibits positive values now just above $2.5 a day.

Robust orderings for the non-extreme component of poverty and the whole period may be obtained at the cost of considering narrower classes of poverty indices and lower values for the maximum value of the poverty line as shown in Fig. 6. Focusing on the subset Π^2 of distribution-sensitive poverty measures, we can conclude that the absolute contribution of non-extreme poverty has declined during that period if we limit the set of admissible values for the poverty line within the range]1.25,2.17] (cf. Fig. 6 (a)). In order to get a robust ordering with respect to the non-extreme

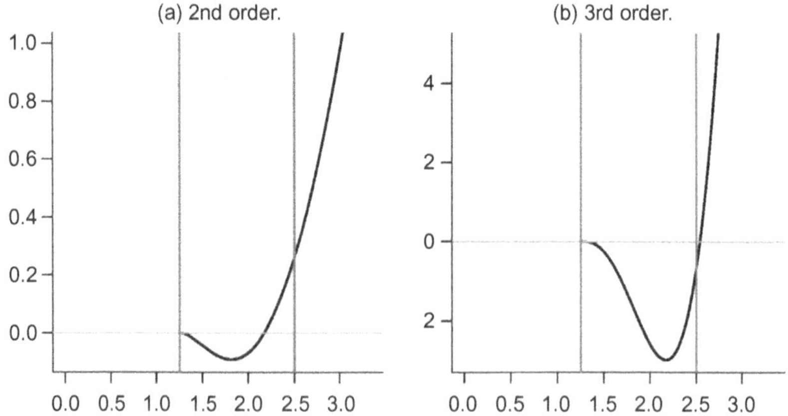

Fig. 6. Generalized Second and Third-Order Dominance Tests: Whole population, 1990–2005.

component of poverty up to the \$2.5 a day poverty line, it is necessary to turn to the subclass Π^3 of poverty indices that exhibit decreasing returns to Pigou–Dalton transfers. Fig. 6(b) then shows that the non-extreme component of poverty has declined during the period whatever the chosen poverty index within Π^3 and the poverty line within the interval]1.25, 2.53].

As these results may be driven by the two most populated countries of our sample, namely China and India, we also perform our generalized dominance tests when the Chinese and Indian populations are alternatively excluded from the generated income distributions. We do not report the figures referring to the usual poverty dominance tests, but omitting either of these two countries leaves unaffected the conclusion that overall poverty has regularly declined in a robust manner considering poverty lines below the \$2.5 a day threshold. Regarding the contribution of non-extreme poverty, while the exclusion of India (Fig. 7(b)) does not change our results from a qualitative point of view, omitting China (Fig. 7(a)) does not make it possible to conclude any more that the burden of non-extreme poverty has unambiguously alleviated during the subperiod 1995–2005 considering the whole set of monotone poverty indices Π^1. Turning to the second or third orders of dominance still yields non-conclusive results, so that it can be concluded that the assessment of changes in the contribution of non-extreme poverty between 1995 and 2005 for the non-Chinese population

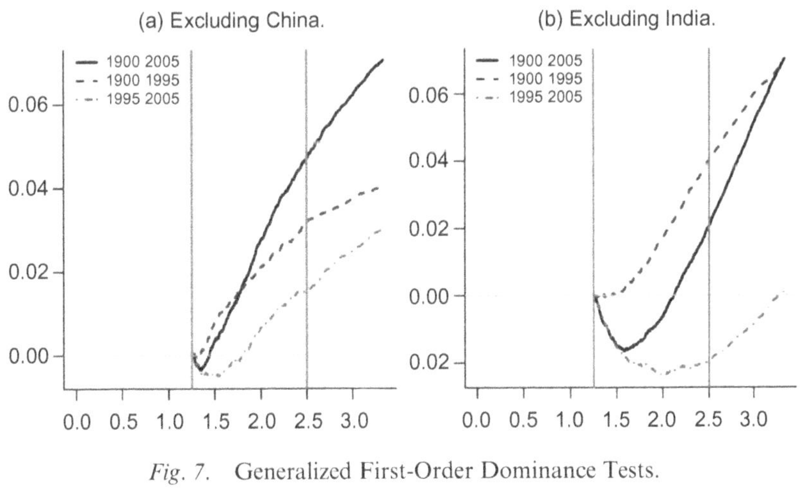

Fig. 7. Generalized First-Order Dominance Tests.

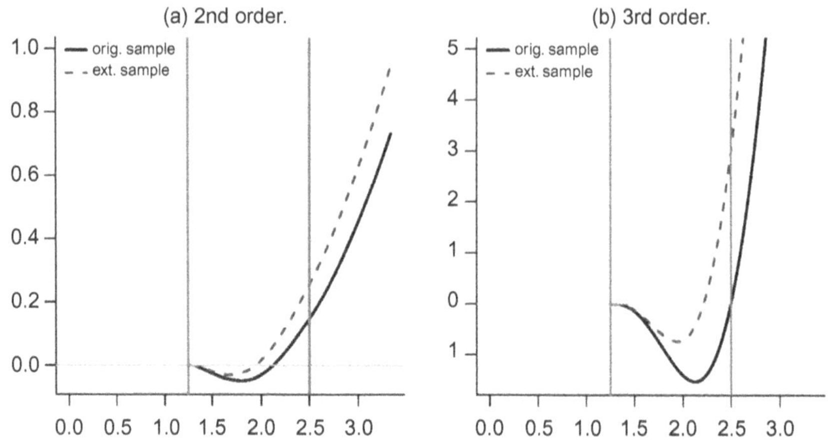

Fig. 8. Generalized Second and Third-Order Dominance Tests: Excluding China, 1995–2005.

heavily depends on the aggregation procedure of individual poverty situations[16] (Fig. 8).

Along the previous paragraphs, we have put forward that the \$1.25 a day threshold chosen by the World Bank as the extreme poverty line was the subject of a unanimous agreement. Here, we try to assess the robustness of the results presented in Fig. 5 to the choice of the extreme poverty line when that bound is arbitrarily chosen within the \$1–\$1.5 interval. For this purpose, we first focus on Eq. (12) of Proposition 3 since it may be the most disqualifying condition. However, since empirical studies of poverty involves working with discrete income distributions, Eq. (12) may hardly be satisfied with empirical pdfs. To circumvent that problem we perform an estimation of each year's pdf using kernel density estimations.[17] The resulting curves are plotted on the top panels of Fig. 9. For the 1995–2005 decline of the non-extreme component of poverty to be robust to the choice of the lower bound within the interval [1,1.5], we should observe the curve corresponding to the 2005 pdf to be nowhere above the curve relating to the 1995 pdf in this interval. Figs. 9(a) and (b) show that this condition is fulfilled with the original sample as well as with the extended sample. However, the differences in generalized dominance curves depicted on the bottom panels of Fig. 9 indicate a failure to satisfy Eq. (11) of Proposition 3. Consequently, the estimated distributions for the year 1995 and 2005 do not make it possible to conclude in a robust manner that

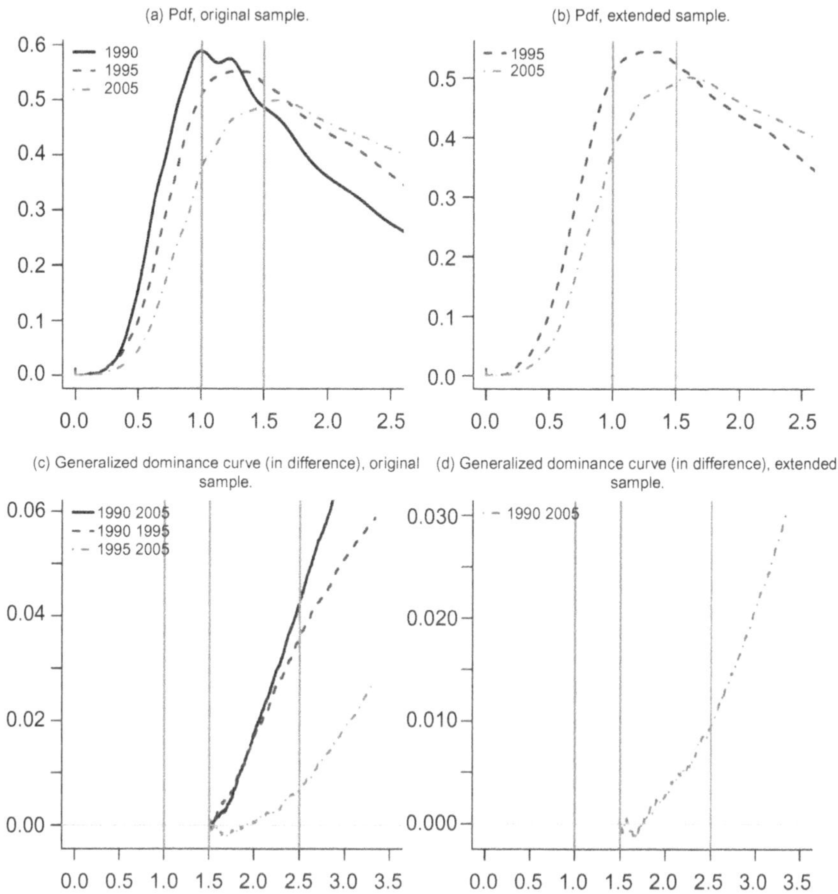

Fig. 9. The Generalized First-Order Dominance Test with Uncertain Lower Bound: Whole Population.

the contribution of non-extreme poverty has declined during the period considering extreme poverty thresholds somewhere between \$1 and \$1.5 a day, poverty lines between \$1.5 and \$2.5 a day and poverty measures that are within the set of monotone poverty indices Π^1. Fig. 9(a) also shows that this contribution for the period 1990–1995 is contingent to the choice of the extreme poverty line as the pdfs cross within the interval [1,1.5]. Finally, the generalized dominance curve, expressed in difference, for the whole period 1990–2005 (cf. Fig. 9(c)), is consistent with an increase in the non-extreme component of poverty, but although the 1990 and 2005 pdfs do not cross within the interval [1,1.5], they are not ordered in the appropriate manner to support this conclusion.

It deserves to be noted that our results are not necessarily as fragile as the previous dominance checks seem to indicate since the difference in pdfs can be used to extend below \$1.25 the range of values for extreme poverty. For instance, using the kernel density estimates of Fig. 9 and the initial checks of Fig. 5, so that the \$1.25 a day threshold is now regarded as the maximum value for the lower bound v, it is at least possible to conclude that the 1995–2005 decline is robust for each extreme poverty threshold within the interval [0.2,1.25].

CONCLUSION

Assessing progresses with respect to the objective of poverty alleviation is a difficult exercise since poverty evaluation involves value judgments that may endlessly be questioned. Stochastic dominance techniques are very powerful tools to circumvent such problems and it is regretful that they are not widely used in poverty evaluations produced by national statistical agencies and multilateral institutions in spite of the ease of their implementation. In the present paper, we show that the scope of dominance procedure usages for the analysis of poverty can be extended to the study of poverty changes over income intervals that correspond to convex subsets of the poverty domain. More specifically, we show how robust orderings can be obtained for comparisons of the absolute contribution to total poverty of population subgroups defined with respect to income intervals. From our point of view, putting the focus on limited portions of the poverty domain may notably be justified when the chosen interval is defined with respect to administrative thresholds that determine the access to specific social services or more generally when different income levels within the poverty domain imply significantly different poverty alleviation strategies. The proposed procedures then make it possible to provide orderings for the poverty component that corresponds to the chosen income interval for different values of its upper and lower bounds as well as different classes of additive poverty indices. As the proposed generalized dominance procedures can be implemented using Foster et al.'s (1984) family of poverty indices, our theoretical work can be seen as a generalization of Foster and Shorrocks's (1988a) results.

As an illustration of the procedures described in Section "Poverty Measurement and Generalized Dominance Conditions," we have considered the changes in the contribution of the non-extreme poor to monetary poverty during the period 1990–2005 for low and middle income countries, non-extreme poverty being defined as living with an income less that $2.5 a day but above $1.25 a day. Previous estimations of extreme poverty and overall poverty by Chen and Ravallion (2010) showed an increase in the share of individuals in a state of moderate poverty during that period alongside a decrease in extreme and overall poverty. Chen and Ravallion (2004) already noted this "bunching up" process for the period 1980–2000. Building a synthetic income distribution for the years 1990, 1995, and 2005 using PovcalNet's data and Shorrocks and Wan's (2008) procedure, we report extreme-poverty component estimates that indicate an increase of both the absolute and relative burden of moderate between 1990 and 2005 using the headcount, poverty gap and squared poverty gap indices. While this general result proved to be robust for the identification (i.e., to the choice of the poverty line) and the aggregation procedures (i.e., the choice of the poverty index) considering the limited subset of poverty indices that comply with transfer sensitivity, we show that the increase observed between 1990 and 1995 as well as the subsequent alleviation between 1995 and 2005 are ethically robust considering any member from the broad class of monotone poverty indices. We also point out the crucial role of China's economic progress during the period in shaping these results. Finally, it is worth noting that our results hinge on the chosen value of $1.25 a day for the extreme poverty line since non-conclusive results are obtained when that threshold is lifted up to $1.5 a day.

As noted earlier, this is not bad news for the developing world since it indicates that extreme poverty reduction has really been given priority in global poverty reduction strategies during the last decades. Households in moderate poverty may also have climbed the income ladder during the same period but the pace of poverty reduction for these households seems to have been slower than for the extreme poor so that we do not observe a uniform reduction of poverty along the poverty domain. Consequently, the burden of poverty tends to shift from extreme poverty to non-extreme poverty and will logically call for different anti-poverty strategies in order to reach the long-term objective of eradicating poverty since multiple poverty traps are likely to impede the improvement of the living conditions of the poor.

NOTES

1. Chen and Ravallion (2004) already noted that the number of individuals living with incomes between \$1 and \$2 a day had risen during the period 1980–2000.

2. The priority of the bottom poor with respect to the richest poor is an idea that is challenged by Bourguignon and Fields (1997). Indeed, considering poverty indices that are not continuous at the poverty line should be regarded as desirable when individual poverty is the cumulative effect of being poor and experiencing a given income gap with respect to the poverty line. Discontinuity at the poverty line expresses the social cost of being poor. Bourguignon and Fields (1997) showed that when that social cost is sufficiently high, then priority can be given for transfers to the richest of the poor.

3. See for instance Foster and Shorrocks (1988a, 1988b), Atkinson (1992), Jenkins and Lambert (1993), Zheng (1999, 2000), Duclos and Makdissi (2004, 2005). Extensions to multidimensional poverty and intertemporal poverty analyses include Bourguignon and Chakravarty (2002), Duclos, Sahn, and Younger (2006) and Bresson and Duclos (2012).

4. A poverty index is said to comply with subgroup-consistency if it provides orderings that are consistent with the ordering observed when comparing subgroups of the two populations under scrutiny. In other words, the overall level of poverty should not increase whenever poverty decreases within some subgroup of the population and is unchanged outside that group. Foster and Shorrocks (1991) have shown that every subgroup-consistent poverty index is an increasing transform of an additive poverty index of the type (1), so that poverty orderings observed with classes of additive poverty indices should also hold for the corresponding classes of subgroup-consistent poverty indices.

5. From a technical point of view, it can be noted that $D^s(x,\nu)$ is simply a Riemann-Liouville integral considering only integers for the order of integration.

6. Since incomes are generally supposed to be non-negative real values, z is also the maximum value for the income shortfall. If we suppose that the wellbeing variable used for the measurement of poverty has a minimum value equal to κ^-, the non-extreme component of the corresponding FGT-type index would then be:

$$C(P^s_{\mathrm{A}}(z);\nu,z) := \int_\nu^z \left(\frac{z-y}{z-\kappa^-}\right)^{s-1} \mathrm{d}F_{\mathrm{A}}(y)$$

7. Though no connection has been made to the best of our knowledge between restricted dominance and the fuzzy approach to poverty measurement, both approaches finally share this idea of complete deprivation for some threshold $x > \kappa^-$.

8. It is worth stressing that within that framework, we may allow for the poverty index to refer to different classes of poverty indices on the different parts of the poverty domain. For instance, we could imagine that transfer sensitivity is required on the non-extreme part of the poverty domain while only monotonicity is assumed for the extreme part.

9. The conditions are however restrictive and so not necessary since we may of course observe overall poverty to decline without having all its components to decrease.

10. For a review of the different approaches and the main issues regarding the estimation of global distributions of income, see Anand and Segal (2008).

11. Careful readers may notice that the first two periods overlap, but we would like to stress that only four distributions are common, that is the Central African Rep. 1992, the Kyrgyz Rep. 1993, Namibia 1993, and Nicaragua 1993. Removing these countries from our sample does not change the results.

12. The exact percentages are respectively 85.2%, 84.8%, and 83.9% for the years 1990, 1990, and 2005.

13. The exact percentages are 89.2% for the year 1995 and 88.6% for the year 2005.

14. Of course, this does not preclude other methodological changes like a modified sampling design or a different coverage of income sources that may affect the shape of the observed income distribution.

15. In 1990, the poverty gap and squared poverty gap indices for low and middle income countries were respectively equal to 37.70 and 23.15 according to PovcalNet. The figures were 32.67 and 19.06 in 1996 and 25.28 and 14.12 in 2005.

16. Our estimations show that a robust decline of non-extreme poverty can be stressed considering the very limited subset Π^6 of poverty indices and poverty lines up to $2 a day.

17. The kernel density estimations for Fig. 9 have been realized using the logarithm of income and a Gaussian kernel with Silverman's rule of thumb. Using alternative procedures for bandwidth selection, like the cross-validation procedure, does not change our results regarding the 1995–2005 period.

ACKNOWLEDGMENTS

The author thanks the anonymous referees for their helpful comments as well as the audience at the fifth meeting of the ECINEQ in Bari and the 2014 CSAE Conference in Oxford. All errors are the author's own.

REFERENCES

Anand, S., & Segal, P. (2008). What do we know about global income inequality. *Journal of Economic Literature*, *46*, 57–94.

Atkinson, A. (1987). On the measurement of poverty. *Econometrica*, *55*, 749–764.

Atkinson, A. (1992). Measuring poverty and differences in family composition. *Economica*, *59*, 1–16.

Blackorby, C., & Donaldson, D. (1980). Ethical indices for the measurement of poverty. *Econometrica*, *48*, 1053–1060.

Bourguignon, F., & Chakravarty, S. (2002). *Multi-dimensional poverty orderings*. Working Paper No. 2002–22. DELTA.

Bourguignon, F., & Fields, G. (1997). Discontinuous losses from poverty, generalized P_{α} measures, and optimal transfers to the poor. *Journal of Public Economics, 63*, 155–175.

Bourguignon, F., & Morrisson, C. (2002). Inequality among world citizens: 1820–1992. *American Economic Review, 92*, 727–744.

Bresson, F. (2009). On the estimation of growth and inequality elasticities of poverty with grouped data. *Review of Income and Wealth, 55*, 266–302.

Bresson, F., & Duclos, J.-Y. (2012). *Intertemporal poverty comparisons*. Document de Recherche 2012–13. LÉO, CNRS – Université d'Orleans.

Chakravarty, S. (1983a). A new index of poverty. *Mathematical Social Sciences, 6*, 307–313.

Chakravarty, S. (1983b). Ethically flexible measures of poverty. *The Canadian Journal of Economics/Revue Canadienne d'Économique, 16*, 74–85.

Chen, S., & Ravallion, M. (2004). How have the world's poorest fared since the early 1980's? *World Bank Research Observer, 19*, 141–169.

Chen, S., & Ravallion, M. (2010). The developing world is poorer than we thought, but no less successful in the fight against poverty. *Quarterly Journal of Economics, 125*, 1577–1625.

Chen, S., & Ravallion, M. (2012). *More relatively-poor people in a less absolutely-poor world.* World Bank Policy Research Working Paper Series 6114. World Bank.

Clark, S., Hemming, R., & Ulph, D. (1981). On indices for the measurement of poverty. *The Economic Journal, 91*, 515–526.

Davidson, R., & Duclos, J.-Y. (2013). Testing for restricted stochastic dominance. *Econometric Reviews, 32*, 84–125.

Dhongde, S., & Minoiu, C. (2010). *Global poverty estimates: Present and future*. Working Paper No. 181. ECINEQ.

Duclos, J.-Y., & Makdissi, P. (2004). Restricted and unrestricted dominance for welfare, inequality, and poverty orderings. *Journal of Public Economic Theory, 6*, 145–164.

Duclos, J.-Y., & Makdissi, P. (2005). Sequential stochastic dominance and the robustness of poverty orderings. *Review of Income and Wealth, 51*, 63–87.

Duclos, J.-Y., Sahn, D., & Younger, S. (2006). Robust multidimensional poverty comparisons. *The Economic Journal, 116*, 943–968.

Fishburn, P. (1976). Continua of stochastic dominance relations for bounded probability distributions. *Journal of Mathematical Economics, 3*, 295–311.

Foster, J., Greer, J., & Thorbecke, E. (1984). A class of decomposable poverty measures. *Econometrica, 52*, 761–766.

Foster, J., & Shorrocks, A. (1987). Transfer sensitive inequality measures. *Review of Economic Studies, 54*, 485–497.

Foster, J., & Shorrocks, A. (1988a). Poverty orderings. *Econometrica – Notes and Comments, 56*, 173–177.

Foster, J., & Shorrocks, A. (1988b). Poverty orderings and welfare dominance. *Social Choice and Welfare, 5*, 179–198.

Foster, J., & Shorrocks, A. (1991). Subgroup consistent poverty indices. *Econometrica, 59*, 687–709.

Jenkins, S., & Lambert, P. (1993). Ranking income distributions when needs differ. *Review of Income and Wealth, 39*, 337–356.

Kakwani, N. (1980). On a class of poverty measures. *Econometrica, 48*, 437–446.

Kolm, S.-C. (1976). Unequal inequalities II. *Journal of Economic Theory, 13*, 82–111.

Maddala, G., & Singh, S. (1977). A flexible functional form for Lorenz curves. *Économie Appliquée, 30*, 481–486.

Milanovic, B. (2002). True world income distribution, 1988 and 1993: First calculation based on household surveys alone. *The Economic Journal*, *112*, 51–92.

Sachs, J. (2005). *The end of poverty: How we can make it happen in our lifetime*. London: Penguin.

Sala-i-Martin, X. (2006). The world distribution of income: Falling poverty and... convergence, period. *Quarterly Journal of Economics*, *121*, 351–397.

Sen, A. (1976). Poverty: An ordinal approach to measurement. *Econometrica*, *44*, 219–231.

Sen, A. (1983). Poor, relatively speaking. *Oxford Economic Papers*, *35*, 153–169.

Shorrocks, A., & Wan, G. (2008). *Ungrouping income distributions: Synthetising samples for inequality and poverty analysis*. Research Paper No. 2008/16. UNU WIDER.

Watts, H. (1968). An economic definition of poverty. In D. P. Moynihan (Ed.), *On understanding poverty*. New York, NY: Basic Books.

Zheng, B. (1997). Aggregate poverty measures. *Journal of Economic Surveys*, *11*, 123–162.

Zheng, B. (1999). On the power of poverty orderings. *Social Choice and Welfare*, *16*, 349–371.

Zheng, B. (2000). Poverty orderings. *Journal of Economic Surveys*, *14*, 427–466.

APPENDIX: PROOFS

The proofs of Propositions 1–4 are partly inspired by Duclos and Makdissi (2004). For the sake of simplicity, demonstrations are performed assuming that the function $\pi^{(s)}(x,z)$ is everywhere differentiable with respect to x on the considered interval. Extending the demonstration to the case where $\pi^{(s)}(x,z)$ is not differentiable at some points is straightforward.

Proof of Propositions 1 and 2

Let first consider first-order dominance, that is the case for $s=1$. Since $\pi(x,z)=0\ \forall x \geq z$, we have $C(P(z);v,z)=C(P(z);v,K^{+})$. Integrating this by parts yields:

$$\int_{v}^{\kappa^{+}} \pi(x,z)f(x)\mathrm{d}x = [\pi(x,z)F(x)]_{v}^{\kappa^{+}} - \int_{v}^{\kappa^{+}} \pi^{(1)}(x,z)F(x)\,\mathrm{d}x \tag{A.1}$$

$$= -\pi(v,z)F(v) - \int_{v}^{\kappa^{+}} \pi^{(1)}(x,z)F(x)\,\mathrm{d}x \tag{A.2}$$

$$= (\pi(\kappa^{+},z) - \pi(v,z))F(v) - \int_{v}^{\kappa^{+}} \pi^{(1)}(x,z)F(x)\,\mathrm{d}x \tag{A.3}$$

$$= \int_{v}^{\kappa^{+}} \pi^{(1)}(x,z)F(v)\mathrm{d}x - \int_{v}^{\kappa^{+}} \pi^{(1)}(x,z)F(x)\,\mathrm{d}x \tag{A.4}$$

$$= \int_{v}^{\kappa^{+}} \pi^{(1)}(x,z)(F(x) - F(v))\,\mathrm{d}x \tag{A.5}$$

$$= \int_{v}^{\kappa^{+}} \pi^{(1)}(x,z)D^{1}(x;v)\,\mathrm{d}x \tag{A.6}$$

since $\pi(\kappa^+,z)=0$. Sufficiency is thus proved for $s=1$. Now assume that for any integer $s \geq 2$:

$$\int_{v}^{\kappa^+} \pi(x,z)f(x)\,\mathrm{d}x = (-1)^s \int_{v}^{\kappa^+} \pi^{(s)}(x,z)D^s(x;v)\,\mathrm{d}x \tag{A.7}$$

We then have:

$$\int_{v}^{\kappa^+} \pi^{(s)}(x,z)D^s(x;v)\,\mathrm{d}x = \left[\pi^{(s)}(x,z)\int_{\kappa^-}^{x} D^s(y;v)\,\mathrm{d}y\right]_{v}^{\kappa^+} - \int_{v}^{\kappa^+} \pi^{(s+1)}(x,z)\int_{\kappa^-}^{x} D^s(y;v)\,\mathrm{d}y\,\mathrm{d}x \tag{A.8}$$

$$= -\pi^{(s)}(v,z)\int_{\kappa^-}^{v} D^s(y;v)\,\mathrm{d}y - \int_{v}^{\kappa^+} \pi^{(s+1)}(x,z)\int_{\kappa^-}^{x} D^s(y;v)\,\mathrm{d}y\,\mathrm{d}x \tag{A.9}$$

$$= \left[\pi^{(s)}(x,z)\right]_{v}^{\kappa^+}\int_{\kappa^-}^{v} D^s(y;v)\,\mathrm{d}y - \int_{v}^{\kappa^+} \pi^{(s+1)}(x,z)\int_{\kappa^-}^{x} D^s(y;v)\,\mathrm{d}y\,\mathrm{d}x \tag{A.10}$$

$$= \int_{v}^{\kappa^+} \pi^{(s+1)}(x,z)\int_{\kappa^-}^{v} D^s(y;v)\,\mathrm{d}y\,\mathrm{d}x - \int_{v}^{\kappa^+} \pi^{(s+1)}(x,z)\int_{\kappa^-}^{x} D^s(y;v)\,\mathrm{d}y\,\mathrm{d}x \tag{A.11}$$

$$= -\int_{v}^{\kappa^+} \pi^{(s+1)}(x,z)\left(\int_{\kappa^-}^{x} D^s(y;v)\,\mathrm{d}y - \int_{\kappa^-}^{v} D^s(y;v)\,\mathrm{d}y\right)\mathrm{d}x \tag{A.12}$$

$$= \int_{v}^{\kappa^+} \pi^{(s+1)}(x,z)\int_{v}^{x} D^s(y;v)\,\mathrm{d}y\,\mathrm{d}x \tag{A.13}$$

as $\pi^{(s)}(\kappa^{+},z)=0$, so that:

$$\int_{v}^{\kappa^{+}} \pi(x,z)f(x)\,\mathrm{d}x = (-1)^{s+1}\int_{v}^{\kappa^{+}} \pi^{(s+1)}(x,z)D^{s+1}(x;v)\,\mathrm{d}x \tag{A.14}$$

It can be seen that Eq. (A.6) complies with Eq. (A.7) and consequently with Eq. (A.14). So, we can recursively see that it holds for any integer s. Necessity is straightforward.

Proof of Proposition 3

It can easily be shown that $\frac{\partial}{\partial v}D^{s}(x,v) = -f(v)$. Then, using Leibnit'z rule, we have $\forall s \geq 2$:

$$\frac{\partial}{\partial v}D^{s}(x,v) = \frac{\partial}{\partial v}\int_{v}^{x} D^{s-1}(y,v)\,\mathrm{d}y \tag{A.15}$$

$$= -D^{s-1}(v,v) + \int_{v}^{x} \frac{\partial}{\partial v}D^{s-1}(y,v)\,\mathrm{d}y \tag{A.16}$$

$$= \int_{v}^{x} \frac{\partial}{\partial v}D^{s-1}(y,v)\,\mathrm{d}y \tag{A.17}$$

since $D^{s-1}(v,v)=0$. Solving recursively this equation, we finally obtain:

$$\frac{\partial}{\partial v}D^{s}(x,v) = \frac{1}{(s-1)!}(x-v)^{s-1}f(v) \tag{A.18}$$

Differentiating Eq. (A.14) with respect to v then yields:

$$\frac{\partial}{\partial v}\int_{v}^{\kappa^{+}} \pi(x,z)f(x)\,\mathrm{d}x = \frac{\partial}{\partial v}(-1)^{s+1}\int_{v}^{\kappa^{+}} \pi^{(s+1)}(x,z)D^{s+1}(x;v)\,\mathrm{d}x \tag{A.19}$$

$$=(-1)^{s+1}\left(-\pi^{(s+1)}(v,z)D^{s+1}(v;v)+\int_{v}^{\kappa^{+}}\pi^{(s+1)}(x,z)\frac{\partial}{\partial v}D^{s+1}(x;v)\,\mathrm{d}x\right) \tag{A.20}$$

$$=(-1)^{s+1}\int_{v}^{\kappa^{+}}\pi^{(s+1)}(x,z)\frac{\partial}{\partial v}D^{s+1}(x;v)\,\mathrm{d}x \tag{A.21}$$

$$=(-1)^{s+1}\int_{v}^{\kappa^{+}}\pi^{(s+1)}(x,z)\frac{1}{s!}(x-v)^{s}f(v)\,\mathrm{d}x \tag{A.22}$$

Proposition 2 implies that, for a given value v, we should have $\Delta D^{s}(x,v)=D_{\mathrm{A}}^{s}(x,v)-D_{\mathrm{B}}^{s}(x,v)\leq 0\ \forall x\in[v,z]$ for non-extreme poverty to be lower for population A when compared with population B. When $x=v$, we necessarily have $D^{s}(v,v)$=0 and so $\Delta D^{s}(x,v)$=0. Consequently, for the dominance condition to be fulfilled after a marginal decrement of the extreme poverty bound, it is necessary for the marginal change $D_{\mathrm{A}}^{s}(v,v-\mathrm{d}v)$ to be lower than the marginal change $D_{\mathrm{B}}^{s}(v,v-\mathrm{d}v)$ where dv is a positive infinitesimal. Eq. (A.22) shows that, whatever the order of dominance s, this condition is fulfilled if and only if $f_{\mathrm{A}}(v)\leq f_{\mathrm{B}}(v)$. This is for necessity.

Regarding sufficiency, it is worth noting that, using Eq. (7):

$$(s-1)!D^{s}(x,v)=\int_{v}^{x}(x-y)^{s-1}\mathrm{d}F(y) \tag{A.23}$$

$$=\int_{v}^{v^{+}}(x-y)^{s-1}\mathrm{d}F(y)+\int_{v^{+}}^{x}(x-y)^{s-1}\mathrm{d}F(y) \tag{A.24}$$

$$=\int_{v}^{v^{+}}(x-y)^{s-1}f(y)\,\mathrm{d}y+(s-1)!D^{s}(x,v^{+}) \tag{A.25}$$

Consequently, if we observe $D^s_A(x, v^+) \leq D^s_B(x, v^+)\ \forall x \in [v^+, z^+]$ and $f_A(v) \leq f_B(v)\ \forall v \in [v^-, v^+]$, we obtain $D^s_A(x, v) \leq D^s_B(x, v)\ \forall x \in [v, z^+]$, $v \in [v^-, v^+]$. ■

Proof of Proposition 4

Let us first consider first-order dominance, that is the case for $s = 1$. Integrating $C(P(z); v, w)$ by parts yields:

$$\int_v^w \pi(x, z) f(x)\, dx = [\pi(x, z)F(x)]_v^w - \int_v^w \pi^{(1)}(x, z)F(x)\, dx \tag{A.26}$$

$$= \pi(w, z)F(w) - \pi(v, z)F(v) - \int_v^w \pi^{(1)}(x, z)F(x)\, dx \tag{A.27}$$

$$= \pi(w, z)(F(w) - F(v)) + \pi(w, z) - \pi(v, z))F(v) - \int_v^w \pi^{(1)}(x, z)F(x)\, dx \tag{A.28}$$

$$= \pi(w, z)D^1(w; v) + [\pi(x, z)]_v^w F(v) - \int_v^w \pi^{(1)}(x, z)F(x)\, dx \tag{A.29}$$

$$= \pi(w, z)D^1(w; v) + \int_v^w \pi^{(1)}(x, z)F(v)\, dx - \int_v^w \pi^{(1)}(x, z)F(x)\, dx \tag{A.30}$$

$$= \pi(w, z)D^1(w; v) - \int_v^w \pi^{(1)}(x, z)(F(x) - F(v))\, dx \tag{A.31}$$

$$= \pi(w, z)D^1(w; v) - \int_v^w \pi^{(1)}(x, z)D^1(x; v)\, dx \tag{A.32}$$

Now assuming that for any integer $s \geq 1$:

$$\int_{v}^{z} \pi(x, z) f(x)\,\mathrm{d}x = (-1)^{s} \int_{v}^{w} \pi^{(s)}(x, z) D^{s}(x; v)\,\mathrm{d}x + \sum_{t=1}^{s} (-1)^{t-1}(w, z) D^{t}(w; v) \tag{A.33}$$

Integrating by parts the first element of the right-hand term in Eq. (A.33), we obtain:

$$\int_{v}^{w} \pi^{(s)}(x, z) D^{s}(x; v)\,\mathrm{d}x = \left[\pi^{(s)}(x, z) \int_{\kappa^{-}}^{x} D^{s}(y; v)\,\mathrm{d}y\right]_{v}^{w} - \int_{v}^{w} \pi^{(s+1)}(x, z) \int_{\kappa^{-}}^{x} D^{s}(y; v)\,\mathrm{d}y\,\mathrm{d}x \tag{A.34}$$

$$= \pi^{(s)}(w, z) \int_{\kappa^{-}}^{w} D^{s}(y; v)\,\mathrm{d}y - \pi^{(s)}(v, z) \int_{\kappa^{-}}^{v} D^{s}(y; v)\,\mathrm{d}y - \int_{v}^{w} \pi^{(s+1)}(x, z) \int_{\kappa^{-}}^{x} D^{s}(y; v)\,\mathrm{d}y\,\mathrm{d}x \tag{A.35}$$

$$= \pi^{(s)}(w, z) \int_{\kappa^{-}}^{w} D^{s}(y; v)\,\mathrm{d}y + \pi^{(s)}(w, z) \int_{\kappa^{-}}^{v} D^{s}(y; v)\,\mathrm{d}y - \pi^{(s)}(w, z) \int_{\kappa^{-}}^{v} D^{s}(y; v)\,\mathrm{d}y \tag{A.36}$$

$$- \pi^{(s)}(v, z) \int_{\kappa^{-}}^{v} D^{s}(y; v)\,\mathrm{d}y - \int_{v}^{w} \pi^{(s+1)}(x, z) \int_{\kappa^{-}}^{x} D^{s}(y; v)\,\mathrm{d}y\,\mathrm{d}x \tag{A.37}$$

$$= \pi^{(s)}(w, z)\left(\int_{\kappa^{-}}^{w} D^{s}(y; v)\,\mathrm{d}y - \int_{\kappa^{-}}^{v} D^{s}(y; v)\,\mathrm{d}y\right) + \left(\pi^{(s)}(w, z) - \pi^{(s)}(v, z)\right) \times \int_{\kappa^{-}}^{v} D^{s}(y; v)\,\mathrm{d}y - \int_{v}^{w} \pi^{(s+1)}(x, z) \int_{\kappa^{-}}^{x} D^{s}(y; v)\,\mathrm{d}y\,\mathrm{d}x \tag{A.38}$$

$$= \pi^{(s)}(w,z)D^{s+1}(w;v) + [\pi^{s}(x,v)]_{v}^{w} \int_{\kappa^-}^{v} D^{s}(y;v)\,\mathrm{d}y - \int_{v}^{w} \pi^{(s+1)}(x,z) \int_{\kappa^-}^{x} D^{s}(y;v)\,\mathrm{d}y\,\mathrm{d}x \tag{A.39}$$

$$= \pi^{(s)}(w,z)D^{s+1}(w;v) + \int_{v}^{w} \pi^{(s+1)}(x,z) \int_{\kappa^-}^{v} D^{s}(y;v)\,\mathrm{d}y\,\mathrm{d}x - \int_{v}^{w} \pi^{(s+1)}(x,z) \int_{\kappa^-}^{x} D^{s}(y;v)\mathrm{d}y\,\mathrm{d}x \tag{A.40}$$

$$= \pi^{(s)}(w,z)D^{s+1}(w;v) - \int_{v}^{w} \pi^{(s+1)}(x,z)\left(\int_{\kappa^-}^{x} D^{s}(y;v)\,\mathrm{d}y - \int_{\kappa^-}^{v} D^{s}(y;v)\,\mathrm{d}y\right)\mathrm{d}x \tag{A.41}$$

$$= \pi^{(s)}(w,z)D^{s+1}(w,;v) - \int_{v}^{w} \pi^{(s+1)}(x,z)D^{s+1}(x;v)\,\mathrm{d}x \tag{A.42}$$

Plugging in that result in Eq. (A.33), we obtain:

$$\int_{v}^{z} \pi(x,z)f(x)\,\mathrm{d}x = (-1)^{s+1} \int_{v}^{w} \pi^{(s+1)}(x,z)D^{s+1}(x;v)\,\mathrm{d}x + \sum_{t=1}^{s+1} (-1)^{t-1}\pi^{t-1}(w,z)D^{t}(w;v) \tag{A.43}$$

The rest of the proof follows by inspection. ■

ARE MASS MEDIA AND ICTS ASSOCIATED WITH INEQUALITY AND POVERTY?

Sanghamitra Bandyopadhyay

ABSTRACT

This paper examines associations of mass media and information and communications technologies (ICTs) with inequality and poverty. It has been found that newspaper circulation has a robust negative association with inequality. Radios and TVs also have a negative association with poverty. ICT expenditures (as a percentage of GDP) have a negative association with poverty. An ICT index is constructed which also has a negative association with poverty. An instrumental variable analysis confirms the robust negative association between newspaper circulation and inequality.

Keywords: Information and communications technologies; mass media; economic development; poverty; inequality

JEL classifications: D30; D80; O1; O57

Economic Well-Being and Inequality: Papers from the Fifth ECINEQ Meeting
Research on Economic Inequality, Volume 22, 185–216

ISSN: 1049-2585/doi:10.1108/S1049-258520140000022005

INTRODUCTION

The rise of mass media as an indispensible accessory of modern society's access to information has been phenomenal. The availability of information is crucial for efficient decision making by citizens and consumers (Stigler, 1961; Stiglitz, 2000). For the voter, information about government actions and political candidates is essential for accurate voting choices. Likewise, consumers and investors require information to purchase products and securities.

Access to information is, however, circumscribed by the instruments that are made available to the citizens. Less developed economies particularly suffer from the lack of adequate communications technologies. While access to communications infrastructure and information is largely asserted to be a prerequisite for growth and productivity, there is little empirical evidence which establishes this fact. This paper empirically investigates the association of Information Communications Technologies (hereafter ICTs) and mass media as instruments of access to information, with inequality and poverty.

The impact of ICTs and telephony is a double-edged innovation – one which results in both driving economic growth and in increasing spatial and individual inequalities. While increasing returns and technological progress are conceptually distinct, both theory and evidence seem to suggest that they often come together and result in a technological lock-in (David, 1985), such that technologies that have an initial advantage tend to endure. Prominent theories on the sources of economic growth reinforce such concerns. The 'weightless' properties of such technologies, with little regard for geographical barriers (Quah, 2001a, 2001b) enhance their rapid spread. These properties, however, due to unequal adoption rates, are predisposed to result in rapid increases in spatial and individual inequalities. Thus, in an LDC context, concentration in telephony and ICT penetration is likely to wedge the urban and the rural areas apart, as well as the rich and poor. Skill-biased technologies such as those engendered by development of ICTs may also result in high wage inequalities – studies of the US increasing wage gap evince that skill-biased technological change (as a consequence of the increasing computerisation of the US work force) is an important driving force of US wage inequality (Acemoglu & Autor, 2010; Autor & Dorn, 2009; Autor, Katz, & Krueger, 1998; Berman, Somanathan, & Tan, 2005; DiNardo & Pischke, 1997; Goldin & Katz, 1996, 2008). The emerging job polarisation is on the rise – ICTs are complementary with human capital and rapid falls in quality-adjusted ICT prices have therefore increased skill demand. There is a large body of literature broadly consistent with this notion.

The task-based theory predicts that ICT improvements increase the demand for the most educated (complementing their non-routine cognitive tasks), reduce demand for the middle educated (as it substitutes for routine tasks) and has ambiguous effects for the least educated. Michaels, Van Reenen, and Natraj (2013) conclude that technical change has raised the relative demand for college educated workers and, consistent with the ICT-based polarisation hypothesis, this increase has come mainly from reducing the relative demand for middle-skilled workers rather than low-skilled workers.

The impact of mass media, however, is less selective on its target audience and not likely to directly accentuate spatial or individual inequalities in the manner of ICTs. Its development and penetration is endogenous in a manner that ICTs are not in that the quality of news generated by the media industry is also dependent on how the government treats the media industry. Deeper media penetration, unlike ICTs, has no unequal effects in its impact. On the other hand, the underdevelopment of media is often a consequence of governments attempting to evade scrutiny from poor delivery or non-delivery of public goods, or government failure. Mass media functions to enhance citizens'' abilities to scrutinise government actions.

I use OLS to show that newspaper circulation is significantly associated with lower inequality. Radios and TVs are also found to be significantly associated with lower poverty.

I obtain mixed results with ICTs and telephony. I find robust evidence for the negative association of ICT expenditures with poverty. I also construct an ICT infrastructure index and I find that its association with inequality varies with the sample chosen – it is positively associated with inequality for the sample with both developed and developing countries, but not robustly associated with inequality for the developing country sample.

To confirm these results, I undertake an instrumental variable (IV) analysis for newspaper circulation, using three different instruments of press freedom and legal rights for information. The results affirm that there exists a negative relationship between inequality and newspaper circulation.

The rest of the paper is organised as follows. In the section 'Mass Media and ICT' the current literature relating to mass media and ICT/telephony is discussed. The section 'Data and Empirical Strategy' discusses the data and presents the empirical strategy and the section 'Associations of Inequality and Poverty with ICTs and Media' presents the results.

The section 'Issues of Endogeneity: Role of mass media' deals with potential endogeneity with an IV analysis. The section 'Conclusion' concludes.

MASS MEDIA AND ICT

Political Accountability

Political Mechanisms

Despite the obvious justifications that mass media creates a more educated and responsive citizen, it is only recently that the political economy literature has seriously begun to address these issues. While most countries have media in some form or another, there is no guarantee that it is a successful vehicle of information. This is affected by a variety of government actions – ranging from policy decisions affecting the regulation and entry and ownership of media on the one hand, to bribery and threats to the media bodies on the other. Besley, Burgess, and Prat (2002) studies the determinants and the consequences of captured media, and found that capture is more likely if there is more state ownership of newspapers and there is greater concentration in ownership of newspapers. Petrova (2008) focussed on media misreporting, and explained media bias by conscious manipulation by media owners or editors and found that it had an impact on public expenditures on education and health. Corneo (2006) finds that a higher concentration in firm ownership is to be likely associated with higher media bias and lower welfare. Baron (2006) also explains persistent media bias that originates with private information obtained by journalists and persists despite profit-maximising news organisations and rivalry with other news organisations.

Corruption

The existence of an active mass media body is usually seen to be associated with an active democracy. A small but growing cross-country literature connects the incidence of a free press and the political framework that accompanies it. There are though countries which are democratic in structure but have low press freedom, especially in the developing world. Brunetti and Weder (2003) and Ahrend (2001) finds robust correlations between press freedom and corruption. Djankov, McLeish, Nenova, and Shleifer (2003) also uncovers robust cross-country evidence of state ownership of the media to be negatively correlated with a number of measures of good governance. Using a panel of 16 Indian states, 1958–1992, Besley and Burgess (2002) find that Indian state governments' provision of public food and calamity relief expenditure is more responsive to falls in food production and crop flood damage in states where newspaper circulation is high. The role of media in moderating business cycles is examined by Shi and Svensson (2002) – using a panel of 123 developed and developing countries over a 21-year period, they indeed find larger political budget cycles in countries where few people have radios.

Greater media outlets on the other hand are found to be encouraging for the emergence of a free press (Besley, Burgess, & Prat, 2002). Competition, though, may result in two different effects. While Besley and Prat argue that more media outlets are an impediment to politicians trying to bribe the media, Mullainathan and Shleifer (2005) argue that greater competition could result in newspapers (or other media forms) printing or broadcasting stories which confirm readers' prior opinions rather than presenting the real facts. Other lines of research investigate governments' incentives to engage in corruption in the presence of independent media bodies (Vaidya, 2005).

The Effect of ICTs

While ICTs are the principal carriers of information, their effect on economic development is more tangible than that of mass media – ICT carries with it technology that directly affects economic productivity and growth.

Growth

Increased investment in ICT has led to significant increases in economic growth (Haacker & Morsinck, 2002; Timmer & van Arky, 2005). The United States, for instance, showed an increase in TFP by one half percentage point per year over the last two decades. Europe's experience with ICT's contribution to economic growth is relatively sporadic. Daveri (2002) reveals that ICT contributions to growth were significant in only 10 countries out of 14 in his study. In only 6 of these, was ICT-related capital-deepening associated with greater aggregate total factor productivity or growth in labour productivity. Among the newly industrialised economies in East Asia, the deepening of ICT has been of significant importance, particularly in production – 28% of their manufacturing exports are ICT products (Kenny, 2003). The contribution of ICT-related capital-deepening in Japan contributed to increasing growth by one half to three quarters.

Inequality
What prominently distinguishes the outcomes of ICTs as different from other forms of information carriers is that on the production front they are pervasively characterised by increasing returns. Arthur (1994) and Krugman (1991) emphasise that the predominance of increasing returns in a certain industry leads to spatial agglomeration, in a manner similar to how technological lock-in sets in. From this point of view, ICTs are no different from other industries – the location of geographic clusters simply reflects the high-skilled and fast-producing nature of the technology. ICT clustering is more pronounced in the EU than in the United States (Koski, Rouvinen, and Yla-Anttila, 2002; Quah, 2001a). Similarly, unequal access to ICTs and thus information, may exacerbate already existing individual inequalities.

Combining all these issues, one is prompted to ask whether ICT investment is just growth spurring or inequality increasing, or both. Some casual empiricism as discussed above suggests both, but its effects are yet to be empirically established. While the phenomenon of spatial agglomeration is clearly understood in the literature, whether it is associated with increasing individual inequalities is not clear.[1] The empirical analysis that follows attempts to uncover any such correlations between various development outcomes discussed above and ICTs.

DATA AND EMPIRICAL STRATEGY

This section discusses the data on ICTs, media, press freedom, the models estimated in the empirical analysis and explains the empirical methodology used. The database has been put together from a variety of sources, each to be described in turn. Tables 1 and 2 present the variable's sources and their summary statistics, respectively.

Measures of Mass Media Penetration

Mass media penetration is measured by using the number of newspapers in circulation, and the ownership of radios, and televisions, per 1,000 people. The principal data source has been the World Bank Indicators database.

Table 1. Variables Used in the Paper and their Sources.

Variable Name	Years	Source
	1994–1997	ICRG
Average quality of the bureaucracy	All years	ICRG
Average Trade ((Export + Import)/GDP)	All years	WDI 2005
Average rule of law	All years	ICRG
Risk Premium	All years	ICRG
Natural Log of GDP, per capita	All years	WDI 2005
Education	All years	WDI 2005
Latin America dummy	All years	–
Africa dummy	All years	–
OECD country dummy	All years	–
The UNCTAD ICT diffusion index	1997	UNCTAD
Gini index	All years	WIDER
Poverty, one dollar a day, headcount ratio	All years	WDI 2005
Poverty, two dollars a day, headcount ratio	All years	WDI 2005
Mobile phones (per 1,000 people)	All years	WDI 2005
Internet Users (per 1,000 people)	All years	WDI 2005
ICT expenditure as a percentage of GDP	All years	WDI 2005
Fax machines (per 1,000 people)	All years	WDI 2005
Telephone mainlines (per 1,000 people)	All years	WDI 2005
Telephone mainlines per employee	All years	WDI 2005
Telephone revenue (per 1,000 people)	All years	WDI 2005
Newspaper circulation (per 1,000 people)	All years	WDI 2005
Radios (per 1,000 people)	All years	WDI 2005
Televisions (per 1,000 people)	All years	WDI 2005
Freedom of Press Index	1994–1997	Freedom House
Right to Information (RTI) Index	1970s onwards	www.rti-rating.org
Reporters Without Borders (RWB) Score	2002 onwards	http://en.rsf.org/

Note: All years refer to the period 1992–1997.

Measures of ICT and Telephony

The data has been compiled from the World Bank indicators dataset (2004). The variables for which I have obtained the maximum coverage for countries are the following:

- Mobile phones (per 1,000 people)
- Internet Users (per 1,000 people)
- ICT expenditure as a percentage of GDP
- Fax machines (per 1,000 people)
- Telephone mainlines (per 1,000 people)

Table 2. Descriptive Statistics.

Variable	Observations	Mean	Std. Dev.	Minimum	Maximum
Panel A: Full sample					
Gini index	491	44.0	12.7	18.1	73.9
ICT index (f1)	166	0.0	0.9	−1.4	2.6
ICT index (f2)	166	−0.1	0.8	−0.8	6.1
Fax	455	10.4	17.0	0.0	127.0
ICT expenditure	258	4.6	2.0	0.3	9.1
Internet users	450	455,735.7	2,677,465	0.0	40,000,000
Mobiles	679	24.8	52.4	0.0	419.4
Newspapers	627	119.2	149.0	0.1	818.8
Radios	684	429.0	477.9	27.9	6,763.8
TVs	676	219.8	197.5	0.5	854.5
Telephone mainlines	506	235.6	230.5	3.2	1,040.1
Mainlines/employee	654	90.6	71.4	6.7	360.7
Mainline revenue	639	982.4	607.9	8.2	4,380.7
Average rule of law	684	4.1	1.4	0.0	6.0
Quality of bureaucracy	684	3.5	1.4	1.0	6.0
Risk premium	684	8.6	1.7	1.0	10.0
Freedom of press index	456	44.5	23.5	5.0	100.0
RWB score	667	2,529.2	2,334.0	50.0	10,900.0
RTI score	371	84.1	19.6	37.0	130.0
Panel B: Developing country sample					
Gini index	311	50.0	11.0	25.5	73.9
Poverty $1/day	99	18.7	19.5	2.0	73.6
Poverty $2/day	99	41.8	27.1	2.0	91.7
ICT index (f1)	66	−0.7	0.4	−1.4	0.2
ICT index (f2)	66	−0.3	0.2	−0.8	0.1
Fax	281	2.5	4.4	0.0	23.6
ICT expenditure	90	3.3	1.4	0.3	7.4
Internet users	261	46,263.5	141,327.7	0.0	1,310,000
Mobiles	475	8.0	19.9	0.0	146.6
Newspapers	429	50.3	62.4	0.1	435.8
Radios	480	288.8	353.4	27.9	6763.8
TVs	472	134.7	136.6	0.5	808.4
Telephone mainlines	372	143.0	151.1	3.2	977.5
Mainlines/employee	455	62.0	48.1	6.7	290.5
Mainline revenue	441	1,033.3	668.6	82.0	4,380.7
Average rule of law	480	3.5	1.2	0.0	6.0
Quality of bureaucracy	480	2.9	1.0	1.0	6.0
Risk premium	480	8.1	1.8	1.0	10.0

- Telephone mainlines per employee
- Telephone revenue (per 1,000 people)
- Number of personal computers per 100,000 people.

There exist a large number of other ICT indicators, but the country coverage dramatically drops, and therefore is not included in the analysis.

To identify the collective effect of the ICT variables, I construct an index of ICT using factor analysis, results of which are presented in Table 3. This technique is a method of data reduction and attempts to describe the indicators as linear combinations of a small number of latent variables. I accept the first factor (f1) to be the general index of ICT and telephony infrastructure (presented later in tables as the ICT index), which takes an eigenvalue of over 5. In performing the factor analysis, the data has been normalised for comparability of the numerical values (e.g. comparing revenues in US dollars to number of personal computers per 1,000 people). For the estimations I mainly use the first factor, and for robustness I use the second factor

Table 3. Factor Analysis.

Panel A: Eigenvalues of the factors of ICT variables obtained using Factor Analysis

Factor	Eigenvalue
Factor1	4.534
Factor2	0.416
Factor3	0.284
Factor4	0.102
Factor5	0.054
Factor6	−0.053
Factor7	−0.109
Factor8	−0.167

Panel B: Factor loadings of the ICT variables obtained using Factor Analysis

Variable	Factor1	Factor2	Factor3	Factor4	Factor5
Mobile phones per 1,000 people	0.721	0.240	−0.175	0.026	−0.134
Internet users per 1,000 people	0.424	0.359	0.298	−0.037	0.083
ICT expenditures as % of GDP	0.776	−0.118	−0.149	−0.076	0.138
Faxes per 1,000 people	0.849	0.125	0.179	0.124	−0.026
Computers per 1,000 people	0.932	0.106	−0.088	−0.144	−0.004
Mainline telephones per 1,000 people	0.888	−0.272	0.092	−0.119	−0.069
Telephone revenue per 1,000 people	0.742	−0.016	−0.212	0.188	0.067
Mainline telephones per employee	0.550	−0.338	0.219	0.092	−0.013

Notes: Average interim Cronbach's alpha (standardised)=0.527. Scale reliability coefficient = 0.899.

f2. I also use The UNCTAD index of ICT diffusion as an alternate indicator of ICT penetration for the year 1997.[2]

Measures of Inequality and Poverty

I use the Gini measure (of income inequality) from the WIID2b database published by UNU-WIDER, which documents annual measures of country Ginis, for each year 1992–1997. I also use two measures of poverty – poverty headcount measured at $1 a day, and $2 dollars a day, also from the World Bank database.

ASSOCIATIONS OF INEQUALITY AND POVERTY WITH ICTS AND MEDIA

In this section, I present the OLS estimates of the correlations of inequality and poverty with ICT infrastructures and mass media. Given that the nature of the impact of any of these outcomes is unknown, I estimate the models using OLS. Tables 4 and 5 present the results with Ginis (inequality) as the dependent variable, for the full sample and developing country samples, respectively and Table 6 presents results with poverty as the dependent variable.

Inequality, and ICTs and Media

In Tables 4 and 5 I present the results of the associations of media and Telephony/ICT variables with levels of inequality, for the full sample and developing country sample, respectively. The dependent variable is the Gini coefficient, obtained from the UNU-WIDER (2005) database (WIID2b) for years 1992–1997. I estimate models both for the full sample of countries, and the developing countries' sample, to observe whether the relationship only holds for LDCs. Figs. 1 and 2 present a scatter plot of the relationship between inequality measured by the Gini index, and newspaper circulation per 1,000 people. There is a clear negative relationship. We also obtain a similar negative relationship between poverty and newspaper circulation, as in Fig. 2. These scatter plots are already suggestive of the results that are obtained in the following analyses.

Table 4. OLS Regressions of the Gini Index 1992–1997, for the Full Sample.

Controls	(1)	(2)	(3) Perotti	(4) Barro	(5) Perotti	(6) Barro
Newspapers	−0.058***	−0.051***	−0.062***	−0.061***	−0.088***	−0.065***
	(0.011)	(0.013)	(0.010)	(0.013)	(0.013)	(0.011)
Radios	0.000	−0.000	−0.001	0.000	−0.001	−0.001
	(0.000)	(0.000)	(0.001)	(0.001)	(0.001)	(0.001)
TVs	−0.040***	−0.039***	−0.024***	−0.043***	−0.035***	−0.030***
	(0.008)	(0.010)	(0.007)	(0.009)	(0.008)	(0.008)
Fax	−0.364**	−0.313*	−0.001			
	(0.161)	(0.174)	(0.155)			
ICT expenditure	0.172	−0.08	−0.88			
	(0.661)	(0.684)	(0.681)			
Internet users	0.000*	0.000**	0.000**			
	(0.0000)	(0.0000)	(0.0000)			
Mobiles	0.019	0.055	−0.0211			
	(0.033)	(0.037)	(0.029)			
ICT index				−0.178		
				(3.082)		
ICT index squared					10.56***	
					(2.758)	
ICT index 2						6.162*
						(3.196)
Quality of bureaucracy	0.263	0.552	1.264	−0.190	1.449*	0.583
	(0.917)	(0.982)	(0.854)	(0.915)	(0.836)	(0.898)
Average rule of law	−3.639***	−2.584***	−1.412	−3.257***	−0.993	−1.078
	(0.854)	(0.904)	(0.874)	(0.904)	(0.818)	(0.882)
Log GDP/capita	3.136**	2.495*	0.578	1.301	3.69***	−0.411
	(1.361)	(1.461)	(1.344)	(1.681)	(1.517)	(1.124)
Education	0.0712	0.104	0.133	0.123	0.383***	0.176
	(0.085)	(0.099)	(0.111)	(0.130)	(0.137)	(0.132)
Average trade	0.029	0.003	0.107***	0.023	0.131***	0.084***
	(0.025)	(0.027)	(0.028)	(0.025)	(0.027)	(0.024)
Risk premium	−0.627	−1.758	−2.14*	−0.697	−1.321	−2.491**
	(1.240)	(1.288)	(1.15)	(1.286)	(1.076)	(1.157)
Telephone mainlines		−0.013*				
		(0.006)				
Africa dummy			10.8***		12.47***	10.73***
			(4.046)		(3.635)	(4.003)
Latin America dummy			13.0***		13.38***	11.9***
			(2.436)		(2.203)	(2.317)
Constant	49.512***	61.114***	55.332***	62.421***	−6.272	66.715***
	(17.883)	(19.16)	(19.424)	(23.399)	(24.99)	(18.099)
N	97	84	97	83	83	83
Adjusted R^2	0.71	0.71	0.78	0.67	0.79	0.76
F-statistic	19.06	15.98	23.79	17.66	20.79	22.12

Note: Heterosdasticity robust standard errors in parentheses.
***Significant at 1% level of significance.
**Significant at 5% level of significance.
*Significant at 10% level of significance.

The basic specification that I am estimating is as follows:

$$\text{GINI}_i = \beta_0 + \beta_1\,\text{NEWS}_i + \beta_2\,\text{RADIO}_i + \beta_3\,\text{TV}_i + \beta_4\,\text{ICT index}_i + \beta_5\,\text{BUREAU}_i + \beta_6\,\text{RULE}_i + \beta_7\,\text{TRADE}_i + \beta_8\,\text{RISK}_i + \varepsilon_i \quad (1)$$

Table 1 lists the abbreviations and the sources of the variables in use. NEWS_i, RADIO_i and TV_i represent the incidence of newspapers, TVs and radios in country i. The ICTindex_i is the index (the first factor, in most cases) that has been estimated using factor analysis in the section 'Measures of ICT and Telephony'.

I include a number of variables as controls which represent the quality of rule of law and institutions, which engender knowledge and information creation and its spread. Rule of law, presented above as RULE, is a variable obtained from the ICRG, which measures the extent of the citizens' capabilities to monitor the extent of corruption. It represents the presence of sound political institutions, a functional legal system and 'provisions for an orderly succession of power'. BUREAU accounts for the quality of bureaucracy in the government, also provided by the ICRG based on evaluations from country experts. It indicates the degree of autonomy (of the bureaucracy) from political pressure. Both variables are typically positively associated with lower values of corruption and knowledge-bias.

In addition to these I include a number of country-level characteristics which act as proxies of determinants of the quality of rule of law and institutions.

TRADE is a proxy for distortions and restrictions of competition in an economy. It measures the exposure of an economy to foreign trade and is defined as the sum of exports and imports as a percentage of GDP. It has been argued that open countries are subject to larger competitive pressure which reduces monopolistic rents (Ades & Di Tella, 1999).[3] I also include a variable collected by the ICRG, an index of expropriation risk, named here as RISK, which is scaled such that high values of RISK indicate low risk of appropriation.

Given these factors, one can conjecture that higher incidence of media variables – such as newspapers, radios and televisions – and higher access to ICTs – such as higher internet usage, and deeper telecommunications' penetration – can be associated with lower levels of inequality. Other country-specific controls are also included. Log of GDP per capita and Literacy measure the level of per capita GDP in 1995 (calculated at purchasing power parity US$), and educational attainment. Both of these act

Table 5. OLS Regressions of the Gini Index 1992–1997, for the Developing Country Sample.

Controls	Barro (1)	Perotti (2)	Barro (3)	Perotti (4)
Newspaper	−0.068**	−0.065*	−0.083**	−0.081**
	(0.310)	(0.034)	(0.032)	(0.034)
Radios	−0.001	−0.001	−0.001	0.000
	(0.001)	(0.001)	(0.001)	(0.000)
TVs	0.002	−0.011	0.007	−0.005
	(0.022)	(0.023)	(0.025)	(0.026)
Fax	0.424	0.026		
	(2.13)	(2.153)		
ICT expenditure	0.321	−1.386		
	(0.936)	(1.319)		
Internet users	0.000	0.000		
	(0.000)	(0.000)		
Mobiles	0.013	0.019		
	(0.139)	(0.135)		
ICT index			1.004	−2.614
			(3.891)	(5.060)
Quality of bureaucracy	2.022*	2.776**	2.246**	2.773**
	(1.039)	(1.201)	(1.010)	(1.188)
Average rule of law	−1.253	−0.536	−1.321	−0.142
	(1.528)	(1.482)	(0.960)	(1.081)
Log GDP/capita	4.433**	−0.618	3.788*	0.076
	(1.808)	(2.678)	(2.135)	(2.793)
Education	−0.062	0.2	0.029	0.184
	(0.088)	(0.172)	(0.129)	(0.195)
Average trade	0.012	0.124**	0.036	0.107**
	(0.034)	(0.057)	(0.026)	(0.048)
Risk premium	−0.083	−0.73	0.149	−0.212
	(1.590)	(1.560)	(1.491)	(1.449)
Africa dummy		14.4*		9.6
		(7.192)		(6.782)
Latin America dummy		15.2**		11.5**
		(5.957)		(5.342)
Constant	24.1	33.8	19.6	20.9
	(22.642)	(23.644)	(28.063)	(33.089)
N	58	58	48	48
Adjusted R^2	0.44	0.49	0.47	0.51
F-statistic	4.46	4.70	5.19	5.04

Note: Heterosdasticity robust standard errors in parentheses.
***Significant at 1% level of significance.
**Significant at 5% level of significance.
*Significant at 10% level of significance.

Table 6. OLS Regressions of Poverty 1992–1997, for the Developing Country Sample.

Dependent Variable	$1 per Day Poverty (1)	$1 per Day Poverty (2)	$1 per Day Poverty (3)	$1 per Day Poverty (4)	$2 per Day Poverty (5)	$2 per Day Poverty (6)	$2 per Day Poverty (7)
Newspapers	0.031	0.127**	0.029	0.036	−0.06	0.007	0.034
	(0.037)	(0.031)	(0.028)	(0.034)	(0.051)	(0.044)	(0.059)
Radios	−0.018*	−0.029**	−0.016*	−0.015*	−0.034**	−0.045***	−0.045***
	(0.008)	(0.006)	(0.007)	(0.008)	(0.014)	(0.013)	(0.013)
TVs	0.059	0.116**	−0.008	−0.026	−0.127**	−0.087**	−0.067***
	(0.051)	(0.033)	(0.021)	(0.025)	(0.042)	(0.037)	(0.032)
Fax	3.753	−3.684			7.426		
	(2.731)	(2.468)			(4.444)		
ICT expenditure	−0.034	3.679			−4.507*		
	(1.534)	(1.789)			(2.292)		
Internet users	0.000	0.000**			0.000*		
	(0.000)	(0.000)			(0.0000)		
Mobiles	−0.076	0.755*			−0.59		
	(0.250)	(0.279)			(0.375)		
ICT index			−1.791	4.791		−9.562	12.274
			(5.559)	(11.170)		(8.049)	(19.144)
Quality of bureaucracy	0.432	−0.766	−2.138**	−1.628	−1.365	−2.707	−1.988
	(1.318)	(0.958)	(0.	(1.390)	(1.731)	(1.535)	(1.996)
Average rule of law	−0.691	−5.334**	−0.058	0.312	5.569	1.857	0.701
	(2.412)	(1.84)		(1.205)	(3.422)	(1.661)	(2.107)
Log GDP/capita	−9.792*	−13.542***	−2.697	−2.210	−2.643	−3.699	−5.815
	(4.462)	(2.845)		(3.121)	(3.462)	(3.449)	(5.549)

Education	−0.334	−1.241***	−0.567**	−0.629**	0.006	−0.875**	−1.107**
	(0.231)	(0.224)		(0.240)	(0.178)	(0.344)	(0.418)
Average trade	−0.105**	−0.238***	−0.089**	−0.092**	−0.109	−0.159***	−0.287***
	(0.044)	(0.050)		(0.033)	(0.067)	(0.042)	(0.108)
Risk premium	−2.256	4.671	−0.749	−1.090	−3.939	0.658	−0.961
	(2.002)	(3.563)		(1.953)	(3.195)	(2.738)	(3.104)
Telephone mainline revenue	0.028**	0.026**					
	(0.012)	(0.008)					
Telephone mainlines/ employee		−0.017					
		(0.015)					
Africa dummy				−0.648			−22.876
				(6.859)			(17.811)
Latin America dummy				1.294			−10.845
				(5.021)			(10.291)
Constant	111.43**	178.77	105.657**	110.579**	123.919**	168.349**	245.095***
	(39.504)	(91.122)		(33.882)	(45.692)	(54.930)	(91.116)
N	25	21	21	21	25	25	21
Adjusted R^2	0.56	0.89	0.63	0.60	0.86	0.87	0.87
F-statistic	3.18	12.17	4.48	3.50	12.60	11.65	12.18

Note: Heterosdasticity robust standard errors in parentheses.
***Significant at 1% level of significance.
**Significant at 5% level of significance.
*Significant at 10% level of significance.

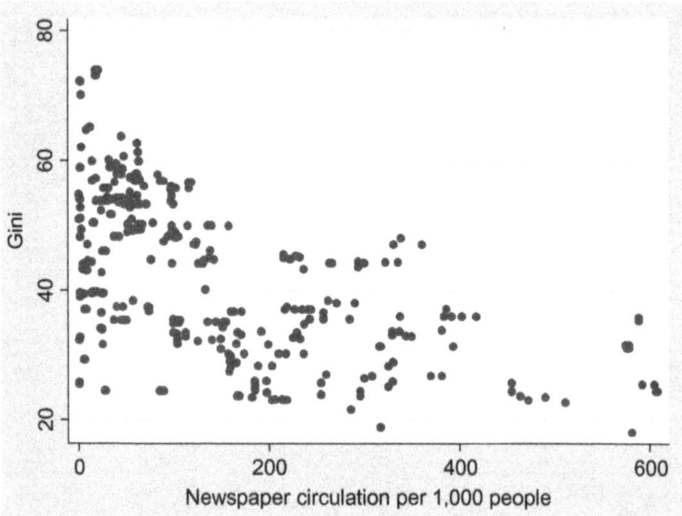

Fig. 1. The Scatter Plot of the Gini Index on Newspaper Circulation per 1,000 People, Full Sample.

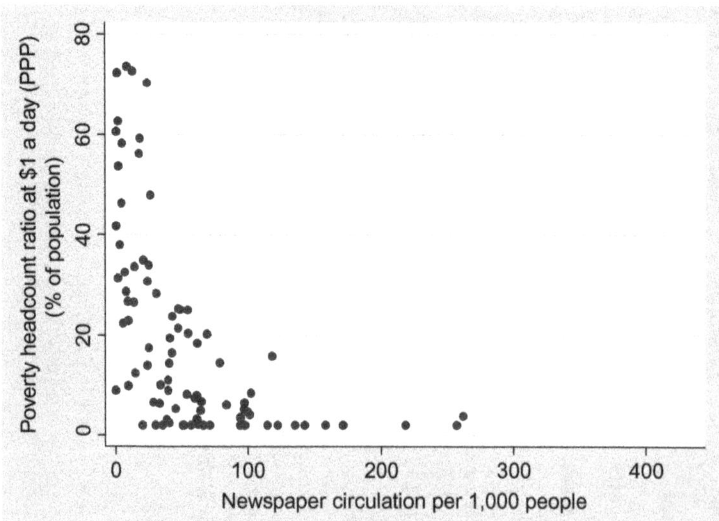

Fig. 2. The Scatter Plot of Poverty $1 a Day on Newspaper Circulation per 1,000 People, Developing Country Sample.

as proxies for external controls – higher levels of GDP per capita and education serve to act to reduce inequality by raising personal incomes.

I envisage the association of any of the media or ICT variables with inequality to be due to media and ICTs facilitating access to information and information technology. Also, societies with higher rule of law indicate the existence of high quality institutions and legal bodies, which can positively affect the impact of ICT and mass media infrastructure on citizen's education or awareness in general. Over time, access to information could translate into higher skills and thereby higher incomes. This impact, if partial across the distribution – that is, positively affects one section of the distribution more than others – may wedge the sections apart, resulting in a rise in inequality. This is often the case in developing countries when access to the knowledge-based technology involved is expensive, and infrastructure-intensive.

The reverse may also happen; the knowledge it engenders, may 'equalise' society on some development outcomes (e.g. awareness about birth control amongst men and women, brought about by national health programmes, brings down household size and thereby raises household per capita income in poor countries). ICTs and media can therefore serve to work either way on the extent of inequality.

Higher international exposure via TRADE makes the economy competitive, and enhances the quicker spread of information and associated technologies, by bringing down the prices of many of these technologies. As discussed earlier with relation to RULE, its effect may be either positive or negative. In addition, I choose two sets of country-specific controls used by Perotti (1996) and Barro (1999) as has been popularly used in the inequality and growth literature (Banerjee & Duflo, 2003). This is because a central concern for the empirical literature is that any of the right hand side variables used as controls could proxy for omitted variables. The choice of the variables entails judgements about causality that are hard to substantiate. Therefore, I use an already established set of controls: those used by Perotti (1996) and those used by Barro (1999). Specifications empirically tested for are repeated with two sets of controls. These specifications are useful benchmarks for two reasons. First, the Perotti specification has been used by most subsequent studies. Second, they represent two extremes, the Perotti specification using the smallest number of control variables and the Barro specification the largest.[4] The Perotti specification excludes most variables (in particular, investment and government spending) through which inequality could be affected. The variables included are male and female education and the purchasing power parity of investment goods, a measure of distortions. Barro, on the other hand, includes a much larger set of variables through which inequality could be affected – investment share of GDP, fertility, education and government spending. The interpretation of the coefficients in two regressions is therefore slightly different. The results presented in Table 4 allow for both sets of controls. To separate out the associations for developing countries only, I estimate the model for both the full sample of countries and the developing country sample separately, presented in Table 5 respectively.

Table 4 presents the estimates for the full sample – Column 1 estimates the basic model, with the individual media and ICT and telephony variables included individually, and the country-level controls BUREAU, RULE, Log of GDP per capita, literacy, TRADE and RISK. It is observed that newspaper circulation, TVs and faxes are negatively and significantly associated with inequality. Telephone mainlines are also negatively and significantly associated with inequality. Of the ICT variables, only the number of internet users is observed to be significant and positively associated with inequality. Inclusion of continent dummies in Column 3, and the Perotti controls, reveals both the Africa and Latin America continent dummies to be significant. I obtain the same results with the Barro controls (results not presented in the table).

For the estimates in columns 4–6, I replace the individual variables with the ICT/telephony index estimated by factor analysis – columns 4 and 5 present the results using the first factor obtained from the factor analysis exercise, with the Barro and Perotti controls; the ICT/telephony index is not significant when included as levels, but is positive and significant when included as a squared variable. Other media variables – newspapers and TVs continue to be negative and significant. I replace the first factor by the second factor obtained from the factor analysis as the ICT index in Column 6 (using Barro controls) – here I obtain a significant and positive coefficient for the ICT index. In all the specifications, the continent dummies are significant.

Table 5 presents the estimates for the developing countries' sample – Columns 1 and 2 present the results for inclusion of the individual media and ICT/telephony variables, with the Barro and Perotti controls respectively. Newspapers are negatively and significantly associated with inequality, but TVs are no longer significant. Continent dummies are significant for both specifications. I replace the individual media and ICT variables with the ICT index in Columns 3 and 4 – I obtain a negative coefficient for the model including the Perotti controls, but it is not significant. I include ICT index (f1) squared and f2 as well, and obtain no significance (result not reported in the table). The same models were tested using the UNCTAD ICT diffusion index as well, and no significant results were obtained (results available from the author).

In both sets of models for the full sample and developing country sample, there have been mixed outcomes for the country-level controls – RULE for the full sample has been negative and significant throughout, likewise mostly for RISK, but not so for the developing country sample. BUREAU has also been positive and significant under some specifications for the developing country sample, while TRADE and literacy even rarely so. Ln GDP for several specifications is positive and significant under both the full sample and developing country sample.

Finally, the results tabulating the regressions of inequality on mass media and ICT indicators in Tables 4 and 5, established two sets of relationships. For the full sample of countries, the ICT index is found to be positively associated with inequality, while for the developing country sample, it is either not significantly associated, or weakly negatively associated with inequality.

To affirm this non-linear relationship between inequality and the ICT index, I plot some kernel regressions of inequality (Ginis) on the ICT index to ascertain the non-linear nature of this relationship. The non-linear relationship between growth and development indicators and inequality is well documented – from Kuznets's inverted U-curve hypothesis, to recent studies on inequality and growth (Banerjee & Duflo, 2003; Quah, 2001a, 2001b). It is well possible that a similar 'stage of development'-specific relationship exists for inequality and the ICT infrastructure index.

Kernel regressions of the Gini on the ICT index are plotted for both f1 and f2 (the first two factors from the factor analysis exercise retained as indices of ICT) in Figs. 3 and 4. I use two types of kernel estimators, the Epanechnikov estimator, and a quartic estimator (not presented) – both reveal similar non-linearities in the relationship between ICT indices and the Gini. For the regression of the Gini on the ICT index first factor, f1 in Fig. 2, it is observed that for lower values of ICT index f1, the relationship is positive, and for higher values of ICT index f1, it is negative. For the regression of the Gini on the ICT index second factor, f2 in Fig. 4 a clearer negative relationship is observed, though this negative relationship often switches to a positive relationship for rising levels of the ICT index f2. This result is also evinced in our regression models earlier when including a ICT (f1) index squared (or f2) term in addition to f1 (or f2).

To summarise the results obtained:

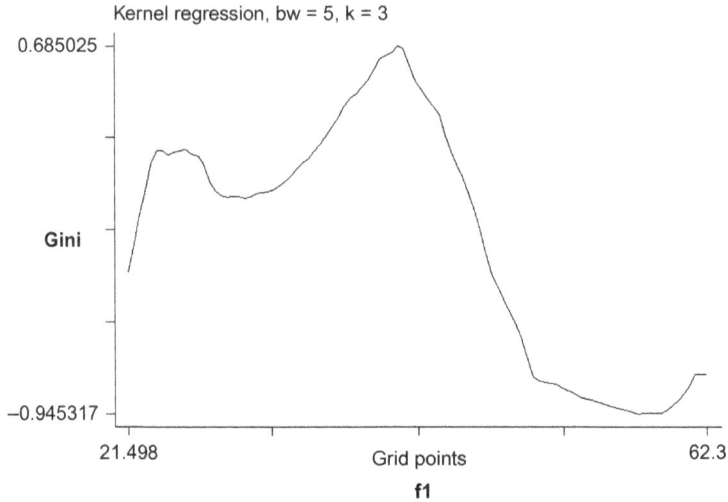

Fig. 3. Kernel Regression of Inequality on the ICT Index f1, Epanechnikov Kernel.

- Inequality is found to be negatively and significantly associated with several media variables, most notably with newspaper circulation. Newspaper circulation is negative and significant under all specifications: for the full sample and developing country sample, and including Perotti and Barro controls. TVs are also found to be negatively associated with inequality, though the level of significance varies with the model and controls included.
- Inequality is also found to be significantly associated with the ICT index under several specifications for the full sample. For the full sample models, it is positive and significant, particularly for the models where it is included as with higher orders, but for the developing country sample it is not significant. The relationship is sensitive to specification, and this could be due to non-linearities in the relationship, as evinced by the kernel regression estimates (Figs. 3 and 4).

Poverty, ICTs and Media

The next relationship that I will be investigating is the association of the media and ICT variables with poverty. The main model estimated is:

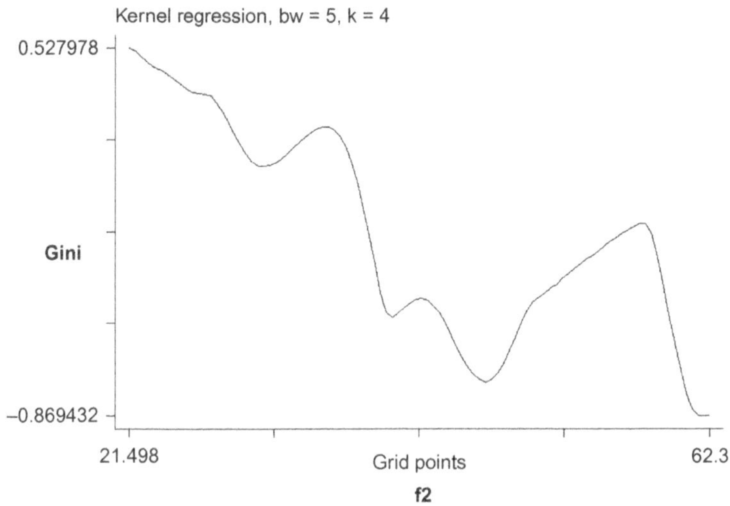

Fig. 4. Kernel Regression of Inequality on the ICT Index f2, Epanechnikov Kernel.

$$\begin{aligned}\text{POVERTY}_i = \beta_0 + \beta_1\,\text{NEWS}_i + \beta_2\,\text{RADIO}_i + \beta_3\,\text{TV}_i + \beta_4\,\text{ICTindex}_i \\ + \beta_5\,\text{BUREAU}_i + \beta_6\,\text{RULE}_i + \beta_7\,\text{TRADE}_i + \beta_8\,\text{RISK}_i + \varepsilon_i\end{aligned} \quad (2)$$

Poverty is measured using two definitions of poverty – the one dollar a day definition (poverty headcount ratio at $1 a day (PPP) (% of population)), and the two dollar a day definition (poverty headcount ratio at $2 a day (PPP) (% of population)) of the World Bank over the years 1992–1997. I also estimated the models with the poverty headcount ratio at the national poverty line (% of population), but due to the number of observations being very low, most specifications did not run. For this analysis I only consider the sample of LDCs (83 countries). Here again I use the same set of controls as determinants of poverty as before, via the same political economy routes. Controls of BUREAU and RULE account for good governance, and provide the institutional set up for growth and economic development. TRADE and RISK ensure the competitiveness required for economic growth and development, thereby lowering levels of poverty. One would expect a negative association of poverty with all of these four controls. Country-level characteristics of log of GDP and literacy are also included, and are expected to be negatively associated with poverty.

In Table 6, Column 1 presents the results of the basic specification with newspaper circulation, radios and TVs as the media variables, and the ICT and telephony individual variables, using the one dollar a day definition of the poverty measure. Due to the small sample size I only include the Perotti controls, and the country-specific characteristics. Newspaper circulation is not significantly associated with poverty – this result holds for all specifications, barring column 2 where it is positively associated with poverty. This result is not observed elsewhere. Radios are however, significant and negative for all models tested. This is observed for all the models presented, and also for any other model that has been tested. TVs are not significant, and this holds for most specifications using the one dollar a day measure of poverty. None of the individual ICT variables are significantly associated with poverty, but telephone revenues are positive and significant. In column 2, I also observe mobile telephony to be negative and significant as well. This is a significant result, as the adoption of mobile telephones by the poor in developing countries is quite high. Most poor households can afford pay-as-you-go mobile telephony due to the competitive rates provided by the service providers. TVs and newspapers are significant and positive – this result is sensitive to the specification, and does not hold for the rest of the results presented. This result also accords with the notion that they are both cost intensive and thus are less affordable by the poorer sections of the income distribution.

In the following two columns, I replace the individual ICT variables with the ICT index – I have tested with both ICT index (f1) and ICT index (f2) factors, and higher order terms (squared terms), the latter are not presented, and it has not been significant in any of the specifications. Radios continue to be negatively and significantly associated with poverty. The continent dummies included in Column 4 are not significant – this is observed for all specifications estimated.

Columns 5 to 7 present the results using the two dollars a day measure of poverty. The negative and significant association of radios and TVs with poverty is observed. This result holds for all specifications tested with the two dollar a day measure of poverty. Of the ICT variables tested, I observe that ICT expenditure as a percentage of GDP to be negative and significant. Internet users are also observed to be negative and significant – this result holds for all specifications. None of the telephony variables are significant. On replacing the individual ICT variables with the ICT index, I do not obtain a significant coefficient. It is possible that the ICT variables that are individually significant are proxying for the level of development.

To summarise our results:

- Radios are significantly and negatively associated with poverty. This result holds for all the models that have been estimated. TVs are also observed to be negative and significant particularly so for the models using $2 a day poverty measure.
- The ICT index is not significantly associated with poverty. Of the individual ICT variables, ICT expenditures are negatively and significantly associated with poverty under some specifications.

ISSUES OF ENDOGENEITY: ROLE OF MASS MEDIA

One major issue to deal with is that of the potential problem of reverse causality between the development outcomes, inequality and poverty, and that of the media and ICT variables. In this section we discuss the potential sources of endogeneity, and then follow it with an IV analysis for the media variable, newspaper circulation (per 1,000 people). Of course, finding an appropriate instrument for either mass media or ICT variables is extremely difficult, but the instruments used below for newspaper circulation, in particular, provide us with some robust IV results.

There are two sources of endogeneity here – both ICT and telephony variables, and mass media, have a two-sided impact upon the development outcomes of inequality and poverty. As discussed earlier, the effect of ICT and telephony variables has a double-edged effect. On the one hand, they have a 'growth' effect: ICT and telephony are infrastructure variables, and thereby contribute to economic growth. In addition, due to the 'weightless' nature of ICTs, their spread is speedy and it disregards physical barriers, enhancing their 'growth effect'. One could therefore expect, on the one hand, the impact of ICTs and telephony to be growth enhancing and poverty reducing (in the medium to long term). On the other hand, there is a distribution-specific effect of ICTs and telephony, in that they are cost intensive for adoption. Even with the competitive prices of ICTs and their weightless nature, in developing countries access to these technologies is out of reach of the poor (though, this is not the case for mobile telephony in LDCs). Therefore, one could conjecture that in industrialised countries, the ICT and telephony penetration facilitates the spread of information, and will likely bring down the extent of income inequality. The same process, though, in developing countries, will push the rich and the poor apart. However, the extent to which the process of inequality increase pans out in developing countries depends upon adoption rates. Adoption and the spread of ICTs and telephony is still relatively slow in LDCs compared to industrialised countries, hence, we may not observe a short-term rise in inequality in LDCs even if ICTs and telephony penetration were to occur.

Similar endogeneity can be envisaged with the case of mass media and the development outcomes of inequality and poverty. Mass media provides crucial information to the median voter and thereby influences decisions on demanding redistributive policies. This brings down inequality. It also creates a more educated society and thereby contributes to economic growth and rising per capita incomes. This also brings down inequality in the long run. One would also expect, however, that the instruments of media (such as newspapers, radios and TVs) themselves are not responsible for creating an educated voter or citizen. It is the nature of the news provider (public or private, national or foreign owned), and the quality of information (unbiased or biased) that is being broadcast that ultimately determines the nature of information provided. On the one hand, media bias (see Djankov et al., 2003) is commonly understood to be less pervasive if the news providing bodies in a country (or region within a country) are competitive – in other words, single bodies such as the state media, in the absence of competing private media bodies are often seen as providing 'propaganda'. On the other hand, in a system where both public and private media bodies co-exist, the news coverage of public bodies is often deemed to be more reliable (e.g. the case of the BBC in the United Kingdom, Doordarshan in India, PBS in the United States).

Irrespective of the number and the ratio of public to private media bodies, what is understood to matter the most is the legal framework which ensures transparency in the provision of information. To this effect, several indicators of the freedom of information and transparency have been compiled by a number of civil society organisations. I use three main indicators of press freedom and transparency as instruments for newspaper circulation. Freedom House has compiled an index of press freedom, and ranks countries according to their index, the Freedom of Press Index, which is an annual survey of media independence in 197 countries and territories. Data for the years 1992 and 1993 are not available (the index starts from 1994), so our variable starts in 1994. In addition, to account for a broader definition of information bias and government actions against a free press, I use the Reporters Without Borders index of press freedom using data on journalists arrested and murdered, in addition to standard indicators of press freedom. Their index starts in 2002 for most countries, otherwise from 2003, and runs till 2010. Given that this is a slow moving variable, I have used the index from 2002 to 2007 (or 2003 to 2008) to represent years 1992 to 1997 (I have used different starting points for the years and the results obtained are identical in terms of their significance). The index covers all countries in the dataset, except for Bahrain. There are two indicators provided, a score and a ranking on the basis of the score – I use of the log of the score provided.

I use a further index of quality of information provided by media, called the Right to Information Index, compiled by the Global Right to Information.[5] The RTI Rating is a system for assessing the strength of the legal framework for guaranteeing the right to information in a given country. The focus of the index is therefore on gauging the legal framework to access information, and not on the 'quality' of implementation of the legal framework. Over time a strong access-to-information law can contribute to advancing openness and help those using it to defend and promote the right of access to information. The index is compiled by using 61 indicators measuring a wide range of international standards and laws on the right to information. For the estimations in the paper, to make the RTI score values comparable to other indicators, I have used the natural logarithmic value of the index.

Results

We now undertake an IV estimation using the three instruments described above. The results of the estimation using Two Stage Least Squares is described in Table 7 for the relationship between inequality and the ICT and media variables. In Table 7, Panel A, I present the first stage results for the determinants of newspaper circulation (per 1,000 households). Here I regress the newspaper circulation on all three instruments, namely the Freedom of Press index, log of RTI index and the log on Reporters Without Borders score alongside the other cross-country controls used in the estimation of Eq. (1). Newspaper circulation is positively and significantly associated with log of RTI index and the log of Reporters Without Borders score instruments for all six regressions, using both Perotti and Barro controls separately. The other controls used are significant at several levels of significance, and in the expected directions. The Cragg–Donald statistic in all six regressions is greater than 10 suggesting that the instruments are not weak (Staiger & Stock, 1997).

I now estimate Eq. (1) as the second stage regression and present the second stage results in Table 7, Panel B. The results are just as strong as in Table 4; in all cases the size of the coefficient for newspapers is greater than before. Due to the small number of observations, I do not present the

Table 7. Instrumental Variable Estimations: First Stage and Second Stage Estimates.

Controls	Perotti	Perotti	Perotti	Barro	Barro	Barro
Panel A: First stage results (Dependent variable: Newspaper circulation)						
	(1)	(2)	(3)	(4)	(5)	(6)
Radios	0.009*	0.009	0.008	0.169***	0.009*	0.008
	(0.005)	(0.007)	(0.005)	(0.051)	(0.005)	(0.005)
TVs	0.077	0.040	0.080	0.161	0.022	0.109
	(1.59)	(0.161)	(0.156)	(0.192)	(0.150)	(0.152)
ICT index	29.804	50.662	0.299	39.358	51.482	
	(29.37)	(33.81)	(0.162)	(37.301)	(33.265)	
ICT index squared		43.821	3.439		41.594	
		(36.04)	(0.799)		(34.786)	
Fax			0.000			0.843
			(0.000)			(1.485)
ICT expenditure			0.098			1.297
			(0.241)			(7.577)
Internet users						0.000
						(0.000)
Mobiles						0.032
						(0.299)
Press freedom	0.246	0.158	1.089	−1.345*	0.317	0.619
	(0.787)	(0.784)	(0.893)	(0.704)	(0.649)	(0.601)
Log RTI index	229.883***	221.652***	241.034***	312.697***	220.007***	226.509***
	(47.860)	(47.956)	(59.220)	(72.084)	(47.108)	(56.990)
Log RPI score	−49.520***	49.968***	−44.050***	−17.757	−48.561***	−51.266***
	(11.49)	(11.41)	(14.596)	(12.322)	(10.596)	(12.039)
Controls	yes	yes	yes	yes	yes	yes
Continent dummies	yes	yes	yes	yes	yes	yes
N	46	46	55	29	46	55
Centred R^2	0.88	0.89	0.89	0.95	0.89	0.96
Anderson's F-statistic p-value	0.000	0.000	0.000	0.000	0.000	0.000
Panel B: Second stage results (Dependent variable: Gini index)						
	(1)	(2)	(3)	(4)	(5)	(6)
Newspapers	−0.125***	−0.134***	−0.115***	−0.116***	−0.128***	−0.112***
	(0.014)	(0.012)	(0.014)	(0.027)	(0.016)	(0.015)
Radios	−0.001*	−0.001**	−0.001**	−0.011*	−0.001**	−0.001**
	(0.000)	(0.000)	(0.000)	(0.006)	(0.000)	(0.000)
TVs	−0.014	−0.024*	−0.026*	0.015	0.008	0.013
	(0.013)	(0.013)	(0.016)	(0.030)	(0.015)	(0.013)
ICT index	1.164	9.343***		3.440	8.962***	
	(1.987)	(2.652)		(3.913)	(3.259)	
ICT index squared		15.271***			17.063***	
		(4.024)			(4.697)	

Table 7. *(Continued)*

Controls	Perotti	Perotti	Perotti	Barro	Barro	Barro
Fax			−0.502***			−0.462***
			(0.141)			(0.144)
ICT expenditure			0.593			0.740
			(0.568)			(0.884)
Internet users			0.00001***			0.00001***
			(0.00000)			(0.00000)
Mobiles			−0.021			−0.029*
			(0.017)			(0.015)
Controls	Yes	Yes	Yes	Yes	Yes	Yes
Continent dummies	Yes	Yes	Yes	Yes	Yes	Yes
N	46	46	55	29	46	55
Centred R^2	0.92	0.95	0.95	0.92	0.93	0.93
F-statistic	108.00	106.42	36.43	13.62	63.00	54.05
Hansen's J statistic p-value	0.008	0.003	0.020	0.006	0.007	0.035
Cragg–Donald statistic	15.30	14.80	18.10	9.90	15.20	18.50

Note: Heterosdasticity robust standard errors in parentheses.
***Significant at 1% level of significance.
**Significant at 5% level of significance.
*Significant at 10% level of significance.

results for the developing country sample. For the same reason the results with poverty are not presented.

CONCLUSION

Mass media and ICTs are two important vehicles of information in developing and developed countries alike. In this paper I present some robust evidence of some associations of ICTs and mass media with inequality and poverty.

I observe that inequality (measured with the Gini index), is negatively associated with newspaper penetration – this is one of the most robust results of all estimates. The ICT and telephony variables and the ICT index have mixed outcomes in their associations with inequality – for the full sample there exists a positive association, and a weak association (mostly negative) for the developing country sample. ICT expenditures as a percentage of GDP are found to have a negative association with inequality. For poverty, the most prominent result observed was the negative association with the incidence of radios and TVs – this result has been robust to all specifications tested, particularly for radios.

I also undertake an IV analysis for the newspaper circulation variable, using three instruments. I continue to find robust evidence that newspaper circulation is robustly negatively associated with inequality. In other words, higher newspaper circulation is found to be associated with lower levels of inequality.

There are several avenues for future research – testing for specific political economy routes of causality for any of these associations will take this literature further. The literature on media capture and bias (Corneo, 2006; Petrova, 2008 for effects of income inequality on media bias, for example) addresses some of the issues that are tested here. Causality related to the effects of information infrastructures on inequality and poverty requires micro-level empirical surveys, which the cross-country macro-approach adopted in this paper can only partially address. Country-specific micro-studies will therefore allow researchers to test for causality.

The role of ICTs in developing countries is much discussed in policy spheres; studies which examine the micro-level impact of these infrastructures will shed light on their effectiveness on local level welfare. With the role of media bias being much studied in a cross-country context, more research on its impact in developing countries in particular, in light of their weak legal institutions would contribute to the developing country literature specifically.

With the empirical literature on relationships between information infrastructures and development outcomes still at its early stages, the evidence obtained in this paper is convincing that there exists a significant association between media and communications infrastructures, and inequality and poverty.

NOTES

1. Some work in this area has been done on the impact of ICTs on wage inequalities in the United States (see Autor et al., 1998).
2. The results using the UNCTAD index are not presented in the paper and are available from the author.
3. A large number of cross-country studies investigating differential development outcomes, have often included the extent of cultural diversification as a possible determinant of differential growth and development outcomes. It is purported to affect corruption in particular by impeding competitiveness. Ethnic fragmentation has been included in several specifications but has not shown up to be significant and hence is not presented.

4. The list of variables included in both specifications are as follows: Perotti: Log (GDP (1990), PPP I (1990), male education (1990), female education (1990). Barro: Log (GDP (1990)), Log (GDP (1990)) squared, government consumption (1990–1995), secondary and higher education (1990), fertility (1990), 1/30*(terms of trade (1995)-terms of trade (1990)), rule of law, democracy (1990), democracy (1990) squared, inflation (1990–1995) and investment share (1990–1995).

5. The source of this RTI Index is http://www.rti-rating.org/country_data.php

REFERENCES

Acemoglu, D., & Autor, D. (2010). Skills, tasks and technologies: Implications for employment and earnings. In D. Card & O. Ashenfelter (Eds.), *Handbook of labor economics* (Vol. 4). Princeton, NJ: Princeton University Press.

Ades, A., & Di Tella, R. (1999). Rents, competition and corruption. *American Economic Review*, *89*(4), 982–993.

Ahrend, R. (2001). *Press freedom, human capital and corruption*. DELTA Working Paper No. 2002–11.

Arthur, B. W. (1994). *Increasing returns and path dependence in the economy*. Ann Arbor, MI: University of Michigan Press.

Autor, D., & Dorn, D. (2009). *Inequality and specialization: the growth of low-skill service jobs in the United States*. NBER Working Paper 15150.

Autor, D., Katz, L. F., & Krueger, A. B. (1998). Computing inequality: How computers have changed the labour market. *Quarterly Journal of Economics*, *113*(4), 1169–1214.

Baron, D. (2006). Persistent media bias. *Journal of Public Economics*, *90*(1–2), 1–36.

Barro, R. J. (1999). *Inequality, growth, and investment*. Working Paper 7038, National Bureau of Economic Research, March.

Banerjee, A., & Duflo, E. (2003). Inequality and growth: What does the data say? *Journal of Economic Growth*, *8*, 267–299.

Berman, E., Somanathan, R., & Tan, H. (2005). Is skill-biased technological change here yet? Evidence from Indian manufacturing in the 1990s. *Annales d'Economie et de Statistique*, *79–80*, 299–321.

Besley, T., & Burgess, R. (2002). The political economy of government responsiveness: Theory and evidence from India. *Quarterly Journal of Economics*, *117*(4), 1415–1451.

Besley, T., Burgess, R., & Prat, A. (2002). Mass media and political accountability. In R. Islam (Ed.), *The right to know: Institutions and the media* (pp. 45–60). Washington, DC: World Bank.

Brunetti, A., & Weder, B. (2003). A free press is bad news for corruption. *Journal of Public Economics*, *87*(7–8), 1801–1824.

Corneo, G. (2006). Media capture in a democracy: The role of wealth concentration. *Journal of Public Economics*, *90*(1–2), 37–58.

Daveri, F. (2002). The new economy in Europe: 1992–2001. *Oxford Review of Economic Policy*, *18*(3), 345–362.

David, P. A. (1985). Clio and the economics of QWERTY. *American Economic Review*, *75*(2), 332–337.

DiNardo, J. E., & Pischke, J.-S. (1997). The returns to computer use revisited: Have pencils changed the wage structure too? *Quarterly Journal of Economics*, *112*(1), 291–303.

Djankov, S., McLeish, C., Nenova, T., & Shleifer, A. (2003). Who owns the media? *Journal of Law and Economics*, *46*(2), 341–381.

Goldin, C., & Katz, L. F. (1996). Technology, skill and wage structure: Insights from the past. *American Economic Review*, *86*(2), 252–257.

Goldin, C., & Katz, L. F. (2008). *The race between education and technology*. Cambridge, MA: Harvard University Press.

Haacker, M., & Morsinck, J. (2002). *You say you want a revolution: Information technology and growth*. IMF Working Paper No. #WP/02/70.

Kenny, C. (2003). The internet and economic growth in LDCs: A case for managing expectations. *Oxford Development Studies*, *31*(1), 99–113.

Koski, H., Rouvinen, P., & Yla-Anttila, P. (2002). ICT clusters in Europe: The great central banana and small Nordic potato. *Information Economics and Policy*, *14*(2), 145–165.

Krugman, P. (1991). Increasing returns and economic geography. *Journal of Political Economy*, *99*(3), 483–499.

Michaels, G., Van Reenen, J., & Natraj, A. (2013). Has ICT polarized skill demand? Evidence from eleven countries over 25 years. *Review of Economics and Statistics*, *96*(1), 60–77.

Mullainathan, S., & Shleifer, A. (2005). The market for news. *American Economic Review*, *95*(4), 1031–1053.

Perotti, R. (1996). Growth, income distribution and democracy. *Journal of Economic Growth*, *1*(2), 149–187.

Petrova, M. (2008). Inequality and media capture. *Journal of Public Economics*, *92*(1–2), 183–212.

Quah, D. (2001a). ICT clusters in development: Theory and evidence. *EIB Papers*, *6*(1), 85–100.

Quah, D. (2001b). The weightless economy in economic development. In M. Pohjola (Ed.), *Information technology, productivity, and economic growth: International evidence* (pp. 72–96). Oxford: Oxford University Press.

Shi, M., & Svensson, J. (2002). *Conditional political budget cycles*. CEPR Discussion Paper, No. 3352.

Staiger, D., & Stock, J. H. (1997). Instrumental variables regression with weak instruments. *Econometrica*, *65*, 557–586.

Stigler, G. (1961). The economics of information. *Journal of Political Economy*, *69*(3), 213–225.

Stiglitz, J. E. (2000). The contributions of the economics of information to twentieth century economics. *Quarterly Journal of Economics*, *115*(4), 1441–1478.

Timmer, M. P., & van Arky, B. (2005). Does information and communication technology drive EU-US productivity growth differentials? *Oxford Economic Papers*, *57*(4), 693–716.

UNU-WIDER. (2005). *World Income Inequality Database-WIID v2.0c*. Helsinki: World Institute for Development Economics Research, United Nations University.

Vaidya, S. (2005). Corruption in the media's gaze. *European Journal of Political Economy*, *21*(3), 667–687.

World Bank. (2004). *World Bank national indicators' dataset*. World Bank. Retrieved from http://data.worldbank.org/indicator

APPENDIX: COUNTRIES USED IN THE ANALYSES

Algeria	El Salvador	Korea, Republic	Poland	Uruguay
Angola	Ethiopia	Kuwait	Portugal	Venezuela
Argentina	Finland	Lebanon	Qatar	Vietnam
Australia	France	Liberia	Romania	Yemen
Austria	Gabon	Libya	Russian Federation	Yugoslavia
Bahamas	Gambia	Luxembourg	Saudi Arabia	Zaire/ DRC
Bahrain	Germany	Madagascar	Senegal	Zambia
Bangladesh	Ghana	Malawi	Sierra Leone	Zimbabwe
Belgium	Greece	Malaysia	Singapore	
Bolivia	Guatemala	Mali	Slovakia	
Botswana	Guinea	Malta	Somalia	
Brazil	Guinea-Bissau	Mexico	South Africa	
Brunei	Guyana	Mongolia	Spain	
Bulgaria	Haiti	Morocco	Sri Lanka	
Burkina Faso	Honduras	Mozambique	Sudan	
Cameroon	Hong Kong	Myanmar	Suriname	
Canada	Hungary	Namibia	Sweden	
Chile	Iceland	Netherlands	Switzerland	
China	India	New Zealand	Syria	
Colombia	Indonesia	Nicaragua	Taiwan	
Congo	Iran	Niger	Tanzania	
Costa Rica	Iraq	Nigeria	Thailand	
Cote d'Ivoire	Ireland	Norway	Togo	
Cuba	Israel	Oman	Trinidad and Tobago	
Cyprus	Italy	Pakistan	Tunisia	
Czech Republic	Jamaica	Panama	Turkey	
Denmark	Japan	Papua New Guinea	UAE	
Dominican Republic	Jordan	Paraguay	Uganda	
Ecuador	Kenya	Peru	United Kingdom	
Egypt	Korea, DPR	Philippines	United States	

The developing country sample consists of the following countries:

Algeria	Gambia	Morocco	Yemen
Angola	Ghana	Mozambique	Zaire/DRC
Argentina	Guatemala	Myanmar	Zambia
Bahamas	Guinea	Namibia	Zimbabwe
Bahrain	Guinea-Bissau	Nicaragua	
Bangladesh	Guyana	Niger	
Bolivia	Haiti	Nigeria	
Botswana	Honduras	Oman	
Brazil	India	Pakistan	
Brunei	Indonesia	Panama	
Burkina Faso	Iran	Papua New Guinea	
Cameroon	Iraq	Paraguay	
Chile	Jamaica	Peru	
China	Jordan	Philippines	
Colombia	Kenya	Qatar	
Congo	Kuwait	Saudi Arabia	
Costa Rica	Lebanon	Senegal	
Cote d'Ivoire	Liberia	South Africa	
Cuba	Libya	Sri Lanka	
Dominican Republic	Madagascar	Surinam	
Ecuador	Malawi	Syria	
Egypt	Malaysia	Thailand	
El Salvador	Mali	Trinidad and Tobago	
Ethiopia	Malta	UAE	
Gabon	Mexico	Venezuela	

SOCIOECONOMIC INEQUALITY IN HAPPINESS IN THE UNITED STATES

Shiyi Chen and Buhong Zheng

ABSTRACT

This paper applies a recently developed method of ranking socioeconomic inequality in health to ranking U.S. happiness from 1994 to 2012 using the GSS data. We also compare happiness between subgroups as decomposed by gender, race, and age. We establish and test a monotone condition of happiness – a richer person is likely to be happier. Under the monotone condition, standard tools of welfare and inequality ranking can be applied straightforwardly.

Keywords: Socioeconomic status; happiness inequality; health inequality; social gradients in health outcomes; income-happiness matrix; Lorenz dominance

JEL classification: D63

Economic Well-Being and Inequality: Papers from the Fifth ECINEQ Meeting
Research on Economic Inequality, Volume 22, 217–236

ISSN: 1049-2585/doi:10.1108/S1049-258520140000022006

INTRODUCTION

A nation's gross domestic product (GDP) has traditionally been used as the all-important indicator of the nation's aggregate well-being. Increasingly, this practice has been criticized for not fully reflecting the many dimensions of well-being (see, e.g., Costanza, Hart, Posner, & Talbert, 2009) and alternative approaches have been developed. One such new approach is the multidimensional measurement of well-being in which well-being is measured over several selected dimensions such as income, health, and education levels of individual citizens. The best known example of the approach is the Human Development Index (HDI) that was developed by UNDP (United Nations Development Programme) in the early 1990s as a measure "to shift the focus of development economics from national income accounting to people-centered policies." The HDI is a simple average over achievements in health, education, and standard of living, and it treats the three components as equally important in reporting each nation's human development/well-being. Besides the obvious issue of properly weighting the different dimensions, a not-less-serious challenge in the multidimensional approach lies in the selection of dimensions to be included in the index in the first place.

Another approach that has recently attracted attention is to view happiness as a gauge of subjective well-being and, consequently, measure the distribution of happiness in a society (see, e.g., Dutta & Foster, 2013; Stevenson & Wolfers, 2008; Veenhoven, 2005). The idea of using happiness as a measure of well-being is rooted in the understanding that "utility can be interpreted in terms of happiness" (Dutta & Foster, 2013) and, thus, it is meaningful to aggregate happiness and evaluate the distribution of it across societies and over time. Compared with the multidimensional approach, the happiness approach has the apparent advantage of not having to choose among different dimensions of well-being. The difficulty in using the approach, however, is that happiness is measured as a subjective self-assessed and self-reported categorical data and as such the traditional measures of welfare and inequality may not be directly applicable. For example, in the General Social Survey (GSS), respondents are asked the question "taken all together, how would you say things are these days, would you say that you are very happy, pretty happy, or not too happy." To compute the traditional inequality indices using the GSS data, one has to convert the ordinal happiness data into numerical scales. For example, Stevenson and Wolfers (2008) assigned 1, 2, and 3 to the three levels of happiness. Although van Pragg (1991) made an argument for cardinalizing happiness in this way since "when choosing between different categories, respondents have a numerical scale in mind," it is still difficult to justify the specific values that are assigned. Indeed, a different set of values such as (1,3,5) or (−1,0,1) should be equally as appealing (or as unappealing) as (1,2,3). It seems that using (1,2,3) is purely a matter of convenience.

The issue encountered in measuring happiness inequality is the same as that encountered in measuring health inequality which has received substantial attention in the last decade. A growing literature has been devoted to the measurement of health inequality with ordinal data. In the context of measuring an individual's health status, while cardinal data for specific health indicators such as blood pressure and BMI are often available, overall health assessment has almost always been represented in categorical format. For example, both the US National Health Interview Survey (NHIS) and the Canadian National Population Health Survey (NPHS) adopt a five-level health rating system: poor, fair, good, very good, and excellent. Traditionally, researchers have assigned integers 1 through 5 (again out of convenience) to the five levels (e.g., Deaton & Paxson, 1998) and then compute inequality of distributions among the multiples of these five numbers. Clearly, inequality comparison between different health distributions may critically hinge upon the five numbers used (1 through 5 or 2 through 6). Allison and Foster (2004) argued convincingly that the analytical tools developed for measuring income distributions such as Lorenz curve and Gini index are no longer suitable for analyzing distributions with ordinal data. They pointed out that since the mean is sensitive to the numbers used for health levels, the reference point for measuring health inequality should be replaced with a different reference point such as the median which is not sensitive to the values assigned. Allison and Foster (2004) introduced a set of new axioms to facilitate their development of a dominance condition for ranking distributions with ordinal data.

A significant amount of the literature on health inequality measurement, however, concerns a different but related issue – the measurement of "socioeconomic inequality in health" (Wagstaff, Paci, & van Doorslaer, 1991). This branch of the literature is interested in measuring the extent to which inequality in health is due to the existence of unequal socioeconomic statuses. An important stipulation in this literature is the "social gradients in health" hypothesis – a richer person or a person with a higher social status tends to be healthier. Over the last half century, this hypothesis has been repeatedly debated and tested. It is now generally accepted as a valid fact of life (e.g., Marmot, 2003) and is often referred to as the "monotone" assumption in the measurement literature. Under the monotone assumption, Zheng (2011) developed a robust approach to evaluate socioeconomic inequality in health. The robustness lies in the fact that the approach does not rely on any numerical scales assigned to the health levels as long as the health value for a better health level is larger than a less-healthy level. The approach does not introduce any new notion of inequality but rather adopts standard definitions of inequality and, hence, theorems and interpretations from income inequality measurement can be carried over in a straightforward manner.

The purpose of this paper is to apply the approach developed for measuring socioeconomic inequality in health to the measurement of happiness distribution and socioeconomic inequality in happiness. To implement the approach, it is necessary to first define and validate a monotone assumption on the relationship between happiness and socioeconomic status – which can also be referred to as "social gradients in happiness" – a richer person or a person with a higher social status tends to be happier. While a strong correlation has been repeatedly confirmed by empirical studies (e.g., Clark, Frijters, & Shields, 2008; research surveyed by DeNeve & Cooper, 1999), the monotone assumption requires much more than a simple regression outcome. In this paper, we formally test the monotone hypothesis in happiness in the United States using the GSS data. We found strong support for the hypothesis. It is important to note that the condition for our monotone assumption does not depend on the numerical scales that happiness levels are assigned.

The rest of the paper is organized as follows. The next section describes the monotone assumption and the approach for measuring happiness distribution and socioeconomic inequality in happiness. The section "Results" tests the monotone hypothesis using the GSS data and then ranks happiness distribution and happiness inequality in the United States from 1994 to 2012. We also decompose the U.S. population into subgroups by gender, race, and age (working vs. retired), and compare happiness between the subgroups. The final section concludes.

THE METHOD

At the heart of the method is an income-happiness matrix. The matrix documents the relationship between the socioeconomic status (often represented by income class) and the level of happiness. Assume there are $m \geq 2$ levels of happiness and $n \geq 2$ socioeconomic (income) classes. Let h_j be the value of the jth happiness level and assume that the values of happiness satisfy $0 < h_1 \le h_2 \le \ldots \le h_m$. The proportion of population in the ith socioeconomic class is π_i with $\sum_{i=1}^{n} \pi_i = 1$; the collection of π_i's, denoted as $\{\pi_i\}$, is referred to as a socioeconomic structure. An income-happiness matrix is:

$$A_{n \times m} = |\alpha_{ij}|_{n \times m} = \begin{bmatrix} \alpha_{11} & \cdots & \alpha_{1m} \\ \vdots & \alpha_{ij} & \vdots \\ \alpha_{n1} & \cdots & \alpha_{nm} \end{bmatrix} \tag{1}$$

with $a_{ij} \ge 0$ and $\sum_{j=1}^{m} \alpha_{ij} = 1$ for all $i = 1, 2\ldots, n$. Each row of the matrix represents the prospect of happiness for the corresponding socioeconomic class. For example, if the first row of A is (0.5,0.3,0.1), these numbers would mean that within the lowest socioeconomic class, 50% of them are "not too happy," 30% of them are "pretty happy," and 10% of them are "very happy."

The monotone assumption is derived from the observation that, holding everything else the same, a richer person is likely to be happier. An individual randomly drawn from socioeconomic class i faces a prospect of happiness $(\alpha_{i1}, \alpha_{i2}, \ldots, \alpha_{im})$ and, given happiness values h_i's, his expected level of happiness is:

$$e_i =: \sum_{j=1}^{m} \alpha_{ij} h_j$$

To say that a person from a higher socioeconomic class t tends to be happier than a person from a lower socioeconomic class s is equivalent to requiring:

$$e_s =: \sum_{j=1}^{m} \alpha_{sj} h_j \le \sum_{j=1}^{m} \alpha_{tj} h_j := e_t, s \le t \tag{2}$$

Since Abel's partial sum formula gives:

$$\sum_{j=1}^{m} \alpha_{sj} h_s = \left(\sum_{j=1}^{m} \alpha_{sj} \right) h_1 + \left(\sum_{j=2}^{m} \alpha_{sj} \right) (h_2 - h_1) + \cdots + \alpha_{sm} (h_m - h_{m-1})$$

and $h_i \leq h_j$ for all $i \leq j$ with $h_1 > 0$ by assumption, it follows that $e_s \leq e_t$ for all possible values of h_i's if and only if:

$$\sum_{j=k}^{m} \alpha_{sj} \leq \sum_{j=k}^{m} \alpha_{tj} \quad \text{for all } k = 1, 2, \ldots, m$$

or

$$\sum_{j=1}^{k} \alpha_{sj} \geq \sum_{j=1}^{k} \alpha_{tj} \quad \text{for all } k = 1, 2, \ldots, m \tag{3}$$

since $\sum_{j=1}^{m} \alpha_{sj} = \sum_{j=1}^{m} \alpha_{tj} = 1$.

Condition (3) constitutes the requirement of our monotone assumption – it is a second-degree stochastic dominance condition (row t second-degree stochastic dominates row s). Clearly, this condition is robust to how happiness is valuated since it does not contain any h_j. The only requirement used in deriving the condition is $0 < h_1 \leq h_2 \leq \cdots \leq h_m$ which is certainly a reasonable assumption. Compared with all other tests of income-happiness relationship documented in the literature, the monotone assumption we define in this paper is the strongest since it holds for all possible valuations of happiness satisfying $h_1 \leq h_2 \leq \cdots \leq h_m$.[1] One important objective of the paper is to empirically test whether this robust (and some would say it is too strong) condition can indeed be satisfied empirically.

For a given socioeconomic structure $\{\pi_i\}$ and an income-happiness matrix $A_{n \times m}$, the vector of expected happiness is:

$$\mathbf{e}(A) = \left(\sum_{j=1}^{m} \alpha_{1j} h_j, \ \sum_{j=1}^{m} \alpha_{2j} h_j, \ldots, \sum_{j=1}^{m} \alpha_{nj} h_j \right)$$

Different income-happiness matrices lead to different vectors of expected happiness. The issue now at hand is to compare between these vectors for a given socioeconomic structure. We are interested in both welfare and inequality implications of different income and happiness connections; welfare comparison tells which matrix yields greater aggregate happiness and inequality comparison reveals which matrix leads to a more equalized distribution of happiness. The tools we use for both comparisons are standard in the literature of income distribution measurement: for welfare comparison we use rank dominance and generalized Lorenz dominance; for inequality comparison we resort to Lorenz dominance. Consequently, our results can be easily interpreted.

As shown by Zheng (2011), for a given socioeconomic structure matrix $\{\pi_i\}$, vector $\mathbf{e}(A)$ rank dominates vector $\mathbf{e}(B)$ with $B = |\beta_{ij}|_{n \times m}$ for all possible values of happiness satisfying $0 < h_1 \leq h_2 \leq \cdots \leq h_m$ if and only if:

$$\sum_{j=1}^{k} \pi_i \alpha_{ij} \leq \sum_{j=1}^{k} \pi_i \beta_{ij} \tag{4}$$

for all $k = 1, 2, \ldots, m$ and all $i = 1, 2, \ldots, n$; $\mathbf{e}(A)$ generalized Lorenz dominates $\mathbf{e}(B)$ for all possible values of happiness $0 < h_1 \leq h_2 \leq \cdots \leq h_m$ if and only if:

$$\sum_{i=1}^{l} \sum_{j=1}^{k} \pi_i \alpha_{ij} \leq \sum_{i=1}^{l} \sum_{j=1}^{k} \pi_i \beta_{ij} \tag{5}$$

for all $k = 1, 2, \ldots, m$ and all $l = 1, 2, \ldots, n$; $\mathbf{e}(A)$ generalized super-Lorenz dominates $\mathbf{e}(B)$ if and only if:

$$\sum_{t=1}^{l} \sum_{i=1}^{t} \sum_{j=1}^{k} \pi_i \alpha_{ij} \leq \sum_{t=1}^{l} \sum_{i=1}^{t} \sum_{j=1}^{k} \pi_i \beta_{ij} \tag{6}$$

for all $k = 1, 2, \ldots, m$ and all $l = 1, 2, \ldots, n$.

If we multiply all elements in row i of A by π_i for $i = 1, 2, \ldots, n$, then the above conditions simply compare the upper left $l \times k$ values of $|\pi_i \alpha_{ij}|_{n \times m}$ and $|\pi_i \beta_{ij}|_{n \times m}$ for all possible k and l combinations when they are properly cumulated. Specifically, for the rank dominance condition, each row is cumulated eastbound and the cumulated values are compared cell-wise between the two matrices. For generalized Lorenz dominance, the cumulated values used in rank dominance are further cumulated column-wise southbound. The resulting matrices are again cumulated column-wise southbound when implementing the generalized super-Lorenz dominance condition.

Inequality comparisons between $\mathbf{e}(A)$ and $\mathbf{e}(B)$ are carried out for two classes of inequality measures: relative inequality measures (doubling all incomes leaves income inequality unchanged) and absolute inequality measures (adding \$10 to all incomes leaves income inequality unchanged).

The dominance conditions for the relative class are relative Lorenz dominance and relative super-Lorenz dominance (the latter is implied by the former), the dominance conditions for the absolute class are absolute Lorenz dominance and absolute super-Lorenz dominance (the latter is also implied by the former). These conditions are given below and the details of implementation are found in the work by Zheng (2011):

(1) **e**(A) relative Lorenz dominates **e**(B) if:

$$\alpha_l^s\beta_n^t + \alpha_l^t\beta_n^s \geq \alpha_n^t\beta_l^s + \alpha_n^s\beta_l^t \tag{7}$$

for all $s \leq t = 1, 2, \ldots, m$ and all $l = 1, 2, \ldots, n-1$.

(2) **e**(A) absolute Lorenz dominates **e**(B) if and only if:

$$\tilde{\pi}_l\alpha_n^k - \alpha_l^k \leq \tilde{\pi}_l\beta_n^k - \beta_l^k \tag{8}$$

for all $k = 2, \ldots, m$ and $l = 1, 2, \ldots, n-1$.

(3) **e**(A) and **e**(B), then **e**(A) relative super-Lorenz dominates e(B) if:

$$\tilde{\alpha}_l^s\beta_n^t + \tilde{\alpha}_l^t\beta_n^s \geq \alpha_n^t\tilde{\beta}_l^s + \alpha_n^s\tilde{\beta}_l^t \tag{9}$$

for all $s \leq t = 1, 2, \ldots, m$ and all $l = 1, 2, \ldots, n-1$.

(4) **e**(A) absolute super-Lorenz dominates **e**(B) if and only if:

$$\hat{\pi}_l\alpha_n^k - \tilde{\alpha}_l^k \leq \hat{\pi}_l\beta_n^k - \tilde{\beta}_l^k \tag{10}$$

for all $k = 2, \ldots, m$ and $l = 1, 2, \ldots, n-1$. The additional notations involved are: $\alpha_l^k = \sum_{j=k}^{m}\sum_{i=1}^{l}\pi_i\alpha_{ij}$, $\beta_l^k = \sum_{j=k}^{m}\sum_{i=1}^{l}\pi_i\beta_{ij}$, $\tilde{\pi}_l = \sum_{i=1}^{l}\pi_i$, $\tilde{\alpha}_l^k = \sum_{i=1}^{l}\alpha_i^k$, $\tilde{\beta}_l^k = \sum_{i=1}^{l}\beta_i^k$, and $\hat{\pi}_l = \sum_{i=1}^{l}\tilde{\pi}_i$.

Since the dominance conditions will necessarily produce incomplete rankings, we will also use two summary indices to aid our comparisons – one for welfare comparisons and one for inequality comparisons. For any income-happiness matrix A with socioeconomic structure $\{\pi_i\}$, its level of welfare can be measure by:

$$W(A) = \frac{m\sum_{i=1}^{n}(n-i+1)\pi_i - S(A)}{(m-1)\sum_{i=1}^{n}(n-i+1)\pi_i} \tag{11}$$

where $S(A)$ is the sum of all elements of the generalized-Lorenz-matrix $|\sum_{i=1}^{l}\sum_{j=1}^{k}\pi_i\alpha_{ij}|_{n\times m}$ that is associated with A. The level of absolute inequality associated with A can be measured by:

$$I(A) = \frac{S'(A)}{(m-1)\pi_n \sum_{i=1}^{n-1}(n-i)\pi_i} \tag{12}$$

where $S'(A)$ is the sum of all elements of the absolute-Lorenz-matrix $|\tilde{\pi}_l\alpha_n^k - \alpha_l^k|_{(n-1)\times(m-1)}$ that is associated with A.

THE RESULTS

The GSS has been conducted in the United States annually since 1972 (with a few gap years). The most recent year that the data are available is 2012. The survey collects answers to a set of demographic, behavioral, and attitudinal questions, plus some topics of special interest. We utilize the GSS data to analyze distributions of happiness and to compare socioeconomic inequality in happiness in recent years. To carry out the comparisons, we need to use both income and happiness variables. We test all even years between 1994 and 2012 (inclusive); the sample size ranges from 1,173 to 2,627. In each year, there are eight sets of inflation-adjusted income variables that group individuals into income intervals. But only variable INCOM06 – respondent's family income in current dollars – enables us to group families into income quintiles (income quintile cutoffs are available from the Current Population Survey (CPS) web site). We use family income to indicate a respondent's socioeconomic status without considering family size and structure.

Happiness in the United States: From 1994 to 2012

After dividing each sample into five groups (by income quintiles and thus $\pi_1 = \pi_2 = \pi_3 = \pi_4 = \pi_5 = 0.2$), we construct the income-happiness matrix by tallying up frequency distributions in each income quintile for all levels of happiness. Table 1 reports all 10 years' income-happiness matrices. In each

Table 1. Income-Happiness Matrices.

1994	*NTH*	*PH*	*VH*	1996	*NTH*	*PH*	*VH*
Q_1	18.97	62.84	18.19	Q_1	20.37	57.23	22.40
Q_2	12.19	61.21	26.60	Q_2	10.68	61.34	27.98
Q_3	8.96	60.22	30.83	Q_3	9.99	58.12	31.90
Q_4	7.33	58.42	34.25	Q_4	7.25	57.91	34.84
Q_5	6.38	50.56	43.06	Q_5	4.57	53.96	41.46
1998	*NTH*	*PH*	*VH*	2000	*NTH*	*PH*	*VH*
Q_1	22.01	55.68	22.31	Q_1	18.70	59.88	21.42
Q_2	12.11	59.94	27.95	Q_2	8.35	60.52	31.13
Q_3	8.40	58.98	32.62	Q_3	6.24	60.16	33.61
Q_4	3.90	56.86	39.23	Q_4	4.94	55.12	39.94
Q_5	3.19	48.90	47.91	Q_5	3.50	47.98	48.52
2002	*NTH*	*PH*	*VH*	2004	*NTH*	*PH*	*VH*
Q_1	20.07	59.90	20.02	Q_1	19.20	58.51	22.29
Q_2	11.40	59.29	29.31	Q_2	15.40	56.80	27.80
Q_3	8.94	56.20	34.86	Q_3	9.29	58.28	32.43
Q_4	6.86	58.06	35.07	Q_4	7.32	46.54	46.14
Q_5	5.54	53.67	40.79	Q_5	6.69	51.16	42.15
2006	*NTH*	*PH*	*VH*	2008	*NTH*	*PH*	*VH*
Q_1	22.33	55.46	22.21	Q_1	26.77	52.49	20.74
Q_2	12.63	63.89	23.48	Q_2	18.54	58.51	22.95
Q_3	9.39	57.34	33.28	Q_3	14.03	51.66	34.31
Q_4	5.58	53.77	40.65	Q_4	5.61	57.27	37.12
Q_5	4.47	48.80	46.74	Q_5	3.12	54.89	42.00
2010	*NTH*	*PH*	*VH*	2012	*NTH*	*PH*	*VH*
Q_1	24.34	56.30	19.36	Q_1	21.78	54.91	23.31
Q_2	14.83	64.16	21.01	Q_2	14.78	58.87	26.35
Q_3	12.82	58.88	28.30	Q_3	7.31	58.79	33.91
Q_4	9.31	55.87	34.82	Q_4	8.81	54.99	36.21
Q_5	5.30	59.12	35.58	Q_5	5.17	50.73	44.10

matrix, Q_i stands for the *i*th income quintile, *NTH* stands for "not too happy," *PH* is "pretty happy," and *VH* is "very happy."

Our first task is to test the monotone assumption, or the social-gradients-in-happiness hypothesis. The hypothesis requires that each row in each matrix second-degree stochastic dominates the row above it. For example, for the first two rows in the 1994 matrix, the condition is satisfied since $12.19 < 18.97$ and $12.19 + 61.21 < 18.97 + 62.84$ (no need to check the cumulations of all three numbers in each row since they are all summed up to 1). It is easy to verify that of the 10 matrices, the monotone condition is unequivocally satisfied by eight of them (1994, 1996, 1998, 2000, 2002, 2006, 2008, and 2010). Two years' matrices (2004 and 2012) slightly violate the assumption and each violates at one cell: in 2004, it is between row 4 and row 5 in the second happiness level ($6.69 < 7.32$ but $6.69 + 51.16 > 7.32 + 46.54$); in 2012, it is between row 3 and row 4 in the lowest happiness level ($8.81 > 7.31$). Since we do not perform statistical analysis, we have no way to tell whether the violation is statistically significant. But by the size of the violation, we suspect it could be well within the statistical boundary of measurement error. For this consideration, we include the two years in our comparisons below.

These matrices provide a strong support for the existence of the social-gradients-in-happiness assertion. The significance of our test lies in the fact that our approach is happiness-scaling free – the results are robust to any valuations of the happiness levels as long as they preserve the ordinal order that a higher level of happiness carries a larger value.

With the monotone assumption being largely verified, we turn to welfare ranking of happiness distributions: we aim at addressing the issue that which year's income-happiness matrix yields the highest aggregate (expected) happiness for the United States. Table 1 reports the results of the pair-wise comparisons among the 10 years. In the table, R stands for rank dominance, GL is generalized Lorenz dominance and GSL is generalized Super-Lorenz dominance. Recall that R compares the matrices cumulated row-wise eastbound, GL compares the matrices used in R that have been further cumulated column-wise southbound, and GSL is applied to further column-wise southbound cumulations. Of course, one could cumulate the matrices further in this manner and carry out additional comparisons. But these further steps require the imposition of additional restrictions on the happiness values (see Zheng, 2011 for more exposition). For this reason, we limit our rankings to the three levels listed above. It is useful to note that these relationships are nested: R implies GL, which further implies GSL. Thus, in the table we only list the lowest level at which dominance holds.

Table 2 summarizes pair-wise welfare ranking of happiness for every other year between 1994 and 2012 (inclusive). In the table, each year (row year) in the first column compares with each year (column year) in the first row and the resulting comparisons are given in the upper right triangle. If a row year rank dominates a column year, the lowest level of dominance is reported. For example, 1996 rank dominates 2010, an "R" is recorded (and both GL and GSL will hold as well). If a row year is dominated by a column year, then a notation "$\sim$" is added in front of the level of dominance.

Table 2. Socioeconomic Ranking of Happiness between 1994 and 2012.

	1996	1998	2000	2002	2004	2006	2008	2010	2012
1994	×	×	~*R*	×	×	×	×	×	×
1996		×	×	×	×	×	*GL*	*R*	×
1998			×	×	×	×	*GL*	*R*	×
2000				*GL*	×	*GL*	*GL*	*R*	×
2002					×	×	×	*GL*	×
2004						×	*GL*	*GL*	×
2006							*GL*	*R*	×
2008								×	~*GL*
2010									~*R*

For example, 1994 is rank dominated by 2000, then "~*R*" is recorded for the comparison. A "×" is recorded if the two years cannot be ranked by the three levels of dominance.

A tabulation of the table indicates that we are able to rank 16 out of 45 pair-wise comparisons: rank dominance (*R*) ranks six pairs, generalized Lorenz dominance (*GL*) picks up 10 more pairs while generalized super-Lorenz dominance (*GSL*) picks up nothing additional.

To see more clearly the pattern, we list in Table 3 the years that a given Year welfare dominates (under "Less Welfare Than") and is dominated (under "More Welfare Than") by any one or more of the three levels of dominance. From Table 3, we can draw several conclusions on the welfare ranking of happiness between 1994 and 2012. First, year 2000 seems to have the highest aggregate happiness as measured by different levels of dominance criteria. It dominates five other years (1994, 2002, 2006, 2008, and 2010) and crosses with four other years (1996, 1998, 2004, and 2012); the welfare indices reported in Table 3 indicates that 2000 has a higher aggregate value than the four crossing years. It also appears that year 2010 has the lowest level of aggregate happiness as it is dominated by all other years except 1994 and 2008; 2008 and 2010 cross at all levels of dominance considered but the indices in Table 3 indicate that 2010 has a lower value than 2008. The years 2000 and 2010 as the highest and lowest levels of aggregate happiness match well with what we have experienced: year 2000 was at the euphoric peak of the dot-com bubble and year 2010 was in the wake of heart-wrenching financial crisis. Year 2008 – right in the midst of the financial crisis – appears also to be close to the bottom of happiness ranking. All other years fall somewhere between 2000 and 2010/2008. The summary welfare indices reported in Table 4 present a complete ranking: it follows a more-or-less *N* pattern – aggregate happiness increases gradually

Table 3. Welfare Ranking Statistics.

Less welfare than	2000	2000	2000		2000		2000	2012 2006 2004 2000 1998 1996	2012 2006 2004 2002 2000 1998 1996	
Year	1994	1996	1998	2000	2002	2004	2006	2008	2010	2012
More welfare than		2008 2010	2008 2010	1994 2002 2006 2008 2010	2010	2008 2010	2008 2010			2008 2010

Table 4. Socioeconomic Indices of Happiness.

1994	1996	1998	2000	2002	2004	2006	2008	2010	2012
0.570	0.579	0.584	0.601	0.580	0.583	0.576	0.550	0.543	0.576

from 1994 and reaches its peak in 2000 and then declines gradually to the bottom year 2008/2010 and then tips up in 2012. This pattern again roughly confirms our experience of the period.

Inequality comparisons are quite different from welfare comparisons. Table 5 summarizes inequality-in-happiness comparisons among the 10 years. Of 45 pair-wise comparisons, 11 can be ranked by at least one of the four dominance conditions (absolute Lorenz dominance *AL*, relative Lorenz dominance *RL*, absolute super-Lorenz dominance *ASL*, and relative super-Lorenz dominance *RSL*). Also to see more clearly the years that each year dominates and dominated, Table 6 lists two groups of the years for that purpose. From Table 6, we can draw two conclusions. First, it does not appear there is a link between inequality ordering and welfare ordering: there are pairs of years that inequality and welfare rankings move in the same direction (1996 vs. 2008 and 2008 vs. 2012) where lower inequality is accompanied by higher welfare, in more pairs the directions are opposite (e.g., 1994 vs. 2000, 1996 vs. 2008, 2000 vs. 2002) where lower inequality is in tandem also with lower welfare. Second, the years 2000 and 2008/2010 are now much less clear to associate with the highest or lowest-inequality

Table 5. Socioeconomic Ranking of Inequality in Happiness between 1994 and 2012.

	1996	1998	2000	2002	2004	2006	2008	2010	2012
1994	×	×	*AL*	×	×	×	×	×	×
1996		*AL* RL	×	×	×	*AL* RL	*AL* RL	×	*ASL*
1998			×	×	×	×	×	~*ASL* ~*RSL*	~*AL* ~*RL*
2000				~*ASL*	×	×	×	×	×
2002					×	×	×	×	×
2004						×	×	×	×
2006							×	×	~*ASL* ~*RSL*
2008								~*AL* ~*RSL*	~*ASL* ~*RSL*
2010									×

Table 6. Inequality Ranking Statistics.

Year	1994	1996	1998	2000	2002	2004	2006	2008	2010	2012
More unequal than			2012 2010 1996	2002 1994			2012 1996	2012 2010		1996
Less unequal than	2000	1998 2006 2008 2012			2000			1996	1998	1998 2006 2008

Table 7. Socioeconomic Indices of Absolute Inequality in Happiness.

1994	1996	1998	2000	2002	2004	2006	2008	2010	2012
0.219	0.200	0.271	0.242	0.202	0.228	0.273	0.292	0.225	0.227

years. The summary indices of inequality do not indicate a clear time trend either (Table 7). They however show that year 1996 as the year with the lowest inequality in happiness and 2008 as the year with the highest inequality – it is also the year with the lowest welfare. It is interesting to see that the financial crisis may not only lower the level of happiness, it also stirs up unevenness in happiness.

Happiness Comparisons of Subgroups by Gender, Race, and Age

There are reasons to believe that people from different groups may possess different associations between socioeconomic status and the level of happiness. For example, a man and a woman from the same socioeconomic class may be quite different in reporting their levels of happiness since they may face very different circumstances and bear very different responsibilities. Similarly, a retired individual may be quite different in assessing quality of life than a working individual who may have many obligations (tuitions to pay for children's education and/or aging parents to take care of) that a retired individual may not have, even though both individuals belong to the same socioeconomic class (say, upper middle class). It is therefore useful to decompose the socioeconomic status – happiness relationship along the line of different population subgroups. In this section, we compare and contrast that relationship between subpopulations by gender, race, and age, respectively. To preserve space we conduct the analyses only for 2000 and 2010 – the supposedly peak and bottom years for aggregate happiness. We form these subgroups by the characteristics of the respondents: both gender and race are straightforward, the age subgroups are formed by those respondents aged between 20 and 60 (working subgroup) and those above 60 (retired subgroup).

A potentially serious problem in this decomposition exercise is that samples for some subpopulations may be getting too small. To test the monotone assumption and the different welfare and inequality ranking conditions, we need sufficiently large samples to estimate each income-happiness matrix which has 15 cells to tabulate. Small sample sizes may introduce too much variability in the calculations – this is indeed confirmed in the subgroups of black and retired subgroups. Notwithstanding this problem, we go ahead with our decomposition and hope we can revisit the issues with larger samples some day in the future.

Table 8 reports the income-happiness matrices for male and female subgroups in 2000 and 2010. The first task is to verify the satisfaction of the monotone assumption by the two matrices in both years. The male group clearly exhibits the pattern of social gradients in happiness but the female group slightly violates the assumption in each year. Again the lack of statistical inference makes it difficult to judge whether the violation is purely a sampling noise or reflects a fundamental problem. Although female group "almost" welfare dominates the male group in both years, a clear dominance is not achieved by neither generalized Lorenz dominance nor generalized super-Lorenz dominance. But the welfare index shows that the female

Table 8. Decomposition by Gender.

Male	*NTH*	*PH*	*VH*	Female	*NTH*	*PH*	*VH*
				2000			
Q_1	20.52	57.34	22.14	Q_1	17.75	61.20	21.05
Q_2	8.57	61.72	29.71	Q_2	8.14	59.40	32.47
Q_3	8.31	61.36	30.33	Q_3	4.19	58.96	36.85
Q_4	4.84	56.44	38.72	Q_4	5.07	53.71	41.22
Q_5	2.90	51.09	46.01	Q_5	4.21	44.32	51.47
$W(Male) = 0.590$				$W(Female) = 0.610$			
$I(Male) = 0.2391$				$I(Female) = 0.249$			
				2010			
Q_1	25.59	54.68	19.73	Q_1	23.61	57.24	19.14
Q_2	19.60	60.16	20.24	Q_2	10.43	67.86	21.71
Q_3	13.23	58.05	28.72	Q_3	12.49	59.57	27.94
Q_4	12.88	56.45	30.67	Q_4	5.59	55.27	39.15
Q_5	6.19	63.10	30.71	Q_5	4.30	54.68	41.02
$W(Male) = 0.527$				$W(Female) = 0.558$			
$I(Male) = 0.195$				$I(Female) = 0.262$			

group has more aggregate happiness than the male group – this seems to be a sensible conclusion. As for inequality comparisons, again both relative Lorenz and absolute Lorenz dominance conditions (and their super versions) fail to clearly rank between the two subgroups in each year. The summary indices reveal that female group's happiness is more unequal than the male group in both years. So the female group is happier than the male group but the level of happiness is also more uneven than the male group.

Table 9 documents the results for the white and black population subgroups. The monotone assumption is satisfied by the white subgroup but it is now more seriously violated by the black subgroup. The violation is more pronounced maybe mainly due to the much smaller sample sizes of the black subgroup. But interestingly, in year 2000, the white group generalized Lorenz dominates the black group – the former has more aggregate happiness than the latter. There is no inequality ranking between the two groups – even the summary indices do not agree between the two years.

Finally Table 10 documents welfare and inequality comparisons by age. Again small sample sizes for the retired group generates a lot of noises as in verifying the monotone assumption. The working group clearly satisfies the monotone assumption in both years. Interestingly, the retired group

Table 9. Decomposition by Race.

White	*NTH*	*PH*	*VH*	Black	*NTH*	*PH*	*VH*
			2000				
Q_1	16.30	60.69	23.01	Q_1	24.29	58.74	16.96
Q_2	8.13	59.95	31.92	Q_2	8.87	59.19	31.94
Q_3	5.01	61.35	33.64	Q_3	11.25	60.27	28.47
Q_4	3.61	55.02	41.37	Q_4	7.62	50.78	41.60
Q_5	2.57	46.33	51.09	Q_5	8.49	57.61	33.92
$W(White) = 0.613$				$W(Black) = 0.567$			
$I(White) = 0.244$				$I(Black) = 0.191$			
			2010				
Q_1	23.47	58.64	17.89	Q_1	26.78	52.95	20.27
Q_2	15.00	62.70	22.30	Q_2	18.35	65.51	16.14
Q_3	13.09	58.32	28.59	Q_3	11.96	59.28	28.75
Q_4	6.67	54.38	38.95	Q_4	29.57	53.81	16.62
Q_5	3.65	61.01	35.35	Q_5	0.00	45.86	54.14
$W(White) = 0.548$				$W(Black) = 0.512$			
$I(White) = 0.249$				$I(Black) = 0.276$			

Table 10. Decomposition by Age.

Working	*NTH*	*PH*	*VH*	Retired	*NTH*	*PH*	*VH*
			2000				
Q_1	19.87	58.85	21.26	Q_1	15.75	62.74	21.52
Q_2	8.79	64.17	27.04	Q_2	5.84	44.88	49.28
Q_3	6.01	59.92	34.07	Q_3	8.62	57.29	34.09
Q_4	3.77	56.02	40.22	Q_4	11.45	47.72	40.83
Q_5	3.74	49.36	46.90	Q_5	2.84	33.85	63.31
$W(Working) = 0.593$				$W(Retired) = 0.633$			
$I(Working) = 0.254$				$I(Retired) = 0.238$			
			2010				
Q_1	25.11	56.15	18.73	Q_1	23.18	56.61	20.21
Q_2	16.03	65.12	18.85	Q_2	10.91	61.98	27.11
Q_3	13.12	59.12	27.76	Q_3	11.73	58.62	29.65
Q_4	8.60	55.78	35.62	Q_4	13.05	54.57	32.38
Q_5	4.65	58.34	37.00	Q_5	8.02	59.61	32.37
$W(Working) = 0.537$				$W(Retired) = 0.556$			
$I(Working) = 0.254$				$I(Retired) = 0.144$			

dominates the working group in 2000 both in welfare and inequality – the retired people are happier than the people still at work and their happiness is also more evenly distributed. In 2010, only welfare dominance holds between the two groups while inequality dominance is now slightly violated. Summary indices confirm that in both years the retired people are happier and also enjoy happiness more evenly compared with people still relying on paychecks.

CONCLUSIONS

Seeking an alternative and supplemental indicator to GDP as a measure of aggregate well-being for a nation has generated several lines of new research. Happiness, as a self-reported assessment of individual's utility, has been argued to reflect other aspects of individual well-being that income cannot capture. As a result of this understanding, it is a meaningful exercise to aggregate happiness in a society and evaluate the distribution of it across individuals. In light of the close association between an individual's socioeconomic status and the level of happiness, a related issue that needs to be examined is how socioeconomic structure (often is proxied by income distribution) affects happiness aggregation and happiness distribution. In other words, to what extent that the level of happiness and the inequality of happiness are determined by the socioeconomic structure.

The objective of this paper has been to apply a method recently developed in measuring socioeconomic inequality in health to measuring happiness distribution. The level of happiness and the self-reported health status have much in common: both are subjective and both are reported as categorical values. In practice, researchers often assign specific but arbitrary numbers to the different categories. The new method proposed in measuring socioeconomic inequality in health (Zheng, 2011) does not hinge on what numbers are assigned to the categories. The method, however, does require a monotone condition or the so-called social gradients in health outcomes – a richer person tends to have better health – which has been repeatedly verified in the health literature. In applying the method to measuring happiness, a first task is to establish and verify a similar monotone assumption for happiness or a social gradients in happiness – a richer person tends to be happier. Once this assumption is upheld, happiness aggregation between different happiness distributions is rank ordered via rank dominance, generalized Lorenz dominance and an extension (generalized super-Lorenz dominance) – standard tools in measuring income distributions. The socioeconomic inequality in happiness is studied through relative and absolute Lorenz dominances and their extensions.

We apply the method to the GSS data and examine happiness and its distribution between 1994 and 2012 (the most recent year that the data are available). We also apply the method to rank and compare happiness between subpopulations by gender (male vs. female), race (white vs. black) and age (working vs. retired) in two years (2000 and 2010). First, we test the monotone assumption for each year. The monotone condition (3) is clearly satisfied by eight years and for the reaming two years (2004 and 2012) the condition is slightly violated. The monotone condition fares less well in population subgroups. This, we believe, has much to do with the small samples that we have. In testing the monotone condition, each year and each subgroup's data need to be divided to estimate 15 cells in each matrix. For some subgroups, there are just not enough data to do the job. For example, there are only 277 data points in the 2010 black subpopulation. But for large subpopulations such as whites and the working group, the monotone assumption has been shown to be valid.

The incomplete rankings of happiness distributions between 1994 and 2012 by the method, together with complete rankings by the summary indices, indicate that the year 2000 is likely to be the year with highest aggregate socioeconomic happiness while the year 2010 seems to be the year (or one of two years) with the lowest level of happiness. The pattern for socioeconomic inequality in happiness is less apparent. The summary indices calculated from the matrices confirm that 2000 and 2010 as the two years with the maximum and minimum levels of aggregate happiness; 1996 and 2008 are the two years with the lowest and highest levels of inequality. Summary indices also indicate that female group has both a higher level of welfare and a higher level of inequality in happiness than the male group; the white group has a higher level of happiness than the black group; the retired people are happier and share happiness more evenly than the grumpy working class.

NOTE

1. Some writers (e.g., Lane, 2000) believe that happiness has diminishing marginal utility and, thus, it may be reasonable to assume the scale of happiness is concave, i.e., $h_i - h_{i-1} \geq h_{i-1} - h_{i-2}$. But some (Desai, 2007) believe that the scale ought to convex. In this paper, we do not want to side with either side of the debate; we allow for all possible scaling, concave and convex alike.

REFERENCES

Allison, R. A., & Foster, J. E. (2004). Measuring health inequality using qualitative data. *Journal of Health Economics*, *23*, 505–524.

Clark, A. E., Frijters, P., & Shields, M. A. (2008). Relative income, happiness, and utility: An explanation for the Easterlin paradox and other puzzles. *Journal of Economic Literature*, *46*, 95–144.

Costanza, R., Hart, M., Posner, S., & Talbert, J. (2009). *Beyond GDP: The need for new measures of progress*. Pardee Paper No. 4. Pardee Center for the Study of the Longer-Range Future, Boston, MA.

Deaton, A., & Paxson, C. (1998). Aging and inequality in income and health. *American Economic Review (Papers and Proceedings)*, *88*, 248–253.

DeNeve, K., & Cooper, H. M. (1999). The happy personality: A meta-analysis of 137 personality traits of subjective well-being. *Psychological Bulletin*, *125*, 197–229.

Desai, R. (2007, November). *The political economy of poverty reduction. Scaling up anti-poverty programs in the developing world.* Working Paper No. 2. The Brookings Institution, Wolfensohn Center for Development, Washington, DC. Retrieved from http://www.brookings.edu/~/media/research/files/papers/2007/11/poverty%20desai/11_poverty_desai.pdf

Dutta, I., & Foster, J. E. (2013). Inequality of happiness in the U.S. 1972–2010. *Review of Income and Wealth*, *59*, 393–415.

Lane, R. E. (2000). Diminishing returns to income, companionship – and happiness. *Journal of Happiness Studies*, *1*, 103–119.

Marmot, M. (2003). Understanding social inequalities in health. *Perspectives in Biology and Medicine*, *46*(Suppl.), S9–S23.

Stevenson, B., & Wolfers, J. (2008). Happiness inequality in the United States. *Journal of Legal Studies*, *37*, S33–S79.

van Pragg, B. M. S. (1991). Ordinal and cardinal utility: An integration of the two dimensions in the welfare concept. *Journal of Econometrics*, *50*, 69–89.

Veenhoven, R. (2005). Return of inequality in modern society? Test by dispersion of life satisfaction across time and nations. *Journal of Happiness Studies*, *6*, 457–487.

Wagstaff, A., Paci, P., & van Doorslaer, E. (1991). On the measurement of inequalities in health. *Social Science and Medicine*, *33*, 545–557.

Zheng, B. (2011). A new approach to measure socioeconomic inequality in health. *Journal of Economic Inequality*, *9*, 555–577.

CROSS-COUNTRY INTERGENERATIONAL STATUS MOBILITY: IS THERE A GREAT GATSBY CURVE?

John A. Bishop, Haiyong Liu and Juan Gabriel Rodríguez

ABSTRACT

Countries with greater income inequality also tend to have less intergenerational mobility. This relationship, as referred by Krueger (2012), is called "The Great Gatsby Curve." Criticisms on this curve have brought to notice several limitations of previous studies: a few number of observations; short gap of time between measured inequality and immobility; heterogeneous databases; and model-based estimates of immobility. To correct for some of these limitations, we test for the impact of past income inequality on intergenerational social status persistence using the International Social Survey Program (2009). In accordance with previous studies, we find a positive relationship between these two variables, though the relatively poor model fit suggests the presence of other factors. In this respect, we find that past economic freedom has a negative

Economic Well-Being and Inequality: Papers from the Fifth ECINEQ Meeting
Research on Economic Inequality, Volume 22, 237–249

ISSN: 1049-2585/doi:10.1108/S1049-258520140000022007

and significant impact on social status persistence, while previous growth is not significant.

Keywords: Intergenerational mobility; income inequality

JEL classifications: I3; D3

INTRODUCTION

The "Great Gatsby Curve" is the name given by Alan Krueger (2012) to the relationship between intergenerational earnings elasticity's and income inequality. Corak (2013a) described the Great Gatsby Curve as the tendency of countries with higher income inequality to be countries where a greater fraction of economic advantage and disadvantage is passed on from parents to children. The debate on this proposal has spread to the blogs of Paul Krugman and Greg Mankiw as well as the popular press (*NPR News Hour, Economist Magazine and the National Review*). Krueger (2013) has further stimulated the debate by projecting that growing income inequality would lead to a substantial decline in future social mobility in the United States. But, why is the Great Gatsby Curve raising so much debate?

It is often argued that income inequality is fine as long as there is income mobility. Therefore, if the Great Gatsby curve holds true, countries would not compensate for income inequality through income mobility. The greater the distance in a country between a high and a low income, the harder it would be to go from the latter to the former or vice versa. Unfortunately, the few number of observations available for the intergenerational elasticity of earnings allows only a correlation analysis. Thus, Corak (2013a) recognized that the Great Gatsby Curve is not a causal relationship.[1] Worse still, the elasticity estimates come from independent studies which consider databases with different levels of reliability and measures of income defined in a different way across countries. Another difficulty worth mentioning is that elasticity estimates are generally based on models. Ideally, the analyses should use real data from adults and their parents when they were children. However, many countries do not conduct studies tracking children's income as they grow older, so researchers must estimate childhood income using an algorithm obtained from a separate data set and compare the result against actual adult–child income.

In addition to these technical problems, there are other important criticisms. Because the reasoning behind the Great Gatsby Curve is that past inequality diminishes current opportunities, the temporal gap between both, inequality and intergenerational elasticity of earnings, should be sufficiently large. Otherwise, the Great Gatsby Curve would just reflect that intergenerational immobility and cross-sectional inequality are related to each other because they shared common factors (Björklund & Jäntti, 1997; Solon, 2004). For example, the Great Gatsby Curve in the work of Corak (2013b) and Krueger (2013) is calculated from inequality data for 1985, and intergenerational income mobility measures for cohorts of children born during the early to mid-1960s with adult outcomes measured in the mid to late 1990s. That is, the temporal gap considered is approximately one decade. This gap does not seem to be sufficiently large to avoid the fact that common factors to both variables might drive the estimation of the curve. Finally, Clark (2014) using surname data suggests that the relationship between inequality and mobility disappears over sufficiently long time periods.

In this paper, we try to palliate these shortcomings. First, the largest number of observations used in the analysis of the Great Gatsby Curve is, as far as we are aware, 22 countries (Corak, 2013b). By exploiting the module Social Inequality Survey IV (2009) of the International Social Survey Program (ISSP), we are able to extend the analysis to 39 countries. Second, the ISSP is the result of a cross-national collaboration so the databases are homogeneous and the measures of income are similar across countries. Third, the surveys in the module Social Inequality Survey IV (2009) ask respondents both their current position in the social status hierarchy as well as the position of the family they grew up in. Finally, we use the Gini coefficient for circa 1990, while the intergenerational elasticity in status is measured in 2009. Hence, the temporal gap considered in this study is almost two decades. Accordingly, elasticity estimates are based on individual perceptions of status mobility, rather than models. In principle, the Great Gatsby Curve refers to the impact of past income inequality on intergenerational income persistence rather than intergenerational status immobility. For this reason, we will ask the related question: Is there a Social Status Great Gatsby Curve?

Apart from testing for the Social Status Great Gatsby Curve, we also test for a second hypothesis: greater economic freedom enhances intergenerational mobility. By limiting nepotism and launching meritocracy in society, economic freedom could be a significant source of intergenerational mobility. Taking advantage of the existence of the Fraser Economic Freedom Index for 1990,[2] we evaluate the impact of this dimension in intergenerational mobility as well. The obtained results are: past inequality has a significant and positive effect on the intergenerational elasticity of social status, but this factor alone is far from explaining the whole variability of this elasticity. Interestingly enough, we find that past economic freedom is also important, namely, it has a significant and negative effect on social status persistence. Meanwhile, previous growth does not seem to exert any influence on social status mobility.

In the next section, we briefly compare the intergenerational elasticity of earnings with the alternative measure used in this paper, the intergenerational elasticity of social status. Then, in the section "Data," the data are presented and the intergenerational elasticity of social status is calculated for all the countries in the sample. The section "Empirical Results" presents and comments the results on the Social Status Great Gatsby Curve and the Economic Freedom Hypothesis. The final section concludes.

ESTIMATION OF THE INTERGENERATIONAL ELASTICITY

The elasticity of intergenerational mobility denotes the persistence in the values of relevant variables like income, earnings, wealth, status, education attainment, consumption, or occupations between parents and children. Thus, in the canonical Galton (1869) regression of a child's outcome (y_{it}) on the parent's outcome (y_{it-1}):[3]

$$\ln y_{it} = \alpha + \beta \ln y_{it-1} + \varepsilon_{it} \quad (1)$$

the constant term α captures the trend in average outcomes across generations due to changes in technology, labor market institutions, international trade, and the like. The error term ε_{it} represents all other influences on the child's adult outcome not correlated with parental outcome. And the coefficient β, called intergenerational elasticity, measures the degree of persistence in a family's outcome across generations. The higher the value of β, the larger the capacity of parent's outcome to predict children's achievement. Accordingly, $1 - \beta$ is a measure of intergenerational mobility.[4]

This model which applies only to quantitative variables can be easily estimated by least squares. However, note that the intergenerational elasticity offers an overall average measure of the degree of immobility without saying anything about the direction of change. Cross-country differences may reflect differences not only in the degree of upward mobility, but also in the magnitude of downward mobility. In addition, this approach does not allow us to study mobility of subgroups across the full distribution, that is, the percentile of the child's variable conditional on the percentile of the parent's variable.

Bearing in mind all these premises, we follow this approach to estimate the elasticity of intergenerational mobility in social status. In principle, the Great Gatsby Curve refers to the effect that past income inequality has on intergenerational income persistence.[5] Therefore, because we analyze here the individual's current position in the social status hierarchy in comparison with the position of the family that he grew up in, we actually ask: Is there a Social Status Great Gatsby Curve?

DATA

The ISSP is a cross-national collaboration of survey's covering topics of interest to social science research. To date, the data consists of 26 modules, beginning with six countries in the 1985 Role of Government module to as many as 40 countries in later surveys. Module topics include religion, citizenship, health, environment, and social inequality, among others. We are primarily interested in the social inequality modules. These began in 1987 and were repeated for 1992, 1997, and 2009. In the first three modules the survey asked the respondent to report their individual perceptions of upward or downward mobility within the past 10 years. Importantly, this survey question was modified for 2009 and now asks one's individual perception of mobility relative to the family you grew up in. This provides the measure of *intergenerational* social mobility for our study.

The Social Inequality IV (2009) module includes 40 countries, 39 of which are included in our study (reasons for excluding the United States are discussed below). Sample sizes vary from 1,335 responses (China) to 233 responses (Estonia) with the median number of responses for a country being more than 500 responses. As a legacy of earlier surveys, "East" and "West" Germany were surveyed separately; we construct separate mean responses for each region and create "Germany" as a population weighted average. We address the separation of Great Britain and Northern Ireland in a similar manner.

Fig. 1 provides the actual social status questions. Respondents are asked to place themselves on a ladder scale from 1 to 10. They are then asked to

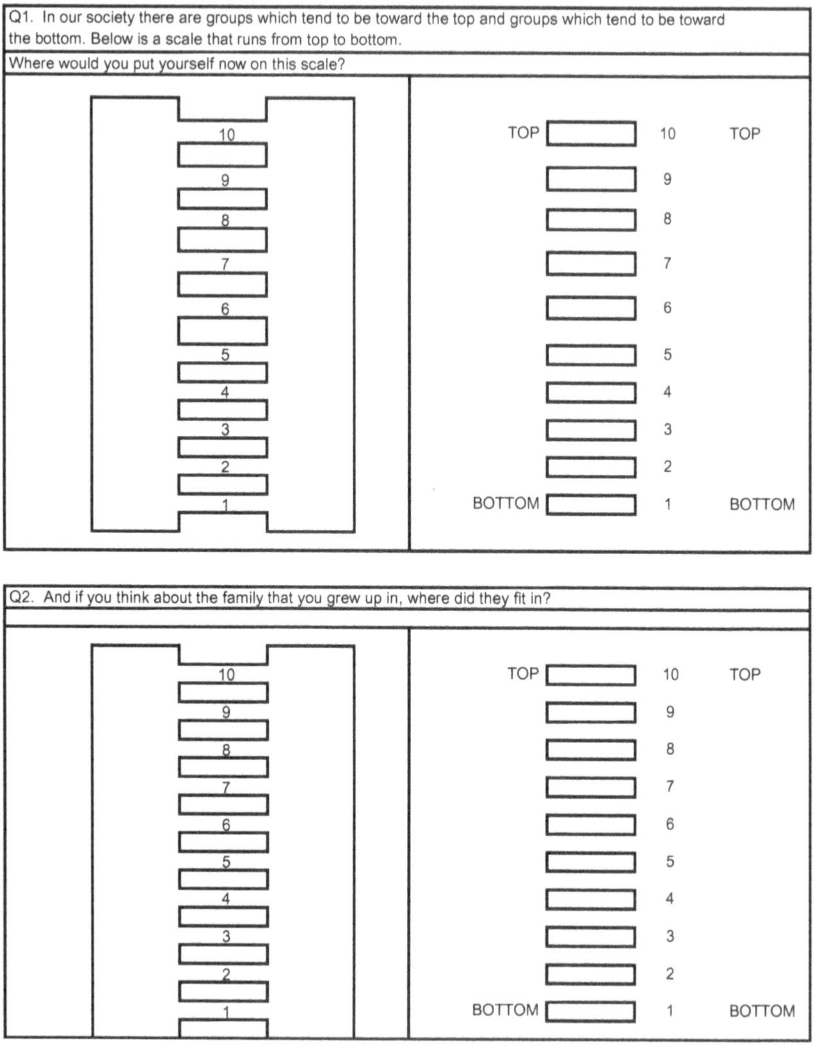

Fig. 1. Social Mobility Questions in the ISSP Social Inequality Module (2009).

place the families they grew up in on the same scale. We measure social mobility by the relationship between these two positions.

In order to summarize the social mobility data, Table 1 provides differences in the current position relative to the family of birth. The 39 countries

Table 1. Net Change in Position: Current versus Family Grew up in.

Position	<−3	−3	−2	−1	None	+1	+2	+3	>+3	Average
High income	2.07	2.71	5.92	10.30	37.16	18.84	13.57	5.79	3.64	0.40
Middle income	2.69	3.16	6.28	8.40	35.71	18.63	14.74	6.67	2.43	0.42
Low income	5.57	4.94	8.44	11.15	37.26	14.88	9.33	4.51	3.93	−0.04
All countries	3.79	3.831	7.10	10.43	37.00	16.96	11.76	5.32	1.54	0.37

Notes: "None" implies percent who report no change in social status relative to "family they grew up in"; "−1" implies moved down one position (out of 10); "+1" implies moved up one position; and, "±3" implies moved 3 or more places relative to the family they grew up in.

in our sample are sorted by GDP per capita into high-, middle-, and low-income groups. In the center of the table is "NONE," implying no change in current position relative to parental family position. Surprisingly, we find little difference in the degree of social stability across income groups – in each case about 36–37% of respondents report no change in social status. Roughly speaking, regardless of income level, about one-third of respondents report no status change, one-third move up or down by one position, and one-third move up or down by more than one position. While we cannot strictly say that social mobility does not vary by the level of country income, the lack of mobility difference across income groups is noteworthy. Finally, we detect a small positive bias (see "average" column) in the responses of middle and upper income respondents – more people say they moved up than down in a zero sum process. Low-income countries report no such bias as the net position change is reported as −0.04.[6]

Inequality and Social Status

We follow Corak and summarize social status mobility with the status elasticities (see the section "Estimation of the Intergenerational Elasticity"). Table 2 reports the social status elasticities for 39 countries. The average status elasticity for our 39 countries is 0.46 which is 40% larger than Corak's (2013a) earning elasticity.[7] The United States is included in *Social Inequality IV* but its elasticity is not reported in Table 2. We exclude the United States from our analysis because it's estimated social status elasticity is negative, oddly implying that high status persons come from low-status families. The United States is the only country with a negative elasticity. To follow up on this issue, we also estimated the 10 year status mobility elasticity using the related question in *Social Inequality III*. Again,

Table 2. Cross-Country Social Status Persistence Elasticity (Ordered Lowest to Highest).

Rank	Country	Social Elasticity (2009)	Gini (1990)	Freedom Index (1990)
1	Latvia	0.234	22.5	47
2	Germany	0.285	25.6	64
3	Austria	0.299	23.6	55
4	Switzerland	0.311	33.8	73
5	Republic of Korea	0.313	33.6	50
6	Croatia	0.327	22.8	24
7	Australia	0.366	26.6	63
8	New Zealand	0.367	31.8	63
9	Iceland	0.368	33.1	49
10	Norway	0.373	22.2	48
11	China	0.376	32.4	39
12	Denmark	0.389	22.6	48
13	Taiwan	0.393	31.2	62
14	Hungary	0.397	27.3	30
15	Estonia	0.400	23.0	56
16	Ukraine	0.408	23.3	34
17	France	0.413	29.0	55
18	Sweden	0.413	20.9	47
19	Slovenia	0.426	23.6	38
20	Spain	0.455	33.7	47
21	Japan	0.457	30.4	69
22	Belgium	0.472	27.4	59
23	Argentina	0.473	46.6	43
24	Cyprus	0.489	29.0	36
25	Finland	0.489	20.9	48
26	Poland	0.491	26.9	28
27	United Kingdom	0.519	35.4	67
28	Russian Federation	0.532	23.8	9
29	Venezuela, RB	0.542	43.8	55
30	Italy	0.544	29.7	50
31	Turkey	0.576	43.6	48
32	Chile	0.580	55.3	56
33	Czech Republic	0.585	23.2	52
34	Israel	0.608	32.9	31
35	Portugal	0.637	32.9	43
36	Bulgaria	0.647	23.4	18
37	Slovak Republic	0.675	19.5	49
38	Philippines	0.677	40.6	58
39	South Africa	0.716	63.0	46

we find the US 10 year status elasticity is negative while all other countries have positive status elasticities. Perhaps the idea of social status is repugnant to Americans – in any case we do not include the United States in our sample.

The countries are presented from the lowest elasticity (least social persistence) to highest elasticity (greatest social persistence). Note that an elasticity of "0" implies no relationship between parental family position and current position while an elasticity of "1" suggests that family position perfectly predicts current position. The elasticities range from 0.234 in Latvia to 0.716 in South Africa. Germany and Austria are among the countries with the lowest persistence, Sweden and Japan are in the middle, and the Slovak Republic and the Philippines along with South Africa are the countries with the highest social persistence.

In order to test the Great Gatsby Hypothesis with social status mobility, we need lagged Gini values. Table 1 provides Gini coefficients collected from the World Bank and the OECD. In the same manner as Corak, we use Gini values lagged 20 years, or circa 1990. For the former socialist countries of Eastern Europe, the first Gini values available are from 1993. The lagged Gini values vary from a low of 19.5 in the Slovak Republic to 63.0 in South Africa. It is interesting to note that the Slovak Republic has one of the smallest lagged Gini values while South Africa has one of the highest.

In addition to the lagged Gini values, which we use to test the Great Gatsby Hypothesis, Table 2 also includes the Fraser Economic Freedom Index. While the Great Gatsby Hypothesis implies higher lagged Gini values lead to more social persistence we test a second hypothesis that greater economic freedom allows greater social mobility.

Given the data used to estimate the intergenerational elasticity of social status, it is worth commenting one potential limitation of this study. In principle, it is possible that people measure intergenerational status mobility in different latent scales so our measure, individual perception of intergenerational status mobility, could be biased. However, it is interesting to note that the literature on happiness which is mainly based on reported life satisfaction, has found little evidence of reporting bias in practice (see Beegle, Himelein, & Ravallion, 2012; Clark, Fleche, & Senik, 2012 and references therein). In accordance with this finding and to make our measure consistent with the previous literature, which focuses on a more objective measurable outcome, such as income or earnings, we assume that reporting biases are negligible.

EMPIRICAL RESULTS

Fig. 2 and Table 3 present the social mobility Great Gatsby Curve. While we find a positive and significant relationship between the lagged Gini coefficient the model fit is very poor ($R^2 = 0.18$ compared to Corak's model,

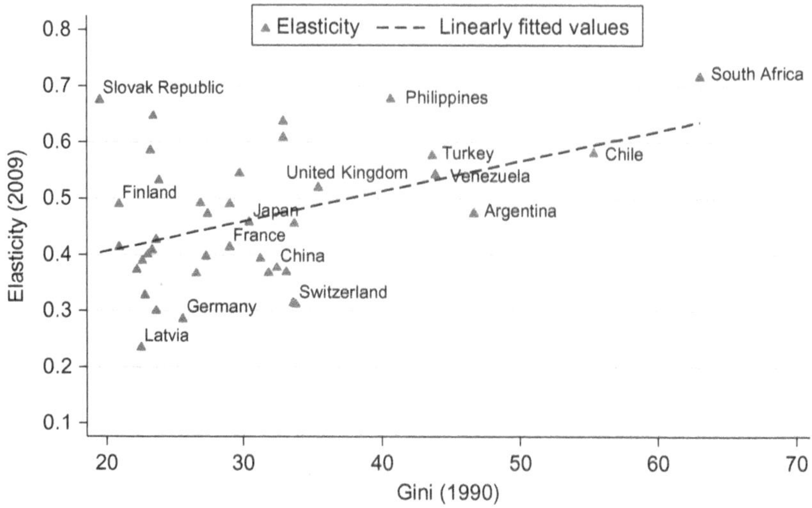

Fig. 2. Social Mobility Great Gatsby Curve.

Table 3. Social Status Persistence Regressions.

Explanatory	Dependent Variable: Social Status Elasticity (2009)			
	Model 1	Model 2	Model 3	Model 4
Gini (1990)	0.005*	0.007*	0.006*	0.006*
	(0.002)	(0.002)	(0.002)	(0.002)
Freedom Index (1990)	–	–	−0.003*	−0.003*
			(0.001)	(0.001)
GDP Growth (1995–2008)	–	–	–	−0.005
				(0.013)
Eastern Europe	–	0.072	–	–
		(0.040)		
Intercept	0.299	0.229	0.403	0.428
Observations	39	39	39	39
R^2	0.18	0.24	0.28	0.28

Note: Standard errors in parenthesis.
*Significant at 10%, **significant at 5%, ***significant at 1%.

$R^2 = 0.76$). Furthermore, the magnitude of the lagged Gini effect is about four times smaller in the social mobility case as opposed to Coraks' results (0.005 vs. 0.022). Of course, Corak is measuring father–son earnings elasticity and we are measuring self-reported social mobility for all respondents.

Table 3 further investigates the determinants of the relationship by introducing additional control variables. In particular, we would like to address several issues. First, of the 39 countries in our sample, 11 are former socialist countries of Eastern Europe. In most cases these countries experienced a significant increase in their Gini coefficients over time. Second, we hypothesize that social mobility is directly related to economic freedom – a country with a poor record of economic freedom will not generate opportunities for its citizens to rise in the social status distribution. We estimate the effect of economic freedom on social status mobility using the Fraser Institute Index of Economic Freedom (see Table 2). Finally, we control directly for the effect of economic growth on social status mobility using the change in GDP per capita between 1995 and 2008.

The first column in Table 3 presents the Great Gatsby Curve estimation results (as shown in Fig. 1). Model 2 controls for the 11 Eastern European countries. We find that the Eastern Europe indicator variable is positive, but with a p-value that is just above 0.10; however, adding the Eastern Europe control does improve R^2 to 0.24. Next, we test the hypothesis that economic freedom is negatively related to social status persistence. Model 3 confirms our conjecture – the negative sign for the Freedom variable indicates that social persistence declines with an increase in the degree of economic freedom. Importantly, controlling for economic freedom does not change the positive relationship between the lagged Gini coefficient and social status persistence. This implies that both factors influence social mobility; high degrees of inequality and the lack of economic freedom both hinder social mobility. Finally, Model 4 controls for GDP growth between 1995 and 2008. Here we find that growth has no significant impact on social mobility.

CONCLUSIONS

This paper addresses two hypotheses, the Social Status Great Gatsby Hypothesis – higher inequality leads to less social mobility, and the Economic Freedom Hypothesis – greater Economic Freedom leads to greater social mobility. Using data on 39 countries from the ISSP Social

Inequality Survey (2009), our estimation results are consistent with both of these hypotheses: intergenerational elasticity of social status is positively affected by economic inequality and negatively affected by economic freedom. However, growth is found not to have any influence on social status mobility. Despite these results, the relatively poor fit of the model suggests that other factors yet uncovered could be also explaining differences in social status mobility across countries.

NOTES

1. Corak believes it is "too glib to dismiss it by simply saying correlation does not imply causation." In his view, the Great Gatsby Curve summarizes the "whole host of ways that inequality of incomes affects children" (2013a, p. 7).
2. See Gwartney, Lawson, and Block (1996).
3. To enable a broader set of cross-country comparisons, the literature has typically focused on the outcomes of fathers and sons since the analysis needed to address the changing role of women in the labor force is more complicated. Since we are measuring social status, not earnings, we include females in our analysis.
4. See Mulligan (1997) for a detailed description of this model.
5. There are two potential advantages of using self-reported social status persistence as opposed to earnings persistence. First, the inherent randomness of earnings is greater than that of social status (see Clark, 2014). Earnings depend on occupational choice and the short-run volatility of the economy, while status is quite stable over time. Second, parental earnings are usually declared at the particular moment when the survey takes place, while reported parental status usually reflects a whole-life (long-term) position in the labor market.
6. Most countries report values close to ± 0.5, however China reports a +1 while the Ukraine reports a -1.
7. This is consistent with Clark's (2014) argument that status is less subject to random shocks than earnings. Our estimates are smaller than "Clark's Rule" of 0.75.

REFERENCES

Beegle, K., Himelein, K., & Ravallion, M. (2012). Frame-of-reference bias in subjective welfare. *Journal of Economic Behavior and Organization*, *81*, 556–570.

Björklund, A., & Jäntti, M. (1997). Intergenerational income mobility in Sweden compared to the United States. *American Economic Review*, *87*, 1009–1018.

Clark, A., Fleche, S., & Senik, C. (2012). *The great happiness moderation*. IZA Discussion Paper No. 6761, Bonn, Germany.

Clark, G. (2014). *The son also rises: Surnames and the history of social mobility*. Princeton, NJ: Princeton University Press.

Corak, M. (2013a). Income inequality, equality of opportunity, and intergenerational mobility. *Journal of Economic Perspectives*, *27*, 79–102.

Corak, M. (2013b). Inequality from generation to generation: The United States in comparison. In R. Rycroft (Ed.), *The economics of inequality, poverty, and discrimination in the 21st century*. Santa Barbara, CA: ABC-CLIO.

Galton, F. (1869). *Hereditary genius: An inquiry into its laws and consequences*. London: Macmillan.

Gwartney, J., Lawson, R., & Block, W. (1996). *Economic freedom in the world, 1975–1995*. Vancouver, BC: Fraser Institute.

Krueger, A. (2012). *The rise and consequences of inequality. Presentation made to the Center for American Progress*. Retrieved from http://www.americanprogress.org/events/%20/2012/01/12/17181/the-rise-and-consequences-of-inequality/. Accessed on January 12.

Krueger, A. (2013). Land of hope and dreams: Rock and roll, economics, and rebuilding the middle class. Presentation made at the Rock and Roll Hall of Fame in Cleveland, OH. Retrieved from http://www.whitehouse.gov/sites/default/files/docs/hope_and_dreams_-_final.pdf. Accessed on June 12.

Mulligan, C. B. (1997). *Parental priorities and economic inequality*. Chicago, IL: University of Chicago Press.

Solon, G. (2004). A model of intergenerational mobility variation over time and place. In M. Corak (Ed.), *Generational income mobility in North America and Europe*. Cambridge, MA: Cambridge University Press.

PERCEPTION OF INCOME INEQUALITY: A MULTIDIMENSIONAL SCALING STUDY

Barbara Jancewicz

ABSTRACT

Existing research shows that popular income inequality measures fail to reflect their respondents' perceptions of income inequality. However, most of the current literature focuses on what is negative, telling us what individuals do not perceive. This paper presents an alternative methodology to help uncover actual perceptions of inequality, how people perceive inequality instead of how they don't. Multidimensional scaling, a statistical tool for visualizing dissimilarity data as a low-dimensional map, is used on results of a simple grouping task with a given distribution set. The outcome is a perception map that presents respondents' answers spatially, which enables additional insight into respondents' thinking. The map created by the respondents' replies, presented in this paper, indicates that their decisions are driven by two factors: what the biggest gap in incomes of a given distribution is and whether some groups have equal incomes. The result additionally validates multidimensional scaling as

Economic Well-Being and Inequality: Papers from the Fifth ECINEQ Meeting
Research on Economic Inequality, Volume 22, 251–272

ISSN: 1049-2585/doi:10.1108/S1049-258520140000022008

a tool for measuring income inequality perception and opens new ways of improving inequality perception questionnaires.

Keywords: Income inequality; inequality; inequality axioms; questionnaire experiments; transfer principle; income transformations

JEL classification: D63

INTRODUCTION

Following the seminal work of Amiel and Cowell (1992, 1999), there has been extensive research on how people perceive and define inequality (e.g., Amiel & Cowell, 2002; Amiel, Cowell, & Gaertner, 2012; Ballano & Ruiz-Castillo, 1993; Gaertner & Namazie, 2003; Harrison & Seidl, 1994; Traub, Seidl, & Schmidt, 2009). However, these results focus on how respondents do not perceive inequality, instead of revealing how they do. This is because most researchers only test whether people support certain rules or measures. Hence, when respondents do not express support for classical income inequality measures or axioms, we have very little information about why. Other studies have given respondents choices from a small set of very broad categories (Devooght, 2003), failing to identify precise preferences. Therefore we still have only a very vague idea about how respondents perceive inequality.

This paper presents a new methodology for investigating perceptions of income inequality. It explores respondents' views and uses multidimensional scaling to present results as a perception map. However, for such an analysis we need to have information about relationships between all the pairs of distributions included in the study. This means requiring $n(n-1)/2$ pairwise comparisons, where n is the number of examples. For instance, to evaluate 10 distributions we would need to ask 45 questions. We can avoid this by asking respondents to perform a grouping task on a set of examples. Having all the relevant examples in one map allows us to test existing hypotheses and construct new ones, based on the respondents' answers. Another advantage of this methodology is the simplicity of the questionnaire when compared to other possibilities.

The paper is organized as follows. The next section describes the methodology used. The section "Results" presents the most important empirical results and suggests a way they can be interpreted. The section "Discussion" provides discussion and conclusions.

MATERIALS AND METHODS

Views on income inequality were collected in the form of a questionnaire with research methodology similar to the one used by Amiel and Cowell (1999). The survey was conducted in October 2013 at the Institute of Sociology, University of Warsaw at the beginning of a statistics lecture. First-year students at the start of their academic year were chosen to participate in this research, because they possess basic mathematical skills but are not yet influenced by courses in statistics or economics. Altogether 113 questionnaires were collected. The survey was anonymous and its completion took less than 15 minutes. In general it was well received by the respondents and there was very little missing data.

The structure of the questionnaire was created with simplicity and ease of completion in mind, since respondents tend to be less concentrated during surveys conducted in class. The questionnaire consisted only of an introduction and six questions (the questionnaire itself is included in the appendix). Respondents received a one-page introductory sheet and a set of 10 cards in random order. Each card presented one income distribution in the form of a bar chart, as shown in Fig. 1. Respondents were instructed on how to interpret those charts, despite the fact that pre-tests showed that they were very intuitive to read.[1] In each bar chart there were five equally sized income groups and each was characterized by their income, presented in the form of stacks of coins. The amount of stacks roughly corresponded to the level of earnings in Poland, so that respondents could easily imagine the situations presented. The introduction on how to read the charts was followed by questions about the most and least unequal distributions. Afterwards respondents were asked to group the examples according to their similarity in income inequality. They could create as many groups as they wanted, but each distribution could belong only to one group. Finally, there were three background questions including: respondents' sex (34.5% males), major (17.7% studied other topics beside sociology), and whether they lived in Warsaw (46%) or its surroundings (17.7%) before joining the University.

Most researchers choose examples for their studies according to income inequality axioms (Amiel & Cowell, 1999; Gaertner & Namazie, 2003;

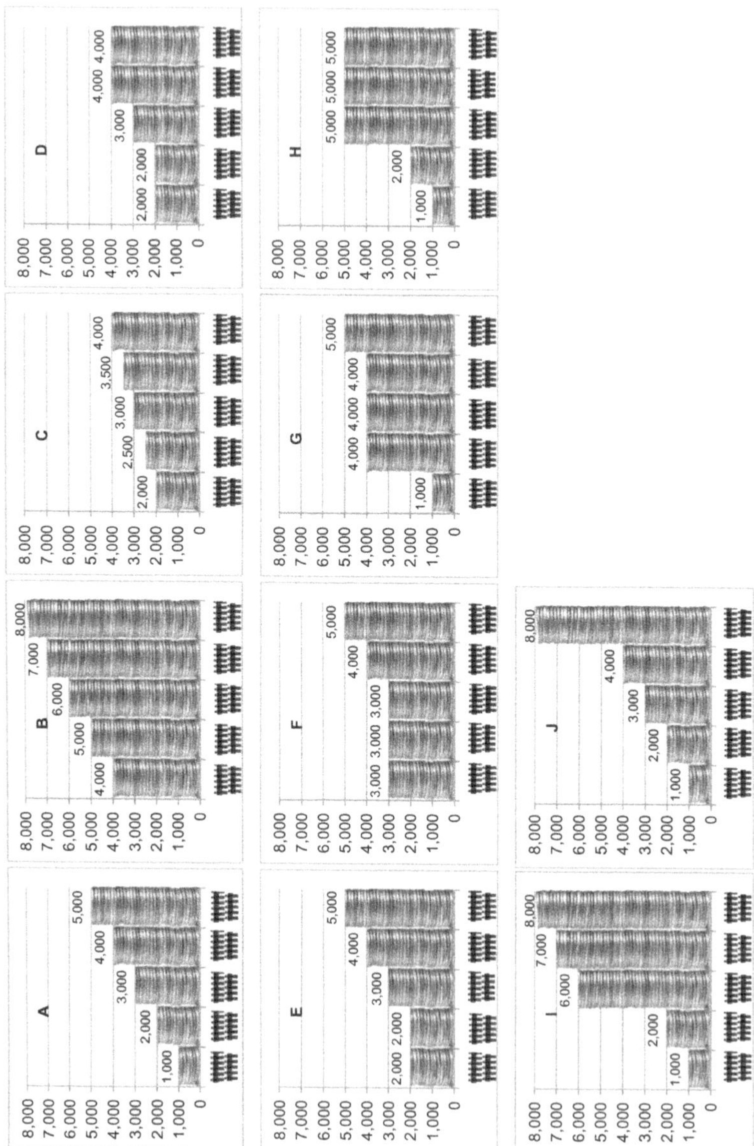

Fig. 1. Distributions Used in the Survey.

Harrison & Seidl, 1994). However, this is only one criterion amongst others available: real-life distributions, inequality measures, income inequality axioms, respondents' answers from previous research, and of course one's own hypotheses. The choice of examples for this study was partially guided by answers from a set of qualitative interviews[2] conducted in 2012 and, for comparability's sake, axioms such as the principle of transfers,[3] scale and translation invariance.[4] Three examples were constructed according to these axioms (one for each). The remaining examples were then created either by modifying incomes of the highest- and lowest-income groups or by flattening selected parts of the distribution. We aimed at constructing easily comprehensible examples, thus each one is in some way regular. The created set of distributions is presented in Fig. 1 and their basic characteristics can be found in Table 1.

The use of multidimensional scaling aims at representing a set of objects as points in a low-dimensional space, so that distances between these points correspond as closely as possible to given differences between the objects analyzed (Borg & Groenen, 2005; Borg, Groenen, & Mair, 2013; Cox & Cox, 2001). This method was created for psychometrics and currently is a technique used in marketing and psychological research. The most basic and popular example of how multidimensional scaling works is based on a geographical map. Imagine that we are interested in marking

Table 1. Selected Characteristics of Distributions Used in the Survey.

Example	Minimum	Maximum	P80/20[a]	Mean	Variance	Income Gap 1−2	Biggest Income Gap	Gini Coefficient	Theil Index
A	1,000	5,000	5	3,000	2,500,000	1,000	1,000	0.267	0.120
B	4,000	8,000	2	6,000	2,500,000	1,000	1,000	0.133	0.028
C	2,000	4,000	2	3,000	625,000	500	500	0.133	0.028
D	2,000	4,000	2	3,000	1,000,000	0	1,000	0.160	0.045
E	2,000	5,000	2.5	3,200	1,700,000	0	1,000	0.200	0.066
F	3,000	5,000	1.667	3,600	800,000	0	1,000	0.111	0.024
G	1,000	5,000	5	3,600	2,300,000	3,000	3,000	0.178	0.090
H	1,000	5,000	5	3,600	3,800,000	1,000	3,000	0.244	0.137
I	1,000	8,000	8	4,800	9,700,000	1,000	4,000	0.317	0.198
J	1,000	8,000	8	3,600	7,300,000	1,000	4,000	0.356	0.211

Note: Income gap 1−2 means the difference in incomes between the first and the second group (the one that has lowest and second lowest income). The biggest income gap has the biggest difference between neighboring income groups that exists in the given distribution.

[a]In examples used in the study the income ratio of 20% best and 20% worst income groups is simply a maximum/minimum ratio.

a position of several cities. However, we do not possess the locations of these cities, but we do have the distances between them. Multidimensional scaling is able to retrieve the original configuration of these cities just with the information about how far they are from one another. What will be lost though is the north–south orientation of the map, since we only have information of locations of these cities in relation to each other. Therefore, the resulting map can be rotated freely to find the best angle. Empirical examples are rarely as well represented as cities, since the data often contain errors and some topics are not appropriate to be represented in a low-dimensional Euclidean space. Only dissimilarities which meet the conditions of a distance function, with some approximation, can be shown on a map with little error. Thus, one of the aims of our study is to verify whether income perception data can be reasonably represented in a perception map. A multidimensional scaling algorithm creates a configuration of points that matches given data as closely as possible, using a STRESS function as measurement. The STRESS function calculates the extent of differences between distances on the map and source dissimilarities (more precisely, it is the normalized sum of squared differences between them). The result of multidimensional scaling is a configuration for which the STRESS function returns the lowest result. Multidimensional scaling can be used to visualize, explore, and verify structural hypotheses, without, however, the possibility of assessing statistical significance. Multidimensional scaling is often used by psychologists and market researchers, since it allows us to discover what governs people's perceptions, even when respondents are not completely conscious of the rules they are using when evaluating certain objects.

RESULTS

Analysis of the respondents' answers shows that their choices of the least and the most unequal distributions only partially match the results of classical income inequality measures. On one hand example F, most often selected by respondents as the least unequal (69% of the sample, as presented in Table 2), is indeed the least unequal according to measures such as Gini, Theil, P80/20, and others. However on the other hand, the frequency with which respondents chose example B (12.4%) and C (52.2%) shows that they view them as significantly different distributions.[5] This result is in conflict with scale invariance that is assumed by the most popular income inequality measures. Scale invariance implies that multiplying

Table 2. Distributions Chosen as the Least Unequal, Corresponding Percentages, and Selected Characteristics.[a]

Least Unequal	Percent of Cases	P80/20	Variance	Biggest Income Gap	Gini Coefficient	Theil Index
A	5.3	5	2,500,000	1,000	0.2666667	0.120
B	12.4	2	2,500,000	1,000	0.1333333	0.028
C	52.2	2	625,000	500	0.1333333	0.028
D	32.7	2	1,000,000	1,000	0.16	0.045
E	2.7	2.5	1,700,000	1,000	0.2	0.066
F	69.0	1.666667	800,000	1,000	0.1111111	0.024
G	5.3	5	2,300,000	3,000	0.1777778	0.090
H	3.5	5	3,800,000	3,000	0.2444444	0.137
N = 113	183.2	–	–	–	–	–

[a]Percentages sum to over 100% because respondents could choose more than one distribution as the least unequal.

incomes by a constant does not influence the inequality level, since income shares remain the same. Distribution B can be created by doubling all incomes in distribution C. Hence, according to scale invariance, these two distributions are identical, while according to over 43.4% of our sample, they are not.[6] In summary, respondents agree with the most popular income inequality measures from which example F is the least unequal, yet their answers do not support perceiving income distributions as income shares.

The two distributions chosen as the most unequal are indeed such according to popular income inequality measures, yet according to the respondents, their order is different. Table 3 shows that distribution I is chosen most often, as the most unequal. Example I shows a society divided into two parts, one with small incomes (earning 1,000 and 2,000 zloty, which is equivalent to 240 and 480 euro) and the second one with high incomes (6,000–8,000 zloty, equivalent to 1,440 and 1,920 euro). According to income inequality measures like Gini's coefficient, Theil's index, or Atkinson's measure, an even more unequal distribution is when high incomes are received by the smallest possible group. Such a situation is closer to example J, where four groups form the low-income part of the distribution (1,000–4,000 zloty, which is 240 to 960 euro), while the last group earns a high income of 8,000 zloty (1,920 euro). Nevertheless, distribution J was chosen by the respondents slightly less often than example I. In general, both of the most unequal examples were selected by a huge majority of respondents as such, yet the indication which one of them is

Table 3. Distributions Chosen as the Most Unequal, Corresponding Percentages and Selected Characteristics.[a]

Most Unequal	Percent of Cases	P80/20	Variance	Biggest Income Gap	Gini Coefficient	Theil Index
A	6.2	5	2,500,000	1,000	0.2666667	0.120
B	3.5	2	2,500,000	1,000	0.1333333	0.028
G	8.0	5	2,300,000	3,000	0.1777778	0.090
H	18.6	5	3,800,000	3,000	0.2444444	0.137
I	76.1	8	9,700,000	4,000	0.3166667	0.198
J	74.3	8	7,300,000	4,000	0.3555556	0.211
N = 113	186.7	–	–	–	–	–

[a]Percentages sum to over 100% because respondents could choose more than one distribution as the least unequal.

more unequal goes against suggestions of popular income inequality measures.

Applying logistic regression to the study results[7] shows that answers to the "least unequal distribution" question are best predicted by the variance of incomes. In case of the most unequal distribution, however, the prediction is not that obvious. If one uses model fitting, Theil's measure and variance come out as the best predictors, while the distribution's minimum and biggest income gap have the highest regression coefficients. In addition, there is no apparent dependency between the choice of the least and most unequal distributions.[8] Overall, it seems that variance might be considered the best predictor of choices regarding the least and most unequal distributions. However, further studies are recommended, because such predictions are highly dependent on the example set used in the study.

Respondents were asked to group examples by their similarity in income inequality. They could create any number of groups, even keeping each distribution separate from the others, but one example could only belong to one group. That way for each individual we obtained a similarity matrix: distributions belonging to the same group were considered similar (distance equal to zero), while examples in other groups were considered dissimilar (distance equal to 1). Taking an average from all respondents, produced a matrix of frequencies with which distributions were put into separate groups. This data was used in the Multidimensional Scaling analysis[9] creating a perception map presented in Fig. 2.

The perception map presents frequencies with which two distributions were considered similar with good accuracy.[10] In an ideal situation, if

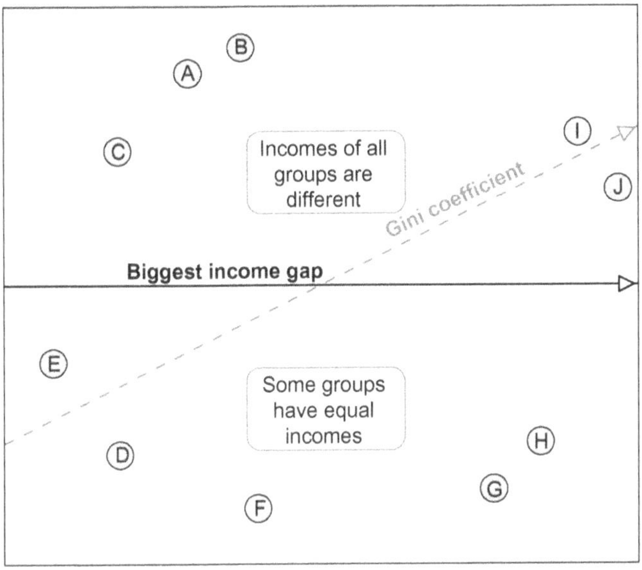

Fig. 2. A Perception Map of Income Distributions, Used in the Survey, with an Interpretation. *Note*: Obtained result was rotated by 24° to make biggest income gap axis horizontal. *Source*: Produced by the Multidimensional Scaling Procedure, based on respondents' grouping of received examples by similarity in income inequality.

two points lay further away from each other on a perception map, it means that they were placed in separate groups more often. This allows us to interpret the distances between points and the whole configuration in terms of respondent's answers. One of the techniques often used to aid perception map interpretation is an OLS regression. We use point's locations as predictors of variables we consider important for respondent's answers. That is a standard procedure for finding and placing axis on a perception map (Borg & Groenen, 2005). The better the prediction expressed with R^2, the stronger is the dependency between a variable and the configuration of points on the perception map. Hence, if a variable is strongly dependent on a point's configuration, we can suspect there is a significant relationship between the variable and respondent's views.

Out of all characteristics described in Table 1, the strongest dependency was with the biggest income gap ($R^2 = 0.912$). Thus, a corresponding axis was placed on the perception map and the map was rotated to make it horizontal. Dependencies between the points' locations and income inequality measures, such as P80/20 (R^2 = 0.786), Variance (R^2 = 0.773), Theil measure (R^2 = 0.7), and Gini coefficient[11] (R^2 = 0.557) were also strong. The general directions of axes which were created by those measures appeared very similar: from the left to the right of Fig. 2. The Gini coefficient was added as an example and for reference, since the axis corresponding to other measures lay between the Gini and the biggest income gap axis. For this reason, income inequality measures do not seem to explain the second dimension of the perception map. However, upon closer inspection it is apparent that all the distributions below the biggest income gap axis contain groups with equal incomes, while those above do not. Hence, the location of income distributions in the perception map seems to be best explained by the biggest income gap between neighboring groups and whether there are some groups with equal incomes.

Consequently, analyzed examples are divided into four categories. The first one with regular increases in incomes is formed by examples C, A, and B. There are small income gaps, but every group has a different income. The second category consists of examples I and J with regular increases in incomes broken by one huge gap of 4,000 zloty (960 euro). The third category, composed of distributions G and H, is characterized by a huge gap and equal incomes of three high-earning groups. The last category is somewhat less interconnected, with bigger distances between its members. It consists of examples E, D, and F, where the latter lies in the direction of the GH category, with which it shares the fact of having three equal incomes. This category is characterized by a lack of a big income gap, and equal incomes concentrated at the bottom of the distribution. In short, respondents' answers suggest that the size of the biggest income gap and existence of equal income groups were the most important characteristics of analyzed distributions.

Again it seems that respondents' answers are only partially in line with popular income inequality measures. The existence of equal income groups is often connected with low inequality and so is the lack of huge income gaps. However, most income inequality measures take into consideration many more factors and weigh their importance differently, yielding different results. Nevertheless, there is a significant dependency between the respondents' perception map and measures such as P80/20, Variance, Theil, and others. In conclusion, respondents' perception of inequality and popular income inequality measures are strongly connected, but they are not the same.

DISCUSSION

The main aim of this research was to test a new methodology and see whether it will allow us to discover how respondents perceive inequality. This goal was achieved. A consistent perception map was created with little error and its dimensions can be reasonably interpreted based on a distribution's characteristics. When analyzing only income inequality axioms, the results are similar to those obtained by other studies: that the support, when taking into consideration specific pairs of examples, is relatively small. However, when one looks at dependencies between all the examples, respondents' answers are strongly connected with income inequality measures. Furthermore, creating the perception map helped in understanding the respondents and allowed for further interpretations. In short, we gained additional insights into people's views on income inequality.

Our results are in accordance with those of other researchers who used the axiomatic approach. For example, Amiel's and Cowell's study (1999, p. 48) showed support for scale independence at 51%, while 57% of our respondents have put the two corresponding distributions (B and C) in one group, which can also be seen as expressing support. Other studies found different support for those axioms, yet as a general rule it was rather small. For instance, Ballano and Ruiz-Castillo (1993) found this support to be 44%, Harrison and Seidl found it to be 37–39% (1994). It is expected, though, that the percentage of those who found the two distributions similar will be higher than of those who found them the same. In general, responses collected are consistent with results obtained in previous studies, further validating the outcome of the study.

The study has shown that respondents' answers can be best described by the size of the biggest income gap in a distribution and whether or not there are groups with exactly equal incomes. Respondents divided the examples into roughly four groups characterized by different levels of these factors. There is a significant connection between income inequality measures (P80/20, Variance, Theil index, Gini coefficient) and respondents' groupings, yet these measures are not the best predictors of responses obtained. Similar conclusions can be drawn from an analysis of the distributions selected as the most and least unequal, where respondents' answers were only partially in agreement with income inequality measures. Therefore we can say that people's responses were guided by certain characteristics of distributions that are correlated with income inequality measures.

The implications of the study presented are twofold. First of all, we have a new tool that can be used to measure perception of income inequality: a perception map obtained by multidimensional scaling analysis. This method could be used to verify already conducted research in order to see whether there are some additional insights behind them. Secondly, when choosing examples for other research, researchers should note whether, besides the variable that is of researchers' interest, there are differences in the biggest income gap and the amount of people with equal incomes. Also it is worth remembering that, in this study, examples concerning doubling/halving incomes, or adding a constant to every income, were considered similar. This means that numerical questions concerning scale (multiplying incomes) and translation (adding constant to incomes) invariance are very prone to errors, since for the respondents they all seem similar (although not exactly the same). All in all, this methodology is worth further testing and results obtained so far can aid scientists in constructing examples for their research.

Finally, a number of limitations should be considered, which would also be a recommendation for future work. First of all, a small, unrepresentative sample was used. The methodology should be tested on bigger samples, both to see whether results obtained from larger and diversified groups would also be consistent and representable through an MDS procedure, and to check if results would be similar to those from the original research group. Secondly, income distributions were presented as bar charts. It would be valuable to assess the effects that different graphical representations of income distributions have on respondents' answers. Thirdly, we asked respondents to group income distributions, so the results obtained could be compared to answers to numerical questions in other studies, while it was shown that responses to verbal formulation of the same problems can differ significantly (Amiel & Cowell, 1999). Fourthly, the set of income distributions used in the study is necessarily limited, which limits possibilities of exploration and interpretation. Further research might use the same methodology to evaluate different sets of examples, for example, those already used in another, more traditional study. In conclusion, there are many ways in which the findings of this paper can be expanded and used in future research.

NOTES

1. Ten income distributions were selected for the study instead of the 15 used in pre-tests, as they showed that presenting too many cards resulted in lack of careful analysis. Pre-tests consisted of two parts: first the respondent was asked to answer

the questionnaire and talk out loud what they are thinking, if they were able to. Afterwards there was a short discussion on how they filled out the questions, whether everything was understandable, what their views on income inequality are and so on. Most respondents faced with 15 examples said, that they didn't pay careful attention to each one of the distributions presented, because they felt overwhelmed. Also, when observing the respondent completing the task, one could see that with 15 examples they rarely laid examples out on the table, to see all of them simultaneously (which often happened with 10 examples), but tended to flip through the pile.

2. The interviewees were undergraduate students finishing their first course in statistics.

3. Pigou–Dalton's principle of transfers states that any transfer from a richer person to a poorer one will decrease inequality, as long as such a transfer will not reverse donor's and recipient's positions.

4. Scale invariance assumes that multiplying all incomes by a positive constant does not alter inequality. Translation invariance claims the same about equal additions and is considered to be an axiom rivalling scale invariance.

5. Both examples B and C were selected by 10.6% of respondents.

6. 43.4% of respondents chose only C or only B as least unequal. 46% selected neither of them as least unequal, so we do not know, whether they perceive them as the same or different.

7. Logistic regression with random effects, performed in STATA. The Xtlogit command was used on a data set of pairs respondent-distribution, with binary variables "most unequal" and "least unequal." There were 10 observations for each respondent (one per example evaluated) and the set was configured similarly to panel data sets, with the id of a respondent serving as a grouping variable. Due to colinearity issues, a separate logistic regression was performed for each predicting variable.

8. Crosstabulation of both answers is available in the appendix.

9. The PROXSCAL algorithm (implemented in SPSS) was used. Two-dimensional results were chosen by checking changes of STRESS measure in different dimensionalities (4 to 1 was tested) with different start options (all yielded similar results). Subsequently, the best result was obtained through 1,000 random starts; a final normalized STRESS of 0.03105 was obtained. Data was treated as measured on the ratio scale, maximum iterations were set to 1,000, minimal STRESS and difference in STRESS to 0.00001. The Shepard's diagram reported moderate underrepresentation of middle sized distances, yet with no degeneracy.

10. The same analysis performed on 100 sets of random data (with exactly the same options selected) had an average normalized Raw STRESS of 0.10922. Accuracy of 0.03105 obtained for the data from the study is reasonably low in comparison. In terms of Pearson's correlation, the dependency between source dissimilarities and distances in the map is 0.916.

11. Theil's measure had stronger dependency of $R^2 = 0.7$, yet the Gini coefficient was chosen due to its widespread recognizability.

REFERENCES

Amiel, Y., & Cowell, F. A. (1992). Measurement of income inequality: Experimental test by questionnaire. *Journal of Public Economics*, *47*, 3–26.

Amiel, Y., & Cowell, F. A. (1999). *Thinking about inequality*. Cambridge, MA: Cambridge University Press.

Amiel, Y., & Cowell, F. A. (2002). Attitudes towards risk and inequality: A questionnaire-experimental approach. In F. Andersson & H. Holm (Eds.), *Experimental economics: Financial markets, auctions, and decision making* (pp. 85–115). Dordrecht: Kluwer Academic Publishers.

Amiel, Y., Cowell, F. A., & Gaertner, W. (2012). Distributional orderings: An approach with seven flavours. *Theory and Decision*, *73*, 381–399.

Ballano, C., & Ruiz-Castillo, U. J. (1993). Searching by questionnaire for the meaning of income inequality. *Revista Española de Economía*, *10*(2), 233–259.

Borg, I., & Groenen, P. J. F. (2005). *Modern multidimensional scaling: Theory and applications*. New York, NY: Springer.

Borg, I., Groenen, P. J. F., & Mair, P. (2013). *Applied multidimensional scaling*. New York, NY: Springer.

Cox, T., & Cox, M. (2001). *Multidimensional scaling*. London: Chapman&Hall/CRC.

Devooght, K. (2003). Measuring inequality by counting complaints: Theory and empirics. *Economics and Philosophy*, *19*(2), 241–263.

Gaertner, W., & Namazie, C. (2003). Income inequality, risk, and the transfer principle: A questionnaire-experimental investigation. *Mathematical Social Sciences*, *45*(2), 229–245.

Harrison, E., & Seidl, C. (1994). Perceptional inequality and preferential judgements: An empirical examination of distributional axioms. *Public Choice*, *79*(1–2), 61–81.

Traub, S., Seidl, C., & Schmidt, U. (2009). An experimental study on individual choice, social welfare, and social preferences. *European Economic Review*, *53*(4), 385–400.

APPENDIX

Table A1. Dissimilarity Matrix – Frequencies with Which Two Distributions Were Put in Different Groups.

	A	B	C	D	E	F	G	H	I	J
A	0	0.28	0.42	0.92	0.78	0.96	0.94	0.95	0.94	0.9
B		0	0.43	0.93	0.86	0.92	0.95	0.97	0.94	0.92
C			0	0.74	0.84	0.78	0.96	0.97	0.97	0.95
D				0	0.5	0.55	0.87	0.88	0.96	0.96
E					0	0.69	0.89	0.92	0.96	0.95
F						0	0.71	0.74	0.98	0.95
G							0	0.25	0.88	0.93
H								0	0.78	0.86
I									0	0.27
J										0

Table A2. Frequencies of Choices Regarding the Most and Least Unequal Distribution.

Total Responses $N = 439$		Most Unequal						
		A	B	G	H	I	J	Total
Within groups of most unequal distribution chosen								
Least unequal	A	0.0%	0.0%	0.0%	10.0%	2.4%	1.8%	2.9%
	B	0.0%	9.1%	4.5%	12.0%	7.7%	7.1%	6.8%
	C	31.6%	27.3%	40.9%	32.0%	29.6%	30.4%	28.5%
	D	21.1%	18.2%	22.7%	18.0%	17.2%	20.8%	17.9%
	E	0.0%	0.0%	0.0%	2.0%	1.8%	1.2%	1.4%
	F	36.8%	27.3%	31.8%	22.0%	37.3%	35.1%	37.7%
	G	5.3%	9.1%	0.0%	2.0%	2.4%	1.8%	2.9%
	H	5.3%	9.1%	0.0%	2.0%	1.8%	1.8%	1.9%
	Total	100.0%	100.0%	100.0%	100.0%	100.0%	100.0%	100.0%
	Count	19	11	22	50	169	168	439

Total Responses $N = 439$		Most Unequal							
		A	B	G	H	I	J	Total	Count
Within groups of least unequal distribution chosen									
Least unequal	A	0.0%	0.0%	0.0%	41.7%	33.3%	25.0%	100.0%	12
	B	0.0%	3.0%	3.0%	18.2%	39.4%	36.4%	100.0%	33
	C	4.4%	2.2%	6.7%	11.9%	37.0%	37.8%	100.0%	135
	D	4.8%	2.4%	6.0%	10.7%	34.5%	41.7%	100.0%	84
	E	0.0%	0.0%	0.0%	16.7%	50.0%	33.3%	100.0%	6
	F	4.7%	2.0%	4.7%	7.3%	42.0%	39.3%	100.0%	150
	G	10.0%	10.0%	0.0%	10.0%	40.0%	30.0%	100.0%	10
	H	11.1%	11.1%	0.0%	11.1%	33.3%	33.3%	100.0%	9
	Total	3.3%	1.9%	4.3%	10.0%	40.8%	39.8%	100.0%	439

Table A3. Logistic Regressions Predicting the Choice of the Most Unequal Distribution.

Predicted: Most Unequal	Variable			Constant			Model	
Variable name	Odds ratio	Coefficient	Standard error	Odds ratio	Coefficient	Standard error	σ_{υ}	Log likelihood
Theil	13.1013	2.5727	0.1892	0.0433	−3.1396	0.2396	0.63276	−268.3
Variance	7.6832	2.0390	0.1381	0.0843	−2.4737	0.1792	0.67261	−278.9
Biggest income gap	14.1021	2.6463	0.2170	0.0357	−3.3337	0.2740	0.33903	−284.5
Gini	10.2096	2.3233	0.1669	0.0586	−2.8366	0.2010	0.37325	−295.4
Maximum	4.5601	1.5174	0.1000	0.1136	−2.1752	0.1291	0.00002	−377.0
Minimum	0.0677	−2.6926	0.2922	0.0605	−2.8046	0.2299	0.00086	−418.7
P80/20	0.2708	−1.3065	0.4890	0.1690	−1.7778	0.1770	0.00046	−521.3
Mean	1.5471	0.4364	0.0678	0.2165	−1.5302	0.0799	0.00047	−524.3
First income gap	1.3637	0.3102	0.0697	0.2228	−1.5013	0.0782	0.00046	−534.6

Note: Logistic regression with random effects for panel style data for data set consisting of pairs respondent-distribution with binary variable "most unequal." Due to colinearity issues, a separate model was used for each predicting variable.

Table A4. Logistic Regressions Predicting the Choice of the Least Unequal Distribution.

Predicted: Least Unequal	Variable			Constant			Model	
Variable name	Odds ratio	Coefficient	Standard error	Odds ratio	Coefficient	Standard error	σ_υ	Log likelihood
Variance	0.0104	−4.5678	0.3815	0.0192	−3.9505	0.2833	0.00068	−371.9
Gini	0.0844	−2.4719	0.2183	0.0597	−2.8189	0.2002	0.00060	−384.3
Theil	0.0788	−2.5414	0.2435	0.0570	−2.8647	0.2181	0.00099	−392.7
Biggest income gap	0.1643	−1.8062	0.2095	0.1001	−2.3014	0.1724	0.00049	−439.6
P80/20	2.2640	0.8171	0.0672	0.1910	−1.6554	0.0872	0.00067	−457.2
First income gap	0.2566	−1.3602	0.1418	0.1469	−1.9181	0.1093	0.00049	−471.5
Maximum	0.3093	−1.1735	0.1383	0.1542	−1.8696	0.1118	0.00047	−477.2
Minimum	2.0290	0.7075	0.0729	0.1924	−1.6481	0.0863	0.00051	−489.9
Mean	0.6076	−0.4983	0.1059	0.2087	−1.5668	0.0828	0.00047	−523.9

Note: Logistic regression with random effects for panel style data for data set consisting of pairs respondent-distribution with binary variable "most unequal." Due to colinearity issues, a separate model was used for each predicting variable.

Table A5. Ordinary Least Squares Regressions Predicting Points Location on the Perception Map.

	R^2	Adjusted R^2	Coefficients			Significance		
			Constant	Dimension 1	Dimension 2	Constant	Dimension 1	Dimension 2
Biggest income gap	0.912	0.887	1,950.000	2,659.724	−0.639	0.000	0.000	0.998
P80/20	0.786	0.725	4.117	4.194	1.425	0.000	0.002	0.150
Variance	0.773	0.703	3,222,500	4,873,350	2,218,217	0.000	0.003	0.085
Theil	0.7	0.614	0.095	0.112	0.038	0.000	0.006	0.237
Maximum	0.655	0.556	5,700.000	1,946.677	1,895.027	0.000	0.032	0.039
Gini	0.557	0.43	0.210	0.110	0.063	0.000	0.035	0.189
First income gap	0.33	0.139	850.000	1,021.682	14.062	0.014	0.106	0.981
Minimum	0.276	0.069	1,800.000	−1,077.324	167.382	0.001	0.151	0.813
Mean	0.258	0.047	3,740.000	636.430	771.180	0.000	0.344	0.267

THE QUESTIONNAIRE (OWN TRANSLATION)

Income Inequality Questionnaire

The aim of this study is getting to know your views on income inequality, so we can evaluate its levels. There are no "wrong" answers, since we are interested only in your attitudes. The questionnaire is anonymous. We would like to thank you for your participation.

Along with the questionnaire you have received 10 cards with income distributions. **These examples describe countries** similar according to their economic development, where – like in Poland – **the currency is Polish zloty**. The population of each country is divided in *five equal groups*, which means the number of people in every group is the same. The coin stacks in the charts represent **after-tax income received by each member of a given group**. For example, graph A presents a country where one fifth (20%) of the population receives 1,000 zloty monthly, the next one fifth earns 2,000 zloty, etc.

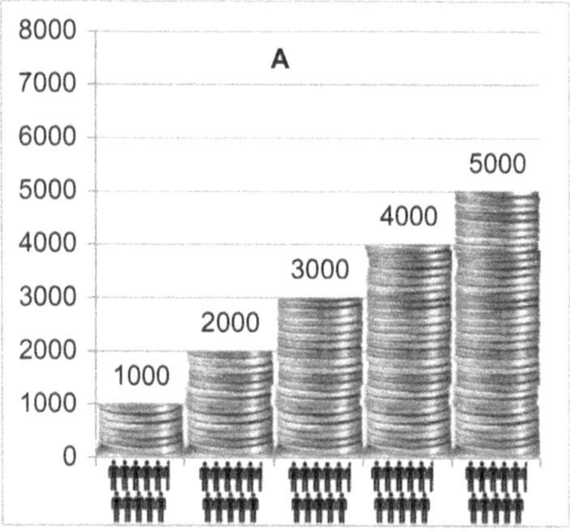

1. Which example is characterized by the **lowest income inequality**? [you can choose more than one distribution]

   .... [please write the symbol of the distribution chosen]

2. Which example is characterized by the **highest income inequality**? [you can choose more than one distribution]

   .... [please write the symbol of the distribution chosen]

3. **Please group the examples according to their similarity in income inequality.** You can create as many or as little groups as you wish. Each example can belong to one group only. You can create groups that consist of only one example.

   Please write down the groups created, by naming the symbols of examples belonging to each group (the order of the groups is unimportant).

   - ....
   - ....
   - ....
   - ....
   - ....
   - ....
   - ....
   - ....
   - ....
   - ....

4. Are you male or female? M F

5. What is or was your major?
   - ○ Sociology (IS UW)
   - ○ ....
   - ○ ....

6. Where did you live before University?
   - ○ In Warsaw
   - ○ Near Warsaw (up to 50 km)
   - ○ In Poland, further than 50 km from Warsaw
   - ○ Abroad

Thank you for your participation!

We will be thankful for any comments or suggestions, please write them here:

....

....

POLARIZATION OF TIME AND INCOME – A MULTIDIMENSIONAL ANALYSIS FOR GERMANY

Joachim Merz and Bettina Scherg

ABSTRACT

A growing polarization of society accompanied by an erosion of the middle class is receiving increasing attention in recent German economic and social policy discussion. Our study contributes to this discussion in two ways: First, on a theoretical level we propose extended multidimensional polarization indices based on a constant elasticity of substitution (CES)-type well-being function and present a new measure to multidimensional polarization, the mean minimum polarization gap, 2DGAP. This polarization intensity measure provides transparency with regard to each single attribute, which is important for targeted policies, while at the same time respecting their interdependent relations. Second, in an empirical application, time is incorporated, in addition to the traditional income measure, as a fundamental resource for any activity. In particular, genuine personal leisure time will account for social participation in the sense of social inclusion/exclusion and Amartya Sen's capability approach.

Instead of arbitrarily choosing the attribute parameters in the CES well-being function, the interdependent relations of time and income are

Economic Well-Being and Inequality: Papers from the Fifth ECINEQ Meeting
Research on Economic Inequality, Volume 22, 273–321

ISSN: 1049-2585/doi:10.1108/S1049-258520140000022009

evaluated by the German population. With the German Socio-Economic Panel (GSOEP) and detailed time use diary data from the German Time Use Surveys (GTUSs) 1991/1992 and 2001/2002, we quantify available and extended multidimensional polarization measures as well as our new approach to measuring the polarization of the working poor and affluent in Germany.

There are three prominent empirical results: Genuine personal leisure time in addition to income is an important and significant polarization attribute. Compensation is of economic and statistical significance. The new minimum 2DGAP approach reveals that multidimensional polarization increased in the 1990s in Germany.

Keywords: Interdependent multidimensional time and income polarization; minimum multidimensional polarization gap (2DGAP); working poor and affluent; CES well-being function; German Socio-Economic Panel; German Time Use Surveys 1991/92 and 2001/02

JEL classifications: I32; D31; J22

INTRODUCTION

A growing polarization in society accompanied by an erosion of the middle class is receiving greater attention in recent economic and social policy discussion in Germany. This drifting apart has many far-reaching consequences for the economy and for the quality of life in general and requires engagement on many levels. If this complex topic is examined from an economic perspective, the question is about a growing income gap, which means that "the rich get richer and the poor get poorer" (Grabka & Frick, 2008). Though the case is important and there is a large literature about inequality and in particular income inequality with a focus on the poor, there are only a few theoretical and empirical studies which explicitly investigate both poles of income distribution (but see the approaches discussed below). Even less-empirical evidence and fewer theoretical approaches about polarization can be found when not only income but also a multidimensional approach to economic well-being is considered, though multidimensional approaches have proven to be important for extended poverty studies (Alkire & Foster, 2011; Atkinson, 2003; Bourguignon & Chakravarty, 2003; Chakravarty, 2009; Chakravarty & Silber, 2008).

Our study contributes to the polarization discussion with respect to interdependent multidimensional (IMD) theoretical measurement and its empirical application in two ways:

First, we propose a methodology using extended multidimensional polarization indices based on a constant elasticity of substitution (CES)-type well-being function, and we present new well-being measures of multidimensional polarization, and in particular the new mean minimum polarization gap 2DGAP, a shortest way to escape poverty or to leave affluence. This unique polarization intensity measure provides transparency with regard to each single attribute *and* ensures at the same time their interdependent relations.

Second, since polarization has both an economic and a social dimension, in the empirical application we respect both and argue that – in addition to the traditional income measure – time as a fundamental resource for any activity should be incorporated into multidimensional analysis. Genuine personal leisure time in particular will account for the social participation aspect in the sense of social inclusion/exclusion and Amartya Sen's capability approach (e.g., Sen, 1999, 1985). The interdependent relations of time and income via the polarization attribute parameters in the CES well-being function will be estimated and evaluated by the German population instead of arbitrarily assigning them values (as in Bourguignon & Chakravarty, 2003 or Maasoumi & Lugo, 2008; Lugo & Maasoumi, 2009).

This empirical application is based on the German Socio-Economic Panel (GSOEP) with additional detailed time use diary data from two available German Time Use Surveys (GTUSs) 1991/1992 and 2001/2002. We quantify available and extended polarization measures as well as our new approaches to polarization development over that decade in Germany according to time and income. In addition to one-value multidimensional polarization indices quantified and discussed in our study, we argue that our new transparent multidimensional polarization 2DGAP components have empirical significance for Germany and are important for targeted policies aiming to overcome polarization.

Current approaches to polarization measurement can be divided into two strands, regardless of whether they are unidimensional or multidimensional. One strand, based on Foster and Wolfson (2010), considers bipolarity with two income groups, one above and one below the income median. This family of measures includes the unidimensional indices of Foster and Wolfson (2010) and Wang and Tsui (2000) as well as the multidimensional extension of Scheicher (2010). The second strand, which is based on the work of Esteban and Ray (1994), relies on a separation of the income distribution into several groups and defines polarization by inequality within the groups and the distance between the groups. This family of polarization measurements includes the unidimensional measure by Esteban and Ray (1994), Esteban, Gradín, and Ray (2007), and Duclos, Esteban, and Ray (2004), as well as the multidimensional approach of Gigliarano and Mosler (2009). In the following we only briefly characterize these multidimensional approaches; the respective formulas can be found in the appendix.

Gigliarano and Mosler (2009) construct a class of multidimensional polarization measures by decomposing different inequality measures and measuring the relative sizes of various groups. Polarization is then described as inequality within groups and as inequality between groups. This measure is a multidimensional extension of the earlier group approach of Esteban and Ray (1994). Scheicher's (2010) multidimensional polarization index is based on individual middle class attribute distances to middle class thresholds. For each individual the single attribute distances are summed up so as to provide individual mean distances of the poor and of the affluent, which are then aggregated. An advantage is certainly the incorporation of multiple attributes and this was an inspiration for our following proposal. However, since the attributes could have different dimensions (euros for income and minutes for time, say), it is difficult to provide a convincing and comprehensive argument in favor just of adding up. While the approach of Gigliarano and Mosler allows a substitution of attributes, the distance measure by Scheicher does not include a substitution parameter.[1]

Though the multidimensional approach is obviously the virtue of these approaches, because of the differences in the attribute dimensionalities, it is necessary to find a combined "umbrella" that aggregates the single polarization attributes and respects their interdependence. The contribution of this paper will be to fill that gap.

This study is the multidimensional polarization extension of our minimum 2DGAP approach and application recently proposed for multidimensional poverty studies (Merz & Rathjen, 2014b).

The remainder of this paper is organized in a theoretical and an application part as follows. The next section is about the identification and aggregation of multidimensional polarization (MDP, see "Multidimensional Polarization: Identification and Aggregation"), and the specification of the multidimensional CES well-being function (see "Multidimensional Polarization: Multidimensional CES Well-Being Function"). The section "Multidimensional Polarization: New Indices Based on a Multidimensional

(CES) Well-Being Function" proposes our new well-being measures of IMD polarization. The section "Minimum Multidimensional Polarization Gap (2DGAP)" introduces the minimum multidimensional polarization gap (2DGAP) with transparent attribute contributions in the compensation context.

The entire application part consists of different sections which build on each other. Section "Multidimensional Time and Income Polarization in Germany – Justification of Attributes and Polarization Threshold Line Concept" justifies time and income as the two most important multidimensional polarization attributes, describes their expected interdependence, and discusses the polarization threshold lines concepts. Section "Multidimensional Time and Income Polarization in Germany – Data and Empirical Threshold Lines" describes the database and the empirical polarization threshold lines. Section "Multidimensional Time and Income Polarization in Germany – Headcount Ratios, Well-Being Gap, and Minimum 2DGAP Results" provides polarization results based on measures reported in the literature and in particular on the results of our new (CES) well-being gap and minimum 2DGAP IMD polarization indices. Section "Multidimensional Time and Income Polarization in Germany – Results for Socio-Demographic Groups" is about the importance of polarization for various socio-demographic groups. The last section provides a conclusion.

There are three prominent empirical results for Germany: First, genuine personal leisure time, in addition to income, appears to be an important and significant polarization attribute. Second, compensation between these two attributes, evaluated by the German population, is found to be of economic and statistical significance. Third, as shown by the new minimum 2DGAP approach, multidimensional polarization significantly increased in Germany over the decade 1991/1992–2001/2002.

MULTIDIMENSIONAL POLARIZATION: IDENTIFICATION, AGGREGATION AND MULTIDIMENSIONAL CES WELL-BEING FUNCTION

Multidimensional Polarization: Identification and Aggregation

To define multidimensional polarization, we mainly build on the multidimensional poverty discussion (Deutsch & Silber, 2005; Kakwani & Silber,

2008). In *multidimensional poverty identification* (Bourguignon & Chakravarty, 2003), there are two approaches. In the so-called *union approach (strong focus axiom)*, a person is judged to be multidimensional poor as soon she or he is deprived in at least one dimension (see Fig. 1(b) for the two-dimension case, the shaded area with the corresponding poverty thresholds z_1 and z_2). The *intersection approach*, by contrast, judges an individual to be multidimensional poor when she or he is deprived in all dimensions (Fig. 1(a)). Intermediate concepts are conceivable as well.

The selection of the union, intersection, or intermediate approach ultimately depends on the relationship between poverty dimensions. Given

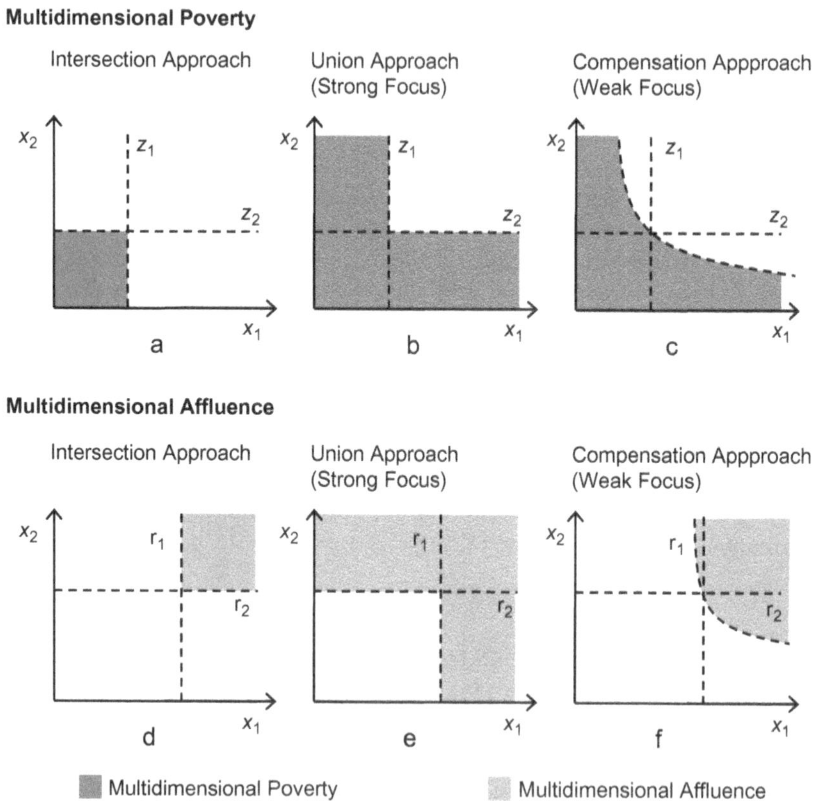

Fig. 1. Identification of Multidimensional Polarization. *Note*: x_1 and x_2 are the quantities of the first and second dimension, z_1 and z_2 are the corresponding poverty and r_1 and r_2 the corresponding affluence dimension thresholds. *Source*: Own figure.

a substitutive situation the intersection approach is preferable. If a complementary relation is given, then the union approach would be appropriate.

Since the union and intersection approaches seem to be too rigid as identification strategies for most cases, an intermediate approach would be most appropriate (Lugo & Maasoumi, 2009). It allows compensation (weak focus axiom) for all ranges in one dimension given poverty in the other (Fig. 1(c)). In the *compensation approach* thus, besides being poor in both dimensions (intersection), a person is multidimensional poor when she or he cannot compensate poverty in one dimension by the other nonpoverty dimension.

The empirical question is whether and to which extent a poverty gap in one dimension might be compensated for by higher quantities in the other one. If a gap in one dimension can be compensated by another's dimension quantity above the dimension threshold, then a person is off poverty (Fig. 1(c), unshaded area). Thus, the multidimensional poverty line in the two-dimensional case runs through the intersection of the dimension thresholds $z=(z_1, z_2)$ dividing the poor (shaded areas in Fig. 1(a–c)) and the nonpoor (unshaded areas in Fig. 1(a–c)).

We extend multidimensional poverty identification to *multidimensional polarization* in a similar though not identical way to poverty. We identify the other pole of the distribution, the affluent, by mirroring the poverty areas along the single affluence thresholds $r=(r_1, r_2)$ (Fig. 1(d–f)). The kind of relationships between dimensions does not change with respect to the intermediate, union, and compensation ranges. Fig. 1 also allows the identification of unidimensional polarization with regard to the x_1 dimension (poor to the left of z_1, affluent to the right of r_1) and to the x_2 dimension (poor below z_2, affluent above r_2).

In the following we focus on the compensation approach (weak focus axiom), where the grade of compensation will be evaluated empirically by the German population. For the compensation approach, Fig. 2 illustrates the poverty *and* the affluence situation (two-dimensional case). Again, the shaded areas in Fig. 2 describe the poor under the poverty line and the affluent above the affluence line. Take for example the affluence compensation above the income threshold (right of r_1 in Fig. 2). The time deficit (being below the time affluence line r_2) is considered to be compensated by a high income above the multidimensional affluence line to be assigned IMD affluent. The time deficit, however, is considered to be not compensated by high income below the multidimensional affluence line; there is no more multidimensional affluence.

The poverty and affluence lines (in the two-dimension case) can be interpreted as *multidimensional isopolarization contours*, which are isoquants of

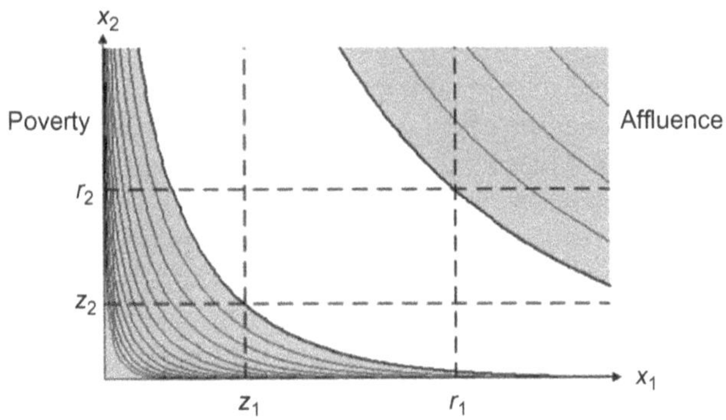

Fig. 2. Multidimensional Isopolarization Contours – Compensation Approach (Weak Focus Axiom) in the Two-Dimension Case. *Source*: Own figure.

an underlying well-being function, a function which comprises all polarization attributes and evaluates their interdependent relation. This well-being function is specified in the next section.

To measure the multidimensional polarization for a population, the possible interdependence of attributes has to be specified by the aggregation across the dimensions for each individual well-being index as well as the aggregation across individuals obtaining a poverty measure; see the development for our approach in the section "Multidimensional Polarization: New Indices Based on a Multidimensional (CES) Well-Being Function."

Multidimensional Polarization: Multidimensional CES Well-Being Function

Following the compensation approach, this section specifies a particular multidimensional well-being function, a CES function, whose multidimensional isopolarization contours, as described above, identifies the individuals in the polarization poles, both the poor and the affluent. The CES well-being function accounts for the interdependence of the polarization attributes and will be the key element in our new multidimensional polarization indices (described in the next section) and the foundation for our new minimum 2DGAP polarization approach.

Our CES-type well-being function with its individual well-being indicator V_i (weak focus axiom) is based on the multidimensional poverty approach by Merz and Rathjen (2014a) and evaluates the interdependence of dimensions by

$$V_i = \gamma[w_1(x_{1i})^{-\rho} + w_2(x_{2i})^{-\rho}]^{\frac{\upsilon}{-\rho}} \tag{1}$$

with the substitution elasticity $\sigma = 1/(1+\rho)$ measuring the curvature of the isoquants, ρ as a substitution parameter of the isopolarization contours with $\rho \neq 0$, γ as a constant, υ as returns to scale, x_{1i} and x_{2i} as the polarization attribute quantities, and the coefficients w_1 and $w_2 = 1 - w_1$ as distribution and weighting parameters describing the skewness of the isopolarization contours.

The degree of substitution between genuine personal leisure time and income is measured by the Hicks' elasticity of substitution as the relative change in the proportion of the two attributes dependent on the relative change of the corresponding marginal rate of substitution. With the CES function, the intersections of all isoquants with a ray from the origin have the same marginal rate of substitution. Substitution/compensation, however, is different between different rays from the origin, which allows different degrees of substitution with different time and income ratios.

Compared to other specifications the CES function has the virtue that the elasticity of substitution/compensation can be estimated empirically and is not restricted to a certain value, like a value of one as with the Cobb–Douglas function (a special case of the more general CES function). Since in our empirical application we estimate the CES by a log-Taylor approximation, the results can even be interpreted as being a more flexible specification like a translog one.[2]

Following the CES well-being compensation approach to quantifying the interdependence of the polarization attributes, the aggregated *multidimensional poverty line* and the aggregated *multidimensional affluence line* will be defined at their respective thresholds by

$$V_z = \gamma[w_1(z_1)^{-\rho} + w_2(z_2)^{-\rho}]^{\frac{\upsilon}{-\rho}} \text{ and } V_r = \gamma[w_1(r_1)^{-\rho} + w_2(r_2)^{-\rho}]^{\frac{\upsilon}{-\rho}} \tag{2}$$

resulting in the two isopolarization contours, the isopoverty and the isoaffluence contours, which cross the poverty threshold intersection at $z = (z_1, z_2)$, or respectively the affluence threshold intersection at $r = (r_1, r_2)$. All individuals with their calculated multidimensional well-being $V_x = V(x_{i1}, x_{i2})$ below the isopoverty line are assigned to be poor, above the isoaffluence line to be affluent, and together assigned to be polarized (see again Fig. 2).

MULTIDIMENSIONAL POLARIZATION: NEW INDICES BASED ON A MULTIDIMENSIONAL (CES) WELL-BEING FUNCTION

We propose a new straightforward measurement approach to multidimensional polarization which respects the interdependence of the attributes based on the above compensation perspective by a multidimensional well-being function like our CES function. With regard to the aggregation of individual well-beings to a multidimensional polarization index for a population, we follow the so-called "shortfall of well-being" aggregate approach used also by Lugo and Maasoumi (2009) for the multidimensional *poverty* aggregation of well-being levels. In our empirical application in particular we follow this well-being level approach rather than the "well-being of shortfalls" component approach based on the relative differences between individual attributes and their thresholds.

Multidimensional Well-Being Polarization (Median)

The first multidimensional polarization measure is the multidimensional well-being extension of the unidimensional Wang and Tsui (2000) polarization measure which considers polarization poles below and above the respective medians. Our *multidimensional well-being polarization index (median)* (weak focus axiom) P_{median} measures the polarization intensity as a mean relative well-being gap with respect to the median, and is defined (for the two-dimensional case) by

$$P_{\text{median}} = \frac{1}{n}\sum_{i=1}^{n}\left[\left|\frac{V(x_{i1}, x_{i2}) - V(m_1, m_2)}{V(m_1, m_2)}\right|\right]^{\alpha} \tag{3}$$

where $V(.)$ is a (CES) well-being function as in Eq. (1), m_i is the median value of the polarization attributes, and n is the population size. The greater the distance from the median well-being to the individual well-being, the greater is this index. In contrast to Wang and Tsui (2000), who relate α to the interval [0, 1], we follow the Foster, Greer, and Thorbecke (1984) idea of α describing here a polarization aversion index, with $\alpha = 1$ as the relative well-being distance to the median, and $\alpha = 2$ (or $\alpha \geq 1$) for a greater polarization sensitivity with greater weights for larger gaps.

Multidimensional Well-Being Polarization (Poverty and Affluence Threshold Lines)

Whereas the last index comprises all gaps below and above the well-being median, the next well-being measure considers the individual gaps with respect to distinct poverty and affluence threshold lines.[3]

Our *multidimensional well-being polarization index (poverty and affluence threshold lines)* P_{all} is the sum of a mean relative poverty and a mean relative affluence well-being gap under the weak focus axiom as defined by

$$P_{\text{all}} = \frac{1}{n}\sum_{i=1}^{n}\left[\max\left(\frac{V(z_1, z_2) - V(x_{1i}, x_{2i})}{V(z_1, z_2)}, 0\right)\right]^{\alpha} + \frac{1}{n}\sum_{i=1}^{n}\left[\max\left(\frac{V(x_{i1}, x_{i2}) - V(r_1, r_2)}{V(x_{i1}, x_{i2})}, 0\right)\right]^{\beta} \quad (4)$$

The exponents α and β serve as polarization aversion coefficients, with $\alpha=0$ and $\beta=0$ delivering the multidimensional polarization headcount ratios. With $\alpha=1$ and $\beta=1$ an average relative polarization gap in well-being units is measured, and with $\alpha>1$ and $\beta>1$ a higher aversion against strong polarization (which may be different for the poor and the affluent) is reflected. The proposed polarization index Eq. (4) has its origins in a multidimensional Foster et al. (1984) poverty index under the weak focus axiom according to well-being units (Lugo & Maasoumi, 2009; Merz & Rathjen, 2014a, 2014b).

The construction principle of this index – which transfers gap measures from poverty analysis to the analysis of the affluent – reveals a general problem of measuring any gap for the affluent. Whereas a poverty gap is restricted to the maximum interval z, the affluence gap would be unbounded. If the affluence part were specified in the same manner as the poverty part, then a reference to the affluence threshold $V(r_1, r_2)$ might deliver values greater than one (further implications are discussed, e.g., in Peichl, Schaefer, & Scheicher, 2010). Thus, the second part of our multidimensional polarization index refers to the individual situation $V(x_{i1}, x_{i2})$ ensuring affluence percentage ratios in the interval [0, 1].

Though both index parts have a different reference, for both parts a larger index characterizes an increasing polarization as increasing mean distances within the multidimensional poles.

Since in both parts of the multidimensional polarization index (Eq. (4)), the average is related to the whole population (n), relatively small values have to be expected in an empirical application. A more intuitively appropriate average would be related to only the poor or affluent population numbers. The *multidimensional well-being polarization index (poverty and affluence threshold lines)* P_{poles} then is defined by

$$P_{\text{poles}} = \frac{1}{n_{\text{poor}}} \sum_{i \in \text{poor}}^{n_{\text{poor}}} \left[\frac{V(z_1, z_2) - V(x_{i1}, x_{12})}{V(z_1, z_2)} \right]^{\alpha} + \frac{1}{n_{\text{rich}}} \sum_{i \in \text{rich}}^{n_{\text{rich}}} \left[\frac{V(x_{i1}, x_{i2}) - V(r_1, r_2)}{V(x_{i1}, x_{i2})} \right]^{\beta} \quad (5)$$

with exponents α and β greater than or equal to one. Our polarization index (Eq. (5)) respects well-being units, whereas the unidimensional Scheicher (2010) polarization index refers to income units.

With regard not to relative but absolute deviations, the respective *multidimensional well-being polarization index (poverty and affluence contour)* in *absolute well-being deviations* then is

$$P_{\text{all, abs}} = \frac{1}{n} \sum_{i=1}^{n} [\max(V(z_1, z_2) - V(x_{1i}, x_{2i}), 0)]^{\alpha} + \frac{1}{n} \sum_{i=1}^{n} [\max(V(x_{i1}, x_{i2}) - V(r_1, r_2), 0)]^{\beta} \quad (6)$$

and

$$P_{\text{poles, abs}} = \frac{1}{n_{\text{poor}}} \sum_{i \in \text{poor}}^{n_{\text{poor}}} [V(z_1, z_2) - V(x_{i1}, x_{12})]^{\alpha} + \frac{1}{n_{\text{rich}}} \sum_{i \in \text{rich}}^{n_{\text{rich}}} [V(x_{i1}, x_{i2}) - V(r_1, r_2)]^{\beta} \quad (7)$$

with an analogous interpretation as the relative indices Eqs. (4) and (5).

Multidimensional Well-Being Polarization Asymmetry

The building blocks of our multidimensional well-being polarization index allows a characterization of the polarization asymmetry between the poverty part and the affluence part. This asymmetry might be described by a *multidimensional well-being polarization gap ratio* between the poverty and affluence gaps for the different relative mean concepts by

$$P_{\text{all, ratio}} = \left\{ \frac{1}{n} \sum_{i=1}^{n} \left[\max\left(\frac{V(z_1, z_2) - V(x_{1i}, x_{2i})}{V(z_1, z_2)}, 0 \right) \right]^{\alpha} \right\} \Bigg/ \left\{ \frac{1}{n} \sum_{i=1}^{n} \left[\max\left(\frac{V(x_{i1}, x_{i2}) - V(r_1, r_2)}{V(x_{i1}, x_{i2})}, 0 \right) \right]^{\beta} \right\} \tag{8}$$

and

$$P_{\text{poles, ratio}} = \left\{ \frac{1}{n_{\text{poor}}} \sum_{i \in \text{poor}}^{n_{\text{poor}}} \left[\frac{V(z_1, z_2) - V(x_{i1}, x_{12})}{V(z_1, z_2)} \right]^{\alpha} \right\} \Bigg/ \left\{ \frac{1}{n_{\text{rich}}} \sum_{i \in \text{rich}}^{n_{\text{rich}}} \left[\frac{V(x_{i1}, x_{i2}) - V(r_1, r_2)}{V(x_{i1}, x_{i2})} \right]^{\beta} \right\} \tag{9}$$

and in a similar way for the absolute gaps of Eqs. (6) and (7) as

$$P_{\text{all, ratio, abs}} = \left\{ \frac{1}{n} \sum_{i=1}^{n} [\max(V(z_1, z_2) - V(x_{1i}, x_{2i}), 0)]^{\alpha} \right\} \Bigg/ \left\{ \frac{1}{n} \sum_{i=1}^{n} [\max(V(x_{i1}, x_{i2}) - V(r_1, r_2), 0)]^{\beta} \right\} \tag{10}$$

and

$$P_{\text{poles, ratio, abs}} = \left\{ \frac{1}{n_{\text{poor}}} \sum_{i \in \text{poor}}^{n_{\text{poor}}} [V(z_1, z_2) - V(x_{i1}, x_{12})]^{\alpha} \right\} \Bigg/ \left\{ \frac{1}{n_{\text{rich}}} \sum_{i \in \text{rich}}^{n_{\text{rich}}} [V(x_{i1}, x_{i2}) - V(r_1, r_2)]^{\beta} \right\} \tag{11}$$

Larger *multidimensional well-being polarization gap ratios* than a value of one describe a greater asymmetry between the pole gaps.

MINIMUM MULTIDIMENSIONAL POLARIZATION GAP (2DGAP)

Multidimensional polarization by the compensation approach, as so far discussed, is captured by a multidimensional well-being function which is at the heart of our new polarization indices described above. The virtue of measuring multidimensional well-being and any well-being gap by a CES-type or other type well-being function is that it respects and quantifies the interdependence of multiple well-being attributes by a one-value well-being index. However, such an aggregation of dimensions into a single well-being value is questionable if it is still measuring "multidimensional" poverty, affluence, or polarization, since the single attributes are no longer transparent. Transparency for the single attributes in the multidimensional approach is however desirable in a manner which allows a targeted policy aimed at the specific attributes of poverty, affluence, or polarization.

The main motivation for developing the multidimensional polarization 2DGAP is thus to "disentangle" the single attributes of a well-being gap to obtain a unique multidimensional intensity measure with transparent single attributes. This approach extends the minimum poverty 2DGAP concept proposed in Merz and Rathjen (2014b) to the multidimensional polarization case.

In the polarization case, both poles of a distribution with their respective poverty threshold and affluence threshold contours are of interest. Fig. 3 (top) shows the CES well-being graph and describes the two-dimensional poverty and affluence case: $V_z = V(z_1, z_2)$ is the well-being contour at the poverty threshold $z = (z_1, z_2)$, and $V_i = V(x_{1i}, x_{2i})$ is the individual well-being contour at $x_i = (x_{i1}, x_{i2})$. The difference $V_z - V_i$ is the multidimensional poverty well-being gap. In an analogous way $V_i^r - V_r$ defines the multidimensional affluence well-being gap for a rich person with $V_i^r = V(x_{i1}^r, x_{i2}^r)$ and $V_r = V(r_1, r_2)$ as the affluence threshold.

The mapping of the multidimensional well-being on its (two) single dimensional input space now allows for another attractive integrated approach for describing multidimensional polarization intensity while disentangling the single attribute contributions. It consists of a unique distance between an individual situation and the poverty or, respectively, the affluence threshold.

As an illustration, consider the two-dimensional case from the compensation approach and its attribute space as in Fig. 3 (at the bottom) and regard first the poverty situation at $x = (x_1, x_2)$ for an individual. With respect to both dimensions there is a fan of distances from that point

$x=(x_1,x_2)$ to the IMD isopoverty threshold. Indeed, each distance yields the same well-being difference $V_z - V_i$. However, each distance requires that different single attribute input mixtures need to be overcome in order to escape multidimensional poverty.

The *shortest* path between $x=(x_1,x_2)$ and the corresponding point $p=(p_1,p_2)$ at the isopoverty threshold contour is shown in Fig. 3. It requires a minimum input mixture in the sense of an optimized compensation intensity, a minimum combined input "length," in order to escape multidimensional poverty. A natural measure for that length is the Euclidian distance of the single attributes $c=[a^2+b^2]^{0.5}$ with their components a and b as the single poverty attribute gap intensities.

The same approach will be used for a shortest path from a multidimensional affluent individual situation to the isoaffluence line. It is the minimum combined input length necessary to lose multidimensional affluence.

Following the proposed minimum 2DGAP for the poverty case in Merz and Rathjen (2014b), we call this shortest distance c the *minimum multidimensional poverty/affluence 2DGAP* (for two polarization dimensions).

The solution for the shortest (or closest) length is characterized by the orthogonal path from a poor individual $x=(x_1,x_2)$ to the tangent at $p=(p_1,p_2)$ for the poverty case of the CES-type isothreshold line by

$$\begin{aligned} c = \|c\| &= [a^2+b^2]^{0,5} = [(p_1-x_1)^2+(p_2-x_2)^2]^{0,5} \\ &= [(p_1-x_1)^2+(f(p_1|V_z)-x_2)^2]^{0,5} = \min! \end{aligned} \tag{12}$$

where $f(p_1|V_z)$ is the isothreshold contour with regard to the ordinate values x_2 (say, time) of the CES multidimensional well-being function

$$f(p_1|V_z) = \left(\left(\left(\frac{V_z}{\gamma}\right)^{-\frac{\rho}{\nu}} - w_1 p_1{}^{-\rho}\right) \Big/ w_2\right)^{-\frac{1}{\rho}} \tag{13}$$

The solution p_1 of the minimizing problem then allows calculation of c by Eq. (12) for a given $x=(x_1,x_2)$. Since the proposed CES well-being function is well behaved, there is always a unique solution for the minimum 2DGAP (distance c).

Because of the quadratic distances in Eq. (12), the solution procedure for the affluence situation is similar to the poverty situation. The solution p_1, respectively $p^r=(p_1^r, p_2^r)$ in the affluent case, of the nonlinear Eq. (12) (see also Fig. 3) then allows calculating c again by Eq. (12) for a single poor $x=(x_1, x_2)$ or a single affluent $x_i^r=(x_{i1}^r, x_{i2}^r)$ individual.

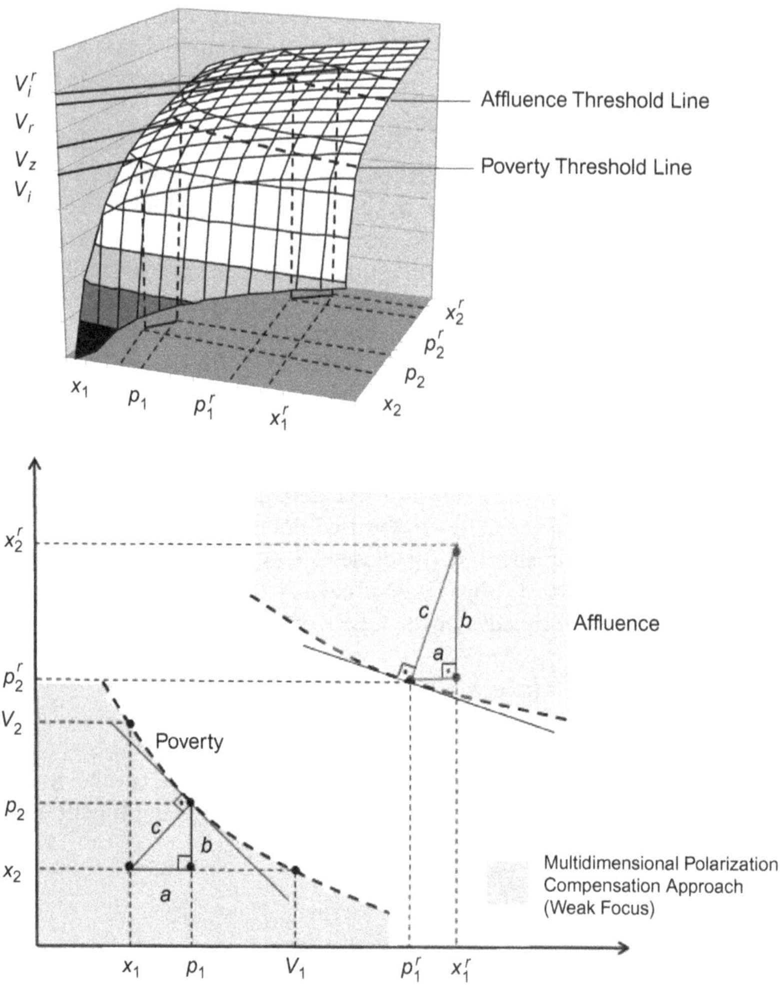

Fig. 3. Multidimensional Polarization: Well-Being Gap and Minimum 2DGAP. *Source*: Own illustration.

Single Poverty/Affluence Attribute Gaps

Once $p=(p_1, p_2=f(p_1|V_z))$ is found, the single poverty and affluence *attribute gaps* can be calculated by

$$a=p_1-x_1 \text{ and } b=f(p_1)-x_2 \tag{14}$$

Relative Minimum 2DGAP

For the *poverty case* the 2DGAP might be defined relative to the maximum 2DGAP distance $c_{\max}$, which is the distance from the origin (0,0) to the respective orthogonal slope of the IMD isopoverty threshold:

$$c_{\text{rel}} = \frac{c}{c_{\max}} \text{ where } c_{\max} = \|c_{\max}\| = [(p_1)^2 + (f(p_1, V_z))^2]^{0,5} = \min! \qquad (15)$$

with its corresponding relative single poverty attribute gap intensities:

$$a_{\text{rel}} = \frac{a}{p_1 | a_{\max}} \text{ and } b_{\text{rel}} = \frac{b}{f(p_1, V_z) | b_{\max}} \qquad (16)$$

However, for the *affluence case*, as already discussed, there is no comparable genuine maximum distance since any affluence well-being or 2DGAP gap faces the problem of an open top interval.

A possible relative minimum affluence 2DGAP relating to the isoaffluence line precludes direct comparisons to poverty pole measures. Relating it to the overall median for both pole minimum 2DGAPs would have a comparable reference but would not deliver transparent single attribute components.

Aggregation and Mean Minimum Polarization 2DGAP

To retain the polarization single attribute contributions in the multidimensional approach, we propose a straightforward aggregation by the sum of the respective minimum 2DGAP pole means, the *mean minimum polarization 2DGAP*:

$$C = \frac{1}{n_{\text{poor}}} \sum_{i \in \text{poor}}^{n} c_i + \frac{1}{n_{\text{rich}}} \sum_{i \in \text{rich}}^{n} c_i \qquad (17)$$

with its single aggregated components[4]

$$A = \frac{1}{n_{\text{poor}}} \sum_{i \in \text{poor}}^{n} a_i + \frac{1}{n_{\text{rich}}} \sum_{i \in \text{rich}}^{n} a_i, \; B = \frac{1}{n_{\text{poor}}} \sum_{i \in \text{poor}}^{n} b_i + \frac{1}{n_{\text{rich}}} \sum_{i \in \text{rich}}^{n} b_i \qquad (18)$$

The Benefit: Transparency of Single Attributes of Multidimensional Polarization

The minimum 2DGAP distance c itself measures the shortest multidimensional gap as the shortest length of all dimensional gap intensities in combined attribute units but without direct interpretation in terms of, say, money or time units. However, this is the benefit of our proposed approach: both sides (attributes) of the right-angled triangle (a and b) are measurable and interpretable in the single dimension, say, income in money units (euros) and time in time units (minutes). This information and transparency then allows targeted single-dimension antipolarization policies while respecting its multidimensional interdependence. We briefly discuss such polarization policies in our concluding section.

The n-*Dimensional Case*

The minimum 2DGAP can be extended to the n-dimensional case, called minimum NDGAP, by a multivariate minimum search, where the slopes of the NDGAP linear distance are subject to the orthogonality of the n-dimensional tangents to their respective isothreshold contours.

Input Distance Function Approach and Minimum 2DGAP

Another input-related gap measurement is the input distance function (IDF) approach (Anderson, Crawford, & Leicester, 2008; Deutsch & Silber, 2005; Malmquist, 1953). It is a measure of efficiency where all input factors would have to be changed proportionally by a certain value to achieve a total (technical and allocative) economically efficient output.[5] This measurement requires that the slope (marginal rate of substitution) of the output level isoquants is identical at any crossing point with a given input vector at a given fixed allocative input price ratio. Then the IDF is an appropriate scaling ratio along the input vector, an arrow from the input space origin with a fixed input factor ratio, to efficiently achieve a certain output level.[6]

With respect to multidimensional poverty (Deutsch & Silber, 2005), the IDF approach can be interpreted and adapted as a standard of living gap measure in the input (resource) space. The farther the resource vector is below from a well-being (utility) frontier, the lower is the standard of living. In particular, the IDF approach describes the proportional increase of the multidimensional poverty attributes (time and income, say) to reach the efficient allocation at the multidimensional poverty isoquant. Thereby, this is the important difference to our minimum 2DGAP intensity, the individual input price ratio (individually evaluated time and income) from a budget constraint with regard to the optimal allocation at the individual situation remains constant also at the crossing point of the input vector and the poverty isoquant.

Take as an example the wage rate as the price for income (working hours). In case of a higher wage offer for a working poor, a constant price ratio in the IDF approach would require foregoing a better paid working situation to escape poverty.

A poverty gap measured by our minimum 2DGAP approach, however, provides a *minimum* gap from the individual situation to the multidimensional threshold isoquant while respecting the attribute compensation. The minimum 2DGAP thereby allows a changing input factor ratio and a changing individual price ratio on the path to the multidimensional poverty threshold isoquant. In contrast to the IDF approach, this would allow an individual, for example, to take advantage of better-paid jobs to escape poverty.

In brief, whereas with the IDF gap the individual situation (slope of the individual budget line of the optimal allocation ratio of time and income) remains constant, the 2DGAP allows a changing individual situation and allocation to achieve the poverty respectively affluence frontier led by the minimum compensation as evaluated by, in our study, the German population.

MULTIDIMENSIONAL TIME AND INCOME POLARIZATION IN GERMANY – JUSTIFICATION OF ATTRIBUTES AND POLARIZATION THRESHOLD LINE CONCEPT

The empirical application part of our study is about multidimensional polarization in Germany. Some empirical polarization findings for Germany are already available (see Goebel, Gorning, & Häußermann, 2010; Grabka & Frick, 2008); they are however primarily based on unidimensional income polarization. Merz (2006) and Merz and Zwick (2005) analyze unidimensional income polarization of the self-employed as freelancers or entrepreneurs in particular. Scheicher (2009) provides empirical results based on his multidimensional approach with working hours and income as polarization attributes. Education and income are the polarization attributes of the Gigliarano and Mosler (2009) multidimensional analysis according to their group-specific approach.

Though the available German results show, roughly speaking, some increasing polarization, mainly in the decade 2001–2009, the empirical results with our new polarization measures, polarization attributes, and type and periods of data are obviously new.

In the empirical part of this study, this section justifies time and income as multidimensional polarization attributes and their expected interdependence, and discusses the polarization threshold lines concept. The next section describes the database and the empirical polarization threshold lines. Section "Multidimensional Time and Income Polarization in Germany – Headcount Ratios, Well-Being Gap, and Minimum 2DGAP Results" provides polarization results based on other measures found in the literature as well as the results of our new (CES) well-being gap and minimum 2DGAP IMD polarization indices. Section "Multidimensional Time and Income Polarization in Germany – Results for Socio-Demographic Groups" is about the degree of polarization for various socio-demographic groups.

A general remark to the empirical part: since our study is an extension of our multidimensional time and income poverty study (Merz & Rathjen, 2014a, 2014b), further in-depth empirical justifications and information are available there concerning the variables under investigation, time and income, and all further empirical definitions regarding poverty. These will not be elaborated on in this study.

Time and Income as Multidimensional Polarization Attributes

To understand poverty in a broader sense, empirical multidimensional poverty studies incorporate various poverty attributes. An example is the European Union Laeken social inclusion/exclusion indicator set with educational disadvantages, health inequalities, unemployment, and worklessness as poverty dimensions (Atkinson, 2003). Whereas these and a number of other attributes are broadly accepted and discussed in the context of economic and social policies combating poverty, a simple mirror image of affluence is obviously misleading in many aspects.

Why Use Income as a Polarization Dimension?

Income is the traditional and most-widely accepted poverty attribute and typically the focus of much policy-making. The affluent are commonly defined as controlling a large amount of material resources, in particular income and wealth. Thus, income is a natural candidate as a polarization dimension for both poles.

Why Use Time as a Polarization Dimension?

We argue that, in addition to income as a fundamental material resource, time, though immaterial, is a similar fundamental resource and should be incorporated as a second attribute to better understand societal polarization. Time is important for individual well-being simply by allowing or prohibiting desired everyday activities for the poor and the affluent alike. The importance of the time dimension for poverty studies is stressed meanwhile by other studies (see the discussion in Bittman, 1999; Burchardt, 2008; Goodin, Rice, Parpo, & Eriksson, 2008; Harvey & Mukhopadhyay, 2007 or Merz & Rathjen, 2014a; Vickery, 1977).

Time as an enabling factor is also a condition for social participation, or social inclusion/exclusion, which is an important aspect in the extended poverty discussion (Sen, 1999, 1985). We are also convinced that social participation has a similar importance for the affluent if they are to lead an integrated social life.

Instead of a broad leisure time concept we propose *genuine personal leisure time* as being essential to the multidimensional approach. Time poverty occurs when genuine personal leisure time – which is defined as the time left after all paid and unpaid, market and nonmarket obligations have been met – is below a given threshold level and does not allow or limits social participation in society (see Merz & Rathjen, 2014a for further discussion). Correspondingly, time affluence occurs when genuine personal leisure time is above a given threshold level.

Why Interdependent Time and Income Polarization?

Time availability restricts both market and nonmarket activities. Thus the more time is spent for income-related activities; the less is available for leisure, and vice versa. This trade-off is well-known and is central to optimal allocation theory in microeconomics and Becker's (1965) household production function approach. The microeconomic reference should only illustrate the general competing time–income interdependence; however, the individual time–income optimal allocation admittedly is not in the focus of our analysis.

As discussed above, the trade-off will be quantified in our study by a CES well-being function with time and income as weighted input factors. Instead of arbitrarily chosen trade-off weights and situations with different compensation degrees, we let the German population (through survey data) identify the degree of interdependence and substitution between income and genuine personal leisure time.

Income, Time, and Multidimensional Poverty and Affluence Threshold Line Concepts

Single poverty threshold lines z_i and single affluence lines r_i ($i = 1, 2$) identify the poor and the affluent respectively, and the respective multidimensional well-being thresholds and finally the set of individuals in our polarization analysis. Yet, empirical analysis requires concrete values.

Income: Poverty and Affluence Threshold Line Concept

Income poverty studies commonly use monthly household net equivalence income with equivalence scales like the OECD scale.[7] Conventional income-based poverty studies in the European Union identify a person as income poor if her or his net equivalence income is below 60% of the median income of all households (Bundesregierung, 2005, p. XV). As a result, the 60% median line of the monthly household net equivalence income is adopted in this study as the *income poverty line*. For the sake of comparison, all subsequent income information for 1991/1992 is adjusted to 2001/2002 price levels.

Whereas there is common agreement about the income poverty line, there is a longstanding and still open discussion about a respective affluence line. The German government explicitly focused for the first time on affluence in addition to poverty in their first "Poverty and Affluence Report" (Bundesregierung, 2002), which was followed by three further government reports (Bundesregierung, 2005, 2011, 2013). During that period, top incomes experienced increasing attention not only in Germany (Atkinson & Piketty, 2007; Dell, 2007 with German income tax microdata from 1891 to 1998, Merz, Hirschel, & Zwick, 2005 with German income tax microdata from 1992 to 2003). Several affluence lines were proposed in this literature, including an affluence line as a multiple of an income fraction, such as 200% or 150% of mean median income, or as a top income percentile.

As a pragmatic approach, we are choosing 150% as the cut-off for the median monthly household net equivalence income affluence threshold line, whiche is supported, e.g., by the polarization studies of Goebel et al. (2010) or Grabka & Frick (2008) from the German Economic Institute.

Time: Poverty and Affluence Threshold Line Concept
Compared to income, the discussion about time poverty or even time affluence is still in its infancy. Bittman (1999) mentions a 50% time poverty line. To be consistent to our income poverty and affluence line, we chose 60% of the median genuine personal leisure time as defining an individual which is time poor, and 150% of the median as the time affluence threshold line. Admittedly, such threshold lines are certainly debatable.

MULTIDIMENSIONAL TIME AND INCOME POLARIZATION IN GERMANY – DATA AND EMPIRICAL THRESHOLD LINES

Data: GSOEP 2002 and GTUS 1991/1992 and 2001/2002

The German Socio-Economic Panel (GSOEP)
The GSOEP provides representative individual longitudinal data for all persons older than 16 years living in German households. The representative panel study started in 1984 and provides annual subjective as well as objective information about individual living conditions in Germany (for details, see Wagner, Frick, & Schupp, 2007). In particular, the GSOEP asks about satisfaction with regard to different topics, such as income, as well as general questions about life satisfaction. The 11-point scale regarding general satisfaction information is used for our CES well-being estimation and refers to the recent happiness/satisfaction literature (Clark, Frijters, & Shields, 2008; Sen, 2008; Frey & Stutzer, 2005).

Since appropriate well-being data are only available in the GSOEP, we use the GSOEP 2002 for the CES well-being estimation. Although in principle we could use the GSOEP for further analyses, we prefer to use time use diary data from the GTUSs from 1991/1992 and 2001/2002 (with no appropriate well-being information) since the time use diaries provide more in-depth information.

GTUSs 1991/1992 and 2001/2002
The German Federal Statistical Office conducted two large representative time use surveys, the GTUSs 1991/1992 and 2001/2002 (Ehling, 2003;

Ehling, Holz, & Kahle, 2001). In these surveys all respondents in a household older than 11 years noted their everyday routines in diaries in their own words for two working days and a Saturday or Sunday. Personal and household questionnaires also provided socio-economic background information. The final available data for our analysis comprised 6,774 households with 15,366 persons and 30,732 diaries for 1991/1992, and 5,144 households with 11,908 persons and 35,685 diaries for 2001/2002.

Empirical Time, Income, and Well-Being Multidimensional Poverty and Affluence Threshold Lines, Germany, 1991/1992 and 2001/2002

The time and income single poverty and affluence threshold lines are summarized in Table 1.[8] All income data are adjusted for price inflation.

The *median income*, and as a result the income poverty and affluence thresholds, increased by 19.2% to 1322.59 euros in the 10-year period between 1991/1992 and 2001/2002.

The *median time*, and again the time poverty and affluence thresholds, increased somewhat less by 17.0% to 310 minutes per day within that 10-year period.

Concerning the empirical well-being and isopolarization thresholds an estimation of the CES well-being function is necessary. With the GSOEP-reported general life satisfaction data on an 11-point scale,[9] an estimation of individual well-being requires rather a type of ordered response

Table 1. Income, Time, and Well-Being Multidimensional Poverty and Affluence Lines, Germany 1991/1992 and 2001/2002.

	1991/1992	2001/2002
Median net equivalence income (in euros per month and 2002 prices)	1109.64	1322.58
Median personal leisure time (in minutes per day)	265	310
Income poverty line (=60% median net equivalence income)	665.78	793.55
Time poverty line (=60% median personal leisure time)	159	186
Well-being poor $V^{\text{poor}} = f(I^{\text{poor}}, L^{\text{poor}})$	6.704	6.827
Income affluence line (=150% of median)	1664.46	1983.97
Time affluence line (=150% of median)	397.50	465.00
Well-being rich $V^{\text{rich}} = f(I^{\text{rich}}, L^{\text{rich}})$	7.402	7.538

Source: Own calculations with data from GTUS 1991/1992 and 2001/2002. The time and income poverty lines and affluence lines by GTUS data are calculated for the total population for the median income, and the median genuine personal leisure time for the available population older than 11 years.

modeling. The Kmenta (1967) Taylor series approach, however, allows a simple OLS estimation of the log-transformed nonlinear CES well-being function (see Merz & Rathjen, 2014a) and results in the CES well-being function

$$V = f(I, L) = 3.550 \cdot (0.519 \cdot I^{0.297} + 0.481 \cdot L^{0.297})^{\frac{0.108}{0.297}} \tag{19}$$

with $I = x_{i1}$ for income and $L = x_{i2}$ for genuine personal leisure time. Significantly estimated coefficients together with the fulfillment of further consistency rules quantify the relevance of substitution/compensation between time and income. The population-based evaluation[10] of the substitution/compensation between genuine time and income yields a substitution elasticity of $\sigma = 1.422$, which shows an easier substitution than in the Cobb–Douglas type ($\sigma = 1$) situation.[11] For comparison reasons, the 1991/1992 well-being function is specified by the same estimated parameters as in 2001/2002.

The evaluated *well-being poverty threshold line* at the intersection of the single time and income thresholds in Eq. (19) has a well-being level of 6.704 in 1991/1992 and 6.827 in 2001/2002. By contrast, the evaluated *well-being affluence threshold line* at the intersection of the single time and income thresholds yields a well-being level of 7.402 in 1991/1992 and 7.538 in 2001/2002.

Thus, the CES results suggest a slight increase in overall well-being over the 10-year period. The estimated input coefficients, the weight w for income and $(1 - w)$ for personal leisure, indicate a relative importance of income. However, the evaluated time contribution is not that far away from a balanced 50% situation and reflects the importance of time.

MULTIDIMENSIONAL TIME AND INCOME POLARIZATION IN GERMANY – HEADCOUNT RATIOS, WELL-BEING GAP, AND MINIMUM 2DGAP RESULTS

Overall Multidimensional Polarization Results: Headcount Ratios and Well-Being Gaps

Our analysis concentrates on the economically active population. With regard to the working poor, we shed light on a situation where despite governmental efforts poverty still exists. Similarly, we regard the economically active affluent without taking any further wealth situation into account. Thus, we will focus for both distributional poles on those who are economically active with more than five daily working hours.[12]

We identify the poor and the affluent by their headcount ratios subdivided in six multidimensional regimes for both available years (Fig. 4). The regimes identify unidimensional time and income polarization as well as IMD time and income polarization with their compensation regimes. Table 2 provides unidimensional and multidimensional polarization well-being results of our respective indices as well as of indices from the literature. With a focus on our new well-being indices, we only briefly summarize some results of the literature indices. Together with their formulas, they are discussed in more detail in Merz and Scherg (2013).

Unidimensional Polarization Results

Table 2 and Fig. 4 summarize the unidimensional income and time results. The combined *time* polarization situation is less selective than the *income* polarization situation; the still divergent poverty and affluence developments only result in a significantly increased median specific polarization (Wang and Tsui). All other polarization measures (Foster and Wolfson; Esteban, Gradín, and Ray; Scheicher) are insignificant with respect to time. However with respect to income, all these measures (except Scheicher) describe a significant income polarization decrease.

Multidimensional Well-Being Results

The discussed *compensation approach (weak focus axiom)* allows substitution between time and income and respects the interdependence of the polarization dimensions. New results of our *well-being multidimensional polarization measures* and components over that decade in Germany are presented (IMD results in Fig. 4 and Table 2). We regard P_{median} (Eq. (3)) which is related to the median P_{poles} (Eq. (4)), which in turn is related to the poverty and affluence lines, and $P_{\text{poles, ratio}}$ (Eq. (9)) which measures the asymmetry of both pole gaps. We divide the discussion with respect to the poverty and the affluence poles, and then discuss them combined.

IMD Poverty: The *headcount ratios* of the multidimensional poor (Fig. 4 top, regimes P1, P2, P3) declined slightly from 12.6% in 1991/1992 to 12.2% in 2001/2002. Though the change is not significant, the absolute level of the working poor in both years is still remarkable. Regime P3 is of particular importance as even an income above the poverty threshold is assigned not to compensate time poverty for 9.3% and 8.7%, respectively,

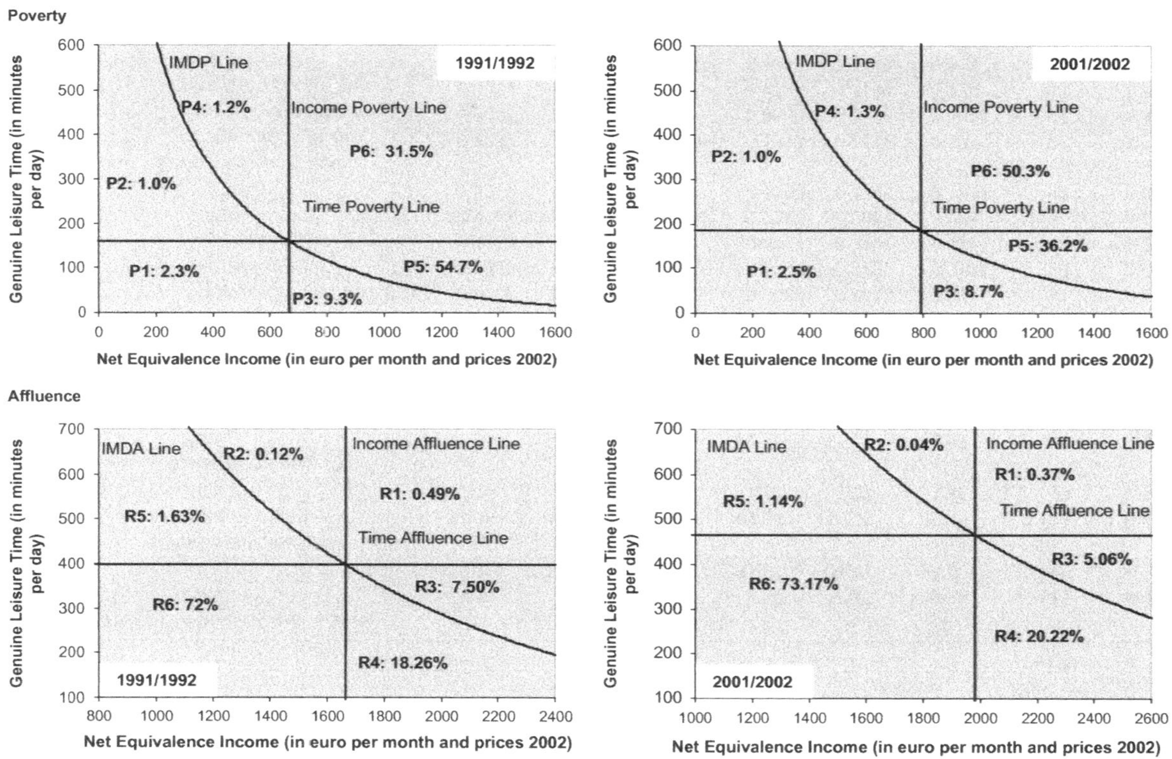

Fig. 4. Multidimensional Polarization Headcount Ratios in Different Poverty and Affluence Regimes for Germany 1991/1992 and 2001/2002. *Note*: IMDP (IMDA) line is the multidimensional time and income isopoverty/isoaffluence threshold based on the GTUS 2002 CES estimates. *Source*: Own calculations with GTUS 1991/1992 and 2001/2002, economically active population.

Table 2. IMD and Unidimensional Time and Income Polarization Headcount Ratios and Well-Being Measures: 1991/1992 and 2001/2002, Germany.

		1991/1992			2001/2002				
		Index	95% confidence interval		Index	95% confidence interval		Ratio 1991/1992 =100	Diff. test[a] *p*-values
Headcount ratio (%)	Unidimensional income								
	Poor	4.19	3.79	4.58	4.82	4.35	5.28	115	0.043*
	Rich	26.25	25.39	27.12	25.65	24.71	26.6	98	0.361
	Unidimensional time								
	Poor	43.06	42.09	44.03	47.34	46.26	48.43	110	0.000***
	Rich	2.24	1.95	2.53	1.55	1.28	1.82	69	0.000***
	Multidimensional IMD[b]								
	Poor	12.55	11.9	13.2	12.16	11.45	12.87	97	0.425
	Rich	8.11	7.57	8.65	5.47	4.97	5.96	67	0.000***
	Poor and rich	20.66	19.81	21.50	17.63	16.85	18.41	85	0.000***
Polarization	Unidimensional income								
	Foster and Wolfson	0.0996	0.0969	0.1023	0.0908	0.0878	0.9386	91	0.000***
	Esteban, Gradín, and Ray	0.0506	0.0498	0.0516	0.0458	0.0445	0.047	91	0.000***
	Gap Wang, and Tsui	0.4356	0.4257	0.4455	0.3894	0.3801	0.3988	89	0.000***
	Gap Scheicher	0.4104	0.4017	0.419	0.4034	0.3941	0.4127	98	0.286
	Poor	0.1905	0.1749	0.2061	0.2215	0.2063	0.2366	116	0.005**
	Affluent	0.2199	0.2134	0.2263	0.1820	0.1745	0.1895	83	0.000***
	Unidimensional time								
	Foster and Wolfson	0.1239	0.1201	0.1276	0.1214	0.1172	0.1255	98	0.379
	Esteban, Gradín, and Ray	0.0608	0.0596	0.0619	0.0600	0.0586	0.0614	99	0.357
	Gap Wang, and Tsui	0.4074	0.4022	0.4125	0.4205	0.4149	0.426	103	0.000***
	Gap Scheicher	0.5115	0.5033	0.5197	0.5073	0.4987	0.5158	99	0.484

Poor	0.4037	0.3956	0.4118	0.3899	0.3818	0.3980	97	0.018*
Rich	0.1078	0.0964	0.1192	0.1174	0.0989	0.1359	109	0.388
Multidimensional								
Scheicher (Gap)	223.64	214.91	232.38	224.02	214.83	233.22	100	0.953
Multidimensional IMD								
*P*median (%)	3.28	3.23	3.34	3.09	3.03	3.15	94	0.000***
*P*poles (%)	5.20	5.02	5.39	4.87	4.65	5.08	94	0.020*
Poor	3.49	3.28	0.37	3.35	0.31	3.59	96	0.394
Rich	1.72	1.61	1.83	1.52	0.14	1.64	88	0.018*
*P*poles, ratio	2.03			2.2				

Source: GTUS 1991/1992 and 2001/2002, own calculations, weighted data.

Notes: IMD: Interdependent Multidimensional compensation approach; Affluence: CES well-being at 150% of income respective time median (CES well-being (1991/1992) = 7.402, CES well-being (2001/2002) = 7.538).

[a]Two-sample difference in means test with variance inhomogeneity and unequal variances; *** = significant on the 0.1% level; ** = significant on the 1% level; * = significant on the 5% level.

[b]IMD: Interdependent Multidimensional compensation approach; Poverty: CES well-being at 60% of income respective time median (CES well-being (1991/1992) = 6.704, CES well-being (2001/2002) = 6.827).

of the economically active population. Regime P3 is also the prominent poverty regime in the multidimensional perspective. A detailed discussion of time and income multidimensional *poverty* development (compensation approach, weak focus axiom) with the same data is provided by Merz and Rathjen (2014a).

IMD Affluence: There is a significant reduction in multidimensional affluence by *headcount ratios* from 1991/1992 to 2001/2002 from 8.1% to 5.5% (Table 2 and Fig. 4 bottom, regimes R1, R2, R3). The prominent regime in both years is regime R4. These individuals (18.26% respectively 20.22%) are assigned not to be multidimensional affluent though income rich but time poor; their time deficit is assigned not to be compensated by high income. In contrast, regime R3 individuals (only 7.50% respectively 5.06%) are assigned to be compensated their time deficit by their high income; they are multidimensional affluent.

Furthermore, whereas this group and regime decreases from 7.5% to 5.06% in 2001/2002, regime R4 developed in the opposite direction, from 18.26% to 20.22%. Thus, the headcount ratio of the income but not time affluent increased in Germany over that decade. Notably, there is only less than a half percent of the economically active population which is affluent in both attributes and both years (regime R1).

IMD Polarization: Now regard the combined poverty and affluence situation. The IMD polarization *headcount ratio* decreases significantly from a remarkable 20.7% in 1991/1992 to 17.6% in 2001/2002. Of specific interest and empirical importance are regimes with time deficits (Table 3): for poverty, where the time deficit is assigned not to be compensated even by above poverty threshold income (regime P3); for affluence, where the time deficit is assigned to be compensated by above affluence threshold income (regime R3). These regimes show the highest IMD polarization headcount ratios for both years and emphasize the importance of genuine personal leisure time for the German population.

IMD polarization well-being intensity decreases significantly over that decade if the common polarization threshold is the median (P_{median}). However, if the isopoverty and isoaffluence thresholds are farther from the median, then the multidimensional polarization decrease is only of minor significance (P_{poles}). This indicates particular differences between the lower and upper middle classes relatively close to the median.

Thus, based on the compensation evaluation of the German population with a CES well-being function, time and income polarization only declined in the 1990s when both distributional poles were measured with respect to the median time and income values.

If differences to median pole thresholds are regarded, which pole is driving the polarization measure? An answer is given by our *multidimensional well-being polarization gap ratio,* $P_{\text{poles, ratio}}$ (Eq. (9)), which measures the *pole asymmetry*. The mean well-being poverty gap is more than twice as large as the mean well-being affluence gap, and, the pole asymmetry grew. The dominance of the poverty well-being gap might be explained as follows. First, less than 1% is considered affluent in both dimensions (possibly due to underreporting) and are expected to be not far away from the IMD affluence line, which results in small well-being differences. Second, and a related reason, instead of being affluent in both dimensions it is expected instead that high income together with high working hours restricts genuine personal leisure time. Relatively high regime R4 headcount ratios (Fig. 4) support this argument.

To summarize the overall situation, the *unidimensional* consideration of income and time suggests a decrease in income polarization and a slight increase in time polarization in Germany over the decade. Concerning the single poles, time as well income poverty increases whereas income affluence decreases. Therefore, there is no definite evidence of an increasing bipolarity of income and time distribution if the unidimensional measures are regarded separately.

The proposed *IMD* polarization well-being approach however provides such a combined analysis. The results up to now show, only with respect to the median but not to the specific poverty and affluence lines, a significant overall decrease in IMD time and income polarization.

Multidimensional Polarization by the Minimum 2DGAP

The 2DGAP results so far discussed embrace the interdependence of time and income under the CES well-being shield. However, and in particular for targeted policy analysis, one might argue that the single polarization attributes suffer from a lack of transparency when only a one-value indicator is given. Our proposed multidimensional polarization 2DGAP measure, developed in section "Minimum Multidimensional Polarization Gap (2DGAP)" above, in fact provides such a single time and income polarization contribution while respecting the assigned attribute compensations.

Table 3 shows polarization results as *mean minimum 2DGAPs* (Eq. (17)) with the disentangled income and genuine personal leisure time components (Eq. (18)) for 1991/1992 and 2001/2002 overall and divided for the respective poverty and affluence regimes. In addition, Table 3 presents

Table 3. Multidimensional Polarization: Mean Minimum 2DGAP of IMD Time and Income, Regime-Specific Headcount Ratios, and Mean Well-Being Gaps 1991/1992 and 2001/2002, Germany[a].

		Headcount Ratio				Well-Being Gap				2DGAP: Mean Minimum 2DGAP c				2DGAP: Mean Minimum Income 2DGAP a (in €)				2DGAP: Mean Minimum Time 2DGAP b (in minutes per day)			
	Year	1991	2001	Index 1991 =100	Diff. test[e]	1991	2001	Index 1991 =100	Diff. test	1991	2001	Index 1991 =100	Diff. test	1991	2001	Index 1991 =100	Diff. test	1991	2001	Index 1991 =100	Diff. test
Poor	P1[b]	2.28	2.46	107		0.2593	0 3435	131	***	106.48	152.21	143	***	50.52	72.09	143	***	92.85	133.11	144	***
	P2[c]	1.04	1.02	98		0.0932	0.1080	18		56.32	74.75	133	*	35.51	46.67	131		43.19	57.82	134	*
	P3[d]	9.27	8.69	94		0.2186	0.1864	86	**	34.54	44.10	128	***	7.64	10.71	140	***	33.58	42.66	127	***
	IMD poor	12.9	12.17	97		0.2160	0.2116	95		49.38	68.50	139	***	17.72	26.11	147	***	45.11	62.20	138	***
Rich	R1	0.49	0.37	76		0.1831	0.1639	88		188.66	204.65	108		36.26	40.30	111		183.98	199.59	108	
	R2	0.12	0.04	33	*	0.0291	0.0557	21		39.79	95.74	241	*	16.30	46.04	282	*	36.27	83.92	231	*
	R3	7.50	5.06	67	***	0.1296	0.1146	85	*	86.42	90.96	105		9.85	9.76	99		85.63	90.30	105	
	IMD rich	8.11	5.47	67	***	0.1314	0.11752	92	*	91.92	98.73	107		11.55	12.09	107		90.87	97.69	108	
Rich and Poor	P1 + R1	2.77	2.83	102		0.4424	0.5075	114	**	295.14	356.86	121	***	86.78	112.39	130	***	276.56	332.7	120	***
	P2 + R2	1.16	1.06	91		0.1223	0.1638	141	**	96.11	170.49	177	***	51.81	92.71	179	***	79.46	141.74	178	***
	P3 + R3	16.77	13.75	82	***	0.3483	0.3010	86	***	120.96	135.06	117	***	17.49	20.47	117	***	119.21	132.96	112	***
	IMD P + IMD R	**20.70**	**17.64**	**85**	***	**0.3473**	**0.3291**	**94**	*	**141.30**	**167.23**	**118**	***	**29.27**	**38.56**	**132**	***	**135.98**	**159.89**	**118**	***

Source: Own calculations with GTUS 1991/1992 and 2001/2002, economically active population.

Notes: Poverty: CES well-being at 60% of income respective time median (CES well-being in 1991/1992 = 6.704, CES well-being in 2001/2002 = 6.827); IMD: interdependent multidimensional compensation approach; Affluence: CES well-being at 150% of income respective time median (CES well-being in 1991/1992 = 7.402, CES well-being in 2001/2002 = 7.538).

[a]Poor describes multidimensional poverty, Rich multidimensional affluence, and Rich & Poor multidimensional polarization in respective regimes; Headcount Ratio as P_{all} of Eq. (4) with $\alpha = \beta = 0$; Mean well-being gap as P_{poles} of Eq. (5) with $\alpha = \beta = 1$.

[b]P1/R1: regime of income *and* time poor/rich individuals.

[c]P2: regime of income poor individuals but not time poor.

[d]P3: regime of time poor individuals but not income poor; R2: regime of time rich individuals but not income rich; R3: regime of income rich individuals but not time rich.

[e]Two-sample difference in means test with variance inhomogeneity and unequal variances; *** = significant at the 1% level; ** = significant at the 5% level; * = significant at the 10% level.

regime-specific mean well-being gaps as the underlying one-value well-being indicator, and further regime-specific polarization headcount ratios.

2DGAP Overall (C) (see the last line of Table 3): The *mean multidimensional polarization 2DGAP* (*C*, Eq. (17)) increased significantly by 18% starting at 141.30 in 1991/1992. Thus, respecting the compensation between genuine personal leisure time and income as evaluated by the German population, polarization increased in the 1990s, a remarkable result.

Of particular interest are its mean components for income and time (*A* and *B* of Eq. (18)) under compensation:

2DGAP Income Component (A): The summarized mean minimum *income 2DGA*P component increases from €29.27 to €38.58 (2DGAP *a*). Though the mean income gap is small, the relative monetary increase of 32% is remarkable and highly significant. There is an asymmetry with a stronger poverty than affluence intensity: the poverty income component (€17.72) is greater than the affluence income component (€11.55). This might be an indication for an antipoverty policy instead of a policy to tax higher income in an effort to successfully decrease polarization.

2DGAP Time Component (B): The summarized mean minimum *time 2DGAP* component of the poverty and affluence gaps (2DGAP *b*) increased significantly from 136 minutes per day to 150 minutes of genuine personal leisure time by 18%. The asymmetry between the poor and the affluent mean minimum time gap component is remarkable. The affluence time gap in 1991/1992 is twice as large as the poor time gap in 1991/1992. It is reduced to a 1.6 multiple in 2001/2002. A steeper mean minimum 2DGAP *c* for the affluent with a higher time–income relation indicates the importance of the compensated time deficits (regime R3, Fig. 4). By some contrast, the less steep mean minimum 2DGAP *c* for the poor with a lower time–income relation indicates the importance of the time situation below the income threshold.

Overall, though genuine personal leisure time is an important contribution to well-being polarization, the significant overall 2DGAP polarization growth is mainly due to the significant growth of the income 2DGAP component.

2DGAP polarization regimes: The minimum polarization gaps (2DGAP) measure the poverty and affluence intensities. The strongest polarization intensity is given for the intersection of time and income poverty together and for each respective pole separately (Table 3, regimes P1, R1 and IMD poor and IMD rich). Those individuals face poverty or affluence beyond any compensation. This holds for the combined 2DGAP *C* as well as for the single income (2DGAP *A*) and time (2DGAP *B*) components.

The strongest gap growth rate is seen in the R2 regime for the affluent based, however, on a relatively low headcount ratio. Individuals there are multidimensional affluent though income is below the affluence income threshold; less income there is assigned to be compensated by time affluence. Further results concerning the single income and time 2DGAP components can be found in Table 3.

The 2DGAP results, different for various regimes, show different combinations of different time–income compensation and stress the differences to escape poverty or to leave affluence by the shortest way.

Polarization centers: The mean minimum 2DGAP can also describe polarization centers. In particular, a polarization center is the starting point (x_{1c}, x_{2c}) of the mean minimum 2DGAP (Table 4).[13]

At the polarization center the relation B/A of the 2DGAP poverty intensity components illustrates the compensation there. For 2001/2002 poverty, the slope at the IMD isopoverty line where c is crossing (= marginal rate of substitution) is $c'_{\perp} = -A/B = -0.42$. Thus the assigned amount of time to compensate one euro income locally is about 0.42 minutes; that is, it is less than a 1:1 compensation; 0.42 minutes are enough to compensate one euro, which highlights the particular importance of time. For 2001/2002 affluence, the comparable slope is 0.12; that is, 0.12 minutes are enough to compensate one euro, which highlights the even stronger time importance for the affluent.

Fig. 5 illustrates the positions of the mean minimum 2DGAP and their polarization centers for 1991/1992 (black) and 2001/2002 (gray). Three results illustrate the numerical findings: first, the mean gaps are relatively small, thus the poverty and affluence positions are relatively near their respective thresholds. Second, there is a particular move of the mean affluence gap to higher income over the decade. Third, relatively steep rising mean gaps pinpoint the importance of the time component.

Table 4. Multidimensional Polarization Centers 1991/1992 and 2001/2002, Germany.

2DGAP components	1991/1992		2001/2002	
	Poor	Rich	Poor	Rich
Income (x_{1c}) (€)	656.72	2818.95	735.98	3344.46
Time (x_{2c}) (minutes)	109	224	131	56

Source: Own calculations with GTUS 1991/1992 and 2001/2002, economically active population.

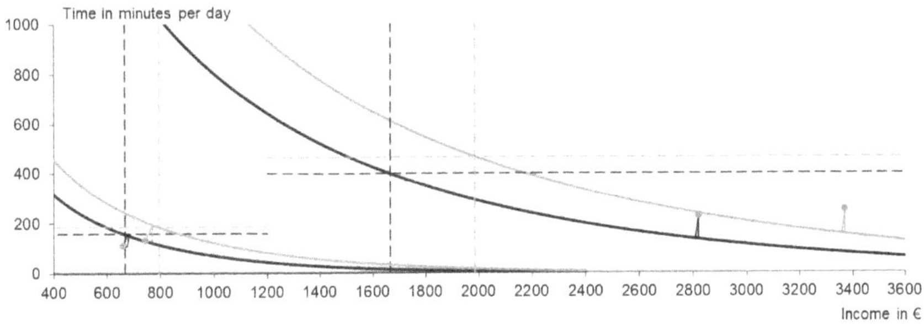

Fig. 5. Multidimensional Polarization: Mean Minimum Multidimensional Polarization Pole Gaps (2DGAP *c*) and Polarization Centers 1991/1992 and 2001/2002 (gray). *Source*: Own calculations with GTUS 1991/1992 and 2001/2002, economically active population.

The Kernel densities of the poverty and affluence gap distributions for 1991/1992 and 2001/2002 shown in Fig. 6 illustrate the different pole distributions of the minimum 2DGAP *c* measure. The affluent pole distributions are more right-skewed than the poor pole distributions and characterize situations farther away from their polarization threshold.

Multidimensional Polarization Well-Being and Minimum 2DGAP Results Compared

A last remark is about differences between well-being and minimum 2DGAP results. The mean minimum polarization gaps (2DGAP) indicate a significant increase in multidimensional time and income polarization, whereas the well-being polarization gaps indicate some decreasing polarization, which is however significant only for the median reference and of minor importance for the pole threshold specific measure (P_{poles}).

One explanation is the following: Any well-being difference is described by two respective contours as isoquants in the 2D attribute space. There, a fan of multitude gaps describes the differences from one individual situation to the isopoverty or the isoaffluence line. Yet, there is only a one-value well-being gap, which covers the whole area between the individual isoquant and the respective isothreshold. However, the indefinite number of possible distances (gaps) between a single situation and the isopoverty or the isoaffluence line results in a fuzzy overall well-being situation. The minimum 2DGAP approach, by contrast, builds on a unique well-defined multidimensional shortest distance from the individual situation to the respective threshold with interpretable polarization components. So, the

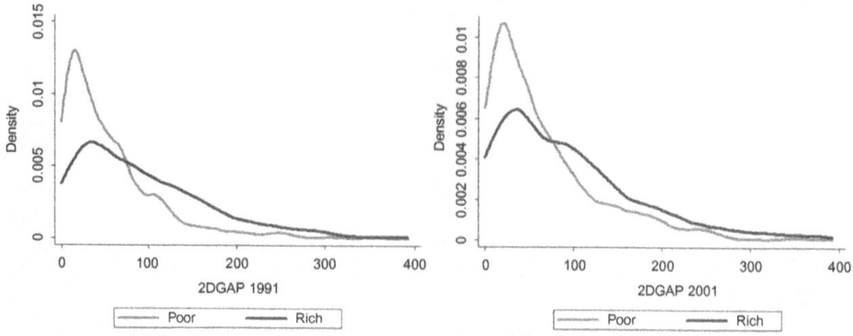

Fig. 6. Kernel Densities of Minimum Multidimensional Polarization Pole Gaps (2DGAP *c*) 1991/1992 and 2001/2002, Germany. *Source*: Own calculations with GTUS 1991/1992 and 2001/2002, economically active population.

"fuzziness" of the well-being gap might be the reason for different well-being gap and minimum 2DGAP results.

To summarize the 2DGAP multidimensional polarization results, with highly significant results we face a strong case for an increased IMD time and income polarization intensity for Germany between 1991/1992 and 2001/2002.

MULTIDIMENSIONAL TIME AND INCOME POLARIZATION IN GERMANY – RESULTS FOR SOCIO-DEMOGRAPHIC GROUPS

It is to be expected that different individual resources and limitations will result in a different polarization situation for different socio-economic and socio-demographic groups. Finally, for those groups which experience attention in the public discussion, Table 5 presents polarization headcount ratios, mean IMDP well-being gaps (compensation approach, weak focus), and mean minimum multidimensional 2DGAPs with their income and time components respecting compensation. The 2001/2002 information also provides indices that describe the development since 1991/1992 in Germany (detailed results are given in the Appendix, Tables 4b,c, including information for the single poles in our downloadable discussion paper Merz & Scherg, 2013).

Table 5. Multidimensional Polarization in Socio-Economic Groups of IMD Time and Income Polarization 2001/2002, Germany.

	Polarization Headcount Ratio						Well-Being Gap		Multidimensional Polarization Minimum 2DGAP					
	Income	Index 1991 =100	Time	Index 1991 =100	IMD[a]	Index 1991 =100	Mean	Index 1991 =100	Mean *c*	Index 1991 =100	Mean *a* Income (€)	Index 1991 =100	Mean *b* Time (min.)	Index 1991 =100
Gender														
Male	29.84	99	47.29	115	17.76	92	0.3525	103	182.97	134	40.51	152	175.34	133
Female	31.55	99	51.65	98	17.40	76	0.2845	80	135.34	92	33.88	105	128.46	91
Age														
12–17	17.05	76	40.57	103	17.90	135	0.2846	114	158.86	89	69.38	105	140.47	86
18–24	20.32	79	38.45	95	14.65	81	0.2776	84	158.23	111	45.83	126	148.90	111
25–44	28.79	101	50.92	109	17.97	84	0.3171	95	157.61	117	37.47	136	150.20	116
45–65	36.16	97	49.75	109	18.16	86	0.3520	95	174.20	120	36.08	130	167.79	120
>65	54.33	139	59.91	151	20.65	84	0.2662	45	189.54	110	55.76	283	175.89	103
Education														
A-Level	45.86	107	52.52	114	19.07	76	0.3579	97	172.75	113	36.81	113	166.35	115
Vocational dipl.	33.50	71	48.46	104	18.46	70	0.2919	74	163.61	115	37.92	134	156.19	114
Second. school II	24.92	93	49.54	107	18.33	85	0.3212	96	167.12	117	42.47	130	158.45	116
Second. school I	22.90	87	45.16	103	15.08	91	0.3217	100	155.57	127	32.79	135	149.65	126
No certificate	28.69	219	48.84	158	17.64	145	0.2595	54	131.82	63	32.41	95	126.62	63
Occupation														
Self-employed	52.88	100	59.44	114	33.95	96	0.4563	95	240.22	129	59.59	168	227.72	128
Liberal. Prof.	59.84	–	49.64	–	28.29	–	0.4278	–	230.50	–	50.67	–	220.54	–
Entrepreneur	48.16	–	66.11	–	37.79	–	0.4510	–	231.47	–	62.20	–	218.11	–
Civil servant	53.22	97	47.83	124	18.97	82	0.3220	80	135.19	104	16.37	84	133.84	104
White-collar	33.88	102	50.14	103	14.34	69	0.2886	88	130.23	103	24.43	72	126.69	104
Blue-collar	15.41	78	46.35	110	14.95	85	0.2561	88	155.62	127	37.06	124	149.97	128

Table 5. *(Continued)*

	Polarization Headcount Ratio						Well-Being Gap		Multidimensional Polarization Minimum 2DGAP					
	Income	Index 1991 =100	Time	Index 1991 =100	IMD[a]	Index 1991 =100	Mean	Index 1991 =100	Mean *c*	Index 1991 =100	Mean *a* Income (€)	Index 1991 =100	Mean *b* Time (min.)	Index 1991 =100
Working hours														
<20	21.70	75	47.74	116	22.24	105	0.2597	88	170.52	112	44.65	94	162.31	116
21–38	24.74	71	44.03	107	13.62	78	0.2745	82	151.23	112	31.58	115	145.84	112
39–40	27.98	115	47.70	103	14.23	71	0.3001	102	151.38	130	31.14	118	146.37	131
41–44	32.57	149	50.91	113	16.84	90	0.3508	78	187.05	100	36.04	106	182.01	100
>45	46.75	106	60.99	115	27.9	92	0.4024	91	187.40	115	45.74	163	177.82	113
HH – size														
Single-H H	30.13	132	50.40	122	15.88	81	0.3067	88	178.73	109	36.52	77	172.49	123
Couple 0 kids	56.07	110	46.82	108	18.17	69	0.3294	90	150.37	106	26.76	112	145.84	106
Couple 1 kid	23.95	136	47.47	102	14.04	95	0.2780	94	127.73	98	31.69	106	122.67	98
Couple 2 kids	14.61	97	49.36	97	16.34	78	0.2833	85	146.62	97	42.85	148	138.69	94
Couple >2 kids	20.94	114	57.65	100	31.68	118	0.2973	96	191.76	147	84.28	294	170.43	135
Single par. 1 kid	31.18	121	40.46	78	22.23	105	0.3337	90	232.64	133	65.03	145	218.50	132
Single par. >1k id	22.96	81	51.77	82	17.43	40	0.2491	119	146.09	151	47.44	114	135.88	158
Other structure	25.96	73	50.99	120	17.46	96	0.3693	102	160.14	129	52.63	212	148.68	124
Region														
West Germany	32.98	90	46.43	110	16.26	87	0.3193	85	161.59	121	36.16	141	154.57	120
East Germany	19.38	114	59.77	114	23.65	93	0.3536	113	191.00	126	46.06	128	182.51	126

Source: Own calculations with GTUS 1991/1992 and 2001/2002, economically active population.
[a]IMD: Interdependent Multidimensional polarization compensation approach.

There are many interesting individual results given the compensation evaluation by the German society. To be brief, we will focus on selected results, in particular with regard to our new multidimensional 2DGAP polarization measure and its components, which describe the polarization intensity concerning income (in euros) and genuine personal leisure time (in minutes).

Gender: Females are affected more often than males by poverty or affluence referring to unidimensional income and time polarization. In contrast, males face a deeper multidimensional polarization gap (2DGAP *c*) overall *and* with respect to income and time. And, the 2DGAP polarization increased the most (2DGAP *a, b, c*) between 1991/1992 to 2001/2002 for males.

Age: Individuals who are over 65 years old and who are still working more than five daily hours are the group with the highest unidimensional polarization headcount ratios in the poles as well as under the IMD polarization regimes. The older the individuals are, the deeper are the polarization gaps (2DGAP *c*), too. The importance of age for both distributional poles is remarkable and underlines a particular erosion of the middle class for the elderly.

Education: Individuals with an A level (*Abitur*) – in contrast to all other educational levels – show the most intense polarization. The higher the education level, the higher is the headcount ratio of the affluent (Merz & Scherg, 2013, Appendix Table 4b). Secondary schooling is connected with the fastest polarization growth, which in contrast to A-level education is driven by a prominent poverty pole importance.

Occupation: The self-employed are remarkably more often affected by income (52.88%), time (59.44%), and IMD polarization (33.95%) than any other occupational group. Subdividing the self-employed into the liberal professions (architects, lawyers, physicians, etc.) and entrepreneurs reveals that the high percentages should be traced back to the high percentages of entrepreneurs with regard to time and IMD polarization, however not for the reverse income polarization. Furthermore, polarization intensity measured by multidimensional gaps show the highest spread for the self-employed (2DGAP *c*) and in particular for genuine personal leisure time (2DGAP *b*). Finally, multidimensional polarization grew fastest for the self-employed, followed by blue-collar workers.

For the self-employed, one notable result is that since two-thirds of the self-employed in the two poles under IMD polarization are found at the poverty pole, the deprived situation is of particular importance for the self-employed despite the relatively dominant affluence gap contribution (see Merz & Scherg, 2013, Appendix Tables 4b,c). This underpins and is in line with the self-employed multidimensional time and income *poverty* results of Merz and Rathjen (2011).

Working Hours: The highest polarization headcount ratios and the largest IMD polarization intensity (2DGAP *c*) are found for those with the most weekly working hours.

Household/Family Structure: The IMD polarization headcount ratio for couples with two or more children is the highest among the family groups, the polarization is strongest for single parents with children (2DGAP *c*). As to be expected, single parents with children also show the relatively highest time gap. Further analysis show that this is mainly due to the poverty pole. They faced a strong polarization increase by 33% (2DGAP *c*) over that decade. The increase is even stronger for single parents with more children (51%) and pinpoints growing difficulties for single parents.

Region: Though unidimensional income and time poverty headcount ratios are higher in the old German states, this is not the case for the multidimensional situation. The relative number of individuals in the distributional poles is higher in the new German states (23.65% vs. 16.26% in the old German states) and the polarization intensity overall and with regard to income and time is greater in the new than in the old German states.

To summarize: As expected, different socio-demographic groups show different unidimensional and multidimensional polarization and different polarization growth depending on gender, age, education, family structure, and geographic region. Notably, multidimensional polarization of time and income of the self-employed as well single parents deserves specific attention.

Our quantification of multidimensional time and income polarization for various socio-demographic groups in Germany is important to detect groups of specific concern. It is expected that many further factors will be needed to explain and to formulate targeted policies. This discussion has to be postponed until further research has been done.

CONCLUDING REMARKS

This study contributes to the conceptual refinement of multidimensional polarization by using new methodological approaches which provide new empirical results. In particular, we propose a CES well-being function to capture interdependence/compensation/substitution between polarization attributes. This is the basis for new well-being polarization measures and for the new minimum multidimensional polarization (2DGAP) approach. In particular, the 2DGAP approach disentangles the single polarization attributes *and* ensures at the same time that compensation between the polarization attributes is accounted for. This is important for the development of targeted economic and social policies.

The empirical application uses genuine personal leisure time in addition to income as polarization attributes in order to supplement the traditional use of income in polarization indices with social participation aspects. This is done by using the German time use diary data for the period 1991/1992 to 2001/2002. Beyond unidimensional and multidimensional polarization results of measures found in the literature, we develop new findings about polarization while accounting for compensation, which is not given an arbitrary value but instead one which is estimated and evaluated by the German population.

There are three prominent empirical results for Germany: First, genuine personal leisure time, in addition to income, appears to be an important and significant polarization attribute. Second, compensation between these two attributes, evaluated by the German population, is found to be of economic and statistical significance. Third, as shown by the new minimum 2DGAP approach, multidimensional polarization significantly increased in Germany over the decade 1991/1992–2001/2002.

In particular, the *IMD polarization headcount ratio* decreases significantly from a remarkable 20.7% in 1991/1992 to 17.6% in 2001/2002. Of specific interest and empirical importance are regimes with time deficits (Table 3): for poverty, where the time deficit is assigned not to be compensated even by above poverty threshold income (regime P3); for affluence, where the time deficit is assigned to be compensated by above affluence threshold income (regime R3). These regimes show the highest IMD polarization headcount ratios for both years and emphasize the importance of genuine personal leisure time for the German population.

IMD polarization well-being intensity decreases significantly over that decade if the common polarization threshold is the median. However, if the isopoverty and isoaffluence thresholds are farther from the median, then the multidimensional polarization well-being intensity decrease is only of minor significance. This indicates particular differences between the lower and upper middle classes relatively close to the median. The *new minimum 2DGAP polarization* measure, however, shows a significant increase of multidimensional time and income polarization intensity by 18%. The disentangled components increased significantly for income (32%) and less distinct but also significantly for genuine personal leisure time (18%). With regard to polarization regimes, the strongest multidimensional polarization 2DGAP intensity is given for the intersection of time and income for the poverty as well as for the affluence pole.

The starting point of the overall mean minimum 2DGAP intensity can be interpreted as a *polarization center*. For the poverty pole this center is in the intersection of time as well income poverty. For the affluence pole this center is in the regime where the time deficit is assigned to be not compensated by above affluence threshold income. The polarization centers thus show time deficits in both poles and highlights the strong importance of genuine personal leisure time for the multidimensional polarization in Germany that time period.

We argue that some differences in well-being and minimum 2DGAP intensity results are due to the "fuzziness" of the well-being gap. In summary, with highly significant minimum 2DGAP results we face a strong case for an increased IMD time and income polarization intensity for Germany between 1991/1992 and 2001/2002.

Further results for socio-demographic groups show greater polarization for the self-employed and increasingly for single parents than for differences based on gender, age, or geographic region.

These and all other findings in this study stress the relevance of genuine personal leisure time with its social participation aspect as an important polarization dimension both for the poor and for the affluent. Economic and social policy will probably deal differently with the poverty and affluence pole when a reduction in polarization is sought. However, more detailed information about both the poor and the affluent is needed to understand polarization trends; and this is what our contribution provides to a certain extent.

Obviously, data both contribute to and restrict the explanatory power of any analysis. In our case it is questionable whether available survey data would describe in sufficient detail the situation of the affluent and in particular the high income affluent. Compulsory income tax data, which arguably provides the most meaningful information about high income individuals, showed an increased unidimensional income polarization in Germany during the same period of analysis (Merz, 2006). This is an indication that the increase of the multidimensional time and income polarization gap described in our study would probably have been even greater if more detailed data had been available.

NOTES

1. For a more in-depth discussion of unidimensional and multidimensional polarization indices, see Merz and Scherg (2013).

2. For a further discussion, reasoning and justification of the CES well-being function with multidimensional poverty application, the reader is referred to Merz and Rathjen (2014a).

3. It is an extension of the Scheicher (2010) index, which for each individual gap only sums up attribute values without any compensation possibilities.

4. The aggregation of the single poverty attributes a and b and of the 2DGAP c over all individuals might not result in the joint aggregate condition $c=(a^2+b^2)^{0.5}$. With two degrees of freedom, one remaining component (a, b, or c) is computable from the other aggregates. In our application, alternative computations of the respective remaining components have shown close accordance with the orthogonal condition.

5. The distance value is one if the input factors result exactly in a certain output level (total economically efficient situation). Depending on the definition of the input arrow length's relation, a distance value different to one requires more or less input factor quantities (in a fixed relation) to be efficient.

6. Imagine an individual two-dimensional input situation ($x=(x_1,x_2)$) below a multidimensional well-being threshold with its respective individual optimal allocation at x and regard the input space of a linear homogeneous output function (e.g., Cobb–Douglas well-being function). Then a distance function value of 1.5 (times the length of x) requires 50% more of both inputs x_1 and x_2 to achieve the poverty threshold isoquant in an efficient way.

7. With a weight 1 for a household head, a weight of 0.5 for additional household members aged 15 years or older and a weight of 0.3 for all others.

8. As mentioned, income is defined as monthly net equivalence income. Time is personal genuine leisure time, which is detailed in the individual time use diaries and includes one of the main categories "Contact, Conversations, Sociality" or "Media Use, Free-time Activities" in GTUS 1991/1992 and the categories "Social Life and Entertainment," "Participation in Athletic Activities, e.g., Outdoor Activities," "Hobbies and Games," and "Mass Media" in GTUS 2001/2002.

9. GSOEP 2002 question 11 in the personal questionnaire.

10. Our CES well-being function estimates are based on the working population because the economically active population actually experiences both work and leisure and therefore its judgment of the trade-off between the two dimensions is probably more appropriate.

11. Perfect substitution: ($\rho=-1$, $\sigma=\infty$), Cobb–Douglas case with ($\rho=0$, $\sigma=1$), no substitution at all (complementary input factors, $\rho=\infty$, $\sigma=0$).

12. A graphical inspection of the time and income situations is found in our discussion paper, Merz and Scherg (2013).

13. It is calculated by an iterative process via 2DGAP mean components and the orthogonal requirement.

ACKNOWLEDGMENT

We thank the participants of the ECINEQ 2013 conference in Bari, Italy, for their helpful comments.

REFERENCES

Alkire, S., & Foster, J. (2011). Counting and multidimensional poverty measurement. *Journal of Public Economics*, *95*(7–8), 476–487.

Anderson, G., Crawford, I., & Leicester, A. (2008). Efficiency analysis and the lower convex hull approach. In N. Kakwani & J. Silber (Eds.), *Quantitative approaches to multidimensional poverty measurement* (pp. 176–191). New York, NY: Palgrave, Macmillan.

Atkinson, A. B. (2003). Multidimensional deprivation: Contrasting social welfare and counting approaches. *Journal of Economic Inequality*, *1*, 51–65.

Atkinson, A. B., & Piketty, T. (Eds.). (2007). *Top incomes over the 20th century a contrast between continental European and English speaking countries*. Oxford: Oxford University Press.

Becker, G. S. (1965). A theory of the allocation of time. *Economic Journal*, *75*, 493–517.

Bittman, M. (1999). *Social participation and family welfare: The money and time cost of leisure*. SPRC Discussion Paper No. 95, Sydney, Australia.

Bourguignon, F., & Chakravarty, S. R. (2003). The measurement of multidimensional poverty. *Journal of Economic Inequality*, *1*(1), 25–49.

Bundesregierung. (2002, 2005, 2011, 2013). Lebenslagen in Deutschland, Der erste (zweite, dritte, vierte) Armuts- und Reichtumsbericht der Bundesregierung, Bundesministerium für Gesundheit und Soziale Sicherung, Berlin, Germany.

Burchardt, T. (2008). *Time and income poverty, centre for analysis of social exclusion*. London, UK: London School of Economics.

Chakravarty, S. R. (2009). *Inequality, polarization and poverty: Advances in distributional analysis*. New York, NY: Springer-Verlag.

Chakravarty, S. R., & Silber, J. (2008). Measuring multidimensional poverty: The axiomatic approach. In N. Kakwani & J. Silber (Eds.), *Quantitative approaches to multidimensional poverty measurement* (pp. 192–209). New York, NY: Palgrave Macmillan.

Clark, A. E., Frijters, P., & Shields, M. (2008). Relative income, happiness and utility: An explanation for the Easterlin Paradox and other puzzles. *Journal of Economic Literature*, *46*, 95–144.

Dell, F. (2007). Top incomes in Germany throughout the twentieth century: 1891–1998. In A. B. Atkinson & T. Piketty (Eds.), *Top incomes over the twentieth century* (pp. 365–425). Oxford: Oxford University Press.

Deutsch, J., & Silber, J. (2005). Measuring multidimensional poverty: An empirical comparison of various approaches. *The Review of Income and Wealth*, *51*(1), 145–174.

Duclos, J.-Y., Esteban, J.-M., & Ray, D. (2004). Polarization: Concepts, measurement, estimation. *Econometrica*, *72*(6), 1737–1772.

Ehling, M. (2003, August). *Erhebungen zur Zeitverwendung 1991–92 und 2001–02. Skizzierung des methodischen Vorgehens*. In Wirtschaft und Statistik – Sonderausgabe anlässlich des 54. Weltkongresses des Internationalen Statistischen Instituts vom 13. bis 20. Berlin, Germany, pp. 85–87.

Ehling, M., Holz, E., & Kahle, I. (2001). Erhebungsdesign der Zeitbudgeterhebung 2001/2002. *Wirtschaft und Statistik*, *6*, 427–436.

Esteban, J.-M., Gradín, C., & Ray, D. (2007). An extension of a measure of polarization, with an application to the income distribution of five OECD countries. *Journal of Economic Inequality*, *5*(1), 1–19.

Esteban, J.-M., & Ray, D. (1994). On the measurement of polarization. *Econometrica*, *62*(4), 819–851.

Foster, J., Greer, J., & Thorbecke, E. (1984). A class of decomposable poverty measures. *Econometrica*, *52*(3), 761–766.

Foster, J., & Wolfson, M. C. (2010). Polarization and the decline of the middle class: Canada and the U.S. *Journal of Economic Inequality*, *8*(2), 247–273.

Frey, B. S., & Stutzer, A. (2005). Happiness research: State and prospects. *Review of Social Economy*, *82*(2), 207–228.

Gigliarano, C., & Mosler, K. (2009). Constructing indices of multivariate polarization. *Journal of Economic Inequality*, *7*(4), 435–460.

Goebel, J., Gorning, M., & Häußermann, H. (2010). *Polarisierung der Einkommen: Die Mittelschicht verliert*. Berlin, Germany: Wochenbericht des DIW Berlin. Nr. 24/2010.

Goodin, R., Rice, J., Parpo, A., & Eriksson, L. (2008). *Discretionary time: A new measure of freedom*. Cambridge, UK: Cambridge University Press.

Grabka, M., & Frick, J. R. (2008). *Schrumpfende Mittelschicht – Anzeichen einer dauerhaften Polarisierung der verfügbaren Einkommen*. Berlin, Germany: Wochenbericht des DIW Berlin. Nr. 10/2008.

Harvey, A. S., & Mukhopadhyay, A. K. (2007). When twenty-four hours is not enough: Time poverty of working parents. *Social Indicators Research*, *82*(1), 57–77.

Kakwani, N., & Silber, J. (2008). *Quantitative approaches to multidimensional poverty measurement*. Basingstoke, UK: Palgrave Macmillan.

Kmenta, J. (1967). On estimation of the CES production function. *International Economic Review*, *8*(2), 180–189.

Lugo, M. A., & Maasoumi, E. (2009). *Multidimensional poverty measures from an information theory perspective*. OPHI Working Paper No. 10, Oxford Poverty & Human Development Initiative, Oxford, UK.

Maasoumi, E., & Lugo, M. A. (2008). The information basis of multivariate poverty assessments. In N. Kakwani & J. Silber (Eds.), *Quantitative approaches to multidimensional poverty measurement* (pp. 1–29). New York, NY: Palgrave Macmillan.

Malmquist, S. (1953). Index numbers and indifference surfaces. *Trabajos Estatistica*, *2*, 209–242.

Merz, J. (2006). Polarisierung der Einkommen von Selbständigen? – Zur Dynamik der Einkommensverteilung von Freiberuflern und Unternehmern. In J. Merz (Ed.), *Fortschritte der Mittelstands Forschung, CREPS-Schriftenreihe* (Vol. 3, pp. 395–415). Münster, Germany: LIT Verlag.

Merz, J., Hirschel, D., & M. Zwick (2005). *Struktur und Verteilung hoher Einkommen – Mikroanalysen auf der Basis der Einkommensteuerstatistik*. Gutachten zum zweiten Armuts- und Reichtumsbericht der Bundesregierung, Lebenslagen in Deutschland, Bundesministerium für Gesundheit und Soziale Sicherung, Berlin, Germany.

Merz, J., & Rathjen, T. (2011). Sind Selbständige zeit- und einkommensarm? – Zur Dynamik interdependenter multidimensionaler Armut mit den deutschen Zeitbudgeterhebungen.

In S. Bekmeier-Feuerhahn, A. Martin, J. Merz, & U. Weisenfeld (Eds.), *Die Dynamik tiefgreifenden Wandels in Gesellschaft, Wirtschaft und Unternehmen* (pp. 219–239). Münster, Germany: LIT Verlag.

Merz, J., & Rathjen, T. (2014a). Time and income poverty – An interdependent multidimensional poverty approach with German time use diary data. forthcoming in *The Review of Income and Wealth, Forthcoming*.

Merz, J., & Rathjen, T. (2014b). Multidimensional time and income poverty: Well-being gap and minimum 2DGAP poverty intensity – German evidence. forthcoming in *Journal of Economic Inequality*. doi:10.1007/s10888-013-9271-6

Merz, J., & Scherg, B. (2013). *Polarization of time and income – A multidimensional approach with well-being gap and minimum 2DGAP: German evidence, Forschungsinstitut Freie Berufe (FFB), Leuphana Universität Lüneburg*. FFB-Discussion Paper No. 95, Lüneburg, Germany. Retrieved from www.leuphana.de/ffb

Merz, J., & Zwick, M. (2005). Hohe Einkommen: Eine Verteilungsanalyse für Freie Berufe, Unternehmer und abhängig Beschäftigte mit Mikrodaten der Einkommensteuer statistik. *Journal of Applied Social Science Studies, 125*(2), 313–328.

Peichl, A., Schaefer, T., & Scheicher, C. (2010). Measuring richness and poverty – A micro data application to Europe and Germany. *The Review of Income and Wealth, 56*(3), 597–619.

Scheicher, C. (2009). *Armut, Reichtum, Umverteilung: Begriff und statistische Messung*. Lohmar, Germany: Eul Verlag.

Scheicher, C. (2010). *Measuring polarization via poverty and affluence*. Köln Discussion Papers in Statistics and Econometrics, No. 2/08, 2nd version June 24, Köln, Germany.

Sen, A. K. (1985). *Commodities and capabilities*. Amsterdam, the Netherlands: North-Holland.

Sen, A. K. (1999). *Development as freedom*. New York, NY: Knopf Publishers.

Sen, A. K. (2008). The economics of happiness and capability. In L. Bruni, F. Comim, & M. Pugno (Eds.), *Capabilities and happiness* (pp. 16–27). Oxford, UK: Oxford University Press.

Vickery, C. (1977). The time-poor: A new look at poverty. *Journal of Human Resources, 12*(1), 27–48.

Wagner, G. G., Frick, J. R., & Schupp, J. (2007). The German Socio-Economic Panel study (GSOEP): Scope, evolution and enhancements. *Journal of Applied Social Science Studies, 127*(1), 139–179.

Wang, Y.-Q., & Tsui, K.-Y. (2000). Polarization orderings and new classes of polarization indices. *Journal of Public Economic Theory, 2*(3), 349–363.

APPENDIX: POLARIZATION MEASURES IN THE LITERATURE

Unidimensional Polarization Measures

Foster and Wolfson (Mimeo 1992, Released 2010)

Income spread:

$$S(q) = \left| \frac{F^{-1}(q) - m}{m} \right| \tag{A.1a}$$

Bipolarity:

$$B(p) = \left| \int_q^{0.5} \frac{F^{-1}(p) - m}{m} \right| \mathrm{d}p \tag{A.1b}$$

$$P^{\mathrm{FW}} = 2 \left| \int_q^{0.5} \frac{F^{-1}(p) - m}{m} \right| \mathrm{d}p \tag{A.1c}$$

where F is the cumulative distribution function of income, q is the population fraction, and m is the median income. This polarization index is closely related to the Gini coefficient

$$P^{\mathrm{FW}} = (G^W - G^B)\frac{\mu}{m} \tag{A.1d}$$

Wang and Tsui (2000)

$$P^{\mathrm{WT}} = \frac{1}{n}\sum_{i=1}^{n} \left| \frac{y_i - m}{m} \right|^{\alpha} \tag{A.2}$$

where $\alpha \in [0, 1]$, m is the median income, y_i is the income of individual i, and n is the number of observations.

Scheicher (2010)

$$P^{\mathrm{S}}_{\mathrm{univ}} = \frac{1}{n_{\mathrm{poor}}} \sum_{i \in \mathrm{poor}} \left| \frac{z - y_i}{z} \right|^{\alpha} + \frac{1}{n_{\mathrm{rich}}} \sum_{i \in \mathrm{poor}} \left| \frac{y_i - r}{y_i} \right|^{\beta} \tag{A.3}$$

where z is the poverty line, r is the affluence line, m is the median, and y_i describes individual income.

Polarization with Separate Groups by Esteban and Ray (1994)

$$P^{ER} = K \sum_{i=1}^{g} \sum_{j=1}^{g} \pi_i^{1+\alpha} \pi_j |\mu_i - \mu_j| \tag{A.4}$$

where π is the population fraction of group i, and μ is the mean income of group i. Thus, if all individuals have the same income, the index will be zero so that the minimum of the index is achieved at minimal inequality. The maximum of the measure is achieved when half of the population has the minimum income and half of the population has the maximum income. Then the measure will be one normalized by a constant K.

Esteban et al. (2007)

$$P^{ERG} = \sum_{i=1}^{g} \sum_{j=1}^{g} \pi_i^{1+\alpha} \pi_j |\mu_i - \mu_j| - \beta \varepsilon (G - G^{\text{grouped}}) \tag{A.5}$$

where β is a weight for measurement error. An advantage of this extended polarization measure is that it is not necessary to classify the groups on the basis of arbitrary income constraints. Only the number of groups has to be chosen, and the group assignment is instead done by a classification algorithm.

Duclos, Esteban, and Ray (2004)

$$P_\alpha^{DER}(F) = \int_y f(y)^\alpha a(y) \mathrm{d}F(y) \text{ with } a(y) \equiv \mu + y(2F(y) - 1) - 2 \int_{-\infty}^{y} x \, \mathrm{d}F(x) \tag{A.6}$$

where F is the distribution function, f the associated density and μ is the income mean, $\alpha \in [0,1]$.

Multidimensional Polarization Measures

Gigliarano and Mosler (2009)

$$P_1^{GM} = \phi\left(\frac{B(X)}{W(X) + c}\right) \cdot S(X) \tag{A.7a}$$

$$P_2^{\mathrm{GM}} = \psi(B(X) - W(X)) \cdot S(X) \quad \text{(A.7b)}$$

$$P_3^{\mathrm{GM}} = \tau\left(\frac{B(X)}{B(X) + W(X) + c}\right) \cdot S(X) \quad \text{(A.7c)}$$

where $B(X)$ is the inequality between the groups, and $W(X)$ is the inequality within the groups. φ, ψ, τ are strictly increasing functions of a specific inequality measure. $S(X)$ is the relative group size, which is measured by an inverse concentration measure like the Herfindahl index. X is a matrix which contains all individuals in the columns and their multiple attributes in the rows. Polarization is measured either via Eqs. (A.7a–c). An increasing inequality or an increasing group size raises polarization, and an increasing inequality within the groups lowers polarization.

Scheicher (2010)

$$\mathrm{d}(y_{ij}, [z_j, r_j]) = \begin{cases} \min\{|y_{ij} - z_j|, |y_{ij} - r_j|\} \ \mathit{if}\ y_{ij} \notin [z_j, r_j] \\ 0 \ \mathit{if}\ y_{ij} \in [z_j, r_j] \end{cases} \quad \text{(A.8a)}$$

where z_j is the poverty line, r_j is the affluence line of attribute j, and y_{ij} stands for the value of the jth attribute of individual i. For aggregation, the single attribute specific distances are summed up over all attributes:

$$\mathrm{d}(y_i, [z, r]) = \sum_j \mathrm{d}(y_{ij}, [z_j, r_j]) \quad \text{(A.8b)}$$

Finally, the mean of all aggregated distances of the poor and the rich individuals given the respective middle class thresholds builds the Scheicher (2010) multidimensional polarization index:

$$P_{\mathrm{mult}}^{\mathrm{S}} = \frac{1}{n} \sum_i \mathrm{d}(y_i, [z, r]) \quad \text{(A.8c)}$$

ON THE MEASUREMENT OF REGIONAL CONVERGENCE IN INEQUALITY AND WELFARE

Adelaide P. S. Duarte, Jacques Silber, João Sousa Andrade and Marta C. N. Simões

ABSTRACT

This paper extends a methodology proposed by Nissanov and Silber (2009) who decomposed the coefficient β used in convergence analysis into three components checking respectively whether there was σ-convergence, whether 'pure mobility' (upward or downward income mobility) was lower among the poor and what the extent of 'residual mobility' (the third component) was.

The present paper extends this analysis by applying it to the analysis of regional per capita income levels but also to that of within regions inequality and regional welfare levels. The empirical illustration uses Portuguese data on average earnings at the level of NUTS3.

Keywords: β-convergence; σ-convergence; inequality; NUTS3; Portugal; welfare

JEL classifications: O18; O47; P46

Economic Well-Being and Inequality: Papers from the Fifth ECINEQ Meeting
Research on Economic Inequality, Volume 22, 323–349

ISSN: 1049-2585/doi:10.1108/S1049-258520140000022010

INTRODUCTION

Following the seminal papers of Barro and Sala-i-Martin (1992) and Mankiw, Romer, and Weil (1992) there is by now a vast literature dealing with the issue of convergence. As stressed by Islam (2003) 'whether income levels of poorer countries of the world are converging to those of richer countries is by itself a question of paramount importance for human welfare'. But Islam (2003) emphasized also the fact that for many economists the concept of convergence was related to the choice between alternative growth theories since convergence was assumed to be an implication of neo-classical growth theory (NCGT) whereas it could not be inferred from new growth theories. This is why testing for convergence has been often considered as being equivalent to testing the validity of these two alternative growth theories. The literature has made a distinction between the concepts of β-convergence and σ-convergence.

The notion of β-convergence may be summarized as follows. The assumption of diminishing returns implies that the marginal productivity of capital will be higher in a capital-poor country so that, if savings rate are similar, poorer economies will have a higher growth rate. In other words one may expect a negative correlation between the initial income level and the subsequent growth rate which is exactly what β-convergence is all about.

There is however an alternative approach to this issue of convergence (e.g. see Friedman, 1992; Quah, 1993), one that argues that convergence should be tested by checking whether there is a decrease over time in the dispersion of income levels and/or growth rate across countries, hence the idea of σ-convergence.

The literature has also made a distinction between conditional and unconditional convergence. Whereas, as mentioned previously, NCGT implies that countries with access to identical technologies should converge to a common income level, hence the notion of unconditional convergence, Rodrik (2011) argues that 'there is no tendency for poor countries to grow faster than rich ones, over any reasonable long time horizon for which we have data. Whatever convergence one can find is conditional: it depends on policies, institutions and other country-specific circumstances. The only exceptions to the rule seem to be states/regions within a unified economy such as the United States (Barro & Sala-i-Martin, 1991)'.

The convergence literature is evidently somehow related with checking the existence of pro-poor growth although the latter is rather based on the use of individual income data. This literature on pro-poor growth takes generally an anonymous approach since it ignores the identity of individuals, when comparing two income distributions. Among the exceptions one may cite the works of Fields, Cichello, Freije, Menéndez, and Newhouse (2003), Grimm (2007) and Nissanov and Silber (2009). The latter study borrowed tools commonly used in convergence analysis to check whether growth was pro-poor. More precisely it suggested a breakdown of the coefficients of the traditional β-convergence analysis into three components. The first one amounts in fact to checking whether there was σ-convergence. The second component allows one to check whether 'pure mobility' was higher or lower among the poor, the term 'pure' referring to upward as well as to downward income mobility. Finally the third element of this breakdown measures what the authors called 'residual mobility'.

The present paper extends the analysis proposed by Nissanov and Silber (2009) in so far as it suggests applying it not only to the analysis of regional per capita income levels but also to that of within regions inequality and of regional welfare levels. The empirical illustration uses Portuguese data at the level of NUTS3. Portugal is an interesting case to examine because it experienced for the period under analysis two distinct episodes of economic growth, a more uneven income distribution and an uneven location of economic activities, population and human capital in its territory. A priori, we cannot tell how the Portuguese NUTS3 behaved in the process of β-convergence in terms of per capita incomes, within regions inequalities or in terms of welfare levels of the various regions. Portugal joined the European Union in 1986 and experienced a vibrant growth until 1999, with an annual real GDP per capita growth rate of 3.7% for the period 1985–1999, while EU-15 registered for the same period a growth rate of 2.1%. That growth came to a halt by 2002 and a long episode of sluggish growth followed and still goes on. For the period 2000–2006 the annual real GDP per capita growth rate was 0.79% for Portugal and 1.62% for EU-15. So the Portuguese output level stopped converging to the output level of EU-15 (EU-27), by this period.[1] For 1986 the Portuguese real GDP per capita was 51.1% relative to EU-15 and for 2006 it was 65.4%. Meanwhile, Portugal has become one of EU member-states with the most uneven income distribution. At the regional level (continental) Portugal is characterized by a concentration of its economic activities (industry and services), population and human capital on the coastal area with littoral regions usually recording better economic performances than other areas.

The paper is organized as follows. The next section presents the methodology and the subsequent section gives the results of the empirical illustration based on Portuguese data. Concluding comments are given in the final section.

THE METHODOLOGY

Measuring the Regional Convergence of Per Capita Incomes

Let y_i^t be the average income in region i at time t. The regression checking for β-convergence of the average regional incomes is then expressed as:

$$\ln\left(\frac{y_i^t}{y_i^{t-1}}\right) = \alpha + \beta \ln\left(y_i^{t-1}\right) + u_i^t \tag{1}$$

Therefore, if β is negative one will have detected convergence of incomes.

If additional explanatory variables are included in Eq. (1), one talks about conditional β-convergence.

Nissanov and Silber (2009) suggested to decompose the coefficients β into two components, measuring respectively anonymous growth and the amount of re-ranking that takes place during the period examined.

Let x_i^t be the average income in the region that had rank i at time $(t-1)$ that would have been observed at time t, had this region kept the original rank i it had at time $(t-1)$. The dependent variable in the β-convergence regression may therefore be expressed as

$$\ln\left(\frac{y_i^t}{y_i^{t-1}}\right) = \ln\left(\frac{x_i^t}{y_i^{t-1}}\right) + \ln\left(\frac{y_i^t}{x_i^t}\right) \tag{2}$$

We can then estimate two separate regressions. The first one will be expressed as

$$\ln\left(\frac{x_i^t}{y_i^{t-1}}\right) = \alpha_1 + \beta_1 \ln\left(y_i^{t-1}\right) + u_{i1}^t \tag{3}$$

A negative sign of β_1 implies that the lower the income, the higher the anonymous growth rates, which clearly implies that there was σ-convergence.

The second regression will be expressed as

$$\ln\left(\frac{y_i^t}{x_i^t}\right) = \alpha_2 + \beta_2 \ln\left(y_i^{t-1}\right) + u_{i2}^t \tag{4}$$

Here a negative sign of β_2 implies that the lower the income, the greater the improvement in relative income ranking. But the coefficient β_2 remains subject to Galton's fallacy (see Friedman, 1992) because the ranking of high incomes is more likely to decrease than increase, the opposite being true for low incomes, so that this alone could explain the negative sign of the coefficient β_2. To tackle this issue Nissanov and Silber (2009) decomposed the coefficient β_2 into two subcomponents and, as a consequence, the coefficient β is broken down into three components.

Let us therefore rewrite Eq. (2) as

$$\ln\left(\frac{y_i^t}{y_i^{t-1}}\right) = \ln\left(\frac{x_i^t}{y_i^{t-1}}\right) + \left|\ln\left(\frac{y_i^t}{x_i^t}\right)\right| + \left\{\ln\left(\frac{y_i^t}{x_i^t}\right) - \left|\ln\left(\frac{y_i^t}{x_i^t}\right)\right|\right\} \tag{5}$$

and estimate three separate regressions:

The first one is the same as Eq. (3).

The second one is expressed as

$$\left|\ln\left(\frac{y_i^t}{x_i^t}\right)\right| = \alpha_3 + \beta_3 \ln\left(y_i^{t-1}\right) + u_{i3}^t \tag{6}$$

The third one is written as

$$\left[\ln\left(\frac{y_i^t}{x_i^t}\right) - \left|\ln\left(\frac{y_i^t}{x_i^t}\right)\right|\right] = \alpha_4 + \beta_4 \ln\left(y_i^{t-1}\right) + u_{i4}^t \tag{7}$$

The first regression (Eq. (3)) will check as before for the presence of regional σ-convergence (decrease in inequality).

The second regression (Eq. (6)) will check whether the degree of 'pure mobility' is greater, the poorer the region (the lower, its average income). Note that the expression 'pure' means that the change in the regional income may be an increase or a decrease.

The third regression (Eq. (7)) is a residual regression and it checks again for the presence of 're-ranking'. Note, however, that in Eq. (7) the dependent variable $[\ln(y_i^t/x_i^t) - |\ln(y_i^t/x_i^t)|]$ will be equal to zero when there was an improvement in the ranking of the region and negative when there was 'deterioration' in the ranking of the region. Clearly the probability of a rank improvement is a priori higher for low than high regional incomes so that in this third regression one may expect the coefficient β_4 to be negative, whereas a priori we do not know whether the coefficients β_3 and β_1 will be negative. Galton's fallacy remains thus clearly an issue for the third regression.

Needless to say, we do not have to express Eqs. (1)–(7) in logarithmic terms and may start with the following regression:

$$\left(y_i^t - y_i^{t-1}\right) = \gamma + \delta\left(y_i^{t-1}\right) + v_i^t \tag{8}$$

If the coefficient δ in Eq. (8) is negative, it implies that the lower the original per capita income in region i, the higher the increase in \$ terms of this per capita income between times $t-1$ and t, whereas Eq. (1), with a coefficient β negative, implied that the lower the original per capita income in region i, the higher the rate of growth in this per capita income between times $t-1$ and t.

Using the technique previously described, we may then decompose Eq. (8) into three different regressions.

$$\left(x_i^t - y_i^{t-1}\right) = \gamma_1 + \delta_1\left(y_i^{t-1}\right) + v_{i1}^t \tag{9}$$

$$\left|\left(y_i^t - x_i^t\right)\right| = \gamma_3 + \delta_3\left(y_i^{t-1}\right) + v_{i3}^t \tag{10}$$

$$\left[\left(y_i^t - x_i^t\right) - \left|\left(y_i^t - x_i^t\right)\right|\right] = \gamma_4 + \delta_4\left(y_i^{t-1}\right) + v_{i4}^t \tag{11}$$

If δ_1 is negative, Eq. (9) which takes an anonymous approach to the β-convergence issue implies, like Eq. (3), a decrease in (absolute) inequality over time since the \$ increase in per capita income will be higher the lower this original per capita income. Eq. (9) therefore checks, like Eq. (3), whether there was σ-convergence between times $t-1$ and t.

If δ_3 is negative, Eq. (10) implies that the lower the level of per capita income in a given region at time $t-1$, the higher the change in absolute value in \$ terms in this per capita income between times $t-1$ and t.

Eq. (11), a residual regression, checks for the presence of 're-ranking'. Like in Eq. (7) the dependent variable in Eq. (11) will be equal to zero when there was an improvement in the ranking of the region and negative when there was 'deterioration' in the ranking of the region. Since the probability of a rank improvement is a priori higher for low than high regional incomes, one may expect the coefficient δ_4 to be negative, whereas a priori we do not know whether the coefficients δ_3 and δ_1 will be negative. Here again (in Eq. (11)) Galton's fallacy remains an issue.

Measuring the Regional Convergence of within Regions Inequalities and of Welfare Levels of the Various Regions

Let now I_i^t be some measure of the within region i income inequality at time t, such as the Gini, the Atkinson or some generalized entropy index. Following Ravallion (2003) we can check for β-convergence of these within regions inequalities by implementing the following regression:

$$\left(I_i^t - I_i^{t-1}\right) = \lambda + \rho\left(I_i^{t-1}\right) + v_i^{\prime t} \tag{12}$$

One can then say that if ρ turns out to be negative and significant there has been over time a convergence of the within regions income inequalities.

Here also if additional explanatory variables are included in Eq. (12), it checks whether there has been a conditional β-convergence of the within regions inequalities.

It is also possible to apply to Eq. (12) the decomposition technique suggested by Nissanov and Silber (2009) in their analysis of the β-convergence of incomes and presented in Eqs. (8)–(11). Eq. (12) will then be broken down into three components. And we can estimate two separate regressions.

Let J_i^t be the degree of inequality within the region that had rank i at time $(t-1)$ that would have been observed at time t, had this region kept the original rank i it had at time $(t-1)$, as far as within regions inequality is concerned.

The first one will be expressed as:

$$\left(J_i^t - I_i^{t-1}\right) = \lambda_1 + \rho_1\left(I_i^{t-1}\right) + v_{i1}^{\prime t} \tag{13}$$

A negative sign of ρ_1 implies that the lower (higher) the level of inequality at time $t-1$ in a region with rank i, as far as the ranking of within regions inequalities is concerned, the higher the difference between the within region inequalities of the regions that had this rank i at times $t-1$ and t. In other words, Eq. (13) takes an anonymous approach to the β-convergence of the within regions inequality and a negative and significant sign of the coefficient ρ_1 implies therefore that there was σ-convergence of the within regions inequalities over time, that is, that the dispersion of these inequalities decreased over time.

The second regression will be expressed as:

$$\left(I_i^t - J_i^t\right) = \lambda_2 + \rho_2\left(I_i^{t-1}\right) + v_{i2}^{\prime t} \tag{14}$$

Here a negative sign of ρ_2 implies that the lower the within region inequality, the greater the improvement between times $t-1$ and t in the ranking of the region, as far as the ranking of these within regions inequalities is concerned. Since here also the ranking of regions with a high (low) degree of inequality is more likely to decrease (increase) than that of regions with a low (high) degree of inequality, we face again the issue of Galton's fallacy. Therefore, here also, we can decompose Eq. (14) into two separate regressions. We first write that:

$$\left(I_i^t - I_i^{t-1}\right) = \left(J_i^t - I_i^{t-1}\right) + |\left(I_i^t - J_i^t\right)| + \{\left(I_i^t - J_i^t\right) - |\left(I_i^t - J_i^t\right)|\} \quad (15)$$

and then estimate the following two regressions:

$$|\left(I_i^t - J_i^t\right)| = \lambda_3 + \rho_3\left(I_i^{t-1}\right) + v_{i3}'^t \quad (16)$$

and

$$[\left(I_i^t - J_i^t\right) - |\left(I_i^t - J_i^t\right)|] = \lambda_4 + \rho_4\left(I_i^{t-1}\right) + v_{i4}'^t \quad (17)$$

Eq. (16) checks whether the change in absolute value in the within region inequality between times $t-1$ and t is greater, the lower the original level of within region inequality at time $t-1$.

Eq. (17), a residual regression, checks whether there was 're-ranking' in the within regions inequalities. Here again the dependent variable $[\left(I_i^t - J_i^t\right) - |\left(I_i^t - J_i^t\right)|]$ will be equal to zero when there was an improvement in the ranking of the region and negative when there was 'deterioration' in the ranking of the region. As a consequence, Galton's fallacy remains an issue for Eq. (17).

Following the introduction of Atkinson's (1970) concept of 'equally distributed equivalent level of income',[2] Sen (1974) suggested measuring the welfare W_i^t of a given area[3] i at time t as:

$$W_i^t = y_i^t\left(1 - I_i^t\right) \quad (18)$$

where y_i^t is the average income in area i at time t and I_i^t is a measure of the within area i income inequality at time t, the inequality index selected being one (such as the Gini or Atkinson index) that can be related to a welfare function and varies between 0 and 1.

Following the methodology described previously for analysing the convergence of regional per capita income as well as inequality levels, we can also check for β-convergence of the regional welfare levels defined in Eq. (18) and once again implement a breakdown into three different components.

Decomposing the Degree of Regional Convergence in the Welfare Level of the Various Regions into Per Capita Income and Inequality-Related Components

Using Eq. (18) we may express the welfare in region i at time t as:

$$W_i^t = f\left(y_i^t, I_i^t\right) \tag{19}$$

so that the change in welfare $\Delta W_i^t = \left(W_i^t - W_i^{t-1}\right)$ in region i between time $t-1$ and time t may be expressed as:

$$\Delta W_i^t = g\left(\Delta y_i^t, \Delta I_i^t\right) \tag{20}$$

where $\Delta y_i^t = \left(y_i^t - y_i^{t-1}\right)$ and $\Delta I_{it} = \left(I_t - I_{i,t-1}\right)$.

In what follows, to simplify, we will drop the subscript i.

Using the so-called Shapley decomposition (see Chantreuil & Trannoy, 2013; Sastre & Trannoy, 2002; Shorrocks, 2013, as well as Appendix A1 for more details on this decomposition), we may express the contribution $C_{\Delta y_t}$ of the variation in income between time $t-1$ and time t as

$$\begin{aligned} \boldsymbol{C}_{\Delta y_t} = {} & (1/2)\{\boldsymbol{f}[(\Delta \boldsymbol{y}_t \neq 0);(\Delta \boldsymbol{I}_t \neq 0)] - \boldsymbol{f}[(\Delta \boldsymbol{y}_t = 0);(\Delta \boldsymbol{I}_t \neq 0)]\} \\ & + (1/2)\{\boldsymbol{f}[(\Lambda \boldsymbol{y}_t \neq 0);(\Delta \boldsymbol{I}_t = 0)] - \boldsymbol{f}[(\Delta \boldsymbol{y}_t = 0);(\Delta \boldsymbol{I}_t = 0)]\} \end{aligned} \tag{21}$$

$$\begin{aligned} \leftrightarrow C_{\Delta y_t} = {} & (1/2)\{[W(y_t, I_t) - W(y_{t-1}, I_{t-1})] - [W(y_{t-1}, I_t) - W(y_{t-1}, I_{t-1})]\} \\ & + (1/2)\{[W(y_t, I_{t-1}) - W(y_{t-1}, I_{t-1})] - [W(y_{t-1}, I_{t-1}) - W(y_{t-1}, I_{t-1})]\} \end{aligned} \tag{22}$$

$$\leftrightarrow C_{\Delta y_t} = (1/2)\{y_t(1 - I_t) - y_{t-1}(1 - I_t)\} + (1/2)\{y_t(1 - I_{t-1}) - y_{t-1}(1 - I_{t-1})\} \tag{23}$$

$$\begin{aligned} \leftrightarrow C_{\Delta y_t} & = (y_t - y_{t-1}) - ((I_t + I_{t-1})/2)(y_t - y_{t-1}) \\ & = (y_t - y_{t-1})[1 - ((I_t + I_{t-1})/2)] \end{aligned} \tag{24}$$

We may similarly express the contribution $C_{\Delta I_t}$ of the variation in inequality between time $t-1$ and time t as:

$$C_{\Delta I_t} = (1/2)\{f[(\Delta y_t \neq 0);(\Delta I_t \neq 0)] - f[(\Delta y_t \neq 0);(\Delta I_t = 0)]\} + (1/2)\{f[(\Delta y_t = 0);(\Delta I_t \neq 0)] - f[(\Delta y_t = 0);(\Delta I_t = 0)]\} \quad (25)$$

$$\leftrightarrow C_{\Delta I_t} = (1/2)y_t(I_{t-1} - I_t) + (1/2)y_{t-1}(I_{t-1} - I_t) = -[(y_t + y_{t-1})/2](I_t - I_{t-1}) \quad (26)$$

It is then easy to verify that, as expected:

$$C_{\Delta y_t} + C_{\Delta I_t} = y_t(1 - I_t) - y_{t-1}(1 - I_{t-1}) = (W_t - W_{t-1}) \quad (27)$$

Combining Eqs. (A.1), (24), (28) and (29) we may then estimate two separate regressions. The first one will be written as:

$$C_{\Delta y_t} = (y_t - y_{t-1})[1 - ((I_t + I_{t-1})/2)] = \pi_1 + \mu_1(W_i^{t-1}) + \tau_{1i}^t \quad (28)$$

and will check whether there is β-convergence of the regional levels of welfare, assuming the change over time in welfare is only the consequence of a change in the regional per capita incomes.

The second one will be written as:

$$C_{\Delta I_t} = -[(y_t + y_{t-1})/2](I_t - I_{t-1}) = \pi_2 + \mu_2(W_i^{t-1}) + \tau_{2i}^t \quad (29)$$

and will check whether there is β-convergence of the regional levels of welfare, assuming the change over time in welfare is only the consequence of a change in the inequality of the per capita regional incomes.

Combining Eqs. (A.1), (27), (28) and (29) we evidently may write that:

$$\pi = \pi_1 + \pi_2 \quad (30)$$

and

$$\mu = \mu_1 + \mu_2 \quad (31)$$

Moreover, as before, we may break down the regression given in Eq. (28) into three separate regressions checking:

- whether there was σ-convergence of the regional welfare levels, assuming the change over time in regional welfare was only the consequence of a change in regional per capita incomes;
- whether the change in absolute value in the ranking of the welfare level of the regions between times $t-1$ and t (assuming this change is only the consequence of a change in regional per capita incomes) was greater, the lower the original level of welfare in the region at time $t-1$;
- whether the residual change in the regional welfare levels (assuming this change was only the consequence of a change in regional per capita incomes) was greater, the lower the original level of welfare in the region at time $t-1$.

We can similarly decompose the regression given in Eq. (29) into three separate regressions.

AN EMPIRICAL ILLUSTRATION – PORTUGAL BETWEEN 1985 AND 2006

The methodology described in the previous section has been applied to Portuguese data at the NUTS3 level for the period 1985–2006, we have built a panel database with $N=30$ (NUTS3$_i$, $i=1,\ldots,30$) and $T=8$ (corresponding to a three-year period).

Our econometric strategy favours dynamic General Method of Moments (GMM) panel data methods due to some data characteristics (see Roodman, 2009): (a) some of the dependent variables exhibit time autoregressive dependency; (b) our database has more individuals than time periods. When autoregressive dependency is rejected we use static panel models that address the problem of heterogeneity of the intercepts and finally when these models are rejected we use between models. In the former case we apply two-steps System General Method of Moments (SYS-GMM) estimator (see Arellano, 2003; Arellano & Bond, 1991). This estimator combines two moment conditions (for the difference equation and for the model in levels) and it is more efficient than the first-difference GMM estimator. As a consequence we solve also a problem of covariate endogeneity. We have tested the validity of the instruments and we included in the results the over-identifying restrictions test (Sargan) that has as null the over-identifying is valid. Additionally, we have included the tests for auto-correlation of order 1 and 2 (AR1, AR2). These are the original Arellano and Bond m1 and m2 tests under the null of no autocorrelation in the first-difference residuals. The AR1 test usually rejects the null and the non-rejection of AR2 is a condition for consistent GMM estimation. Wald test results are also reported, it is a joint test for the null of the regressors, excluding the constant term.

We apply static panel methods following a well-known econometric strategy that addresses the issue of heterogeneity of the intercepts by considering whether the unit specific coefficients are time invariant or random. In the former case, Pooled OLS is estimated against Fixed Effects (FE) under the null of intercepts homogeneity by using the F test. In the latter case, Random Effects (RE) model is estimated against FE under the null of RE consistency by using the Hausman test. Finally, when none of these models is retained we apply the Between Model, but note that it discards time series information of our data meaning that we lose information (Verbeek, 2008).

Arellano robust standard errors (see Arellano, 1987), were calculated for all panel estimations and real average earnings and welfare levels were transformed in logs in all estimations (ln y_i and ln W_i), respectively.

Table 1 is a summary statistics table for the variables of our database (see Appendix B). One may note that the coefficients of variation are high especially for the growth rate and for the Atkinson[4] index. The period under study is characterized by a high volatility of the annual real growth

Table 1. NUTS3 Summary Statistics (1985–2006).

	Real Average Earnings (€-2000)	Annual Growth Rate of Real Average Earnings	Gini Index	Atkinson Index
Number of observations	240	210	240	240
Average	887.97	0.022322	0.20430	0.039483
Median	877.42	0.019219	0.19590	0.034873
Minimum	501.80	−0.16390	0.10590	0.012776
Maximum	2069.6	0.24800	0.50200	0.32126
Coefficient of variation	0.24928	1.6660	0.25446	0.69221
Within (each cross-sectional unit) standard deviation	180.12	0.038582	0.041713	0.026334
Between (cross-sectional units) standard deviation	145.29	0.010200	0.034774	0.011906

rate of average earnings of NUTS3. For all the variables standard deviation is higher for within[5] each cross-sectional unit than for between[6] cross-sectional units, which means that differences between individuals are less important than the changes affecting the individuals over time.

Measuring the Regional Convergence of Per Capita Incomes

Table 2 gives the results of the estimation of Eq. (1). In other words if β is found to be negative, one will have detected a convergence of incomes.

The results confirm a priori regional real convergence of average real earnings since the β coefficient is negative (−0.2689) and significant at least at 1%. The average error of the fitted values relative to actual values is 16.6% (ser), revealing the accuracy of the model. We cannot reject at the level of 10% the presence of first order autocorrelation which was expected and we cannot reject the null of no autocorrelation of second order a condition for the validity of the dynamic estimation. The Wald test rejects the null of the model, in this case the null of the regression coefficient besides the constant at least at the 1% level. Finally the Sargan test does not reject the validity of the 22 instruments (with $22 < N = 30$) used in the estimation.

Table 2. Estimation of Eq. (1).

Equation Number	Model	α	$\beta+1$	ser	AR1	AR2	Wald	Sargan
(1)	AB	1.881	0.7311 (0.094)*	0.166	−1.955***	−0.338	(1) = 60.15*	(22) = 29.50

Notes: Equation number refers to equation numbering in the first and second sections and in Appendix A. 'Model' refers to pooled OLS (POLS) or to fixed effects (FE) model or to random effects (RE) model, or to between model (BE) or to the two-step Arellano and Bond System Generalised Method of Moments Estimator (AB); α_i, λ_i and π_i stand for the constant and β_i, ρ_i and μ_i represent the coefficient of the independent variable in the appropriate regression equation, θ indicates the coefficient of the lagged dependent variable; note that for standard β-equations like Eqs. (1) or (A.1), θ equals $(\beta+1)$ or $(\mu+1)$, respectively; standard errors of the coefficients are given in parentheses; ser represents the standard error of the regression; *, ** and *** indicate significance at the 1%, 5% and 10% level, respectively; AR1 and AR2 represent the Arellano–Bond tests for errors autocorrelation of order 1 and 2, respectively, with null the no autocorrelation in the first-difference residuals; Wald is a joint test for the null of the regressors, excluding the constant term; Sargan is the over-identification test for instruments with null the over-identifying is valid. In parentheses the number of regressors without the constant and the number of instruments are reported for the Wald test and for the Sargan test, respectively.

As mentioned previously, Nissanov and Silber (2009) suggested however to decompose the coefficients β into two components, measuring respectively anonymous growth and the amount of re-ranking that takes place during the period examined (see Eqs. (2)–(4)). The coefficient β_2 is subject to Galton's fallacy, hence Nissanov and Silber's (2009) suggestion to decompose this coefficient into two subcomponents (see Eqs. (6) and (7)).

β_1, β_3 and β_4 estimates, statistically significant at 1%, 5% and 10%, are presented jointly in Table 3 along with the models estimated. Recall that β_3 and β_4, for the reasons already addressed in this section, are estimated in the framework of static panel models.[7]

The negative sign of the β_1 estimate in Table 3 confirms the existence of σ-convergence while the positive sign of the estimate β_2[8] (see Appendix B1) implies that the lower the income, the smaller the improvement in relative earnings ranking. This last result clearly indicates a deterioration of mobility among Portuguese NUTS3 regions. Furthermore, after estimating the coefficients β_3 and β_4, the two subcomponents of the coefficient β_2, we concluded that the previous two results were confirmed. σ-convergence is not associated with an improvement in the ranking of the poor Portuguese regions. On the contrary 'pure mobility' is clearly greater for regions with higher earnings.

As far as re-ranking is concerned, one would have a priori expected a negative sign for the coefficient β_4, implying that the probability of a rank improvement would be higher for regions with low average earnings (although Galton's fallacy remains an issue for Eq. (6)). The results of Table 3 indicate however that the re-ranking was not in favour of poorer regions. We can therefore conclude that the decrease in between regions differences in real average earnings that was observed during the period 1985–2006 was not accompanied by an improvement in the ranking of poor regions.

Table 3. σ-Convergence (β_1), Pure Mobility (β_3) and Re-Ranking Estimates (β_4) of Regional Per Capita Incomes.

σ-Convergence	Pure Mobility	Re-Ranking
AB	RE	POLS
−0.301	0.107	0.316
(0.115)*	(0.048)**	(0.120)*

Note: See Table 2.

Measuring the Regional Convergence of within Regions Inequalities and of Regional Welfare Levels

The results of the estimation of Eq. (12) are given in Table 4A (for the Gini index) and Table 4B (for the Atkinson index). As mentioned previously, if the coefficient ρ is negative and significant, it implies that there has been over time a convergence of the within regions income inequalities. Both these tables indeed confirm this result.

We then applied to the study of the convergence of within regions inequality the decomposition technique originally proposed by Nissanov and Silber (2009) to study the convergence of incomes. We report here the results for the coefficients ρ, σ-convergence of the within regions inequalities (ρ_1), pure mobility (ρ_3) and re-ranking. ρ_1, ρ_3 and ρ_4 estimates, statistically significant at 1%, 5% and 10%, are jointly given in Table 5. Recall that ρ_3 and ρ_4, for the reasons already addressed in this section, are

Table 4A. Estimation of Eq. (12) Using the Gini Index.

Equation Number	Model	λ	ρ	ser
(12) (Gini)	FE	0.212 (0.022)*	−1.047 (0.109)*	0.042

Note: See Table 2.

Table 4B. Estimation of Eq. (12) Using the Atkinson Index.

Equation Number	Model	λ	ρ	ser
(12) (Atkin)	FE	0.044 (0.002)*	−1.140 (0.055)*	0.027

Note: See Table 2.

Table 5. σ-Convergence (ρ_1), Pure Mobility (ρ_3) and Re-Ranking (ρ_4) Estimates of within Regions Inequalities.

σ-Convergence Gini FE	σ-Convergence Atkinson POLS	Pure Mobility Gini FE	Re-Ranking Gini POLS
−1.06 (0.087)*	−0.947 (0.048)*	−0.267 (0.066)*	0.280 (0.090)*

Note: See Table 2. Estimates of pure mobility and re-ranking using the Atkinson Index are not reported as they are not statistically significant.

estimated in the framework of static panel models.[9] σ-convergence of within regions inequalities is confirmed using either the Gini index or the Atkinson index, since the coefficient ρ_1 is negative and significant (Table 5).

Since the coefficient ρ_3 is negative and significant (see Table 5), we may conclude that 'pure mobility' of the regions that took place between time $t-1$ and time t, as far as their earnings inequality is concerned and no matter what the direction of these movements, was greater, the lower the original level of within region inequality at time $t-1$, but the ρ_4 estimate is positive which might explain why there is not re-ranking (ρ_2)[10] despite of the sign of the coefficient ρ_3. We may summarize as follows the results of our analysis of the convergence of within regions earnings' inequality. First, there is σ-convergence, that is, the dispersion of regional within regions inequality decreased over time. Second, we did observe pure mobility in the sense already mentioned above. Third, evidence does not support convergence as far as the re-ranking of the regions by level of within regions earnings inequality is concerned.

In Tables 6A and 6B, we present the results of the estimation of Eq. (19), using the Gini and Atkinson indices. Since the coefficient μ is negative and significant, we may conclude that there was a priori β-convergence of the regional welfare levels.

We apply the usual decompositions of the coefficients μ and μ_2 described previously. μ_1, μ_3 and μ_4 estimates are jointly presented in Table 7.[11] We check whether there was σ-convergence of the regional levels of welfare.

Table 6A. Estimation of Eq. (A.1) Using the Gini Index.

Equation Number	Model	π	$\mu+1$	ser	AR1	AR2	Wald	Sargan
(A.1) (Gini)	AB	1.739 (0.285)*	0.743 (0.044)*	0.122	−4.403*	1.557	(1) = 287.3*	(19) = 28.63***

Note: See Table 2. Taking as 5% our critical level we do not reject over-identification of the model.

Table 6B. Estimation of Eq. (A.1) Using the Atkinson Index.

Equation Number	Model	π	μ	ser	AR1	AR2	Wald	Sargan
(A.1) (Atkin)	AB	1.682 (0.445)*	0.759 (0.067)*	0.131	−4.07*	−1.015	(1) = 129.5*	(19) = 29.35***

Note: See Tables 2 and 6A.

Table 7. σ-Convergence (μ_1), Pure Mobility (μ_3) and Re-Ranking (μ_4) Estimates of the Welfare Levels of the Various Regions.

σ-Convergence Gini Index AB	σ-Convergence Atkinson Index AB	Pure Mobility Gini Index BE	Pure Mobility Atkinson Index BE	Re-Ranking Gini Index AB	Re-Ranking Atkinson Index AB
−0.383	−0.320	0.168	0.229	0.197	0.334
(0.102)*	(0.111)*	(0.098)***	(0.089)*	(0.104)***	(0.071)*

Note: See Table 2.

For both indices, the coefficient μ_1 is negative and significant, so we can conclude that over time there was σ-convergence of the regional levels of welfare.

Applying again the decomposition described previously, we present in Table 7 estimates for μ_3 and μ_4. More precisely we check first whether the absolute value of the change in the ranking of the welfare level of a region that took place between times $t-1$ and t was greater, the lower the original level of welfare in the region at time $t-1$. And second we check whether there was a 're-ranking' of the welfare levels of the various regions.

Using the Gini index, the coefficient μ_3 is positive and significant at 10% level confirming that regions with lower levels of welfare did not improve in absolute terms their ranking in terms of welfare.

The results about re-ranking, μ_4, are positive and significant at 1% for both the Gini and the Atkinson indices (AB model). Three main conclusions may therefore be drawn: at the level of Portuguese NUTS3 regions there was σ-convergence of the regional welfare levels for the period under analysis but pure mobility and re-ranking were not observed.

Decomposing the Degree of Regional Convergence in the Welfare Level of the Various Regions into Per Capita Income and Inequality-Related Components

As mentioned previously Eq. (28) checks whether there was β-convergence of the regional levels of welfare, assuming the change over time in welfare is only the consequence of a change in the regional per capita incomes while Eq. (29) checks whether there was β-convergence of the regional levels of welfare, assuming the change over time in welfare was only the consequence of a change in the inequality of the average regional

Table 8A. Estimation of Eq. (28) on the Basis of the Gini Index.

Equation Number	Model	π_1	μ_1	ser
(28) (Gini)	POLS	0.213 (0.042)*	−0.030 (0.006)*	0.027

Note: See Table 2.

Table 8B. Estimation of Eq. (28) on the Basis of the Atkinson Index.

Equation Number	Model	π_1	μ_1	ser
(28) (Atkin)	POLS	0.318 (0.064)*	−0.044 (0.009)*	0.033

Note: See Table 2.

Table 9. Estimation of Eq. (29) on the Basis of the Gini Index.

Equation Number	Model	π_2	μ_2	ser
(29) (Gini)	FE	2.589 (1.009)**	−0.399 (0.155)**	0.392

Note: See Table 2.

earnings.[12] The results for Eq. (28) are given in Tables 8A (when using the Gini index) and 8B (when using the Atkinson index).

Since the coefficient μ_1 is negative and significant, the results of both Tables 8A and 8B confirm the existence of β-convergence of the regional levels of welfare, assuming the change over time in welfare is only the consequence of a change in the regional per capita incomes ($\mu_1 < 0$).

In Table 9 we present the results of the estimation of Eq. (29) when using the Gini index.

Since the coefficient μ_2 is negative, we may conclude, at least when using the Gini index, that there was β-convergence of the regional levels of welfare, assuming the change over time in welfare was only the consequence of a change in the inequality of the per capita regional incomes ($\mu_2 < 0$).[13]

CONCLUDING COMMENTS

In this paper we tried to analyse the extent of regional convergence of Portuguese NUTS3 during the period 1985–2006. We broadened the methodology originally proposed by Nissanov and Silber (2009) by looking not only at the convergence of average regional incomes but also at that of within regions inequality and of regional welfare levels. Additionally, we used panel data information to try to overcome the well-known problem of omitted variable bias encountered by cross-section β-convergence regressions.

Here are our main conclusions. First β-convergence was never rejected, whether we checked for regional convergence of per capita incomes, within regions inequality or regional welfare levels. Similarly in these three cases we also observed σ-convergence. A deterioration of mobility among Portuguese NUTS regions was confirmed except for regional convergence within regions inequality. In the latter case, 'pure mobility' (rank mobility of these inequalities, no matter its direction) was higher for originally less unequal regions. Additionally, re-ranking was never observed for the three dimensions of convergence analysis considered (per capita incomes, within regional inequalities and regional welfare levels).

It therefore seems that we can conclude that in Portugal, during the period 1985–2006, the decrease in differences between regional real average earnings or in within regions inequalities or in regional levels of welfare was not accompanied by an improvement in the ranking of poorer regions in terms of earnings or welfare levels or more unequal regions. Finally we can conclude that both the change in regional average earnings and the change in the within regions inequality in real average earnings inequality, contributed, *ceteris paribus*, to the change in regional welfare levels during the period analysed.

Finally we should stress that we only implemented an unconditional β-convergence analysis and it will be useful to extend the analysis in the future to the case of conditional β-convergence analysis.

NOTES

1. For the period 2008–2012, the Portuguese economic experienced a decrease of the average (annual) real GDP per capita growth rate of 0.056%.
2. A similar concept was introduced by Kolm under the name of 'equal equivalent income', see Kolm (1976a, 1976b).
3. This area could be a nation (state) or a region.
4. We chose 0.5 as value of the parameter that appears in the definition of the Atkinson index.
5. Within estimation replaces original series values by deviations from time means (it is equivalent to subtracting the means from each time series).

6. Between estimation replaces the original series values by the means of each individual (N observations will remain, corresponding to the number of individuals).

7. For detailed information about the econometric results, see Appendix B1.

8. See Appendix B1.

9. For detailed information about the econometric results, see Appendix B2.

10. This coefficient is positive and significant, see Appendix B2, Eq. (14).

11. Recall that μ_3 and μ_4, for the reasons already addressed in section 'An Empirical Illustration – Portugal between 1985 and 2006', are estimated in the framework of static panel models (for detailed information about the econometric results, see Appendix B3).

12. Combining Eqs. (A.1), (27), (28) and (29) we evidently may write that $\pi = \pi_1 + \pi_2$ and $\mu = \mu_1 + \mu_2$. As those equations were estimated by different methods we have not tested these equalities.

13. As for Eq. (29) using the Atkinson index, the null hypothesis of the coefficients was never rejected.

ACKNOWLEDGMENT

Duarte, Simões and Sousa Andrade acknowledge the financial support of the FCT of the Portuguese Ministry of Science and Higher Education under the project PTDC/ECO/71326/2006, while Silber is thankful to the Adar Foundation of the Department of Economics at Bar-Ilan University for its financial support. They also thank an anonymous referee for his/her very valuable comments and suggestions.

REFERENCES

Arellano, M. (1987). Computing robust standard errors for within group estimators. *Oxford Bulletin of Economics and Statistics*, *49*, 431–434.

Arellano, M. (2003). *Panel data econometrics*. Oxford: Oxford University Press.

Arellano, M., & Bond, S. (1991). Some tests of specification for panel data: Monte Carlo evidence and an application to employment equations. *The Review of Economic Studies*, *58*, 277–297.

Atkinson, A. B. (1970). On the measurement of inequality. *Journal of Economic Theory*, *2*, 244–263.

Barro, R., & Sala-i-Martin, X. (1991). Convergence across states and regions. *Brookings Papers on Economic Activity*, *1*, 107–158.

Barro, R. J., & Sala-i-Martin, X. (1992). Convergence. *Journal of Political Economy*, *100*, 223–251.

Chantreuil, F., & Trannoy, A. (2013). Inequality decomposition values: The trade-off between marginality and consistency. *Journal of Economic Inequality*, *11*(1), 83–98.

Fields, G., Cichello, P., Freije, S., Menéndez, M., & Newhouse, D. (2003). For richer or for poorer? Evidence from Indonesia, South Africa, Spain and Venezuela. *Journal of Economic Inequality*, *1*(1), 67–99.

Friedman, M. (1992). Do old fallacies ever die? *Journal of Economic Literature*, *30*, 2129–2132.

Grimm, M. (2007). Removing the anonymity axiom in assessing pro-poor growth. *Journal of Economic Inequality*, *5*(2), 179–197.

Islam, N. (2003). What have we learnt from the convergence debate? *Journal of Economic Surveys*, *17*(3), 309–362.

Kolm, S. C. (1976a). Unequal equalities: I. *Journal of Economic Theory*, *12*, 416–442.

Kolm, S. C. (1976b). Unequal equalities: II. *Journal of Economic Theory*, *13*, 82–111.

Mankiw, N. G., Romer, D. H., & Weil, D. N. (1992). A contribution to the empirics of economic growth. *Quarterly Journal of Economics*, *107*, 407–437.

Nissanov, Z., & Silber, J. (2009). On pro-poor growth and the measurement of convergence. *Economics Letters*, *105*, 270–272.

Quah, D. (1993). Galton's fallacy and tests of the convergence hypothesis. *Scandinavian Journal of Economics*, *95*, 427–443.

Ravallion, M. (2003). Inequality convergence. *Economics Letters*, *80*(3), 351–356.

Rodrik, D. (2011). *Unconditional convergence*. National Bureau of Economic Research, Working Paper No. 17546, Cambridge, MA.

Roodman, D. (2009). How to do xtabond2: An introduction to difference and system GMM in Stata. *Stata Journal*, *9*(1), 86–136.

Sastre, M., & Trannoy, A. (2002). Shapley inequality decomposition by factor components: Some methodological issues. *Journal of Economics*, (Suppl. 9), 51–89.

Sen, A. K. (1974). Information bases of alternative welfare approaches. *Journal of Public Economics*, *3*, 387–403.

Shorrocks, A. F. (2013). Decomposition procedures for distributional analysis: A unified framework based on the Shapley value. *Journal of Economic Inequality*, *11*(1), 99–126.

Verbeek, M. (2008). *A guide to modern econometrics* (3rd ed.). Chichester, UK: Wiley.

APPENDIX A: ON THE CONCEPT OF SHAPLEY DECOMPOSITION

Let $I(a, b)$ be a function depending on two variables a and b. Such a function need not be linear. Although Chantreuil and Trannoy (2013) and Sastre and Trannoy (2002) limited their application of the Shapley value to the decomposition of income inequality, Shorrocks (2013) has shown that such a decomposition could be applied to any function.

The idea of the Shapley value is to consider all the possible sequences allowing us to eliminate the variables a and b. Let us start with the elimination of the variable a. This variable may be the first one or the second one to be eliminated. If it is eliminated first, the function $I(a, b)$ will become equal to $I(a=0;\ b\neq 0)$ since the variable a has been eliminated so that in this case the contribution of a to the function $I(a, b)$ is equal to $I(a\neq 0;\ b\neq 0)-I(a=0;\ b\neq 0)$. If the variable a is the second one to be eliminated, the function I will then be equal to $I(a\neq 0;\ b=0)$. Since both elimination sequences are possible and assuming the probability of these two sequences is the same, we may conclude that the contribution $C(a)$ of the variable a to the function $I(a, b)$ is equal to:

$$\begin{aligned} C(a) = {} & (1/2)\{I(a\neq 0; b\neq 0) - I(a=0; b\neq 0)\} \\ & + (1/2)\{I(a\neq 0; b=0) - I(a=0; b=0)\} \end{aligned} \tag{A.1}$$

Similarly one can prove that the contribution $C(b)$ of the variable b to the function $I(a, b)$ is:

$$\begin{aligned} C(b) = {} & (1/2)\{I(a\neq 0; b\neq 0) - I(a\neq 0; b=0)\} \\ & + (1/2)\{I(a=0; b\neq 0) - I(a=0; b=0)\} \end{aligned} \tag{A.2}$$

Combining Eqs. (A. 1) and (A.2) we observe that:

$$C(a) + C(b) = I(a, b) \tag{A.3}$$

APPENDIX B: DATABASE

Database/Variables	Description/Definition/Source
Quadros de Pessoal database (1985–2007) Except 1999 and 2001	Data from annual compulsory survey conducted by *Ministério do Trabalho e da Solidariedade Social (MTSS), Portugal*, where firms are required to provide information about their workers on items such as monthly compensation, highest schooling level attained, age and monthly hours worked.
Average earnings of employees at Concelhos	Average full earnings of employees that performed complete working hours during the month of October, *Quadros de Pessoal* database.
HCPI (Harmonized Consumer Price Index, 2000 = 1)	*Instituto Nacional de Estatística*, INE, Portugal
Average real earnings of employees at NUTS3	*Authors' own computation – Note* that NUTS3 was *inexistent for the period* 1985–*1994, so real earnings at NUTS3 were* estimated *from data for Concelhos from which* NUTS3 are composed of.
Inequality measures at NUTS3 level – Gini, Atkinson indices (1985–2007)	*Authors' own computation* – Weighted distributions of real earnings were computed from which the inequality measures were derived.
Welfare proxies	*Authors' own computation*
Portuguese Concelhos	Geographic-Administrative units, a total of 308
Portuguese NUTS3	Portuguese Nomenclature for Territorial Units for Statistics, a total 30

APPENDIX B1: ECONOMETRIC RESULTS FOR REGIONAL CONVERGENCE OF PER CAPITA INCOMES

Table B1.1. Estimation of Eq. (3).

Equation Number	Model	α_1	β_1	θ	ser	AR1	AR2	Wald	Sargan
(3)	AB	2.089 (0.775)*	−0.301 (0.115)*	0.050 (0.098)	0.259	−3.510*	0.643	(2) = 40.858*	(4) = 4.433

Note: See Table 2.

Table B1.2. Estimation of Eq. (4).

Equation Number	Model	α_2	β_2	θ	ser	AR1	AR2	Wald	Sargan
(4)	AB	−1.704 (0.858)**	0.255 (0.125)**	0.202 (0.121)***	0.257	−2.847*	−0.321	(2) = 15.08*	(19) = 20.25

Note: See Table 2.

Table B1.3. Estimation of Eq. (6).

Equation Number	Model	α_3	β_3	ser
(6)	RE	−0.545 (0.326)***	0.107 (0.048)**	0.146

Note: See Table 2.

Table B1.4. Estimation of Eq. (7).

Equation Number	Model	α_4	β_4	ser
(7)	POLS	−2.304 (0.825)*	0.316 (0.120)*	0.263

Note: See Table 2.

APPENDIX B2: ECONOMETRIC RESULTS FOR REGIONAL CONVERGENCE OF WITHIN REGIONS INEQUALITIES

Table B2.1A. Estimation of Eq. (13) Using Gini Index.

Equation Number	Model	λ_1	ρ_1	ser
(13)	FE	0.213	−1.06	0.048
(Gini)		(0.017)*	(0.087)*	

Note: See Table 2.

Table B2.1B. Estimation of Eq. (13) Using the Atkinson Index.

Equation Number	Model	λ_1	ρ_1	ser
(13)	POLS	0.037	−0.947	0.028
(Atkin)		(0.002)*	(0.048)*	

Note: See Table 2.

Table B2.2A. Estimation of Eq. (14) Using the Gini Index.

Equation Number	Model	λ_2	ρ_2	ser
(14)	RE	−0.051	0.253	0.061
(Gini)		(0.019)*	(0.091)*	

Note: See Table 2.

Table B2.2B. Estimation of Eq. (14) Using the Atkinson Index.

Equation Number	Model	λ_2	ρ_2	ser
(14)	FE	0.007	−0.177	0.038
(Atkin)		(0.002)*	(0.055)*	

Note: See Table 2.

Table B2.3A. Estimation of Eq. (16) Using the Gini Index.

Equation Number	Model	λ_3	ρ_3	ser
(16)	FE	0.095	−0.267	0.044
(Gini)		(0.013)*	(0.066)*	

Note: See Table 2.

Table B2.4A. Estimation of Eq. (17) Using the Gini Index.

Equation Number	Model	λ_4	ρ_4	ser
(17)	POLS	−0.098	0.280	0.075
(Gini)		(0.021)*	(0.090)*	

Note: See Table 2.

APPENDIX B3: ECONOMETRIC RESULTS FOR THE WELFARE LEVELS OF THE VARIOUS REGIONS

Table B3.1A. Estimation of Eq. (A.2) Using the Gini Index.

Equation Number	Model	π_1	μ_1	θ	ser	AR1	AR2	Wald	Sargan
(A.2)	AB	2.553	−0.383	0.061	0.230	−2.955*	−0.289	(2) = 15.04*	(26) = 28.05
(Gini)		(0.669)*	(0.102)*	(0.089)					

Note: See Table 2.

Table B3.1B. Estimation of Eq. (A.2) Using the Atkinson Index.

Equation Number	Model	π_1	μ_1	θ	ser	AR1	AR2	Wald	Sargan
(A.2)	AB	2.209	−0.320	0.073	0.241	−2.881*	0.739	(2) = 17.99*	(26) = 27.52
(Atkin)		(0.744)*	(0.111)*	(0.065)					

Note: See Table 2.

Table B3.2A. Estimation of Eq. (A.3) Using the Gini Index.

Equation Number	Model	π_2	μ_2	θ	ser	AR1	AR2	Wald	Sargan
(A.3)	AB	−2.175	0.332	0.103	0.232	−0.004*	0.239	(2) = 19.49*	(19) = 21.61
(Gini)		(0.713)*	(0.110)*	(0.102)					

Note: See Table 2.

Table B3.2B. Estimation of Eq. (A.3) Using the Atkinson Index.

Equation Number	Model	π_2	μ_2	θ	ser	AR1	AR2	Wald	Sargan
(A.3)	AB	−2.839	0.420	0.029	0.239	−2.833*	−0.847	(2) = 21.66*	(19) = 17.78
(Atkin)		(0.827)*	(0.124)*	(0.086)					

Note: See Table 2.

Table B3.3A. Estimation of Eq. (A.4) Using the Gini Index.

Equation number	Model	π_3	μ_3	SE reg
(A.4)	BE	−0.922	0.168	0.079
(Gini)		(0.637)	(0.098)***	

Note: See Table 2.

Table B3.3B. Estimation of Eq. (A.4) on the Basis of the Atkinson Index.

Equation Number	Model	π_3	μ_3	Ser
(A.4)	BE	−1.349	0.229	0.070
(Atkin)		(0.597)**	(0.089)*	

Note: See Table 2.

Table B3.4A. Estimation of Eq. (A.5) Using the Gini Index.

Equation Number	Model	π_4	μ_4	θ	ser	AR1	AR2	Wald	Sargan
(A.5)	AB	−1.428	0.197	0.159	0.310	−2.683*	−1.415	(2) = 7.67**	(26) = 27.00
(Gini)		(0.687)**	(0.104)***	(0.074)					

Note: See Table 2.

Table B3.4B. Estimation of Eq. (A.5) Using the Atkinson Index.

Equation Number	Model	π_4	μ_4	θ	ser	AR1	AR2	Wald	Sargan
(A.5)	AB	−2.395	0.334	−0.017	0.304	−2.344**	−0.273	(2) = 23.14*	(19) = 13.41
(Atkin)		(0.489)*	(0.071)*	(0.086)					

Note: See Table 2.

REGIONAL INCOME CONVERGENCE IN PORTUGAL (1991–2002)

Gertrudes Saúde Guerreiro

ABSTRACT

Does the standard of living vary from region to region in Portugal and are spatial units in Portugal converging in income? We observe spatial error dependence between municipalities and estimate spatial econometric models to test convergence. For conditional convergence we conclude that primary sector employment, activity rate, and percentage of active population with higher education are important to distinguish the "steady state" of the regional economies, reflecting the labor market at regional level.

Keywords: Income distribution; regional inequality; regional convergence; spatial econometrics

JEL classifications: C21; E25; R12

Economic Well-Being and Inequality: Papers from the Fifth ECINEQ Meeting
Research on Economic Inequality, Volume 22, 351–381

ISSN: 1049-2585/doi:10.1108/S1049-258520140000022011

INTRODUCTION

Regional imbalances represent an intrinsic characteristic of the Portuguese economy (Guerreiro, 2012). Mateus, Madruga, and Rodrigues (2000) argues that the structural evolution of the European economy has resulted in convergence between countries and divergence between regions. European Union Policy stresses economic and social cohesion, which is fostered by regional convergence.

Our research addresses the problem of inequality from a different perspective than the traditional studies addressing inequality among individuals (see Rodrigues, 1994, 1999, 2008). We address questions such as: Does geography influence the pattern of inequality? Does Portuguese's standard of living depend on the place of residence? Finally, in the growth process are the spatial units that make up Portugal converging in terms of income? Our approach to these questions is to investigate convergence between smaller territorial units, that is, municipalities.

The economic literature differentiates between two typos of convergence, the convergence of income, and the convergence of inequality in income, living conditions, or welfare between people. The study of income convergence (β convergence[1]) uses standard regional or national economic indicators such as Gross Domestic Product per capita (GDPpc).[2] The study of inequality convergence (σ convergence[3]) normally uses indicators like household (or individual) income and/or household consumption, or microeconomic data on households.[4] In this research, we exam both types of convergence. There is an interesting debate in the economic literature and more particularly in convergence studies, regarding these two types of convergence (introduced by Sala-i-Martin, 1990). Sala-i-Martin (1995) states that application of these concepts to real world data reveals that where σ convergence is observed, β convergence is also observed. But Young, Higgins, and Levy (2008), in a study of American counties, showed that β convergence is a necessary but not sufficient condition for σ convergence.

Following this discussion, we test the hypothesis that β convergence is indeed a necessary but not sufficient condition for the existence of σ convergence, through application and analysis of the two concepts in our data set.

Guerreiro (2012) evaluated the convergence of regional income growth using a static analysis. She finds growing inequality between regional incomes over the period 1990–2006. She concludes that this distribution of earnings reflects the current distribution of economic activity in Portugal, which is concentrated in the coastal and metropolitan areas of Lisbon and

Oporto, and also reflects differences in economic specialization and education in each territorial unit.

This paper proposes to address the convergence in wages per worker (over the period 1991–2002) between municipalities and NUTS III[5] regions of mainland Portugal. For NUTS III regions, we evaluate the convergence in the variable GDPpc (which is unavailable for municipalities).

To meet the objectives set out in this paper, we present a brief literature review, a description of the methodology and our sources of data. The spatial autocorrelation analysis follows. Finally, we evaluate and interpret the econometric results of the estimated models. We conclude with a synthesis of results and possible future developments in the context of this work.

LITERATURE REVIEW

In our research, we perform two kinds of analysis that cross two research areas: first, the regional distribution of income inequality (dealt with in a previous paper) and secondly, regional convergence in income growth, dealt with in this paper.

The analysis of convergence as an area of interest has emerged through the work of Barro and Sala-i-Martin (Barro & Sala-i-Martin, 1992; Sala-i-Martin, 1996a, 1996b, among others) based on the neoclassical growth model of Solow (1956) and Swan (1956). These authors study the convergence between countries using international data.

In the last decade, convergence studies have proliferated, particularly those relating to the convergence between countries and/or regions of the European Union, following the successive changes in its composition in terms of member states. These studies evaluate convergence based on GDPpc and some of them aim to evaluate the effectiveness of EU policies, mainly the effects of structural funds in narrowing the gap between member states (e.g., Beugelsdijk & Eijffinger, 2003).

For Portuguese regions, we summarize the findings of several studies published in Table 1.

In all above studies, the convergence analysis is carried out based on the regional GDPpc variable, which reflects the distribution of production between the territorial units making up the country, but tells us nothing about the distribution of income from production between these regions.

In fact, locale of production can be different from the locale where production is allocated. Imagine the example of a small country or region

Table 1. Key Findings of Empirical Studies on Income Convergence in Portugal.

Authors	Data and Spatial Units of Analysis	Major Findings
Soukiazis (2003)	GDPpc (Regio, Eurostat, 2001) by NUTS II regions for the period 1981–1996	The convergence process in GDPpc suggests that absolute convergence is slower than conditional convergence, due to the reallocation of resources (employment by sector of activity) and the concentration of trade flows.
Soukiazis and Antunes (2004)	GDPpc and productivity by NUTS III regions (INE, National Accounts) for the period 1991–2000	Empirical analysis shows that convergence is mainly conditional, rather than absolute, both in terms of GDPpc and productivity.
Freitas and Torres (2005)	GDPpc and Gross Value Added (GVA) per employee (DGREGIO, Eurostat, 2003) by NUTS II regions for 1990 and 2001	The period 1995–2000 shows a divergence between regions, both in terms of GDPpc and GVA per employee. During this period, only Madeira approached the national average in terms of GDPpc. In the extended time period 1990–2001, it is observed that only the Algarve and the North grow faster than the national average for both indicators.
Antunes and Soukiazis (2006)	GDPpc for NUTS III and later separated into only two major regions, inland and coastal	In the process of convergence it is important if the region is on the coast or inland. Coastal regions grow faster in terms of GDPpc. Regional distribution of structural funds is revealed to benefit more in developed coastal regions than in inland regions. However, structural funds have contributed to increased speed of convergence among all regions. The regional convergence in terms of GDPpc is slightly higher in inland regions, which means they become more homogeneous over time, converging to a different "steady state" from that of the coastal area.

"P," consisting of 10 factories and no housing, so no resident population. The factory employees commute daily from their country or region of residence "R" to work in place "P." As such, part of the GDP generated in "P" is distributed in the form of wages to residents in "R," so the regional distribution of production does not coincide with the regional distribution of income, and in particular with respect to wages.

It is this phenomenon that we want to measure, the convergence in the regional distribution of income, and particularly in wages. For the chosen territorial units, that is, NUTS III regions, we compare the convergence in GDPpc growth with the regional convergence of wages. We conduct a further study of convergence in wages, between municipalities in mainland Portugal.

When convergence studies of small territorial units are conducted, location is revealed to be a key component that affects growth patterns in a heterogeneous manner. According to Anselin (1988), the use of regional data implies considering the hypothesis that observations are not independent, as a result of the interrelationships between neighboring regions. As referred to by Ertur, Gallo, and Baumont (2006), Paas, Kuusk, Võrk, and Schlitte (2006), and Buccellato (2007), the spatial component is not negligible. Hence, conventional estimates of convergence may prove to be biased toward the spatial dependence between observations, and many regional studies can be seriously compromised by bias and inefficiency of estimates, due to space interdependence not being considered.

For Portugal, Martinho (2005) and Caleiro and Guerreiro (2005) demonstrate the existence of spatial dependence with regard to some observable variables for smaller territorial units. In the first case there is spatial dependence in the productivity per sector of activity at the level of NUTS III regions, and in the second case, spatial dependence in the relationship between election results and unemployment rate by municipality.

Caleiro and Guerreiro (2005) conclude that despite geographical proximity between Portuguese municipalities, economic distance is great (measured by the purchasing power indicator). In fact, Portugal is characterized by high regional disparities. These authors suggest that study of the distribution of income among families could enrich these results. So we have developed this study in this context.

METHODOLOGY AND INFORMATION SOURCES

In the first phase of our work we measure the convergence between the spatial units in the period of analysis, based on two alternative variables:

- Wages per capita for municipalities and for NUTS III regions;
- GDPpc for NUTS III regions.

Following Sala-i-Martin (1990), σ convergence means a convergence of regional economies via reduction of dispersion (standard deviation (σ)) of GDPpc or wages between regions, over the period considered. The absolute β convergence states that poorer economies tend to grow faster than richer ones which, in our case, means a higher growth rate of wages and/or of GDPpc in poorer geographic units.

Finally conditional β convergence states that the growth rate of an economy is inversely related to the distance that separates this economy from its steady state, and that the steady state differs from economy to economy. In this study, we begin by testing a model of absolute convergence, and at a second stage, we include some explanatory variables in order to distinguish the steady state of small economies under study, to test the hypothesis of conditional convergence.

To obtain a first estimate of the absolute β convergence between the territorial units of the country, we follow the adjustment made by Barro and Sala-i-Martin (1995, 1999) to the Solow model (Solow, 1956):

$$\ln\left(\frac{y_{iT}}{y_{i0}}\right) = \alpha + \beta \ln(y_{i0}) + \varepsilon_{it} \tag{1}$$

where y_{i0} is per capita variable for the territorial unit i, in the first year of the series (year 0); y_{iT} is per capita variable for the territorial unit i, in the last year of the series (year T); α, β are parameters to be estimated by the model, where α is the constant and β is the coefficient of convergence; ε_{it} is error term.

Our dependent variable is growth (in GDPpc or in employee earnings, depending on the model estimated), where we compare the initial and final years of the series, using the information from only these two years, and the independent variable is its value in the initial year of our data series.

For wages we have information about the municipalities, but in the case of GDPpc (INE, National Accounts), we only have data for NUTS III territorial units. Therefore, in the case of wages we estimate the model for municipalities and for NUTS III regions, while in the case of the GDPpc variable we only estimate the model for the NUTS III regions.

For NUTS III regions, with both results we can compare the estimates using each of the variables (earnings and GDPpc), one of our initial goals.

As for conditional β convergence, we again follow the linear model proposed by Barro and Sala-i-Martin (1995, 1999):

$$\ln\left(\frac{y_{iT}}{y_{i0}}\right) = \alpha + \beta \ln(y_{i0}) + \gamma X_{i0}' + \varepsilon_{it} \tag{2}$$

where $\varepsilon \sim$ i.i.d. $(0, \sigma^2 I_n)$; y_{iT} is GDPpc/average salary in region i at time T; α is the constant; β is the coefficient of convergence; X is a matrix with additional explanatory variables (values observed in year 0), and γ the corresponding vector of coefficients.

After a first estimation of the model by the ordinary least squares (OLS) method, we must test the interdependence between spatial units of analysis (municipalities and NUTS III) and decide to what extent the original model should be amended to incorporate this spatial interdependence through a so-called neighbors matrix, which can be build up, for example, based on geographical contiguity.

Spatial dependence can occur when the value assumed by the dependent variable in a given location depends on the value of the same variable in neighboring locations. This dependence arises from the existence of spatial autocorrelation, that is, spatial clusters with similar values to the dependent variable. But spatial dependence can also result from processes of spatial diffusion effects (explanatory variables) (Anselin, 1988, 2002; Caleiro, 2008b). Spatial dependence can indeed take many forms, giving rise to different specifications (models) that include such dependence (see the multiplicity of models proposed in Le Sage, 1998, 1999).

However, most applied work considers only two forms of spatial dependence, coupled with two types of models: spatial dependence in the dependent variable, as synonymous with spatial diffusion, which translates into spatial autoregressive models, and spatial dependence in the errors/residues translated into spatial error models (see Anselin, 2002, 2003a; Caleiro, 2008a).

In any case, application of spatial statistical techniques can be justified (Le Sage, 1998, 1999) if:

- there is a theoretical model that supports the existence of that kind of spatial dependence;
- spatial autocorrelation, detected at the level of clusters in space, is confirmed by specific tests.

To test the spatial interdependence (autocorrelation), we can calculate different statistical tests of spatial correlation, and the Moran's I test is the most widely used (Moran, 1950). In algebraic terms, the global Moran's I statistic is calculated with the following expression (Moran, 1950):

$$I = \frac{n}{\sum_i \sum_j v_{ij}} \frac{\sum_i \sum_j v_{ij}(x_i - \bar{x})(x_j - \bar{x})}{\sum_i (x_i - \bar{x})^2} \tag{3}$$

where n represents the number of units/spatial locations, indexed by j, v_{ij} represents the spatial weights, x the variable of interest, and $\bar{x}$ their average. When the I statistic has a high value and is positive, it means there is positive autocorrelation. If there is no spatial dependence, we have $I = -[1/(n-1)]$.

The same statistics can be calculated for each site (Local Moran's I (I_i)):

$$I_i = \frac{(x_i - \bar{x}) \sum_{i=1}^{n} (x_j - \bar{x})}{\sum_{i=1}^{n} (x_i - \bar{x})^2 / n} \tag{4}$$

$I_i < 0$ indicates a negative local spatial autocorrelation; $I_i = 0$ indicates the absence of local spatial autocorrelation, and $I_i > 0$ indicates positive local spatial autocorrelation.

The definition of neighborhood relations is clearly determinant in calculating levels of spatial correlation. Neighbor relations are usually expressed by a matrix, the spatial weights matrix (W matrix), which is subsequently introduced into the model specification. Construction of the W matrix is typically based on contiguity between the territorial units under study, or alternatively, on the geographical distance (Euclidean distance).

We choose a matrix of spatial weights based on spatial contiguity. In our study, especially with regard to municipalities, this option is fully justified by the small size of spatial units and simultaneously the number of neighborhoods in each unit. In fact, although municipalities are small spatial units, they are also surrounded by other small units, meaning that each municipality has always more than one neighbor (some of them have 8 or 9 neighbors). As such, making an assumption that observational units in close proximity should exhibit effect levels that are similar (Le Sage & Pace, 2009), the spatial contiguity matrix covering a large net of relationships, covers the economic situation of these small units too.

The W matrix based on contiguity results from standardization[6] of a neighborhood's V matrix, which can take many forms. Its simplest form can be defined by: $V = \lfloor v_{ij} \rfloor$, where $v_{ij} = 0$ if location j is not near i (and if $j = i$) and $v_{ij} = 1$ if location j is near i. Considering the locations as neighboring or not depends on previously established criteria, because there are different ways of defining contiguity.

Of the five different ways suggested by Le Sage (1999) to define the presence or absence of contiguity between regions, we highlight those applied by Anselin (2003b):

- Queen contiguity: provided that the territorial units have one point in common in their boundaries, we consider they are neighbors;
- Rook contiguity: to be considered neighbors, the territorial units have an entire limit or boundary in common.

As such, the spatial weights matrix based on queen contiguity always has a denser structure of connectivity; that is, for each land unit, the number of neighbors is greater than in the concept of rook contiguity. Therefore, in the present study, we choose the matrix of queen neighborhoods.[7]

As for the statistical tests of spatial correlation, Moran's I test compares the value of the global variable in any location with its value in all other locations. It is based on a statistical calculation that is roughly the correlation coefficient between the variable values by location, and the average values of this variable presented in neighboring locations (spatial lags), that is, for all $j \neq i$ where $v_{ij} = 1$.

Moran's I test is a diffusion test, indicating the existence (or not) of spatial dependence, giving no indication of possible alternative solutions (Florax & Graaf, 2004). The alternative hypothesis of these tests is that there is spatial correlation, but, if so, there is no indication of what kind of correlation and, hence, which model specification is advised.

Convergence is a dynamic process and spatial lags model cannot fully "capture" the nature of this process. Following Le Sage and Pace (2009) we consider that spatial heterogeneity in convergence can be better represented by a spatial error model (spatial dependence only in the errors).

With regard to the absolute convergence with spatial error dependence, we estimate the following model (specification suggested by Anselin, 1988 adapted to the existence of spatial dependence only in the errors):

- Spatial Error Model

$$\ln\left(\frac{y_{iT}}{y_{i0}}\right) = \alpha + \beta \ln(y_{i0}) + \varepsilon_{it} \text{ and } \varepsilon_{it} = \lambda(W\varepsilon)_{it} + u_{it} \qquad (5)$$

where λ is the coefficient of spatial autocorrelation and W is the regional weight matrix (standardized neighborhood matrix).

Considering also the spatial dependence represented by a spatial error model (Le Sage & Pace, 2009), we estimate the following model of conditional convergence (Anselin, 1988):

- Spatial Error Model:

$$\ln\left(\frac{y_{iT}}{y_{i0}}\right) = \alpha + \beta \ln(y_{i0}) + \gamma X_{i0}^{'} + \varepsilon_{it} \tag{6}$$

$$\varepsilon_{it} = \lambda (W\varepsilon)_{it} + u_{it} \quad u_{it} \sim i.i.d.\,(0, \sigma^2 I_n)$$

where λ is the coefficient of spatial autocorrelation and W is the regional weight matrix (standardized neighborhood matrix).

According to Le Sage (1998) and Anselin (1988), in the estimation of spatial models, the maximum likelihood method must be applied. In fact, in the spatial error model, the coefficient λ measures the degree of spatial autocorrelation among the error terms of neighboring areas, which makes the OLS estimators inefficient. As such, in the present study, we estimate these models using the maximum likelihood method.

To select the additional explanatory variables to include in the matrix X, with which we intend to describe and distinguish the economic base of each territorial unit, we use the same criterion adopted by Guerreiro and Rego (2005). We follow the Territorial Competitiveness Pyramid proposed by Mateus et al. (2000) (Fig. 1), in an attempt to distinguish territorial units based on their competitive conditions, which can be grouped in several areas (the pyramid basis): demographics, labor market, skills, innovation, business dynamics, productive specialization, and infrastructure support.

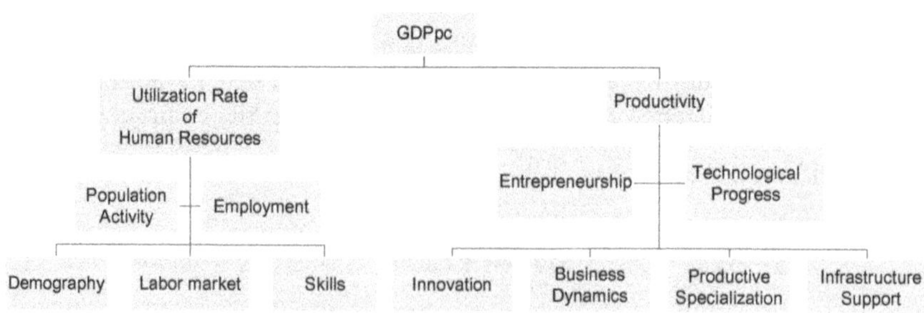

Fig. 1. Territorial Competitiveness Pyramid. *Source*: Adapted from Mateus et al. (2000).

In Table 2 we present the selection of variables by theme, and their choice was subject to the availability of information in official sources (INE, 2008) for the spatial units of analysis.

The information collected for the variables listed in Table 2 refers to the initial year of our data series, namely 1991[8] in an attempt to incorporate in the model, the structural differences that distinguish the territorial units at the starting point of the convergence analysis.

For data analysis and estimation of the models we use the following software: GeoDa (developed by Luc Anselin) and STATA. In collecting information, we access the official (institutional) sources. As such, we used information from two distinct sources:

- National Statistics Institute (INE): National Accounts, Consumer Price Index (CPI), and all the socio-economic information available on Portuguese municipalities and compiled annually in electronic publishing of Portugal in numbers;
- Ministry of Labour and Social Solidarity – Office of Strategy and Planning (DGEEP): information relating to employees' remuneration, by municipality and industry.

The time period chosen for our analysis is primarily the 1990s, 1991/2002 for the dependent variable of employees' remuneration and 1990/2003

Table 2. Explanatory Variables Selected.

Base of Territorial Competitiveness Pyramid	Explanatory Variables (Proxy)
Demography	• Ageing ratio
Labor market	• Activity rate • Unemployment rate
Skills	• Percentage of labor force with higher education • Illiteracy rate
Innovation	Not available for base year (1991)
Business dynamics	Not available for base year (1991)
Productive specialization	Employment structure by sector of activity: • Percentage of population employed in sector I • Percentage of population employed in sector II • Percentage of population employed in sector III
Infrastructure support	Information not collected because we did not consider it relevant in the distinction of spatial units

Source: National Statistics Institute, Census of Population (1991).
Note: Sector I is agricultural sector, sector II is industrial sector, and sector III is the services sector.

for the variable of GDPpc. To avoid bias in the analysis, we excluded the Autonomous Regions (Azores and Madeira), which do not have a spatial relationship of contiguity with other regions.

We choose the municipality as the spatial unit of analysis; however, it raises problems of changes in territorial nomenclature, because during this period new administrative units were created at this level (new municipalities). Thus, for our annual results to be comparable, we use the Nomenclature of Territorial Units for Statistics of 1990 (see appendix), and for subsequent years, we convert the data into the same classification of municipalities.

Employee remuneration for the final year of the series (2002) was deflated, that is, recalculated at constant prices of the initial year of the series (1991). Since we are working according to the income rather than production approach, the deflator used was the CPI. The CPI is calculated by INE only at the level of disaggregation of NUTS II regions (level II of the Nomenclature of Territorial Units for Statistics), so for each municipality the values were deflated by the CPI of the NUTS II region to which each one belongs.

ANALYSIS OF SPATIAL AUTOCORRELATION

Between NUTS III Regions: Regional Growth of GDPpc

Fig. 2 shows the absence of spatial autocorrelation in the growth of regional GDPpc. In fact, Moran's I test for the dependent variable has a value close to zero. As such, there is no need to estimate the spatial error model for the growth of GDPpc among the NUTS III regions.

The GeoDa allows us to perform an analysis of local spatial autocorrelation (Local Indicators of Spatial Association [LISA]), which provides an indicator of spatial autocorrelation for each location individually (Anselin, 2003b). Among the 28 NUTS III regions, only five showed a statistically significant Local Moran I test: Tâmega, Médio Tejo, and Alentejo with a significance level of 5%, and Pinhal Interior Norte and Pinhal Litoral with a significance level of 1%.

Between NUTS III Regions: Regional Growth of Average Monthly Earnings per Worker

In Fig. 3 we analyze spatial autocorrelation of regional wages growth with the Moran's I test for the dependent variable.

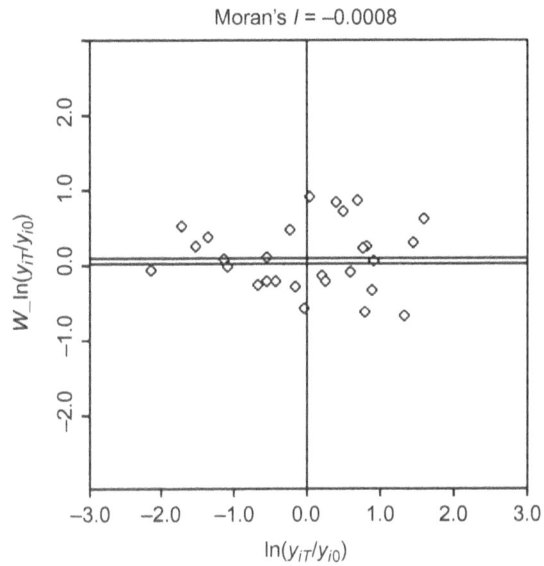

Fig. 2. Moran's *I* in the Growth of Regional GDPpc. *Note*: $W\_\ln(y_{iT}/y_{i0})$ is the growth in the spatially lagged GDPpc and $\ln(y_{iT}/y_{i0})$ is the growth in GDPpc.

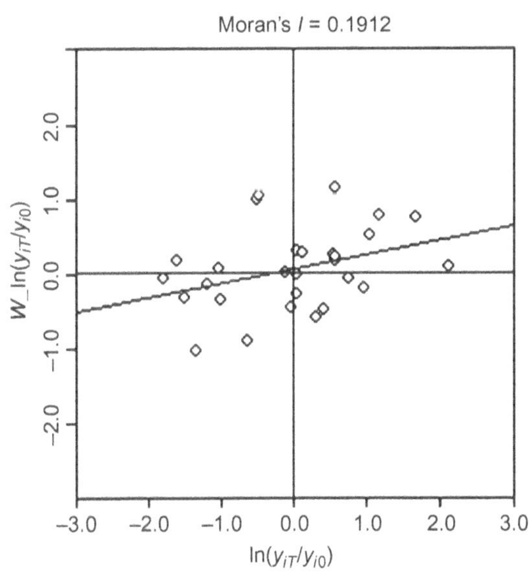

Fig. 3. Moran's *I* in Regional Wages Growth.

The Moran's *I* test for the dependent variable has a low value near zero, but it does not indicate complete absence of spatial correlation, as was the case for GDPpc.

Once again, among the 28 NUTS III regions, only five (but not the same ones identified for GDPpc) present statistically significant Local Moran's *I* tests. The regions of Grande Porto, Entre Douro e Vouga, Oeste, and Baixo Alentejo have a local Moran's *I* statistic with a significance level of 5%, and Baixo Vouga with a significance level of 1%.

Among Municipalities

Fig. 4 presents Moran's *I* statistic for wages growth among municipalities and shows there is autocorrelation between these spatial units.

This is confirmed in Fig. 5, where we repeat the analysis of local spatial autocorrelation (LISA) in terms of remuneration per municipality.

We identify three "clusters" of municipalities with very different characteristics:

- Municipalities in the north-east, near the border with Spain (Montalegre, Cabeceiras de Basto, Boticas, Chaves, Bragança, Vimioso, Miranda do

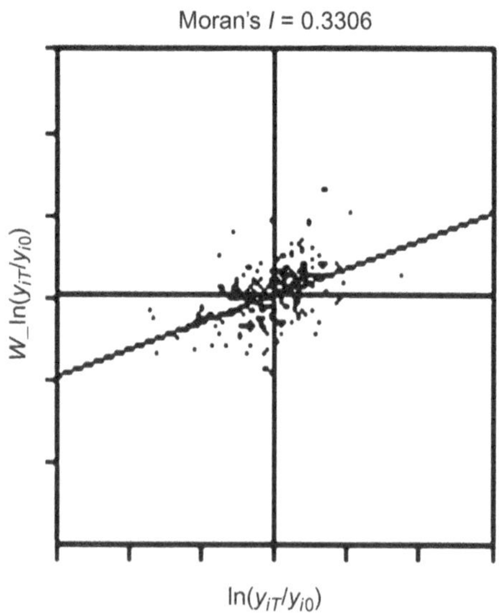

Fig. 4. Moran's *I* for Wages Growth among Municipalities.

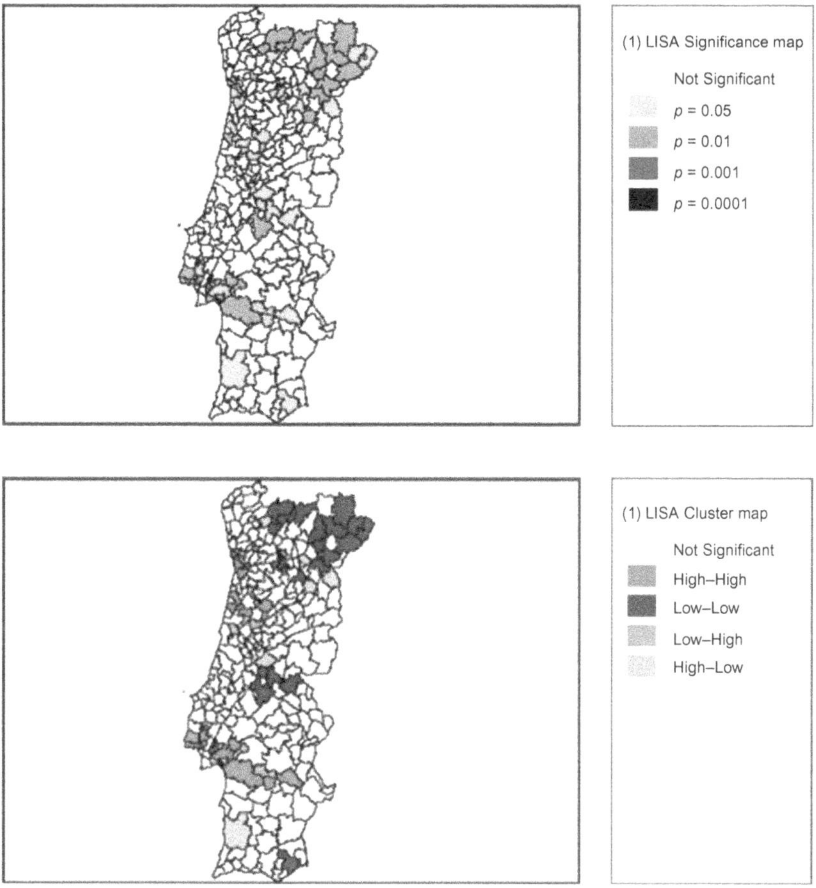

Fig. 5. Significance and Cluster Maps of Local Spatial Autocorrelation for Wages by Municipality.

Douro, Mogadouro, Macedo de Cavaleiros, Mirandela, Vila Flor, and Torre de Moncorvo), with significant local spatial autocorrelation, forming a low–low cluster, with low values for both variables (the dependent variable and lagged dependent variable) and spatially correlated;

- Municipalities of the northern and central coastline, with an extension to the inland center, with significant local spatial autocorrelation, but forming two types of clusters: high–high cluster for the coastal municipalities (Maia, Matosinhos, Porto, Gondomar, Vila Nova de Gaia, and Santa

Maria da Feira in the north, and Vagos, Aveiro, Oliveira de Barro, Anadia, Tondela, and Santa Comba Dão in the center), with high values for the dependent variable and lagged dependent variable; and low–low cluster for the municipalities of the inland center (Nisa, Mação, Vila de Rei, and Abrantes);

- Municipalities that form a track almost from Lisbon to the border with Spain (Cascais, Sintra, Loures, Lisboa, Palmela, Montijo, Alcochete, Alcácer do Sal, Alvito, and Portel), except the municipality of Moura, with significant local spatial autocorrelation forming a high–high cluster, with high values for the dependent variable and lagged dependent.

σ CONVERGENCE

We study the σ convergence between NUTS III regions in GDPpc growth and wages growth (Fig. 6).

We observe a slight decrease in GDPpc dispersion over the period ($\sigma=0.28$ in 1990, $\sigma=0.25$ in 2002, and $\sigma=0.26$ in 2003), but in employee remuneration there is a slight increase in the dispersion ($\sigma=0.11$ in 1991 and $\sigma=0.13$ in 2002[9]). It follows that, although GDPpc distribution has

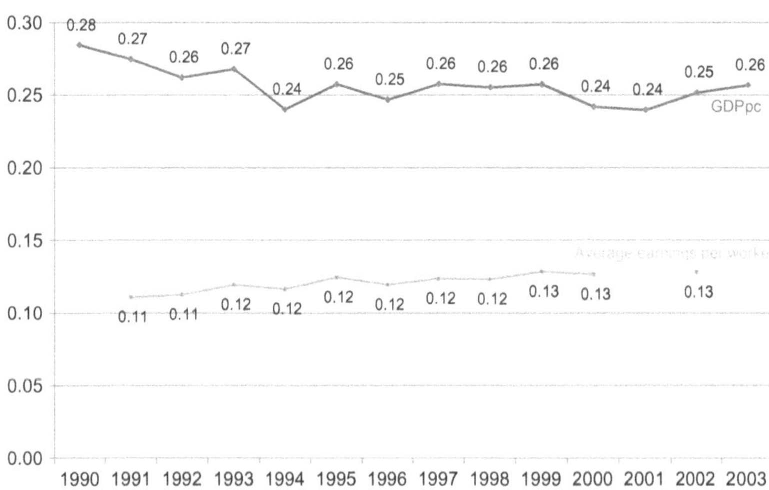

Fig. 6. Dispersion (σ Convergence) of GDPpc and Wages (Average Earnings per Worker) among NUTS III Regions of Mainland Portugal.

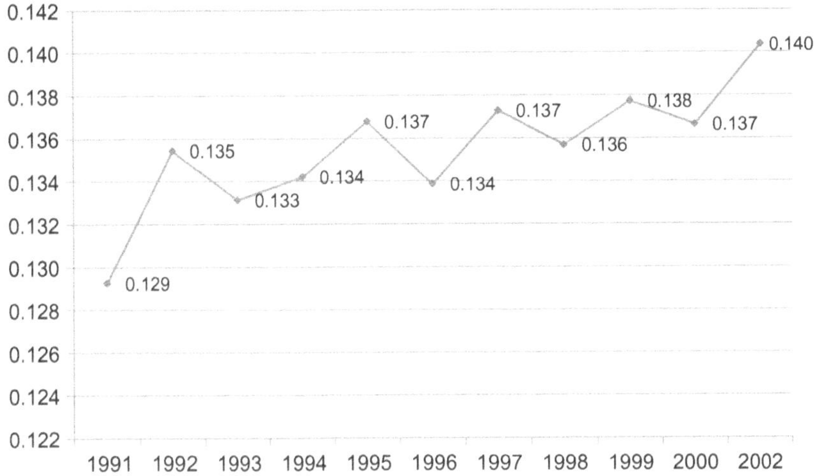

Fig. 7. Dispersion (σ Convergence) in Wages among the Municipalities of Mainland Portugal.

become less unequal among NUTS III regions, the same was not true for wages.

Fig. 7 presents the dispersion in average earnings per worker (or wages or employee remuneration) among mainland municipalities and we observe a clear increase in dispersion over the period of review; in 1991 we note $\sigma = 0.129$ and in 2002 $\sigma = 0.140$.

Guerreiro (2012) concludes that the spatial distribution of employee remuneration was moderately uneven, with a tendency to become increasingly unequal, as the weighted variation coefficient and weighted Gini coefficient increased between 1991 and 2002. This conclusion is confirmed here by the increased dispersion during this period. We do not register σ convergence.

In the next section, we check β convergence in the spatial data series of GDPpc and wages.

β CONVERGENCE: ECONOMETRIC RESULTS

Among NUTS III Regions of Mainland Portugal, in GDPpc Growth

Fig. 8 examines the existence of β convergence among NUTS III regions of mainland Portugal in GDPpc growth between 1990 and 2003. The horizontal axis represents the logarithm of GDPpc in the initial year of our series, 1990, and the vertical axis represents the growth rate of GDPpc between 1990 and 2003.

Fig. 8 shows the inverse relationship between growth and initial value of GDPpc, by indicating the existence of convergence. The corresponding estimation results of absolute and conditional convergence models using the OLS method are in Table 3.

From Table 3 we observe that the β estimated value is negative and statistically significant in both models, indicating convergence between the regions with regard to GDPpc. In the conditional convergence model, all other estimated coefficients are not statistically significant, and nor is the F-statistic. Therefore, contrary to Soukiazis and Antunes (2004)[10] for the period 1995–2000, there are indications that the model of absolute convergence is more appropriate for modeling growth in GDPpc among NUTS III regions for the period 1990–2003.

Among NUTS III Regions of Mainland Portugal, in Wages Growth

Fig. 9 shows that during the period from 1991 to 2002 there was no absolute β convergence of remuneration growth per employee among NUTS III regions, and these spatial units moved away from each other in terms of this indicator.

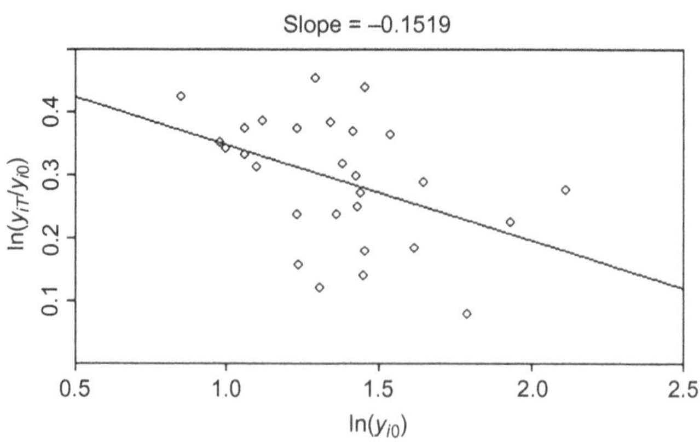

Fig. 8. Convergence among NUTS III Regions in GDPpc Growth between 1990 and 2003.

Table 3. Estimation of Absolute and Conditional β Convergence Models, Applied to GDPpc Growth among NUTS III Regions.

Dependent Variable: *Growth of GDPpc among NUTS III Regions (1990–2003)*		
Explanatory Variables	$\ln\left(\frac{y_{iT}}{y_{i0}}\right) = \alpha + \beta \ln(y_{i0}) + \varepsilon_i$	$\ln\left(\frac{y_{iT}}{y_{i0}}\right) = \alpha + \beta \ln(y_{i0}) + \gamma X'_{i0} + \varepsilon_{it}$
Constant	0.498 (5.698)*	0.445 (0.840)
GDPpc (1990)	−0.152 (−2.430)**	−0.259 (−2.265)**
Ageing ratio		0.001 (0.979)
Activity rate		0.008 (0.764)
Unemployment rate		−0.012 (−1.200)
Employment in sector I		−0.002 (−0.532)
Employment in sector II		−0.003 (−0.868)
Labor force with higher education		0.003 (0.202)
R^2	0.185	0.325
F-statistic	5.907 ($p = 0.022$)	1.377 ($p = 0.268$)
N	28	28
Breuch–Pagan test	0.519 ($p = 0.471$)	3.342 ($p = 0.852$)
Moran's *I* (error)	0.462 ($p = 0.644$)	0.780 ($p = 0.435$)

Notes: We present the results of the more complete conditional convergence model, although other models have been tested with different compositions of the *X* matrix; figures in brackets mean *t* statistic; * indicates that the estimated coefficient is statistically significant for a significance level of 1% and ** significant at 5%.

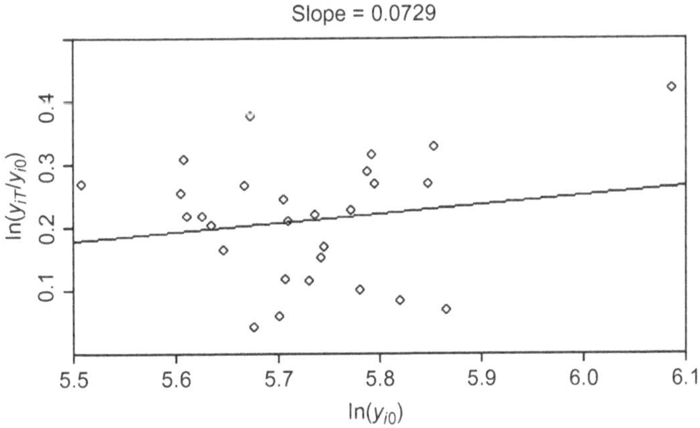

Fig. 9. Convergence among NUTS III Regions in Wages Growth between 1991 and 2002.

Table 4 presents the estimation results of absolute and conditional β convergence models in employee remuneration growth for NUTS III regions in the period 1991–2002, using the OLS estimation method. For conditional convergence, we tested four alternative models: Model A, which includes as explanatory variables, among others, the proportion of people employed in sectors I and II; Models B, C, and D where, in terms of sectorial structure of employment, we include separately the percentage of employed population in sectors I, II, and III, respectively. In our view, models B and D appear more appropriate in terms of convergence of wages in NUTS III regions, because in both the estimated models β is negative and statistically significant, which demonstrates (conditional) convergence in regional employee remuneration levels.

Among Portuguese Municipalities, in Wages Growth

Fig. 10 reveals evidence of absolute β convergence in remuneration per employee growth for the period 1991–2002. In fact, there is an inverse relationship between the initial level of remuneration in each municipality and its growth over this period, with a $\hat{\beta}= -0.1657$.

Table 5 describes the estimation results of absolute and conditional convergence models applied to wages growth for municipalities in the period 1991–2002. We present the results of four alternative conditional convergence models. The difference between the models lies only in the employment structure by sector of activity in the municipality. In model A, we include the percentage of employment in sectors I and II as explanatory variables, and models B, C, and D include each sector separately, respectively, sector I, sector II, and sector III.

All estimated models reveal the existence of convergence between municipalities in earnings throughout the period under review (1991–2002), with $\hat{\beta}<0$ statistically significant. The estimated coefficient for the ageing ratio is not significant in any model, while the estimated coefficients for the activity rate and labor force with higher education are significant in all models.

Fig. 10 and Table 5 lead us to conclude that there is spatial autocorrelation in wages growth among municipalities, because in all the models Moran's I test has a non-zero and significant value. When spatial autocorrelation is included, the convergence in wages growth becomes more evident (greater and more significant in absolute terms). Furthermore, λ assumes a significant estimated value (Table 6).

Table 4. Estimation Results of Absolute and Conditional β Convergence Models among NUTS III Regions, Applied to the Growth in Average Earnings.

Dependent Variable: *Growth in Average Earnings in NUTS III Regions (1991–2002)*

Explanatory Variables	$\ln\left(\frac{y_{iT}}{y_{i0}}\right)=\alpha+\beta\ln(y_{i0})+\varepsilon_i$	Model A (I and II) $\ln\left(\frac{y_{iT}}{y_{i0}}\right)=\alpha+\beta\ln(y_{i0})+\gamma X'_{i0}+\varepsilon_{it}$	Model B (I) $\ln\left(\frac{y_{iT}}{y_{i0}}\right)=\alpha+\beta\ln(y_{i0})+\gamma X'_{i0}+\varepsilon_{it}$	Model C (II) $\ln\left(\frac{y_{iT}}{y_{i0}}\right)=\alpha+\beta\ln(y_{i0})+\gamma X'_{i0}+\varepsilon_{it}$	Model D (III) $\ln\left(\frac{y_{iT}}{y_{i0}}\right)=\alpha+\beta\ln(y_{i0})+\gamma X'_{i0}+\varepsilon_{it}$
Constant	−0.262 (−0.542)	0.875 (1.483)	1.354 (2.806)*	0.847 (1.601)	1.254 (2.281)**
Average earnings (1991)	0.073 (0.087)	−0.167 (−1.569)	−0.237 (−2.487)**	−0.165 (−1.615)	−0.245 (−2.305)**
Ageing ratio		0.000002 (0.007)	−0.00006 (−0.225)	0.000011 (0.041)	0.0000098 (0.327)
Activity rate		0.002 (0.714)	0.003 (1.083)	0.002 (0.777)	0.006 (2.598)**
Unemployment rate		0.003 (0.840)	0.0003 (0.125)	0.003 (0.969)	0.001 (0.414)
Employment in sector I		−0.0002 (−0.118)	−0.002 (−1.683)***		
Employment in sector II		0.002 (1.358)		0.002 (2.239)**	
Employment in sector III					−0.001 (−0.816)
Labor force with higher education		0.017 (3.548)*	0.014 (3.267)*	0.018 (4.577)*	0.005 (3.631)*
R^2	0.028	0.725	0.7	0.725	0.670
F	0.749 (p = 0.395)	7.546 (p = 0.000)	8.168 (p = 0.0001)	9.235 (p = 0.000)	7.108 (p = 0.000)
n	28	28	28	28	28
Breuch–Pagan test	1.589 (p = 0.208)	3.343 (p = 0.765)	8.136 (p = 0.228)	6.776 (p = 0.342)	3.343 (p = 0.765)
Moran's I (error)	2.062 (p = 0.039)	0.758 (p = 0.449)	0.831 (p = 0.406)	0.817 (p = 0.414)	0.651 (p = 0.515)

Notes: Figures in brackets mean t statistic; * indicates that the estimated coefficient is statistically significant for a significance level of 1%; ** significant at 5%, and *** significant at 10%.

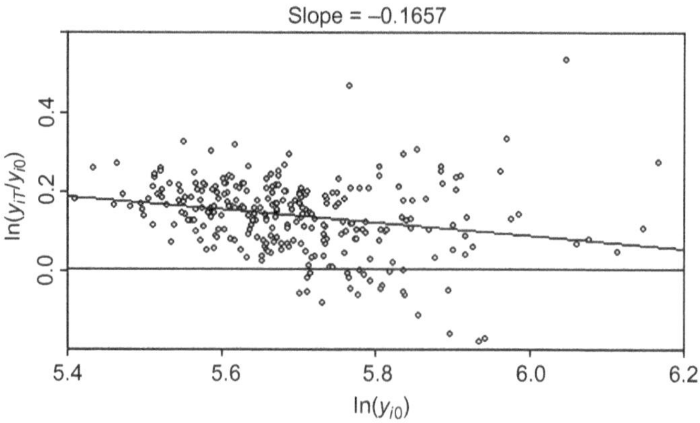

Fig. 10. Convergence between Municipalities in Wages Growth between 1991 and 2002.

For the conditional convergence spatial error model, we obtained the results listed in Table 7.

All estimated models still show the presence of convergence between wages for municipalities throughout the period under review (1991–2002), with $\hat{\beta}<0$ statistically significant, and λ is always positive (positive spatial autocorrelation) and statistically significant, confirming the existence of spatial error dependence. The estimated coefficient of the ageing rate is not significant in any model, while the estimated coefficients of the activity rate and labor force with higher education are significant and positive in all models.

We find that in terms of earnings growth, Portuguese municipalities have been converging, although to different "steady states" (conditional convergence). The main determinants of growth differences between those territorial units, according to our models, are the characteristics of the resident population, both in terms of activity rate and in terms of the active population's level of education (labor force with higher education). In addition, the sectorial structure of employment appears as a determinant of wages growth, with statistically significant estimated coefficients for sectors I and II.

The significance of estimated coefficients for the different variables of matrix X changes due to the correlation between these variables (Table 8).

The ageing rate shows a high correlation with the activity rate and the illiteracy rate, negative in the first case and positive in the second. The

Table 5. Estimation Results of Absolute and Conditional β Convergence Models among Municipalities, Applied to the Growth in Wages.

Dependent Variable: *Growth in Average Earnings in Municipalities (1991–2002)*					
Explanatory Variables	$\ln\left(\frac{y_{iT}}{y_{i0}}\right) = \alpha + \beta\ln(y_{i0}) + \varepsilon_i$	Model A (I and II) $\ln\left(\frac{y_{iT}}{y_{i0}}\right) = \alpha + \beta\ln(y_{i0}) + \gamma X'_{i0} + \varepsilon_{it}$	Model B (I) $\ln\left(\frac{y_{iT}}{y_{i0}}\right) = \alpha + \beta\ln(y_{i0}) + \gamma X'_{i0} + \varepsilon_{it}$	Model C (II) $\ln\left(\frac{y_{iT}}{y_{i0}}\right) = \alpha + \beta\ln(y_{i0}) + \gamma X'_{i0} + \varepsilon_{it}$	Model D (III) $\ln\left(\frac{y_{iT}}{y_{i0}}\right) = \alpha + \beta\ln(y_{i0}) + \gamma X'_{i0} + \varepsilon_{it}$
Constant	1.077 (3.19)*	1.951 (6.96)*	2.015 (7.58)*	1.884 (6.97)*	1.920 (6.82)*
Average earnings (1991)	−0.166 (−2.77)*	−0.373 (−7.82)*	−0.380 (−8.11)*	−0.367 (−7.74)*	−0.375 (−7.59)*
Ageing ratio		0.0002 (1.19)	0.0001 (1.10)	0.0002 (1.32)	0.0002 (1.21)
Activity rate		0.005 (4.92)*	0.005 (5.12)*	0.005 (5.11)*	0.006 (6.48)*
Unemployment rate		0.003 (2.20)**	0.002 (2.00)**	0.003 (2.47)*	0.003 (1.93)**
Employment in sector I		−0.0004 (−0.81)	−0.001 (−2.25)**		
Employment in sector II		0.0004 (0.92)		0.001 (2.39)**	
Employment in sector III					0.00001 (0.03)
Labor force with higher education		0.017 (4.46)*	0.015 (4.60)*	0.018 (6.04)*	0.017 (4.62)*
R^2	0.053	0.445	0.444	0.444	0.433
F	7.65 ($p = 0.006$)	24.51 ($p = 0.000$)	28.72 ($p = 0.000$)	27.29 ($p = 0.000$)	24.26 ($p = 0.000$)
n	275	275	275	275	275
Breuch–Pagan test	86.95 ($p = 0.000$)	3.85 ($p = 0.05$)	4.47 ($p = 0.035$)	3.75 ($p = 0.05$)	6.55 ($p = 0.011$)
Moran's I (error)	10.48 ($p = 0.000$)	4.238 ($p = 0.000$)	4.277 ($p = 0.000$)	4.127 ($p = 0.000$)	4.366 ($p = 0.000$)

Notes: Figures in brackets mean t statistic; * indicates that the estimated coefficient is statistically significant for a significance level of 1% and ** significant at 5%.

Table 6. Estimation Results of the Absolute β Convergence Models for Municipalities, Applied to the Wages Growth.

Explanatory Variables	$\ln\left(\frac{y_{iT}}{y_{i0}}\right) = \alpha + \beta \ln(y_{i0}) + \varepsilon_i$	Spatial Error Model
		$\ln\left(\frac{y_{iT}}{y_{i0}}\right) = \alpha + \beta \ln(y_{i0}) + \varepsilon_{it} \varepsilon_{it} = \lambda (W\varepsilon)_{it} + u_{it}$
Constant	1.077 (3.19)*	1.705 (5.96)*
Average earnings (1991)	−0.166 (−2.77)*	−0.277 (−5.41)*
	–	$\lambda = 0.598$ (9.33)*
	–	Log likelihood = 310.114
	$R^2 = 0.053$	AIC = −616.227
n	275	275

Notes: Figures in brackets mean *t*-value (OLS) and z-value (spatial autocorrelation models); * indicates that the estimated coefficient is statistically significant for a significance level of 1%.

Table 7. Estimation Results of Spatial Error Models for Conditional β Convergence, in Wages Growth, between Municipalities.

Dependent Variable: *Growth in Average Earnings for Municipalities (1991–2002)*

$\ln\left(\frac{y_{iT}}{y_{i0}}\right) = \alpha + \beta \ln(y_{i0}) + \gamma X'_{i0} + \varepsilon_{it};\ \ \varepsilon_{it} = \lambda (W\varepsilon)_{it} + u_{it}; u_{it} \sim \text{i.i.d.}(0, \sigma^2 I_n)$

Explanatory Variables	Model A (I and II)	Model B (I)	Model C (II)	Model D (III)
Constant	2.103 (6.73)*	2.145 (7.21)*	2.039 (6.60)*	2.066 (6.50)*
Average earnings (1991)	−0.391 (−7.54)*	−0.394 (−7.75)*	−0.385 (−7.41)*	−0.390 (−7.27)*
Ageing ratio	0.00009 (0.54)	0.00008 (0.51)	0.00009 (0.51)	0.00006 (0.35)
Activity rate	0.004 (3.74)*	0.004 (3.91)*	0.004 (3.77)*	0.005 (4.40)*
Unemployment rate	0.002 (0.98)	0.001 (0.87)	0.002 (1.14)	0.001 (0.86)
Employment in sector I	−0.0005 (−0.89)	−0.0008 (−1.96)**		
Employment in sector II	0.0004 (0.74)		0.0008 (2.01)**	
Employment in sector III				0.0001 (0.20)
Labor force with higher education	0.014 (3.43)*	0.013 (3.61)*	0.015 (4.80)*	0.014 (3.51)*
λ	0.329 (3.19)*	0.329 (3.25)*	0.331 (3.10)*	0.344 (3.30)*
Log likelihood	351.087	350.836	350.677	348.865
n	275	275	275	275

Notes: Figures in brackets mean *z*-value; * indicates that the estimated coefficient is statistically significant for a significance level of 1% and ** significant at 5%.

Table 8. Correlation Table between Matrix *X* Variables for Municipalities.

	A. Rate	Activ. R.	Unemp. R.	Empi	Empii	Empiii	Illiter.	LFHEduc
A. Rate	1.0000							
Activ. R.	-0.7076	1.0000						
Unemp. R.	0.1777	-0.1321	1.0000					
Empi	0.3390	-0.5503	0.0121	1.0000				
Empii	-0.4003	0.5098	-0.2608	-0.6510	1.0000			
Empiii	0.0395	0.0966	0.2843	-0.4915	-0.3411	1.0000		
Illiter.	0.7362	-0.6962	0.2827	0.6589	-0.5146	-0.2256	1.0000	
LFHEduc	-0.2026	0.3321	0.0170	-0.4960	-0.0512	0.6730	-0.4977	1.0000

activity rate is also negatively correlated with the illiteracy rate and employment in the primary sector. This last variable is even more highly correlated with other two variables, a negative correlation with employment in the secondary sector and positive with the illiteracy rate. On the other hand, the share of employment in the tertiary sector shows a high correlation with the percentage of the labor force with higher education.

CONCLUSIONS

This study confirms spatial correlation (in wages growth) for smaller Portuguese territorial units – municipalities, but we cannot confirm it in GDP and wages growth between NUTS III regions. This implies that spatial correlation applies in intra-regional rather than inter-regional level.

For NUTS III regions, we observed σ convergence in GDPpc growth, but not in wages growth (at the end of the period wages register a greater dispersion). Indeed, when we tested for the existence of absolute β convergence (necessary but not sufficient for σ convergence) we conclude that it occurs only in the growth of GDPpc. We tested further alternative models of conditional β convergence on wages growth between the regions, and it appears to be significant in models which include the sectorial employment structure together with other variables related to the workforce and level of education. It may indeed be decisive for the different regional "steady state"; the weight these sectors play in the economy, partly because during the period under review there was a net transfer of jobs across sectors, especially in regions where the agricultural sector (I) was of major importance in 1991.[11] It is important to note the high significance of the estimated coefficient for the variable of labor force with higher education, demonstrating the importance of this variable as a determinant of growth and convergence of wages.

As regards municipalities, we conclude on the absence of σ convergence in wages over the period of our study, which confirms the results obtained in Guerreiro (2012) when observing the evolution of inequality indexes, as well as the results obtained for NUTS III regions. We therefore conclude there was increased dispersion of wages among Portuguese municipalities, but this does not invalidate the verification of β convergence, which is confirmed by the significance of $\hat{\beta}$ in all estimated models. After confirming the existence of spatial autocorrelation, the models that consider it turn out to be the best, both in terms of absolute and conditional convergence. When spatial autocorrelation is included, the convergence in wages growth becomes more evident (greater and more significant in absolute terms).

With regard to conditional convergence, we follow the same methodology as in the case of NUTS III regions and estimate four alternative models. For conditional convergence we conclude that primary sector employment, activity rate, and percentage of active population with higher education are important to distinguish the "steady state" of the regional economies, reflecting the labor market at regional level.

From a policy-making point of view, the results of our analysis provide support for policies explicitly designed to promote regional growth in the less-developed territories. The existence of spatial spillovers shows the importance of the coordination of regional and municipal policies.

We are aware of several limitations of this paper. The first limitation regards the lack of available statistical information on small territorial units, preventing the processing of Gross Disposable Income (GDI) of Families with this spatial disaggregation. Analysis of regional GDI would give a better picture of the spatial distribution and convergence of income levels by region and municipality. Another possible limitation and possible indication for future developments regards the explanation for the inequality found in spatial distribution of income. We have pointed out some differences in demographic, economic and social indicators between the spatial units, particularly concerning the spatial concentration of economic activity, trying to differentiate regions or municipalities in terms of "steady state," but there is still much more to explore. Finally, in spatial models, we can test other (different) weight matrices.

NOTES

1. The concept of β convergence tells us that when countries or regions are similar (tending toward the same "steady state"), the rate of growth in the future will be as great as the initial delay, that is, poor economies tend to grow faster than rich ones.

2. Barro and Sala-i-Martin (1992, 1995, 1999), Barro (1991), Sala-i-Martin (1990, 1995, 1996a, 1996b) and for Portugal the applied studies of Soukiazis (2003), Soukiazis and Antunes (2004), and Soukiazis and Castro (2004).

3. σ convergence occurs when a group of economies converge toward a decrease in the standard deviation, that is, when the dispersion in real GDPpc decreases over time $\sigma_{t+T} < \sigma_t$.

4. Consider the reference works of Atkinson (1975, 1997), Atkinson, Rainwater, and Smeeding (1995), Cowell (2008a, 2008b), and in Portugal the recent studies of Rodrigues (1994, 1999, 2008).

5. Nomenclature of Territorial Units for Statistics (2002, see appendix).

6. According to Anselin (1988) and Le Sage (1999), standardization or normalization of V matrix is advisable to guarantee that the sum of its columns for each row is equal to 1 ($\sum w_i = 1$) and that the new matrix is not symmetric.

7. We have constructed the rook matrix of neighborhoods and found that the results do not change significantly.

8. Although the data series relating to GDPpc for NUTS III begins in 1990, the 1991 data are more reliable, since it was a year of Population Census.

9. Note that in employee remuneration there is a series break in 2001 beyond the author's control. In fact, the DGEEP, the entity supplying this information, has no data for this year for methodological reasons.

10. Soukiazis and Antunes (2004) carry out estimation of panel data and the composition of the matrix X is not exactly the same as we consider in our work. In addition, these authors do not exclude the autonomous regions of Azores and Madeira. So, their work differs from ours in respect of methodology and sample.

11. Similarly, Ramajo, Márquez, Hewings, and Salinas (2008) and Brasili, Bruno, and Saguatti (2008) consider the weight of the agricultural sector (measured by the share of agricultural to total employment) as an important variable in maintaining the steady state of each economy constant.

ACKNOWLEDGMENTS

The author is pleased to acknowledge financial support from Fundação para a Ciência e a Tecnologia and FEDER/COMPETE (grant PEst-C/EGE/UI4007/2011). The author also gives thanks for the alterations suggested by António Bento Caleiro, John Bishop, and an anonymous referee.

REFERENCES

Anselin, L. (1988). *Spatial econometrics: Methods and models*. Dordrecht, the Netherlands: Kluwer Academic.

Anselin, L. (2002). Under the hood: Issues in the specification and interpretation of spatial regression models. *Agricultural Economics*, *17*(3), 247–267.

Anselin, L. (2003a). Spatial externalities, spatial multipliers and spatial econometrics. *International Regional Science Review*, *26*(2), 153–166.

Anselin, L. (2003b). *GeoDa™ 0.9 user's guide*. Center for Spatially Integrated Social Science, University of Illinois, Urbana-Champaign.

Antunes, M., & Soukiazis, E. (2006). *Two speed regional convergence in Portugal and the importance of structural funds on growth*. Coimbra, Portugal: Faculdade de Economia da Universidade de Coimbra.

Atkinson, A., Rainwater, L., & Smeeding, T. M. (1995). *Income distribution in OECD countries. Evidence from the Luxembourg income study*. Paris, France: OECD.

Atkinson, A. B. (1975). *The economics of inequality*. Oxford: Clarendon Press.

Atkinson, A. B. (1997, March). Bringing income distribution in from the cold. *The Economic Journal*, *107*(441), 297–321.

Barro, J., & Sala-i-Martin, X. (1992). Convergence. *Journal of Political Economy*, *100*(2), 223–251.

Barro, J., & Sala-i-Martin, X. (1995). Economic growth. New York, NY: McGraw-Hill.

Barro, J., & Sala-i-Martin, X. (1999). *Economic growth*. London, UK: The MIT Press.

Barro, R. (1991). Economic growth in a cross section of countries. *Quarterly Journal of Economics*, *106*, 407–443.

Beugelsdijk, M., & Eijffinger, S. (2003). *The effectiveness of structural policy in the European Union: An empirical analysis for the EU-15 during the period 1995–2001*, Discussion Paper No. 3879 of Centre for Economic Policy Research.

Brasili, C., Bruno, F., & Saguatti, A. (2008). A spatial econometric approach to EU regional disparities between economic and geographical periphery. *Statistica, Year LXXII, 3*, 299–316.

Buccellato, T. (2007). *Convergence across Russian regions: A spatial econometrics approach, centre for financial and management studies*. Discussion Paper No. 70. University of London, UK.

Caleiro, A. (2008a). *A spatial viewpoint on fertility by regions in Portugal – Revista Portuguesa de Estudos Regionais* No. 17, 1° Quadrimestre, Portugal.

Caleiro, A. (2008b). *Algumas notas soltas sobre econometria espacial*. Évora, Portugal: Universidade de Évora.

Caleiro, A., & Guerreiro, G. (2005). Understanding the election results in Portugal – A spatial econometrics point of view. *Portuguese Economic Journal*, 4, 207–228.

Cowell, F. A. (2008a). Inequality: Measurement. In S. N. Durlauf & L. E. Blume (Ed.), *The new Palgrave dictionary of economics*. Basingstoke, UK: Palgrave Macmillan.

Cowell, F. A. (2008b). Income distribution and inequality. In J. B. Devis & W. Dolfsma (Ed.), *The Elgar companion to social economics*. Cheltenham, UK: Edward Elgar.

Ertur, C., Gallo, J. L., & Baumont, C. (2006). The European regional convergence process, 1980–1995: Do spatial regimes and spatial dependence matter? *International Regional Science Review 29, 1*(January), 3–34.

Florax, R., & Graaf, T. (2004). The performance of diagnostic tests for spatial dependence in linear regression models: A meta-analysis of simulation studies. In L. Anselin, R. J. G. M. Florax, & S. J. Rey (Ed.), *Advances in spatial econometrics. Methodology, tools and applications*. Berlin: Springer.

Freitas, M., & Torres, F. (coord.). (2005). *Regional convergence in Portugal: Policy impacts (1990–2001)*. In C. Amorim, A. Bongardt, M. Dias, & R. Silva (Eds.), Documentos de Trabalho em Economia (No. 35). Universidade de Aveiro, Departamento de Economia, Gestão e Engenharia Industrial, Aveiro, Portugal.

Guerreiro, G. (2012). *Regional income distribution in Portugal, center for advanced studies in management and economics (CEFAGE-UE)*. Working paper 2012/06, University of Évora, Évora, Portugal.

Guerreiro, G., & Rego, M. (2005, August). Regional delimitation in continental Portugal: What does cluster analysis tell us? Paper presented at the 45th Congress of European Regional Science Association, Amsterdam, the Netherlands.

INE. (2008). *O País em Números – Informação Estatística 1991–2006*, 2008.

Le Sage, J. (1998). Spatial econometrics (circulated for review). University of Toledo, Department of Economics, OH.

Le Sage, J. (1999). The theory and practice of spatial econometrics. University of Toledo, Department of Economics, OH.

Le Sage, J., & Pace, R. K. (2009). *Introduction to spatial econometrics*. Boca Raton, FL: Chapman & Hall.

Martinho, V. (2005). Análise dos Efeitos Espaciais na Produtividade Sectorial entre as Regiões Portuguesas. *Centro de Estudos da União Europeia (CEUNEUROP), Documento de trabalho* (No. 30). Coimbra, Portugal: Faculdade de Economia da Universidade de Coimbra.

Mateus, A., Madruga, P., & Rodrigues, D. (2000). Pirâmide de Competitividade Territorial das Regiões Portuguesas. *Revista de Estudos Regionais*, *2*, 47–78.

Moran, P. A. P. (1950). Notes on continuous stochastic phenomena. *Biometrika*, *37*, 17–23.

Paas, T., Kuusk, A., Võrk, A., & Schlitte, F. (2006). *Modelling regional income convergence in EU-25*. Tartu, Estonia: University of Tartu, HWWA (Hamburgisches Welt-Wirtschafts-Archiv).

Ramajo, J., Márquez, M., Hewings, G., & Salinas, M. (2008). Spatial heterogeneity and interregional spillovers in the European Union: Do cohesion policies encourage convergence across regions? *European Economic Review*, *52*, 551–567.

Rodrigues, C. F. (1994). Repartição do Rendimento e Desigualdade: Portugal nos anos 80. *Estudos de Economia*, *XIV*, 4, 399–428, Instituto Superior de Economia e Gestão (ISEG).

Rodrigues, C. F. (1999). Repartição do Rendimento e Pobreza em Portugal [1994/95] – [Uma Comparação entre o Painel de Agregados Familiares e o Inquérito aos Orçamentos Familiares]. *Revista de Estatística*, No. 10/1ºQ99 (pp. 117–142). Lisboa, Portugal: Instituto Nacional de Estatística (INE).

Rodrigues, C. F. (2008). *Distribuição do Rendimento, Desigualdade e Pobreza: Portugal nos anos 90*. Coimbra, Portugal: Edições Almedina.

Sala-i-Martin, X. (1990). *On growth and states*, PhD. Dissertation, Harvard University, Cambridge, MA.

Sala-i-Martin, X. (1995). *The classical approach to convergence analysis, economics*. Working Paper No. 117, Universitat Pompeu Fabra, Barcelona, Spain.

Sala-i-Martin, X. (1996a). The classical approach to convergence analysis. *The Economic Journal*, *106*, 1019–1036.

Sala-i-Martin, X. (1996b). Regional cohesion: Evidence and theories of regional growth and convergence. *European Economic Review*, *40*, 1325–1352.

Solow, R. M. (1956). A contribution to the theory of economic growth. *The Quarterly Journal of Economics*, *70*(1), 65–94.

Soukiazis, E. (2003). Regional convergence in Portugal. *Centro de Estudos da União Europeia (CEUNEUROP), Documento de trabalho* (No. 14). Coimbra, Portugal: Faculdade de Economia da Universidade de Coimbra.

Soukiazis, E., & Antunes, M. (2004). The evolution of real disparities in Portugal among the NUTS III regions. *An empirical analysis based on the convergence approach, Centro de Estudos da União Europeia (CEUNEUROP), Documento de trabalho* (No. 25). Coimbra, Portugal: Faculdade de Economia da Universidade de Coimbra.

Soukiazis, E., & Castro, V. (2004). How the Maastricht rules affected the convergence process in the European Union. *A panel data analysis, Centro de Estudos da União Europeia (CEUNEUROP), Documento de trabalho* (No. 24). Coimbra: Faculdade de Economia da Universidade de Coimbra.

Swan, T. W. (1956). Economic growth and capital accumulation. *Economic Record*, *32*(November), 334–361.

Young, A. T., Higgins, M. J., & Levy, D. (2008). Sigma convergence versus beta convergence: Evidence from US county-level data. *Journal of Money, Credit and Banking*, *40*(5), 1083–1093.

APPENDIX: NOMENCLATURE OF TERRITORIAL UNITS FOR STATISTICS (2002): NUTS II, NUTS III, AND MUNICIPALITIES

Nomenclaturas Territoriais NUTS II, NUTS III e Concelhos (2002)

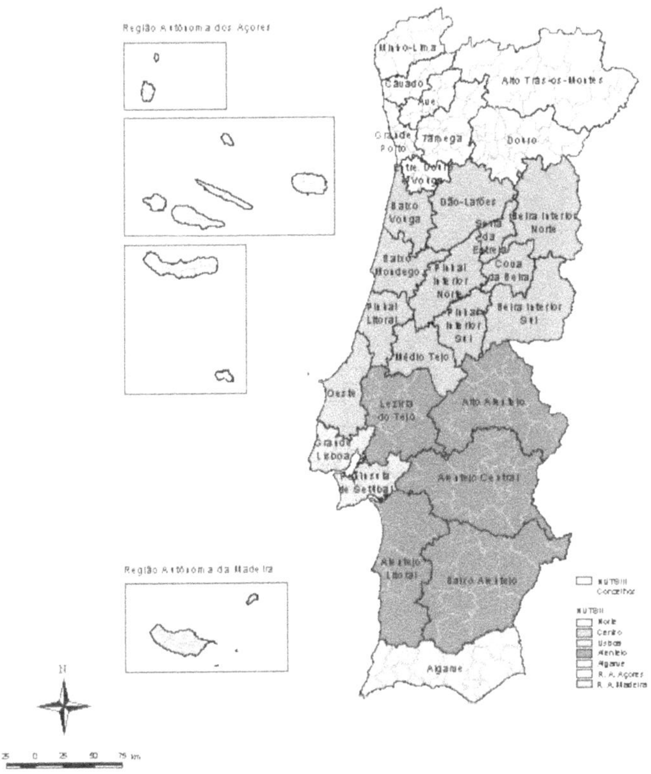

INEQUALITY, WELFARE, AND ORDER STATISTICS

Encarnación M. Parrado-Gallardo,
Elena Bárcena-Martín and Luis J. Imedio-Olmedo

ABSTRACT

In this paper, we use the distributions of order statistics to define functions with the appropriate properties to represent social preferences regarding income distributions. Following the approach of Yaari (1987, 1988), this allows constructing a set of social welfare functions from which the corresponding inequality indices are derived. The obtained measures incorporate diverse normative criteria, with different degrees of preference for equality. The generalized Gini coefficients and the family of indices proposed by Aaberge (2000) are obtained as particular cases. This approach allows interpreting each inequality measure in terms of the statistics computed from a randomly selected sample and the identification of unbiased estimators of the Social Welfare Functions. It also shows that each of the families of inequality indices are obtained from the moments of the order statistics and, therefore, each of the families characterizes any income distribution with finite mean. This characterization is very useful in the case of distributions

Economic Well-Being and Inequality: Papers from the Fifth ECINEQ Meeting
Research on Economic Inequality, Volume 22, 383–399

ISSN: 1049-2585/doi:10.1108/S1049-258520140000022012

with heavy tail and pronounced positive skew that shows only a few potential moments.

Keywords: Inequality aversion; Lorenz curves; order statistic; social preference function; transfers

JEL classifications: C10; D31; I30

INTRODUCTION

When studying the relationship between inequality measures and social welfare functions (SWF) in the context of income distributions following the approach by Yaari (1987, 1988), the distribution functions of the measures that characterizes social preferences[1] have an essential role. These functions incorporate the normative aspects or value judgments that are always present in the evaluation of both magnitudes, welfare and inequality. The properties of the functions of social preferences determine the degree of preference for equality[2] (or inequality aversion) of the measure, thus affecting the behavior of the measure when certain changes take place in the income distribution.

This paper shows that from the distributions of order statistics it is possible to define functions that meet the properties required to represent social preferences about the distribution of income between units in a population. This allows us to build a set of SWFs from which the corresponding inequality indices are derived. The obtained measures incorporate diverse normative criteria with different degrees of preference for equality, and hence a different response to progressive income transfers. The generalized Gini coefficients (Donaldson & Weymark, 1980; Kakwani, 1980, 1983; Weymark, 1981; Yitzhaki, 1983) and the family of indices proposed by Aaberge (2000) are obtained as particular cases, in addition to measures that, in the normative aspect, occupy an intermediate position between the two families.

Although the use of order statistics in the analysis of welfare and of inequality as the starting point to define social preferences functions is rare, there are some results in the literature in this regard. For instance, it is known that the SWFs of the generalized Gini coefficients have a simple interpretation from the first-order statistics (Lambert, 2001, chap. 5, pp. 125–126), while Kleiber and Kotz (2002) use the mean values of these statistics to show that this family of indices characterizes any income distribution with finite mean, except for a factor of proportionality.

Our proposal extends and generalizes this analysis using certain statistical averages of the order statistics, from the minimum to the maximum. The starting point is the definition of a family of social preference functions, whose properties determine the normative characteristics of the corresponding social evaluation functions and their associated inequality measures. Therefore, the approach taken in this paper provides a constructive way to define new measures of welfare and inequality. There exist, in addition, further advantages in our approach. First, it permits obtaining an alternative characterization of distributions that are not determined by their potential moments due to the fact that they only allow a small number of moments. This is the case of empirical income distributions. Since these distributions usually have a heavy tail with a pronounced positive skew, the asymptotic convergence to the Pareto law (Mandelbrot, 1960) is a condition usually required of the theoretical parametric models used to adjust the observed distributions. The models that satisfy this condition, such as the Pareto or Singh-Maddala (1976) models, cannot be characterized from their potential moments.[3] This justifies the interest in alternative procedures to characterize such distributions.

Moreover, in addition to providing diverse distributive criteria in assessing welfare and inequality, the procedure used in this paper allows an intuitive interpretation of each measure in terms of the statistics computed from a randomly selected sample drawn from the population, as well as identifying unbiased estimators of the SWFs.

The paper is structured as follows. In the next section, we present the analytical framework with special reference to the Lorenz curve and, in particular, to the inequality measures that weight the area between the curve and the line of equal distribution. We also examine the relationship between welfare and inequality, as well as issues related to order statistics. The main results are obtained in the next section. Here we define the functions of social preferences, the corresponding SWFs and their associated inequality indices, considering some particular cases. We also show the relationship between the preference functions and the functions that weight the Lorenz differences in the inequality indices, and their policy implications. The final section briefly summarizes the results and includes some comments.

ANALYTICAL FRAMEWORK: PRELIMINARY CONSIDERATIONS

Let us assume that the income distribution is represented by the random variable X, whose range is the positive real numbers $R_0^+ = [0, \infty)$, where $F(\cdot)$ is its distribution function, and $\mu = E(X) = \int_0^\infty x \, dF(x) < \infty$ is its mean income.

Inequality

A common and intuitive way to assess inequality in the income distribution is to weight the deviations between the income perceived by each individual and the mean income, $x-\mu$, or to weight deviations relative to the mean income, $(x-\mu)/\mu$, using a weight function, $\omega(\cdot) : R_0^+ \to R$, which incorporates the value judgments when adding local inequality. This procedure yields inequality measures of the type:

$$\mathrm{I} = \frac{1}{\mu}\int_0^\infty (x-\mu)\omega(x)\,\mathrm{d}F(x) = \frac{1}{\mu}\int_0^1 (F^{-1}(p)-\mu)\lambda(p)\,\mathrm{d}p \qquad (1)$$

where $F^{-1}(p) = \inf\{x : F(x) \geq p\}$, $0 \leq p \leq 1$ is the income of an individual in the pth percentile of the distribution and $\lambda(p) = \omega(F^{-1}(p))$.

The above measures allow a simple geometric interpretation from the Lorenz curve, L($\cdot$), which is associated with the distribution. This curve is defined as:

$$L : [0,1] \to [0,1], \quad L(p) = \frac{1}{\mu}\int_0^{F^{-1}(p)} s\,\mathrm{d}F(s) = \frac{1}{\mu}\int_0^p F^{-1}(t)\,\mathrm{d}t,$$
$$0 \leq p \leq 1, \quad p = F(x) \qquad (2)$$

For each $p = F(x)$, $L(p)$ is the proportion of total income accumulated by the set of units with an income lower than or equal to x. It is clear that for $0 \leq p \leq 1$ we have $L(p) \leq p$, where $L(p) = p$ in the case of perfect equality and $L(p) = 0$ for $0 \leq p < 1$, $L(1) = 1$ if the concentration is maximum. For any distribution, X, the Lorenz curve is increasing and convex, and given the mean income, determines the density function. Hereinafter, $\Lambda = \{F : 0 < \int_0^\infty x \, \mathrm{d}F(x) < \infty\}$ represents the set of distributions with finite mean income, thus supporting the Lorenz curve.

From Eqs. (1) and (2), and integrating by parts, we get:

$$I = \int_0^1 (p - L(p))\pi(p)\,\mathrm{d}p, \quad \pi(p) = \lambda'(p), \quad 0 < p < 1 \tag{3}$$

Each of these indices weights the area between the Lorenz curve and the line of perfect equality.[4] The weight used is what differentiates one index from another.

The best known measure of inequality, the Gini (1914) coefficient, is obtained when $\omega(x) = 2F(x)$, or $\pi(p) = 2$. The generalized Gini coefficients with a positive integer parameter are obtained by weighting the Lorenz differences with $\pi(p) = n(n-1)(1-p)^{n-2}$, $n \geq 2$. If $\pi(p) = np^{n-2}$, $n \geq 2$, we obtain the family of indices proposed by Aaberge (2000).

Welfare and Inequality

In order to establish the relationship between inequality and social welfare, we follow the Yaari approach (1987, 1988). If $F(\cdot)$ is the income distribution and $\phi{:}[0,1] \to R$ is a distribution function[5] that represents the policy maker's evaluation measure, the Yaari social welfare function (YSWF) is given by:

$$W_\phi(F) = \int_{R^+} x\,\mathrm{d}\phi(F(x)) = \int_0^1 F^{-1}(p)\,\mathrm{d}\phi(p) = \int_0^1 \phi'(p)F^{-1}(p)\,\mathrm{d}p \tag{4}$$

Thus, W_ϕ is additive and linear in the incomes and weights them according to the rankings assigned to the individuals in the distribution. The weight attached to the income of an individual with rank p, $0 < p < 1$, is $\phi'(p) \geq 0$. The YSWF W_ϕ can be expressed as a social welfare function associated to a linear measure of inequality of the type defined in Eq. (3). Then,[6]

$$W_\phi(F) = \mu\lfloor 1 - I_\phi(F)\rfloor \tag{5}$$

where

$$I_\phi(F) = \int_0^1 (p - L(p))\pi_\phi(p)\,\mathrm{d}p, \quad \pi_\phi(p) = -\phi''(p) \tag{6}$$

The above two expressions yield an explicit relationship between the YSWFs, $W_\phi(\cdot)$, and their associated inequality indices, $I_\phi(\cdot)$, thus relating the functions of social preferences, $\phi(\cdot)$, and the weighting scheme of the Lorenz differences, $\pi_\phi(\cdot)$.

According to the Blackorby and Donaldson approach (1978), expression (5) is the equally distributed equivalent income,[7] in which case $\mu I_\phi(F)$ measures the loss of social welfare due to inequality.

The function $\phi(\cdot)$ incorporates the normative characteristics of the YSWFs, $W_\phi(\cdot)$, and, consequently, of $I_\phi(\cdot)$. Yaari (1988) shows that the inequality measures show inequality aversion if and only if $\phi'(\cdot)$ is a decreasing function, which is equivalent to the concavity of $\phi(\cdot)$, and this is equivalent to say that the Pigou-Dalton Principle of Transfers[8] (PDPT) is fulfilled. Additionally the Principle of Positional Transfer Sensitivity[9] (PPTS) (see Mehran, 1976; Muliere & Scarsini, 1989; Zoli, 1999) is fulfilled if and only if $\phi'(\cdot)$ is a convex function (equivalently, $\phi'''(p)>0$).

Order Statistics

Let $X_1, X_2, \ldots, X_n$ be a sample of size n, $n \in N$, $n \geq 2$, from a distribution $F(\cdot)$ and define the order statistics, $X_{k:n}$, $k \in \{1, 2, \ldots, n\}$, in the ascending order by:

$$X_{1:n} \leq X_{2:n} \leq \cdots \leq X_{n:n}$$

That is, in each specific realization of the sample, once the values are ordered from lowest to highest, the variable $X_{k:n}$ assigns the value at position k to each sample.

The cumulative distribution function $F_{k:n}(\cdot)$ of $X_{k:n}$ can be written as:

$$F_{k:n}(x) = \sum_{j=k}^{n} \binom{n}{j} (F(x))^j (1 - F(x))^{n-j} \tag{7}$$

If the variable X is continuous and $f(\cdot)$ is its density function, $f(\cdot)=F'(\cdot)$, the density function of $X_{k:n}$ is:

$$f_{k:n}(x) = k \binom{n}{k} (F(x))^{k-1} (1 - F(x))^{n-k} f(x)$$

The mean values of the order statistics are given by the expressions:

$$E(X_{k:n}) = \int_0^{\infty} x \, \mathrm{d}F_{k:n}(x) = k\binom{n}{k} \int_0^1 F^{-1}(p)p^{k-1}(1-p)^{n-k} \, \mathrm{d}p \tag{8}$$

From the above expression it is evident that $E|X_{k:n}| \leq cE|X|$ for some $c > 0$. Consequently, if the distribution $F(\cdot)$ has a finite mean, the existence of the first moment of any order statistic is assured. This property is important because there are distributions, such as heavy-tailed income distributions, for which only a few potential moments exist, and therefore no characterization in terms of (ordinary) moments is feasible. In these cases, it is interesting to analyze whether the distribution can be characterized by the moments of the order statistics, $\{E(X_{k:n})\}_{(k,n) \in N \times N}$, or a subset of them. There is also a recurrence relation between the first moments of order statistics (David, 1981, p. 46)

$$(n-k)E(X_{k:n}) + kE(X_{k+1:n}) = nE(X_{k:n-1})$$

which allows knowing the whole array $\{E(X_{k:n})\}_{(k,n) \in N \times N}$, if we can have one moment (of first order) for each sample size.

The following result characterizes a distribution function with finite mean from the expectations of their order statistics.

Proposition 1.[10] Let X be a random variable with $E|X| < \infty$ and $k(n)$ a positive integer, $1 \leq k(n) \leq n$, then the distribution $F(\cdot)$ is uniquely determined by the sequence $\{E(X_{k(n):n})\}_{n \in N}$.

Based on the previous proposition, in the next section, any element of Λ with continuous distribution function is characterized by certain families of SWFs or their corresponding inequality measures.

WELFARE FUNCTIONS AND INEQUALITY MEASURES GENERATED THROUGH MEAN VALUES OF ORDER STATISTICS

From the distribution functions of order statistics, we can obtain functions with the right properties to be considered functions of social preferences. After specifying these functions, and applying the procedure and the results detailed in the section "Welfare and Inequality," their corresponding SWFs and corresponding inequality measures are identified. These measures are of the type defined in Eq. (1) or (3) applicable to distributions $F \in \Lambda$.

General Case

The interpretation of the generalized Gini coefficient in terms of order statistics starting from the distributions of preferences, $\{\phi_{1:n}(\cdot)\}_n \equiv \{F_{1:n}(F^{-1}(\cdot))\}_n$ proposed by Lambert (2001) might suggest that, in general, the functions $\{F_{k:n}(F^{-1}(\cdot))\}_{2 \leq k \leq n}$ can be preference distributions. Nevertheless, it is found that these functions are increasing in the range (0,1), but not necessarily concave over the whole range.[11] This would result in SWFs and indices of inequality that would not meet the Pigou-Dalton Principle of Transfers (PDPT), a condition that is equivalent to the aversion to inequality of the measures.

However, if for fixed sample size n, $n \geq 2$, we calculate consecutively the arithmetic mean of the functions $\{F_{k:n}(F^{-1}(\cdot))\}_{1 \leq k \leq n}$, we obtain a sequence of functions which have an appropriate behavior to be considered functions of social preferences.

Definition. For each (n,k), $n \geq 2$, $k = 1, 2, \ldots, n$, we consider the function $\phi_{k:n}$:$[0,1] \rightarrow R$ given by:

$$\phi_{k:n}(p) = \frac{1}{k} \sum_{i=1}^{k} F_{i:n}(F^{-1}(p)), \quad 0 \leq p \leq 1, \quad k = 1, 2, \ldots, n \tag{9}$$

It is:

$$\phi_{1:n}(p) = F_{1:n}(F^{-1}(p))$$

$$\phi_{2:n}(p) = \frac{F_{1:n}(F^{-1}(p)) + F_{2:n}(F^{-1}(p))}{2}$$

....

$$\phi_{n-1:n}(p) = \frac{F_{1:n}(F^{-1}(p)) + F_{2:n}(F^{-1}(p)) + \cdots + F_{n-1:n}(F^{-1}(p))}{n-1}$$

$$\phi_{n:n}(p) = \frac{F_{1:n}(F^{-1}(p)) + F_{2:n}(F^{-1}(p)) + \cdots + F_{n-1:n}(F^{-1}(p)) + F_{n:n}(F^{-1}(p))}{n} = p$$

$\phi_{k:n}(\cdot)$ are distribution functions defined over the interval [0,1], they are increasing and strictly concave.

From Eqs. (7) and (9) the function $\phi_{k:n}(\cdot)$ is expressed as:

$$\phi_{k:n}(p) = \frac{1}{k}\sum_{i=1}^{k}\left(\sum_{j=i}^{n}\binom{n}{j}p^j(1-p)^{n-j}\right)$$

It is verified that $\phi_{k:n}(0)=0$, $\phi_{k:n}(1)=1$. Each $\phi_{k:n}(\cdot)$ is strictly increasing and for $1 \leq k \leq n-1$ is strictly concave in the interval (0,1), as its first two derivatives are:

$$\phi'_{k:n}(p) = \frac{1}{k}\sum_{i=1}^{k}\left(i\binom{n}{i}p^{i-1}(1-p)^{n-i}\right)$$

$$\phi''_{k:n}(p) = -(n-k)\binom{n}{k}p^{k-1}(1-p)^{n-k-1} \tag{10}$$

It is evident that $\phi'_{k:n}(p)>0$, $1 \leq k \leq n$; $\phi''_{k:n}(p)<0$, $1 \leq k \leq n-1$, $p \in (0,1)$. Consequently, the following proposition is made.

Proposition 2. Each of the functions $\{\phi_{k:n}(\cdot)\}$, $1 \leq k \leq n$, defined in the interval [0,1] shows the properties required of a function of social preferences, that is, it is increasing and concave.

As a consequence of the previous result, and applying the methodology described in the section the section "Welfare and Inequality," we get the corresponding YSWFs $W_{k:m}(\cdot)$ from the distributions of preferences $\phi_{k:n}(\cdot)$. Their expressions are:

$$\begin{aligned} W_{k:n}(F) &= \int_0^1 F^{-1}(p)\,\mathrm{d}\phi_{k:n}(p) \\ &= E\left(\frac{1}{k}(X_{1:n} + X_{2:n} + \cdots + X_{k:n})\right), \quad k = 1, 2, \ldots, n \end{aligned} \tag{11}$$

Therefore, $W_{k:n}(F)$, $n \geq 2$, $1 \leq k \leq \mathrm{n}$, is the expectation of the arithmetic mean of the k first-order statistics for samples of size n from the distribution $F(\cdot)$. That is, if the level of welfare assigned to any sample of n incomes from $F(\cdot)$ is identified with the mean of their k lower incomes, the welfare of the population is the expectation of those values when considering all possible samples of size n.

The inequality measures underlying the above YSWFs, given Eqs. (5), (6), and (11) are:

$$I_{k:n}(F) = 1 - \frac{W_{k:n}(F)}{\mu} = 1 - \frac{1}{k\mu} E(X_{1:n} + X_{2:n} + \cdots + X_{k:n}), \quad n \geq 2$$

or:

$$I_{k:n}(F) = (n-k)\binom{n}{k} \int_0^1 (p - L(p))p^{k-1}(1-p)^{n-k-1}\mathrm{d}p, \quad n \geq 2 \qquad (12)$$

The indices $\{I_{k:n}(\cdot)\}$ are linear inequality measures of the type defined in Eq. (1) or Eq. (3). They weight Lorenz differences by:

$$\pi_{k:n}(p) = -\phi''_{k:n}(p) = (n-k)\binom{n}{k} p^{k-1}(1-p)^{n-k-1}$$

The welfare loss due to inequality is measured by the corresponding absolute indices, $\mu I_{k:n}(F)$:

$$\mu I_{k:n}(F) = \mu - W_{k:n}(F) = E\left(\overline{X}_n - \frac{1}{k}(X_{1:n} + X_{2:n} + \cdots + X_{k:n})\right)$$

where $\overline{X}_n$ is the sample mean of order n. The above equality indicates that $\overline{X}_n - (X_{1:n} + X_{2:n} + \cdots + X_{k:n})/k$ is an unbiased estimator of $\mu I_{k:n}(F)$. In a particular sample of n incomes, the difference between the mean and the mean of the k lower incomes is a point estimate of the index $\mu I_{k:n}(F)$.

Particular Cases

- The case $k = 1$ has been studied by Lambert (2001), which provides the SWFs corresponding to the family of the generalized Gini coefficient.

- For $k = n - 1$, the functions of social preferences are given by:

$$\phi_{n-1:n}(p) = \frac{\sum_{i=1}^{n-1} F_{i:n}(F^{-1}(p))}{n-1} = \frac{np - F_{n:n}(F^{-1}(p))}{n-1} = \frac{np - p^n}{n-1}, \quad n \geq 2, \quad 0 \leq p \leq 1$$

The corresponding SWFs are expressed by applying Eq. (11) as:

$$W_{n-1:n}(F) = \frac{\sum_{i=1}^{n-1} E(X_{i:n})}{n-1} = \frac{E(n\overline{X}_n - X_{n:n})}{n-1} = \frac{n}{n-1}\mu - \frac{1}{n-1}E(X_{n:n}) \tag{13}$$

Their associated inequality measures are:

$$I_{n-1:n}(F) = 1 - \frac{W_{n-1:n}(F)}{\mu} = 1 - n\int_0^1 L(p)p^{n-2}\,\mathrm{d}p = n\int_0^1 (p - L(p))p^{n-2}\,\mathrm{d}p, \quad n \geq 2$$

$\{I_{n-1:n}(F)\}_n \equiv \{A(n)\}_n$ coincides with the family of indices proposed by Aaberge (2000). For $n = 2$ we get the Gini coefficient. The welfare loss due to inequality is given by the corresponding absolute indices, $\mu I_{n-1:n}(F)$:

$$\mu I_{n-1:n}(F) = \mu - W_{n-1:n}(F) = E\left(\overline{X}_n - \frac{1}{n-1}\sum_{i=1}^{n-1} X_{i:n}\right) \tag{14}$$

The expressions (13) and (14) imply that, in this case, the welfare associated with each set of n incomes is identified with the average obtained by excluding the highest income. The difference between this average and the one of the whole group, including the maximum income, is the welfare loss due to inequality. For the population, the welfare and the cost of inequality is the average that would be obtained by considering all possible sets of n incomes. Moreover, using Proposition 1 again, we can say that any continuous distribution $F \in \Lambda$ is characterized by the sequence of SWFs $\{W_{n-1:n}(F)\}_n$ or by the absolute indices $\{\mu I_{n-1:n}(F)\}_n$. The family of relative indices $\{I_{n-1:n}(F)\}_n$ also determines the distribution F, except for a multiplicative factor.

- If $k = n$, the function of social preferences is:

$$\phi_{n:n}(p) = \frac{1}{n}\sum_{i=1}^{n} F_{i:n}(F^{-1}(p)) = p, \quad n \geq 2$$

That is, $\phi_{n:n}(\cdot)$ is the identity in [0,1], which is strictly increasing but not strictly concave. Hence the resulting SWF shows no aversion to inequality. This SWF identifies the welfare of each income distribution, $F(\cdot)$, with its average income. Indeed, applying Eq. (11) we get:

$$W_{n:n}(F) = \int_0^1 F^{-1}(p)\,\mathrm{d}p = E\left(\frac{1}{n}(X_{1:n} + X_{2:n} + \cdots + X_{n:n})\right) = E(\overline{X}_n) = \mu$$

Consequently, the associated inequality index is zero for any distribution:

$$I_{n:n}(F) = 1 - \frac{W_{n:n}(F)}{\mu} = 0, \quad n \geq 2$$

This does not imply the absence of inequality, but that both the SWF and its corresponding index are indifferent to inequality.

We still have more families of inequality indices and SWFs for the different values of n. Our proposal allows the interpretation of not only known indices, but also a wide range of inequality measures that incorporate diverse normative criteria in terms of order statistics. In general, when the value of n is fixed and k varies, the criteria used in the measurement of welfare and inequality are modified. When k increases, the preference distributions reduce their concavity, and the SWFs therefore show less inequality aversion, form the corresponding to the generalized Gini coefficient, $W_{1:n}(\cdot)$, until indifference, $W_{n:n}(F)=\mu_F$. Consequently, when k increases, the associated inequality measures assign less weight to the inequality corresponding to low incomes and greater weight to the inequality corresponding to high incomes. Indeed, in the expressions of the indices that weight Lorenz differences, expression (12), these weights are:

$$\pi_{1:n}(p) = n(n-1)(1-p)^{n-2}$$

....

$$\pi_{k:n}(p) = (n-k)\binom{n}{k}p^{k-1}(1-p)^{n-k-1}$$

....

$$\pi_{n-1:n}(p) = np^{n-2}$$

$$\pi_{n:n}(p) = 0$$

It is evident that if $n > 2$, $\pi_{1:n}(\cdot)$ is strictly decreasing in the interval [0,1], $\pi_{k:n}(\cdot)$, $1 < k < n-1$, is increasing in $[0,(k-1)/(n-2)]$ and decreasing in the rest of the interval, while $\pi_{n-1:n}(\cdot)$ is strictly increasing. Moreover, $\pi_{n:n}(\cdot)$ assigns a weight of zero to all Lorenz differences.

Fig. 1 displays, for $n = 5$, the distributions of preferences $\{\phi_{k:5}\}_{1 \leq k \leq 5}$ for the SWFs $\{W_{k:5}\}_{1 \leq k \leq 5}$ and the weights $\{\pi_{k:5}\}_{1 \leq k \leq 5}$ of the Lorenz differences corresponding to the indices $\{I_{k:5}\}_{1 \leq k \leq 5}$.

As k increases, the concavity of the function of social preferences decreases (being linear for $k = 5$), while the weight given to inequality in low income diminishes, with income inequality weighing more in intermediate and high incomes. Indeed, $\pi_{1:5}$ is strictly decreasing, $\pi_{2:5}$ is bell-shaped and maximum for $p = 1/3$, $\pi_{3:5}$ is bell-shaped and maximum for $p = 2/3$, and $\pi_{4:5}$ is strictly increasing. For $k = 5$, the SWF is indifferent to inequality and both the weighting and the index are zero.

The above considerations show that given an income distribution, $F \in \Lambda$, the family of SWF $\{W_{k:n}(F)\}_{(k,n)}$ results in a family of inequality indices $\{I_{k:n}(F)\}_{(k,n)}$, which includes the generalized Gini coefficients, $\{I_{1:n}(F)\}_n$, and the Aaberge (2000) indices as subfamilies. The weights of local inequality in both subfamilies of inequality measures are monotonic functions along the distribution so that the greater weight is assigned to one of its ends. However, in our proposal the weights for the Lorenz differences for the indices of the family, $\{I_{k:n}(F)\}_{(k,n)}$, $1 < k < n-1$, are not necessarily monotonic. They can reach their maximum or minimum value at any percentile.

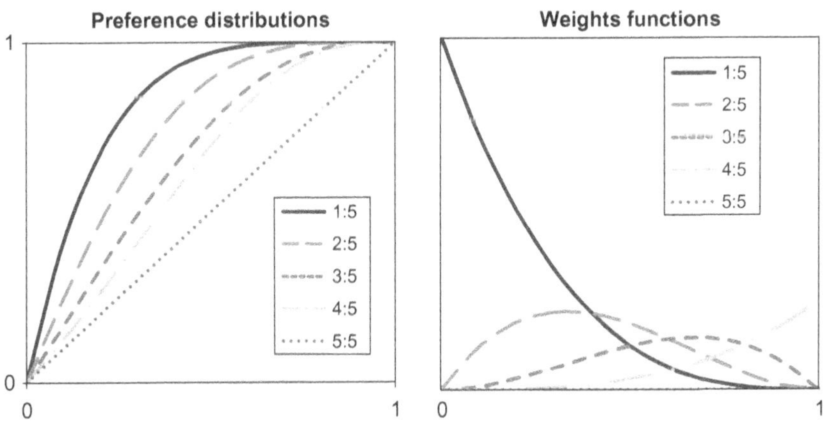

Fig. 1. Distributions of Preferences and Weights of the Lorenz Differences, $n = 5$, $1 \leq k \leq 5$.

We get inequality measures with different attitudes in assessing inequality and welfare, depending on the characteristics of the social preferences distribution, as we mentioned in the section "Welfare and Inequality". As $\phi(\cdot)$ is concave any measure obtained from this function satisfies the PDPT. The fulfillment of the PPTS depends on the convexity of $\phi'(\cdot)$. From expression (10) we observe that the convexity of $\phi'(\cdot)$ is fulfilled if and only if:

$$T(n,k,p) = [(n-2)p - (k-1)] > 0$$

for any $p \in (0, 1)$.

Therefore, the Gini index, $G = I_{1:2}$, does not satisfy the PPTS because $T(2,1,p)=0$, $0 < p < 1$. That is, given a rank difference, the effect over G of any progressive transfer is the same irrespective of the income distribution to which it is applied. However, the generalized Gini coefficient, $G(n)=I_{1:n}$ for $n > 2$, does fulfill this principle since in this case $T(n,1,p)=(n-2)p > 0$, $0 < p < 1$. Other indices exhibit a behavior opposite to the PPTS. That is, a progressive transfer reduces the value of the index but given a difference of ranks, the reduction is greater the higher the individuals involved are in the income distribution. This is the case for the Aaberge indices, $A(n)=I_{n-1:n}$ for $n > 2$, because $T(n,n-1,p)=(n-2)(p-1)<0$, $0<p<1$. There are also indices $I_{k:n}$ whose behavior with respect to this principle is not uniform. For example, for $I_{2:5}$ it is $T(5,2,p)=3p-1$, so that this index satisfies the PPTS if $p > 1/3$ and behaves the opposite for $0 < p < 1/3$. In sum, starting from the functions of social preferences, $\{\phi_{k,n}(\cdot)\}$, we get measures that incorporate diverse normative criteria in the assessment of welfare and inequality.

CONCLUSIONS

The use of order statistics in the definition of SWFs and indices of inequality provides a joint treatment of measures that share common features, but differ from and complement each other from the normative standpoint.

Our approach leads to linear measures that are the result of weighting the differences between the incomes of the distribution and the average income. This is equivalent to weighting the Lorenz differences or inequality accumulated up to each income percentile. The different weighting schemes generate different attitudes in the assessment of inequality and welfare throughout the distribution, depending on the part of the distribution considered, and the degree of inequality aversion of the indices.

The approach adopted in this work not only provides a constructive procedure to define the measures under study, but also proves that, given the average income, certain families of indices characterize the income distribution, and provides a clear statistical interpretation to each SWF and its corresponding index of inequality.

In practice, the appropriate selection of various elements of the set $\{I_{k:n}\}_{(n,k)}$, or $\{W_{k:n}\}_{(n,k)}$, permits applying very different distributional judgments when comparing levels of inequality or welfare associated with different income distributions. Hence, the conclusion in a particular application may be interesting either when a robust result is obtained, or if the outcome is different depending on the index considered, as the properties of the different measures are taken into account.

NOTES

1. From now on we will refer to it as functions of social preferences for sake of simplicity.
2. A SWF shows inequality aversion or preference for equality if it fulfills the Pigou-Dalton Principle of Transfers. That is, if a given income transfer takes place from a richer individual to a poorer one without changing the relative order between both (progressive transfer), the social welfare (inequality) increases (decreases).
3. Even some models used to adjust income distributions, such as the lognormal model, cannot be characterized by the sequence of their moments despite the fact that all of them are finite (Heyde, 1963).
4. Note that $p - L(p)$ is the difference between the share in the total income of the individuals with an income smaller or equal to $x = F^{-1}(p)$, in the case of equally distributed income, and the effective share in the total income in the distribution considered. The function $\pi(\cdot)$ provides a criterion to add this difference along the distribution.
5. We assume it to be a class C^2 function, which is twice continuously differentiable. When necessary, we will admit the existence of higher order derivatives in later results.
6. For a detailed calculation see Imedio-Olmedo and Bárcena-Martín (2007).
7. This refers to a level of income such that if it is equally attached to all the individuals of the population, it will provide an identical level of social welfare, according to the specified SWF, to that of the existing distribution. See Atkinson (1970), Kolm (1976a, 1976b), and Sen (1973).
8. A SWF shows inequality aversion or preference for equality if it fulfills the PDPT. That is, if a given income transfer takes place from a richer individual to

a poorer one without changing the relative order between both (progressive transfer), the social welfare (inequality) increases (decreases).

9. According to PPTS when there is a given difference in ranks among the individuals for whom the transfer takes place, the effect of the transfer is greater when it occurs among individuals in the lower part of the distribution.

10. Huang (1989) proves this result and makes a detailed revision of the literature.

11. For example, $F_{2:n}(F^{-1}(p))=1-(1-p)^n-np(1-p)^{n-1}$ is strictly increasing in (0,1) and strictly convex in $(0,1/(n-1))$.

ACKNOWLEDGMENTS

The authors acknowledge the financial support provided by the Spanish Institute of Fiscal Studies and the Universidad of Málaga. Elena Bárcena acknowledges the financial support provided by the Spanish Ministry of Education through Grant ECO2012-33993. She also thanks the financial support provided by Fundación Ramón Areces, XI Concurso Nacional para la Adjudicación de Ayudas a la Investigación en Ciencias Sociales.

REFERENCES

Aaberge, R. (2000). Characterizations of Lorenz curves and income distributions. *Social Choice and Welfare*, *17*, 639–653.

Atkinson, A. B. (1970). On the measurement of inequality. *Journal of Economic Theory*, *2*, 244–263.

Blackorby, C., & Donaldson, D. (1978). Measures of relative equality and their meaning in terms of social welfare. *Journal of Economic Theory*, *18*, 59–80.

David, H. A. (1981). *Order statistics* (2nd ed.). New York, NY: Wiley.

Donaldson, D., & Weymark, J. A. (1980). A single parameter generalization of the Gini indices of inequality. *Journal of Economic Theory*, *22*, 67–86.

Donaldson, D., & Weymark, J. A. (1983). Ethically flexible indices for income distributions in the continuum. *Journal of Economic Theory*, *29*, 353–358.

Gini, C. (1914). Sulla misura della concentrazione e della variabilità dei caratteri. *Atti del Reale Istituto Veneto di Scienze, Lettere ed Arti*, *73*, 1203–1248.

Heyde, C. C. (1963). On a property of the lognormal distribution. *Journal of the Royal Statistical Society*, *25*(Series B), 392–393.

Huang, J. S. (1989). Moment problem of order statistics. *International Statistical Review*, *57*, 59–66.

Imedio-Olmedo, L. J., & Bárcena Martín, E. (2007). Dos familias numerables de medidas de desigualdad. *Investigaciones Económicas*, *30*, 191–217.

Kakwani, N. C. (1980). On a class of poverty measures. *Econometrica*, *48*, 437–446.

Kleiber, C., & Kotz, S. (2002). A characterization of income distributions in terms of generalized Gini coefficients. *Social Choice and Welfare, 19*, 789–794.
Kolm, S. C. (1976a). Unequal inequalities, I. *Journal of Economic Theory, 12*, 416–442.
Kolm, S. C. (1976b). Unequal inequalities, II. *Journal of Economic Theory, 13*, 82–111.
Lambert, P. J. (2001). *The distribution and redistribution of income*. Manchester: Manchester University Press.
Mandelbrot, B. (1960). The Pareto-Lévy law and the distribution of income. *International Economic Review, 1*, 79–106.
Mehran, F. (1976). Linear measures of inequality. *Econometrica, 44*, 805–809.
Muliere, P. y., & Scarsini, M. (1989). A note on stochastic dominance and inequality measures. *Journal of Economic Theory, 49*, 314–323.
Sen, A. K. (1973). *On economic inequality*. Oxford: Clarendon Press.
Singh, S. K., & Maddala, G. S. (1976). A function for the size distribution of incomes. *Econometrica, 44*, 963–970.
Weymark, J. A. (1981). Generalized Gini inequality indices. *Mathematical Social Sciences, 1*, 409–430.
Yaari, M. E. (1987). The dual theory of choice under risk. *Econometrica, 55*, 99–115.
Yaari, M. E. (1988). A controversial proposal concerning inequality measurement. *Journal of Economic Theory, 44*, 381–397.
Yitzhaki, S. (1983). On an extension of the Gini index. *International Economic Review, 24*, 617–628.
Zoli, C. (1999). Intersecting generalized Lorenz curves and the Gini index. *Social Choice and Welfare, 16*, 183–196.

ON THE MEASUREMENT OF INTERMEDIATE INEQUALITY: A DOMINANCE CRITERION FOR A RAY-INVARIANT NOTION

Francisco Azpitarte and Olga Alonso-Villar

ABSTRACT

This paper introduces a unit-consistent Lorenz dominance criterion that allows ranking income distributions according to centrist measures à la Seidl and Pfingsten (1997). In doing so, it defines α*-Lorenz curves that generalize the absolute Lorenz curve. These curves allow implementing unanimous rankings for a broad set of centrist inequality notions, whereas they become closer and closer to the absolute curve when* α *approaches equity. In addition, this paper provides an empirical illustration of these tools using Australian income data. The results suggest that despite the reduction of relative inequality for Australian-born people between 1999 and 2003, their inequality increased for most centrist value judgments.*

Keywords: Income distribution; Lorenz dominance; intermediate inequality indices; Ray-invariance; Australia

JEL classification: D63

Economic Well-Being and Inequality: Papers from the Fifth ECINEQ Meeting
Research on Economic Inequality, Volume 22, 401–420

ISSN: 1049-2585/doi:10.1108/S1049-258520140000022013

INTRODUCTION

In the literature on income distribution, there is a wide consensus on the properties an inequality measure has to satisfy when using it to compare income distributions having the same mean: Symmetry (S) and the Pigou-Dalton principle of transfers (PD).[1] The former axiom guarantees anonymity, and the latter requires a transfer of income from a richer to a poorer person to decrease inequality.

When comparing two income distributions that differ in their means, another value judgment has to be invoked – the one regarding the type of mean-invariance the index satisfies – and no agreement has been reached with respect to this matter. Most scholars choose relative indexes, which implies that inequality remains unaltered when all incomes increase/decrease by the same proportion (scale invariance). Others opt, instead, for absolute measures so that inequality does not change if all incomes are augmented/diminished by the same amount (translation invariance). However, as Kolm (1976) pointed out, some people believe that an equiproportional increase in all incomes raises income inequality, whereas an equal increment decreases it.[2] He labeled these measures "centrist" (intermediate) and considered "rightist" (relative) and "leftist" (absolute) measures extreme cases of this more general view.

Relative inequality indexes that verify the replication invariance (RI) principle, together with PD and S, are consistent with the (strong) Lorenz dominance criterion (Foster, 1985). In other words, if the Lorenz curve of an income distribution lies at no point below that of another and at some point above, the former distribution will have lower inequality than the latter according to any relative inequality index satisfying the above axioms, which makes Lorenz dominance an attractive tool. Absolute indexes verifying PD, S, and PP are also consistent with a Lorenz-type dominance criterion, in this case given by "absolute" Lorenz curves (Moyes, 1987). However, as opposed to what happens with relative and absolute measures, in the centrist context, there are notions for which no Lorenz dominance criterion has been defined yet.

The literature offers different intermediate inequality notions. Some of them involve nonlinear iso-inequality contours, so that the inequality perception of individuals changes when income increases. Thus, according to the "fair compromise" notion proposed by Krtscha (1994), later generalized by Yoshida (2005) and Zheng (2007b), to keep inequality unaltered, 50% of each extra unit of income should be allocated among individuals preserving their income shares while the remaining 50% should be distributed in equal absolute amounts. This notion is rather challenging because it approaches the absolute view soon when income increases, which makes it difficult for inequality to decrease when analyzing an economy over time (Del Río & Alonso-Villar, 2008). Other notions offered in the literature exhibit instead linear iso-inequality contours and, therefore, they do not allow any change in individuals' value judgments when varying aggregate income (Bossert & Pfingsten, 1990; Chakravarty & Tyagarupananda, 2008; Del Río & Alonso-Villar, 2010; Del Río & Ruiz-Castillo, 2000; Seidl & Pfingsten, 1997). These measures seem plausible for analysis in the short and medium run, bringing a complementary perspective to the former.

In a nonlinear centrist framework, a (weak) Lorenz dominance criterion was first introduced by Yoshida (2005).[3] Later on, Zheng (2007a) proposed a more general class of intermediate Lorenz ordering and showed that Yoshida's dominance criterion is the only one that satisfies unit-consistency (i.e., inequality rankings remain unchanged when all incomes are multiplied by a positive scalar). However, as far as we know, no unit-consistent dominance criterion has been proposed in the literature in a linear centrist framework.[4]

To close this gap, this paper aims to introduce a unit-consistent (strong) Lorenz dominance criterion that allows comparisons among income distributions according to the ray invariance proposed by Seidl and Pfingsten (1997), which is a general centrist notion that has given rise to measures with a clear empirical implementation (Del Río & Alonso-Villar, 2010; Del Río & Ruiz-Castillo, 2000). Consistently with the α-inequality concept proposed by Seidl and Pfingsten (1997), this paper proposes α-Lorenz curves. These curves approach the absolute Lorenz curve when α is close to equity. The advantage of using a Lorenz-type dominance criterion is that it allows the discovery of cases in which one distribution has a higher inequality than another, not only according to a particular index but according to all those indexes consistent with the dominance criterion, which adds robustness to empirical findings. By defining α-Lorenz curves that generalize the absolute Lorenz curve, one can implement unanimous rankings for a broad set of centrist inequality notions.

The α-inequality concept proposed by Seidl and Pfingsten (1997) is rather simple: to keep inequality unaltered, any extra income should be distributed in fixed proportions given by vector α. Based on this idea, Del Río and Ruiz-Castillo (2000) introduced a similar notion but with the advantage of having economic meaning and satisfying the horizontal equity axiom.[5] Their intermediate approach requires considering only those α-rays resulting from linear combinations between the relative and the absolute ray. Thus, when total income increases, inequality remains unchanged if π 100% of the income surplus is allocated preserving income shares in the distribution of reference, v, and $(1-\pi)$ 100% is distributed in equal absolute amounts. This notion approaches the rightist view when π is close to 1 and the leftist view when π is close to 0. Because the centrist notion proposed by Del Río and Ruiz-Castillo (2000) can be seen as a particular case of the α-inequality proposed by the Seidl and Pfingsten (1997), the new dominance criterion is also valid for it.[6]

It is important to note that intermediate measures are not only a theoretical refinement of relative and absolute measures but a helpful tool for applied research because they allow delving deeper into situations in which income growth is accompanied by a decrease in inequality according to the relative Lorenz criterion together with an increase according to the absolute Lorenz criterion.[7] In those cases, several centrist measures can be used to ascertain to what extent relative inequality has decreased and how far the economy is from experiencing a reduction in absolute inequality. In doing so, this paper draws upon the centrist approach proposed by Del Río and Ruiz-Castillo (2000) and uses different π s to ascertain the range of values under which one distribution has lower inequality than another. Thus, we can determine the set of value judgments that would make society prefer one distribution over the other.[8]

As opposed to centrist and leftist inequality indices, rightist indices are cardinally unaffected by the unit of measurement, which has made them very popular. However, as pointed out by Zheng (2007b), to measure inequality it is not necessary to ask for this property but for unit-consistency, which guarantees that rankings are unaffected by the currency unit. In this new scenario, not only relative or rightist measures but also intermediate or centrist measures that satisfy the unit-consistency axiom, as it is the case of the Del Río and Ruiz-Castillo's (2000) notion used in this paper, appear as plausible options for empirical research.[9]

These tools are illustrated by using Australian income data. Between 1999 and 2003, Australian-born individuals witnessed a general increase in their incomes and a reduction in relative inequality together with an increase in absolute inequality. It seems, therefore, convenient to explore inequality in more detail to ascertain whether inequality has also decreased according to most centrist views and how far this group is from reaching a reduction according to a leftist view of inequality. For this purpose, the Lorenz dominance defined in this paper is applied to the ray-invariant notion proposed by Del Río and Ruiz-Castillo (2000).

The paper is structured as follows. The next section presents the intermediate inequality approach followed in this paper and defines a Lorenz-type curve which gives rise to a dominance criterion consistent with this centrist view. The next section offers an empirical illustration of these tools using Australian data. The last section presents main conclusions.

RAY INVARIANCE AND THE LORENZ CRITERION

Let $I:\mathfrak{R}^n \rightarrow \mathfrak{R}$ $(2 \leq n < \infty)$ be a function satisfying the following basic properties:

a) *Symmetry*: $I(x)=I(x\Pi)$, where Π is a permutation matrix.
b) *Replication invariance*: $I(x) = I\underbrace{(x, ..., x)}_{k}$, where $\underbrace{(x, ..., x)}_{k}$ is a k-fold replication of x.
c) *Strict Schur convexity*: $I(Bx) < I(x)$ for all bistochastic matrices B that are not permutation matrices.

This function is labeled as an intermediate or centrist index if $I(ax) > I(x)$ and $I(x + b1^n) < I(x)$, for any $x \in \mathfrak{R}^n_{++}$, $a > 1$ and $b \in \mathfrak{R}_{++}$ where $1^n \equiv \underbrace{(1, ..., 1)}_{n}$.

Because we focus on symmetric indexes, we can restrict our analysis to the set of all possible ordered income distributions $x_1 \leq x_2 \leq \ldots \leq x_n$, denoted by $D \subset \mathfrak{R}^n_{++}$.

The Ray Invariance of Seidl and Pfingsten (1997)

A centrist inequality attitude can be modeled in various ways, depending on the shape of the set of inequality equivalent income distributions (for comparisons of different centrist notions, including both linear and non-linear inequality contours, see Del Río & Alonso-Villar, 2008). In what follows, we present the α-inequality concept proposed by Seidl and Pfingsten (1997) (hereinafter S-P). Accordingly, any extra income should be distributed in fixed proportions (α) in order to keep inequality unaltered.

Let $\alpha \in D$ be a vector of the simplex (i.e., $\sum_{i=1}^{n} \alpha_i = 1$), we require this vector to be weakly Lorenz-dominated by vector $(1^n/n)$.[10] The set of distributions for which α represents an intermediate notion is denoted by

$\Gamma(\alpha) = \{x \in D : \alpha \succ_L v_x\}$, where $\succ_L$ denotes strongly Lorenz dominance and $v_x \equiv \left(\frac{x_1}{\sum_{i=1}^{n} x_i}, \ldots, \frac{x_n}{\sum_{i=1}^{n} x_i} \right)$ is the vector of income shares associated with distribution x.[11] Therefore, this inequality notion requires a certain relationship between the direction of the invariance line, given by α, and distribution x if one wants it to represent an intermediate attitude. In other words, α cannot be used for all distributions but only for those that it strongly Lorenz-dominates. Conversely, given a distribution $x \in D$, not all α vectors are suitable if they are to represent intermediate notions for x. Only those included in the set $\Omega(x) = \left\{ \alpha : \alpha \in D, \ \sum_{i=1}^{n} \alpha_i = 1, \ \alpha \succ_L x \right\}$ are admissible.

Given a distribution $x \in \Gamma(\alpha)$, the corresponding iso-inequality line is defined by $E_\alpha(x) = \{y \in D : y = x + \tau\alpha, \ \tau \in \mathfrak{R}\}$ (for the bi-dimensional case, see Fig. 1). This notion coincides with the absolute view when α is equal to $(1^n/n)$ and the relative view when α is close to v_x. Note that, on the one hand, any distribution in $E_\alpha(x)$ with $\tau < 0$ is less egalitarian in the Lorenz

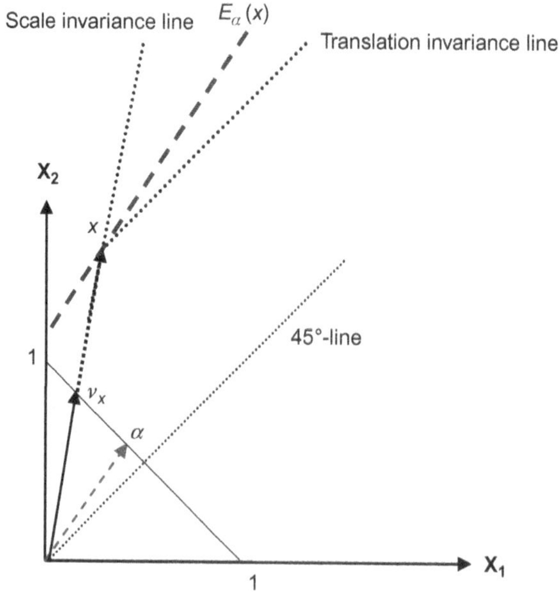

Fig. 1. Ray-Invariance in Seidl and Pfingsten and Scale and Translation Invariances ($n = 2$).

sense than $x + \tau 1^n$ and more egalitarian than λx when $\lambda > 1$. On the other hand, those distributions in $E_\alpha(x)$ having $\tau < 0$ are more equally distributed than $x + \tau 1^n$ and less equally distributed than λx when $0 < \lambda < 1$.

We label an intermediate inequality measure, I_α, ray invariant if $I_\alpha(x) = I_\alpha(x + \tau\alpha)$, where $x \in \Gamma(\alpha)$ and $\tau \in \Re$.[12] We define a binary relation as follows:

$$x \succ_\alpha y : \Leftrightarrow I_\alpha(x) < I_\alpha(y),$$

where $x, y \in \Gamma(\alpha)$.

A New Lorenz Dominance Criterion

Let $\tilde{x}$ denote a distribution obtained through distribution $x \in \Gamma(\alpha)$ allocating its total income among individuals according to income shares given by α (i.e., $\tilde{x} \equiv \alpha \sum_{i=1}^{n} x_i$, see Fig. 2). Using $\tilde{x}$, we construct distribution x_α as the ordered vector resulting from the losses and gains experienced by individuals when moving from distribution x to $\tilde{x}$ (i.e., x_α is obtained from $x - \tilde{x}$).[13]

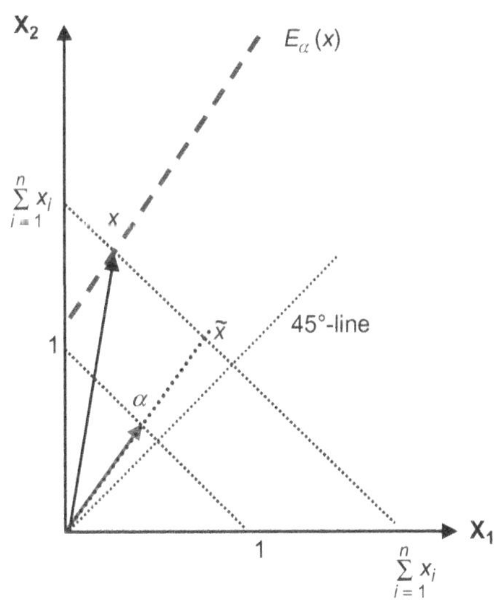

Fig. 2. Constructing Distribution $\tilde{x}$.

Definition. We define the α-Lorenz curve for distribution $x \in \Gamma(\alpha)$ as the generalized Lorenz curve (Shorrocks, 1983) of distribution x_α:

$$L_\alpha(p,x) = GL(p, x_\alpha)$$

for any $P \in (0,1]$ and adopting the convention $L_\alpha(0,x) = 0$ (where the generalized Lorenz curve of a distribution y is $GL\left(\frac{k}{n}, y\right) = \frac{1}{n}\sum_{i=1}^{k} y_i$). This function is convex with respect to p, takes no positive values within the interval (0,1), is equal to zero when p is equal to 0 and 1, and reaches a minimum at a point $p^* = \frac{k^*}{n}$, where k^* represents the individual with the smallest loss (i.e., $(x_\alpha)_{k^*} < 0$ and $(x_\alpha)_{k^*+1} \geq 0$, see Fig. 3). This curve generalizes the absolute Lorenz curve since when α is equal to $(\frac{1}{n}, \ldots, \frac{1}{n})$, the generalized Lorenz curve applied to x_α becomes the generalized Lorenz curve applied to $x - \bar{x}1^n$, that is, the absolute Lorenz curve.[14]

Definition. For any $x,y \in \Gamma(\alpha)$ we define an α-Lorenz-dominance criterion as follows:

$$x \succ_{L\alpha} y : \Leftrightarrow L_\alpha(p,x) \geq L_\alpha(p,y)$$

for all $p \in [0, 1]$ and the strict inequality holds at least once.

The binary relation given by $\succ_{L\alpha}$ allows a partial ordering of income distributions following the α-ray invariance notion proposed by S-P. It is straightforward to prove that according to this ordering, inequality rankings between income distributions remain unchanged when all incomes are multiplied by a (positive) scalar. Therefore, this ordering satisfies the unit-consistency axiom. This property guarantees that one will reach the same conclusion whether income is measured in euros, Australian dollars,

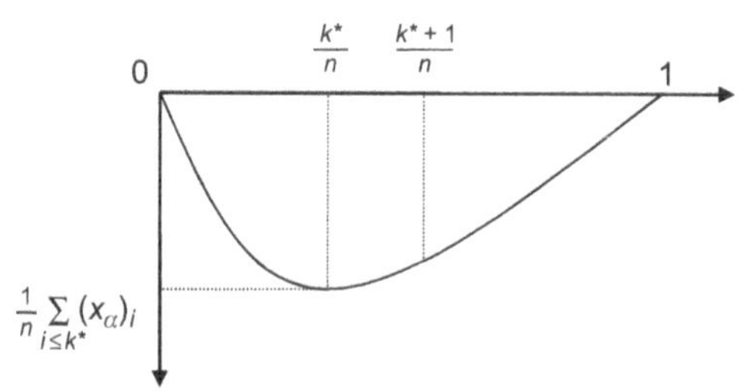

Fig. 3. The α-Lorenz Curve.

American dollars, or whatever other currency unit, which seems a desirable property for empirical analysis.

Proposition. The ranking given by an α-Lorenz curve is consistent with that of any index I_α satisfying symmetry, replication invariance, strict Schur-convexity, and invariance along α-rays. Namely, if $x,y \in \Gamma(\alpha)$, $I_\alpha(x) < I_\alpha(y) \Leftrightarrow x \succ_{L\alpha} y$.

Proof

First, we prove that for any $x,y \in \Gamma(\alpha)$, $I_\alpha(x) < I_\alpha(y) \Rightarrow x \succ_{L\alpha} y$.

Because I_α satisfies symmetry and is α-invariant, we have that $I_\alpha(x) = I_\alpha(x_\alpha) < I_\alpha(y_\alpha) = I_\alpha(y)$. Using Theorem 1 from Dasgupta, Sen, and Starret (1973), the strict Schur-convexity of I_α implies that $(x_\alpha)_1 + \cdots + (x_\alpha)_k \geq (y_\alpha)_1 + \cdots + (y_\alpha)_k$ $\forall k \leq n$ (with strict inequality for at least a k) and $(x_\alpha)_1 + \cdots + (x_\alpha)_n = (y_\alpha)_1 + \cdots + (y_\alpha)_n$. Consequently, $GL(p,x_\alpha) \geq GL(p,y_\alpha)$ (with strict inequality at least once). In other words, $x \succ_{L\alpha} y$.

Second, we prove that for any $x,y \in \Gamma(\alpha)$, $x \succ_{L\alpha} y \Rightarrow I_\alpha(x) < I_\alpha(y)$.

If $x \succ_{L\alpha} y$, then $\frac{1}{n}\left[(x_\alpha)_1 + \cdots + (x_\alpha)_k\right] \geq \frac{1}{n}\left[(y_\alpha)_1 + \cdots + (y_\alpha)_k\right]$ $\forall k \leq n$ (with strict inequality at least once). From the aforementioned theorem, it follows that the value of any strict Schur-convex function evaluated at x_α is lower than at y_α. Consequently, $I_\alpha(x_\alpha) < I_\alpha(y_\alpha)$. Because I_α is α-invariant $I_\alpha(x) = I_\alpha(x_\alpha)$ and $I_\alpha(y_\alpha) = I_\alpha(y)$. Therefore, $I_\alpha(x) < I_\alpha(y)$.

Interpreting α According to Del Río and Ruiz-Castillo (2000)

The ray invariance concept proposed by S-P has no clear economic interpretation – which makes it difficult its use in empirical analyses – and violates the horizontal equity axiom because individuals who have the same income level initially may be treated differently (Zoli, 2003). To solve these problems, Del Río and Ruiz-Castillo (2000) offered a ray-invariant notion that can be considered as a special case of the former. According to their proposal, inequality depends on two parameters, instead of one: the income shares in the distribution of reference that gives rise to the rightist and leftist views, denoted by simplex vector v, and $\pi \in [0,1]$ which is used to define a convex combination between them.[15] Once v and π are fixed, it is possible to calculate the n-dimensional simplex vector $\alpha = \pi v + (1-\pi)\frac{1^n}{n}$ that defines the direction of the ray. The economic meaning of this invariance notion is simple: when total income increases, inequality remains unchanged if π 100% of the income surplus is allocated preserving income shares in the distribution of reference and $(1-\pi)$ 100% is distributed in equal absolute amounts. In other words, α can be interpreted as a convex combination of the value judgments behind the distribution of reference, v, and those behind the equalitarian distribution, $\frac{1^n}{n}$ (see Fig. 4). If we choose a value of π close to 1, the notion represents rightist value judgments while if π is close to 0, the inequality attitude is rather leftist, as compared to the distribution of reference. Note that in our case, the only feasible values of π are those that make α strongly Lorenz-dominate distribution x.

The distribution of reference, v, plays an important role in this approach. Note that vector v does not necessarily have to coincide with vector v_x (as shown in Fig. 4). However, in comparing distribution x and distribution y (which can be assumed to have a higher mean without loss of generality), vector v could be chosen as the income shares of x, that is, $v=v_x$. By using this benchmark, together with the parameter π reflecting the inequality-invariance value judgments of society, it would be possible to determine whether y has a lower inequality than the distribution reached if π 100% of the income gap had been distributed according to income shares in x and $(1-\pi)$ 100% in equal amounts among individuals. Note that, in doing so, the same vector of reference $(v=v_x)$ has to be used for

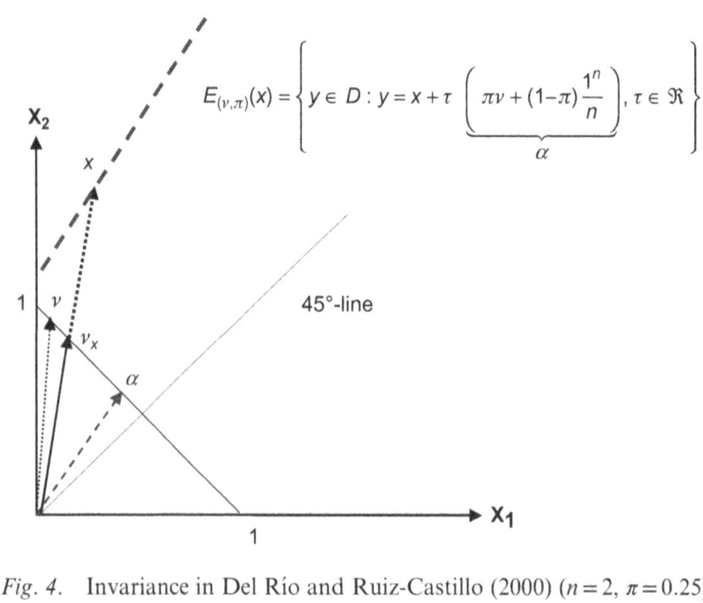

Fig. 4. Invariance in Del Río and Ruiz-Castillo (2000) ($n=2$, $\pi=0.25$).

both distributions x and y (which makes this centrist notion path independent, as explained in Del Río & Alonso-Villar, 2010). It would not be possible to use $v = v_x$ for measuring the inequality level corresponding to x while using $v = v_y$ in the case of distribution y because that would imply that different inequality attitudes would be used for each distribution. In other words, once v and π are chosen, they cannot be changed: the same intermediate notion must be used when comparing any two income distributions. Therefore, when studying the evolution of an economy over time, this approach allows the possibility of taking into account the starting point.

AN ILLUSTRATION: INCOME INEQUALITY IN AUSTRALIA

To illustrate our intermediate dominance criterion, this section provides an empirical analysis using Australian income data between 1999 and 2003.[16] During this period, Australia experienced high and sustainable economic and employment growth, the real economy growing on average almost 4% every year (Australian Bureau of Statistics [ABS], 2011). As will be shown, the evolution of the income distribution of some groups in Australia during this period provides a suitable case for an intermediate inequality analysis.

The data used in our analysis come from the 1999–2000 and 2003–2004 Surveys of Income and Housing Costs (SIHC) conducted by the ABS. We illustrate the use of the new dominance criterion looking at the changes in inequality in the distribution of weekly household disposable income of Australian-born people included in the ABS surveys. This income variable includes any employee cash income received by household members, income from own unincorporated business, investment income, income from government pensions and allowances, and all incomes from other regular sources. Differences in non-income needs across households of different size and composition are considered in the analysis, so household income is converted into household equivalent income using an equivalence scale. In particular, we use the parametric family of equivalence scales introduced by Buhmann, Rainwater, Schmaus, and Smeeding (1988):

$$e(s, \Theta) = s^{\Theta}$$

Table 1. Annual Changes in Mean Income and Income Shares by Income Quintiles in Australia between 1999 and 2003.

Quintile	Absolute Change (AUD $)	Relative Change (%)	Income Shares (%)	
			1999	2003
1	12.89	6.23	7.40	7.76
2	20.37	5.96	12.30	12.73
3	26.13	5.34	17.71	17.97
4	31.43	4.78	24.04	23.83
5	46.28	4.41	38.55	37.71
All	27.43	5.00	100.00	100.00

Note: Equivalent incomes computed assuming a value for Θ equal to 0.5.

where s is the size of the household and $0 \leq \Theta \leq 1$ is the elasticity of the scale rate. Adjusted income values are computed by dividing household income by scale factor s^{Θ}, with different values of Θ being used to check the robustness of the results. Finally, all the estimates are computed using the population weights reported in SIHC to obtain population rather than sample estimates.

Table 1 summarizes the main changes in the distribution of income among natives that took place between 1999 and 2003. In this period, this group witnessed a general increase in weekly incomes, with the mean income growing more than $27 every year, equivalent to an annual rate of growth of 5%. This growth, however, was not uniform across the whole distribution. Thus, the first column in Table 1 suggests that the *absolute* income gains among the top three quintiles were larger than those experienced by the bottom positions, whose mean income grew less than the overall mean. On the contrary, the largest *relative* income growth was for the poorest three quintiles, which grew above the population average, with the growth rate declining as we move up in the distribution. This growth pattern is consistent with the increase in the income share of the three bottom quintiles and the corresponding decline of the share accumulated by the two top quintiles (columns 3 and 4).[17]

These changes in the income distribution have important implications in terms of inequality. The fact that the absolute difference between top and bottom positions widened suggests an increase in absolute inequality. On the contrary, the convergence in the income shares of the groups points toward a reduction in relative inequality. These findings are corroborated in Fig. 5, which shows the absolute and relative Lorenz curves for the 1999 and 2003 income distributions. In the relative case (Fig. 5(a)), the Lorenz

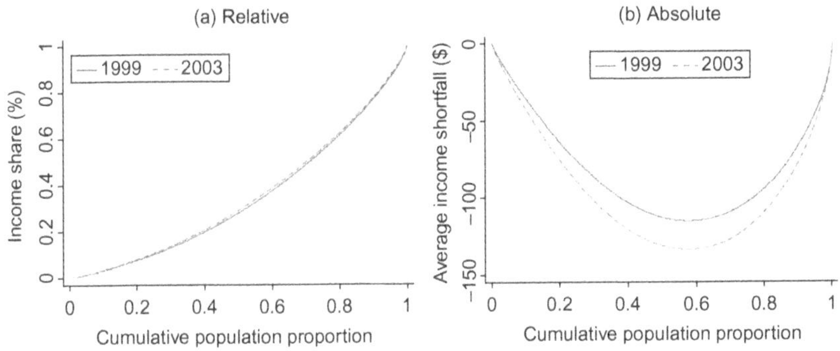

Fig. 5. Absolute and Relative Lorenz Curves for Australia, Years 1999 and 2003 ($\Theta = 0.5$).

curve for 2003 dominates the initial one, which implies that these two distributions will be unambiguously ranked by the class of scale invariant inequality indexes (Foster, 1985). In contrast, the absolute Lorenz curve for 1999 lies above that of 2003 at every point (Fig. 5(b)), so that any inequality measure verifying the translation invariance property would indicate an increase in the level of absolute inequality during this period (Moyes, 1987).[18]

It is important to note that the relative and absolute dominance criteria do not inform us about the changes in inequality for intermediate notions of inequality lying between the "rightist" and "leftist" extreme cases. To deal with this issue, we now use our α-Lorenz curves and the corresponding dominance criterion to compare the 1999 and 2003 distributions adopting centrist notions of inequality. This methodology allows us to search for unambiguous rankings among the classes of intermediate inequality measures. For that purpose, we use the class of inequality indexes consistent with the ray-invariant notion proposed by Del Río and Ruiz-Castillo (2000).

Let x and y denote the income distributions in Australia in 1999 and 2003. Also, let v_x, v_y, and $(1^n/n)$ be the vectors of the simplex associated with the x, y, and egalitarian distributions, respectively. Taking the initial distribution as the distribution of reference, we consider inequality-invariance value judgments, α, of the form:

$$\alpha = \pi v_x + (1 - \pi)\frac{1^n}{n} \tag{1}$$

where $\pi \in [0,1)$. When π is equal to zero, α becomes the absolute ray-invariant notion, whereas when it tends to 1 it leads to the relative ray. Further, for a particular α to represent a centrist attitude, α must Lorenz-dominate both v_x and v_y. This condition holds when π is equal to 0 but it is not fulfilled when π is close to 1 because v_x is Lorenz-dominated by v_y.[19]

We denote by π^M the maximum value of π for which a valid intermediate notion can be derived. For a given vector α, the ordered distributions x_α and y_α defined in the section "A New Lorenz Dominance Criterion" have to be constructed to check for the existence of α-Lorenz dominance. When x and y come from populations of different sizes, this requires the use of replications of the initial distributions to ensure that the vectors are conformable. Notice that this does not impose any limitation on the validity of the analysis because inequality rankings are unaffected by population replication. In fact, for the general class of inequality indexes satisfying the replication invariance principle considered in this paper, the original and replica distributions exhibit exactly the same level of inequality independently of the mean-invariance notion. Furthermore, for any value of π, the invariance value judgment given by α is equivalent to the one obtained for the replicated population because both α vectors have the same Lorenz curve. This means that to keep inequality unaltered, both notions require an analogous allocation of the income growth among individuals.

As an example, Fig. 6 presents the α-Lorenz curves for 1999 and 2003 for an equivalence scale parameter Θ of 0.5 and values of π equal to 0.25, 0.5, 0.87, and 0.9. As the figure shows, it is possible to derive unambiguous rankings of the initial and the final distributions for some centrist notions of inequality. Thus, when π is set equal to 0.25 or 0.5, the curve for 1999 α-Lorenz dominates that of 2003 and, therefore, it follows from our proposition that any inequality index consistent with these centrist attitudes would conclude that income inequality increased during this period. Interestingly, this result does not hold anymore when centrist views that are closer to the relative notion of inequality are considered. For both π equal to 0.87 and 0.9, the α-Lorenz curves for 1999 and 2003 cross multiple times, which implies that no unambiguous ranking of these two distributions can be derived for these attitudes towards inequality.

Table 2 summarizes the main results of the intermediate inequality analysis for different values of the equivalence scale parameter Θ. For each case, the interval $[0,\pi^M]$ represents the values of π for which the α vectors given by (1) are valid notions of intermediate inequality.[20] Further, three sets of centrist notions expressed in terms of π are provided: the values according to which income inequality increased during the period as the

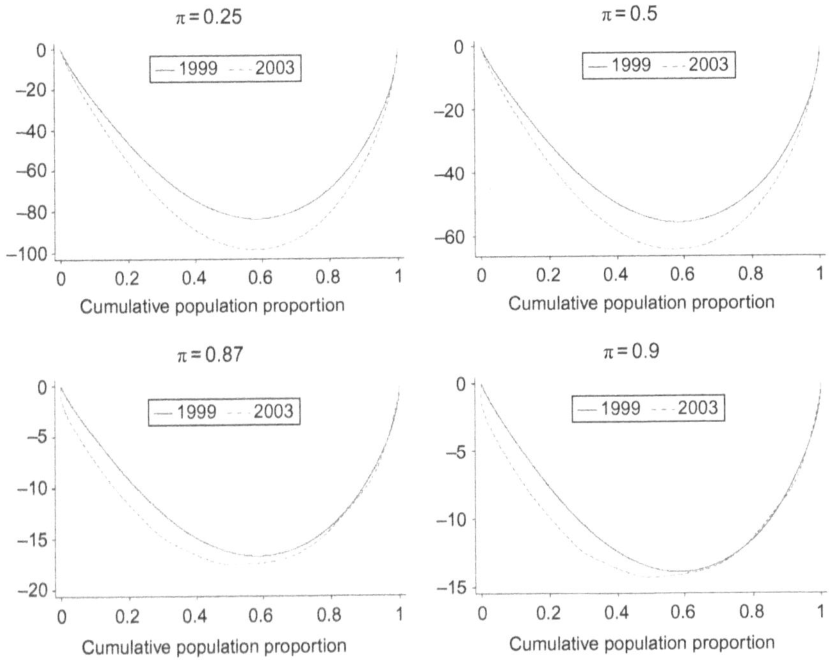

Fig. 6. α-Lorenz Curves for Australia, Years 1999 and 2003 ($\Theta = 0.5$).

Table 2. Intermediate Inequality in Australia: 1999–2003.

Θ	Values of π for which α is a Valid Centrist Notion: $[0,\pi^M]$	Values of π According to which Inequality		
		Increased ($X \succ_{L\alpha} Y$)	Equivalent	Reduced ($Y \succ_{L\alpha} X$)
0	[0,0.91]	[0,0.91]	–	–
0.25	[0,0.92]	[0,0.89]	(0.89,0.92]	–
0.5	[0,0.91]	[0,0.86]	(0.86,0.91]	–
0.75	[0,0.90]	[0,0.82]	(0.82,0.90]	–
1	[0,0.92]	[0,0.80]	(0.80,0.92]	–

distribution in 1999 dominates that in 2003 (labeled in the table as "increased"); those π *s* for which these two distributions cannot be unambiguously ranked (labeled as "equivalent"); and the set of notions for which one could claim income inequality declined from 1999 to 2003 (labeled as "reduced"). Note that some of these sets may be empty because distributions can be ranked according to the α-Lorenz dominance criterion only for those vectors α that represent a valid notion of centrist inequality.

We find that the initial and the final distributions are comparable for most of the centrist notions that can be constructed as a convex combination of the vectors v_x and $(1^n/n)$. Thus π^{M} is around 0.9 for all the equivalence scales considered. Remarkably, our results suggest that income inequality among Australian born-people increased for most of the intermediate value judgments. In fact, inequality increased for all those centrist attitudes that require the equal distribution of at least 9–20%, depending on the value of parameter Θ, of the income gains in order to keep inequality unchanged. Thus, for example, when $\Theta = 0.5$, inequality increases if one judges inequality using centrist views where at most 86% of the income growth is distributed across individuals according to income shares in 1999 (Table 2, column 2) and, consequently, at least 14% of the growth is allocated in equal amounts.

For all the values of Θ but zero, there exists a set of intermediate notions according to which the initial and the final distributions are equivalent in terms of inequality. In the case of $\Theta = 0.5$, for instance, the initial and the final distributions cannot be unambiguously ranked when using invariant notions according to which inequality is maintained if the proportion of the income growth that is equally distributed among individuals ranges between 9% and 14% (Table 2, column 3). For the remaining equivalence scale values, the lower and upper limits of the interval are 8–10% and 11–20%, respectively.

Finally, for none of the values of π for which a valid centrist notion can be defined, we can claim income inequality in Australia actually declined between 1999 and 2003.

CONCLUSIONS

This paper has introduced a unit-consistent dominance criterion that allows ranking income distributions according to the centrist inequality notion proposed by Seidl and Pfingsten (1997). In doing so, it has defined α-Lorenz curves that generalize the absolute Lorenz curve (Moyes, 1987). These curves allow implementing unanimous rankings for a broad set of centrist inequality notions whereas they become closer and closer to the absolute curve when α approaches equity. Our proposal allows finding cases in which one distribution has higher inequality than another not only according to a particular α-index but according to all those α-indexes consistent with our dominance criterion (as also happens with the relative and absolute Lorenz dominance criteria and the indexes verifying the scale invariance and the translation invariance axioms, respectively). We have used this dominance criterion to rank income distributions in Australia between 1999 and 2003 according to the family of centrist notions proposed by Del Río and Ruiz-Castillo (2000), which are particular cases of those proposed by Seidl and Pfingsten (1997). The results show that even though relative inequality decreased during the period for Australian-born people, according to most ray-invariant centrist views of inequality, inequality increased.

NOTES

1. Properties such as normalization, continuity, differentiability, and replication invariance are also commonly invoked.
2. Following Dalton (1920), several reports on questionnaires support this view (see Amiel and Cowell (1992), Harrison and Seidl (1994), and Seidl and Theilen (1994), among others). In particular, Ballano and Ruiz-Castillo (1993) find that 27% of individuals support this perception of inequality.
3. According to this criterion, when moving from an income distribution to another having a higher income, if the Lorenz curve of the latter lies at no point below the former, any inequality index satisfying Schur convexity would say that inequality has not increased. Strict Schur convexity, which is the property behind the Pigou-Dalton principle, would require instead inequality to decrease after this change.
4. As shown by Zheng (2007a), the Lorenz criterion proposed by Pfingsten (1988), which follows a ray-invariant centrist notion, is not unit-consistent.
5. This notion also satisfies path independence, as shown by Del Río and Alonso-Villar (2010).
6. The new criterion is also valid for the intermediate measures proposed by Del Río and Alonso-Villar (2010), which can be seen as extensions of those by Del Río and Ruiz-Castillo (2000).
7. This circumstance is not unusual because when the mean of an income distribution rises, absolute measures are more demanding than relative. This is so because giving an equal amount of income to every individual leads to a more egalitarian distribution than giving to each of them an amount that keeps the original income shares.
8. This approach was used by Del Río and Ruiz-Castillo (2001) to compare income distributions in Spain between 1980 and 1990.
9. As opposed to what happens when using the linear inequality notion proposed by Bossert and Pfingsten (1990), the notion proposed by Del Río and

Ruiz-Castillo (2000) is unaffected by the currency unit, as shown by Del Río and Alonso-Villar (2008).

10. This is consistent with S-P formulation and, at the same time, is compatible with the α-Lorenz curves we will built later on.

11. We require strong dominance here to exclude the case where α coincides with ν_x because in that case the α-Lorenz curve would not be well defined.

12. As opposed to S-P, we consider measures that fulfill strict Schur convexity rather than Schur convexity.

13. As we explained earlier, we discard $\alpha = \nu_x$. The reason is that in that case, $x - \tilde{x}$ would be equal to zero.

14. Although the intermediate Lorenz curve proposed by Yoshida (2005) is not obtained following this type of reasoning, it could be also interpreted as the generalized Lorenz curve of an income distribution transformed according to his intermediate notion: $(x - \bar{x}1^n/\bar{x}\beta)$.

15. Vector ν is assumed to represent an ordered distribution.

16. For studies focusing on earlier periods using other methodologies, see, for example, Saunders, Stott, and Hobbes (1991), Blacklow and Ray (2000), Athanasopoulos and Vahid (2003), and Atkinson and Leigh (2007).

17. Analyzing the top incomes in Australia, Atkinson and Leigh (2007) found that between the 1920s and 1980s top income shares fell for most of the period, while they rose rapidly between the 1980s and 1990s.

18. The dominance results presented in Fig. 5 are not sensitive to the choice of the equivalence scale parameter. Thus, for any value of $\Theta \in [0,1]$, we find that absolute (relative) inequality in Australia increased (decreased) between 1999 and 2003.

19. This comes from the fact that x is Lorenz-dominated by y.

20. Note that for a particular a to represent a centrist attitude, it must strongly Lorenz-dominate both the income distribution of 1999 and 2003.

ACKNOWLEDGMENT

Financial support from the *Ministerio de Ciencia e Innovación* (grants ECO2011-23460, ECO2010-21668-C03-03, and ECO2013-46516-C4-2-R), *Xunta de Galicia* (CN2012/178), and from FEDER is gratefully acknowledged. We want to thank Coral del Río for helpful comments.

REFERENCES

Amiel, Y., & Cowell, F. A. (1992). Measurement of income inequality: Experimental test by questionnaire. *Journal of Public Economics*, *47*, 3–26.

Athanasopoulos, G., & Vahid, F. (2003). Statistical inference and changes in income inequality in Australia. *The Economic Record*, *79*(247), 412–424.

Atkinson, A. B., & Leigh, A. (2007). The distribution of top incomes in Australia. *The Economic Record*, *83*(262), 247–261.

Australian Bureau of Statistics. (2011). *Australian national accounts: National income, expenditure and product*. Table 1. Key National Accounts Aggregates, cat. No. 5206.0.

Ballano, C., & Ruiz-Castillo, J. (1993). Searching by questionnaire for the meaning of income inequality. *Revista Española de Economía*, *10*, 233–259.

Blacklow, P., & Ray, R. (2000). A comparison of income and expenditure inequality estimates: The Australian evidence, 1975–76 to 1993–94. *Australian Economic Review*, *33*, 317–329.

Bossert, W., & Pfingsten, A. (1990). Intermediate inequality, concepts, indices and welfare implications. *Mathematical Social Sciences*, *19*, 117–134.

Buhmann, B., Rainwater, L., Schmaus, G., & Smeeding, T. M. (1988). Equivalence scales, well-being, inequality, and poverty: Sensitivity estimates across ten countries using the Luxembourg Income Study (LIS) database. *Review of Income and Wealth*, *34*(2), 115–142.

Chakravarty, S., & Tyagarupananda, S. (2008). The subgroup decomposable intermediate indices of inequality. *Spanish Economic Review*, *11*(2), 83–97.

Dalton, H. (1920). The measurement of inequality of income. *Economic Journal*, *30*, 348–361.

Dasgupta, P., Sen, A., & Starret, D. (1973). Notes on the measurement of inequality. *Journal of Economic Theory*, *6*, 180–187.

Del Río, C., & Alonso-Villar, O. (2008). Rankings of income distributions: A note on intermediate inequality indices. In J. Bishop & B. Zheng (Eds.), *Inequality and opportunity: Papers from the second ECINEQ society meeting* (Vol. 16, pp. 213–229). Research on Economic Inequality. Emerald Group Publishing Limited.

Del Río, C., & Alonso-Villar, O. (2010). New unit-consistent intermediate inequality indices. *Economic Theory*, *42*(3), 505–521.

Del Río, C., & Ruiz-Castillo, J. (2000). Intermediate inequality and welfare. *Social Choice and Welfare*, *17*, 223–239.

Del Río, C., & Ruiz-Castillo, J. (2001). Intermediate inequality and welfare: The case of Spain 1980–81 to 1990–91. *Review of Income and Wealth*, *47*, 221–237.

Foster, J. E. (1985). Inequality measurement. In H. Peyton Young (Ed.), *Fair allocation. Proceedings of Symposia in Applied Mathematics* (Vol. 33, pp. 31–68). Providence RI: American Mathematical Society.

Harrison, E., & Seidl, C. (1994). Acceptance of distributional axioms: Experimental findings. In W. Eichorn (Ed.), *Models and measurement of welfare and inequality* (pp. 67–99). Berlin: Springer-Verlag.

Kolm, S. C. (1976). Unequal inequalities I. *Journal of Economic Theory*, *12*, 416–442.

Krtscha, M. (1994). A new compromise measure of inequality. In W. Eichorn (Ed.), *Models and measurement of welfare and inequality* (pp. 111–120). Heidelberg: Springer-Verlag.

Moyes, P. (1987). A new concept of Lorenz domination. *Economics Letters*, *23*, 203–207.

Pfingsten, A. (1988). New concepts of Lorenz domination and risk aversion. In P. Kleinschmidt, F. J. Radermacher, W. Schweitzer, & H. Wildemann (Eds.), *Methods of operations research* (Vol. 59, pp. 75–85). Königstein: Hain.

Saunders, P., Stott, H., & Hobbes, G. (1991). Income inequality in Australia and New Zealand: International comparisons and recent trends. *Review of Income and Wealth*, *37*, 63–79.

Seidl, C., & Pfingsten, A. (1997). Ray invariant inequality measures. In S. Zandvakili & D. Slotje (Eds.), *Research on taxation and inequality* (pp. 107–129). Greenwich, CT: JAI Press.

Seidl, C., & Theilen, B. (1994). Stochastic independence of distributional attitudes and social status. A comparison of German and polish data. *European Journal of Political Economy*, *10*, 295–310.

Shorrocks, A. F. (1983). Ranking income distributions. *Economica*, *50*, 3–17.

Yoshida, T. (2005). Social welfare rankings of income distributions. A new parametric concept of intermediate inequality. *Social Choice and Welfare*, *24*, 557–574.

Zheng, B. (2007a). Inequality orderings and unit consistency. *Social Choice and Welfare*, *29*, 515–538.

Zheng, B. (2007b). Unit-consistent decomposable inequality measures. *Economica*, *74*, 97–111.

Zoli, C. (2003). *Characterizing inequality equivalence criteria*. University of Nottingham, Mimeo.

WAGE DISTRIBUTIONS AND THE ACCOUNTING PERIOD: AN ASSESSMENT OF THE SHORROCKS EFFECT

Carsten Schröder

ABSTRACT

When individual or household incomes are collected for administrative or scientific surveys, the accounting period is sometimes a month, sometimes a quarter, and sometimes a year. The accounting period likely affects the shape of the income distribution and the level of measured inequality. The present study systematically explores the sensitivity of inter-temporal and inter-regional inequality comparisons to the length of the accounting period.

Keywords: Inequality; volatility; wage distribution; accounting period; Shorrocks effect

JEL classifications: D3; D31

Economic Well-Being and Inequality: Papers from the Fifth ECINEQ Meeting
Research on Economic Inequality, Volume 22, 421–447

ISSN: 1049-2585/doi:10.1108/S1049-258520140000022014

INTRODUCTION

Normative decisions underlie any empirical analysis of the income distribution. These decisions concern the living standard indicator used (e.g., income or wealth), the unit of analysis (e.g., individual vs. household), the selection of equivalence scales, etc. A vast literature explores the sensitivity of the obtained results to these normative decisions. Little, however, is known about the sensitivity of inequality indices to the length of the period over which income is surveyed: the accounting period (AP). Arguably, extending the accounting period – say from a month to a year – evens out sub-annual income fluctuations, smoothing the income distribution and lowering the extent of inequality. This in turn restricts the comparability of inequality indices from databases where APs differ.

In its influential 2001 report, the Canberra expert group on household income statistics argued that the lack of a uniform AP across micro databases may introduce "an element of non-comparability" (Canberra Group, 2001, p. 48). However, even in highly standardized databases like the Luxembourg Income Study (LIS), maybe the most influential database for cross-country inequality comparisons,[1] a uniform AP is not ensured. The LIS has assembled and harmonized household micro data from numerous countries. The micro data, however, are provided by the national data-collecting institutions, and these institutions define the AP. As a result, there is no uniform AP. As an example, for the United Kingdom, the AP for regular income "is the period covering the last payment received." Usually, this period should be a month for earnings from employment and a quarter/year for capital incomes. For France, the AP is the "twelve months preceding the interview," for Australia "the financial year preceding the date of interview," and for Germany and the United States, the "calendar year" (see the survey information provided at http://www.lisdatacenter.org/ for details). In other databases, APs change over the years. As an example, in the German Income and Expenditure Survey, the AP has been reduced from a year (until 1993) to a quarter.

Shorrocks (1978) has shown under relatively general conditions that inequality and the AP are negatively related.[2] Hence, extending the AP will lower the level of measured inequality. This is because the correlation between incomes from different periods typically is lower than one, so that an extension of the AP evens out sub-annual income fluctuations. As an example, suppose we observe a population of two subjects over two periods. The two-period income stream is (5,10) for the first subject and (9,6) for the second. Any inequality index that satisfies the weak principle of transfers will indicate more inequality in the period-specific distributions, $\begin{pmatrix} 5 \\ 9 \end{pmatrix}$ and $\begin{pmatrix} 10 \\ 6 \end{pmatrix}$, than in the two-period distribution, $\begin{pmatrix} 15 \\ 15 \end{pmatrix}$. This is the so-called "Shorrocks effect."

The theory defines the direction of the Shorrocks effect. Its quantitative strength is an empirical question. The data requirement for a rigorous empirical assessment of the Shorrocks effect, however, is high. Ideally, incomes for different APs should have been collected under ceteris paribus conditions, that is, from the same sample, the same observation period, the same sampling units, and the same income concept. Maybe for this reason, only little is known about the quantitative size of the Shorrocks effect for standard lengths of APs – a month, a quarter, or a year.[3] These studies include Shorrocks (1981), Ruggles and Williams (1989), and Ruggles (1990) for the United States, Morris and Preston (1986), Nolan (1987), and Böheim and Jenkins (2006) for the United Kingdom, Gibson, Huang, and Rozelle (2001) for China, Cantó, Gradin, and Del Río (2006) for Spain, Finkel, Artsev, and Yitzhaki (2006) for Israel, and Detlefsen (2012) and Schröder, Golan, and Yitzhaki (2014) for Germany.

The aforementioned empirical literatures offer mixed results on the quantitative size of the Shorrocks effect.[4] Some studies find sizeable effects. Gibson et al. (2001), for example, find that inequality indices from a monthly AP are up to 1.69 times larger than indices from an annual AP in China. Since the standard AP in datasets from China is a year and thus longer than those of many other countries, the Shorrocks effect offers a plausible explanation for the puzzlingly low inequality estimates for China compared to other areas of the world (Gibson et al., 2001, p. 329). Other studies find rather moderate effects. Böheim and Jenkins (2006), for example, find that short-term "current and annual income measures provide very similar pictures of the income distribution" and conclude: "differences in income distributions between Britain and other nations do not arise because of the different survey measures of income that have been used" (Böheim & Jenkins, 2006, p. 756).

Why is the empirical evidence on the size of the Shorrocks effect so mixed? First of all, the aforementioned studies deal with data from different countries and points in time. Cross-country differences in social security systems or (macro-)economic conditions therefore offer one plausible explanation. For example, the sub-annual volatility of wages in a country that has dipped into a recession is expected to be higher than that of a country that is experiencing a phase of economic stability. The differences in the sub-annual volatility of wages will again be echoed in the magnitude of the Shorrocks effect. Second, the studies exhibit methodological differences. These differences concern the type of data (survey vs. administrative data); the income concept (gross vs. net); the observation unit (household vs. individual); the construction of income aggregates; the choice of inequality indices; etc. To better understand the evidence on the Shorrocks effect, Finkel et al. (2006, p. 177), therefore, conclude that "additional research on different data sets is needed."

The reviews by Cantó et al. (2006) and Schröder (2012) also point to two limitations of existing studies. First, data limitations sometimes lead researchers to seek proxies for short-term incomes. Sometimes, these proxies are "close to ... annual income" (see Cantó et al., 2006, p. 210), which leads to an underestimation of the Shorrocks effect. Second, many of the existing studies do not provide statistical tests on whether the AP changes the conclusions from inter-temporal or inter-regional inequality comparisons. Systematically testing the sensitivity of inequality comparisons to the choice of the AP, however, is important for understanding the information content of comparative inequality analyses that build on data where a uniform AP is not ensured.

In light of the above, this paper makes three contributions. Using a longitudinal administrative survey of persons insured in the German statutory pension system with month-by-month information on individual gross wages, we quantify the Shorrocks effect under the desired ceteris paribus conditions, including an examination of the stability of the effect over a long observation period. Second, we test the sensitivity of inter-temporal and inter-regional comparative inequality analyses to the choice of AP. Third, to understand the results, we complement the inequality analysis with a volatility analysis. In the latter, we provide biannual and sub-annual volatility indices.

Our results can be summarized as follows. Our first result is that the Shorrocks effect can be of sizeable magnitude, yet it depends on the inequality index and varies over time and regions. For example, the Theil index increases up to 16 percent if the AP is shortened from a year to a quarter, whereas the Gini index increases no more than 3 percent. As a result, there is little hope of identifying a general rule for the size of the Shorrocks effect. Our second result is that inter-temporal and inter-regional inequality comparisons are sensitive to the length of the AP. In various cases, the AP is important for the level of significance. In some cases, the choice of the AP can also change the sign of the comparisons. In 1993, as an example, the Theil index from annual wages in the "old" German states of the former West Germany is significantly lower than the Theil index from quarterly wages in the "new" states of the former East Germany. For quarterly wages in the old states and annual wages in the new states, however, the finding reverts. Such reversals arise because of the inter-temporal changes and inter-regional differences in levels of sub-annual wage volatility.

In sum, our empirical examination indicates that a single simple answer to the question "How large is the Shorrocks effect?" does not exist. Instead, the size of the Shorrocks effect varies over time, and it differs over regions and inequality indices. The size of the effect probably also depends on the income concept. Further, our analysis reveals that the results obtained from comparative inequality analysis (e.g., comparisons over time/regions) are sensitive to the accounting period. Both of these findings together suggest that a uniform accounting period is required for a valid comparative inequality analysis.

The paper is organized as follows. The next section introduces the database and outlines the methodological procedure for assessing the AP-inequality nexus. This is followed by the section that provides the empirical results, and the final section concludes.

METHODOLOGICAL CONSIDERATIONS

Data and Data Preparation

Our empirical analysis builds on administrative micro data provided by the Research Data Center of the German Statutory Pension Insurance (Forschungsdatenzentrum der Rentenversicherung). We use the Insurance Account Sample from 2006 (IAS 2006, "Versicherungskontenstichprobe"). IAS 2006 is a panel with biographical information on 60,304 individuals. It is split into two parts. The first part provides time-invariant information on the insured, such as gender and birth year. The second part provides the employment biographies of the insured, particularly information on individual gross wages subject to social insurance contributions and on social security status. Both pieces of information are available for every month of the employment phase.

The main advantage of the IAS is its panel structure combined with the monthly level information on wages. These features allow the construction of quarterly and annual wages by simple aggregation of monthly wages over the course of a year. As an IAS biography contains up to 624 entries for each item (i.e., wages and social security status), we can derive up to 624 monthly, 208 quarterly, and 52 annual wage distributions from these data. This allows an assessment of the Shorrocks effect over a long time horizon under the desired ceteris paribus condition: same sampling units, same observation period, same income concept (individual gross wages subject to social security contributions).

In the empirical examination of the Shorrocks effect, we restrict our attention to the period starting with German reunification in 1991 and ending in 2006. To isolate our results from other factors, we focus on a homogeneous IAS subsample consisting of prime-age insured persons (age cohort 30–50) whose social security status during the twelve months of the year was one of the following: employed subject to social security requirements, marginally employed,[5] or unemployed. The unemployed enter the distributional analysis with a zero wage.[6] With our subsample, we focus on insured persons who are "close" to the labor market. The focus places an artificial limit on the time volatility of wages, as changes in individual wages due to switches into a "non-labor market status" (child care, invalidity, etc.) are not reflected in our data. At the same time, insured persons with a "non-labor market status" frequently maintain this status for years, always implying a wage of zero. Including these persons would lower the level of sub-annual volatility and the magnitude of the Shorrocks effect. Further details on the data, the data preparation, and the working sample composition can be found in Schröder (2012).

For an assessment of the Shorrocks effect, it is important that IAS provides high-quality data on individuals' gross wages. In Germany, nearly all dependent employees are mandatorily covered by federal pension insurance.[7] German law requires their employers to provide the social security institutions (here: the statutory pension insurance) with all the information relevant to determine their social security contributions (and future entitlements). Hence, IAS should provide high-quality information on the monthly gross wages subject to social security contributions.

The main disadvantage of the IAS (and other administrative datasets) is its limited set of socioeconomic variables. This limitation is due to legal reasons. Particularly, IAS lacks information on household composition, on income from other sources (e.g., capital income), and on other household members. These restrictions led us to focus on a narrow income concept: individual gross wages subject to social security contributions. It is not guaranteed that other income sources have the same time variability.[8]

If different income sources exhibit different levels of time variability, the magnitude of the Shorrocks effect changes with the income concept. The question mark on the generalizability of results, however, is no guarantee for the validity of comparative inequality analyses building on data where a uniform AP is not ensured.

Quantification Strategy

We are interested, first, in the quantification of the Shorrocks effect in inequality analyses. Here, we focus on two well-known and frequently used inequality indices, the Gini index, I^{G}, and the Theil index, I^{T}. For both indices and the entire observation period (1991–2006), a three-stage procedure is implemented. First, the index I^{j} is derived for each distribution of annual wages, E_a ($a = 1991, \ldots, 2006$), quarterly wages, $E_{a,q}$ ($q = 1, 2, 3, 4$), and monthly wages, $E_{a,m}$ ($m = 1, \ldots, 12$). This gives 17 values per index and observation period. In a second step, the indices from the quarterly and monthly distributions are averaged over the course of a year, $\bar{I}^{j}_{a,q} = \sum_{q=1}^{4} w_{a,q} I^{j}(E_{a,q})$ and $\bar{I}^{j}_{a,m} = \sum_{m=1}^{12} w_{a,m} I^{j}(E_{a,m})$, using the quarter-specific (month-specific) sum of wages relative to the annual sum of wages as weighting factors, w_a.[9] Third, we divide the average quarterly and monthly index by the annual index, $\bar{I}^{j}_{a,q}/I^{j}_{a}$ and $\bar{I}^{j}_{a,m}/I^{j}_{a}$. This normalization allows an immediate assessment of the magnitude of the Shorrocks effect.

Second, we are interested in the effect of the AP on the volatility of wages. Here we implement two types of analysis. The first type deals with the sensitivity of biannual volatility indices to the length of the AP. This biannual analysis is conducted in the same spirit as the analysis of the Shorrocks effect in the inequality analysis. The second type of analysis deals with the sub-annual volatility of wages: volatility between consecutive quarters or months of a year. This sub-annual analysis provides insights into the source of the Shorrocks effect in the inequality analysis.

Our volatility index is the standard deviation of percentage changes in wages. For our purposes, the standard deviation of percentage changes in wages has an important advantage over other volatility measures (e.g., the magnitude of transitory wages): it does not rely on a particular model of income dynamics and thus permits a clear view of the data (see Dynan, Elmendorf, & Sichel, 2012). Further, because our index builds on percentage changes in wages rather than absolute changes, comparability over periods is ensured.

For assessing biannual wage volatility, the standard deviation of percentage changes in annual wages for the years a and $a+1$ is computed as $V_{a,a+1} = \sqrt{\sum_{i=1}^{N} (v_{a,a+1,i} - \bar{v}_{a,a+1})/(N-1)}$. The term $v_{a,a+1,i} = 100\frac{(E_{a+1,i} - E_{a,i})}{0.5(E_{a+1,i} + E_{a,i})}$ is the percentage change of annual wages for person i, where $E_{a+1,i}$ is the annual wage of i, and $\bar{v}_{a,a+1}$ denotes arithmetic mean of the percentage changes of wages over all persons $i = 1, \ldots, N$. Suppose, instead, that the accounting period is a quarter or a month. The standard deviation of percentage changes in wages for a particular quarter/month of the years a and $a+1$ is $V^{q}_{a,a+1} = \sqrt{\sum_{i=1}^{N} (v^{q}_{a,a+1,i} - \bar{v}^{q}_{a,a+1})/(N-1)}$ and $V^{m}_{a,a+1} = \sqrt{\sum_{i=1}^{N} (v^{m}_{a,a+1,i} - \bar{v}^{m}_{a,a+1})/(N-1)}$. Thus, as with the annual volatility index, the indices are derived from a biannual comparison.

For assessing the sensitivity of biannual wage volatility to the AP, we have implemented a three-step procedure similar to the one for the inequality indices. First, for two consecutive years, we derive one volatility index, $V_{a,a+1}$, from the two annual distributions, E_a and E_{a+1}, four volatility indices ($V^{q}_{a,a+1}$) from each pair of quarterly distributions, $E_{a,q}$ and $E_{a+1,q}$ with $q = 1, \ldots, 4$, and 12 volatility indices ($V^{m}_{a,a+1}$) from each pair of monthly distributions, $E_{a,m}$ and $E_{a+1,m}$ with $m = 1, \ldots, 2$. As an example, the quarterly-level (monthly-level) volatility index $V^{q=1}_{2005,2006}$ ($V^{m=5}_{2005,2006}$) is derived from the two distributions for the first quarter of 2005 and 2006 (May 2005 and May 2006). Second, we compute the weighted mean of the sub-annual indices, $\overline{V}^{q}_{a,a+1} = \sum_{q=1}^{4} w^{q}_{a,a+1} V^{q}_{a,a+1}$ and $\overline{V}^{m}_{a,a+1} = \sum_{m=1}^{12} w^{m}_{a,a+1} V^{m}_{a,a+1}$. The weight $w^{q}_{a,a+1}$ ($w^{m}_{a,a+1}$) is the sum of the wages in the particular quarter (month) over both years divided by the total biannual sum of wages. Third, we normalize the average quarterly and monthly volatility index by the volatility index from the annual distributions, $V_{a,a+1}$.

For assessing the level of sub-annual volatility of wages, we can compare wages between quarters or months. The standard deviation of percentage changes in wages between two consecutive quarters is $V^{q,q+1}_{a} = \sqrt{\sum_{i=1}^{N} (v^{q,q+1}_{a,i} - \bar{v}^{q,q+1}_{a})/(N-1)}$. The term $v^{q,q+1}_{a,i} = 100\frac{(E^{q+1}_{a,i} - E^{q}_{a,i})}{0.5(E^{q+1}_{a,i} + E^{q}_{a,i})}$ is the percentage change of quarterly wages for person i between quarter q and $q+1$, and $\overline{v}_a^{q,q+1}$ is the arithmetic mean of the percentage changes. Following the same logic, the standard deviation of percentage changes in wages between two consecutive months is $V_a^{m,m+1} = \sqrt{\sum_{i=1}^{N}(v_{a,i}^{m,m+1} - \overline{v}_a^{m,m+1})/(N-1)}$. From both indices, we then derive the weighted averages, $\overline{V}_a^{q,q+1} = \sum_{q=1}^{3} w_a^{q,q+1} V_a^{q,q+1}$ and $\overline{V}_a^{m,m+1} = \sum_{m=1}^{11} w_a^{m,m+1} V_a^{m,m+1}$. The weight $w_a^{q,q+1}$ ($w_a^{m,m+1}$) is the sum of the wages in the two quarters or months, $\sum_{i=1}^{N}(E_{a,i}^{q} + E_{a,i}^{q+1})$ or $\sum_{i=1}^{N}(E_{a,i}^{m} + E_{a,i}^{m+1})$, normalized with the wage sum $\sum_{q=1}^{3}\sum_{i=1}^{N}(E_{a,i}^{q} + E_{a,i}^{q+1})$ or $\sum_{m=1}^{11}\sum_{i=1}^{N}(E_{a,i}^{m} + E_{a,i}^{m+1})$.[10]

A bootstrap procedure has been implemented to test for statistical significance of the results. Particularly, we have drawn 1,000 bootstrap samples with replacement from any distribution, and for any bootstrap distribution we have computed the aforementioned distributional indices. From the ordered 1,000 bootstrap indices, the 95 percent bootstrap confidence interval has been derived using the percentile method.[11]

EMPIRICAL ANALYSIS

The empirical analysis is divided into two parts. The first part takes a long-run perspective, studying the sensitivity of inter-temporal trends in inequality and volatility to the AP. The second part takes a regional perspective, studying the sensitivity of inter-regional comparisons of inequality and volatility to the AP.

An Inter-Temporal Perspective

Inequality Patterns

Fig. 1 depicts the inter-trend of wage inequality in Germany. Results are assembled in six separate graphs, one graph per inequality index and AP. The vertical lines represent the 95% bootstrap confidence interval while crosses represent point estimates of the index.

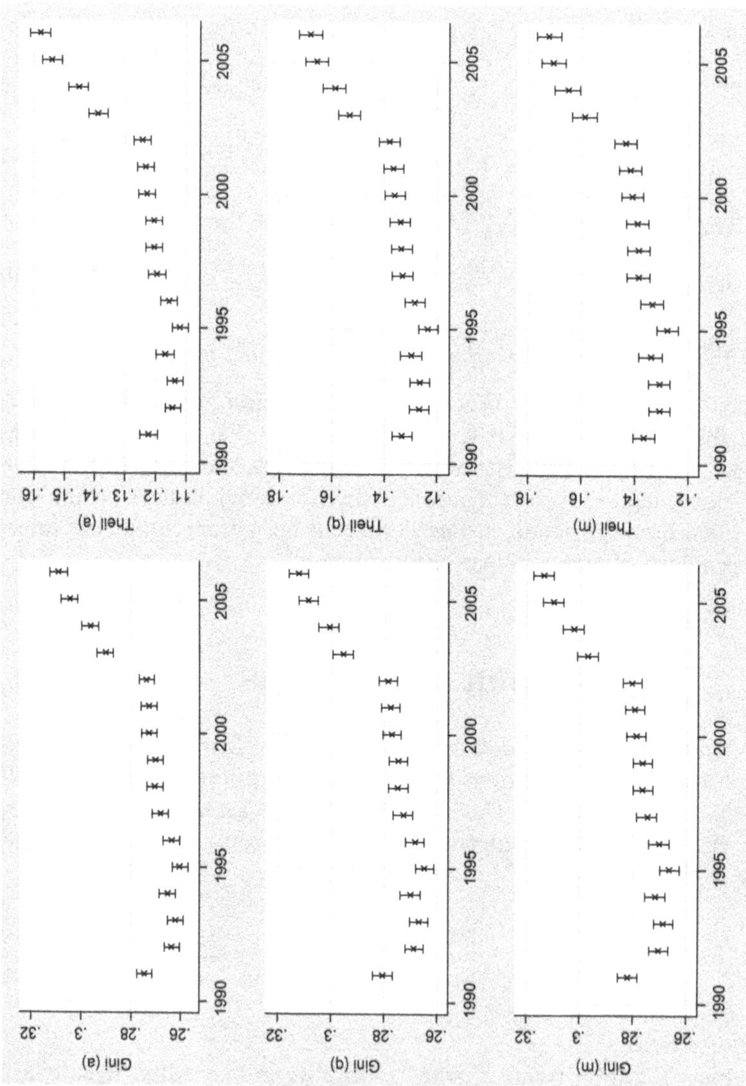

Fig. 1. Inter-Temporal Inequality Patterns and the Accounting Period. *Note*: "a"/"q"/"m" refers to annual/quarterly/monthly income reference period. *Source*: Data from IAS (2006). Own calculations.

The first important message from Fig. 1 is that the length of the AP seems to matter little for inter-temporal patterns of inequality: for all three APs (and both indices), the consistent message is a slight decrease in inequality between 1991 and 1992, followed by a period of stability, and a marked increase from 2003 on. As an example, the point estimate of the Gini index from annual wages declines from 0.275 to 0.264 between 1991 and 1992, varies around 0.26–0.27 until 2002, and then increases, reaching a peak of 0.309 in 2006.[12] The second important message is the sensitivity of the size of the Shorrocks effect to the choice of the inequality index. The Gini index is much more robust to AP variations than the Theil index. This can best be seen by the normalized indices, $\bar{I}^j_{a,q}/I^j_a$ and $I^j_{a,m}/I^j_a$ provided in Fig. 2. For the Gini index, $\bar{I}^G_{a,q}/I^G_a$ varies around 1.0175 and $\bar{I}^G_{a,m}/I^G_a$ around 1.025. In other words, shortening the AP from a year to a quarter/month increases the level of measured inequality by about 1.75/2.5 percent. For the Theil index, the changes are quantitatively larger: $\bar{I}^T_{a,q}/I^T_a \approx 1.11$; $\bar{I}^T_{a,m}/I^T_a \approx 1.15$. Another important observation from Fig. 2 is the time-variability of the normalized indices and hence of the Shorrocks effect: the effect is much smaller in the later years of the observation period than in the early 1990s.

The results from Figs. 1 and 2 suggest that a simple rule of thumb such as "increasing the AP by X percent lowers measured inequality by Y percent" does not exist. Instead, "X" turns out to be index-specific and time-variant. Particularly, its time-variability calls into question the validity of inter-temporal inequality comparisons if a uniform AP is not ensured.

Inter-Temporal Inequality Comparisons and the Accounting Period

We complete the inter-temporal analysis with tests on the sensitivity of inter-temporal inequality comparisons to the length of the AP. The type of analysis that is implemented is as follows: "Suppose annual wages are distributed more unequally in 2005 than in 2004. Do we find the same result for quarterly and monthly wages?" If the answer is "no," then valid inter-temporal inequality comparisons require a uniform AP.

Table 1 provides the test results. For each year and inequality index, a three-digit numerical sequence is provided. The first/second/third digit refers to an inter-temporal inequality comparison that builds on an annual/a quarterly/monthly AP. A significant inter-temporal inequality increase (decrease) is indicated by "+1" ("−1"). A constant inequality level is

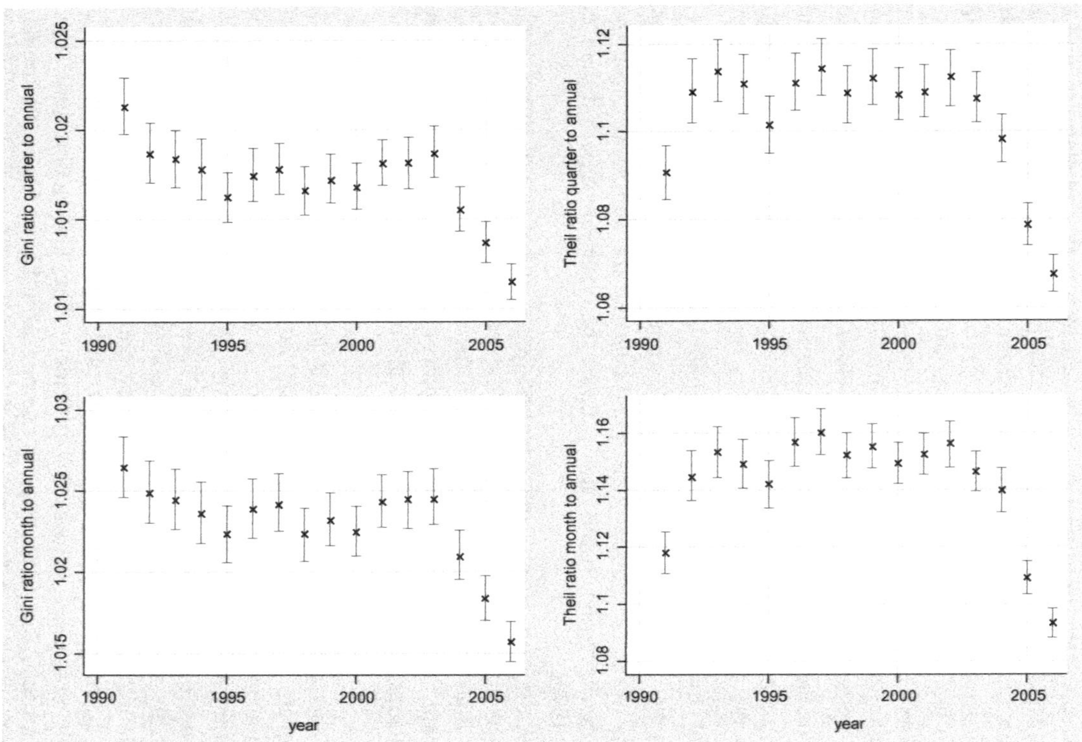

Fig. 2. Ratios of Inequality Indices from Different Accounting Periods. *Note*: Average weighted index from quarterly or monthly distributions relative to index from annual distribution. *Source*: Data from IAS (2006). Own calculations.

Table 1. Inter-Temporal Inequality Comparisons and the Accounting Period.

Index	Period	1991 *aqm*	1992 *aqm*	1993 *aqm*	1994 *aqm*	1995 *aqm*	1996 *Aqm*	1997 *aqm*	1998 *aqm*	1999 *aqm*	2000 *aqm*	2001 *aqm*	2002 *aqm*	2003 *aqm*	2004 *aqm*	2005 *aqm*
Gini	1992	−1 −1 −1														
	1993	−1 −1 −1	000													
	1994	−1 −1 −1	000	000												
	1995	−1 −1 −1	000	000	000											
	1996	−1 −1 −1	000	000	000	000										
	1997	0−10	000	000	000	111	000									
	1998	000	100	111	000	111	100	000								
	1999	000	100	111	000	111	100	000	000							
	2000	000	111	111	100	111	111	000	000	000						
	2001	000	111	111	111	111	111	000	000	000	000					
	2002	000	111	111	111	111	111	000	000	000	000	000				
	2003	111	111	111	111	111	111	111	111	111	111	111	111			
	2004	111	111	111	111	111	111	111	111	111	111	111	111	000		
	2005	111	111	111	111	111	111	111	111	111	111	111	111	111	110	
	2006	111	111	111	111	111	111	111	111	111	111	111	111	111	111	000
Theil	1992	−100														
	1993	−100	000													
	1994	000	000	000												
	1995	−1 −1 −1	000	000	000											
	1996	−100	000	000	000	000										
	1997	000	000	100	000	111	000									
	1998	000	100	100	000	111	000	000								
	1999	000	101	101	000	111	000	000	000							
	2000	000	111	111	100	111	100	000	000	000						
	2001	000	111	111	100	111	110	000	000	000	000					
	2002	000	111	111	111	111	111	000	000	000	000	000				
	2003	111	111	111	111	111	111	111	111	111	111	111	111			
	2004	111	111	111	111	111	111	111	111	111	111	111	111	100		
	2005	111	111	111	111	111	111	111	111	111	111	111	111	111	100	
	2006	111	111	111	111	111	111	111	111	111	111	111	111	111	110	000

Source: Data from IAS (2006).
Notes: "a"/"q"/"m" refers to annual/quarterly/monthly income reference period. "1"/"−1": inter-temporal inequality increase/decrease. "0": change in inequality level is insignificant.

indicated by "0". If the three digits of a sequence do not coincide, a uniform AP seems to be required for valid inter-temporal inequality comparisons.

Most of the 240 sequences suggest that the results from inter-temporal inequality comparisons are robust to variations of the AP. However, six sequences for the Gini index and 15 for the Theil index indicate inconsistencies. For example, take the sequence "100" in column "1996 *aqm*" row "Gini, 1999." The sequence indicates that inequality has significantly increased for an annual AP, but that it remained constant for APs of a quarter or a month. That the number of inconsistencies is larger for the Theil index than for the Gini index is probably due to the fact that the former is more sensitive to changes at the bottom of the distribution. Outright reversals, that is, a significant inter-temporal inequality increase for one AP but a decrease for another AP, do not arise.

Volatility Patterns

The fundamental driver of the Shorrocks effect is the sub-annual volatility of wages. Fig. 3 shows the sub-annual volatility indices from quarterly and the monthly wage distributions, $\overline{V}_a^{q,q+1}$ and $\overline{V}_a^{m,m+1}$. Our first finding is that the volatility index from the quarterly distributions is larger than the index from the monthly distributions: the former varies around 35 percent; the latter around 25 percent. Hence, the sub-annual volatility of wages captured by the standard deviation of percentage changes in wages between two consecutive quarters is larger than the volatility between two consecutive months. Our second finding is that the sub-annual volatility indices from both APs exhibit a similar inter-temporal pattern: after an increase of the index in the early 1990s, it first stabilizes and then decreases in the mid-2000s. The inter-temporal trend of sub-annual volatility thus closely follows the inequality trend (Fig. 1). The pronounced decline in sub-annual volatility in the last observation periods (2002/2003 and on), in particular, explains the declining magnitude of the Shorrocks effect in the inequality analysis, as captured by decreasing normalized inequality indices, $\overline{I}_{a,q}^{\mathrm{G}}/\overline{I}_a^{\mathrm{G}}$, $\overline{I}_{a,m}^{\mathrm{G}}/\overline{I}_a^{\mathrm{G}}$, $\overline{I}_{a,q}^{\mathrm{T}}/I_a^{\mathrm{T}}$, and $\overline{I}_{a,m}^{\mathrm{T}}/I_a^{\mathrm{T}}$.

The sub-annual volatility of wages gives an idea of the mechanics underlying the Shorrocks effect in inequality analyses. However, it is also interesting to study the role of the AP for biannual comparisons of volatility – the Shorrocks effect translated into the world of volatility.

Fig. 4 provides the inter-temporal trends of volatility between two consecutive years, a and $a+1$, for an annual, a quarterly, and a monthly AP (left

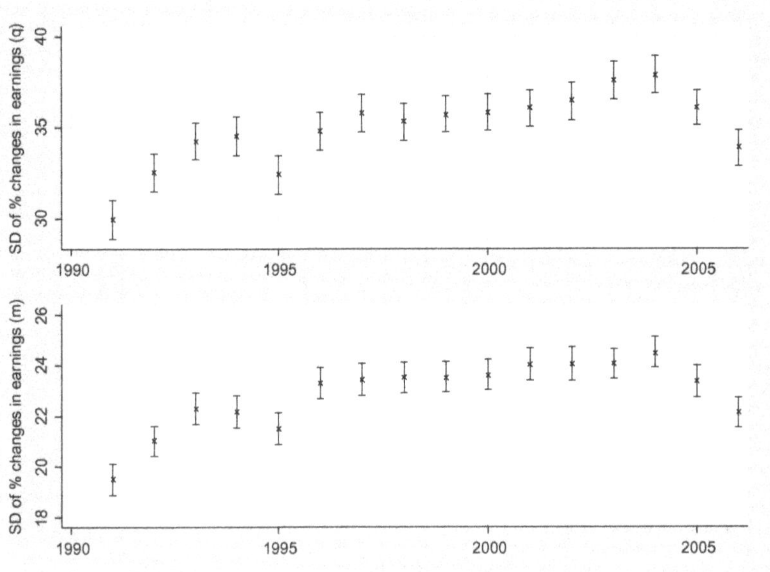

Fig. 3. Sub-Annual Volatility and the Accounting Period. *Notes*: 95% confidence intervals. "a"/"q"/"m" refers to annual/quarterly/monthly income reference period. The abscissa gives the second observation period for the biannual volatility measure. *Source*: Data from IAS (2006). Own calculations.

column), and also the normalized indices, $\overline{V}^{q}_{a,a+1}/V_{a,a+1}$ and $\overline{V}^{m}_{a,a+1}/V_{a,a+1}$ (right column). The abscissa always indicates the second year $(a + 1)$ of the biannual comparison.

The most immediate result from Fig. 4 is the sensitivity of our biannual volatility indices to the AP: shortening the AP increases the level of measured biannual volatility. Short-term variations in wages offer a reasonable explanation. This is because our volatility index builds on percentage changes in individual wages. Suppose the wage of an individual is equal to one in all months of a biannual observation period, except for the fifth month of the first year, a, when it is zero. This gives the following percent changes of wages (in absolute terms): $|v_{a,a+1,i}| = \left|100\frac{(12-11)}{0.5(12+11)}\right| < \left|v^{q=2}_{a,a+1,i}\right| = \left|100\frac{(3-2)}{0.5(3+2)}\right| < \left|v^{m=5}_{a,a+1,i}\right| = \left|100\frac{(1-0)}{0.5(1+0)}\right|$. The inequality means that biannual volatility increases if the AP is shortened. The same inequality holds for

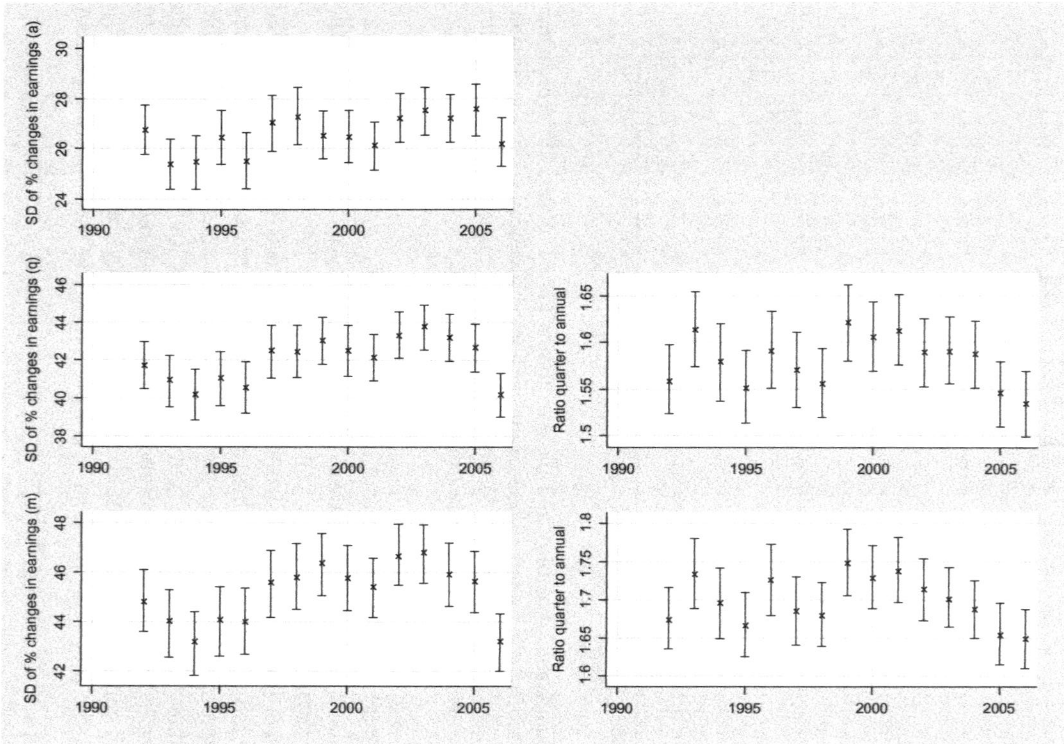

Fig. 4. Biannual Volatility and the Accounting Period. *Notes*: 95% confidence intervals. "a"/"q"/"m" refers to annual/quarterly/monthly income reference period. The abscissa gives the second observation period for the biannual volatility measure. *Source*: Data from IAS (2006). Own calculations.

the average relative changes over the quarters/months: $|v_{a,a+1,i}| = \frac{100}{11.5} < |\overline{v}^{q}_{a,a+1,i}| = \frac{100}{10} < |\overline{v}^{m}_{a,a+1,i}| = \frac{100}{6}$.

Another result from Fig. 4 is that our biannual volatility measure is more sensitive to a reduction of the AP from a year to a quarter compared to a reduction from a quarter to a month. As an example, for 2005–2006, the 95 percent confidence intervals of the volatility indices from the annual/quarterly/monthly distributions are [25.289;27.231], [39.046;41.313], and [41.997;44.322]. We do not believe that this result is akin to a natural law. Instead, all our results should be seen as indications that a uniform accounting period is critical for drawing valid conclusions from comparative distributional analysis.

An Inter-Regional Perspective

We complement the previous inter-temporal analysis with an inter-regional analysis. To do so, we split our working sample in two subsamples: insured persons from the former West German ("old") and East German ("new") states. The central issue we seek to address now is the sensitivity of inter-regional inequality comparisons to the length of the AP.

Inequality Patterns by Regions

Fig. 5 depicts the region-specific trends of inequality indices. The trends are assembled in six separate graphs, one graph per index and AP. Within each graph, a vertical black (gray) line represent the 95% bootstrap confidence interval for the old (new) states and a black (gray) cross the point estimate of the index. Inequality in the old states follows a very similar trend to inequality in Germany as a whole. Again, we see for both indices and all APs a moderate inequality decrease between 1991 and 1992, a period of stability into the early 2000s, and a substantial increase in inequality from 2003 to 2006. The trend for the new states is different: for both indices and all APs, a long phase of rising inequality from 1991 to 2004 was followed by a significant decline in 2005/2006.

Fig. 6 provides the region-specific Shorrocks effects, captured by the normalized inequality ratios. The figure conveys two interesting massages: First, the Shorrocks effect is much larger in the new states than in the old states. As an example, we find a normalized ratio $\overline{I}^{\mathrm{T}}_{a,m}/I^{\mathrm{T}}_{a}$ of about 1.4 for the new states and of <1.2 for the old states. Second, the ratios for the new and old states exhibit different time variability. The difference is most

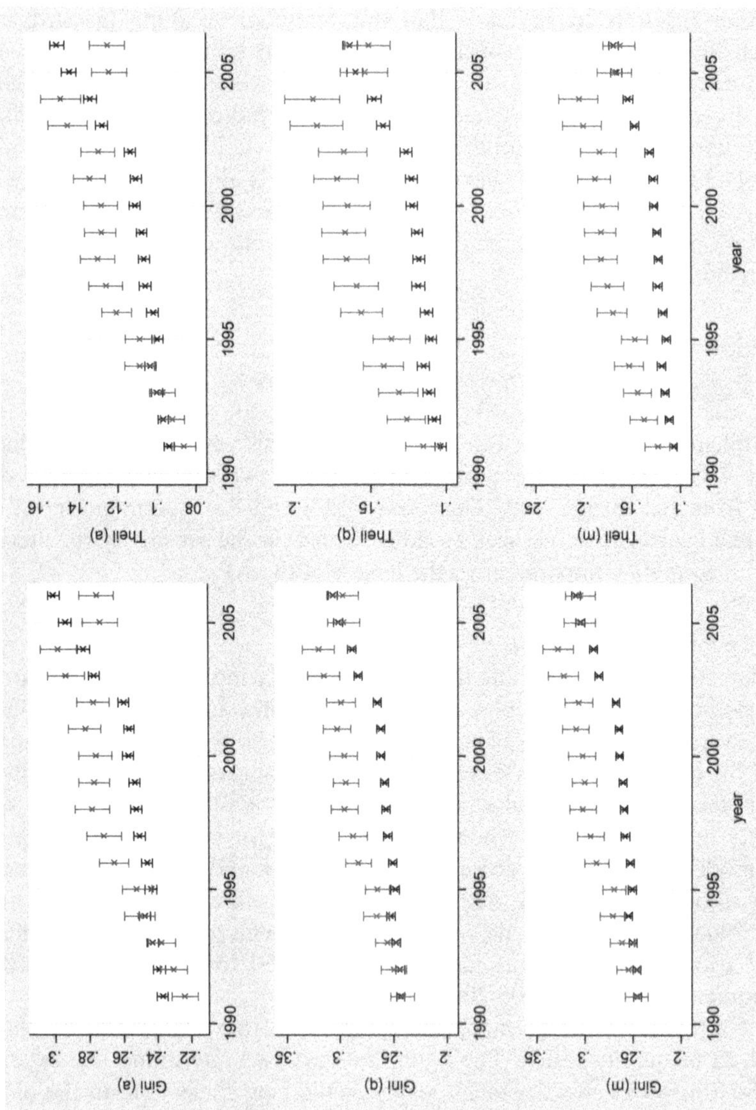

Fig. 5. Inequality and the Accounting Period: Regional Perspective. *Notes:* Black 95% confidence intervals relate to the Old states; gray intervals to the New states. "a"/"q"/"m" refers to annual/quarterly/monthly income reference period. *Source:* Data from IAS (2006). Own calculations.

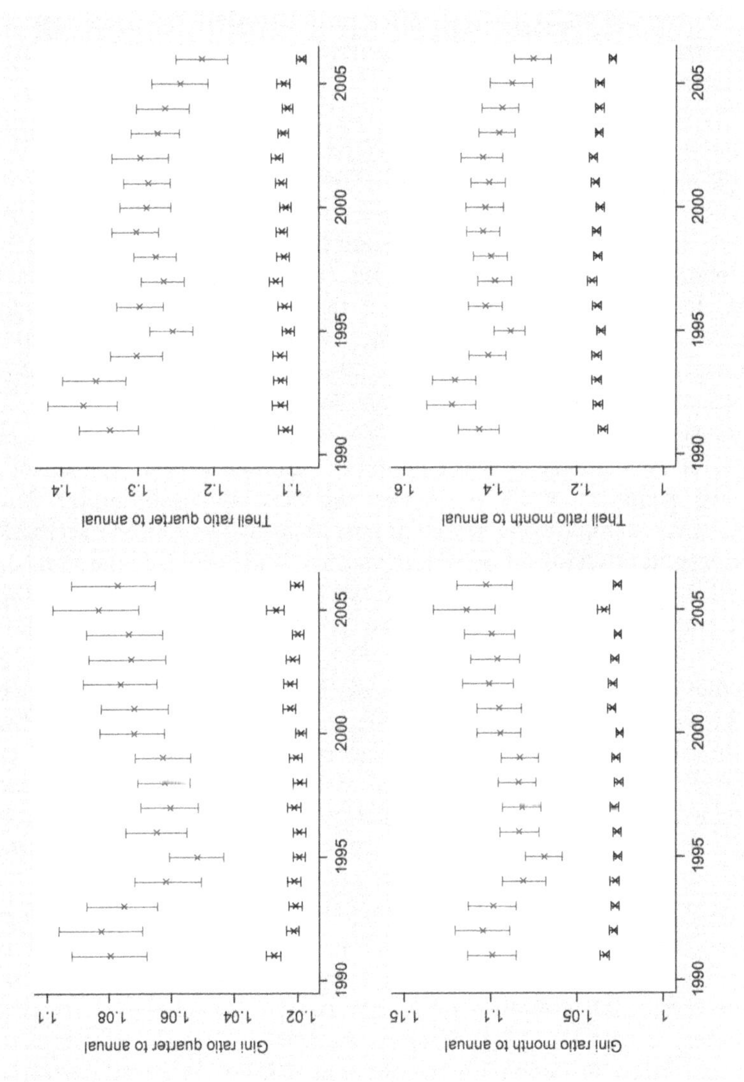

Fig. 6. Ratios of Inequality Indices from Different Accounting Periods: Regional Perspective. *Note*: Average weighted index from quarterly or monthly distributions relative to index from annual distribution. *Source*: Data from IAS (2006). Own calculations.

pronounced for the normalized Theil index. In the new states, the ratio $\bar{I}^{\mathrm{T}}_{a,q}/I^{\mathrm{T}}_{a}$ ($I^{\mathrm{T}}_{a,m}/I^{\mathrm{T}}_{a}$) decreases over the observation period from about 1.35 (>1.4) to about 1.2 (1.3). In the old states, both ratios show almost no variation. As we will see below, the different time variability of the region-specific Shorrocks effects may invalidate inter-regional inequality comparisons if a uniform AP is not ensured.

Inter-Regional Inequality Comparisons and the Accounting Period

The sample split by regions provides the basis for experiments of the following type: "Suppose a uniform annual AP applies to both regions, N (new states) and O (old states), and we find that inequality is significantly higher in region O. Do we find the same result if, in both regions, the AP is shortened? Do we find the same result if the AP is a quarter in the old states and a year in the new states?" The use of non-uniform APs in the two regions may appear artificial, but the situation of a non-uniform AP is what we have to face in many international databases.

Because we have distinguished three APs, nine possible combinations of region-specific APs emerge. For each combination and observation period, we compare inequality levels in the old and new state subsamples. The results from the comparisons are summarized in Table 2. For every AP combination and observation period, a number is provided. If the number is "1" ("−1"), inequality is higher in the old (new) states compared to the new (old) state subsample. If the number is "0," inequality levels do not differ.

Altogether, Table 2 assembles the results in 10 columns. The first nine columns provide the results of the inter-regional inequality comparisons for the nine different AP combinations. The last column reveals whether different AP combinations yield contradictory results ("reversals"), that is, the sign of the inter-regional comparison, changes across the nine possible AP combinations. If the number in the last column is "1" ("0"), this indicates that we find (no) reversal in the particular observation period.

The first three columns of Table 2 provide the results from the regional inequality comparisons for a uniform AP in the old and new states. For example, the column "*OaNa*" ("*OqNq*") summarizes the results for an annual (quarterly) AP in both regions. The general message from the first three columns is that the AP sometimes impacts the significance level of inter-regional inequality comparisons but that it does not cause reversals. The adjacent six columns summarize the results if APs differ across the two regions. For example, the column "*NaOq*" refers to the constellation of an annual AP in the new states and a quarterly AP in the old states. In case of

Table 2. Cross-Regional Inequality Comparisons and the Accounting Period.

Index	Period	*OaNa*	*OqNq*	*OmNm*	*OaNq*	*NaOq*	*OaNm*	*NaOm*	*OqNm*	*NqOm*	Outright Reversal
Gini	1991	1	0	0	0	1	0	1	0	0	0
	1992	0	0	0	0	1	0	1	0	0	0
	1993	0	0	0	0	0	−1	0	0	0	0
	1994	0	0	0	−1	0	−1	0	−1	0	0
	1995	0	−1	−1	−1	0	−1	0	−1	0	0
	1996	−1	−1	−1	−1	−1	−1	0	−1	−1	0
	1997	−1	−1	−1	−1	−1	−1	0	−1	−1	0
	1998	−1	−1	−1	−1	−1	−1	−1	−1	−1	0
	1999	−1	−1	−1	−1	−1	−1	−1	−1	−1	0
	2000	−1	−1	−1	−1	−1	−1	0	−1	−1	0
	2001	−1	−1	−1	−1	−1	−1	−1	−1	−1	0
	2002	−1	−1	−1	−1	0	−1	0	−1	−1	0
	2003	−1	−1	−1	−1	0	−1	0	−1	−1	0
	2004	−1	−1	−1	−1	0	−1	0	−1	−1	0
	2005	1	0	0	0	1	0	1	0	0	0
	2006	1	0	0	0	1	0	1	0	0	0
Theil	1991	0	0	0	−1	1	−1	1	−1	0	1
	1992	0	−1	−1	−1	1	−1	1	−1	0	1
	1993	0	−1	−1	−1	1	−1	1	−1	0	1
	1994	0	−1	−1	−1	0	−1	0	−1	−1	0
	1995	0	−1	−1	−1	0	−1	0	−1	−1	0
	1996	−1	−1	−1	−1	0	−1	0	−1	−1	0
	1997	−1	−1	−1	−1	0	−1	0	−1	−1	0
	1998	−1	−1	−1	−1	0	−1	0	−1	−1	0
	1999	−1	−1	−1	−1	0	−1	0	−1	−1	0
	2000	−1	−1	−1	−1	0	−1	0	−1	−1	0
	2001	−1	−1	−1	−1	0	−1	0	−1	−1	0
	2002	−1	−1	−1	−1	0	−1	0	−1	−1	0
	2003	−1	−1	−1	−1	0	−1	0	−1	−1	0
	2004	−1	−1	−1	−1	0	−1	0	−1	1	0
	2005	1	0	0	0	1	−1	1	0	0	1
	2006	1	0	0	0	1	0	1	0	0	0

Source: Data from IAS (2006).

Notes: "a"/"q"/"m" refers to annual/quarterly/monthly income reference period. "1"/"−1": inequality is higher/lower in the Old compared with the New states. "0": no significant difference in inequality levels.

the Gini index, we never observe a reversal. In case of the Theil index, however, four reversals occur, that is, in the years 1991, 1992, 1993, and 2005. For example, take the year 1991 and the constellation "*OaNq*": if the AP is a year in the old and a quarter in the new states, then the Theil index shows lower inequality in the old states. For the opposite constellation, *NaOq*, however, the Theil index shows higher inequality in the old states. Hence, it is plausible to assume that non-uniform APs can also undermine the validity of cross-country inequality comparisons.

Volatility Patterns by Regions

To better understand the role of the AP for the inter-regional inequality comparisons, Fig. 7 provides the time series of region-specific sub-annual volatility indices. The structure of Fig. 7 is the same as of Fig. 3. However, there are two time series within each graph, one for the old states (black) and one for the new states sample (gray).

The two graphs convey two important messages. First, the sub-annual volatility levels differ pronouncedly in Germany's old and new states. Particularly, the indices for the new states are markedly larger than in the old states. This difference also helps in understanding why the normalized

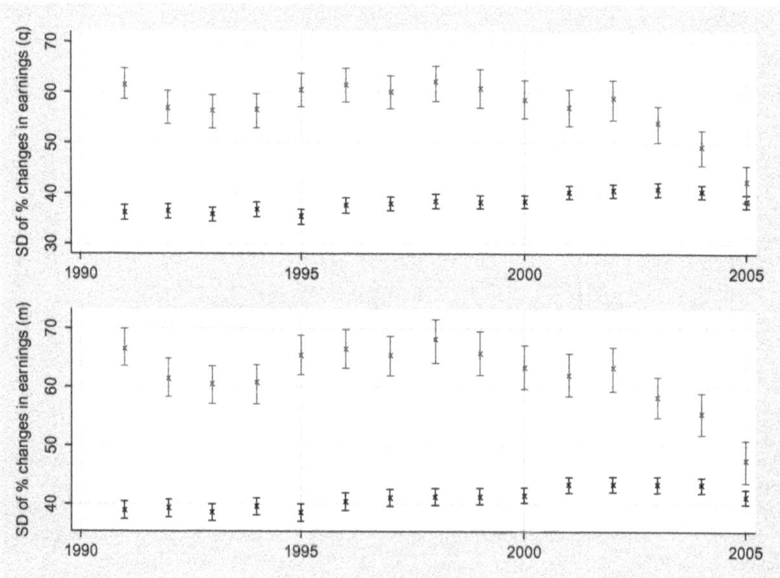

Fig. 7. Sub-Annual Volatility and the Accounting Period: Regional Perspective. *Notes*: Black 95% confidence intervals relate to the Old states; gray intervals to the New states. "a"/"q"/"m" refers to annual/quarterly/monthly income reference period. The abscissa gives the second observation period for the biannual volatility measure. *Source*: Data from IAS (2006). Own calculations.

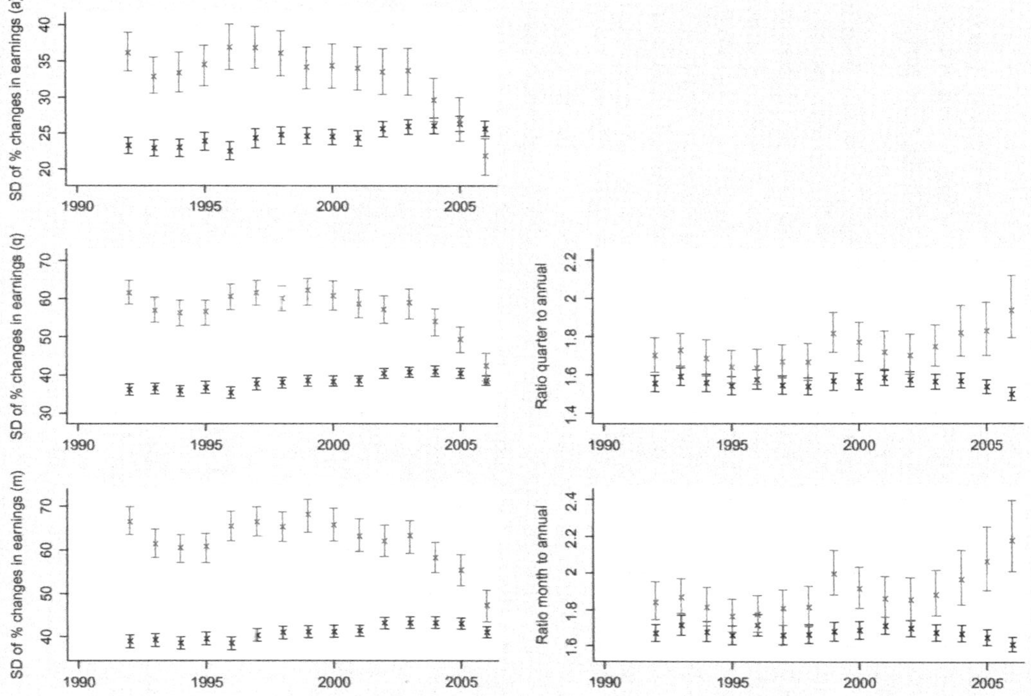

Fig. 8. Biannual Volatility and the Accounting Period: Regional Perspective. *Notes*: Black 95% confidence intervals relate to the Old states; gray intervals to the New states. "a"/"q"/"m" refers to annual/quarterly/monthly income reference period. The abscissa gives the second observation period for the biannual volatility measure. *Source*: Data from IAS (2006). Own calculations.

inequality indices in the new states are larger than in the old states (see Fig. 6). The second message is that the difference in the sub-annual volatility indices over the observation period has become smaller, particularly in recent years. Thus, "projections" on the size of the Shorrocks effect from historical data do not seem well advised.

We conclude the inter-regional analysis with the biannual volatility indices. The time trends of the indices are provided in Fig. 8. Fig. 8 has the same structure as Fig. 4, except that now two region-specific time series are provided in each graph (old states: black; new states: gray).

The graphs in Fig. 8 convey the following messages. First, the biannual volatility indices for the new states are in most cases larger than in the old states. This result holds for all three APs. For example, the 95 percent confidence interval for the standard deviation of percent changes in annual wages in 1995/1996 is [21.313;23.771] in the old states and [33.781;40.073] in the new states. Second, the regional divide in volatility levels diminishes during the observation period: biannual wage volatility trends downwards in the new states and (slightly) upwards in the old states. As a result, for 2005/2006, the index from annual wages in the old states, [24.582;26.705], indicates more biannual volatility than the index in the new states, [19.205;24.407]. Third, biannual volatility indices in both regions increase if the AP is shortened. As for Germany as a whole, the increase is larger if the AP is reduced from a year to a quarter than if it is reduced from a quarter to a month. Fourth, shortening the AP has a stronger effect on measured biannual volatility in the new states (both in absolute and relative terms). Interestingly, the $\overline{V}^q_{a,a+1}/V^q_{a,a+1}$ and the $\overline{V}^m_{a,a+1}/V_{a,a+1}$ have become more and more disparate over the observation period.

CONCLUDING REMARKS

Various household micro datasets are available for studying patterns and trends in inequality. A potential element of non-comparability for distributional analyses is the accounting period, the period over which incomes are surveyed in the data. Even highly standardized international databases do not ensure a uniform accounting period.

The present study indicates that the length of the income accounting period is not without consequence for comparative inequality analyses. Our results show that the strength of the Shorrocks effect varies over time and differs across regions and inequality indices. Thus, "forecasting" the strength of the Shorrocks effect from previous analyses does not seem advisable. Instead, a uniform AP appears to be a key requirement for valid comparative distributional analyses.

NOTES

1. The working paper series of the Luxembourg Income Study lists several hundred inequality-related papers.

2. Wodon and Yitzhaki (2003) provide the formal relationship between the AP and the Gini index. For other distributional aspects, that is, poverty or mobility, theoretical predictions are ambiguous (see Böheim & Jenkins, 2006, and references cited therein).

3. A broad literature studies the relationships between annual and lifetime income distributions. Influential studies include Björklund (1993), Burkhauser and Poupore (1997), and Trede (1998). See Burkhauser and Couch (2009) for a review of the literature. However, this is not the focus of the present study, which focuses on the shorter time horizon of a year, a quarter, or a month.

4. For a detailed summary of the results, see the literature reviews by Cantó et al. (2006), Böheim and Jenkins (2006), and Schröder (2012).

5. Marginal employment is a particular status in the German social security system. Basically, it describes persons with rather low wages.

6. More precisely, the monthly wages of unemployed persons are set to EUR 1, so that all the distributional indices are always defined. An alternative strategy would be the imputation of unemployment benefits. Our strategy should imply higher levels of inequality and sub-annual volatility.

7. Most self-employees and civil servants are not mandatorily insured, their earnings are not contained in IAS.

8. I would like to thank an anonymous Reviewer for detailed comments on the time variability of different income concepts.

9. With our empirical strategy, we follow the theoretical examination by Shorrocks (1978).

10. We derive the changes in wages from three quarterly comparisons – first/second quarter; second/third quarter; third/fourth quarter. The weighting takes into account that in the comparisons the distributions of the first and fourth quarter enter once but the distributions of the second and third quarter enter twice. For the analysis at the monthly level, the first and twelfth months enter once and all other months enter twice.

11. As an alternative to percentile-based confidence intervals, Hall's bootstrap confidence interval (Hall, 1994) is recommended when earnings/incomes are not normally distributed. All our conclusions also hold when Hall's bootstrap confidence interval is derived. The results can be provided by the authors upon request.

12. Since 2003, assessment ceilings in the "new" states have been increased rather moderately, and have been left almost unaltered in the "old" states. Accordingly, the recent rise in inequality is not due to data peculiarities but should reflect changes

in the actual gross earnings distribution. This is reconfirmed by the decomposed estimates by old and new states that follow.

ACKNOWLEDGMENT

All correspondence to: cschroeder@diw.de. I would like to thank the Max Planck Institute for Demographic Research, in particular Joshua Goldstein, and the Kiel Institute for the World Economy for their kind hospitality during research visits from October 2011 to September 2012. Further, I would like to thank the Editors for their professional support, an anonymous Reviewer for her/his most constructive report, and Ralf Himmelreicher of the Research Center of the German Statutory Pension Insurance for guiding me through the data. I also benefited from comments of participants of a research seminar at Hebrew University (2013) and the ECINEQ conference in Bari (2013).

REFERENCES

Björklund, A. (1993). A comparison between actual distributions of annual and lifetime income: Sweden 1951–89. *Review of Income and Wealth*, *39*, 377–386.

Böheim, R., & Jenkins, S. P. (2006). A comparison of current and annual measures of income in the British household panel survey. *Journal of Official Statistics*, *22*, 733–758.

Burkhauser, R., & Couch, K. (2009). Intragenerational inequality and intertemporal mobility. In W. Salverda, B. Nolan, & T. Smeeding (Eds.), *The Oxford handbook of economic inequality*. Oxford: Oxford University Press.

Burkhauser, R., & Poupore, J. (1997). A cross-national comparison of permanent inequality in the United States and Germany. *Review of Economics and Statistics*, *79*, 10–17.

Canberra Group. (2001). *Expert group on household income statistics, final report and recommendations*. Ottawa.

Cantó, O., Gradin, C., & Del Río, C. (2006). Poverty statics and dynamics: Does the accounting period matter? *International Journal of Social Welfare*, *15*, 209–218.

Detlefsen, L. (2012). Earnings inequality: Does the accounting period matter? *Journal of Applied Social Science Studies*, *132*, 297–321.

Dynan, K., Elmendorf, D., & Sichel, D. (2012). The evolution of household income volatility. *The B.E. Journal of Economic Analysis & Policy*, *12*, 1–42.

Finkel, Y., Artsev, Y., & Yitzhaki, S. (2006). Inequality measurement and the time structure of household income in Israel. *Journal of Economic Inequality*, *4*, 153–179.

Gibson, J., Huang, J., & Rozelle, S. (2001). Why is income inequality so low in China compared to other countries? The effect of household survey methods. *Economic Letters*, *71*, 329–333.

Hall, P. (1994). Methodology and theory for the Bootstrap. In R. Engle & D. McFadden (Eds.), *Handbook of econometrics* (Vol. 4, pp. 2341–2381). Amsterdam: Elsevier.

Morris, N., & Preston, I. (1986). Inequality, poverty and the redistribution of income. *Bulletin of Economic Research*, *38*, 277–344.

Nolan, B. (1987). *Income distribution and the macroeconomy*. Cambridge: Cambridge University Press.

Ruggles, P. (1990). *Drawing the line: Alternative poverty measures and their implications for public policy*. Washington, DC: The Urban Institute Press.

Ruggles, P., & Williams, R. (1989). Longitudinal measures of poverty: Accounting for income and assets over time. *Review of Income and Wealth*, 35, 225–244.

Schröder, C. (2012). The sensitivity of distributional measures to the income reference period. *Journal of Income Distribution*, *21*, 77–115.

Schröder, C., Goland, Y., & Yitzhaki, S. (2014). Inequality and the time structure of earnings: Evidence from Germany. *Journal of Economic Inequality*. (online first article). Retrieved from http://link.springer.com/article/10.1007/s10888-013-9260-9#page-1

Shorrocks, A. F. (1978). Income inequality and income mobility. *Journal of Economic Theory*, *19*, 376–393.

Shorrocks, A. F. (1981). Income stability in the United States. In N. A. Klevmarken & J. A. Lybeck (Eds.), *The statics and dynamics of income, Tieto*. Clevedon: Avon.

Trede, M. (1998). The age profile of mobility measures: An application to earnings in West Germany. *Journal of Applied Econometrics*, *13*, 397–409.

Wodon, Q., & Yitzhaki, S. (2003). Inequality and the accounting period. *Economics Bulletin*, *4*, 1–8.

TOURNAMENTS AND SUPERSTAR MODELS: A MIXTURE OF TWO PARETO DISTRIBUTIONS

Abdoul Aziz Junior Ndoye and Michel Lubrano

ABSTRACT

We provide a Bayesian inference for a mixture of two Pareto distributions which is then used to approximate the upper tail of a wage distribution. The model is applied to the data from the CPS Outgoing Rotation Group to analyze the recent structure of top wages in the United States from 1992 through 2009. We find an enormous earnings inequality between the very highest wage earners (the "superstars"), and the other high wage earners. These findings are largely in accordance with the alternative explanations combining the model of superstars and the model of tournaments in hierarchical organization structure. The approach can be used to analyze the recent pay gaps among top executives in large firms so as to exhibit the "superstar" effect.

Keywords: Pareto distribution; superstars; tournament theory; wage inequality

JEL classifications: D03; D33; D41; J31; J33

Economic Well-Being and Inequality: Papers from the Fifth ECINEQ Meeting
Research on Economic Inequality, Volume 22, 449–479

ISSN: 1049-2585/doi:10.1108/S1049-258520140000022015

INTRODUCTION

During the last three decades, the U.S. economic growth has experienced episodes of rapidly changing wage differentials characterized by a marked increase in wage inequality in the upper tail of the distribution. Various competing explanations of these earning inequalities have recently generated a heated debate. Common explanations among others attribute these changes to the increase in the wage premium for skilled relative to unskilled workers, to the changes in labor market institutions and in wage setting norms (Bound & Johnson, 1992; DiNardo, Fortin, & Lemieux, 1996; Katz & Autor, 1999; Mincer, 1993; Murphy & Welch, 1992). The recent empirical literature on the changing distribution of wages,[1] and, on the competitive market for Chief Executive Officers (CEOs) and on high compensations in financial markets[2] are contradicting these textbook explanations. These various explanations suggest that each part of the wage distribution is governed by a different logic, each part requiring different explanations. Burkhauser, Feng, Jenkins, and Larrimore (2008) emphasize that "if income inequality has been substantially increasing since 1993 in the U.S., such increases have been confined to the very upper tail of the income distribution." This makes alternative explanations of inequalities in the upper tail of the U.S. earning distribution a considerable challenge.

Atkinson (2008) suggests to combine the superstars model of Rosen (1981) with the hierarchical model of Simon (1957) and Lydall (1959). In addition, tournament theory[3] gives a supplementary motivation for explaining both the increase of the span of control in large firms and the wage gap of top performers.

In the tournament theory in hierarchical organizations, salaries depend on individual performance and are individually negotiated, so that each worker earns a constant multiple of the salary of the worker in the rank below him. This generates approximately a Pareto tail for the earnings distribution (as shown by Lydall, 1968). Tournament theory leads to high increment of salaries in the top rank making the changing of positions costly and difficult. As a consequence, only a small number of competitors will share prizes generated in multi-period tournaments leading to the "superstar" effect of Rosen (1981).

In the economics of superstars of Rosen (1981), individuals differ in their talents, which are assumed fixed, and small differences in talent may imply large differences in earnings. Adler (1985) extends the "superstar" model of Rosen (1981) and argues that factors other than talent, like popularity and charisma, may also expand the services of superstars. Frank and

Cook (1995) emphasize that the distribution of earnings of superstars stems largely from the growing prevalence of winner-take-all markets, which are in many cases the result of competitive forces. The distribution of earnings is then given by the maximum values generated by the results of many separate competitions. Exceeding a given high threshold value, the distribution takes a generalized Pareto form with a Pareto tail (Embrechts, Kluppelberg, & Mikosch, 1997).

Each type of earnings distribution in both models has a Pareto form, the combination of the two models leads naturally to a mixture of two Pareto distributions. This paper provides Bayesian inference for a mixture of two Pareto distributions in order to approximate the upper tail of a wage distribution. This mixture model is applied to the data from the CPS Outgoing Rotation Group to analyze the recent structure of top wages in the United States from 1992 through 2009. Our results show a rising wage inequality between the very highest wage earners (0.95 quantile) and the other high wage earners. These findings are largely in accordance with the explanations combining the model of superstars and the model of tournaments in hierarchical organization structure.

The remainder of the paper is organized as follows. The next section reviews the tournament theory in the hierarchical organization model of Simon (1957) and Lydall (1959), the superstar model of Rosen (1981) and shows how a mixture of two Pareto distributions emerges. The section "Mixture of Pareto Distributions" provides Bayesian inference for the model represented by a mixture of two Pareto distributions. The section on "Empirical Application" presents a truncated sample procedure and illustrates our approach using the CPS-ORG sample from 1992 to 2009. The last section concludes and points out the inferential statistical problems of a mixture of Pareto.

TOURNAMENTS, SUPERSTARS, HIERARCHIES, AND PARETO DISTRIBUTIONS

Simon (1957) and Lydall (1959) model a pyramidal employment structure where each worker has subordinates and where pay increases by a constant increment as one advances up on the ladder. The ratio between the number of supervisors in each rank and the number of persons below this rank is constant. The structure and the number of jobs are relatively fixed and remunerations are closely dependent on the rank $t \in [1,n]$ in the hierarchy rather than being dependent on the individual performance. If s is a fixed span of control and N_t the total number of subordinates at each rank t, we have the recurrence relation $N_{t+1} = sN_t$. And, the salary of a supervisor of any level in the hierarchy is directly related to the aggregate salary of the persons whom he controls. If the salary of each grade of employee is w_t and i a fixed increment of salary when moving up to the next step of the ladder, the wage structure is given by $w_{t+1} = (1+i)w_t$.

With these assumptions, Lydall (1968) shows that the distribution of earnings in a hierarchical organization can be approximated by a Pareto distribution with exponent α corresponding to the slope of the plot of the logarithm of the number of persons in each grade (log N_t) against the logarithm of the salary appropriate to that grade (log w_t):

$$\alpha = \frac{\log(N_{t+1}/N_t)}{\log(w_{t+1}/w_t)} = \frac{\log s}{\log(1+i)} \tag{1}$$

The Gini index I_G has an analytical expression for the Pareto distribution and depends only on the Pareto coefficient α, so that $I_G = 1/(2\alpha - 1)$, $\alpha > 0.5$. This suggests that, a rise in wage inequality in a hierarchical organization corresponds to a decrease of the Pareto coefficient, α. This can be caused either by an increase in the increment prize i or a decrease in the span of control s.

Tournament Theory and the Hierarchical Model

Rosen (1981) and Lazear and Rosen (1981) show that an optimal tournament dominates other forms of remuneration schemes adopted by firms. In tournament theory, firms are willing to pay extremely large compensation differences to those situated in the top ranks of the hierarchy in order to create adequate incentives for employees. These large pay differences are supposed to induce greater efforts and performances for employees who seek to increase their chances of promotion (Brian, Charles, & James, 1993; Rosen, 1986). The highest rank corresponds to the highest salary, so the main prize of this competition is the top executive's job.

We now introduce the simple assignment model (see Sattinger, 1993; Tervio, 2008 or Gabaix & Landier, 2008) for top rank managers pay in the previous model of large hierarchical organizations. In this tournament model, we consider a set of n ordered positions labeled by t, and determined by the expected talent of managers. The market capitalization of the firm is characterized by its size denoted by S. The manager indexed by its rank t has an expected talent $T(t)$ and receives a total compensation $w(T(t))=w(t)$. If C is the effect of talent on earnings, then $CS^{\gamma}T(t)$ is the firm value generated by the overhead t. For a fixed high compensation, the firm chooses its potential CEO so as to maximize his net impact:

$$\max_{t} \; CS^{\gamma}T(t) - w(t) \tag{2}$$

In a competitive equilibrium, the manager t who is expected to be the most talented is ranked at the top, so that $t=n$. The first order condition implies that the marginal cost $w'(n)$ of the better manager is equal to the marginal benefit that he generates, that is:

$$w'(n) = CS^{\gamma}T'(n) \tag{3}$$

where a small difference in talent, dn, is such that $T'(n)\mathrm{d}n = T(n+\mathrm{d}n) - T(n)$.

In a hierarchical organization, tournaments suggest high compensation differences among the executive ranks of the structure. As a consequence, if the compensation is kept largely fixed at the top, this makes any organizational change costly and any position modification in the structure difficult. This leads to an increase in both the span of control s, and the salary of the top executives.

Gabaix and Landier (2008) develop an assignment model for CEOs' pay across different hierarchical organizations. In their model, CEOs have different talents and are matched to firms in a competitive assignment model. There is a set of N firms, each firm $n \in [1, N]$ has size $S(n)$. It is assumed that each firm has a potential CEO who is optimally chosen using the maximization program 2. In a competitive equilibrium, the classical assignment Eq. (3) holds.

Following extreme value theory, Gabaix and Landier (2008) emphasize that the size of the firm, $S(n)$ and the spacings in the upper tail of the talents, $T'(n)$ follow a Pareto distribution. That is, $S(n) = An^{-\alpha}$, and $T'(n) = -Bn^{\beta-1}$. They solve Eq. (3) and find that the reservation wage of at least one talented CEO is given by:

$$w(n) = \frac{A^{\gamma}BC}{\alpha\gamma - \beta} \times n^{-(\alpha\gamma+\beta)} \tag{4}$$

The reservation wage of talented CEO follows a Pareto distribution with coefficient $(\alpha\gamma + \beta)$. Then, the enormous CEO pay in large pyramidal organizations is consistent with "the superstar effect" of Rosen (1981).

However, Lazear and Rosen (1981)'s tournament theory is different from the superstar theory of Rosen (1981).

Superstars Model and Its Pareto Approximation

The economics of "superstars" has long been employed to explain wages of professional sport players or opera singers. However, in recent years, the superstar model has been employed in many other fields including academic research, scientific work, arts and architecture, financial markets, executives, and others.

Building on the insights of Marshall (1947),[4] Rosen (1981) introduced the superstar model to explain large earnings differentials induced by small differences in talent among performers. According to Rosen (1981) and Adler (1985), the development in communication, manufacturing technology, trade liberalization, and globalization allows to the most talented and popular performers to expand their services and to extract a rent that is related to the extent of the served market. For every superstar who receives a high earning, advanced payment in accordance to his talent or popularity which impacts to the vast audience he is able to reach, there are the others, many of them being nearly as talented, who never manage to even support themselves. This ensures a small number of top performers with extremely high earnings relative to their rivals.

The superstar model of Rosen (1981) is re-interpreted by Frank and Cook (1995) as a winner-take-all market. In a winner-take-all market, Frank and Cook (1995) suggest that runaway professional wages are the result not of a breakdown of competition but of the spread of markets in which the value of production depends primarily on the efforts of only a handful of top players, "superstars" who are paid accordingly. Frank and Cook (1995) emphasized that the distribution of earnings of top performers stems largely from the growing prevalence of winner-take-all markets, which are in many cases the result of competitive forces. In this case, the distribution of earnings is given by the maximum values generated by the results of many separate competitions. Exceeding a given high threshold value w_m, the distribution of earnings takes the form of a Pareto as shown by Embrechts et al. (1997) (or Gabaix & Landier, 2008), with coefficient α

such that the mean income higher than the threshold w_m, $E(w|w \geq w_m)$ is given by:

$$E(w) = w_m \frac{\alpha}{\alpha - 1} \Pi(w \geq w_m), \quad \alpha > 1$$

Atkinson (2008) suggests that a decline in the exponent of the Pareto distribution is the basis for the superstar explanation of rising earnings dispersion.

In the winner-takes-all market, the presence of superstars with significantly higher talent and popularity will reduce the efforts of other competitors. Brown (2011) studies the effects of incentives and strategies created by the presence of a superstar among golf professionals. He finds that the presence of *Tiger Woods* has a negative effect on the top half of the competitor field in terms of ability. This means that the earnings of the second best player depend on the reach of *Tiger Woods* and so on down the range of talents.

Similarly, tournament prizes in hierarchical organizations can create negative incentives, the presence of a talented executive can have a negative impact on the performance of many workers and thus commands a very high salary. This configuration leads to a decrease of the Pareto exponent in the superstar model.

What Do We Observe?

The distribution of earnings in the model of "superstars" (Rosen, 1981) and in the model of tournament in hierarchical organization (Lydall, 1959; Simon, 1957) has a Pareto form and their combination leads to a mixture of two Pareto. In the tournament theory in hierarchical organizations, salaries depend on individual performance and are individually negotiated. Lydall (1968) shows that for a fixed span of control, c, and a fixed increment of salary, i, the distribution of earnings can be approximated by a Pareto distribution with an exponent equal to $\ln(c)/\ln(1+i)$. The superstars theory of Rosen (1981) is re-interpreted by Frank and Cook (1995) as the "winner-takes-all" markets. In this model, extreme values theory suggests that for a sufficiently high threshold, the distribution of earnings takes a generalized Pareto form which has a Pareto tail (see for instance Embrechts et al., 1997). Using a reparametrization, a random variable of the generalized Pareto distribution can be transformed into that of the Pareto distribution. In addition, Gabaix and Landier (2008) provide a competitive assignment equilibrium model of CEO pay. Matching CEOs with different talents, they find a very small dispersion in CEO talent, which nonetheless justifies large pay differences. This exhibits the "superstars" effect. They demonstrate that the distribution of CEO pay takes a Frechet form which behaves like a Pareto for very high earnings. However, the superstar models leads in theory to a lower Pareto coefficient than the hierarchical model. For a given dataset, we observe two types of top wage formation. We can successfully test these models using a mixture of two Pareto distributions with significantly different Pareto parameters to distinguish the high wage earners and the very highest wage earners.

MIXTURE OF PARETO DISTRIBUTIONS

The Pareto density is very well documented in the literature (see, e.g., the review by Arnold, 2008, and the references quoted in). Mixtures of Pareto densities are on the contrary very scarcely covered and most of the time only particular cases are considered. Nadarajah (2006) considers the case of a mixture of two Pareto with a common scale parameter which is in fact equivalent to the double Pareto of Reed and Jorgenson (2004). Nair (2007) explores the properties of Pareto II mixtures for modelling income distribution and reliability analysis. However, he has constrained parameters for inference (see also Noor & Aslam, 2012). Bee, Benedetti, and Espa (2013) consider an unconstrained model of two Pareto I mixture. They report that the EM algorithm does not work in this case, confirming that inference for Pareto mixtures is not a simple task. We shall first review the Pareto process and Bayesian inference for this process. We will then investigate how Bayesian inference can be implemented for a mixture of two Pareto distributions.

Pareto Processes

A random variable Y is said to be distributed according to a Pareto law if its density is equal to:

$$f(y|\alpha, y_m) = \alpha y_m^{\alpha} y^{-(\alpha+1)} \Pi(y > y_m), \quad y_m > 0, \quad \alpha > 0$$

where $\Pi(\cdot)$ is the indicator function, y_m is a scale parameter and α a shape parameter, which is known as the tail index. The support of the Pareto density is defined over $[y_m, \infty)$, which means that the support of the density depends on a parameter. The first two moments are:

$$E(y) = \frac{\alpha}{\alpha - 1} y_m \quad \mathrm{Var}(y) = \frac{\alpha}{(\alpha - 1)^2(\alpha - 2)} y_m^2$$

and exist only for $\alpha > 1$ and $\alpha > 2$, respectively. The cumulative distribution is:

$$F(y) = (1 - y_m^{\alpha} y^{-\alpha}) \Pi(y > y_m)$$

Two sufficient statistics are provided by Min(y) and $\sum \log(y_i/y_m)$. Classical estimates are obtained by taking $\hat{y}_m = \mathrm{Min}(y)$ and $\hat{\alpha} = n / \sum \log(y_i/y_m)$.[5]

This is the Type I Pareto. The Pareto family is rather rich. Four variants are commonly reported and are particular cases of the Feller-Pareto distribution FP$(\mu, \sigma, \gamma, \alpha)$ which is obtained as the ratio of two Gamma distributions U_1 and U_2 with:

$$W = \mu + \sigma \left(\frac{U_1}{U_2} \right)^{\gamma}$$

where $U_1 \sim \Gamma(1, 1)$ and $U_2 \sim \Gamma(\alpha, 1)$. The Pareto I corresponds to FP$(y_m, y_m, 1, \alpha)$. Simple Bayesian inference is not available for the Pareto II–IV as underlined by Arnold (2008). So that in practice, only the Pareto I is commonly used.

Bayesian Inference for the Pareto I Process

Bayesian inference for the Pareto process was treated in a number of papers, starting with Lwin (1972) and Arnold and Press (1983). Arnold (2008) details a Gibbs sampler after a re-parametrization in $\tau = 1/y_m$, where τ is called a precision parameter. This parametrization is convenient for Bayesian inference because both a Pareto prior on τ and a Gamma prior on α are natural conjugates when the other parameter is considered as fixed. The conditional posterior of τ is itself a Pareto density, while the conditional posterior of α is a Gamma density. However, a Pareto prior on τ is difficult to interpret while a prior on y_m has a natural sample interpretation. It is possible to keep the usual parametrization of the Pareto process if we choose the prior on y_m as a power function density.

Power Functions

A random variable X is said to have a power function distribution if its probability density function is defined as

$$p(x) = \alpha x_m^{-\alpha} x^{\alpha-1} \Pi(x < x_m), \quad \alpha > 0, \quad x_m > 0$$

It is an increasing function of x when $\alpha > 1$ (decreasing when $0 < \alpha < 1$) and is defined over $[0, x_m]$. Its moments are:

$$E(x) = \frac{\alpha}{\alpha+1} x_m \quad \mathrm{Var}(x) = \frac{\alpha}{(\alpha+1)^2(\alpha+2)} x_m^2$$

and always exist, contrary to the Pareto process. The cumulative distribution function is:

$$F(x) = x_m^{-\alpha} x^{\alpha} \Pi(x < x_m)$$

Two sufficient statistics are provided by Max(y) and $\sum \log(y_i/y_m)$.[6] If x has a power function distribution in (α, x_m), then $y = 1/x$ is distributed according to a Pareto(α, y_m) where $y_m = 1/x_m$. We have chosen to present separately this distribution even if it corresponds to a simple transformation of the Pareto I because we shall use its properties and moments to elicit a prior information.

Likelihood Function and Prior Densities

Let us consider a sample $(y_1, \ldots, y_n)$ of n observations of the Pareto random variable Y. The likelihood function of this sample is:

$$L(y; \alpha, y_m) = \alpha^n y_m^{\alpha n} \prod y_i^{-(\alpha+1)} \Pi(y_{(1)} > y_m)$$

where $y_{(1)}$ is the first order statistics, that is, the minimum of the sample. It is convenient to rewrite this likelihood function as:

$$L(y; \alpha, y_m) = \alpha^n \ \exp\Big\{ -(\alpha+1) \sum \log(y_i) + \alpha n \log(y_m) \Big\} \Pi(y_{(1)} > y_m)$$

It is clear that the Pareto distribution does not belong to the exponential family when its two parameters are unknown, just because the support depends on one of the parameters. However, from this writing, we can find that $y_{(1)}$ and $\sum \log(y_i)$ are two sufficient statistics. And, conditionally on y_m known, the Pareto does belong to the exponential family. Following Arnold and Press (1983), we propose to use an independent prior $p(\alpha, y_m) = p(\alpha)p(y_m)$. We shall discuss and justify this choice in a separate subsection.

When y_m is known, $\log(y/y_m)$ is distributed according to an exponential distribution. In this case, the natural conjugate prior for α is the Gamma density with ν_0 degrees of freedom and as scale parameter α_0:

$$p(\alpha|\nu_0, \alpha_0) \propto \alpha^{\nu_0 - 1} \exp(-\alpha\alpha_0), \quad E(\alpha) = \nu_0/\alpha_0, \quad \mathrm{Var}(\alpha) = \nu_0/\alpha_0^2$$

A non-informative prior corresponds to letting the prior parameters go to the limit of their domain of definition with $\alpha_0 = 0$ and $\nu_0 = 0$:

$$p(\alpha) \propto \frac{1}{\alpha}$$

When α is known, it is also possible to find a convenient conjugate prior for y_m. As we adopt the same parameterization as given by Arnold and Press (1983), the conjugate prior is a Power function distribution with shape parameter α_0 and scale parameter y_{m0}:

$$p(y_m|\gamma_0, y_{m0}) = \gamma_0 y_{m0}^{-\gamma_0} y_m^{\gamma_0 - 1} \Pi(y_m < y_{m0})$$

A non-informative prior is obtained for $\gamma_0 = 0$, and letting y_{m0} go to infinity:

$$p(y_m) \propto \frac{1}{y_m}$$

Alternative Prior Distributions

From a probabilistic point of view, the natural way of specifying a prior is to consider a joint prior on all the parameters. A joint prior in a natural conjugate prior is a convenient tool as it combines easily with the sufficient statistics of the sample. It leads to simple posteriors in the linear regression model. An independent prior on the regression parameter might lead to more complicated posteriors in this simple model (see, e.g., Drèze, 1977). However, a joint natural conjugate prior has a tendency to hide possible conflicts between the sample and the prior information, whereas an independent prior would not. Following Bauwens (1991), a joint natural conjugate prior can lead to some pathologies in the case of partial non-informativeness.

We are here in a special case with the Pareto I process. It has two parameters, a shape parameter α and a scale parameter y_m which is in fact a minimum bound of the observations. Since this parameter depends on the support of the density, the Pareto process does not belong to the exponential family, except when the minimum bound is fixed. Despite this pathology, Lwin (1972) managed to propose a joint prior density for (α,y_m) which combines nicely with the sample. However, this prior has some particular features that can make it not attractive. First, it is parameterized as $p(\alpha, y_m)=p(\alpha)p(y_m|\alpha)$. In the Pareto process, it is more natural to start eliciting a prior on y_m in terms of a boundary and then independently eliciting a prior on the shape parameter α, for instance in terms of a Gini coefficient, $1/(2\alpha-1)$. Second, as amply underlined by Arnold and Press (1983), when using this joint prior, the marginal posterior density of y_m is unbounded with no sample information being able to remove this feature. On the contrary, with independent priors on α and y_m, first the marginal posteriors have simpler expressions (even if their evaluation requires numerical integration) and second, a slight prior information on y_m removes the unboundedness of the marginal posterior of y_m as we shall see below. Another advantage of these independent priors on α and y_m is that they combine easily with the likelihood function, leading to simple conditional posterior densities leading to a simple Gibbs sampler algorithm for inference in a mixture of two Pareto densities. Finally, we should note that Arnold, Castillo, and Sarabia (1998) have proposed for many models and in particular for the Pareto process a specific bivariate prior that has the independent priors of Arnold and Press (1983, 1989) and the bivariate prior of Lwin (1972), as particular cases (see also Arnold, Castillo, & Sarabia, 1999; Arnold, Castillo, & Sarabia, 2001). This prior is very convenient for comparing the influence of the different parametrizations. From the application reported by Arnold and Press (1989), there does not seem to be a major difference.

Alternative Parametrizations

The parametrization for inference in the Pareto process is not a settled matter. Arnold and Press (1983) adopt the parameterization α, y_m and note that with this parametrization the joint prior of Lwin (1972) leads to an unbounded marginal posterior of y_m at the boundary zero. They note that a reparametrization in $\tau = 1/y_m$ would solve the problem. However, they argue that the natural parametrization in y_m is much easier both to elicit and to interpret. As a matter of fact, and especially when in a mixture of two Pareto densities, a marginal prior on y_m is easy to elicit in terms of a minimum bound first and then in terms of a point of discontinuity between the two Pareto members. Once the support of the two Pareto members is elicited, it is easier to elicit the two α's in terms of a Gini coefficient for each member. For the single Pareto I, Arnold and Press (1989) adopt the parametrization $\tau = 1/y_m$ together with a modified Lwin's (1972) prior in $\alpha|y_m$ and τ and note that using this parametrization, the pathological behavior of the original Lwin's (1972) prior disappears. However, they maintain their criticism against the use of a joint prior on α and τ instead of two independent priors on each parameter. Arnold (2008) adopts the parametrization in $x > y_m$ for presenting the process and detailing Bayesian inference with independent priors using a Gibbs sampler. Introducing the conditionally conjugate priors of Arnold et al. (1998), they turn to the parametrization in terms of τ without much discussion. We could conclude that the parametrization in τ is more convenient for the modified Lwin's prior (Arnold & Press, 1989) while the parametrization in y_m is more convenient when using independent marginal priors in the context of mixtures.

Joint Posterior Densities

Arnold and Press (1983) have conducted Bayesian inference when both α and y_m are unknown. They derived analytical expressions for the two marginal densities of α and y_m, using independent informative priors. Those marginals do not belong to any class of known densities as we have:

$$p(\alpha|y) \propto \left(\alpha + \frac{\gamma_0}{n}\right)^{-1} \alpha^{n+\nu_0-1} \exp\left(-\alpha\left(\alpha_0 + \sum \log(y_i) - n \log \min(y_{m0}, y_{(1)})\right)\right)$$

$$p(y_m|y) \propto y_m^{\gamma_0 - 1}\left(1 - \frac{n}{\alpha_0 + \sum \log y_i} \log y_m\right)^{n+\nu_0} \Pi(y_m < \min(y_{(1)}, y_{m0})$$

The sole point of interest of these posteriors is to point out that the marginal posterior of y_m is ill-behaved when $\gamma_0 \leq 1$. So, we are obliged to have an informative prior on y_m.

Integrating these two posteriors for finding moments for instance is a cumbersome task (Arnold & Press, 1983, provide approximations). So, as it is possible to find well-defined conditional posteriors, a Gibbs sampler is the privileged route.

Conditional Posteriors

The conditional posterior of α given y_m is:

$$p(\alpha|y_m, y) \propto \alpha^{n+\nu_0-1} \exp\left(-\alpha\left(\sum \log(y_i) + \alpha_0 - n \log(y_m)\right)\right)$$

This is a Gamma density $G(a_*, v_*)$ where:

$$\nu_* = \nu_0 + n \quad \alpha_* = \alpha_0 + \sum \log(y_i/y_m)$$

The conditional posterior of y_m given α is obtained by neglecting all the elements which are independent of y_m in the product of the likelihood function times the prior:

$$p(y_m|y, \alpha) \propto y_m^{\alpha n+\gamma_0-1} \Pi(y_m < y_i) \Pi(y_m < y_{m0})$$

We identify a Power function density $PF(g_*, y_{m*})$ with parameters:

$$\gamma_* = \gamma_0 + n\alpha \quad y_{m*} = \mathrm{Max}(\mathrm{Min}(y_i), y_{m0})$$

We note that the support of the conditional posterior density y_{m*} depends on the minimum value of the sample and on the value of y_{m0}. Collecting these results, inference on α and y_m is conducted using a Gibbs sampler. If y_m were given, inference would rely only on the Gamma posterior density $p(\alpha|y_m, y)$.

Motivations for Considering a Mixture of Two Pareto Distributions

We now analyze the statistical characterization of a mixture of two Pareto I distributions. As we have seen earlier, this model is justified by the use of a combination of tournament and superstars theories for high wage formation. This is the joint model sketched by Atkinson (2008, pp. 93–95). Of course, a Pareto concerns only the upper tail of the income distribution (which is here our main interest). We have truncated the lower incomes and even more. We could have considered hybrid mixtures of lognormal and Pareto distributions. Harrison (1981) for instance considers both the lognormal and the Pareto distribution to analyze the earning distribution in the United Kingdom for 1972 coming from the New Earnings Survey. But he estimates separately these two distributions, considering truncated data. We have tried to implement an hybrid lognormal-Pareto mixture, but we could identify only one Pareto tail. So, the resulting statistical model was not in coherence with our economic model, certainly because one of the lognormal tails played the role of a Pareto tail. Mitzenmacher (2004) shows that a lognormal distribution can exhibit a Pareto tail by expanding its shape parameter, σ^2.

Mixtures of Two Pareto Distributions

A mixture of two distributions for the random variable Y consists in considering two random variables: the observed values of Y and an unobserved random variable Z which is assumed to follow a binomial process that allocates the observations between the two regimes. The conditional distribution of observation y_i given the value of z_i is simplify:

$$y_i|z_i = j \sim f_j(y|\theta_j)$$

If we now consider the marginal distribution of Y, when Z is integrated out, we have the usual mixture formulation:

$$f_Y(y|\theta) = pf_1(y|\theta_1) + (1-p)f_2(y|\theta_2)$$

with a probability mixing weight p. The conditional probability that $z_i = j$, with $j = 1, 2$, given each observation y_i is obtained as a normalized ratio:

$$P(z_i = 1|Y = y) = \frac{pf_1(y|\theta_1)}{pf_1(y|\theta_1) + (1-p)f_2(y|\theta_2)}$$

This formulation corresponds to the general case where every observation has the same marginal probability p of belonging to the first member. It is used to build a Gibbs sampler in a Bayesian framework or an EM algorithm in a classical framework.

A Pareto mixture is a slightly different case, as the support of each member depends on a parameter. In a Bayesian framework, Noor and Aslam (2012) propose to analyze the following two-member rescaled Pareto II mixture:

$$f(y|\alpha_1, \alpha_2, \lambda, p) = p\alpha_1 \frac{\lambda^{\alpha_1}}{(\lambda + y)^{(\alpha_1 + 1)}} \Pi(y > 0) + (1 - p)\alpha_2 \frac{\lambda^{\alpha_2}}{(\lambda + y)^{(\alpha_2 + 1)}} \Pi(y > 0)$$

But we note that in this formulation the two members have the same support where y and λ are just restricted to be positive. Moreover, Noor and Aslam (2012) assume that λ is known, so that their final model is a particular case of a mixture of two Pareto I densities.

The type of mixture we are interested in is slightly different and more general as we consider the case with different shape and scale parameters as given by Bee et al. (2013):

$$f(y|\alpha_1, \alpha_2, y_{m1}, y_{m2}, p) = p\alpha_1 \frac{y_{m1}^{\alpha_1}}{y^{(\alpha_1 + 1)}} \Pi(y > y_{m1}) + (1 - p)\alpha_2 \frac{y_{m2}^{\alpha_2}}{y^{(\alpha_2 + 1)}} \Pi(y > y_{m2}) \quad (5)$$

In Eq. (5) the two components have a different support, so it is natural to assume for instance that $y_{m2} > y_{m1}$, even if y_{m2} could be as close as possible from y_{m1} which thus corresponds to the minimum observation of the complete sample (this is also the assumption made by Bee et al., 2013). In this framework, the first member is concerned with observations greater than y_{m1} while the second component corresponds to observations greater than y_{m2}. So, any observation y_i such that $y_{m1} < y_i < y_{m2}$ belongs to the first regime with probability 1 and not with probability p. It is not surprising that under these conditions, Bee et al. (2013) report that the usual EM algorithm does not work for estimating the five parameters of Eq. (5) and works only when y_{m2} is known. Bee et al. (2013) proved that in the bivariate case, the EM algorithm does not update the value found for the estimation of y_{m2}. In the M step, the objective function is not differentiable in y_{m2}.

This motivates our concern for presenting first a Gibbs sampler when y_{m2} is fixed and given a priori. We shall then try to investigate the case where both y_{m1} and y_{m2} are unknown in order to see if a prior information on y_{m2} is enough in order to get convergence of the Gibbs sampler.

Remark:

The mixture we consider is that of Bee et al.'s (2013) and implicitly also that of Atkinson's (2008, pp. 93–95). However, as we suppose that $y_{m2} > y_{m1}$, we could have also consider a hybrid mixture of a Pareto I and a generalized Pareto. The argument might be derived from Pickands (1975) and extreme value theory. The generalized Pareto that Pickands (1975) (see also Arnold, 2008) considers is:

$$f(x|\beta,\sigma) = \frac{1}{\sigma}\left(1+\beta\frac{x}{\sigma}\right)^{-(1+\beta)/\beta}\Pi(x>0,\beta x>\sigma), \quad \beta, \quad \sigma>0$$

It also corresponds to a particular case of the Pareto II which is:

$$f(x|\alpha,\sigma,y_{m2}) = \frac{\alpha}{\sigma}\left[1+\frac{x-y_{m2}}{\sigma}\right]^{-(\alpha+1)}\Pi(x>y_{m2})$$

and that it collapses down to the Pareto I for $\sigma = y_{m2}$. This density is not convenient for inference as it is not possible to find sufficient statistics as underlined by Arnold and Press (1983). So, a mixture combining a Pareto I and a Pareto II would not be a convenient model. We prefer to stick to the original model of Bee et al. (2013).

For the moment, let us give in Fig. 1 a graphical representation of Eq. (5) with $p = 0.80$, $\alpha_1 = 3$, $y_{m1} = 30$, $\alpha_2 = 1$, and $y_{m2} = 80$. A mixture of two densities is usually a smooth function of y. The very particular shape of the Pareto and the fact that its support is parameter dependent produce a discontinuity in the graph which is well present here at $y = y_{m2}$. The height of the discontinuity depends on the value of $1-p$. So, a small jump is coherent with a large p.

Bayesian Inference for y_{m2} *Known*

If y_{m2} is known, we have a conceptual simplification of the problem. We are in one of the cases investigated by Bee et al. (2013) in a classical framework. Let us consider an observation y_i. If $y_i < y_{m2}$, then for sure, this observation belongs to the first component of the mixture. If $y_i > y_{m2}$, there

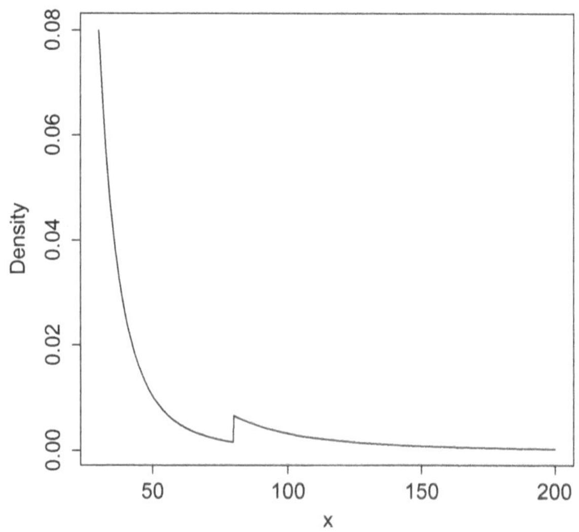

Fig. 1. Mixture of Two Pareto.

is a certain probability that it belongs to the first regime and a complementary probability that it belongs to the second regime. The probability $P(z_i = j|Y = y_i)$ can be computed only for the observations for which $y_i > y_{m2}$. Consequently, the random allocation of the observations between the two regimes which is at the heart of the usual Gibbs sampler in mixture problems can only be applied for that part of the sample. Because the support of the density depends on the parameters, we have a different sample allocation, different from the usual algorithm.

As in the usual framework, we introduce a Beta prior on p with prior parameters n_{o1} and n_{o2}. The prior moments of p are:

$$E(p) = \frac{n_{o1}}{n_{o1} + n_{o2}} \quad \mathrm{Var}(p) = \frac{n_{o1} n_{o2}}{(n_{o1} + n_{o2})^2 (n_{o1} + n_{o2} + 1)}$$

The posterior density of p is also a Beta density with posterior parameters $n_{o1} + n_1$ and $n_{o2} + n_2$. n_1 and n_2 are the number of observations that conditionally on z fall into each regime. n_{1_r} represents the number of observations that are randomly allocated to the first regime as a function of z, while n_{1_s} represents the number of observations that are for sure allocated to the first regime because they are lower than y_{m2}, so that $n_1 = n_{1s} + n_{1r}$. We propose the following algorithm:

Gibbs Sampler Algorithm with y_{m2} *Known*

1. Fix a value for the total number of draws m, fix a value for y_{m2}, select a starting value for p, and compute the following starting values $y_{m1} = y_{(1)}$, $\alpha_1 = \hat{\alpha}(y_{m1})$, $\alpha_2 = \hat{\alpha}(y_{m2})$.
2. Determine the vector of observations $y_{1s}|y<y_{m2}$ that belong for sure to the first regime. The Gibbs sampler will run only for the remaining vector of observations $y_{12}|y>y_{m2}$ as y_{m2} is given and fixed.
3. Start the loop on j, the Gibbs iterations.
4. For the remaining observations, simulate the sample allocation $z^{(j)}$ where each element is drawn according to a Binomial$(z_i|p_i)$ with base probability:

$$p_i = \frac{p^{(j-1)} f_1(y_{12i}|\alpha_1^{(j-1)}, y_{m1}^{(j-1)})}{p^{(j-1)} f_1(y_{12i}|\alpha_1^{(j-1)}, y_{m1}^{(j-1)}) + (1 - p^{(j-1)}) f_2(y_{12i}|\alpha_2^{(j-1)}, y_{m2}^{(j-1)})}$$

5. Select the sub-sample separation $y_{1r}^{(j)}$ and $y_{2r}^{(j)}$ among the y_{12}.
6. Form the first regime allocation $y_1^{(j)} = (y_{1s}, y_{1r}^{(j)})$ which is partially fixed and the second regime allocation $y_2^{(j)} = y_{2r}^{(j)}$ which is random.
7. Compute $n_1^{(j)} = n_{1s}^{(j)} + n_{1r}^{(j)}$ and $n_2^{(j)}$.
8. Draw $p^{(j)} \sim \text{Beta}(n_1^{(j)} + n_{o1}, n_2^{(j)} + n_{o2})$.
9. Draw $y_{m1}^{(j)} \sim \text{Power}(n_1^{(j)} * \alpha_1^{(j-1)} + \gamma_1^o, \text{Max}(\text{Min}(y_1^{(j)}), y_{mo_1}))$.
10. Draw $\alpha_1^{(j)} \sim \text{Gamma}(\alpha_1^o + \sum \log(y_1^{(j)}/y_{m1}^{(j)}), \nu_{01} + n_1)$.
11. Draw $\alpha_2^{(j)} \sim \text{Gamma}(\alpha_2^o + \sum \log(y_2^{(j)}/y_{m2}^{(j)}), \nu_{02} + n_2)$.
12. $j = j+1$ End of loop.

As a check, we have simulated a sample of size $n = 1{,}000$ with $y_{m1} = 30$, $y_{m2} = 80$, $\alpha_1 = 3$, $\alpha_2 = 2$, and $p = 0.80$. We have chosen a rather weak prior information with $y_{mo} = (30, 80)$ and $\gamma_o = (1, 1)$ for the Power prior on y_m and $\nu_o = (5, 5)$, $\alpha_o = (1, 2)$ for the Gamma prior on α and $n_o = (1, 1)$ for the Beta prior on p. We took 3,000 + 500 draws for the Gibbs. We get $E(\alpha_1|y) = 2.98$, (0.15), $E(\alpha_2|y) = 2.10$, (0.17), $E(y_{m1}|y) = 30.01$, (0.012), and $E(p|y) = 0.83$, (0.016), which all are close to the values used for the generating process. The algorithm converges without any problem, as checked with CUMSUM graphs.

Bayesian Inference for Both y_{m1} *and* y_{m2} *Unknown*

Considering y_{m2} as a random parameter modifies slightly the previous algorithm. The observations that belong for sure to the first component of the mixture, $y_{1s}|y<y_{m2}$ have to be determined at each iteration, for each random value of y_{m2}. So once y_{m2} is drawn, the algorithm follows the same logic.

General Gibbs Sampler Algorithm

1. Fix a value for the total number of draws m, fix a value for y_{m2}, select a starting value for p, and compute the following starting values $y_{m1} = y_{(1)}$, $\alpha_1 = \hat{\alpha}(y_{m1})$, $\alpha_2 = \hat{\alpha}(y_{m2})$.
2. Start the loop on j, the Gibbs iterations.
3. Determine the observations $y_{1s}|y<y_{m2}$ that belong for sure to the first regime for a given draw of y_{m2}. Determine the remaining observations $y_{12}|y>y_{m2}$.
4. For the remaining observations y_{12}, simulate the sample allocation $z^{(j)}$ where each element is drawn according to a Binomial($z_i|p_i$) with base probability:

$$p_i = \frac{p^{(j-1)} f_1(y_{12i}|\alpha_1^{(j-1)}, y_{m1}^{(j-1)})}{p^{(j-1)} f_1(y_{12i}|\alpha_1^{(j-1)}, y_{m1}^{(j-1)}) + (1-p^{(j-1)}) f_2(y_{12i}|\alpha_2^{(j-1)}, y_{m2}^{(j-1)})}$$

5. Select the sub-sample separation $y_{1r}^{(j)}$ and $y_{2r}^{(j)}$ among the y_{12}.
6. Form the first regime allocation $y_1^{(j)} = (y_{1s}, y_{1r}^{(j)})$ and the second regime allocation $y_2^{(j)} = y_{2r}^{(j)}$.
7. Compute $n_1^{(j)} = n_{1s}^{(j)} + n_{1r}^{(j)}$ and $n_2^{(j)}$.
8. Draw $p^{(j)} \sim \text{Beta}(n_1^{(j)} + n_{o1}, n_2^{(j)} + n_{o2})$.
9. Draw $y_{m1}^{(j)} \sim \text{Power}(n_1^{(j)} * \alpha_1^{(j-1)} + \gamma_1^o, \text{Max}(\text{Min}(y_1^{(j)}), y_{mo_1}))$.
10. Draw $y_{m2}^{(j)} \sim \text{Power}(n_2^{(j)} * \alpha_2^{(j-1)} + \gamma_2^o, \text{Max}(\text{Min}(y_2^{(j)}), y_{mo_2}))$.
11. Draw $\alpha_1^{(j)} \sim \text{Gamma}(\alpha_1^o + \sum \log(y_1^{(j)}/y_{m1}^{(j)}), \nu_{01} + n_1)$.
12. Draw $\alpha_2^{(j)} \sim \text{Gamma}(\alpha_2^o + \sum \log(y_2^{(j)}/y_{m2}^{(j)}), \nu_{02} + n_2)$.
13. $j = j+1$ End of loop.

Using the same parameters to draw the random sample and the same prior information as before, we manage to have a similar convergence of the algorithm. Again with 3,000 + 500 draws for the Gibbs, we get

$E(\alpha_1|y) = 3.09$, (0.16), $E(\alpha_2|y) = 2.13$, (0.16), $E(y_{m1}|y) = 29.99$, (0.012), $E(y_{m2}|y) = 80.05$, (0.41), and $E(p|y) = 0.80$, (0.015). Of course, there is more uncertainty for the estimation of y_{m2} than for y_{m1}. This is why at least a weak prior information is needed.

We have now to explore the role of the prior information to insure a proper behavior of the posterior density of the scale parameters y_m. First of all, in order to have a proper posterior, we must have $\gamma_1^o, \gamma_2^o > 1$, so as to avoid having a sample configuration where the Power function could have a shape parameter lower than 1, leading to a bimodal posterior (see Arnold & Press, 1983 for a similar result). Second, apparently any value for y_{mo1} between 0 and $\text{Min}(y_i)$ can be chosen without any influence on the results. This is due to the way one part of the observations in regime 1 is chosen and to the expression for the conditional posterior density of y_{m1}. Choosing a $y_{mo1} > \text{Min}(y_i)$ does have an influence on the posterior results and eventually leads to an abnormal termination of the algorithm. The case of y_{mo2} is of course more delicate. For values of y_{mo2}, greater than the value used for generating the data, the algorithm either does not converge or converges to wrong values. For values of y_{mo2} lower than that used for generating the data, the algorithm converges to reasonable values and seems to be rather insensitive to the choice of y_{mo2}, provided this choice is not too far from the truth (between 50 and 80 in our case). The other priors seem to play only a minor role. These simulation examples are rather encouraging, especially when comparing them to the usual EM algorithm (see Fig. 2 below).

Eliciting Prior Information

It is very difficult to estimate a mixture without prior information and the usual practice consists in computing sample moments and using them to provide identical information for each mixture component, at the cost of favoring label switching. For a Pareto mixture, we have some extra tools, one of which being the graph of $\log(1-\hat{F})$ versus $\log(y)$. A natural estimate for the cumulative distribution F is very easy to obtain. The Pareto distribution belongs to the power family and thus its log is an affine function of $\log(y)$. The regression of $\log(1-\hat{F})$ over $\log(y)$ is a common device to estimate the Pareto coefficient. The situation is slightly more complex here as the complementary cumulative distribution is given by:

$$1 - F(y) = p(y_{m1}^{\alpha_1} y^{-\alpha_1})\Pi(y > y_{m1}) + (1-p)(y_{m2}^{\alpha_2} y^{-\alpha_2})\Pi(y > y_{m2})$$

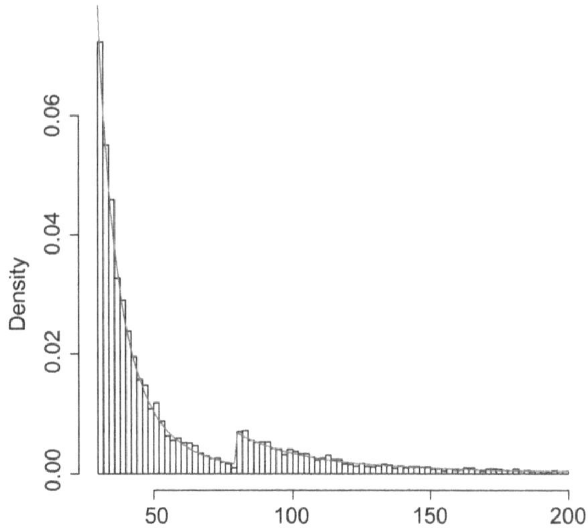

Fig. 2. Fitting a Mixture of Two Pareto Distributions.

Taking the log of this expression of course is not similar to taking the log of the complementary distribution of a single Pareto because we have a sum of two elements. So, we cannot infer the same type of information as we could derive from the same graph corresponding to a single Pareto process. However, we can infer information on the localization of y_{m2}. This can be checked with our simulated sample as shown in Fig. 3. The vertical line corresponds to $x = \log(80)$. There is a clear kink in the curve corresponding to y_{m2}. So, this type of graph can be used to determine a prior value for y_{m2} which is a crucial information as we have shown before. But it cannot be used to extract further information on the value of the Pareto coefficients.

EMPIRICAL APPLICATION: TOP EARNINGS INEQUALITY IN THE UNITED STATES 1992–2009

Over the past two decades, the United States experienced a sharp rise in wage inequality accompanied by large increase in wage differentials in the upper tail. We illustrate the approach developed above by approximating the upper tail of the U.S. wage distribution by a mixture of two Pareto distributions.

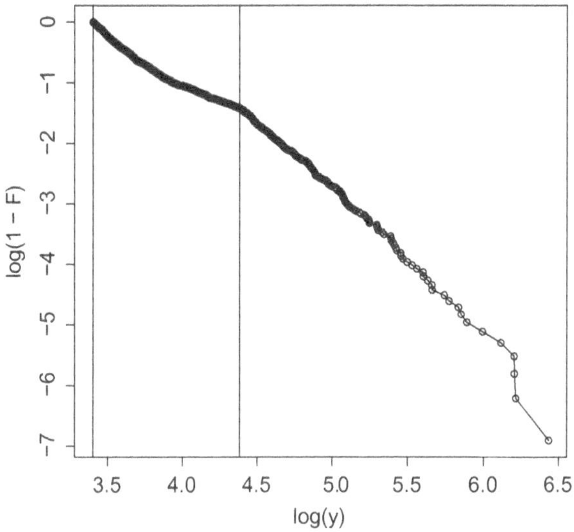

Fig. 3. A Log-Log Plot of the Complementary Cumulative Distribution of *Y*.

The Data

This paper uses the Current Population Surveys (CPS),[7] Outgoing Rotation Groups (ORG).[8] We take the monthly earnings files for January 1992 through May 2009. We decide to focus our attention on three years (1992, 2001, 2009) to cover the main features of the recent period and their evolution. We use the weekly wage divided by the number of hours worked in order to get an homogeneous definition of hourly wages.[9] We deflate these wages by the annual average CPI which values are respectively 140.2, 177.1, and 214.5 for these three years.

Between 1992 and 2009, we have a constant rise of real wage together with a sharp increase in inequality in the upper tail at the end of the period. As displayed in Table 1, we should notice that the number of respondents in 2009 is much lower (by 20%) than in 1992 and 2001. This might create a selection bias. However, we shall see in Table 2 that when we restrict our attention to the upper tail, the number of respondents becomes quite comparable over the different samples.

In Fig. 4, we display a non-parametric estimate of the wage density, which is characterized by a heavy right tail. Even if it is difficult to have a precise estimate of this tail, we can have a glance at the huge difference contained in the 2009 data.

Table 1. Hourly Real Wage Dispersion for the U.S. Recent Period.

	1992	2001	2009
Mean	18.00	20.05	24.49
Median	14.52	15.53	15.62
$q_{0.75}$	22.21	24.22	26.49
$q_{0.90}$	31.37	36.01	46.12
$q_{0.95}$	39.75	46.57	67.25
$q_{0.99}$	63.32	77.62	144.23
Gini	0.352	0.369	0.455
N	62,107	63,409	47,837
% of Female	53.03	52.43	52.34

Table 2. Top Wage Dispersion in the Upper Tail of the U.S. Wage Distribution.

	1992		2001		2009	
Min	25.80	(0.828)	24.55	(0.764)	22.20	(0.673)
q_{25}	28.67	(0.868)	28.52	(0.823)	27.00	(0.755)
Mean	39.83	(0.951)	41.42	(0.931)	49.26	(0.913)
Median	33.10	(0.912)	33.76	(0.881)	34.60	(0.836)
q_{75}	41.99	(0.958)	43.66	(0.939)	50.48	(0.918)
q_{90}	55.17	(0.985)	58.23	(0.977)	75.00	(0.967)
q_{95}	65.33	(0.992)	72.76	(0.988)	110.55	(0.984)
q_{99}	122.31	(0.998)	141.30	(0.998)	278.05	(0.997)
Gini	0.214		0.240		0.352	
N	11,079		14,945		15,634	
% of Female	46.65		45.10		45.60	

Note: In parenthesis, we have given the position of the left number in the original un-truncated distribution of hourly wages.

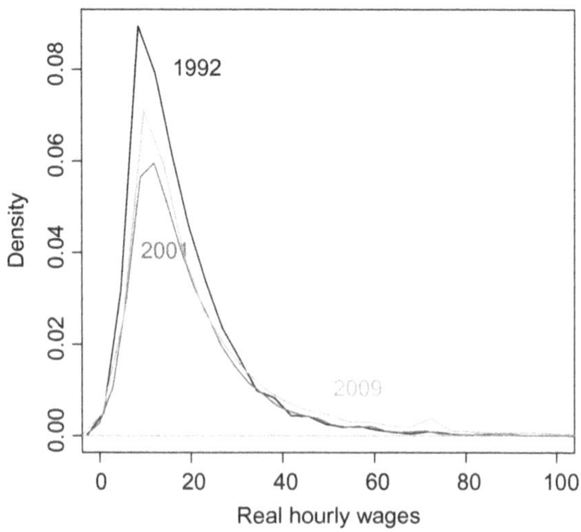

Fig. 4. Real Wage Density Estimates.

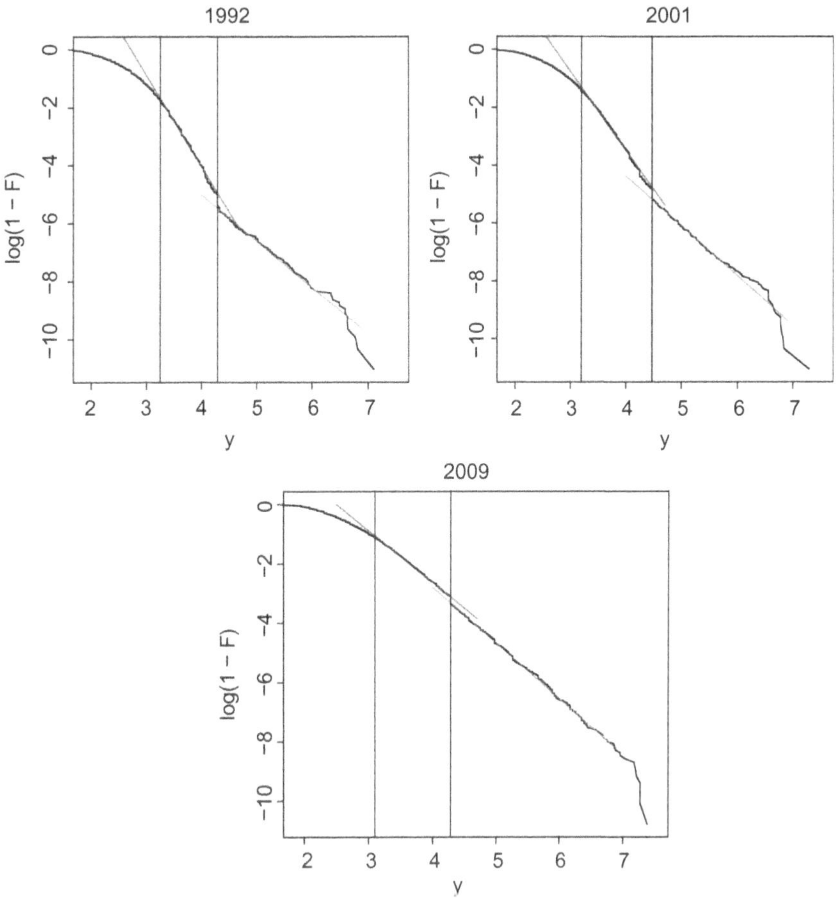

Fig. 5. Power Tails in the ORG Wages for 1992, 2001, and 2009.

In Fig. 5, we have plotted the complementary cumulative distribution function $\log(1-F)$ on the $\log(y)$ for the same three years. From these graphs, we can extract two pieces of information: the first point at which we have to cut our sample (y_{m1}) in order to use a Pareto model and then at which point there can be a change in the Pareto coefficients. This graphical information is translated into numerical values in Table 3. We note that with this graphical method, the number of superstars as reported in the last column of Table 3 is very small, compared to the total sample size, except

Table 3. Cutting Points for the Pareto Tails in the Complete Distribution.

Years	y_{m1}	$Pr(y<y_{m1})$	y_{m2}	$Pr(y<y_{m2})$	n_2
1992	exp(3.25)	0.83	exp(4.29)	0.996	273
2001	exp(3.20)	0.76	exp(4.47)	0.995	346
2009	exp(3.10)	0.67	exp(4.28)	0.966	1,637
2009	exp(3.10)	0.67	exp(4.58)	0.980	936

perhaps for 2009. However, we propose for this year two different prior for y_{m2} as we were obliged to modify it during the estimation due to a contradiction between the sample and the prior information.

At the discontinuous point, Fig. 5 shows a large number of observations (high wage earners) which could illustrate the impact of tournaments in hierarchical organizations, that is, the difficulty of changing a position in the hierarchy.

Modeling the Upper Tail of the U.S. Wage Distribution

We summarize the information contained in the truncated samples that we shall use (dropping all the observations lower than y_{m1}) in Table 2. The first quartile (in the truncated distribution) and the median remain constant over time. The distribution is changing over time only after $q_{0.75}$, for the highest hourly wages.

We elicit prior information in the following way. We assume that the Pareto coefficient is lower for the superstar model than for the hierarchical model which means, $\alpha_{o2}<\alpha_{o1}$. The number of superstars is assumed to be lower than the number of overheads while the mean wage of the former is greater than that of the latter. So we assume that y_{mo2} is strictly greater than y_{mo1}. We have chosen the value of y_{mo2} following the indications provided in Fig. 5. The role of p is now ambiguous as it is both the total proportion of observations in regime 1 and it plays also a role in determining the proportion of observations in regime 1 that are greater than y_{m2}. So we put a prior expectation of 0.50. All this motivates the selection of the following prior information. The prior value for y_{mo} is different among the three samples and given in Table 3. We have in contrast taken the same prior information for the different samples concerning the other parameters (see Table 4 below).

Table 4. Hyperparameters and Resulting Prior Moments.

	Hyperparameter	γ_{o1}	γ_{o2}	α_{o1}	ν_{o1}	α_{o2}	ν_{o2}	n_{o1}	n_{o2}
	Value	100	100	10	30	15	30	100	100
	Parameter	y_{m1}	y_{m2}	α_1		α_2		p	
1992	Mean	25.54	72.24	3.00		2.00		0.50	
	S.D.	(0.25)	(0.72)	(0.55)		(0.37)		(0.035)	
2001	Mean	24.29	86.49	3.00		2.00		0.50	
	S.D.	(0.24)	(0.86)	(0.55)		(0.37)		(0.035)	
2009	Mean	21.98	71.53	3.00		2.00		0.50	
	S.D.	(0.22)	(0.71)	(0.55)		(0.37)		(0.035)	
2009	Mean	21.98	94.64	3.00		2.00		0.50	
	S.D.	(0.22)	(0.94)	(0.55)		(0.37)		(0.035)	

Note: Prior moments for y_{m1} and y_{m2} were computed using the information contained in Table 3 together with the values of γ_{o1} and γ_{o2}.

Table 5. Posterior Inference for Mixture of Two Pareto Distributions and Corresponding Gini Indices.

	y_{m1}	y_{m2}	α_1	α_2	p	π	I_{G_1}	I_{G_2}
1992	25.80	73.18	3.08	1.50	0.978	0.013	0.194	0.509
	(0.001)	(0.25)	(0.032)	(0.14)	(0.002)	(0.001)	(0.0024)	(0.076)
2001	24.55	87.36	2.46	1.23	0.988	0.006	0.255	0.691
	(0.001)	(–)	(0.021)	(0.13)	(0.001)	(0.001)	(0.003)	(0.12)
2009	22.19	95.91	2.42	1.76	0.980	0.014	0.268	0.400
	(0.001)	(0.16)	(0.31)	(0.016)	(0.002)	(0.002)	(0.043)	(0.0049)

Notes: π is the proportion of superstars computed as the mean number of superstars n_2 divided by the sample size n. Results for 2001 were obtained with a fixed y_{m2}. Otherwise, the algorithm did not converge.

We use 5,000 draws for the main chain plus 500 draws to warm up the chain. The algorithm seems still to converge quite well, but we were obliged to consider y_{mo2} as known for 2001. The posterior mean of each parameter with the posterior standard error in parentheses are summarized in Table 5. Using the Gibbs output, we have computed a Gini index for each group of the mixture, corresponding to each of the α:

$$I_{G_k} = \sum_{t=1}^{m} \frac{1}{2\alpha_k^{(t)} - 1} \tag{6}$$

Table 6. Posterior Mean Wages for the Two Groups.

	High Wage Earners	Superstars
1992	37.58	210.59
	(0.14)	(11.51)
2001	39.97	299.62
	(0.16)	(22.72)
2009	47.59	163.15
	(0.28)	(14.05)

Notes: Standard deviations are given between parenthesis. These figures are computed inside the Gibbs loop, using the sample separation. If it were computed using the posterior draws of α and y_m, for values of α getting close to 1, the resulting estimates would have been very unstable and thus unreliable.

imposing the restriction $\alpha_k^{(t)} > 1$ for the evaluation. Inequality is greater in the second group (superstars) for 1992 and 2001. The implied Gini steadily increases over time, which is coherent with the literature. The mean wage of the first group increases as reported in Table 6. When we turn to the superstars group, the situation is more contrasted. First, their number, as detected in the sample, is very small, less than 2% of the truncated sample representing 145, 84, and 224 persons. Their mean wages has increased a lot in 2001, but has dropped in 2009. Inequality which was much higher than in the first group and also increasing in 2001, suddenly dropped to a much lower level in 2009 after the financial crisis. Table 6 shows a remarkable differences of the mean wages between the two groups.

CONCLUSION AND DISCUSSION

The distribution of earnings takes a Pareto form in the model of tournament in hierarchical organizations and in the model of "superstars." This paper has provided a Bayesian inference for a mixture of two Pareto distributions to approximate the upper tail of a wage distribution. This mixture model is applied to the data from the CPS Outgoing Rotation Group to analyze the recent structure of top wages in the United States from 1992 through 2009. We find enormous wage disparities between two groups: the very highest wage earners ("superstars") and the other high wage earners. These findings are largely in line with the recent literature explaining wage inequalities in the upper tail of wage distributions, as the recent pay differences of executives among large firms.

Inference for mixture of Pareto distributions is very scarcely covered, as underlined by Bee et al. (2013) the EM algorithm cannot be applied if the largest of the two parameters is not known. Bayesian inference for a mixture of Pareto is sensitive to the choice of prior information. This paper has provided a careful elicitation procedure on the parameter's priors of the mixture.

NOTES

1. Atkinson (2008) argues that "a constantly rising demand for more educated and more skilled workers does not lead to a constantly rising wage premium, but to a stable wage differential, and countries that adjust more rapidly will see, on a continuing basis, smaller wage differences". Lubrano and Ndoye (2014) find that most of the recent changes in U.S. between 1992 to 2009 have occurred at the top decile, and, the decline in unionization had a weak impact.
2. Tervio (2008) shows that the rise in earnings dispersion in large U.S. firm is largely due to the increase in the span of control of firms and to the tremendous rise in CEOs pay (see also Fox, 2009; Gabaix & Landier, 2008).
3. Tournament theory was first introduced by Lazear and Rosen (1981). It describes a competition between executives. Their pay is determined by their rank in the hierarchy which is determined by their personal performances. High wages are seen as a prize for the winners of the tournament.
4. Marshall (1947) first pointed out the idea of superstar.
5. In the sequel, we shall use the notation $\hat{\alpha}(y_m)$. We mean that $\hat{\alpha}$ is computed using $\sum \log(y_i/y_m)$ where y_i is restricted to the sub-sample $y_i > y_m$.
6. It is simple to draw random numbers using the inverse transform method with $x = x_m u^{1/\alpha}$ and $u \sim U(0, 1)$. For a Pareto process, we have $y = y_m u^{-1/\alpha}$.
7. The CPS is the monthly household survey conducted by the Bureau of Labour Statistics to measure labour force participation and employment. 50-60,000 households per month are queried. This is not really a panel survey since households are not followed if they move. They include the March CPS file and the Outgoing Rotation Group (ORG) files.
8. The ORG files correspond to the set of every household that enters the CPS interviewed each month for 4 consecutive months, and then ignored for 8 months.
9. The ORG files are often used because they include a direct observation of the hourly wage, which thus has not to be computed as the ratio between the weekly wage and the number of worked hours. However, many individuals did not answer to that question, so we prefer to compute a ratio in order to keep the maximum number of observations. And anyway, apart from a few aberrant values, our ratio series gave similar figures as the one given by the hourly series. Atkinson (2008, p. 401) reports different bibliographic sources showing that the ORG data are the most accurate to study the evolution of the U.S. wage structure.

ACKNOWLEDGMENTS

We are grateful to Anthony Atkinson and Stephen Bazen for pointing out several references, data sources and providing stimulating comments. We benefited also from comments of Karim Abadir and Christian Robert. We thank an anonymous referee for constructive comments. Of course, the usual disclaimers apply.

REFERENCES

Adler, M. (1985). Stardom and talent. *American Economic Review*, *75*(1), 208–212.

Arnold, B. C. (2008). Pareto and generalized Pareto distributions. In D. Chotikapanich (Ed.), *Modeling income distributions and Lorenz curves* (pp. 145–199). New York, NY: Springer.

Arnold, B., Castillo, E., & Sarabia, J. (1998). Bayesian analysis for classical distributions using conditionally specified priors. *Sankhya, Series B*, *60*, 228–245.

Arnold, B., Castillo, E., & Sarabia, J. (1999). *Conditional specification of statistical models*. Springer Series in Statistics. New York, NY: Springer Verlag.

Arnold, B., Castillo, E., & Sarabia, J. (2001). Conditionally specified distributions: An introduction (with discussion). *Statistical Science*, *16*, 151–169.

Arnold, B., & Press, S. (1983). Bayesian inference for Pareto populations. *Journal of Econometrics*, *21*, 287–306.

Arnold, B., & Press, S. (1989). Bayesian estimation and prediction for Pareto data. *Journal of the American Statistical Association*, *84*, 1079–1084.

Atkinson, A. B. (2008). *The changing distribution of earnings in OECD countries*. Oxford: Oxford University Press.

Bauwens, L. (1991). The "pathology" of the natural conjugate prior density in the regression model. *Annals of Economics and Statistics/Annales d'Économie et de Statistique*, *23*, 49–64.

Bee, M., Benedetti, R., & Espa, G. (2013). On maximum likelihood estimation of a Pareto mixture. *Computational Statistics*, *28*(1), 161–178

Bound, J., & Johnson, G. (1992). Changes in the structure of wages in the 1980's: An evaluation of alternative explanations. *American Economic Review*, *82*(3), 371–392.

Brian, G., Charles, A. O. I., & James, W. (1993). Top executive pay: Tournament or teamwork? *Journal of Labor Economics*, *11*(4), 606–628.

Brown, J. (2011). Quitters never win: The (adverse) incentive effect of competing with superstars. *Journal of Political Economy*, *119*(5), 982–1013.

Burkhauser, R. V., Feng, S., Jenkins, S. P., & Larrimore, J. (2008). *Estimating trends in US income inequality using the current population survey: The importance of controlling for censoring*. Working Paper No. 14247, NBER.

DiNardo, J., Fortin, N., & Lemieux, T. (1996). Labor market institutions and the distribution of wages, 1973–1992: A semiparametric approach. *Econometrica*, *64*(5), 1001–1044.

Drèze, J. H. (1977). Bayesian regression analysis using poly-t densities. *Journal of Econometrics*, *6*(3), 329–354.

Embrechts, P., Kluppelberg, C., & Mikosch, T. (1997). *Modelling extremal events*. Berlin: Springer Verlag.

Fox, J. T. (2009). Firm-size wage gaps, job responsibility, and hierarchical matching. *Journal of Labor Economics*, *27*(1), 83–126.

Frank, R. H., & Cook, P. J. (1995). *The winner take-all society*. New York, NY: Free Press.

Gabaix, X., & Landier, A. (2008). Why has CEO pay increased so much? *Quarterly Journal of Economics*, *123*, 49–100.

Harrison, A. (1981). Earnings by size: A tale of two distributions. *The Review of Economic Studies*, *48*(4), 621–631.

Katz, L. F., & Autor, D. H. (1999). Changes in the wage structure and earnings inequality. In O. Ashenfelter & D. Card (Eds.), *Handbook of labor economics* (Vol. 3, pp. 1463–1555). Amsterdam: Elsevier.

Lazear, E. P., & Rosen, S. (1981). Rank-order tournaments as optimum labor contracts. *Journal of Political Economy*, *89*, 841–864.

Lubrano, M., & Ndoye, A. A. J. (2014). Bayesian unconditional quantile regression: An analysis of recent expansions in wage structure and earnings inequality in the U.S. 1992–2009. *Scottish Journal of Political Economy*, *61*(2), 129–153.

Lwin, T. (1972). Estimating the tail of the Paretian law. *Scandinavian Actuarial Journal*, *55*, 170–178.

Lydall, H. F. (1959). The distribution of employment incomes. *Econometrica*, *27*(1), 110–115.

Lydall, H. F. (1968). *The structure of earnings*. Oxford: Clarendon Press.

Marshall, A. (1947). *Principles of economics* (8th ed.). New York, NY: MacMillan.

Mincer, J. (1993). Human capital, technology, and the wage structure: What do time series show? In J. Mincer (Ed.), *Studies in human capital*. Brookeld, VT: Edward Elgar Publishing.

Mitzenmacher, M. (2004). A brief history of generative models for power law and lognormal distributions. *Internet Mathematics*, *1*(2), 226–251.

Murphy, K., & Welch, F. (1992). The structure of wages. *Quarterly Journal of Economics*, *107*, 285–326.

Nadarajah, S. (2006). Information matrices for laplace and pareto mixtures. *Computational Statistics and Data Analysis*, *50*, 950–966. Retrieved from www.elsevier.com/locate/csda

Nair, M. T. (2007). *On finite mixture of Pareto and Beta distributions*. PhD thesis, Department of Statistics, Cochin University of Science and Technology, Cochin, Kerala.

Noor, F., & Aslam, M. (2012). Bayesian analysis of two parameter pareto mixture using censoring. *International Journal of Physical Sciences*, *7*(44), 5878–5891.

Pickands, J. (1975). Statistical inference using extreme order statistics. *The Annals of Statistics*, *3*(1), 119–131.

Reed, W. J., & Jorgenson, M. (2004). The double pareto-lognormal distribution – A new parametric model for size distributions. *Communications in Statistics – Theory and Methods*, *33*(8), 1733–1753.

Rosen, S. (1981). The economics of superstars. *The American Economic Review*, *71*(5), 845–858.

Rosen, S. (1986). Prizes and incentives in elimination tournaments. *American Economic Review*, *76*, 701–715.

Sattinger, M. (1993). Assignment models of the distribution of earnings. *Journal of Economic Literature*, *31*, 831–880.

Simon, H. A. (1957). The compensation of executives. *Sociometry*, *20*, 32–35.

Tervio, M. (2008). The difference that CEOs make: An assignment model approach. *American Economic Review*, *98*(3), 642–648.

DETERMINANTS OF ACTIVE INCOME INEQUALITY FOR NON-WAGE EARNERS IN CAMEROON

Simon Alain Song Ntamack

ABSTRACT

Inequality is an essential factor for the alleviation of poverty. In Cameroon, most of the households derive their livelihoods from non-wage income and a better understanding of how different variables affect income inequality is a way to reduce those inequalities and improve social welfare. Studies carried out so far barely make out the determinants among non-wage earners. This study sets out to identify these determinants, using the regression-based decomposition technique and data obtained from the 2005 Employment and Informal Sector Survey (EISS) undertaken by the National Statistic Institute (INS) in Cameroon. Results show that the total inequality of an hourly active income ensues from the ratio of age/experience and unobserved individual heterogeneity among non-wage earners.

Keywords: Inequality; active income; non-wage earner; Shapley decomposition; human capital

JEL classifications: D31; C71; J32

Economic Well-Being and Inequality: Papers from the Fifth ECINEQ Meeting
Research on Economic Inequality, Volume 22, 481–501

ISSN: 1049-2585/doi:10.1108/S1049-258520140000022016

INTRODUCTION

Why are some people better paid than others, who have same abilities and same skills as them? Likewise, why does some or a great part of income from agriculture and other informal activities go to unworthy people? What should be the role of training and other production techniques in pulling the population out of poverty and improving the redistribution of the income?

These questions made researchers put on their thinking cap. Indeed, for several decades now, economics and other social sciences are trying to figure out the inequality of incomes[1] using regression models (Fields, 2003). This reviewed interest is subsequent to a consensus that inequality of incomes has a significant influence on poverty alleviation both at the theoretical and empirical level (Fields, 2001). The inequality level often presented as an explanatory variable of other economic phenomena (relationship between growth and inequality), and a factor of convergence toward a more or less equal society. It is considered as an index revealing economic and social progress (Atkinson, 2002).

Several researchers use various techniques to analyze the causes of inequality in developing countries. These studies give decision makers the elements to understand the origins of inequality within their society. The decomposition of inequality into sources of income helps us understand that one particular source can be at the origin of observed inequalities. With reliable information, decision makers can take measures, aiming precisely, at improving the redistribution of income and the capacity of the different layers of the population in creating income. Despite the influence of income inequality in poverty alleviation, it's astonishing to note that there is just too little knowledge of the causes and reasons that determine the levels of income inequalities; the reasons for the changes in the redistribution of income within a population, a country (Kanbur, 2000) or various countries (Qureshi & Wan, 2008).

International comparisons are strained by the difficulty to take into account different subsets of incomes. In developing countries, income inequality remains relatively high due to greater disparities between regions, genders, ethnicities, and education. In many countries, a lack of adequate government policy and resources to help the poor also contribute to poor distributions of income. Sub-Saharan Africa appears as the region with the most important or accentuated inequalities of incomes, behind Latin America and the Caribbean (World Bank, 2005). However, most evaluations attached to inequalities of incomes in Sub-Saharan Africa rest on the consumption per capita. The income approach is often excluded in developing countries because most surveys reveal households expenses to be superior to incomes, thus leading to an underestimation of incomes (Fambon, 2005). This difference leads to an overestimation of the inequalities gap between Africa and the rest of the world (see Milanovic, 2005).

In Cameroon, as in many developing countries, the social range of the balance sheet of adjustment programs put in place by the government, with the support of international financial institutions, was proven to be widely negative, making it imperious to seriously take into consideration the social aspect. Between 1986 and 1994, a serious economic crisis struck the country as a result of the changes in the world commodity market. This was followed in 1993 by a reduction of about 60% of the salary of civil servants, as well as several losses of jobs in various sectors of the economy (Mbonji, 1999). This economic crisis combined to the FCFA devaluation in January 1994 deteriorated the purchasing power of households. In this context, a particular attention must be granted to the underprivileged social layers of Cameroonian community, whose vulnerability is associated to the process of economic growth.

The World Bank and IMF have elaborated new approaches to support programs of reform and adjustment in countries with low income. The objective of the new generation of economic and social policies considered by the Cameroonian government has two aspects. On one hand, it aims to consolidate passed efforts in order to put up the increase rate, and on the other hand it aims to reinforce the social sphere and boost good economic performances that could result into a net improvement of the living conditions of the population. Documents were then elaborated, pinpointing the major strategic axes of poverty alleviation in order to improve the living conditions of households while facilitating their access to basic infrastructures.

Based on the results of the *Cameroonian Household Surveys,* the decomposition of labor income makes it possible to bring out the considerable gaps between the rich and the poor and between the urban zone and the rural zone (MINEFI/DSCN, 2002). It also indicates that inequality slightly retreated between 1996 and 2001. Inequality measures show that while in 1996 the ratio of total expenditures between the poorest quintile and the richest quintile was 1:7, in 2001 this ratio was 1:8. The Gini index calculated on per capita expenditure based on a purchasing power parity marginally increased between 1996 from 0.427 to 0.472 (Fambon, 2006). For rural areas, Gini index worsened from 0.345 in 1996 to 0.369 in 2001, and that for urban areas ameliorated from 0.449 in 1996 to 0.406 in 2001

(INS, 2005). A comparison with other countries shows that the Gini index for Nigeria was around 0.506 in 2003, while in Ghana, Central African Republic, and Zambia it was 0.407, 0.613, and 0.526, respectively (World Bank, 2003).

Applying the regression-based inequality decomposition approach using Shapley value decomposition rule to explore determinants of income inequality in Cameroon using the 2007 Cameroon household consumption survey, Baye and Epo (2011) indicate that education is the main contributor to inequality.

Although active income constitutes the main component of household's income, the analysis of inequality based on the differences of the active income often ignore those of non-wage earners, self-employed, social welfare transfers, and legacy. Yet, the majority of workers in the world are non-wage earners (BIT, 1998; Fields, 2007), and the inequalities of income drawn from their activities would largely exceed that of wage earners because these incomes are often unequally distributed. These earnings vary because of the heterogeneous character of each activity (Parker, 1999), the difference in human capital (INSEE, 2006), technical or geographical factors (Boyd, 1991), or because of various discriminations against certain groups of the populations in the execution of their activities (Butler & Wilson, 1988).

The monthly average income drawn from the exercise of Cameroonians' main activities is estimated to be 26,800 FCFA (INS, 2005). By decomposition of various sectors, it appears that civil servants earn about 124,300 FCFA in the public administration, 137,400 FCFA in public and parapublic enterprises, with important differences within the sub-sector, and 103,600 FCFA in the private formal sector. The distribution of active income is more unequal among non-civil servants, veiling an important disparity, averaging 27,300 FCFA in informal non-agricultural activities and 11,100 FCFA in agricultural activities (INS, 2005, 2011).

Given the importance of labor market in household income, household consumptions, and poverty[2] alleviation, knowing the various factors that determine inequalities would permit us to better understand the level at which issues like gender, ethnicity, geographical region, or variables whose distribution depends on public policies such as access to education affect household welfare. This would permit decision makers to choose and know which opportunities can be developed.

Cameroon offers an interesting panel to examine the various determinants of income inequality, especially for non-wage earners. Although non-wage earners tend to use simple technology and have low capital intensity, some are highly dynamic, with innovations taking place in inputs, processes, and output, allowing them to adapt to new circumstances and exploit market opportunities. Often reduced as being part of the informal sector (Roubaud, 1994), income activities for non-wage earners engender serious problems due to the reliability of their estimations, the diversity of their status, and the variability of their working hours; making it more delicate to choose an indicator (DIAL/DSCN, 1993). Likewise, numerous inequalities characterize the distribution of these acceptable gains at the cost of a derisory hourly productivity.

The present research aims to arrive at a better understanding of the mechanisms of the determination of inequalities in incomes among non-waged employees in Cameroon. Being an important source of income for households, active income appears like one of the main components of inequality distribution. In the explanation of inequalities, several views are generally taken into consideration. One of the most recurrent themes in economics establishes a theoretical and empirical relation between growth, inequalities, and poverty. Most works related to the analysis of inequality were based on traditional techniques. Recent theoretical and empirical studies highlight the relationship between economic growth, inequality, and poverty, insisting particularly on the impact of growth on poverty and inequality (Dollar & Kraay, 2002; Ravallion & Chen, 1997).

Using the cooperative game theory concept inspired from Shapley value, Montaud (2002) showed that inequalities of income among Burkina-Faso households were lessening while wage income produced by non-agricultural capital were rising. According to Fambon (2005), the study of the relationship between economic growth, poverty, and inequality of incomes using the static decomposition of Kakwani (1993) shows that as time goes by, poverty in Cameroon would quickly increase the phenomenon of inequality. No matter the type of analysis, the phenomenon of income inequality is felt more severely in rural areas than in urban areas, and by women than by men, hereby translating how fragile rural zones and women are with regard to economic growth (Kakwani, 1993, 1997; Lachaud, 1997; Datt & Ravallion, 1992). Existing works on the causes of income inequalities base their study on either sources of income (Fei, Ranis, & Kuo, 1978; Pyatt, Chen, & Fei, 1980; Shorrocks, 1982) or sub-group decomposition techniques (Armor, 1973; Oaxaca, 1973; Shorrocks, 1984). In both cases, the decomposition is statistical in nature because in its construction, a range of variables liable to influence policies put in place were excluded. With both techniques thus, if the decomposition by sub-group helps to appreciate the variation of income between subsets, and the decomposition of inequality measured by sources permits to understand how a source of decomposition can generate inequalities in incomes distribution (Epo, Baye, & Manga, 2011).

Several works have taken the liberty to go beyond the existing static decomposition to examine the factor of inequality in dynamic context. Decomposition based on regression proposed by Fields (2003) permits us to evaluate how analysis of inequality in incomes is explained by different explanatory factors. This technique combines the analysis regression of income to the decomposition by source of income according to Shorrocks, by which the sources of income of the second stage of the decomposition analysis are determined by the first phase of the regression on income. It permits, in addition, to go beyond simple changes in the decomposition of inequalities in terms of income components and in sub groups. Inequalities can then be explained by any factor included in the regression of income or of consumption, as well as politics variables. According to Kanbur (2000), it permits us to explore different sectors in which the understanding of inequalities is relatively low (the reasons for inequalities within a country, as well as at different levels of aggregation within groups that are generally defined as the demography of households, education, regions, or ethnic groups).

METHODOLOGY

This section attempts to explain the methodological technique for the identification of microeconomic determinants of inequalities in labor income. It therefore presupposes to have reliable data at disposal and suitable tools whose exploitation might help pertinent analysis.

DATA

The principal data source used in this study comes from the Employment and Informal Sector Survey (EISS) carried out by the National Institute of Statistics in 2005. It was comprised of 8,536 households which highlighted 22,668 individuals with workers, drawn from a national base covering a diversity of workers of both sexes, aged above 15 years.[3] The EISS delivers precise information to appreciate the unequal distribution of active income particularly relating to the professional status, the schedules of work, the monthly incomes, and individual characteristics (sex, age, level of education, matrimonial status, etc.). In this paper, the analysis is done at the individual level.

The dependent variable used in this analysis will be the hourly income earned by the respondents through income-generating activities. In fact, the volume of work offered is different from one individual to another and monthly income seems to be an obvious determinant of inequality. Explanatory variables are education, gender, the area of residence (two categories), experience or the sector of job activity (three categories), etc. From this set of information, it is possible to appreciate the relative inequality of active income distribution. Admittedly, the analysis would be better if it takes into account the characteristics of non-wage earners enterprises (stock of capital, labor, other inputs, geographical location, specific workplace, etc.), unfortunately the lack of information makes it difficult. These individual characteristics could have been useful for public policies.

Descriptive statistics (Table 1) indicate that non-wage earning activities are mostly practiced in urban areas (70.70%) by individuals with primary level of education (average schooling years 5.21). The majority of non-wage earners are a relatively young population (35 years on average), female (55.39%), single (50.7%), working in the agricultural sector (44.39%), small industries (18.78%), services (36.81%), and practicing Christian religion (71.9%) non-wage earners need to justify at least nine years of working experience.

Table 1. Descriptive Statistics.

Variable	Mean	Standard Deviation
Log hourly income	0.013123	0.1257566
Education[a]	5.210332	3.897131
Age	35.30682	15.2391
Sex (1 = male)	0.446919	0.49719
Household size	6.011185	3.755297
Experience	9.089858	10.9794
Formal sector (1 = yes and 0 = no)	0.080474	0.27204
Urban (1 = yes and 0 = no)	0.707014	0.45515
Activities by sector		
Agro-pastoral activities	0.443981	0.496875
Industrial activities	0.187867	0.390625
Services	0.368152	0.482326

[a]Endogenous variable.
Source: Constructed from raw data (EESI, 2005).

Table 2. Regional Repartition of Employment.

Employment Status	Areas of Location				
	Coast	Forest	Sahel	Mountain	Total
Unemployed	2,414	2,973	1,508	829	7,724
Wage earner	1,526	1,725	678	465	4,394
Non-wage earner	2,728	2,966	2,893	1,963	10,550
Total	6,668	7,664	5,079	3,257	22,668

Source: Constructed from raw data (EESI, 2005).

The breakdown of individual workers by source of income is given in Table 2. Regardless of the zone in which they are, the regional repartition of employment status shows that the majority is made up of non-wage earners. However, relatively few non-wage earners are located in the forest and coastal zone, which include two major cities, namely Yaoundé and Douala, administrative and economics headquarters respectively.

In Cameroon, non-wage earners spend an average of 40 hours per week on income-generating activities and there are no statutory daily hour limits. Income generated from such activities is used for smoothening in the household. If wages are generally well reported using classic information including income by source at the individual level, it is not the same for non-wage income. The survey gives reliable non-wage income from a direct declaration of the self-employed individuals involved in any economic activities.

The *regression model* will then identify explanatory factors that justify the dependent variable, and thereon carry out an inequality analysis. To generate reliable parameter estimates needed for the inequality decomposition exercise, we define our econometric model as:

$$\ln Y = \beta X + \varepsilon \tag{1}$$

where $\ln Y$ is an $n \times 1$ vector of the logarithm for hourly active income declared by the individual, X is an $n \times M$ matrix of individual's characteristics (age, education, household size, residence, etc.), β is a $M \times 1$ vector of coefficients and is an $n \times 1$ vector of residuals, a sample observations $\{\ln y_i, X_i, i = 1,2,\ldots, n\}$ can be used to estimate the model.

The vector β can be interpreted as the effect (or "price") of the independent variables on income. The income-generating function specification admits that income is affected by human capital, social capital, and specific endowments (see Becker, 1964; Card, 2001; Mincer, 1974 for human capital and Fafchamps & Minten, 2002; Glaeser, Laibson, & Sacerdote, 2002 for social capital). In this semi-logarithmic non-wage income equation/model, if ε is distributed according to standard properties, then the estimated β by Least Squares (OLS) method leads to the return on education. However it is necessary to admit bias in this estimation due to some problems that it generates.

For example, social environment and community factors have a direct effect on the active income earned by individuals carrying out an economic activity, and an indirect effect following their level of education. On one hand, active income of an individual i is observed if and only if it is higher than an alternative income. This does not suggest that the non-wage earners constitute a random sample of the working population as a whole. On the contrary, it is better to think that non-wage earners as well as employees are subjects to particular characteristics. The education's rate of return could possibly find itself affected, so estimation using observed labor income has to take into account the left censured data as demonstrated by Heckman (1976, 1979). A potential instrument[4] is then needed in order to consistently estimate effects of education on individual income.

In order to correct sample selection bias in the labor market, it would be necessary to consider a probabilistic model inspired by Bourguignon, Fournier, and Gurgand (2007), from the generalization of Heckman's (1979) model. The decision to participate comprises several options, amongst which the individual must necessarily make a choice. The interpretation of this variable consists in measuring the propensity of choosing one of the options: *to be a non-wage earner*, *to be a wage-earner* or *to be unemployed*, and retaining the alternative which maximizes its utility in terms of profit. By doing so, an evaluation is done on the potential profits or, more precisely, the unobserved productivity of each individual, including those who perceive a different form of remuneration. Furthermore, to make sure that the results are not influenced by endogeneity bias, some variables are clustered on the regional level, which is theoretically a fine instrument for the focus variable.

The estimate of Eq. (1) using the OLS method is correct only if explanatory variables are not correlated with non-observed factors. Some of the income co-variants could be considered for example as endogenous after long periods of time. Thus, the household size could be affected by the level of contributions brought in by the head of household, while the level of education of an individual in a household would depend also on a certain number of decisions taken within the household and other communal constraints. However, the choice of an instrument is not easy, and according to the period of analysis, some characteristics could be considered as exogenous. In order to correct this endogeneity bias, the most frequently used solution (Gourieroux, 1989, p. 197) is to arrange correctly the S_i variable and its square using the Two-Stage Least Squares (2SLS) method.

In order to identify the determinants of the level of income inequalities, the second step consists of computing the marginal contributions of each source that explains active income of non-wage earners. The marginal contribution of different sources in the determination of income inequalities is calculated following a regression-based inequality decomposition technique, which possesses a number of important advantages over traditional inequality decompositions by income source (Shorrocks, 1982).

Since the econometric results yield estimates of the income sources attributed to individual variables, they allow us to make use of decomposition by income sources (or factor endowments). Regression coefficients are then used to construct factor inequality weights for each variable in the regression by exploiting the analogy of Shorrocks' (1982) inequality decomposition by income source (Fields, 2003). By construction, the total income from a given income source is the sum of these estimated flows income source (plus the predicted regression residual): $\hat{y} = x\hat{\beta}$.

If the active income drawn from its m attribute is given by the expression $\hat{y}^m = x\hat{\beta}^m$, it follows that the total income of individual i is written as $yi = \sum_{m=1}^{q+1} \hat{y}_i^m$. The relative contribution of income factor components to total inequality becomes: $s^m = \hat{\beta}^m \left(\frac{\sum_{m=1}^{q+1} \hat{y}_i^m}{I(y)} \right)$ wherein $\hat{\beta}^m$ is the estimated coefficient associated to m, sources of income, and $I(y)$ the index for total inequality. We can therefore decompose all indexes of inequality which could be written as a weighted average of active income.

Using $I(\cdot)$ as a measure of inequality, the overall income inequality can then be decomposed into the contribution of the constant term $I(y_0)$, the contribution of the estimated income sources $I(\tilde{y})$ and the contribution of the predicted residual (for detailed explanations, see Baye & Epo, 2011).

RESULTS AND RECOMMENDATIONS

Table 3 presents determinants of income that have been corrected from endogeneity and selectivity bias. It appears that an hourly return on

Table 3. Determinants of Active Incomes for Non-Wage Earners.

Variable	Corrected Endogeneity Bias	Corrected Selectivity Bias
Endogenous variables		
Education[a]	0.0028229 (0.0003362)***	0.0013484 (0.0004434)***
Exogenous variables		
Age	0.0004444 (0.0003266)	0.0018238 (0.0004241)***
Age squared	1.53e-06 (3.78e-06)	−0.0000132 (4.75e-06)***
Sex (male = 1)	0.009009 (0.0022591)***	0.0076338 (0.0022726)***
Size of household	0.0007239 (0.000306)**	0.000706 (0.0003057)**
Job experience	−0.0000429 (0.0001267)	−0.000057 (0.0001266)
Urban (1 = yes and 0 = no)	−0.0005372 (0.0029302)	0.2376 (0.02724)***
Formal sector (1 = yes and 0 = no)	0.0315416 (0.0055137)***	0.0311525 (0.0055078)***
Activities by sector		
Agro-pastoral activities	−0.0032413 (0.0034522)	−0.002324 (0.0034528)
Services	−0.0017858 (0.003809)	−0.0022915 (0.0038058)
Residual complement of education	−0.0011011 (0.0011357)	−0.0006035 (0.0011386)
Mills ratio		0.1026944 (0.0201716)***
Constant	−0.0197111 (0.0104261)*	−0.0902183 (0.0173277)***
R-square	0.0194	0.0218
Adjusted/R-square	0.0184	0.0207
F-stat [1% relative bias]	0.0000	0.0000
Number of observations	10,550	10,550

[a]Endogenous variable.
Source: Constructed from raw data (EESI, 2005).
Notes: Significance level: (***) 1%, (**) 5%, (*) 10%. The standard deviations are noted in brackets.

education attains 0.3%. The corrective least square method provides convergent estimators and considerably improves the explanatory power of the global model. Every non-wage earner's productivity has an increasing function regarding the level of competence, that is, the human capital obtained by the individual. Education thus makes it possible for the non-wage earners to accumulate competencies (human capital), entailing higher remunerations. Similarly, the influence of age and job experience on the active income is statistically and significantly positive for non-wage earners.

The importance of human capital in the explanation of hourly active income of non-wage earners can be appreciated before and during the active life. In addition, the length of studies has significant and statistical boosting effects on the non-wage earners' active income. The positive coefficient of the rate of return of an additional year of study indicates therefore that workers perceive higher incomes when they have been educated. This result corroborates the importance of human capital in the distribution of active income (Mincer, 1974), especially those carried out using Cameroonian data

(Abessolo, 1997; Ajab-Amin & Awung, 2005; Fomba Kamga, 2008; Song Ntamack, 2012). However they contrast with the works of Tafah-Edokat (1998) in Cameroon and Psacharopoulos (1994).

Table 3 also hosts non-synthetic variables that correlate positively with hourly active income welfare. These variables are sex of the worker, household size, working in the formal sector and living in urban area. Working in the formal sector implies having a steady source of income, as well as other advantages like being able to borrow money and to have an adequate insurance policy. These tend to positively impact on non-wage earners' active income and economic well-being.

To decompose measured income inequality by sources, we calculated contributions of different estimated factors using the analytical approach and the Shapley value approach (Table 4). The difference between the analytical approach and the Shapley value approach is that, while the former computes inequality by the Gini index as the product of the income shares and the coefficients of concentration, the latter is based on a set of axioms (Shorrocks, 1999) and have the merit of computing the weighted marginal

Table 4. Decomposition of Total Inequality by Estimated Income Sources.

Variables	Shapley Value Approach
Endogenous variables	
Education[a]	0.000079 (0.000181)
Exogenous variables	
Age	0.005055 (0.011624)
Age squared	0.426891 (0.981519)
Sex (male = 1)	0.000024 (0.000054)
Size of household	0.000278 (0.000639)
Job experience	0.002577 (0.005926)
Urban (1 = yes and 0 = no)	0.000013 (0.000030)
Formal sector (1 = yes and 0 = no)	0.000005 (0.000012)
Activities by sector	
Agro-pastoral activities	0.000039 (0.000090)
Services	0.000007 (0.000015)
Residual complement of education	−0.000036 (−0.000082)
Mills ratio	−0.000006 (−0.000013)
Constant	
Regression residual	0.000003 (0.000007)
Total	0.434929 (1.000000)

[a]Endogenous variable.

Source: Constructed from raw data (EESI, 2005).

Notes: Values in brackets are the relative contributions.

contributions of an estimated source of income in various coalitions of non-wage earners (Epo et al., 2011).

Nevertheless, we focus our comments on the results obtained from the Shapley value approach. The weighted contributions exactly sum up to the considered inequality measure. Taking into consideration Shapley value, factors that largely explain inequality for non-wage earners as per active incomes are the link between age and job experience of individual. The relative contribution for age each hour is 0.51%. Other factors that explain observed inequality are square of age, gender, household size, working in urban area and being in the formal sector. The sum of their relative is above 98%.

Although the contribution of education is positive, it is relatively weak as compared to other parameters. This may be explained by the fact that, education certainly permits non-wage earners to improve their productive capacities. Nevertheless, it reduces with time because the relative contribution that explains inequality associated to the acquisition of job know-how is more important. Its contribution enables us to appreciate the proportions of the regressed variables that explain total inequality.

The variables represented here would averagely explain more than 43.49% of the total hourly inequality. Thus, individuals or policy makers would be able to choose which parameters to interact with in order resolve the problem of gaps in active income. It is, however, possible to improve the margin of reliability in the suppression of inequality in income activities by improving the collection and the processing of data. Other sources that contributed in explaining hourly inequality are working in the formal sector, household size, and male sex. The estimated income source for education reveals the key role human capital plays over time in enhancing well-being and exacerbating inequality.

Appendix C presents marginal contributions. It is all about measuring the variation of a precise factor and evaluating its impact on measured inequality. Thus, with the weighted average of the marginal contribution of a variable such as education of about 0.000181, and the total inequality (0.434929), about 0.000109 is obtained in the first stage, that is, in the absence of other regressed parameters of hourly active income and the predicted residual. When other sources that explain inequality are taken into consideration, the marginal contribution of education drops to 0.000069. Policywise, this may indicate the importance of targeting professional training as well as skill acquisition, especially through the combination of policy efforts with other sources that help contribute to the welfare of non-wage earners in inequality reduction. The promotion of education will therefore tend to increase the equity in the determination of incomes, though some environmental conditions strive to reinforce inequalities.

The marginal contribution of the age-experience couple presents a progressive and even positive trend, when the effects of other sources are progressively taken into consideration. This observation reinforces the idea according to which the age-experience relation constitutes an essential factor in the acquisition of knowledge and contributes towards increasing the hourly productivity of non-wage earners, and therefore their possibilities of gains as well as their utility.

Variables as size of household, working within the formal sector and residing in an urban area, taken individually (stage 1), possess respectively, very weak weighted impacts. Notwithstanding, whereas the impact of the size of the household progressively reduces to the point of becoming negative, the two other factors also decrease, starting from the stage six and seven respectively. They however constitute important inputs as to understanding inequality outcomes among non-wage earners.

CONCLUDING REMARKS

This paper analyzed microeconomic determinants of hourly active income, for non-wage earners, and computed the contributions of these sources in explaining observed inequality among non-wage earners. Sample selection bias and potential biases due to endogeneity and heterogeneity are resolved.

The level of hourly income inequality is primarily determined by human capital endowments like education and the age-experience relationship. The joint contribution of education and age-experience couple in accounting for total inequality was relatively important, indicating the key role human capital characteristics play in explaining observed inequality in the distribution of hourly active income. These variables constitute essential factor in acquisition of knowledge which contribute towards increasing productivity, income, and utility. Consequently, building skills among actors in the non-wage sector seems most appropriate for workers in this sector to move away from subsistence income-generating activities, and gradually progress towards added value activities and jobs that have higher marginal returns for the workers. Estimated income sources such as education, household size and working in the formal sector were prominent in accounting for measured income inequality. Urban residency also largely contributed to measured income inequality. In a developing country setting like Cameroon, these value added jobs are in the formal or semi-formal sector. This will contribute towards the inclusion of these groups of workers into the normal economy sphere, enabling them to benefit from advantages like social security and health insurance which in turn consolidates their human capital acquisition and therefore welfare.

NOTES

1. Literature employs several concepts for revenue. "Income" expresses a receptive unit from all sources; "profit" indicates a financial benefit that is realized when the amount of revenue gained from a business activity exceeds the expenses. Meanwhile "wages" defines a remuneration based on a fixed time period. Various receptive units include families, households, and employees. To avoid referring repeatedly to income or benefit or wages between households or families or individuals, the following discussion is built around active income among individuals.
2. The analysis of the evolution of the impact of poverty can't permit on its own an accurate appreciation of the progress realized in the alleviation of poverty. This analysis is supposed to be completed by another based on the evolution of inequalities of incomes distribution in order to have a complete view of monetary poverty dynamics. As a matter of facts, it may happen that in a situation of low inequalities in incomes distribution or a high concentration of populations around the poverty line; the impact of poverty may be ameliorated.
3. This limit is fixed at the international rules of age for which education ceases to be obligatory in most of the countries (see convention n° 138 of International Labor Organization concerning the minimum age of work).
4. See Appendix A.

ACKNOWLEDGMENTS

I would like to thank Epo Ngah Boniface and Ngo Ntamack Kerly for comments and discussions. I also want to express my gratitude to the REMA Centre for Research in Applied Microeconomics and to the reading committee.

REFERENCES

Abessolo, Y. A. (1997). *Capital humain, salaires et segmentation du marché du travail en économie sous-développée: Le cas du Cameroun.* Thèse nouveau régime en Economie (342 p.). Bordeaux 4, Faculté des sciences économiques et de gestion.

Ajab-Amin, A., & Awung, W. J. (2005, November 25–26). Economic analysis of private returns to investment in education in Cameroon. *Regional conference on education in West Africa: Constraints and opportunities*, Organized by Cornell/CREA/INRA/ Ministry of Education, Senegal, Dakar, Senegal.

Armor, D. J. (1973). The double standard: A reply. *Public Interest*, (n 30), 113–119.

Atkinson, T. (2002). La distribution des revenus dans les pays de l'OCDE au 20e siècle. *Revue française d'économie*, *17*(1), 3–31.

Baye, F. M., & Epo, B. N. (2011). Inequality decomposition by regressed-income sources in Cameroon. Paper presented at the IARIW-Statistics conference on Measuring National Income, Wealth, Poverty, and Inequality in African Countries SSA, South Africa, September 28–October 1. Retrieved from www.iariw.org

Becker, G. S. (1964). *Human capital*. New York, NY: NBER.

BIT. (1998). Mesure du revenu de l'emploi. *Rapport I de la XVIième Conférence Internationale des Statisticiens du Travail*, Genève.

Bourguignon, F., Fournier, M., & Gurgand, M. (2007). Selection bias corrections based on the multinomial logit model: Monte Carlo comparisons. *Journal of Economic Surveys*, *21*(1), 174–205.

Boyd, R. L. (1991). Inequality in the earnings of self-employed African and Asian Americans. *Sociological Perspectives*, 34(4), 447–472.

Butler, J. S., & Wilson, K. L. (1988). Entrepreneurial enclaves: An exposition into the Afro-American experience. *National Journal of Sociology*, *2*, 127–166.

Card, D. (2001). Estimating the return to schooling: Progress on some persistent econometric problems. *Econometrica*, *69*(5), 1127–1160.

Datt, G., & Ravallion, M. (1992). Growth and redistribution components of changes in poverty measures: A decomposition with applications to Brazil and India in the 1980s. *Journal of Development Economics*, *38*, 275–295.

DIAL/DSCN. (1993, Novembre). *Le secteur informel à Yaoundé, Principaux résultats, Enquête 1–2–3 phase2*, 29 p.

Dollar, D., & Kraay, A. (2002). Growth is good for the poor. *Journal of Economic Growth*, *7*(3), 195–225.

EESI. (2005). *Enquête Emploi Secteur Informel*. INS-Cameroun.

Epo, N. B., Baye, F. M., & Manga, T. A. N. (2011). *Explaining spatial and inter-temporal sources of poverty, inequality and gender disparities in Cameroon: A regression-based decomposition analysis*. Poverty Monitoring and Measurement Analysis (PMMA) Working Paper No. 2011–15. Partnership For Economic Policy Research Network. Retrieved from www.pep-net.org

Fafchamps, M., & Minten, B. (2002). Returns to social network capital among traders. *Oxford Economic Papers*, *54*, 173–206.

Fambon, S. (2005). Croissance économique, pauvreté et inégalité des revenus au Cameroun. *Revue d'économie du développement*, *19*(1), 91–122.

Fambon, S. (2006, 12–13 October). Poverty profiles for Cameroon. AERC discussion paper. *Poverty, income distribution and labour markets in Sub-Saharan Africa dissemination conference*, Addis Ababa, Ethiopia.

Fei, J., Ranis, G., & Kuo, S. (1978). Growth and the family distribution of income by factor components. *Quarterly Journal of Economics*, *92*(1), 17–53.

Fields, G. S. (2001). *Distribution and development: a new look at the developing world*. New York, NY: Russell Sage Foundation.

Fields, G. S. (2003). Accounting for income inequality and its change: A new method with application to the distribution of earnings in the United States. In S. W. Polachek (Ed.), *Worker well-being and public policy* (pp. 1–38). Oxford: Elsevier Science Ltd.

Fields, G. S. (2007). *Labor market policy in developing countries: A selective review of the literature and needs for the future*. ILR Collection Working Papers. Cornell University ILR School.

Fomba Kamga, B. (2008). *Contrat de Travail et Fonctionnement du Marché du Travail au Cameroun*. Thèse Ph.D en Sciences Economiques non publiée, Université de Yaoundé II-Soa.

Glaeser, E. L., Laibson, D. I., & Sacerdote, B. I. (2002). The economic approach to social capital. *Economic Journal, 112*, 437–458.

Gourieroux, C. (1989). *Econométrie des variables qualitative* (2nd ed.). Paris: Economica.

Heckman, J. (1976). The common structure of statistical models of truncation, sample selection and limited dependent variables and a sample estimator for such models. *Annals of Economic and Social Measurement*, 5(4), 475–492.

Heckman, J. (1979). Sample selection bias as a specification error. *Econometrica, 47*(1), 153–161.

INS. (2005, Décembre). *Enquête sur l'emploi et le secteur informel au Cameroun (EESI) en 2005*. Rapport principal.

INS. (2011, Octobre). *Deuxième Enquête sur l'emploi et le secteur informel au Cameroun (EESI 2) en 2010*. Rapport principal.

INSEE. (2006). *Les revenus d'activité des indépendants*. Collection Références, Juin.

Kakwani, N. (1993). Poverty and economic growth with application to Cote d'Ivoire. *Review of Income and Wealth, 39*, 121–139.

Kakwani, N. (1997). *On measuring growth and inequality components of poverty with application to Thailand*. Discussion paper. School of Economics, The University of New South Wales.

Kanbur, R. (2000). Income distribution and development. In A. B. Atkinson & F. Bourguignon (Eds.), *Handbook of income distribution* (Vol. 1, pp. 791–841). Amsterdam: Elsevier.

Lachaud, J.-P. (1997). Croissance économique, pauvrette et inégalité des revenus en Afrique subsaharienne: Analyse comparative, Bordeaux. DT/11, Universite´ Montesquieu-Bordeaux IV, Centre d'économie du développement.

Mbonji, E. (1999). Les 'déflatés' du développement. De la tradition de dépendance à l'autogestion. *Bulletin de l'APAD, 18*. Retrieved from http://apad.revues.org/455

Milanovic, B. (2005). *Worlds apart: Global and international inequality, 1950–2000*. Princeton, NJ: Princeton University Press.

Mincer, J. (1974). *Schooling, experience and earnings*. New York, NY: Columbia University Press for the NBER.

MINEFI/DSCN. (2002). *Conditions de vie des populations et profil de pauvreté au Cameroun en 2001*. Rapport principal de l'ECAM II, Août.

Montaud, J.-M. (2002). *Ajustement structurel et inégalités des revenus en Afrique: une analyse de décomposition appliquée au Burkina-Faso*. Documents de travail 75, Groupe d'Economie du Développement de l'Université Montesquieu Bordeaux IV.

Oaxaca, R. L. (1973). Male-female wage differentials in urban labour markets. *International Economic Review, 14*(3), 693–709.

Parker, S. C. (1999). The inequality of employment and self-employment incomes: A decomposition analysis for the U.K. *Review of Income and Wealth*, *45*(2), 263–274.

Psacharopoulos, G. (1994). Returns to investment in education: A global update. *World Development*, *22*(9), 1325–1343.

Pyatt, G., Chen, C.-N., & Fei, J. (1980). The distribution of income by factor components. *Quarterly Journal of Economics*, *95*(3), 451–473.

Qureshi, M. S., & Wan, G. (2008). Distributional consequences of globalization: Empirical evidence from panel data. *Journal of Development Studies*, *44*(10), 1424–1449.

Roubaud, F. (1994). Le marché du travail à Yaoundé, 1983–1993. La décennie perdue. *Tiers-Monde*, *35*(140), 751–778.

Ravallion, M., & Chen, S. (1997). What can new survey data tell us about recent change in distribution and poverty. *World Bank, Economic Review*, *11*(2), 357–381.

Shorrocks, A. F. (1999). *Decomposition procedures for distributional analysis: A unified framework based on the Shapley value* (Mimeo). University of Essex.

Shorrocks, T. (1982). Inequality decomposition by factor component. *Econometrica*, *50*(1), 193–211.

Shorrocks, T. (1984). Inequality decomposition by population subgroup. *Econometrica*, *52*(6), 1369–1385.

Song Ntamack, S. A. (2012). Education, experience and profits: An application on the job of non wage-earners. *International Journal of Business and Management*, *7*(4), 57–68.

Tafah-Edokat, E. O. (1998). *Rates of return to education: A case of Cameroon* (mimeo). Department of Economics, University of Yaounde II-Soa.

World Bank. (2003). *2002 development indicators* (pp. 74–75). Washington, DC: World Bank Express.

World Bank. (2005). *World development report: Equity and development*. Washington, DC: World Bank.

APPENDIX A: EQUATION TO PREDICT THE COMPLEMENT RESIDUAL OF EDUCATION

	Source	*SS*	*df*	*MS*	
	Model	*24,904.6273*	*3*	*8,301.5424*	*Number of observations = 22,668*
	Residual	*428,340.315*	*22,668*	*18.899590*	*F(3, 22,668) = 439.24*
	Total	*428,340.315*	*22,668*	*19.995806*	*Probability > F = 0.0000*
					R^2=0.0549
					Adjusted R^2=0.0548
					Root MSE = 4.3474
Education[a]	Coefficient		Standard error		$P > \|t\|$
Religion	2.358357		0.0984212		0.000
Household-conditions	1.859412		0.0718783		0.000
Physical handicap	−0.695380		0.1406002		0.000
Constant	3.836702		0.1406002		0.000

[a]Endogenous variable.

Source: Constructed from raw data (EESI, 2005).

APPENDIX B: PARTICIPATION IN THE LABOR MARKET: RESULTS OF ESTIMATES

Multinomial logistic regression				*Number of observations = 22,529*
				LR $Chi^2(34)$ =10,773.90
				Prob > Chi^2=0.0000
Log likelihood = −1,8057.078				*Pseudo R^2=0.2298*
	Coefficient	Standard Error	*t*-Student	$P > \|z\|$
Wage earners				
Age	0.4625	0.0102	45.42	0.000
Age squared	−0.0054	0.0001	−40.08	0.000
Sex	1.8255	0.0475	38.40	0.000
Handicap	−1.0171	0.1120	−9.08	0.000
Marital status				
Married	0.1232	0.1436	0.86	0.391
Level of education				
Higher education	1.2430	0.0954	13.03	0.000
Secondary education	0.9963	0.0933	10.68	0.000
Primary education	1.1684	0.1116	10.46	0.000
Uneducated	–	–	–	–
Constant	−9.7506	0.2400	−40.62	0.000
Non-wage earners				
Age	0.2248	0.0053	42.30	0.000
Age squared	−0.0024	0.0001	−37.50	0.000
Sex	0.4551	0.0349	13.03	0.000
Handicap	−1.0448	0.0788	−13.26	0.000
Marital status				
Married	1.5852	0.1087	14.58	0.000
Level of education				
Higher education	0.5445	0.0553	9.85	0.000
Secondary education	−0.5354	0.0552	−9.70	0.000
Primary education	−1.8132	0.1013	−17.90	0.000
Uneducated	–	–	–	–
Constant	−3.4122	0.1441	−23.68	0.000

Note: Socio-professional Category = without employment is the bases outcome.
Source: Constructed from raw data (EESI, 2005).

APPENDIX C: THE MARGINAL CONTRIBUTIONS OF THE DIFFERENT ESTIMATED SOURCES OF ACTIVE HOURLY INCOME BASED ON SHAPLEY'S APPROACH ON VALUE

Source	Level_1	Level_2	Level_3	Level_4	Level_5	Level_6	Level_7	Level_8	Level_9	Level_10	Level_11	Level_12	Level_13
Endogenous variables													
Education[a]	0.000109	0.000069	0.000041	0.000021	0.000006	−0.000005	−0.000013	−0.000019	−0.000022	−0.000025	−0.000027	−0.000028	−0.000028
Exogenous variables													
Age	0.000421	0.000421	0.000421	0.000421	0.000421	0.000421	0.000421	0.000421	0.000421	0.000421	0.000421	0.000421	0.000421
Age squared	0.032893	0.032860	0.032839	0.032827	0.032821	0.032819	0.032819	0.032822	0.032827	0.032832	0.032838	0.032844	0.032849
Sex (male = 1)	0.000012	0.000006	0.000003	0.000002	0.000001	0.000000	0.000000	0.000000	0.000000	−0.000000	−0.000000	−0.000000	−0.000000
Size of household	0.000100	0.000068	0.000047	0.000032	0.000021	0.000013	0.000008	0.000004	0.000001	−0.000002	−0.000003	−0.000005	−0.000006
Job experience	0.000262	0.000230	0.000210	0.000198	0.000191	0.000187	0.000185	0.000185	0.000185	0.000186	0.000187	0.000186	0.000185
Urban (1 = yes and 0 = no)	0.000010	0.000004	0.000002	0.000001	0.000000	−0.000000	−0.000000	−0.000001	−0.000001	−0.000001	−0.000001	−0.000001	−0.000001
Formal sector (1 = yes and 0 = no)	0.000004	0.000002	0.000001	0.000000	0.000000	0.000000	−0.000000	−0.000000	−0.000000	−0.000000	−0.000000	−0.000000	−0.000000
Activities by sector													
Industrial activities	Ref	Ref	Ref	Ref	Ref	Ref	Ref	Ref	Ref	Ref	Ref	Ref	Ref
Agro-pastorals activities	0.000012	0.000004	0.000002	0.000001	0.000002	0.000002	0.000002	0.000002	0.000002	0.000002	0.000002	0.000002	0.000002
Services	0.000012	0.000004	0.000001	0.000000	−0.000001	−0.000001	−0.000001	−0.000001	−0.000001	−0.000001	−0.000001	−0.000001	−0.000001
Residual complement of education	0.000019	0.000009	0.000003	−0.000001	−0.000003	−0.000005	−0.000006	−0.000007	−0.000008	−0.000009	−0.000009	−0.000010	−0.000010
Mills ratio	0.000003	0.000001	0.000000	−0.000000	−0.000001	−0.000001	−0.000001	−0.000001	−0.000001	−0.000001	−0.000001	−0.000001	−0.000001
Residual regression	0.000001	0.000000	0.000000	0.000000	0.000000	0.000000	0.000000	0.000000	0.000000	0.000000	0.000000	0.000000	0.000000

[a]Endogenous variable.

Note: Ref = *Industrial Activities is the base outcome for Activities by Sector*.

Source: Constructed from raw data (EESI, 2005).